The Vanished Musicians

EXILE STUDIES

VOL. 14

Edited by
FRANZISKA MEYER

A series founded by
ALEXANDER STEPHAN

PETER LANG
Oxford · Bern · Berlin · Bruxelles · Frankfurt am Main · New York · Wien

Albrecht Dümling

THE VANISHED MUSICIANS

Jewish Refugees in Australia

Translated from the German by Diana K. Weekes

PETER LANG

Oxford · Bern · Berlin · Bruxelles · Frankfurt am Main · New York · Wien

Bibliographic information published by Die Deutsche Nationalbibliothek
Die Deutsche Nationalbibliothek lists this publication in the Deutsche
Nationalbibliografie; detailed bibliographic data is available
on the Internet at http://dnb.d-nb.de.

A catalogue record for this book is available from the British Library.

Library of Congress Cataloging-in-Publication Data

Dümling, Albrecht.
  The vanished musicians : Jewish refugees in Australia / Albrecht Dümling.
     pages cm. -- (Exile studies ; 14)
  Includes bibliographical references and index.
  ISBN 978-3-03-431951-5 (alk. paper)
  1. Jews--Australia--Music--History and criticism. 2. Jewish musicians--Australia.
  3. Jewish refugees--Australia. I. Title.
  ML3776.D86 2015
  780.89'924094--dc23
                                  2015036088

Note: English translation of *Die verschwundenen Musiker. Jüdische Flüchtlinge in
Australien*, Cologne: Böhlau, 2011. Translated by Diana K. Weekes.

Cover image: Weintraubs Syncopators © Atelier Lili Baruch, Berlin (Evelyn
Klopfer, Sydney).

Second revised printing

ISSN 1072-0626
ISBN 978-3-0343-1951-5 (print) • ISBN 978-3-0343-9588-4 (ePub)
ISBN 978-3-0353-0816-7 (ePDF) • ISBN 978-3-0343-9587-7 (Mobi)

© Peter Lang AG, European Academic Publishers, Bern 2016, 2016(r)
Hochfeldstrasse 32, CH-3012 Bern, Switzerland
info@peterlang.com, www.peterlang.com, www.peterlang.net

All rights reserved.
All parts of this publication are protected by copyright.
Any utilisation outside the strict limits of the copyright law, without
the permission of the publisher, is forbidden and liable to prosecution.
This applies in particular to reproductions, translations, microfilming,
and storage and processing in electronic retrieval systems.

This publication has been peer reviewed.

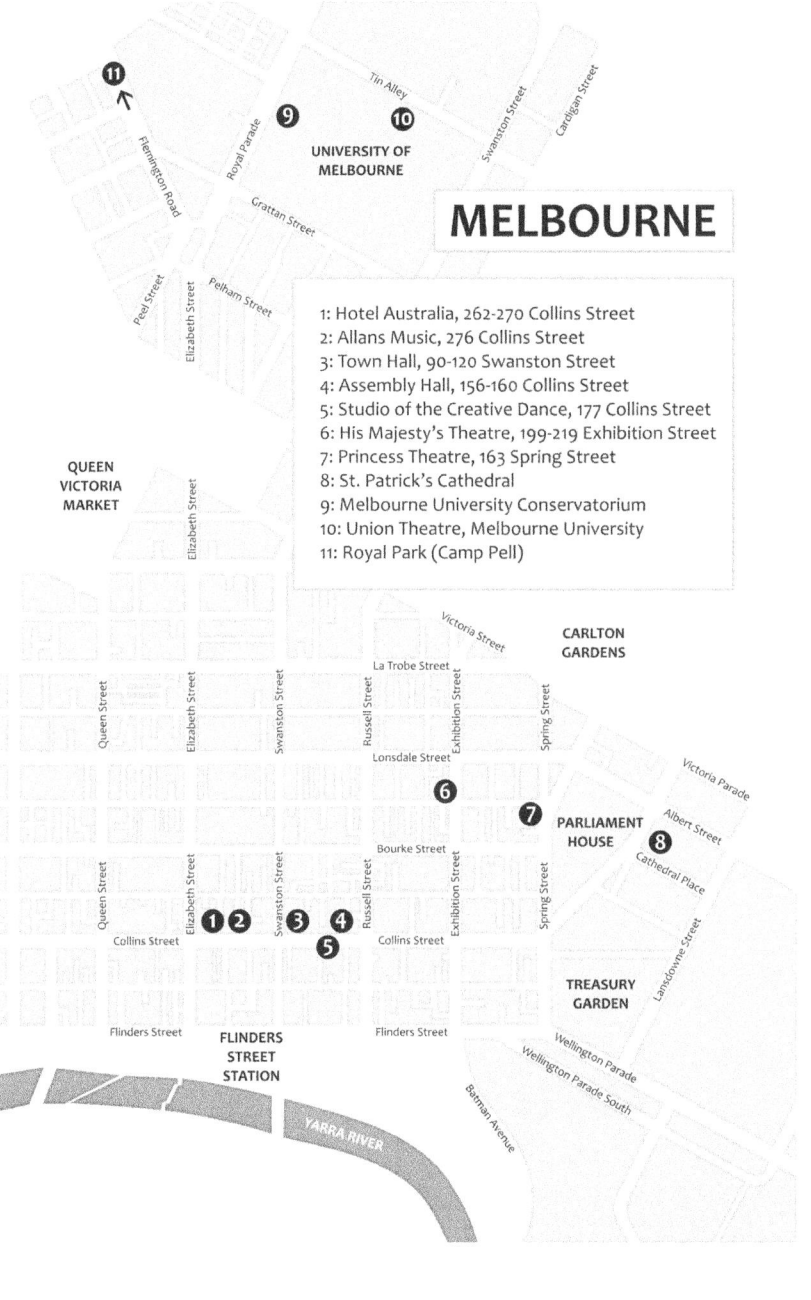

SYDNEY

- PORT JACKSON (SYDNEY HARBOUR)
- HARBOUR BRIDGE
- BENNELONG POINT
- JONES BAY
- PYRMONT BAY
- SYDNEY COVE
- SYDNEY OPERA HOUSE
- Pirrama Road
- DARLING HARBOUR
- Bridge Street
- Conservatorium Street
- George Street
- Pitt Street
- Phillip Street
- Macquarie Street
- ROYAL BOTANIC GARDEN
- Martin Place
- Elizabeth St.
- Phillip Street
- King Street
- George Street
- HYDE PARK
- THE DOMAIN
- Pitt Street
- Castlereagh Street
- Elizabeth Street
- William Street
- DARLING HARBOUR
- Liverpool St.
- George Street
- Liverpool Street
- Oxford Street

1: Dunera Museum, Jones Bay Wharf, 28-32 Pirrama Road, Pyrmont
2: Prince's Restaurant, 42-46 Martin Place (MLC Building)
3: Nicholson's Musical Centre, 416 George Street
4: Sydney Town Hall, 483 George Street
5: Music Palings, 338 George Street
6: The Music Lounge (Klopfer), 563 George Street
7: The Great Synagogue, 166 Castlereagh Street
8: St James' Hall, 171 Phillip Street (Mercury Theatre)
9: Sydney Conservatorium of Music, 1 Conservatorium Street
10: 10a Challis Avenue, Potts Point (Stefan Weintraub)
11: 35 Selsdon Flats, 16 Macleay Street, Potts Point (Emanuel and Addy Fisher)
12: 141 Brougham St., Kings Cross (Marcel Lorber)
13: 35 Darlinghurst Road, Kings Cross (Ernst Norbert Kaufmann)
14: 51 Roslyn Gardens, Potts Point (Sydney John Kay)
15: Maccabean Hall, 148 Darlinghurst Road (now Sydney Jewish Museum)
16: 479 New South Head Road, Double Bay (Walter Dullo)
17: 10 William St., Double Bay (Kurt Herweg)
18: 7 Windsor House, Stafford St., Double Bay (Theodor Schoenberger)
19: Temple Emanuel, 5 Ocean Street, Woollahra

Contents

List of Figures	xvii
Acknowledgements	xxiii
List of Abbreviations	xxvii

CHAPTER 1
Australia: So Far, and Yet so Near	1

CHAPTER 2
'Oh sacred Art': On the Status of Music	9
The Jewish Bourgeoisie and the Music Profession	9
More German than the Germans: Jews in Berlin	14
Women in the Music Profession	19
Acculturation through Music	20
The Blue Danube: Jews in Vienna	23
Women Musicians	26
Vocation or Hobby?	27
'In the Prater, Trees are Blooming again': The Leopoldstadt District	28

CHAPTER 3
Failed Integration: Getting out of Germany, 1933–1937	31
The 'Cleansing' of Musical Life	31
Jazz: Object of Hate	39
Race and Religion	42
'Flying like foam ...': From Kulturbund Deutscher Juden to Jüdischer Kulturbund	46
Early Escape	51

CHAPTER 4
On the Other Side of the World 53
Spirit of Adventure? Off to Australia as Musicians 53
Celebrities on Tour: Jascha and Tossy Spivakovsky 60
No Opportunities in Germany, even as a 'Half Jew' 63
Refuge Britain 72
Arrival with the Royal Grand Opera Company 75

CHAPTER 5
Mixed Feelings: Australian Reactions to German Racial Politics 81

CHAPTER 6
'Muss i denn, muss i denn zum Städtele hinaus?': Persecution and Flight 89
Berlin 1938 89
The Ghettoisation of Musicians 90
'My nature is not to join in hate but to join in love' 93
'An infinitely tougher regime': Vienna after the Anschluss 95
Political Refugees 106
'Musicians Unsuitable': Immigration Policy in
Britain and Australia 108
'There's a ship, the black freighter': Ways of Escape, 1938 111
Direct Travellers to Australia 111
Via Britain 115
Via France 118
Via Luxembourg 121
Further Detours (India, Singapore) 122

CHAPTER 7
After Kristallnacht 129
Detour via Sachsenhausen 129
Bach Fugues and the Volga Boat Song: Organist in Singapore 134
'Protective Custody' in Dachau 137
Ultimate Destination Australia 143

Transit via Britain	143
Urgently Sought: Guarantors for Australia	148
'Larino, safe haven': The Kindertransports	154
'Where everybody goes': New Attractions in Singapore	156
'Song of the Moldau': Escape from Prague and Budapest	159

CHAPTER 8

The Refugee Problem from an Australian Perspective — 165

Thorold Waters and the *Australian Musical News*	165
'I'm absolutely plagued by refugees': Bernard Heinze and the ABC	167
'The fickle nature of the Australian musical public': Handling the Immigrants	170
Final Negotiations: Official Immigration Policy	176
'You will be all right': Arrival in Australia	183

CHAPTER 9

Under Union Scrutiny: The Weintraubs Syncopators — 191

The Fight for Jobs	191
'Somewhere in the World': Jazz Stars on Tour	196
From Concert Tour to Immigration	200
'My Melancholy Baby': Prince's Restaurant	206
Waiting for Residence Permits	211

CHAPTER 10

'Down with the fifth column!': Britain during the War — 217

'Collar the lot!' The Internment of 'Enemy Aliens'	219
'My luggage went into the ocean': The *Arandora Star* and *Dunera*	222

CHAPTER 11

Interned and Defamed in Australia — 227

The Hour of Denunciation	227
Ousted by Competitors: The Fate of the Weintraubs	235

CHAPTER 12

'In corrugated iron huts': Deported to Hay and Tatura

'I came here a stranger': Arrival at the Camp	253
'Hay Days': Music behind Barbed Wire	255
'It is hope that keeps us going': Meeting Place Tatura	269
New Perspectives	282

CHAPTER 13

Snow White in Uniform: The Music Revue *Sergeant Snow White*

'A funny looking crowd': The Eighth Australian Employment Company	283
'Some Day My Prince Will Come': Walt Disney's Snow White Film	289
Jew-ropeans in Australia: The Revue Text	293
Blue Danube, Brown Spree: Viennese Melodies instead of German Music	300
'Sounds of Europe'	303

CHAPTER 14

The Year 1945: Lost and Found

	307
Remigration or Naturalisation?	307
'Deported to Poland': Bad News from Europe	310
Stages of Integration	314
Ironing or Music? Deciding on a Vocation	317

CHAPTER 15

'The cultivated enthusiasm of a handful of missionaries': The Genesis of Musica Viva Australia

	325
Richard Goldner's Sydney Musica Viva	330
The Rebirth	339

CHAPTER 16

Between Adjustment and Self-Assertion: Refugee Contributions to Australian Musical Life

	345
Conductors	345

Orchestral Musicians	357
Choirs	361
Soloists	363
Opera	374
Synagogues	379
Ballet and Dance Theatre	384
Popular Music	387
Music Education	391
Music Critics	393

CHAPTER 17

'Land of Mine': New Compositions for a New Australia	401
'The Back of Beyond': Film Music Pioneers	402
'Vereinsamt' ['Loneliness']: Composing in Secret	405
'Dear land we love': New Beginnings	411
Moses Mendelssohn's Legacy: Felix Werder	414
The Art of Adaptation: George Dreyfus	417
Two Diametrically Opposed Concepts of Music	423

CHAPTER 18

'Happily ever after': Hidden Contributions to Cultural Diversity	429
Notes	439
Short Biographies	483
Ship Arrivals	533
Sources and Bibliography	537
Glossary	557
Index	559
About the Translator	572

Figures

Figure 1:	Portrait of Walter Andreas Dullo, Berlin 1932. (Author's Archive)	32
Figure 2:	The Weintraubs Syncopators around 1930, photographed by Lili Baruch, Berlin. (Evelyn Klopfer, Sydney)	41
Figure 3:	The Spivakovsky-Kurtz Trio with Tossy Spivakovsky, violin, Jascha Spivakowsky, piano, and Edmund Kurtz, violoncello. (Michael Spivakovsky, Melbourne)	61
Figure 4:	Last entries from the diary written by Walter Andreas Dullo's mother for her son and his young wife Annemarie, before their departure to Australia. (Author's Archive)	70
Figure 5:	'Personal Statement and Declaration' of Walter Dullo, completed on 11 September 1937. (NAA: A12508, 21/963)	71
Figure 6:	The Reichsmusikkammer refuses Werner Baer's application for membership. (Bundesarchiv, former BDC, RK R 1, Picture 2754)	91
Figure 7:	Questionnaire of the Emigration Department of the Welfare Centre of the Viennese Kultusgemeinde, completed by Kapellmeister and pianist Adolf Brenner on 20 May 1938. (CAHJP, A/W 2590, 28)	103
Figure 8:	Questionnaire of the Emigration Department of the Welfare Centre of the Viennese Kultusgemeinde for Richard Goldner. (CAHJP, A/W 2590, 74)	105

Figure 9:	German Passport of Alphons Silbermann, issued on 23 May 1938 at the German General Consulate Amsterdam. (NAA: A435, 1947/4/4169)	118
Figure 10:	German Passport of Werner Baer, issued in Berlin on 29 November 1938. (NAA: A435, 1945/4/1221)	131
Figure 11:	'Personal Statement and Declaration' for the violinist Ellen Byk-Cohn. (NAA: A12508, 21/741)	153
Figure 12:	Programme for a Celebrity Concert of the Melbourne Symphony Orchestra on 23 May 1936 at the Melbourne Town Hall. (Michael Spivakovsky, Melbourne)	172
Figure 13:	On 17 April 1940, as Business Manager of the 'Winetraubs Comedy Melodians' Horst Graff applied for permission to travel to Canberra for a charity concert. (NAA: C123, 1213)	237
Figure 14:	From the Peruvian Passport of John Kurt Kaiser, issued on 28 March 1934 in Zurich. (NAA: A435, 1946/4/1792)	244
Figure 15:	Handwritten programme for a concert with light classical tunes on 12 December 1940 at the Hay internment camp. (Tanya Makin, Melbourne)	259
Figure 16:	Handwritten programme for Christmas concerts of the Stadlen Choir on 25 and 26 December 1940 at the Hay internment camp. (Felix Edelmann, Vienna)	264
Figure 17:	Invitation to the programme *Tatura Melody 1940*, presented by Hans Blau on 3 November 1940. (Ilse Blair, Melbourne)	272
Figure 18:	The concert pianist Peter Stadlen applied for registration in Tatura on 16 September 1941. (NAA: B6531, AUSTRIAN/STADLEN PETER)	279
Figure 19:	Like many other refugees the conductor Henry Krips joined the Australian army. (NAA: B884, N319603)	284

Figures

Figure 20:	Programme for the Christmas Concert on 26 December 1943 at the Masonic Hall in Tocumwal (Victoria). (Felix Edelmann, Vienna)	288
Figure 21:	All members of the 'Viennese Orchestra' that played in July 1945 in the small town of Albury belonged to the 8th Australian Employment Company. (Charles Reither, Jr, Melbourne)	289
Figure 22:	For the programme of the revue Erwin Fabian depicted Snow White as a combination of man and woman, soldier and dancer. (Ilse Blair, Melbourne)	295
Figure 23:	Invitation to the 'Sergeant Snowwhite' revue with a woodcarving by Erwin Fabian. (Ilse Blair, Melbourne)	296
Figure 24:	Men and 'women', led by Hans Blau as Maurice Chevalier, join for the Can-Can. (Ilse Blair, Melbourne)	300
Figure 25:	Günter Hirschberg was forced by National Security Regulations to register in September 1941. (NAA: ST1233/1, N32842)	309
Figure 26:	The Kapellmeister, pianist and arranger Hans Bader. (Lisa Vinnic, Melbourne)	314
Figure 27:	Application Form for Membership for the Musicians' Union of Australia, completed by John K. Kay on 16 March 1944. (Noel Butlin Archives Centre, Australian National University: Musicians' Union of Australia, E156-2-3)	319
Figure 28:	Certificate of Naturalization for Majer Pietruschka. (Tanya Makin, Melbourne)	322
Figure 29:	The conductor Kurt Herweg prepares a recording for the animated cartoon 'Christmas Bells'. (NAA: SP1426/4, 1)	350

Figure 30:	The conductor Hermann Schildberger with his Camberwell Philharmonic Society. In uniform, the tenor soloist Hans Edelmann. (Felix Edelmann, Vienna)	352
Figure 31:	The conductor Henry Krips with his family on the cover of the *Australian Musical News*, 1950. (Author's Archive)	354
Figure 32:	The violinist Charles Reither, here with his saxophone. (Charles Reither, Jr, Melbourne)	361
Figure 33:	Programme for a concert for the military on 1 December 1944. (Michael Spivakovsky, Melbourne)	364
Figure 34:	Jascha Spivakovsky with his powerful hands at the concert grand. (Michael Spivakovsky, Melbourne)	366
Figure 35:	The pianist Robert Kolben, publicity picture for the ABC. (NAA, SP1011/1, 2810)	369
Figure 36:	The cellist Otti Veit. (Kurt R. Eisner, Melbourne)	371
Figure 37:	The singer Lily Kolos, photographed by Margaret Michaelis. (Karla Sperling, Sydney)	373
Figure 38:	A versatile radio-man: Werner Baer composing in his office. (NAA: SP1011/1, 952)	413
Figure 39:	The composer George Dreyfus in October 2009 with the author in Berlin. (Author's Archive)	422
Figure 40:	The composer Felix Werder in 2008 in his apartment in Camberwell/Melbourne. (Author's Archive)	428
Figure 41:	Sydney John Kay around 1960 with his tape-recorder in London. (Anthony Kay, Sydney)	435
Figure 42:	The second generation of the Weintraubs Syncopators: Tony Kay, son of Sydney John Kay, and Michael Fisher, son of Manny Fisher, in December 2007 on the occasion of the Weintraubs Revue in Berlin. (Author's Archive)	437

Figures xxi

Musical Examples

Example 1:	J.S. Bach, *Largo* from Concerto in D minor, for 2 violins and orchestra, BWV 1043 (Helmut Kickton)	226
Example 2:	Ray Martin, *Hay Days* (Lippmann Archives, Sydney)	257
Example 3:	Werner Baer/Hans Blau, 'The Ballad of the "Un"-forgotten Israelites' (Author's Archive)	275
Example 4:	George Dreyfus, *Theme from Rush*	405
Example 5:	Boas Bischofswerder, *Phantasia Judaica*. Bars 9–11 (Archive of Australian Judaica Sydney)	407
Example 6:	George Dreyfus, Symphony No. 1 (Allans Music Melbourne)	419
Example 7:	George Dreyfus, *Sextet for Didjeridu and Wind Quintet* (Dobson 1978, p. 132)	421
Example 8:	Felix Werder, *Banker – A Music-Theatre* (Author's Archive)	425

Acknowledgements

This book could not have appeared without the generous help of a great number of people who contributed in many different ways. I should like to thank Mary-Clare Adam-Murwitz, Tel Aviv; Elizabeth Allum, Sydney; Shirley Apthorp, Berlin; Henri Aram, Sydney; Suzanne Baker, Sydney; Sybil Baer (*d.*), Sydney; Anthony Berg, Sydney; Ilse Blair, Melbourne; Fred Blanks (*d.*), Sydney; Bern Brent, Canberra; John Burgan, Berlin; John Carmody, Sydney; Heinrich Blömeke, Singapore; Nicholas Chlumecky (*d.*), USA; Isabella, Eva and Fiona Colin, Melbourne; Kurt Collinet, Cologne; Carolyn Connor, National Archives Canberra; Susan Course, Melbourne; Roger Covell, Sydney; Ronald Cragg, Sydney; Marianne Dacy, Archive of Australian Judaica, Sydney; George Dreyfus, Melbourne; Kay Dreyfus, Melbourne; Catherine Duncan-Copillet (*d.*), Paris; Eric Eckstein (*d.*), Melbourne; Felix Edelmann, Vienna; Susie Ehrmann, Melbourne; Kurt R. Eisner, Melbourne; Andy Factor, Melbourne; June Factor, Melbourne; Susan Faine, Jewish Museum Melbourne; Denis Farrington, Melbourne; Sophie Fetthauer, Hamburg; Kurt Fichman, Melbourne; Addy and Emanuel Fisher (*d.*), Sydney; Michael Fisher, Zurich; Louis Fouvy and Jeanette McArthur, Kew Philharmonic Society; Erwin (*d.*) and Ellen Frenkel, Melbourne; Charmian Gadd, Sydney; Susanne Gabor (*d.*), Melbourne; Peter Goldner, Sydney; Brigitte Goldstein, Albuquerque, New Mexico; Dorothy Graff, Melbourne; Eric Gross (*d.*), Sydney; Primavera Gruber, Orpheus Trust, Vienna; Werner Grünzweig, Academy of Arts, Berlin; Hans-Heinrich Gurland (*d.*), Hildesheim; Sandra Hacker, Melbourne; Werner Hanak, Jewish Museum Vienna; Ellen Harnisch, Kassenärztliche Vereinigung Berlin; Eddy Helfgott, Sydney; Lynne Heller, University of Music and Performing Arts, Vienna; Robyn Holmes, National Library of Australia; Anthony Kay, Sydney; Bernard Keeffe, London; Julie Kerner (*d.*), Sydney; Evelyn Klopfer, Sydney; Arthur and Lurline Knee, Tatura; Robert Kolben (*d.*), Munich; Michael Karbaum, GEMA, Munich; Manuel Krönung, Heidelberg; Gerald Krug, Sydney; Sylvia Krutsch, Melbourne; Rudi Laqueur (*d.*), Melbourne;

Klaus (*d.*) and Uyen Loewald, Canberra; Andrew McCredie (*d.*), Adelaide–Melbourne; Tanya Makin, Melbourne; Celia Male, London; Marlene Norst (*d.*), Sydney; Klaus Neumann, Melbourne; Rosemary Pattenden, Cambridge; David Pear, Brisbane–Canberra–London; Jutta Raab Hansen, Hamburg; Leonard and Therese Radic, Melbourne; Uwe Radok (*d.*), Coffs Harbour, Australia; Charles and Derrick Reither, Melbourne; Harry Rich, Sydney; Karl Rössel, Cologne; Leo Rosner, Melbourne; Leo Roth (*d.*), Berlin; Suzanne Rutland, Sydney; Dietmar Schenk, Berlin University of the Arts; Michael Schildberger (*d.*), Melbourne; Rainer Schildberger, Berlin; Robert Schindel, Vienna; Annie Schlebaum, Sydney; Wilhelmina Schoenzeler, London; Beate Schröder-Nauenburg (*d.*), Dresden; Benjamin Segaloff, Melbourne; Mike Sondheim (*d.*), Melbourne; Karla and Tamara Sperling, Sydney; Michael Spivakovsky, Melbourne; Joseph Toltz, Sydney; Peter Tregear, Melbourne; Walter Veit, Melbourne; Lisa Vinnic, Melbourne; Ruth Voorhis, Canada; Eva Wagner (*d.*), Sydney; Harry Weiss, Sydney; Heidrun Weiss, Vienna Israelite Community; Felix Werder (*d.*), Melbourne; Frank Werther, Cottles Bridge, Australia; Klaus Wilczynski, Berlin; Hannah and Madeleine Wurzburger, London; Kenneth R. Ward, Britain; and Ivor Zetler, Sydney.

I am especially grateful to Wolfgang Benz, former Director of the Center for Research on Antisemitism of the Technical University of Berlin, who was the driving force behind a multi-year project of the Deutsche Forschungsgemeinschaft on German-speaking musical exiles in Australia. A Harold White Fellowship of the National Library of Australia enabled me to work in Canberra for four months. From the start, George Dreyfus accompanied the project with a keen interest and tireless support. Last but not least, I express my thanks to the Alfred Toepfer Foundation, Hamburg, whose award of the KAIROS Prize and a grant for the printing costs made it possible to complete this book.

When I presented the original German edition in several Australian cities in November 2011, many people expressed the wish for an English translation. Barry Humphries wrote: 'Is there any chance that this book will be translated into English? It should be.' Diana Weekes, a former senior lecturer in keyboard at the University of Adelaide, who personally knew many of the musicians portrayed in the book, took the initiative

Acknowledgements

and started translating in late 2011, completing the work in 2015. For her commitment and accommodation I thank her very sincerely. To Franziska Meyer (University of Nottingham) I owe a special debt of gratitude for her exceptional diligence in preparing the English edition. I am grateful to John Richardson for his judicious language editing. Sally Phillips' contribution was crucial at a late stage, and Karen Adler made helpful suggestions throughout. I also thank the publishers, in particular Laurel Plapp, for the excellent collaboration.

This book is an abbreviated and amended version of the German edition. I wish to express my gratitude to Michael Fisher, Zurich; Dieter Rosenkranz, Berlin; and Eva Rieger, Vaduz, for their significant contribution to the realisation of this edition and especially to the Henkell Family Fund (Hans Henkell, Melbourne) and the Council of Christians and Jews, Victoria (Albert Isaacs, Melbourne) for their generous financial support.

Abbreviations

ABC	Australian Broadcasting Commission
AJH	*Australian Jewish Herald*
AM	Order of Australia
AJR	*Australian Music Maker and Dance Band News*
AMN	*Australian Musical News*
BDC	Berlin Document Center
CAHJP	The Central Archives for the History of the Jewish People, Jerusalem
CIB	Commonwealth Investigation Branch
DÖW	Dokumentationsarchiv des österreichischen Widerstands [Documentation Centre of Austrian Resistance], Vienna
GDR	German Democratic Republic
ISCM	International Society for Contemporary Music
JR	*Jüdische Rundschau*
KCR	*The Kitchener Camp Review*
LexM	Online-Lexikon verfolgter Musiker und Musikerinnen der NS-Zeit [Lexicon of Nazi-persecuted musicians], Universität Hamburg
MPI	Military Police Investigation
MSO	Melbourne Symphony Orchestra
NAA	National Archives of Australia
NSW	New South Wales
NWT	*Neues Wiener Tagblatt*
OBE	Order of the British Empire
RM	Reichsmark
RMK	Reichsmusikkammer
TNA	The National Archives, Kew
SMH	*Sydney Morning Herald*
SSO	Sydney Symphony Orchestra

ST   *The Straits Times* (Singapore)
VSO   Victorian Symphony Orchestra
ZA   Zentrum für Antisemitismusforschung der Technischen Universität Berlin [Center for Research on Antisemitism, Technical University Berlin]

CHAPTER 1

Australia: So Far, and Yet so Near

For a long time, Australia was for me just a distant continent on the other side of the globe; the exotic homeland of Antipodeans as well as koalas, emus and kangaroos. But all that changed when, in April 1992, the telephone rang in Berlin and a powerful voice roared through the receiver: 'This is George Dreyfus, a composer from Australia!' He was in the city, had read my book on Brecht and music with interest, and now wanted to talk to me about it. Good heavens, I thought, they even know my book in Australia! Surprisingly, when we met the next day near the Philharmonie, it turned out that, apart from our similar musical and literary interests, we had something else in common: George Dreyfus also came from Wuppertal. Born in 1928, he had moved to Berlin before a Kindertransport took him to Australia, thereby saving him from Nazi persecution. I heard at first-hand the story of his flight and integration into a foreign culture. A little later, the Melbourne composer sent me his autobiography, which gave me a better picture. There I learnt not only about the discrimination against his family under the Nazis, but also about his difficult start in a new environment.

He explained how hard it had been for his father to accept Australia as his new homeland: at his age, he had been too deeply rooted in German culture to readjust. An enthusiastic Wagnerian, his close connection to the fatherland was typical of many German Jews, including the former Minister for Foreign Affairs, Walter Rathenau, to whom George Dreyfus had just dedicated an opera. Whereas up to now the composer's music theatre had met with little response in Australia, a company in Germany was interested in staging his new work. It goes without saying that I attended the premiere in Kassel in June 1993. The first Australian opera to be launched in Europe, *Rathenau* caused a sensation. After this performance, I found the composer's wittily written biography even more gripping. In order to introduce more friends to the life and work of George Dreyfus, our society, *musica reanimata*, arranged a lecture-recital by the German-Australian in the Konzerthaus on the Gendarmenmarkt in Berlin in November 1993. This was probably the very first event in Germany to focus on the distant 'Down Under' as a place of refuge for German-speaking musicians. Thus, chance presented me with a topic which, until then, had hardly been explored.

For Jewish musicians who fled from Germany after 1933, Australia was no dream destination: many of them just landed or were stranded there. Dreyfus mentioned his composer colleague Felix Werder, a born Berliner who also lived in Melbourne. Encouraged by the German scholar Walter Veit at Monash University, I raised the topic with the Deutsche Forschungsgemeinschaft (DFG) [German Research Foundation] and the suggestion fell on fertile ground. In the European summer of 1995, with the support of the DFG and the musicologist Andrew McCredie, I was able to undertake a lecture tour on 'Brecht and Music', as well as on the musical politics of the Nazi regime, at the Universities of Adelaide, Melbourne, Canberra, Sydney, Brisbane and Townsville. In the Barossa Valley near Adelaide, I found traces of Prussian Lutherans who had settled in this fertile region as early as 1838. In Canberra I came across the historian Klaus Loewald, who fled from Hitler to Britain and was deported from there to Australia in 1940 on the ship *Dunera*. Over lunch in the modern High Court building, overlooking the artificial Lake Burley Griffin, he told me of the terrible voyage followed by his internment in the desert camp at Hay. Here, in spite of the heat and sandstorms, the imprisoned men had made music and even given concerts of a very high standard. He had been particularly impressed by the pianist Peter Stadlen. This name stopped me in my tracks, because in 1988 I had met Stadlen in Vienna, where he was lecturing about exiled musicians from Austria; at the time, he had only briefly mentioned his own fate.[1] A chapter of music history that had been forgotten both in Germany and Australia was opening up.

After my return, I reported my discoveries and meetings in various newspaper and journal articles. My perspective changed: instead of shaking their heads over this exotic subject, it suddenly seemed as though almost the whole world was thinking about Australia. I met Jörg Süßenbach, who was preparing a film about the Weintraubs Syncopators.[2] This Berlin jazz band had been just as famous in the 1920s as their singing colleagues, the

CHAPTER 1: *So Far, and Yet so Near*

Comedy Harmonists; in the 1930 cult film *The Blue Angel*, they accompanied Marlene Dietrich in songs like 'Falling in Love Again'. As a result of the Nazi racial persecution, these musicians had to leave Germany. In 1937, they landed in Australia, where they were suspected of being spies and defamed. Internment followed, and finally the sad end of the band.

The Berlin Philharmonic was also interested in Australia, as several of their musicians had strong ties with this continent.[3] In September 1995, the Sydney Symphony Orchestra (SSO) performed in Berlin. I kept discovering Australians living in Germany's capital, for example the critic and colleague Shirley Apthorp, who lived just a few streets away from me. In October 1995, the composer Felix Werder, whom I had visited shortly before in his small house in the Melbourne suburb of Hawthorn, came to visit his home city. Professor McCredie, too, travelled to Berlin. Our discussions gave rise to the idea of organising an Australia conference in Germany. I also invited Klaus Loewald, who accepted immediately because, at the same time as he received my invitation, he learnt of Peter Stadlen's death in London.

The conference on the theme 'Exiled Musicians in Australia' took place in May 1996 in the Dresden Centre for Contemporary Music. George Dreyfus was also in Germany, as his new opera *Marx Sisters* had premiered in Bielefeld the previous month. The Australian experts Andrew McCredie, Wolfgang Benz, Johannes H. Voigt and Gerhard Stilz took the tram from Dresden's main station to the exclusive suburb that subsequently became the subject matter of Uwe Tellkamp's novel, *Der Turm* (2008) [*The Tower*]. This smart residential area where the conference was to take place had nothing to do with Australia, or at least so I thought – until we got out of the tram at the Mordgrundbrücke station. This rang a bell, for I had just been reading about the opera *Mordgrundbruck* by the Australian immigrant Carl Püttmann.[4] Were there secret ties between Dresden and the Antipodes? The music sociologist Alphons Silbermann spoke critically at the conference about the years he had spent as a refugee in Australia. Felix Werder also expressed scepticism about the musical culture in his new country. On the other hand, Klaus Loewald's lecture, dedicated to Peter Stadlen, was much more positive. In two concerts, we were also able to experience the very different styles of the German-Australian composers George Dreyfus and Felix Werder.

This Dresden conference became the nucleus of a research project that began in 2000 at the Center for Research on Antisemitism. In July and August of that year, the project took me to Australia, where the Olympics were underway. But I was more interested in the past than in the enthusiastic sporting present; for example, in the fate of the German-Russian pianist Jascha Spivakovsky who, once a star, had fled to Australia and been forgotten. His son still lives in the huge mansion high above the Yarra River in the prestigious Melbourne suburb of Toorak, its enormous music room housing the concert grands that Spivakovsky brought from Germany. In a little house in St Kilda I visited Ilse Blair, a lively old lady who spoke in fluent German of her two former husbands, Werner Baer and Hans Blau, two very different musicians. She showed me concert programmes and newspaper cuttings with the names of other refugee musicians. In his study, Rabbi John Levi talked about the old vinyl records of Jewish music that Hermann Schildberger, a former organist at his synagogue, had brought from Berlin to Melbourne. Needless to say, I also visited George Dreyfus and Felix Werder again. In the beach paradise of Noosa in Queensland, I met Brett Dean, who had given up a permanent position as a violist with the Berlin Philharmonic to work as a composer in his homeland. In a hotel near Sydney Harbour Bridge, the conductor Markus Stenz told me of his plans for the Melbourne Symphony Orchestra (MSO). Shortly before my return home, a gala concert was given at Government House in Sydney (not far from the famous Opera House) by Musica Viva, that great chamber music organisation founded by German-speaking refugees in 1945. My research topic was gradually taking shape.

Australia used the interest generated by the Olympics to strengthen its own economic and tourism ties with Europe. In January 2001, to mark the Centenary of Federation in Australia, the German President, Johannes Rau, spoke of the close partnership and friendship between Germany and Australia. In February 2001, the Potsdam Australia Centre – founded in 1995 as a joint initiative of the Australian Prime Minister Paul Keating and the Brandenburg Prime Minister Manfred Stolpe – held a symposium, 'Movements and Harmonies: Musical Bridges between Australia and Germany'. The speakers included the Australian conductor Simone Young, who at that time was working regularly with Daniel Barenboim at the Berlin State Opera. At this event, I presented the recently published proceedings of the Dresden conference.[5]

As more and more gaps were filled, the picture became more detailed and colourful. When I travelled to Australia again in March 2003, the Berlin emigrant violinist 'Max' Pietruschka's daughter took me by car to the little town of Tatura, north of Melbourne, where many refugees were interned during the war; today it houses a lovingly created museum. Loewald had already referred me to the National Archives in Canberra, which proved to be an inexhaustible source. Here I examined immigration and military documents, and discovered references to the accusations of espionage that were brought against the Weintraubs Syncopators. Research on the vanished musicians was not easy, however, because on their arrival they often took up other occupations. To avoid rejection, they concealed their true identities. There were doubles with the same name, or people changed their names, which further covered their tracks. Often I had to follow several false leads before I found one of 'my' musicians.

My archival research was supplemented by personal meetings and discussions, during which new names would emerge that were not entered in any register. In Sydney, the ever helpful Sybil Baer gave a vivid description of her husband Werner Baer, a passionate musician to the last, who switched effortlessly between classical and light music. Julie Kerner, still lively at the age of ninety-three, remembered her mother, the Viennese singer Leonie Feigl. The physician Harry Rich, also from Vienna, talked about his piano teacher, Marcel Lorber, whose studio was barely heated even in winter, while Fred Blanks, who fled to Australia as Friedrich Mayer, described his development as a music critic.

By chance I came across a pianist called Robert Kolben. Could this be the musician from Munich who had so passionately championed the compositions of Viktor Ullmann, murdered in Auschwitz? After my return to Germany, I phoned Kolben and discovered that they were the same person: in his youth he had indeed lived in Australia. In a comprehensive interview, he told me all about this time. Similarly, by chance I came across the Jewish cantor Leo Roth, who had also come to Australia as a refugee. I have the Berlin physician Peter Hauber to thank for my introduction to Mary-Clare Adam, who lives in Israel and whose Australian mother, the pianist Mary Baillie, supported German Jewish refugees.

In 2004, a fellowship from the National Library of Australia enabled me to spend several months on this distant continent. A room was reserved for me in one of the residential colleges attached to the Australian National University in Canberra, but then Klaus Loewald wrote to me saying that there was room in his house. I accepted this generous offer and went to stay with him and his Vietnamese wife, Uyen, whom he had told me about in Dresden. After his internment in Australia and his subsequent military service, Loewald had joined his parents in the USA and studied political science at Berkeley. In response to the Nazi persecution of the Jews, he wanted to contribute to international relations as a diplomat. He also studied for several semesters in his home city, Berlin, where he simultaneously worked as a translator for Willy Brandt. His first posting was at the American Embassy in Saigon during the Vietnam War, which put him in a difficult situation. Through his wife-to-be, he had made contact with the Vietnamese resistance and therefore had to leave his position. He married Uyen, re-entered the diplomatic service, left it again on account of political differences, and finally came to Australia to take up a chair in American History.

Throughout all this, Loewald never lost his ties to his German roots. They named their daughter Pamina on account of his love for Mozart's *The Magic Flute*, and Thomas Mann influenced the choice of name for their son, Tonio. I was allowed to live in Tonio's former room in Canberra. I would arrive back there in the evening after my work in the National Library or the National Archives. When we spoke in German about Beethoven or Hermann Hesse, with the air-conditioning humming in the background, Klaus Loewald was happy. On the walls hung Vietnamese wood carvings and pictures of the West Prussian city of Danzig, whence the Loewalds had moved to Berlin. As a farewell gift, Klaus provided me with a valuable bequest: a set of diaries bound in light brown leather, in which his friend Walter Dullo's mother had described her son's early years in Berlin. It was a present rich in associations: during my research on Dullo nine years earlier, I had first come across Klaus Loewald. This wise and warm-hearted man was already ill in 2004. He died a few months after my return to Germany.

It was during my stay in Canberra that plans emerged for this book, and for further archival research in Berlin, Vienna and London.[6] Here I came across the names of more musicians whose fate it was to end up in Australia. On the whole they were not prominent artists like Jascha

Spivakovsky or the Weintraubs Syncopators, but lesser-known people who were not granted the opportunity to flee to the USA. In other words, they were the norm, what Wolfgang Benz called the 'exile of the ordinary people'.[7] In researching the *Snow White* revue, performed in 1943 by Melbourne's Jewish refugees, I stumbled across the name of the reviewer: Catherine Duncan. I remembered having run across a woman with this name years ago at a lecture in Nijmegen, the Netherlands and, through enquiries at the Joris Ivens Foundation, obtained her Paris address. In subsequent correspondence, the then ninety-year-old confirmed that, as a young Australian actress and author, she had been greatly impressed by this German Jewish revue. It was very different from Australian theatre productions both in tempo and its specific brand of humour.

The final incentive for the completion of this book was the award of the European Cultural Prize KAIROS from the Alfred Toepfer Foundation at the beginning of 2007. In my acceptance speech in the Hamburg Playhouse, I talked about Walter Dullo and the vision of German culture that he brought to Australia, one which led him – together with Richard Goldner – to found Musica Viva Australia, today the world's largest chamber music organisation. Like many refugee artists, Dullo (who was born in Königsberg, East Prussia) regarded German not only as the language of a nation, but as a common medium for many different peoples, the language of the Enlightenment and its universal ideals, the language of Kant, Lessing and Moses Mendelssohn. For him, it was closely related to the sound world of Mozart and Beethoven. During my meetings with these survivors, I was mortified to note that some of them cherished such ideals more highly than do most Germans. This was yet another reason to pursue these vanishing traces. The work had to be done while witnesses were still alive. The history of the refugee musicians in Australia consists of many individual memories that have never been presented as a coherent record, fragments of a mosaic that has never been pieced together. They are documents of failure as well as of astounding endurance, all of them belonging to the collective memory of humankind.

CHAPTER 2

'Oh sacred Art': On the Status of Music

> Oh sacred Art, how oft in hours blighted,
> While into life's untamed cycle hurled,
> Hast thou my heart to warm love reignited
> To transport me into a better world!
>
> — FRANZ VON SCHOBER[1]

The Jewish Bourgeoisie and the Music Profession

The musicians who escaped Hitler's Germany and found refuge in Australia were mostly from Jewish families. The Nazis had progressively escalated measures to deprive non-'Aryans' of their rights and finally ostracised them completely. Their numbers included far more musicians than those who were politically persecuted, a fact that is explained by the high standing in which musical education and *Bildung* [culture] were held by German and Austrian Jewry. They valued the art of music, glorified by Franz Schubert in his famous setting of Franz von Schober's poem 'An die Musik' ['To Music'], as a particularly suitable means of approaching German culture, as a key to the German soul.

The music profession, however, never guaranteed a secure existence. Among the middle classes in particular, there were numerous transitional stages between music as a hobby and music as a vocation, so it was not always clear who was a real musician, especially as the level of professionalism would often vary within a single lifetime. For example, in view of the uncertainties of an artistic existence, Robert Schumann's father urged his son to enter the legal profession. Similarly, Dr Andreas Wilhelm Dullo was cautious and hesitant when he discovered that his son was exceptionally musical. In spite of his own artistic ambitions, he had chosen law and economics, been appointed head of the Bureau of Statistics in Königsberg and subsequently become mayor of Offenbach in 1907. Thus, it was with mixed feelings that he watched the development of his only son, Walter Andreas, who began to compose at the age of eleven. Walter's father encouraged these tendencies by taking his son to concerts and letting him have piano lessons; at the same time, however, he hoped that his son would not take music too seriously but treat it as an enjoyable hobby, as he had his own art and painting.

Walter Andreas's ('Adi's') growing interest in music was recorded sympathetically by his mother, Alice, who was Jewish. In December 1915, she wrote in her diary about her thirteen-year-old son:

> In his free time he does a lot of composing. He finished 'Das Heiligtum' ['The Sanctuary'] at Christmas. He immediately started on something new: a piece for piano and violin. He plays the piano accompaniment while whistling the violin part. Then he writes it down quickly. When he's eating or out walking he will suddenly call out: 'I've got another motif!' and hurry in to play it, to find the accompaniment and harmonies for it and to develop it.

When Walter heard the Schumann Piano Quintet at a concert, he saved up his pocket money for weeks on end in order to buy the score. Nothing was more important to him than music. In the light of his talent, his parents sent the sixteen-year-old to Dr Hoch's Conservatory in neighbouring Frankfurt am Main. When his piano teacher saw his pupil's compositions, he was so impressed that he discussed it with his superior:

> Herr Franzen showed Adi's compositions to the director [whereupon] he, Herr v. Bausznern, expressed the desire to speak to Adi's parents. We visited him in April. He said that he considered Adi's productive ability to be very promising; that Adi had a rare sense of style and a healthy originality; the purity of his nature was particularly pleasing; he should dedicate himself completely to music and start theory lessons immediately.

Although the well-known composer Waldemar von Bausznern wanted to teach the young man himself, Adi's father allowed only one theory lesson a month. This rendered the intensive training necessary for a career as a composer impossible. The teacher's enthusiasm also declined; accordingly,

CHAPTER 2: *On the Status of Music*

after his matriculation, Walter Dullo decided to study mathematics. This seemed reasonable, especially as the November Revolution cost his father his position as mayor after twelve years in office.

However, when the mathematics student attended a piano recital by the young Erich Riebensahm in Berlin in 1923, it became abundantly clear to him that his whole life revolved around music. His mother noted: 'And now the self-confidence of his inner artistic being is suddenly bursting forth like a force freed from shackles, and all rational objections simply fade away to nothing in the face of this powerful inner calling'.[2] Since piano playing was now once again the young man's centre of interest, he wanted to transfer to Leonid Kreutzer's class at the Berlin Hochschule für Musik [Academy of Music]. His father remained sceptical and wrote to his wife:

> You know what depressing circumstances I endured during my youth, and how it was my life's ambition to work myself up to a higher level of economic security and culture. I succeeded, but my most ardent desire to see our children and family established at this high level for generations to come will perhaps no longer be fulfilled.[3]

Nevertheless, he did not oppose the endeavours of his son, who did in fact begin piano studies with Kreutzer after passing the entrance exam in October 1924. Walter made progress, but he felt that his teacher did not really understand him. When the young pianist Grete Sultan raved about her tuition with the German-American Leschetizky student Richard Buhlig, Dullo left the Hochschule at the end of the Semester (April 1926) and went to study privately with Buhlig. His parents approved of this decision after meeting the new teacher, about whom Alice wrote: 'Wise, inspiring, spirited and strong: a highly sympathetic impression. An artist through and through. [...] May this teacher make Adi happy and put him on the right path!'[4]

The young pianist was therefore all the more deeply hurt when a year later Buhlig told him that he was born to be a musician, but not a concert artist. With that, his life's dream was shattered. Meanwhile, his father, now a staff member in the German Ministry of Internal Affairs in Berlin and district chairman of the German Democratic Party in Wilmersdorf, had found a flat for the family in a prime location on Hohenzollerndamm. Since a future in music apparently no longer seemed viable, he persuaded his son to take up something that could earn him a living, adding that through his connections he could arrange a career in the civil service. Walter gave in. In a radical move, he did not touch the piano again for years and ended all his friendships with musicians, in order to throw himself completely into his legal studies. Jews had exceptionally good opportunities in this profession: according to the census taken in June 1933, more than 16 per cent of all German lawyers were of Jewish descent.[5] Once he had passed his articled clerk examinations on 12 January 1933, this vocation also seemed to be open to Walter Dullo. Music had been suppressed, but had not disappeared from his consciousness by any means.

Considering the secure circumstances in which Walter Dullo grew up, a musical career – as his father rightly guessed – would have meant taking a very high risk, especially as musicians were not spared by the massive unemployment during the Great Depression of the 1930s.[6] Like Dullo, Alphons Silbermann, the only son of the Cologne printer Salomon Silbermann, was unable to embrace the music vocation of which he dreamt. Although he went to the opera with his parents and, in keeping with bourgeois practice, received piano lessons from the age of nine,[7] these were not regarded as preparation for a career in music. His parents belonged to the assimilated Jewish middle class, and wanted eventually to leave the printing business to their son. 'For why should one slave away building up a business if one can't leave it to one's only son as partner and successor?' The father described the music profession as 'hare-brained'.[8] Alphons Silbermann followed his father's advice and was enrolled in the law faculty at Cologne University in April 1927. During his legal studies, which he completed with his articles and doctorate, he was allowed to take lessons in piano, conducting and composition, to be a music critic, and to work as a repetiteur for months on end at the Cologne Opera – on the side. 'To his great dismay he never became a conductor, never even came anywhere near a conductor's podium.'[9]

The electrical engineer Moritz Kaiser, also from a German Jewish family, was born in Peru and around 1900 moved to Leipzig, where he and his brother founded Kaiser Bros Corporation, a firm that manufactured electric motors for gramophones. He gave the first of his three sons three names – Kurt Ned John – names which were unusual even for cosmopolitan Leipzig. Did Moritz Kaiser suspect that his son would not remain long in Germany? Could the name 'Ned' refer to the Australian folk hero Ned Kelly, the subject of the world's first feature film that was made in 1906, the year of Kaiser's birth? While still at the State Schiller-Gymnasium [Secondary School] in Gohlis, Kurt Kaiser was already passionate about music and presumably he also listened to gramophone records. His mother could well have told him about Robert Schumann, since she grew up next door to the house in Zwickau where the composer was born. But his father forced his son to study engineering, which he began at the Polytechnic University in Berlin in 1925. One year later, he and a friend formed a jazz band – his passion for music would prevail.

The son of a Berlin businessman, Rudolf Theodor Werther experienced a similar conflict between reason and inclination. Originally from Breslau and now living on Kurfürstendamm, his parents enabled their son to have nine years of tuition in piano, harmony and composition at the Klindworth-Scharwenka Conservatory. After matriculating, however, he studied economics and history at his father's behest. In 1918, he continued his studies at Berlin's Friedrich Wilhelm University, supplementing them with private piano tuition from the famous teacher Moritz Mayer-Mahr. Like Dullo, Werther began composing early; he regularly attended the opera and was passionate about Wagner and Strauss. Nonetheless, there was little indication that he would later make music his career.

Thus a twin-track education was always the norm whenever the music profession was not regarded as a secure livelihood. On account of his sonorous baritone voice, the Posen-born Martin Krutsch was advised by his singing teacher to study music but, as the young man suffered from performance anxiety, he decided to study medicine and train as a Jewish cantor. He worked as a doctor in Berlin and eventually became chief cantor at the new synagogue on Prinzregentenstraße, where his rich voice was highly acclaimed. Hermann Schildberger, from Berlin, received private tuition in piano and organ, but then studied law, selecting a topic on music copyright law for his doctorate in Greifswald. At the Universities of Berlin, Frankfurt am Main, Würzburg and Greifswald, he chose musicology as his minor and took additional lessons in music theory and counterpoint. Schildberger persisted in this dual approach. After his first state examinations in law, he earned his living as a music and theatre critic[10] and as an authorised signatory for the Weichmann silk company in Gleiwitz, Upper Silesia. In 1927, he returned to Berlin, where he worked both as an assistant judge and as musical director of the Jewish Reform Congregation. As in the case of Alphons Silbermann, his many talents were to prove an advantage during his exile.

More German than the Germans: Jews in Berlin

Most Jews in the German empire lived in large cities, above all in Berlin. The Prussian Emancipation Laws of 1812 had extended citizenship to Jews. Between the founding of the German empire and the First World War, the capital city's population grew rapidly. Whereas in 1871 there had been 36,000 Jews in Greater Berlin, by 1910 there were already 142,000. As the non-Jewish population was growing at the same pace, the percentage of Jews in the Berlin population remained unchanged: in both 1871 and 1910 it was 4.3 per cent.[11] As most Jews were part of the educated middle class, they played a significant role in the artistic and economic development of the city. In 1877, Leopold Ullstein founded the Ullstein Publishing Company, which became the largest newspaper and book publishing house in the world. Other companies founded by Jews included Mosse Publishers, which launched the *Berliner Tageblatt* in 1872, and the large Tietz and Wertheim department stores. In the main, Berlin Jews represented liberal positions and were closely aligned to the Central-Verein deutscher Bürger jüdischen Glaubens [Central Association of German Citizens of Jewish Faith], founded in 1893. In hardly any other city was their acculturation as successful as in Berlin, which also boasted the largest number of so-called mixed marriages between Christians and Jews.[12] The Weimar Republic, in which artists and intellectuals like Albert Einstein, Lise Meitner, Else Lasker-Schüler, Alfred Kerr, Kurt Tucholsky, Max Reinhardt, Elisabeth Bergner, Arnold Schönberg, Bruno Walter and Otto Klemperer played active roles, was the 'high point of the German Jewish relationship'.[13] Whereas the universities often remained closed to non-Aryan professors, this was not the case at the Berlin Hochschule für Musik, founded by Joseph

Joachim. Highly respected teachers like Franz Schreker, Artur Schnabel, Siegfried Ochs, Emanuel Feuermann and Carl Flesch all taught there.

In 1933, there were roughly 160,000 Jews in Berlin (in 1925, the number had reached 172,672[14]), who lived predominantly in middle-class suburbs: 27,000 in Charlottenburg, 26,600 in Wilmersdorf, 24,400 in Mitte and 18,000 in Prenzlauer Berg. Their presence was much less marked in the traditional working-class suburbs of Wedding (3,500) and Neukölln (2,900).[15] The Scheunenviertel ['Barn Quarter'] near Alexanderplatz, the reserve of Eastern European Jews, was by no means representative of Berlin Jewry. Rather, their social standing is better reflected in the many handsome tombs in Weißensee, the biggest Jewish cemetery in Europe.

The Berlin Jews' strong emphasis on education was also revealed in their representation among Gymnasium students, which was well above average. Although in 1905 Jews made up 4.6 per cent of the Berlin population, 25.2 per cent of Gymnasium students and a full 31.2 per cent in girls' secondary schools were of Jewish descent.[16] In addition, the proportion of Jewish students at Berlin universities (16.7 per cent in the academic year 1911–1912) far outweighed the percentage of Jews in the community, where the less well-off in particular were urged to study.[17] It was the same with music, which in well-to-do families was usually regarded as part of a general education, but not as a serious professional career. Members of the lower classes had fewer scruples about studying music, as this actually offered them the chance to improve their situation, to be transported into a 'better world'.

Werner Baer had the good fortune to be the younger of two brothers. As the elder son took over the family textile business, Werner was allowed to embark on a career in music. In 1914, when he was born, an emperor still reigned in Germany. No-one suspected that just a few months later a world war would radically change the living conditions of all Germans. The parents' shop for menswear and boyswear was located at 5 Rosenthaler Straße in Berlin's old city centre, not in today's popular precinct around the Hackescher Markt, but at the northern end, not far from Rosenthaler Platz. Alfred Döblin describes this area in his novel *Berlin Alexanderplatz*. It opens with Döblin's protagonist Franz Biberkopf alighting from the tram there, not far from where the Baers' generously proportioned home stood at 9–9a Schönhauser Allee.[18]

Werner's father, Robert Baer, was born in Berlin; his mother Lucie, who was five years younger, came from Landsberg an der Warthe. They named their eldest son Fritz Bernhard in memory of grandfather Bernhard Baer, who had come to Berlin as a pedlar but, thanks to his diligence, quickly moved up in the world. He founded the clothing business.[19] Werner Felix, the younger son, owed his middle name to his maternal grandfather and was said to have inherited his musicality from his mother. This talent was recognised during the final war years when, like most Berliners, the Baers were surviving mainly on potatoes. At that time, only Fritz was having piano lessons,[20] but when the piano tuner came to the house, he discovered that the younger boy had perfect pitch. By now Werner was also playing by ear the pieces that Fritz was learning, so their parents decided to give him piano lessons as well. When Mrs Baer took Werner, aged six, to the State Opera for the first time, Mozart's *Così fan tutte* was being performed – a crucial experience that accounted for his love of opera. As Werner later remembered, at first he was only captivated by the music, but after that he was so shocked by the fate of the women betrayed by their lovers that he had to be taken home.[21]

Baer started school in 1920, the year of his first visit to the opera. One year later, disaster struck the family: his father, who had fought in the war, died suddenly, and his widowed mother took over the business. Because she needed the help of her sixteen-year-old son Fritz, he had to leave school. Werner, however, was allowed to continue with his piano lessons in spite of the inflation; at the age of twelve, he began playing the organ and regularly went to operas and concerts, buying standing-room tickets. He played the organ for school church services and occasionally had his own compositions performed by the school orchestra. His parents never treated him as a genius, but made sure that he played outside like all the other children. Baer was forever grateful to his first organ teacher, Dr Arnold Dreyer, for his substantial support.[22] Dreyer was a church music director who taught music at the Sophien-Gymnasium; a composer of choral and organ music, he appointed Werner leader of the school orchestra and sent for him whenever scores from the school library had to be arranged for strings.[23] Thus, even in his early years, Werner Baer was acquiring practical experience as a pianist, composer, arranger and conductor.

By the time he matriculated in 1932, the economic climate had so deteriorated that the family had to give up their large flat in the Schönhauser Allee. Mrs Baer and her sons moved into the building in Rosenthaler Straße that housed the business. They probably lived in cramped conditions as grandmother Bertha Baer, now widowed, also had to be accommodated. After her death, they found a large sum of money under her bed: banknotes that she had hidden away for emergencies but which were now only worthless paper.

There are various sources of information for Werner Baer's musical education.[24] He himself mentions the piano teachers Georg Bertram and Fritz Masbach and the organ teacher Arnold Dreyer.[25] He says that he learnt theory and composition from Gustav Bumcke, a sought-after theory and saxophone teacher at the Stern Conservatory, who had himself studied with Max Bruch and Engelbert Humperdinck. Later, Artur Schnabel is even supposed to have given Baer piano lessons; but Schnabel left Berlin in May 1933. According to Baer himself, he studied at the Hochschule für Musik and the Stern Conservatory from 1930 until 1935, though his name is missing from the records at both these institutions. He then had to give up his music studies as a result of growing racial persecution.[26] However, his skills as a pianist and organist were such that he was able to earn a good living. As a pianist, he accompanied well-known singers and, since he was familiar with light music, he also performed in clubs such as the Barberina and Ambassador, and in the Adlon, Eden and Bristol hotels.[27]

Sometimes it is not easy to establish exactly when the decision was made to become a professional musician. Born in Breslau, Stefan Weintraub did not pursue music when he left school; instead, he began an apprenticeship in pharmaceutical sales. After his national service, he became a representative for several pharmaceutical companies. In the face of war and revolution, studies in music were out of the question. What counted was the ability to earn a secure living. Stefan Weintraub only indulged his passion on the side by learning piano and percussion. Similarly, Horst Graff had little opportunity at first to expand his musical inclinations. His father, Hermann Graff, had moved from a village in West Prussia to the then independent town of Charlottenburg, where he set up a manufacturing and haberdashery business on the Wilmersdorfer Straße. In December 1905, he opened the Graff & Heyn store on the same site,[28] the first department store in Charlottenburg – the Wertheim department store (the biggest in Europe) had opened its doors on Leipziger Platz in central Berlin in 1894, followed by the equally splendid Tietz store on Alexanderplatz in 1904. In early 1912, the Graff & Heyn building was demolished to make way for a new one. Possibly owing to the construction costs, the owners had to sell it to Adolf Jandorf, the proprietor of KaDeWe or *Kaufhaus des Westens* [Department Store of the West], and the name was changed to Jandorf & Co. After the war, Hermann Graff seems to have continued to lose money, as his son Horst left school and became the buyer for a machine factory. In 1924, Horst Graff began to study business at the Polytechnic University in Berlin. At the same time, he received a musical education: he played clarinet, alto saxophone, flute, oboe and trumpet. He was particularly interested in American jazz, and was one of the first people in Berlin to buy an alto saxophone. In the same year (1924), Graff met Stefan Weintraub, who was equally obsessed with jazz, and they decided to form a band. One of its members was the chemistry student Julius Ansco Bruinier, who played cello, trumpet, saxophone and sousaphone and also performed successfully as a whistler.[29] The decision to name the band after the drummer was made by drawing lots.

The 'Tanzkapelle Stefan Weintraub' made a successful debut at the Berlin Brüdervereinshaus [Jewish Fraternity Building] and soon performed under the name 'Weintraubs Syncopaters'. The misspelling of the unusual second word was in use for a long time. On 28 March 1929, a special performance was held at the State Theatre on the Gendarmenmarkt in honour of the recently deceased actor Albert Steinrück. The programme records an illustrious crowd of artists: Werner Krauss, Carola Neher, Heinrich George, Eleonore v. Mendelssohn, Tilla Durieux, Conrad Veidt, Max Pallenberg, Max Hansen, Rosa Valetti, Elisabeth Bergner, Fritzi Massary, Käthe Dorsch, Alexander Granach, Fritz Kortner, Paul Wegener, Rudolf Forster, Kurt Gerron, Veit Harlan, Trude Hesterberg, Hans Albers, Kurt Goetz, Marlene Dietrich, Hilde Körber, Lucie Mannheim, Asta Nielsen, Henny Porten, Alfred Braun, Paul Grätz and the Weintraubs Syncopaters. When Walter Mehring's play *Der Kaufmann von Berlin* [The Merchant of Berlin] had its scandalous premiere later that year, on 6 September at the Piscator Theatre, 'Orchestra: Weintraubs Syncopators' was printed on the programme – a name that already enjoyed cult status among fans of jazz and dance music.

Women in the Music Profession

Although middle-class Jews usually regarded music as an important part of their sons' general education and not as a serious future profession, they were more willing to allow their daughters to follow a musical career. Examples include the Berlin-born Ellen Cohn who, after attending higher girls' schools and studying violin at the Stern Conservatory (with Issay Barmas) and the Klindworth–Scharwenka Conservatory, performed under the name Ellen Byk, and the businessman's daughter Lisbeth Caspary from Königsberg, who began violin studies at the Berlin Hochschule für Musik in October 1900. When health problems forced Caspary to interrupt her studies in the summer of 1903, her teacher gave her a glowing reference:

> Miss Lisbeth Caspary has made significant progress during the last year of her studies at the Berlin Hochschule für Musik. What distinguishes Miss Caspary's talent – apart from her well-developed finger technique – is, above all, her lively musicianship which, together with her careful and intelligent reading of the composer's intentions, renders her playing both intellectually stimulating and moving.

The director of the Hochschule, Joseph Joachim, considered the young violinist suited to a teaching career: 'As she appears to be both intelligent and serious, I think that given her current abilities she would also make a successful teacher.' He would be delighted, the director continued, if Lisbeth Caspary were to continue her studies in Berlin at a later stage.

Marianne Kahn hailed from a very prosperous lawyer's family in Mannheim and was supported by her parents in her vocal studies; she later became a professional singer and was known as Madame Mathy. Similarly Otti Veit, who was born in Emmendingen, Baden, met little resistance when she wanted to become a musician. She came from a musical family: her grandfather, Simon Veit, had been leader of the congregation and cantor at the Emmendingen synagogue for decades and her father, the timber merchant Berthold Veit, was a gifted pianist. His daughter, who loved to reminisce about her grandfather's beautiful voice, began to receive cello lessons at the age of seven. In 1934, after matriculation, she moved to Berlin where she continued her studies with Nicolai Graudan, principal cellist of the Berlin Philharmonic and one of the greats in his field.

Acculturation through Music

While well-established middle-class Jews seldom allowed their sons to study music, for the less well-to-do, music represented a welcome means of assimilation or acculturation. Many Eastern European Jews had come to Berlin not only for economic and political reasons, but because of their love of music, in particular German music, which for them was not just a nationalistically narrow concept, but a broad and universal idea harking back to the vision of Johann Joachim Quantz, Frederick the Great's flute teacher, who once described German musical taste as 'eclectic'.[30] This 'sacred art' represented 'a better world', and one that was open to foreign influences.

The furniture dealer Salomon Frischer had moved with his wife, Feigel, from Chrzanow in Poland to the flourishing town of Charlottenburg. He went regularly from his flat in Krumme Straße to the nearby Municipal Opera and fostered a love of music in his three children. Charlotte, the eldest, received tuition in piano and voice, Adolf played the cello and Emanuel, three years younger, played the violin. When the children finished their schooling, however, despite their musical talents, their parents wanted them to study ordinary professions. Adolf Frischer completed his apprenticeship in the fur trade with Heymann & Felsenburg at the Spittelmarkt; his brother Emanuel began to study medicine. Music was at first just a secondary occupation. Adolf took lessons from the Russian cellist Edmund Kurtz before changing to the double bass, which he played regularly at night in the elegant Ciro-Bar on Kurfürstendamm, in the Bianco-Bachicha Tango Orchestra, or with the Polish violinist and band leader Paul Godwin. Earlier, Emanuel had heard the Weintraubs Syncopators and been so fascinated by them that he formed his own band with schoolmates at the Schiller-Oberschule [secondary school]; it was called the Charles Jazz Syncopators after the pianist. Sometimes the Frischer brothers also played dance music with the multi-talented Werner Baer.[31] Meanwhile, Emanuel Frischer had turned to the trumpet, which he had mastered so well that he was engaged by well-known band leaders such as Dajos Béla, Paul Godwin and Marek Weber. His life's dream was fulfilled when in 1933 he was invited to play trumpet with the famous Weintraubs Syncopators as successor to Ady Rosner. He gave up his medical studies and became a professional musician.

Almost all the members of the band were of Jewish heritage, and some of them had only just moved to Berlin. In 1925, Kurt Ned John Kaiser had begun his studies in engineering at the Polytechnic University in Berlin, and in 1926 he founded the dance band Sid Kay's Fellows with his school friend Siegmund Friedmann, who also hailed from Leipzig.[32] The band's name featured Siegmund as 'Sid' and his tall colleague (who went by his third name, John) as 'Kay'. In the Weimar Republic, 'Kaiser' was no longer popular, while English names were regarded as chic – especially for jazz bands. (Jazz fan Ludwig Rüth now called himself Lewis Ruth and the painter Georg Ehrenfried Groß, who was equally passionate about jazz, became George Grosz.) Sid Kay's Fellows gained their early experience playing for student dances, and in 1929, after the Lewis Ruth Band's success in *The Threepenny Opera* and other theatre productions, they were offered a concert tour to Frankfurt, Vienna and Budapest; a year later they became the regular dance band at the smart Haus Vaterland on Potsdamer Platz. Meanwhile, despite this success, Kaiser had left Sid Kay's Fellows because he was drawn to the Weintraubs Syncopators, who had risen far more rapidly from student outfit to high-profile band. From 1927, the former drummer with Sid Kay's Fellows played trombone with the Weintraubs Syncopators. In view of the sensational success of this band, Kaiser abandoned his engineering studies in order to dedicate himself completely to music. In 1928, apart from him and the founding members Stefan Weintraub (drums) and Horst Graff (clarinet, alto sax and violin), the band comprised tenor saxophonist Freddy Wise, pianist and arranger Friedrich Hollaender, tuba and bass player Ansco Bruinier, and Cyril Schulvater, who was responsible for banjo, guitar and orchestration. Cyril 'Baby' Schulvater, son of a

German Jewish hotel owner, was born in Johannesburg, South Africa, and had trained as a commercial artist.

If the father in a Jewish family was a musician or cantor, it was more likely that the children would take up music as a career. Russian cantor Zemach Schoenberger, who lived in the Prussian province of Posen, was so impressed with his son Theodor Isadore's talent that he sent him to Berlin to study music. His piano teachers at the Stern Conservatory were Heinrich Ehrlich and Felix Dreyschock, while Friedrich Gernsheim tutored him in theory. At the age of twenty-two, Theodor Schoenberger had made such progress that he himself was allowed to teach piano at the Stern Conservatory. The composer Friedrich Hollaender, for a while pianist with the Weintraubs Syncopators, was one of Schoenberger's most famous students.

After the turn of the century, Germany's capital also became the new home for other Russian musicians of Jewish descent, for example the family of synagogue cantor David Spivak and his wife Rahel, for whom music-making was a traditional occupation – their name, after all, meant 'singer'.[33] All nine children showed unusual musicality from an early age: Clara (the eldest) and Adolf with their beautiful voices, Albert and Jascha with their piano playing. The family moved from Smila, near Kiev, to Odessa on the Black Sea, where Isaac ('Issy') and the youngest, Nathan ('Tossy') were born, both of whom learnt the violin. The home of many famous musicians, Odessa was, however, a centre of antisemitic pogroms; in 1905, at least 400 Jews were murdered in riots, and many more Jewish homes and dwellings were devastated. In 1908, in the face of such threats, the Spivakovsky (in German: spelt Spiwakowsky) family moved to Charlottenburg, where they found a flat at 60 Sybelstraße. Here the children could continue their musical studies without interruption, for the most part at the Klindworth–Scharwenka Conservatory. Having already started piano lessons in Russia at the age of three, Jascha now went to Moritz Mayer-Mahr who had been a pupil of Franz Liszt, Clara Schumann and Anton Rubinstein, while Issy was taught by Issay Barmas, a former student of Joachim. Because his younger brother Tossy soon caught up with him on the violin, Issy switched to studying cello with Hugo Becker. In 1910, the fourteen-year-old Jascha was awarded the Blüthner Prize by a jury consisting of Ossip Gabrilowitsch,

Leopold Godowsky and Ferruccio Busoni, and soon afterwards his brother Albert received the same award. Tossy then transferred to the Hochschule für Musik, where Willy Hess, another Joachim student, took him under his wing. As a result of their outstanding talent, all the above-mentioned members of this Russian Jewish family became professional musicians.

In this context, mention must be made of one more Russian: Majer Pietruschka, who was born in Opatow, near Minsk. His father, a fur trader, was an ardent admirer of the last tsar. The news of the tsar's murder is said to have shocked him so deeply that he took his own life. After that, all of his nine children were sent abroad. Majer went first to Warsaw and then to Łódź, where he played in the symphony orchestra. From 1919 onwards, he continued his musical education in Berlin, where he became a violinist with a silent film orchestra that he eventually conducted. When the orchestra disbanded at the beginning of the sound film era, Pietruschka formed his own salon orchestra and performed at Jewish weddings and other functions. While making recordings of Jewish music, he became acquainted with Boas Bischofswerder,[34] who was born near Warsaw and had trained as an opera singer before becoming a cantor. In Berlin, Bischofswerder worked first in the little orthodox Wolfenstein synagogue in Düppelstraße, Steglitz, and then as cantor and finally principal cantor at the Beth-Zion Synagogue in Brunnenstraße. Bischofswerder was an expert in synagogue music; he wrote articles and books on the subject and maintained regular contact with the choral director of the synagogue on Kottbusser Ufer, the multi-talented Arno Nadel.

The Blue Danube: Jews in Vienna

Equally as striking as the high proportion of Jews among persecuted musicians was their preference for the capital cities of Vienna and Berlin. They were either born in these cities, or spent a significant part of their lives there. Migrating Jews were attracted to these metropolises not just on account of their size, but because of the high quality of their musical life, the foundations for which had been laid by the former aristocracy and the church. Berlin and Vienna became focal points for Jewish immigration and were therefore able to raise their profiles as European music centres.

The migration of Jews to Vienna began relatively late, but then all the more rapidly. In 1830, Vienna's population of around 318,000 included 16,040 Jews (just under 4 per cent).[35] By 1869, the number of inhabitants had almost doubled (607,000) and the number of Jews had risen to over 40,000, equal to 6.6 per cent of the population. By 1890, the population had doubled again, while the Jewish percentage had shot up to 8.8 per cent. The percentage of Jews in Vienna increased in both real and relative terms, whereas in Berlin it hardly ever rose above 4.3 per cent. The 175,000 Jews living in the city in 1910 were predominantly immigrants from Eastern Europe; only a fifth of them had been born in Vienna. By 1934, the Jewish community numbered 176,034, now 9.4 per cent of the total population.[36] Many residents saw the high proportion of new arrivals as a threat to the social fabric; the growing antisemitism of spokesmen like Karl Lueger and Georg von Schoenerer strongly influenced the young Adolf Hitler.

The educational drive of Viennese Jews was so unusually strong that here, too, the proportion in secondary and tertiary education far outweighed their share of the total population. From 1870 to 1900, between 24 and 30 per cent of Viennese high school pupils, and between 20 and 34 per cent of university students, were of Jewish descent. The proportion of Jews was even higher among medical students and in the various fields of instrumental music. Thus, in the first decade of the twentieth century, at the Konservatorium der Gesellschaft der Musikfreunde [Conservatory of the Society of the Friends of Music], the proportion of Jewish piano students hovered between 32 and 38 per cent, and that of violinists between 23 and 31 per cent. 'In relation to their numbers, almost three times as many Jews as non-Jews received a musical education.'[37]

The bank director Jacob Langer from Moravian Prerau, who lived with his wife Melanie Mulli (from the well-known Gallia family) at No. 1 Lobkowitzplatz, belonged to the acculturated Viennese Jewry. Their furniture was designed by Adolf Loos, a friend of the family. At home, their son, Peter Langer was exposed to his young mother's piano playing as well as a lot of chamber music, and was given piano lessons from an early age.

The view from the house of the State Opera and, just opposite, the Palais Lobkowitz, where Beethoven was often a guest, might have provided a further incentive. Peter Langer appeared as soloist in the Mozart Piano Concerto in D minor, K. 466, in the Mozart-Saal of the Konzerthaus at the age of eighteen but, instead of music, he studied law, in which he obtained a doctorate. Having emigrated from Galician Lemberg, Adolf Ehrenfeld also chose to study law but, at the same time, he attended lectures in musicology (by Egon Wellesz and Robert Lach) and art history at the University of Vienna. In addition, alongside his main occupation as an associate lawyer, he took conducting lessons from Felix Weingartner and was for a time deputy conductor of the Philharmonic Society.

The merchant Friedrich Fleischer had moved to Vienna from Pilsen, Bohemia. His son Oskar played various instruments, in particular the violin, and became a professional musician. However, Oskar Fleischer was unable to make much of a living, so he continued to stay with his parents, who ran a wholesale egg business in the Fifteenth District. Hugo and Berta Steiner had also come from Moravian Prerau to Vienna, where their son Paul was born in 1901. In the same year, the family moved to Innsbruck. Paul Steiner began his tertiary music studies in oboe and violin there before continuing at the conservatories in Vienna and, for a while, in Breslau. By 1918, he was already active as an orchestral musician and soon formed his own band, with which he toured abroad.

Young men from the bourgeoisie often had to overcome parental opposition if they wanted a musical career. The Viennese doctor and Catholic convert Josef Krips, however, was willing to take the risk and allowed both his sons, Josef and Heinrich, to follow a musical career. Both studied composition and conducting, and both became conductors: Josef Krips in Karlsruhe and at the Vienna State Opera, and Heinrich Krips in Innsbruck and Salzburg. The lawyer Max Stadlen also allowed his son to study music. Peter Stadlen wanted to become a pianist, and attended Paul Weingarten's class at the Vienna Music Academy, complemented by harmony lessons with Joseph Marx. In 1929, he transferred to the Berlin Hochschule, where Leonid Kreutzer (with whom Walter Dullo had been unable to get along) became his teacher. Stadlen supplemented this with tuition in composition (Walter Gmeindl) and conducting (Julius Prüwer). The fact that his studies came to an end in 1933 can be explained not only by Hitler's rise to power, but by the death of his father. Peter Stadlen was now vulnerable to the risks associated with a musical career. The conductor Adolf Brenner discovered just how dangerous these were. As the son of a private official from Budapest, he had grown up in comfortable circumstances in a splendid art nouveau house, the so-called Cottage-Hof in Karl-Beck-Gasse, opposite the Schubert Park in Währing. Music was in the air, as Karl-Beck-Gasse was named after the author of a poem that inspired Johann Strauß to write his famous waltz, 'The Blue Danube'. (The author died in Währing.) Brenner enrolled in the same year as Stadlen at the Vienna Music Academy, where he studied harmony (Emil Prohaska), piano (Franz Moser) and counterpoint (Joseph Marx). After 1924, he turned his attention to subjects like choir rehearsal, accompanying and sight-reading. In 1927, he left the Academy before graduating in order to take up a conducting career.

Women Musicians

In Vienna, as in Berlin, the music profession was more accessible to the daughters of middle-class families than to their sons. During her marriage to the patent attorney Felix Hitschmann, Maximilian Forst's sister Stella had a daughter, Eva, who proved to be musically gifted. Although the marriage quickly broke down, Stella's new husband, the stockbroker Dr Fritz Steiner encouraged his talented stepdaughter. After her matriculation, Eva Hitschmann was allowed to embark on vocal studies at the New Viennese Conservatorium. In keeping with the general attitude towards women in those days, it was taken for granted that, when they married, the husband would provide financial security. For the same reason, the businessman Josef Stern and his wife Emma, who lived in the Sixth Viennese District, agreed to their daughter Gertrud learning the piano without giving the matter any further thought. At eight years of age, she became a pupil at the Music Academy, where she completed her *Reifeprüfung* [final examination] with Hedwig Andrásffy and Alexander Manhart in June 1936. A year later, Gertrud Stern married a lawyer, Dr Arnold Hacker, and after that she gave piano lessons. The life of Leonie Schlesinger, who at barely eighteen had married the businessman Leopold Feigl, confirms that a musical education improved women's opportunities for social advancement. Her husband was involved in the oil industry and she moved with him to Baku, where her son Ernst was born. In 1908, when her husband was appointed the representative for the Rothschild Bank in St Petersburg, the family moved into a large house on Nevsky Prospect. When war broke out, she was in Vienna where, on account of the political turmoil in Russia, she decided to stay – especially as the Rothschilds were able to arrange a position for her husband with the Shell Company in the Austrian capital. In Vienna, Leonie Feigl took more singing lessons from the vocal teacher and composer Marie Brossement. After appearances with the Brossement students (among them the soprano Lotte Schöne, who later worked at the State Opera), from 1918 on she gave lieder recitals at the Konzerthaus. As well as lieder by Brahms and Wolf, Leonie Feigl favoured the works of Russian composers, which she sang in the original language. The mezzo-soprano was now active as a singing teacher, and her salon in their large and beautiful flat on the corner of Geylinggasse in Hietzing was regularly attended by the composer and poet Franz Mittler,[38] the librettist Fritz Lunzer[39] and the composer Richard Stöhr. Like Leopold Suchsland and Robert Fanta, Stöhr also dedicated several songs to the hostess.

Vocation or Hobby?

In the case of some refugees who became professional musicians in Australia, it is difficult to determine whether they always had this vocation in mind. Hans Holzbauer was a clarinettist and saxophonist in Australia. The family lived in Vienna's Seventh District where his father dealt in women's millinery and later in groceries. It is quite possible that for his son, music developed gradually into a vocation.

Hans Edelmann probably never had any training as a professional musician. His father, Owse Leb Edelmann, had come from Lithuania to Vienna, where in 1903 he married the non-Jewish Julie Lemberger and gave up his activity as a Jewish cantor. Under the name of Leo Edelmann, however, he used his musicality and fine ear to become a piano dealer and tuner. After his early death, Julie Edelmann continued to run the business on the corner of Piaristengasse in the bustling Josefstädter Straße, not far from the Josefstadt Theatre. Their son Hans worked in the book trade, but continued to live at home, where he heard piano music and piano tuning every day. This environment might very well account for the fact that he loved to sing and later performed as a solo tenor.

Similarly, the music profession did not seem to offer enough security for Prague-born Friedrich Kramer. Although he studied the violin in Vienna, he first chose a commercial career. Under his name, the 1929 Viennese telephone book lists a vinegar wholesaling business in the Sixth District, and a private flat in the Thirteenth District. Officially registered as a salesman, in January 1930 he entered the profession 'Travelling Salesman' in his new passport. Later, however, he must have decided on a musical career, as the official 1938 address book lists him as 'Fritz Kramer, *Kapellmeister*, XIII. Lainzer Str. 74'. In the meantime, our man seems to have earned the right to accept employment as a conductor.[40]

'In the Prater, Trees are Blooming again': The Leopoldstadt District

Jews from Eastern Europe often lived in Leopoldstadt, Vienna's Second District. This large island between the Danube and the Danube Canal was named after the art connoisseur Emperor Leopold I, who initiated the development of green spaces like the Augarten and Prater. In 1775, his great-grandson Joseph II opened the parklands to the general public and allowed Jewish settlement there. This attracted a great many Jews from the eastern parts of the Habsburg monarchy as well as from Poland, Romania and Russia, who settled where the east European railway lines ended: travellers from Bohemia landed at Northwest station, those from Krakow and Brünn at North station. In 1852, Arnold Schönberg's father, Samuel Schönberg, was among these newcomers; he began as a shoemaker's apprentice and later opened his own shoe shop. At the end of the nineteenth century, the businessman Josef Lorber and his wife Chaje Ruchel arrived from Galicia; they had married in Jaroslau and found a new home in Rembrandtstraße, where their son Marcel was born.[41] Hans Bader was the son of a livestock trader from the Moravian town of Pohrlitz who moved to Vienna in 1912 and found a flat opposite the Volksprater in the Second District. With various jobs and finally a lighting retail business, he was able to finance his son's vocational education and later his violin and conducting lessons.

Leopoldstadt was home to the Prater orchestras that made such a deep impression on Arnold Schönberg, and also to the Jewish chants in the synagogues. The so-called 'polnische Schul' (Polish synagogue) in Leopoldsgasse was a squat building that stood out from the surrounding tenement houses with its highly decorative, oriental façade and little tower.[42] The principal cantor at this orthodox synagogue, Emanuel Frenkel, was born in Simisne, Romania. Just when he and his wife Hanni moved to Vienna has not yet been firmly established. The Viennese registration office only registered their flat from September 1923. When their son Erwin was born in 1921, the family might have been living as subtenants in rented accommodation. Erwin had his first piano lessons at the age of six; at eight he was already a soloist with the synagogue choir, and by age fourteen he was conducting. The singer Israel Jankel Portnoj was also an Eastern European Jew. He moved early from Podberez'ye in the Vilnius region to Vienna, where he married. The young couple found their first flat in the Second District, where their son Heinrich was born, followed by his four siblings Alexander, Erich, Margarete and Ernst. Like Erwin Frenkel, Heinrich Portnoj had inherited his musicality from his father. Unlike the principal cantor's son, however, he showed a preference for Western European art music. Accordingly, he was destined to move out of Leopoldstadt.

Many musically gifted Jews came from far and wide to Vienna, where they hoped to find financial security for themselves and a good education for their children. Among them was the Russian Isaac Stiwelband from Odessa, who arrived in Leopoldstadt in 1905 with his wife Anute and his son Mischa. He began as a factory hand and gradually advanced from businessman to hotelier so that he could send his gifted son to the gymnasium and later to the Conservatory of the Society of the Friends of Music. According to this institution's annual records, Mischa Stiwelband was exempted from school fees and received a scholarship. As a Russian, he did not have to do national service, and from 1917 he was able to earn his living as an orchestral musician. Richard Goldner was born in Czaiora (Craiova), Romania, the son of Jewish businessman Avram Beer Goldner and his wife Bertha. In spite of their deep poverty, Richard received his first violin lessons and soon afterwards was teaching his schoolmates. When his father found work in a paper mill owned by Joseph Kraus, brother of the writer Karl Kraus, their financial circumstances improved and Richard was allowed to transfer to a better violin teacher, Maurice Stierer. In spite of this, he started to study architecture. Apparently Richard Goldner first wanted to establish whether he could earn a good living with serious music. After entering Simon Pullman's chamber music class at the New Viennese Conservatorium, he worked as a deputy in various orchestras. He only gave up architecture when Pullman arranged a grant for his further music study.

CHAPTER 3

Failed Integration: Getting out of Germany, 1933–1937

The 'Cleansing' of Musical Life

Adolf Hitler regarded his takeover as a cultural revolution like the one envisaged by the young Richard Wagner. After seizing power, the plan was to carry out a fundamental 'cleansing' of musical life. For years, the Nazi Party (NSDAP) and the Kampfbund für deutsche Kultur [Combat League for German Culture] had demanded the removal of Jews and 'cultural Bolsheviks' from public office. The new government implemented these demands. Those affected included, for example, Walter Dullo, who had passed his first state law examinations on 12 January 1933 and taken his first position in Havelberg on 19 February. Two weeks later, the Reichstag fire, for which the Communists were blamed, was used to unleash a wave of brutal persecutions. Because Dullo's mother was active in the peace movement, she too came under suspicion. Alice Dullo noted in her diary:

> Communists, pacifists and Jews are being persecuted and arrested, with terrible cruelty. House searches all over the place and confiscation of 'illegal material'. At our place too, on 13 March, an examination of the World Peace League's documents; they found nothing suspicious. But the League has to cease its activities. Our telephone is under police surveillance; letters are opened at the post office.

On 12 April, her son received an official letter:

> You are required immediately to provide official assurance that none of your grandparents is of Jewish descent (in the racial, not in the religious sense). If you are unable to deliver such clarification, you will be required to take leave of absence over and above your annual leave.

Figure 1: Portrait of Walter Andreas Dullo, Berlin 1932. (Author's Archive)

When the young lawyer replied that he could confirm non-Jewish heritage for his paternal grandparents, but not for his maternal ancestors, he received notification of extended leave of absence by return of post. Although he advised the ministry that the Dullos had been Prussian civil servants for centuries and that his mother's Jewish family had lived for many generations in Germany, he was notified of his dismissal from the civil service in June. This was based on the Civil Service Restoration Act of 7 April 1933. One of the implementing regulations stipulated that even people with only one Jewish grandparent were regarded as non-Aryan. As the son of an Aryan father and non-Aryan mother, Walter Dullo was of non-Aryan heritage. He received his definitive letter of dismissal in August: 'In accordance with § 3 of the Civil Service Restoration Act of 7 April, the Right Honourable Prussian Minister for Justice has dismissed you from the judicial service as of 14 August with immediate effect.' Having expected to earn a secure living in the unloved legal service, Dullo now had nowhere to go. His father, since 1928 Director of the Traffic Advertising Association, had already had to restrict the family's lifestyle. In September 1932, the Dullos had moved out of their large flat at 111 Hohenzollerndamm to a less expensive domicile at 5 Goßlerstraße in Friedenau, which since then had also been Walter Dullo's address. After the abrupt end to his legal career, he had to find a new job, and all the more urgently because in the meantime his father's pension had been reduced and he was prohibited from earning any supplementary income.[1]

The situation was hardly less dire for Alphons Silbermann, who had passed his first state law examinations with distinction in Cologne before being awarded his doctorate in 1933. Although at this point his doctoral supervisor, Hans Kelsen – the only unbaptised Jewish professor in the Cologne law faculty – had not yet fled the country and was still dean, Silbermann's superior in the district court where Silbermann began as a clerk was a staunch Nazi. Once their party was in charge, SA men stormed the law courts 'in order to gather up the "Jewish vermin" so that they would no longer defile Aryan legal institutions'.[2] Alphons Silbermann was able to escape through the back entrance. He hurried home, packed a few things and took the train to Utrecht the same day.

The new rulers had their own definition of German music as art by Aryans for Aryans. This 'sacred art' no longer represented a realm of freedom, but was a privilege as part of the ethnicity. Given the model intended for music in racial education, 'cleansing' in this sector was particularly thorough. Only pure Aryans could be employed in cultural institutions. Because – according to the *Völkischer Beobachter* of 11 January 1933 – the Berlin opera houses performed 'operas with harlots and negroes and Jew musicians – with a few Germans to balance things up', they were called harshly to account.[3] When the opera houses celebrated the fiftieth anniversary of Richard Wagner's death on 13 February with new productions of *The Flying Dutchman* and *Tannhäuser* using modern stage sets and costumes, it was seen as 'a brazen assault on Wagner and German culture'.[4] In spite of such attacks, thanks to Hermann Göring, Prime Minister of Prussia, the State Opera Unter den Linden was able to retain a degree of autonomy under its director, Heinz Tietjen. However, further concerts with Otto Klemperer, conductor of the unpopular *Tannhäuser*, were cancelled 'for reasons of public safety'. The Municipal Opera was more vulnerable: on 13 March, SA men invaded the premises and the director, Carl Ebert, who had staged *The Flying Dutchman*, was given leave of absence. Conductors Paul Breisach and Fritz Stiedry and the non-Aryan artistic consultant Berthold Goldschmidt were banned from the house.[5]

Although the 'cleansing' of the Berlin opera houses also affected visiting non-Aryans like the conductor Maurice Abravanel, its target was artists with long-term contracts. Kurt Emmanuel Prerauer had been an assistant conductor at the State Opera since October 1925 and hence had worked on the world premiere of Alban Berg's *Wozzeck*. When the *Generalmusikdirektor* [Director of Music] Leo Blech returned to the State Opera in 1926, he had appointed Prerauer as his personal assistant. Prerauer prepared numerous opera performances, organised rehearsals and played the piano for them. According to the Stage Yearbook, when the State Opera had to reduce the number of repetiteurs from fifteen (1930) to seven (1933), Prerauer – as one of the most qualified – was not dismissed. He even played the piano in concerts. On 4 February 1933, a few days after Hitler seized power, the Staatskapelle under Erich Kleiber performed a new work by Jaromir Weinberger, his *Introduction, Passacaglia and Fugue for organ and orchestra*. To prepare for the difficult solo part, Prerauer had thoroughly acquainted himself with the new organ at the State Opera and even taken private organ lessons.

After the scandal of the *Tannhäuser* performance, it also became increasingly difficult for Kurt Prerauer to continue his work. Whereas Leo Blech, despite being Jewish, had been allowed to stay on account of his many years of experience, it was not possible to keep on his assistant at the State Opera – or Klemperer, the conductor Fritz Zweig, one of the stage managers, the singers Tilly de Garmo, Lotte Schöne and Marcel Noé, and three other repetiteur colleagues.[6] Apparently even before the Civil Service Restoration Act came into force, Prerauer feared that he would be dismissed. On 1 April (his thirty-second birthday), when Jewish businesses were boycotted in every German city, he received a glowing reference from Leo Blech, who praised his assistant as a model of reliability.[7]

With his commitment and enthusiasm, Prerauer had never given cause for any complaint, but only for praise and gratitude. In a short letter dated 31 May, even Wilhelm Furtwängler described the artist as 'a truly outstanding musician' and wrote that he regretted that the State Opera had to dispense with his collaboration on account of the new laws. Senior director Franz Ludwig Hörth, whose position as professor at the Berlin Hochschule für Musik was also threatened,[8] used the letterhead of the Director-General for a reference written on 18 June, in which he described Prerauer as a very capable and artistically sensitive colleague of good character; as an example of Prerauer's diligence, Hörth emphasised his involvement with the new organ. On 24 June, Director-General Heinz Tietjen confirmed that Kurt Prerauer, employed by the State Opera from 1 October 1925 until the end of the 1932–1933 season, had proved himself to be an exceptionally talented musician who had been liked by all his superiors on account of his distinguished conduct. By the time Tietjen wrote this reference, Prerauer had already left Berlin. He had given up the room in Kantstraße, Charlottenburg, which in the end he was renting as a subtenant.[9] He had also lost his forthcoming engagement as repetiteur for the Bayreuth *Festspiele*, allegedly at the insistence of Winifred Wagner. On 18 June, Kurt Prerauer arrived in Harwich, and the following day received his British Certificate of Registration.[10]

Berlin-born conductor Hans Zander, who worked until 1931 as assistant to Kurt Singer, Director of the Municipal Opera, and later held a similar job at the State Opera, also lost his position in June 1933 on racial grounds.[11] He had made his debut as a conductor with *Fidelio* at the age of twenty-four before becoming an opera teacher at the Berlin Hochschule für Musik and artistic director and *Kapellmeister* at the Municipal Opera. Zander's departure was also deplored by his prominent colleagues. Bruno Walter certified that he had known Zander for years as a highly capable opera conductor and musician, and Wilhelm Furtwängler also recommended Zander as a first-class artist.[12] Werner Baer had also been active at the opera,[13] as he later stated in a questionnaire: 'Worked under another name at the Municipal Opera in Berlin, originally encouraged by high-ranking musicians to follow a musical career.' He may have chosen a pseudonym to conceal either his youth, the fact he was still a student or that he was

Jewish. He must have begun this work before 1933, for which by his own account he studied orchestral parts and also conducted. Although Baer was not a member of any political party, he was close to socialist youth groups.[14] When the Führer was confirmed as Chancellor at the last election on 5 March 1933 and his supporters marched through the streets, it was a horrible experience for the young musician, and one with a long-lasting effect.[15] A few days later, on 11 March, the SA invaded the Municipal Opera. Baer's part-time employment must have ceased by then at the latest. Soon after that, the young musician fled to the Netherlands, where he performed as a pianist in restaurants and bars. After six months, he returned to Berlin, since he had not obtained a work permit;[16] moreover, he did not want to leave his mother alone.[17] Baer continued his musical education. He earned his living as an organist at several Berlin synagogues, and then as a pianist for the Jüdischer Kulturbund [Jewish Culture League]. As he later wrote, he began this work 'when it became clear to me that, because of "racial" discrimination, I would no longer be able to pursue the career that I had already started, as an opera conductor'.[18]

At that time, non-Aryan musicians were dismissed from almost all German theatres. Adolf Brenner lost his job as Kapellmeister at the Regensburg Municipal Theatre on 1 April 1933. He had begun his conducting career in two places rich with tradition – Gotha-Sondershausen, Thuringia, and the Bach city, Arnstadt – before being appointed second Kapellmeister in Regensburg in September 1931.[19] It was a time of economic austerity and cutbacks. When symphony concerts ceased, owing to the global financial crisis, two positions were cut from the twenty-six-piece theatre orchestra.[20] Instead of symphony concerts, they now put on 'musical morning galas', for example on 27 September 1931, a recital by the visiting artist Tossy Spivakovsky (advertised as 'the world famous Russian violinist'), and on 8 November a performance by the violinist Alma Prihoda-Rosé, Gustav Mahler's niece. Popular operettas replaced the more intellectually and financially challenging operas. Like the chief Kapellmeister Anton Bayer, the assistant Kapellmeister also had to conduct predominantly works of light entertainment, whereby he was given Viennese operettas and *Singspiele* [musical comedies]. In his first Regensburg season, Brenner took on *Majestät läßt bitten* by Rideamus/Walter Kollo, *Hanni geht tanzen* (Robert Bodanzky/Edmund Eysler), *Der Graf von Luxemburg* (Franz Lehár) and the musical comedies *Das Kaiserliebchen* (Heinrich Berté) and *Zwei Alte Wiener* (Eysler). The Eysler *Singspiel* was dismissed in the *Regensburger Anzeiger* as 'a fairly harmless affair': 'As for the good faith of the operetta public, it is hard to imagine it being any more naïve than this.' On the other hand, Brenner's performance as a conductor was praised. Together with the stage director, Willi Stadler, he had 'at least provided the right touch', so that there was 'a friendly reception from the full house, which showed genuine gratitude and appreciation for the work of the performers'.[21] Since the public liked Eysler's melodies, Brenner also put on his operetta *Der Frauenfresser* in the same season. The critics praised *Der Graf von Luxemburg* even more highly than they had the Eysler: 'Adolf Brenner and his orchestra tackled the Lehár with the warm sensitivity that this conductor's deeply emotional music-making deserves.'[22] In the 1932–1933 season, the second Kapellmeister was also able to conduct the musical comedy *Im weißen Rössl* (Ralph Benatzky), as well as the operettas *Czárdásfürstin* (Emmerich Kálmán), *Morgen geht's uns gut?* (Benatzky), *Die Königin* (Oscar Straus) and *Dolly* (Hugo Hirsch). Then, in April 1933, his work ended prematurely. Unlike Klemperer, Prerauer and Zander in Berlin, Bremer had devoted himself solely to popular music in Regensburg. Nonetheless, the work ban against non-Aryans affected him in the same way as his Berlin colleagues. On 1 April, he vacated his sublet room at 31 Von-der-Tann-Straße (at Becker's)[23] and then left Germany altogether. In Vienna he found accommodation with his mother in Karl-Beck-Gasse, where he provided for their living by giving private lessons in piano and theory.

Non-Aryan musicians who were not permanently employed by orchestras, opera houses or tertiary institutions were still allowed to appear as long as the Reichsmusikkammer [RMK, Reich Chamber of Music], founded in 1933, did not have any Aryan paragraph. In the first year of the Nazi dictatorship, there were still no official *Berufsverbote* [work bans] against them; eventually, however, organised protest rallies were staged as expressions of spontaneous public anger and did not spare stars like Bruno Walter and Artur Schnabel. Disturbed by the growing nationalism, Schnabel had already resigned his professorship at the Berlin Hochschule für Musik in

1931; in the face of increasing restrictions, he left Germany in May 1933 and moved to Italy, where he continued his masterclasses at Lake Como. Many of his students followed, including the Melbourne pianists Julia Mary Baillie and Nancy Weir.

The year 1933 was also a turning point for the pianist and conductor Kurt Herweg. He was born Kurt Hirsch in Landshut, Lower Bavaria. His family came from Znin, south of Bromberg in the Prussian administrative region of Posen.[24] They had moved from this district city (whose 31,568 inhabitants included 313 Israelites in 1890[25]) to Landshut, where Jews were a tiny minority: in 1895, there were only seventeen Jews among 20,554 inhabitants. The young Kurt Hirsch served the fatherland as a German citizen: from December 1916 until February 1919 he fought in France and Serbia and received a medal for service at the front. In 1919, he adopted the stage name 'Kurt Herweg'. In changing his name, he was following in the footsteps of his uncle, Franz Arnold, a successful actor and stage writer. One of Arnold's plays – the farce *Der keusche Lebemann* [The Chaste Playboy] – was premiered at the Munich Volkstheater in 1921. According to Kurt Herweg-Hirsch himself, he studied at the Music Academy in Munich, and began conducting at the age of nineteen. He was also active as a pianist and composer until his musical career in Germany ended in 1933.[26]

The German conservatories were now accepting only a few Jewish students. The Law Against the Overcrowding of German Schools and Colleges, enacted on 20 April 1933, meant that non-Aryan admissions were reduced to a number corresponding to their share of the population. As a result of the first implementation of this regulation, the proportion of newly matriculated Jewish students was restricted to 1.5 per cent of the total student population, which reduced the high percentage of Jewish music students. Adolf Faktor was also affected by this discrimination. His father had moved from Poland to Germany in 1919, married in Plauen, Vogtland in 1923, and opened an embroidery business in the neighbouring city of Falkenstein. When his sons Adolf and Hillel showed great musical talent, he bought two violins for them. Since there was no suitable violin teacher in Falkenstein, they received their first lessons from a trumpet player. The brothers soon appeared as child prodigies, but attempts to get Adolf Faktor into the Leipzig Conservatory failed owing to the restrictions mentioned above. In Berlin, it was no different for the young Karl Josef Berg, a violinist who played in the school orchestra and also composed. 'Hitler prevented me from pursuing a musical career.'[27] Karl was the only Jew in his class at the Augusta-Gymnasium in Charlottenburg, where the political circumstances had become unbearable for him: some of the teachers were already coming to work in SA uniforms.[28] In 1934, he began training as an accountant at Hahn Works Berlin, a large extruded metals foundry owned by one of the founders of the Jewish Reform Congregation.[29] Since Karl Berg had already been to Britain and wanted to improve his English, he went to London in April 1936, the start of his exile.

Heinrich Max Adler, born in Lichtenberg, Berlin, would probably also have studied music under more favourable circumstances but, as things stood, he began an apprenticeship at the large Nathan Israel department store in Spandauer Straße, not far from the Rote Rathaus, and pursued music as a hobby. The situation was no better at the universities: Walter Dullo's sister Eleonore was relegated. Similarly, all staff of Jewish descent fell victim to the 'cleansing'. At the Berlin Hochschule für Musik, then the most prestigious educational institution, the Combat League for German Culture began 'mopping up'.[30]

Jazz: Object of Hate

Those in power saw jazz, the widespread Afro-American musical genre, as a particularly dangerous example of *Rassenschande* [racial defilement]. Moreover, studies in the USA had attempted to prove that blacks were 'racially inferior'.[31] In 1930, the Nazi cultural politician Hans Severus Ziegler (a Hitler loyalist living in Weimar) had issued a decree for Thuringia, 'Against Negro Culture, for the German People', which effectively militated against Ernst Krenek's opera *Jonny spielt auf* [*Jonny Strikes Up the Band*]; the main protagonist of this opera was a black jazz musician who fell in love with a white woman. When Dr Hoch's Conservatory in Frankfurt am Main introduced jazz as a subject this, too, was viewed as scandalous.

The Weintraubs Syncopators, at that time the most high-profile and highly paid German jazz band,[32] were also defamed. At the beginning of 1933, they could still appear in the UFA production of *Heut kommt's drauf an*, in which Hans Albers played the band leader Hannes Eckmann, who with his Eckmann Boys (represented by the Weintraubs) had produced hits such as Walter Jurmann's 'Mein Gorilla hat 'ne Villa im Zoo'.[33] The subsequent UFA film *Gruß und Kuß, Veronika* was the end of the band's film career, especially as Goebbels had dismissed the film *Der blaue Engel* [*The Blue Angel*], as 'filth'.[34] In any case, because jazz was now seen as highly problematic, German promoters no longer wanted to risk inviting a jazz band that consisted almost entirely of non-Aryans. In 1933, the Weintraubs went on an extended tour of Europe that took them to, among other places, Copenhagen, Warsaw and finally Switzerland.

The Weintraubs' recordings were produced by the firms Lindström, Odeon and Electrola. In January 1933, they were still able to record John Kaiser's arrangements for *Der blaue Engel*. Such recordings could be sourced from specialist stores such as the Berlin music store Alberti, 34 Rankestraße, off the Kurfürstendamm, in the immediate vicinity of the Frasquita dance palace, the Ciro-Bar, and the Carlton and Femina clubs. In the early 1920s, the Hungarian Victor Gustav Alberti had opened this music business in association with the Alrobi publishing group; they concentrated on popular and film music, and the record shop specialised in imports. In the field of jazz, the music house (in association with Electrola) brought out their own 'Alberti Special Record' series for licensed pressings. In Berlin, Alberti's was known as '*the* shop for jazz fans and jazz musicians', and as a Mecca for swing fans.[35] On 30 January 1933, Victor Alberti happened to be in Prague when he was warned not to return to Germany[36] and moved to Budapest.[37] In April, he had to give up his position as deputy treasurer for the German Association of Music Publishers. After his departure, the shop was not closed, but taken over by a relative, Nikolaus Weiß. People could still buy foreign hits and jazz in Rankestraße, which is why Hans Brückner fulminated against Alberti in the journal *Deutsches Podium*,[38] and why the SS publication *Das Schwarze Korps* continued to abuse the firm in November 1937 by referring to it as 'a musical pig-sty'.[39]

Figure 2: The Weintraubs Syncopators around 1930, photographed by Lili Baruch, Berlin. With handwritten dedication to Friedrich Klopfer, manager of the Viennese record shop of His Master's Voice, and signed by Stefan Weintraub, Horst Graff, Kurt Kaiser, Baby Schulvater, Arno Olewski, Ansco Bruinier and Georg Haentzschel. (Evelyn Klopfer, Sydney)

Since 1928, Mátyás Seiber had run the jazz course at Dr Hoch's Conservatory in Frankfurt, the first of its kind in Europe. Clarinettist Walter Würzburger had been one of Seiber's students since 1932. He was the son of Siegfried Würzburger, a private music teacher, synagogue organist and director of a music school in Frankfurt. Like his father, Walter had perfect pitch and had taken early lessons in saxophone, clarinet and piano. At the Musterschule [model school], a progressive secondary school in Frankfurt, he had taken part in the Brecht–Weill school opera *Der Jasager* [He Said Yes]. At that time, almost a fifth of the pupils at the Musterschule were of Jewish descent, among them Würzburger's classmates Heinz Rothschild and Arthur Hirsch, who had written operettas for their school. Although Walter Würzburger was known to be apolitical, it came as a shock to him when the new government dismissed his teacher and closed down the jazz class. In 1933, the young musician fled to Paris, taking little more than his clarinet and saxophone.[40] He was known there as *Monsieur Anglais* on account of his good knowledge of English. He played music in the streets and in various jazz bands, provided that he had a work permit, and slept during the day in order to get through his evening performances. Occasionally he toured with a band in Luxembourg, where in 1935 he was visited by his father and brother, Karlrobert. Given that jazz was so hated by the Nazis, Würzburger regarded it as a kind of resistance, as an element of freedom.

Race and Religion

Until this time, many persecuted musicians saw themselves first and foremost as Germans rather than Jews. Their parents, who frequently still had Jewish names, often demonstrated their acculturation by choosing German first names for their children.[41] In doing so, the older generation confirmed its belief in social integration, which now seemed open to their descendants. For example, Salomon and Bella Silbermann, who lived in Catholic Cologne, named their son after Saint Alphons.[42] Boas Bischofswerder clung to the Orthodox faith, but decided on Felix and

Manfred for his two sons; in the same year, Owse Leb and Julie Edelmann chose the name Hans. Salomon and Feigel Frischer called their children Adolf and Emanuel. Isidor Jankel Portnoy and Rosa were the parents of a Heinrich. Chiel Faktor and his wife Dobra chose Adolf Abraham Josef. In those days, the names Adolf,[43] Fritz,[44] Günther, Hans,[45] Heinrich,[46] Kurt,[47] Richard[48] and Werner[49] seem to have been particularly popular among German Jews, whereby 'Adolf' was associated with German and Swedish kings, or with various archbishops, certainly not with the future Führer.

Patriotism was often stronger among assimilated Jews than among non-Jewish Germans. Alphons Silbermann recalled visits from his uncle Sigmund, who proudly wore an Iron Cross on his chest: 'That capacious little word "our" cropped up constantly in conversations; for one spoke of "our king", "our soldiers", and "our war" as if one stood patriotically alongside "our kaiser" or "our Hindenburg" as indispensable elements.'[50] Jews were able to prove their loyalty to the fatherland by doing military service, so they joined the Reichswehr in disproportionate numbers. Kurt Herweg-Hirsch, for example, also became a member of the Reich Federation of Jewish Front Soldiers, founded in February 1919 in memory of the 85,000 Jewish soldiers who had fought for the Germans during the First World War; 12,000 of them had died an 'heroic death for the Fatherland'. Fritz Coper joined the cavalry in 1912 and fought from 1914 to 1918, a year longer than his brother Willy. Stefan Weintraub served from 1916 to 1918, and on his discharge received the Iron Cross. Defeat came as no less of a shock to Jewish soldiers than to non-Jewish. After the war, the father of popular Viennese musician Hans Blau never wanted to hear the march of his Hochmeister Regiment again; he once boxed his son's ears when he heard him playing it.[51] Some retained their respect for uniforms; looking back, Adolf Faktor confessed that he had initially admired the dashing outfits of the Hitler Youth.[52] Because of their patriotic sentiment, even Hitler's speeches at first made an impression on assimilated Jews like Emanuel Frischer.

As a sign of their acculturation, many Jews converted to Christianity, either under pressure or voluntarily. In 1933, there were 300,000 non-Aryan Christians[53] as against just under 500,000 Jews in the German Reich.[54] In any case, liberal Jewry had adopted many elements of Christian worship, including the German language and use of the organ. Like Hermann Schildberger, Walter Hirschberg's family as well as Dr Alfred Peyser and his daughter, Dora, all belonged to the Berlin Reform Congregation.[55] The rabbis of this congregation wore a cassock, like evangelical pastors. Some liberal congregations, such as the Friedenstempel [Temple of Peace], abolished the physical separation of men and women. As with many non-Jews of that generation, disinterest in religion was also spreading among the Jews. When questioned about his religion, Werner Baer replied that until 1938 he had not been interested in such topics. That said, he had been employed as the principal organist at a liberal synagogue since 1934. George Dreyfus expressed similar views: 'In Germany we were never a very Jewish family.'[56] Ilse Blair remarked that the Ten Commandments were enough for her second husband, Hans Blau. The violinist Lisbeth Cohn was not religious either, according to her daughter-in-law, but attended synagogue on the important religious holidays.[57]

Because German Jews' desire for acculturation was stronger than their religious interests, mixed marriages were common. About 35,000 marriages between Jews and non-Jews took place in 1933. There were also mixed marriages between Christians and converted Jews.[58] The Lutheran Andreas Dullo had married Alice Japha, who came from a Jewish family; she converted to Christianity, and their son was baptised and brought up as a Christian. Another mixed marriage was that between Meinhardt Adam and his non-Jewish wife Katharina Schmidt. The Munich-born Max Meyer became a Catholic and married a Catholic.[59] Where they lived, in St Gregor near Oberammergau, the two Meyers were regularly seen at Mass. The son of a Jewish cantor, Hans Edelmann left the Israelite religious congregation in Vienna in 1936 and became a Roman Catholic in order to marry the Catholic Helene Hammerschmied.

Alphons Silbermann wrote of his life experiences around 1930: 'The Jew boy Silbermann is still able to go about his activities without any hindrance; no boycott, no discrimination, no unpleasantness stands in his way.'[60] Zionist ideas were foreign to him: 'He is so fully caught up in the mentality and habitus of the assimilated Jewish bourgeoisie – which advocates separating politics and the Jewish question – that he cannot grasp the talk of his cousin Berthold, a devoted Zionist who is preparing to move to Palestine.'⁶¹ At the beginning of Nazi rule, there were still no coherent procedures for dealing with non-Aryans, who were more likely to be tolerated in the big cities than in the country or smaller towns like Schwäbisch-Gmünd. Here, Fritz Mayer suffered growing discrimination at school from about 1933 onwards. Some pupils threw stones at him, and called out 'Jew, Jew'. In Australia, where he became known as the music critic Fred Blanks, he recalled these incidents. Such experiences had taught the eighteen-year-old what antisemitism was, and what tolerance was. Those stones 'boosted my education in politics, ethics, morality and self-protection, none of them subjects in the school curriculum'.⁶² In 1935, Mayer left the hated institution in his home town and transferred to a Jewish school in Stuttgart. The Wuppertal-Elberfeld businessman Alfred Dreyfus also considered it safer, under the circumstances, to move to Berlin. In 1935, he sold his business and acquired a villa in Berlin's elegant suburb, Dahlem. Jews were less hampered in Berlin than in smaller towns and cities.

At first, many of the old-established Jewish families were unaffected by Nazi rhetoric; they regarded themselves as an integral part of German society and anything but outsiders. Theatre director Kurt Singer's daughter remembered that 'the German Jews of the Weimar Republic were more German than Jewish; they were first and foremost Germans, and so connected with German culture that nothing in the world could separate them from it, not even the Nazis'.⁶³ Families of mixed marriages were especially well integrated into German culture. For Walter Dullo, son of an Aryan father and a Jewish mother, who had been brought up in the Lutheran faith, it was all the more frightening to be called a 'half Jew'. It was only Nazi race laws that forced him into this outsider role. For him, as for many assimilated Jews, the new laws were intended to invalidate the integration that had taken place over such a long period of time. 'We were forced to be Jews', commented Ilse Blair. 'The German Jews were not religious at all – until Hitler came along.' George Dreyfus also recalled that his parents only began to reflect on the heritage of their forbears when they were under external pressure. The Nuremberg Race Laws of 1935 had caused this exclusionary effect: 'In counterpoint to the Nuremberg laws, Jews started feeling more Jewish.'⁶⁴ Similarly, Alphons Silbermann acknowledged that his interest in things Jewish was awakened 'extremely late', and that it was 'elicited by the mark of a person who must be taken to be a Jew, a mark stamped on him by the non-Jewish world and the source of hurt of all kinds'.[65]

'Flying like foam ...': From Kulturbund Deutscher Juden to Jüdischer Kulturbund

An important part in this disintegration process was played by an organisation that was founded in the summer of 1933 for a very different purpose, namely to find opportunities for unemployed Jewish artists and scientists to appear in public. In a first description of the project, one of its initiators, the former opera director Kurt Singer, suggested the name Deutschjüdischer Kulturbund [German Jewish Culture League],[66] based on the idea of a common culture. State Commissioner Hans Hinkel promptly changed the name to Kulturbund Deutscher Juden [Culture League of German Jews], but otherwise agreed with the proposal; for he anticipated that this organisation would give him the opportunity to 'cleanse' theatres, orchestras and other state institutions by removing non-Aryans. He welcomed the fact that those affected were organising a safety net for themselves and for other artists who had been dismissed and were prepared to do without public advertising. Hence, they contributed to the ghettoisation of a cultural life organised by non-Aryans. According to Werner Baer, with the Culture League the many Jews still in Berlin at the time were creating a 'city within a city'.[67]

When the Kulturbund Deutscher Juden was founded on 15 July 1933 in Kurt Singer's flat, Hans Zander became administrative director; as was formerly the case at the Municipal Opera, he was again at Singer's side. According to the statutes, the purpose of the Kulturbund was 'to look after the artistic and scientific interests of the Jewish population and to harness them in providing work for Jewish artists and scientists'. In addition, it was to organise for its members 'in particular theatre performances and concerts, lectures and art exhibitions whose artistic and scientific content was as a matter of principle to be provided by Jews'.[68] Basically, although only non-Aryans could attend these performances, in terms of content there were no thoughts of any restrictions, let alone ghettoisation. In spite of all the new regulations, the Kulturbund wanted to demonstrate – at least in cultural terms – the close connection between the Jewish population and Germany itself, as the theatre critic Julius Bab emphasised in August 1933: 'They can ban us from an active social life in Germany, but not from its spiritual life, or from the world in which we have put down roots and prospered for more than five generations'.[69] This was also the position taken by Hermann Schildberger, whose admission to the bar had been revoked in June 1933,[70] but who continued to work as a choral conductor for the Jewish Reform Congregation.[71] It was a stroke of luck that Hans Lachmann-Mosse, chairman of the Jewish Reform Congregation's liturgical commission and proprietor of Mosse Publishers, shared his interest in new media and modern music. Mosse's generous support had enabled Schildberger to bring out his revised Reform liturgy in three volumes between 1928 and 1932, whereby he scored almost all sections of the comparatively slim prayer book for singing. The recordings of this liturgy were a special attraction. For a three-year period, Schildberger was given the opportunity to work as producer and director in Lindström's modern recording studio with some of the best musicians in Germany, including the tenor Joseph Schmidt and the contralto Paula Salomon-Lindberg.

Apart from the use of the organ, the Reform liturgy specified the use of the German language and mixed congregational singing. The Berlin Reform Congregation used compositions by Louis Lewandowski, who borrowed heavily from Mendelssohn, and set some of the liturgical texts to well-known secular melodies. Thus, besides compositions by Lewandowski and Sulzer, Schildberger's recording project included works by Handel, Beethoven, Schubert, Schumann and Bruckner. A striking example is the modification for liturgical use of the penultimate song from Schumann's *Dichterliebe* song cycle based on poems by Heinrich Heine. Heine's poem reads:

> From olden tales it flings out
> A beckoning white hand;

It sings out and it rings out
From an enchanted land

Where blossoms tall and slender
In the gold-lit eventide
Look up with eyes as tender
As the eyes of a loving bride –

The last verse runs: 'Ah, could I only go there/And free my heart of pain,/And banish all my woe there,/Be free and blest again!' With bitter realism, however, the final lines expose the dream as a romantic illusion: 'Ah, land of bliss undying,/I see it oft in dreams./When dawn comes, it goes flying/Like foam in the morning beams.'[72]

For the new Reform liturgy, Schildberger gave Heine's poetic vision of a magic land a religious twist. Through radical abbreviation he transformed Schumann's great, three-part melody into a simple, strophic song and set it to a text about greeting the Sabbath as a day of peace, represented by a festively adorned bride. We can speculate about why Schildberger chose this particular song from Schumann's *Dichterliebe* for liturgical purposes. Was this free adaption of the famous Heine setting meant to remind people of a particularly successful example of German Jewish cultural symbiosis? From today's perspective, however, it is the poet's question mark which Schumann links with this melody that resonates more powerfully than any certainty of faith expressed by the text.

The Jewish Reform Congregation and Hans Lachmann-Mosse were very pleased with the recordings. Actually, they were intended above all to provide an artistically attractive liturgy for Jewish rural congregations, which had neither choirs nor organists. But Lachmann-Mosse used the records in his own synagogue, even though the Berlin Jewish Reform Congregation already had an organ and a choirmaster by the name of Hermann Schildberger. During his exile in the USA, George Mosse recalled how, every Sunday in the synagogue, his father would sit on a podium behind a curtain, wind up the gramophone and change the records.[73] The new recordings were even positively reviewed by the press. In the *Berliner Tageblatt* the respected critic Dr Alfred Einstein wrote:

[...] the 114 different pieces of music that make up the Jewish Reform Congregation's liturgy have all been recorded on disc, and produced by Lindström. Under the direction of Hermann Schildberger, around 100 people, soloists and choir members, worked together to create what is so far the most comprehensive of all recordings [...] With good equipment properly used the illusion is perfect. And not just the illusion, but the sanctity of the religious service. This innovation represents a spiritual and artistic gain for all congregations.[74]

The recording project made Hermann Schildberger famous well beyond Berlin's Jewry. From 1931, he also led the Collegium Musicum of the Reform Congregation's youth community, which put on, for example, operatic evenings with music by Scarlatti, Gluck, Mozart, Bizet, Smetana and Verdi. As a member of the commission of musical experts of the Jewish Community of Berlin, Schildberger was a founding member of the Kulturbund and head of its music section until 1934. At this time, it had not been realised that State Commissioner Hans Hinkel intended to use the Kulturbund to gradually force non-Aryan artists out of German musical life. Because there could no longer be any German Jews, since Jews were now classified as a foreign race, on Hinkel's instructions the Kulturbund Deutscher Juden was renamed the Jüdischer Kulturbund in Deutschland [Jewish Culture League in Germany]. Composers like Bach, Beethoven, Schumann, Brahms and Wagner had to be removed from the Kulturbund's programmes; Jews could listen only to Jewish music. With the exception of the Zionists, the majority of German Jews deplored this regulation as a terrible restriction, as expulsion from Paradise.[75]

Kulturbünde [Culture Leagues] had also been founded in other cities like Hamburg, where Max Kurt Behrens, formerly a conductor at the Volksoper, now found a new field of activity. Salo Max Tichauer joined the Kulturbund in Breslau. A soldier during the First World War, after the war he became a violinist in various light entertainment bands and as a result joined several German musicians' associations in 1919. In 1923, he and his group were invited to perform on one of the ocean liners run by United States Lines.[76] On his return, Tichauer married in 1925 and then performed in various venues in Germany. In 1933, however, as a Jew he lost his membership of the Musicians' Association. He worked for a while in Poland, and possibly even in his home town of Kattowitz [Katowice] which had been attached to Poland, contrary to the result of the plebiscite in 1922. Apparently he had no luck there either, because in 1934 Tichauer returned to Germany where, in the meantime, the Reichsmusikkammer was implementing the new regulations. Therefore, Salo Tichauer decided to change his vocation. In Breslau, he joined the Reich Federation of Jewish Front Soldiers and the Jewish Culture League, and he ran a delicatessen until December 1938.

Nevertheless, the Kulturbund in Berlin offered the most comprehensive programme. This was why, after the cancellation of his recent engagements, Kurt Herweg-Hirsch moved to the capital, where, for example, he accompanied Hedi Haas in a *chanson* recital for the Kulturbund in March 1935.[77] In the same year, the multi-talented Werner Baer became the pianist for the Kulturbund's Cabaret, which was directed by the actor Max Ehrlich, once star of the Cabaret of Comedians. In spite of the looming danger, Ehrlich returned to Berlin after his successful tours abroad. In October, he founded the Cabaret and found attractive accommodation for it in the Café Leon at 156 Kurfürstendamm, next to the current Schaubühne am Lehniner Platz. Designed by Erich Mendelsohn, this was the building in which Kurt Robitscheck had opened the Cabaret of Comedians in 1928. Here too, the Kulturbund's Cabaret quickly became an institution. Drawn by the star Max Ehrlich, at first many non-Jewish people attended the performances until identity checks were introduced. Even the Gestapo (for whom several boxes were always reserved) was said to have snapped up the tickets.[78] The public wanted light entertainment 'as we have enough *tsoris* [troubles]'.[79] With support from Willy Rosen, Max Ehrlich fulfilled this need with flying colours. Musical revue hits came in rapid succession, like *Kunterbunt* [Motley] (December 1935), *Herr Direktor – bitte Vorschuß!* [Director – an advance please!] (February 1936), *Vorhang auf!* [Curtain up!] (October 1936) and *Bitte einsteigen!* [All aboard!] (March 1937). Werner Baer advanced from pianist to musical director, which meant that he also had to compose songs and write music for sketches.[80] As audiences grew, the Cabaret had to move to bigger halls and finally to the main Kulturbund theatre on Kommandantenstraße. At the same time, Baer was also the pianist for the Kulturbund's orchestra,[81] conducted by Joseph Rosenstock, and for the Sid Kay's Fellows. This jazz band had last been employed by a dance cabaret in Dresden; but because six of its ten members were Jewish, they, like the Weintraubs Syncopators, received no further engagements.[82] Siegmund Friedmann, who later called himself Shabtai Petrushka, immediately applied to the Berlin Kulturbund, which allowed the band, which now consisted of twelve to fifteen players, to continue working under the same name.

Early Escape

Despite all the restrictions, the Kulturbund offered racially persecuted artists an opportunity to earn a living, with the result that many of them put off the idea of emigrating and remained in Germany. That said, the exodus had begun even before this organisation was established. Like Kurt Prerauer, who arrived in England in June 1933, after the new government assumed power, the principal cantor Boas Bischofswerder left the country as quickly as possible. Apparently he had considered emigrating even earlier, as in October 1932, Professor Richard Hagel from the Academy of Church and School Music testified to his brilliance as a singer. Bischofswerder's recordings of ritualistic Jewish works and his own compositions, which the press had singled out for their 'typically Russian–Jewish timbre', had convinced Hagel of his extraordinary talent and high artistic standards.[83] Possibly with emigration in mind, the cantor presented the music critic Hans Heinz Stuckenschmidt with records and asked for a critical opinion. In a letter dated 24 January 1933, the latter replied that Bischofswerder possessed not only a beautiful, strong and versatile voice, but also a profound knowledge of the Jewish musical tradition, adding that there were very few cantors with these abilities and knowledge. The renowned critic wished the young man every success for the future, and expressed the hope that his letter would be of some assistance.

Bischofswerder arrived in London with his wife Helene on 24 July in order to make preparations for the whole family to move.[84] To this end, he contacted the Association of Chazanim of Federated Synagogues, established in 1887 to help Jewish refugees from Eastern Europe[85] and he was offered a position as cantor at the Orthodox synagogue in Great Garden Street, in London's East End.[86] After asking the Jewish Refugees Committee in Bloomsbury House to submit an application for entry for him, the Bischofswerders spent the waiting period in Antwerp. On 15 September, after all the necessary formalities had been completed and the application approved, they were officially able to travel to Britain with their two sons, eleven-year-old Felix and four-year-old Manfred. As his residence permit was valid until September 1935, Bischofswerder became cantor at said synagogue, and later President of the Chazanim Association, whose main office was also located in Great Garden Street. When his residence permit expired, the Jewish Refugees Committee requested an extension; initially it was approved for only one year, but in September 1936 it was converted to a permanent residence permit. Bischofswerder sent his two sons to schools in London and acquired two flats. Three years after their escape, this family of four seemed to have found a new home.

CHAPTER 4

On the Other Side of the World

Spirit of Adventure? Off to Australia as Musicians

Today, Australia is one of the favourite long-distance holiday destinations for Germans; in this huge country they experience a vast and unspoilt natural landscape found hardly anywhere else in the world. Here they can fulfil their dreams of freedom and adventure in a way that is no longer possible in what was once the 'Wild West'. Australia's positive image – illustrated by the 2000 Sydney Olympics, with its colourful pictures of sportspeople – would be unthinkable without the development of aviation. However, when this distant continent could be reached only after several months at sea, 'down under' was the epitome of remoteness and isolation. Australia was therefore sometimes designated as *The Never Never*.[1]

Because of this isolation, from 1788 to 1854 the Australian colonies of New South Wales and Victoria were used by the British as penal colonies for convicts in order to relieve overcrowded British jails. In this way, more than 160,000 people came to this sparsely populated land. In 1835, the Prussian state developed similar plans for deportation to Australia, although they never came to fruition.[2] Only gradually, and with some hesitation, did free settlers arrive, often under duress. For musicians, conditions there were far worse than in Europe; hence, as a rule they headed for Australia only if they had no other alternatives. For a while, the nineteenth-century gold rush was a source of lucrative guest performances, as in the gold-rush cities of the USA or the Brazilian rubber centres of the Amazon; but such tours seldom turned into permanent emigration.

The first creative non-indigenous musician in New South Wales, the Irish composer and violinist William Vincent Wallace (1812–1865) left Ireland on account of financial problems. From 1836, he gave concerts in

Sydney, where he was celebrated as 'the Australian Paganini'. He prepared for a lengthy stay and, together with his wife, he founded a music school – a sensation in this land of pioneers, where the settlers' musical life was otherwise largely limited to military music. Two years later, however, Wallace had to leave the country again to escape his debts. He left his family, went to Chile and lived an unsettled life until in 1846 he finally achieved success in London with his opera *Maritana*. Did coming to Sydney to escape his creditors make Wallace an exiled musician? Do financial problems qualify someone for this honorary title? Or is his two-year residence in Australia to be judged merely as a failed emigration? The question is difficult to answer as it is unclear whether Wallace wanted to settle permanently in Sydney, or whether – putting aside his new financial problems – he always intended to return to Europe.

Five years later, the Jewish composer and musicologist Isaac Nathan (1792–1864) came from London to New South Wales, also to escape from his creditors, and he decided to stay. He had completed a solid musical training, prided himself on his acquaintanceship with Lord Byron and became the authoritative musical personality in the colony. Nathan used the lack of cultural institutions for his own pioneering musical projects. In Sydney, he founded a vocal school, became choir director at the cathedral, opened a music printing business, and composed Australia's first operas and had them performed. Nathan was conscious of his central role in the establishment of a new musical culture. Unlike many subsequent generations of migrant musicians, he did not set out merely to bring British culture to the colony. He wanted to develop something independent by combining European and Australian traditions, so he became interested in the music of the Aboriginal people. Even if it cannot be said that there was a genuine understanding, his intention was nevertheless remarkable. Whereas his operas failed to gain acceptance, his patriotic odes made him famous, one example being his elegy for the German-born explorer Ludwig Leichhardt, who never returned from his last expedition.[3]

Isaac Nathan was definitely not an exiled musician, but an emigrant: he adapted to his new environment and never returned to Britain. In contrast to the convicts, who had been incarcerated and deported to Australia, often for minor offences, he himself decided on this distant country. That said, there are many more cases in which not even those affected could unequivocally differentiate between exile and emigration. The feeling of isolation and longing for the homeland crops up time and again in the diaries of the early settlers. 'In these circumstances it was understandable and natural that they should cling with a certain desperation to every custom, however trivial, that made them feel kinship with the society from which they felt themselves exiles.'[4] A quick glance at the preponderance of Victorian buildings in Melbourne or Adelaide, or at the place and street names, confirms this adherence to traditions that might create the illusion of still being in Britain. In relation to the early settlers, the notion of exile put forward by Roger Covell denotes the feeling of being excluded from the culture they had brought with them, however diverse their motives for leaving their homeland.

In this sense, the Old Lutherans were also 'exiles'. From 1838 onwards, they had moved mostly from Prussia's rural districts to the convict-free colony of South Australia. In spite of, or indeed perhaps because of, the distance, they tenaciously clung to their own customs. The reason for their exile was the unification of Lutheran and Reformist congregations decreed by King Friedrich Wilhelm III. In order to maintain their religious beliefs, whole communities, together with their pastors, risked the long journey from Europe to South Australia. They settled in the fertile Barossa Valley and founded villages whose names reminded them of their former homeland (Grünberg, Langmeil, Gnadenfrei, Klemzig, Lobethal, etc). These refugees retained their culture, language, liturgy and Lutheran chorales. Their newly built churches and organs were modelled on familiar designs, so that an old, established culture was transplanted to new surroundings. In the almost uninhabited rural communities, this was possible with very little adaptation to an otherwise characteristically English environment. Although the Prussian Lutherans were prepared to remain permanently in Australia, they were not emigrants in the classic sense. These people could be seen as exiles, in the sense described by Roger Covell, inasmuch as they were forcibly separated from their home environment. They were also exiled in the religious sense, finding themselves in an in-between state somewhere between an earthly and a heavenly homeland.

The political exiles who left Germany after the failure of the 1848 Revolution were more willing to integrate and assimilate. One of them, the Berlin-born composer Carl Linger (1810–1862) had already written two operas in addition to symphonies and masses by the time he arrived in South Australia in 1849. Linger stayed in the main city, Adelaide, where he worked his way up from arduous beginnings as a dance musician and piano tuner to a renowned music teacher and conductor. He became famous for his patriotic *Song of Australia*, which won a composition competition in 1859. Three years later, he died in Adelaide a highly respected man. By then, despite his German heritage, Carl Linger was recognised as an Australian musician. Thus, for him, exile turned into emigration.

Isaac Nathan may have shown a remarkable curiosity; however, the Aboriginal people were repressed and disenfranchised right from the start, as Australia was to be reserved for white settlers. Although consistent with the 'White Australia Policy' that had been officially introduced in 1901, German immigration ended with the First World War. Just as in Britain the royal family changed its name from Saxe-Coburg-Gotha to Windsor, in Australia the language of the enemy and German place names were prohibited. The Lutherans' hope of practising their traditions more freely than in their homeland proved to be an illusion. Hugo Wertheim from Hesse, whose Melbourne factory employed 300 workers and produced 2,000 pianos a year, was suspected of pro-German activity. A new 'language test', originally developed to keep out unwanted Polish Jews, gave the immigration authorities every opportunity to reject undesirable persons. For example, in 1934, the writer Egon Erwin Kisch, a representative of Prague's German Jewish culture, was prevented from entering the country because, in spite of his polyglot linguistic abilities, he did not speak Gaelic. Kisch has described this outrageous discrimination in his book, *Landung in Australien* [*Australian Landfall*] (1937).[5]

Jews who wished to leave Germany after 1933 were also familiar with this restrictive immigration policy. A comprehensive article on Australia in the magazine *Jüdische Auswanderung* [Jewish Emigration], published by the Hilfsverein der Juden in Deutschland [Aid Association of Jews in Germany], emphasised Australian nationalism and mentioned its slogan '*One* continent, *one* language, *one* people' (reminiscent of similar slogans in Hitler's Germany) as well as the defensiveness of its trade unions. As a result, Australian immigration policy was geared to prevent any mass immigration, but would allow individual immigration – now that the economic crisis was almost completely over – as long as a guarantee was given that the immigrant would assimilate quickly – for which a command of English was the main prerequisite – and also that his [sic] occupation would prove useful to the country'.[6]

Interesting in this context are reflections on 'The Social Foundations of Australian Culture', as they highlight the enormous role played by sport and film, 'while the intellectual problems of art and science are paid little attention'. The average Australian newspaper contained 'basically little more than sports commentary, film reviews and social news. There is little about politics and business and almost nothing about art and science'.[7] 'For other freelance professions such as writers, editors, actors or musicians, the prospects are generally very poor, which is partly to do with Australia's small population, and partly with the superficiality of culture, as described above.'

For German intellectuals, unlike today's tourists, Australia was never a dream destination. While adventurers gladly followed in the path of Ludwig Leichhardt, or sought out unusual natural phenomena described in books by Hans Bertram (*Flug in die Hölle* [Flying to Hell], 1933), Kurt Faber (*Als Landstreicher durch Australien* [Tramping around Australia], 1933), Heinz Geck (*Umweg über Australien* [Detour via Australia], 1937), Kurt Heyd (*Christophs Abenteuer in Australien* [Christopher's Adventures in Australia], 1935), A.E. Johann (*Kängeruhs, Kopra und Korallen* [Kangeroos, Copra and Corals], 1936) or Joseph M. Velter (*Australien kreuz und quer* [Criss-Crossing Australia], 1931),[8] musicians and music lovers were hardly interested in being sent into the desert. Rather, talented Australian musicians had always moved in the other direction, to London, Vienna, Leipzig or Berlin. For them, going overseas was quite natural.[9] For example, the pianist Ernest Hutcheson and the composer Alfred Hill both studied at the Leipzig Conservatory, while the composer Percy Grainger attended Dr Hoch's Conservatory in Frankfurt. The Melbourne-born violinist Johann Kruse, of German extraction, was a pupil of Joseph Joachim and the first Australian instrumentalist to achieve recognition in Europe;[10] according to the critic Thorold Waters, he was the greatest violinist Australia had ever produced.[11] With the First World War, these German–Australian cultural ties came to an almost complete standstill. Although the violinist and conductor Bernard Heinze, the violinist Alma Moodie, and the pianists Julia Mary Baillie and Nancy Weir all studied in Berlin after 1918, this focus on German culture was no longer regarded as politically appropriate. There was a shift towards where Australian culture was supposed to have had its roots: London. Australian artists were only considered to be properly trained if they had received at least some of their training there; and they were only regarded as really successful if the English public and the London press had paid tribute by way of recognition. This rule of thumb was to retain its validity well into the twentieth century.[12]

The musicians who were forced to leave Germany and Austria by the Nazis knew about the poor work conditions in Australia, and sought refuge in other countries first. After 1918, few Germans or Austrians had relocated to Australia to earn a living. The soprano Alice Orff-Solscher was one of these exceptions; Carl Orff's first wife had come to Melbourne in 1930 as guest of the piano-manufacturing Wertheim family.[13] There she was discovered by the conductor Bernard Heinze, Director of the University Conservatorium; he put her in charge of the opera department, and together they staged *Carmen*, *Faust* and *Tosca*.[14] Another exception was the conductor, music writer and composer Gerhard von Keußler, who made the long journey to Australia in 1932. Although he enjoyed great fame in Europe (witness the special issues dedicated to him by periodicals), Keußler had sought in vain for a long-term appointment. In the face of Germany's devastating unemployment, he must have regarded any further efforts as pointless, which would explain why he took this unusual step. When he arrived in Melbourne on the *Heidelberg* on 18 May 1932, the *Argus* newspaper welcomed him under the headline 'Musical Conductor's Visit' as a conductor and composer who wanted to complete an oratorio in Australia before returning to Germany. In truth, the artist was looking for a long-term position. Although the economic crisis had also led to restrictions in Melbourne, in 1933, on the initiative of Bernard Heinze, the newly established Melbourne Symphony Orchestra asked him to conduct one of their symphony concerts. It was a great success,[15] and as a result he (a Lutheran) was offered a temporary position as Musical Director at St Patrick's, Melbourne's Catholic Cathedral.[16] This would hardly have been possible without the approval of Irish-born Archbishop Daniel Mannix.[17] Above all, they wanted Keußler to take charge of the comprehensive musical activities that were planned to celebrate Melbourne's centenary. The visiting artist completed this task with flying colours and, in December 1934, his *Praeludium Solemne* for organ and orchestra, dedicated to the Archbishop, was premiered in St Patrick's Cathedral.[18] In the same year, he was made an honorary member of the British Music Society. Although his employment at the Cathedral terminated in accordance with the contract in July 1935,[19] Keußler conducted several more symphony concerts in Melbourne Town Hall, which were enthusiastically received. He, too, was pleased with the result:

> The lucky star under which all this took place was consistent with Australia's 'heavenly warmth'. When I was officially invited by several prominent people – through one or two of their customary 'Letters to the Editor' – to remain in Australia for good, I replied publicly in the same way, saying that I would gladly come to Australia again one day, but with a return ticket in my pocket.[20]

A year after Alice Orff-Solscher, Keußler also went back to Germany, where working conditions had improved for musicians who were 'unencumbered' on political or racial grounds.[21] This was largely due to the establishment of the Reichsmusikkammer, something that Keußler had eagerly anticipated:[22] it led to a significant decrease in unemployment, and greatly improved the social situation for musicians – at the expense of non-Aryans.[23] The new beginning in Germany was promising: in 1936, the Prussian Academy of Arts gave Keußler a composition masterclass that he was allowed to lead until 1945. In spite of his friendship with Peter Raabe, the President of the Reichsmusikkammer, Keußler was expelled from the RMK in 1939, probably on account of his protests against the Nazis' Jewish policies, which meant being banned from performing.[24] Thus, the Berlin premiere of his symphonic fantasy for orchestra, *Australia* on 10 May 1939 was one of the last Keußler concerts in Hitler's Germany. The composer's thoughts now turned longingly towards that distant land where he had been so celebrated. In an autobiographical sketch from 1940, he describes his twelve months at St Patrick's Cathedral as 'the best working year of my life'. He even attempted to return to Australia but, in view of the war, this was impossible. At the time, in crass contrast to this self-evaluation, the musicologist Ernst Bücken maintained that Keußler had been 'dismissed from his positions' in Australia on account of being German.[25] In fact, this musician in particular had suffered surprisingly little from the widespread anti-German sentiment after the First World War.

Celebrities on Tour: Jascha and Tossy Spivakovsky

Gerhard von Keußler had not come to Australia for racial or political reasons, but for economic reasons. The brothers Jascha and Tossy Spivakovsky did not arrive as refugees either. Quite the contrary; they were celebrated stars touring as guest artists. For Jascha, Australia was no *terra incognita* as he had already completed a very successful tour there in 1921–1922. In the *Australian Musical News*, the pianist was characterised as a young man brimming with vitality who gave no less than seventy-five concerts in seven months. Several London reviews had helped him to secure this engagement. 'We have seldom heard a more brilliant performance', praised the *Daily Telegraph*; and the *Daily Chronicle* wrote about his 'overwhelming passion'.[26] Although the Tait concert agency had advertised the pianist as a musical sensation, the reaction of the Sydney public was initially reserved. By the time of his third concert, the spell was broken; the enthusiastic reception was unlike anything Australia had ever experienced at a piano recital. One of the Melbourne papers said Jascha Spivakovsky was 'probably the most satisfying all-round performer this generation has heard'.[27] After his first appearance in Melbourne, Nellie Melba (Australia's most famous musician) sent the pianist a letter in which she confessed: 'I consider you one of the greatest pianists in the world.'[28]

The pianist returned to Australia for a second tour in 1929, now accompanied by his young wife, Leonore. The millionaire's daughter from Adelaide had got to know the young artist on his first tour, and had fallen in love with him. A few years later, at the age of seventeen, she had travelled to Berlin with her parents and married the pianist there. On his second tour, he gave the first Australian performances of several works, including Mussorgsky's *Pictures at an Exhibition* and Max Reger's monumental *Variations on a Theme of Johann Sebastian Bach*.

Figure 3: The Spivakovsky–Kurtz Trio with Tossy Spivakovsky, violin, Jascha Spivakovsky, piano, and Edmund Kurtz, violoncello (from left). (Michael Spivakovsky, Melbourne)

On 27 January 1933, Jascha Spivakovsky set out from Berlin on his third Australian tour, this time together with his youngest brother Tossy and the cellist Edmund Kurtz; in 1930 they had formed the Spivakovsky–Kurtz Trio. In January 1926, at the age of eighteen, Tossy Spivakovsky had been appointed concertmaster of the Berlin Philharmonic Orchestra. At an all-Tchaikovsky evening by the orchestra on 14 November 1930, Jascha and Tossy played the piano and violin concertos one after the other at the Philharmonie; it was a unique occasion. The brothers were heard regularly in the Beethovensaal of the Philharmonie, either individually or together. When they boarded the *Oronsay* with Edmund Kurtz in Naples on 12 March 1933, the situation in Germany had drastically deteriorated. For Russian Jews like the Spivakovskys, Hitler's Germany no longer offered a professional future. Jascha and Tossy were travelling on Soviet passports, whereas Edmund Kurtz and Jascha's wife Leonore had German papers; but they all decided not to return to Berlin. This meant that they also had to accept the inevitable loss of their assets; just prior to their departure, Jascha had moved into a new flat at 24 Berchtesgadener Straße, Berlin Schöneberg.

By January 1933, the *Australian Musical News* was advertising the Spivakovsky-Kurtz Trio as the best instrumental trio ever to have visited the southern hemisphere.[29] The magazine also mentioned Edmund Kurtz's brother, the conductor Efrem Kurtz, who had already made a successful visit to Australia.[30] W.M.R. Mandeville, Director of the agency Celebrity Concerts Ltd, emphasised in the accompanying material that the tour, limited to fifty-two concerts,[31] had only come about after lengthy negotiations. In the past, even the promise of extraordinarily high fees had failed to lure such prominent artists to travel so far. This time, the decisive factors were the pianist's love of Australia, and that Leonore Spivakovsky wanted to visit relatives and friends. Hence, the comprehensive concert programme contained photographs not only of the three artists, but also of Jascha's wife.

The programme had been printed at a stage when all the parties assumed that this would be a regular concert tour. In the meantime, however, the musicians had already made the decision to stay longer in Australia. As the pianist had been a member of the Australian Musicians' Union since 1929, and therefore had no need to be afraid of the organisation that otherwise treated overseas artists with utter scepticism, the tour started under favourable conditions. In April, the six-month residence permit issued on their arrival had already been extended to twelve months. The newcomers received substantial assistance from Jascha's parents-in-law, who had emigrated to Australia from Odessa, and from Bernard Heinze, the Director of the University Conservatorium, who knew and appreciated the pianist. Founded in 1895 by the Scottish-born Francis Ormond, the Conservatorium belonged to the University of Melbourne and delivered courses both in practical music skills and academic studies,[32] a combination at that time unique in the British Empire. According to Thérèse Radic, they were attended mainly by aspiring young female piano teachers: '[the Conservatorium's] reputation was that of a piano-oriented, female teacher-producing factory'. In Australia, the study of music was regarded as a woman's domain.[33] The institution offered the Spivakovsky brothers masterclasses for three years, whereupon their residence permits were extended for a further three years in February 1934.[34] Edmund Kurtz, who had returned to Europe, also received a position at the Melbourne University Conservatorium in 1935.

Jascha Spivakovsky also gained entry permits for his parents and for his brothers, Adolf and Issy. Adolf Spivakovsky was living with his German wife Paula in Berlin Charlottenburg[35] and, in February 1934, they travelled from the Anhalter Bahnhof [station] to Marseilles; from there the *Orsova* took them to Australia via the Suez Canal and Colombo. On 6 March, the ship docked in Fremantle, Western Australia, and four days later the small party came ashore in Adelaide.[36] After three months in South Australia, they moved on to Melbourne, where Adolf was also soon appointed to a position at the Conservatorium. Issy initially worked at Melbourne's Wesley College as 'visiting violin master'[37] before being appointed teacher of violin, viola and cello at Scotch College, one of the largest schools in the country.

In August, the *Australian Musical News* announced that the three members of the famous piano trio wanted to settle in Melbourne, at least for the next few years.[38] The Spivakovskys did in fact prepare themselves for a longer stay. With the help of Jascha's parents-in-law, with whom they had lived for a while in Magill, Adelaide, they acquired a splendid mansion with forty-five rooms in Toorak, Melbourne's most prestigious suburb. From 1935 onwards, Jascha Spivakovsky dwelt high above the Yarra River in Edzell House, 76 St Georges Road, with his wife, her parents and his own parents. At the centre of the house was an enormous music room with two grand pianos, one of them the Blüthner Prize won in Berlin. The pianist's lifestyle there was much more lavish than it had been in Germany. Not even the Villa Aurora, the famous Los Angeles home of Lion Feuchtwanger, who likewise fled Berlin in 1933, could compare with Edzell House in Melbourne.[39] Exile began for the pianist in fairytale luxury; but it was not to remain that way.

No Opportunities in Germany, even as a 'Half Jew'

Musicians who could not come to Australia as easily as the members of the Spivakovsky–Kurtz Trio hesitated before making the long voyage. Those who were not fortunate enough to have a job or an engagement already lined up first made efforts to find another destination. They had to be in dire need to choose Australia. Walter Andreas Dullo was. Following his dismissal as a trainee civil servant in April 1933, he initially wanted to emigrate to Spain, where he intended to become a music critic or a photographer. From his mother's diaries, we gather that in August Dullo auditioned with Julius Bab for a position with the Kulturbund Deutscher Juden, but without success: 'Rejection; impossible; hundreds of similar requests, no money.' His father then advised him to use the time to begin a doctorate, but Dullo did not want to do this and preferred to occupy himself with music, even though he had not touched the piano for years. 'He is quietly reading through scores and writing music for hours at a stretch. He is writing cadenzas for the Mozart piano concertos; judging by a few hints, he seems to have composed these himself.' His mother was happy that 'Adi [... was] once again in his element, music'.

In December, the offer to become a legal adviser near Lörrach provided a ray of hope; but when Dullo had to give up this position after only six months, his thoughts turned once more to emigration, especially since one of his sister Nora's friends, Dora Peyser, had gone to Australia at the end of 1934.[40] Nevertheless, he did not pursue these ideas seriously while there were still job offers (however unattractive) in Berlin. After applying in vain for a position with a travel bureau, Dullo worked first in a financial services office, and finally as an estate agent. None of these positions, however, offered him any long-term prospects. On 6 May 1935, his mother wrote:

> Thoughts of emigration have been constantly weighing on our mind – in case there is no possibility of employment for Adi in Germany. The sad thing is that Europe is almost closed to German emigrants on account of the high unemployment in all the European countries; there are no work permits for foreigners, not even in North America.

Thus their thoughts now turned again to more distant countries. 'The best chances for work appear to be in Brazil and South Africa: Cape Town and Johannesburg, where many of our friends are going.'[41] With an eye to emigration, Walter Dullo began to study English.

His mother read the Nuremberg Race Laws of 1935 very carefully. In November, she noted some of the provisions in her diary, like Paragraph 4, which states that Jews cannot be German citizens and have no voting rights. As by this time her son had become engaged to a so-called 'full Jew'

[*Volljüdin*], his boyhood friend Annemarie Deutsch, his mother wanted to check what racial status the marriage would have according to the new laws:

> § 2: A Jewish Mischling [individual of mixed Jewish and non-Jewish blood] is one who is descended from one or two grandparents who were racially full Jews [...].
>
> § 5: A Jew is also one who is descended from at least three full Jewish grandparents, if (a) he belonged to the Jewish religious community at the time this law was issued [...], (b) he was married to a Jewish person or married one subsequently.[42]

Alice Dullo also copied out the following passage:

> Marriages between Jews and subjects of the state of Germany or related blood are forbidden. Marriages nevertheless concluded are invalid, even if concluded abroad to circumvent this Law. Any person who violates the prohibition under Article 1 will be punished with a prison sentence.[43]

Henceforth, before any marriage could take place, a certificate of racial identity was needed:

> Before the marriage, every engaged person must produce a certificate of racial identity to prove that there is no obstacle to the marriage under §6.
>
> §6: A marriage shall not take place if there is any likelihood of issue that will endanger the purity of the German blood.

These pseudo-theoretical racial discussions, which had hitherto been meaningless to the family, take up several pages in the diary. Alice Dullo now made it clear to her son that her own father, who was Jewish before his marriage, 'married a full Jew who had been baptised, so that Mama (although she came from a Christian home) would be regarded as a Jew'. Since her own husband, Dr Andreas Dullo, was a 'pure Aryan, our three children are Halb-Mischlinge [Nazi classification for Germans of mixed race], and have it best under this law: they are allowed to marry Jews or Aryans'. The conclusion drawn from this discussion, which bordered on the absurd, was: 'therefore nothing stands in the way of Adi's marriage to Annemarie'.

The question of where the young couple would emigrate to, and what their professions would be, was still undecided. South Africa was often discussed as that was where the bride's sister, Erika Deutsch, was to go. Then again, they thought of New York and Istanbul, where friends were living. Another friend of the family brought a pamphlet from the Hilfsverein with details about employment and career opportunities in South America. Walter's mother noted: 'Important for Adi.' There was unfavourable news from down under: 'Dora Peyser writes from Australia that it is difficult to earn a living there; one takes a great risk, you have to come yourself and look for a job.'[44] They were at least clear about one thing: one could hardly survive abroad as a lawyer. 'Adi now wants to learn something practical in order to be able to earn a living overseas with Annemarie.' Walter Dullo talked to his father about finances and also began to study business management. Besides this, in October 1936, he began a massage course (at first only the theory). Concurrently, every day from 10 a.m. to 2 p.m. he, and four other participants, attended a course given by a Swiss Jewish confectioner.

Surprisingly, on 8 December, Walter Dullo heard from his Jewish travel bureau that emigration to the USA and South Africa was more difficult than to Australia because of the required documents and guarantees. 'It is easy to enter as a tourist, without a visa; no-one has been turned away, especially if they bring money with them.' In general, Australia was a flourishing country. 'Adi is leaning towards it the most', noted his mother; 'it seems to be the most sensible'. Lying awake at night, she tried to console herself with these thoughts, even though she knew that 'Australia means: *never* seeing him again'. The Never Never Land. Nevertheless, her son wrote again to Dora Peyser to ask about practical details such as guarantees and freight. Would it be possible to go as a tourist with lots of household goods?

Dora Peyser was the daughter of Dr Alfred Peyser, chair of the Jewish Reform Congregation; two years younger than Walter Dullo, she now became his most important source of information. A former secretary to the social reformer Alice Salomon, she had gained her highly regarded doctorate at the Berlin University with a thesis on social philosophy. Later, in Australia, Dora Peyser summarised her research on aid as a group phenomenon in a book, *The Strong and the Weak*,[45] and put her findings into practice as an active social worker. Peyser knew what she was talking about; for, alongside her studies, she also had had to look after her brother Thomas, who arrived with her in Melbourne on the ship *Bendigo* in November 1934. As Dora Peyser soon moved to Sydney, Walter Dullo also focused on this city.

His preparations for emigration had now reached the concrete stage. In February 1937, Dullo received the necessary emigration questionnaire from the Australian office in London. Further requirements included a medical certificate, a police certificate of good conduct, an English curriculum vitae and copies of references in English, as well as an accompanying letter stating the applicant's intended occupation in Australia. Once they had all the necessary documents, on 12 March the applications were 'sent airmail with a lot of pictures and documents; cost 8 marks'. Once this was done, they could prepare for the wedding. The official in the Schmargendorf registry office checked all the papers and then objected: 'There are three evangelical grandparents and only one of Jewish birth, so you are three-quarters Aryan, and cannot marry a Jew. No, I cannot accept the banns.'[46] Although the young groom pointed out that his evangelical grandmother, Japha, was 100 per cent Jewish, that his mother was therefore a 'full Jew' and he himself a 50 per cent Mischling, the official stuck to his 'No'. Walter's mother commented on the event as follows:

> The amazing thing is that all the Germans want an Aryan grandmother by hook or by crook in order to retain their positions and privileges, while Adi is fighting furiously for his Jewish grandmother (if only dear Ohan knew this!) in order to marry his true love.

Since there was no chance of being married in the Berlin district of Schmargendorf, the couple went a week later to publish the banns in Friedenau. They were relieved when the registrar there accepted their marriage. 'When they emerged from the Town Hall and went through the market square, happy and relieved of their anxiety, they met Mama in the square and told her of their victory. Great joy all round!'[47] Over the next few days, the young couple visited friends like the artist Käthe Kollwitz and the pianist Grete Sultan; then the official wedding ceremony took place on 9 June 1937 in Friedenau Town Hall. Afterwards, they took the S-Bahn [overground train] to Grunewald station in order to celebrate with the bride's parents. Presents were piled up on the grand piano, among them a lot of musical scores and records. In spite of retraining as a masseur and confectioner in preparation for their emigration, classical music still remained Walter Dullo's great passion.

Three days before the wedding, the landing permit arrived from Australia, along with authorisation to import cash to the considerable amount of 8,000 Reichsmark (RM) that had been provided by an uncle. Alice Dullo was thinking of the forthcoming departure when she made her wedding speech as a tribute to the bridal couple. 'Today I become the old Mrs Dullo, since a new Mrs Dullo has now appeared. We will both now proudly bear this worthy title.'[48] The best wedding present, she said, was the immigration permit for Australia that had just arrived, because for both of them it solved the urgent question of the future. Walter and Annemarie Dullo now had a clear, firm goal in sight.

As emigration was associated with physical separation from their homeland, Alice Dullo once again invoked her son's ancestry:

> *Heimat!* [Home!] For you, that is the whole of Germany. For you, home is first of all Königsberg in East Prussia, where you were born in your grandparents' house; where you played on the beach beside the Baltic Sea. Home is also Offenbach, where you spent your entire boyhood and school years, and made lifelong friends; home is Berlin, where you spent your early manhood, your developmental and student years, where you established friendships and found your love.

But the feeling for *Heimat*, his mother continued, was not restricted to these places. 'Many cities, old cathedrals and art institutions, the mountains of South Germany, the forests, the rivers, German music, German poetry – they are also *Heimat*.' Heimat, in this sense, can be transplanted, even into exile. Therefore, in her wedding speech, his mother stressed:

> Your two souls are so thoroughly soaked in *German culture*[49] that you will never be parted from it. Home is also your German emotional life: intimate family relations, Christmas, holidays, being quietly immersed in books, pictures, music, in everything that is beautiful and great. That lives so strongly in you as a couple that you will take it with you far away, and it will never be lost.

Even if the first years in Australia were to be difficult, this need not destroy their spiritual and intellectual values. In spite of all the persecution by the Hitler regime, Alice Dullo felt herself to be all the more connected to German culture. She also expected this from the young couple:

> In spite of all the necessary adjustment, you will keep the roots of our fatherland alive in your innermost being, and even if we all wish that you make a proper new home there, we still hope that overseas you will be the *bearers of German culture and German character*[50] in the truest sense. Even if, from an overall perspective, we regard this cruel fact – that a part of German youth is being cast out from the fatherland, and that families are being torn apart – as a potential act of providence, we believe that fate has chosen you to radiate German culture from the deep fullness of your youth into a distant country that is young and still developing, and to experience the uplifting effect of your character.

Walter's mother hoped that, as outcasts and victims of persecution, her son and Annemarie would be all the more successful as ambassadors for German culture and 'the other Germany'.

Just a few days after the wedding, Walter Dullo bought the tickets. A cargo vessel of the Hamburg–American Line was to take him and his young wife on the seven-week voyage to Australia. On 7 July, their German passports showed: 'The bearer of this passport is an emigrant.'[51] Before their departure, Walter earned some extra money as a masseur, and took leave of absence from his compulsory military service. Their cargo crates, in which they had stowed kitchen utensils for their own pastry shop, were collected on 17 July; among their belongings were a brand new granite rolling mill, books, music, old letters and Walter's large picture postcard collection – lovely reminders of Germany. The jewels in the crown, however, were the gramophone and the records of classical music that he had received at the wedding.

On Friday 23 July, Walter and Annemarie Dullo travelled to Hamburg, accompanied by their parents; their ship, the 6,200 ton *Rendsburg*, left for Australia the following day: they were the only passengers on board. The long journey began through the English Channel, first towards Antwerp, where a transit visa was stamped in their passports on 29 July. Then they sailed past France, Portugal and the African continent until at last the ship docked on 11 September in Port Adelaide, South Australia. There Walter Dullo had to fill out the 'Personal Statement and Declaration' form that included questions about his nationality and race. He gave 'German' as

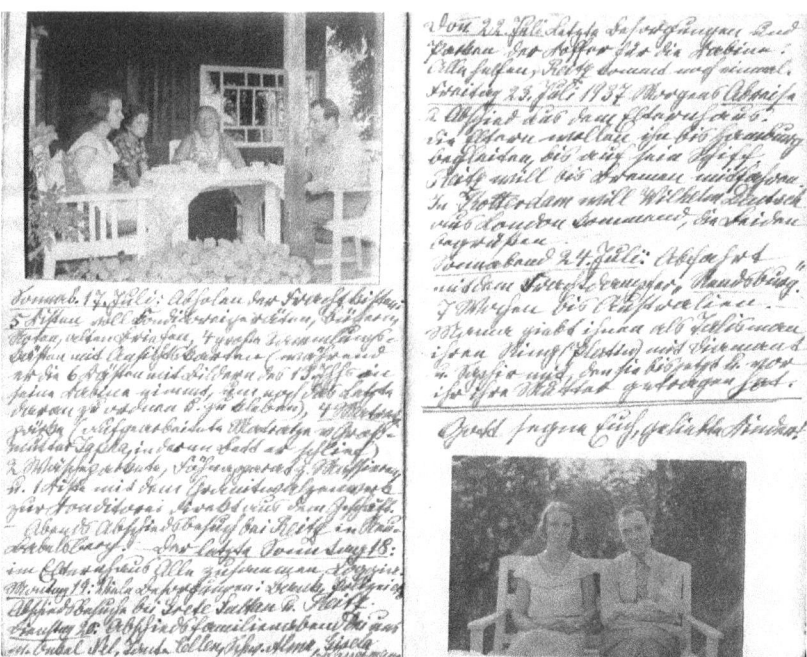

Figure 4: Last entries from the diary written by Walter Andreas Dullo's mother for her son and his young wife Annemarie, before their departure to Australia: 'God bless you, beloved children!' (Author's Archive)

his nationality, and 'European' as his race. He answered Question 14, 'Do you intend to settle in Australia?' with a clear 'Yes'. Their entry as tourists was no longer an option. He had no relatives in Australia, but he did have a friend: Dora Peyser. For Question 12, 'Intended occupation in Australia', he wrote: 'Massage or pastry cooking'.

The *Rendsburg* continued on to Sydney, where the thirty-four-year-old Walter and his twenty-five-year-old wife Annemarie went ashore on 24 September. A new life had begun for them, far away from their native Berlin, and far removed from Walter Dullo's real purpose in life: music. But there was, after all, a faint glimmer of hope. Shortly before the wedding, Dullo had received a letter of recommendation to a family of musicians who had been living in Australia for some years: the Spivakovskys.

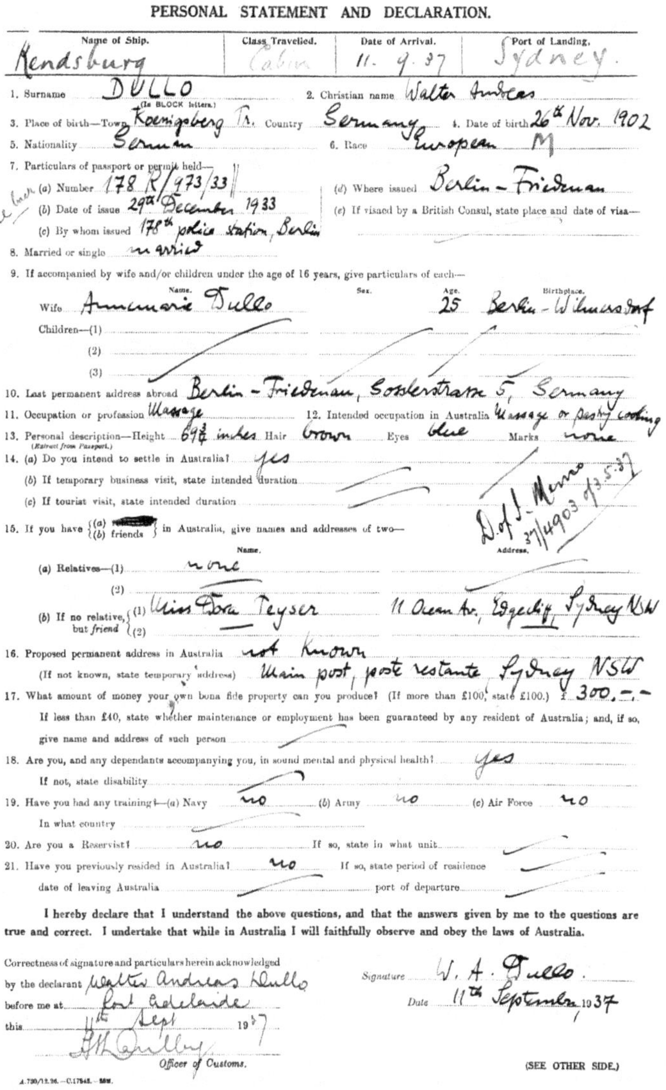

Figure 5: 'Personal Statement and Declaration' of Walter Dullo, completed on 11 September 1937. As his 'race' he states 'European', as future profession 'Massage or Pastry cooking', as friend he names Dora Peyser. (NAA: A12508, 21/963)

Refuge Britain

Britain was attractive to musicians as its musical life was similar to that of Germany. On the other hand, refugees in the British Isles were seldom able to obtain a work permit. Earlier leniency towards foreigners had disappeared after the First World War. The 'Alien Restriction Act' of 1919 and the 'Aliens Order' introduced a year later meant that immigrants were restricted to those who could prove that they had a secure income. Thereupon, thousands of the approximately 60,000 Germans who had lived in Britain until then left the country.[52] Once 'asylum rights' had been abolished,[53] the British government could make decisions about the intake of migrants at its own discretion. In contrast to the USA, there was no limit to the number of immigrants, but a quota system was introduced for various professions. Thus, the total number of foreign inhabitants was reduced from 0.8 per cent (1911) to 0.44 per cent (1931).[54] Indeed, Britain was now mainly a country of emigration.

In spite of these restrictions, which conformed to British interests rather than humanitarian considerations, at the start of the Hitler regime the British Passport Control Office in Berlin experienced a rush of Jews wishing to emigrate. On 29 March 1933, the incumbent officer, Captain Frank E. Foley, reported to his superiors: 'This office is overwhelmed with applications from Jews to proceed to Palestine, to England, to anywhere in the British Empire.'[55] Although Foley wanted to be generous – like his colleague in Frankfurt am Main, Consul-General R. T. Smallbones[56] – the selection criteria proved a difficult hurdle to overcome. Germany's neighbours: France, the Netherlands, Austria and Czechoslovakia offered the refugees better chances. Whereas in the first fifteen months of the Nazi regime France took around 21,000 refugees, Britain accepted only about 2,000.[57] In the first year of the Hitler dictatorship only 300–400 refugees were let in.[58]

In those days, Britain could more or less only be reached by ship through Harwich, Dover and Folkestone. Many inhabitants of the islands took pride in their splendid isolation from mainland Europe, to which they often still fancied they were superior. On arrival, everyone was interrogated by an immigration officer who enquired about occupation and financial security in the host country. This information was crucial, as immigration officers were entitled to refuse entry to new arrivals.[59] As a rule, the officials viewed potential immigrant musicians sceptically and unsympathetically. They then referred to the unions, who would not issue work permits for foreigners. Musicians were only allowed to stay for three months if they promised that, during this time, they would undertake 'no employment, either paid or unpaid'.[60] Therefore, on arriving in England on 18 June 1933,[61] Kurt Prerauer described himself as a tourist, and accordingly gave 'Visitor' as his profession on the Certificate of Registration.[62] Apparently it had become clear to him that he would not receive a work permit, despite his positive references from Leo Blech, Wilhelm Furtwängler and Heinz Tietjen. According to his papers, he was only allowed to work for a few days in April 1934. The entry 'Occupation: Musical assistant (operatic) from 16.4.34 to 22.4.34' refers to his collaboration on the London rehearsals for *Wozzeck*, under Adrian Boult. Prerauer had been drawn to this job because of his participation in the world premiere of Berg's opera in Berlin. Like other refugee musicians, he is likely to have earned his living by giving private lessons and working as a repetiteur or coach for singers and instrumentalists, although such activities had to be undertaken unofficially.[63]

The opera singer Fritz Coper also left Germany in the summer of 1933, unlike his brother Willy, who remained in Berlin.[64] In his autobiographical sketch, compiled in 1942 in Australia when he applied for naturalisation, he wrote: 'In January 1933 with the coming of the Nazi regime I lost every possibility of carrying on with my work because of being a Jew.'[65] In July, he fled to Czechoslovakia, where he appeared as a singer in various cities. Then he looked for work in Hungary and Yugoslavia before finally coming to England in April 1936. On his arrival in Folkestone, he answered the question about his occupation by saying that he did not have one: thus his Certificate of Registration shows 'No occupation'.[66] Coper hid from the authorities the fact that he was looking for work. No doubt he mentioned the Jewish Welfare Committee, which would take care of his income. At that stage, London's Woburn House, where the administration was located, was the most important point of contact for refugees from

Hitler's Germany.⁶⁷ This organisation did, in fact, help Fritz Coper with his job search. The Central Synagogue in Great Portland Street engaged him as a singer, and the Reform synagogue in the West End employed him as its choirmaster. Coper was issued with a work permit, but like all other refugees he had to extend his entry permit every three months, and send his passport in to the Home Office.

There were no restrictions for people who came to study, or at least not if they were financially secure. In 1936, Karl Josef Berg was able to continue the accountancy studies that he had begun in Berlin. After completing the course, however, it proved impossible for him to obtain a permanent residence permit. Similar problems were experienced by the young cellist Otti Veit, whose teacher, Nicolai Graudan, was a foreign Jew. His contract as principal cellist with the Berlin Philharmonic was extended at the end of 1934, though under less favourable conditions.⁶⁸ Graudan then made an effort to find a position in London, and moved there in the summer of 1935. Otti Veit followed him. At a London reception given by the Graudans, she met the Berlin mining engineering student Kurt Eisner, her future husband. In 1938, when Graudan decided to move to the USA, Otti transferred to the Royal College of Music, where her teachers were Ivor Jones and the Australian Laurie Kennedy, who was then principal cellist with the London Philharmonic. Concert programmes show that she participated in several concerts at the College. After completing her studies, the young cellist, like most of the refugees, was unable to obtain a work permit as a musician and became a language teacher. Seventeen-year-old Günter Hirschberg had come to Britain in April 1937 under the auspices of a German–British Exchange Programme for children. When he finished his schooling, he enrolled to study theology at the University of London and at Jews' College. Although his parents, whom he periodically visited, had to remain in Berlin, their son was satisfied to be establishing a second home in England.

Kurt Herweg-Hirsch had obtained his German passport⁶⁹ in Berlin Schöneberg on 28 May 1935. This showed his family name: 'Hirsch', his stage name: 'Herweg', his occupation: 'Kapellmeister' and, as a mark of identification, a broken nose. The passport also indicates that Herweg-Hirsch left Germany and travelled to England on 1 July 1936. Two days later, he arrived in Harwich, where he pledged to the immigration officer not to undertake any work, paid or unpaid. As his passport showed, he was only able to come under these conditions. Luckily, Herweg was able to live with an aunt. He also had other relatives living in Britain: his uncle, Franz Arnold, and two of his mother's nieces, the actress Lilli Palmer and her sister, the dancer Hilda Palmer. They must have been partly responsible for Herweg being employed as a pianist for the Rippman School of Dancing, and as a composer for a theatre troupe, the Pepler Mime Group. Although his residence permit could only be extended every three months on condition that he did not undertake any paid or unpaid work, Herweg was also active as a singing teacher and as an arranger and conductor for the BBC. Alongside second-hand bookshops and publishers, Radio in Britain was one of the few small enclaves where exceptions were made regarding work permits.[70] All the experience that Herweg gathered there was to help him during his later stay in Australia.

If, unlike Kurt Herweg, the refugees were unable to stay with friends or relatives, they lived mainly in simple guest houses and furnished rooms, preferably in London's northern or north-western suburbs. The more affluent rented flats in the Hampstead area which, with its many parks, was comparable to districts like Tiergarten or Grunewald in Berlin. Apart from the support given by Jewish aid organisations, refugees in Britain were relatively isolated. There was little understanding of their situation. The press reported in detail on German musical life and on guest performances by German soloists, orchestras and opera houses,[71] but tended to ignore the persecution of Jewish musicians. On the contrary, the refugees also met with antisemitism in Britain.[72]

Arrival with the Royal Grand Opera Company

In 1934, Kurt Prerauer received an offer to be the accompanist for Melbourne soprano Florence Austral on a concert tour of the Netherlands.[73] Famous above all for her Wagner interpretations, in the interwar years this artist was the best known Australian singer internationally since Melba. Prerauer had certainly already heard Austral sing, as in November 1930 she appeared as a visiting artist in the role of Brünnhilde at the Berlin State Opera. Because of her German pronunciation, however, her contract was not extended. Prerauer was only later to learn that, at the time, the singer had just been diagnosed with multiple sclerosis.[74] Surprisingly, this Australian connection through Florence Austral was to have even wider ramifications: immediately after their tour of the Netherlands, the English impresario Sir Benjamin Fuller invited Prerauer to travel to Australia as one of three conductors for his Royal Grand Opera Company. Because in his youth he had accompanied his father on a minstrel and vaudeville show that toured Australia and New Zealand, Fuller knew the region. Since these guest performances had been successful, he had settled with his brother in Sydney, where he worked his way up from popular entertainment to 'high art'. He had already started to present Italian operas in 1916. With his Royal Grand Opera Company, he claimed nothing less than that he was laying the foundation for a permanent opera company in Australia. In addition to Prerauer, Fuller also engaged the conductors Maurice Abravanel and Robert Ainsworth for this ambitious project.[75] 'A trio of maestros of experience, talent and high reputation.'[76] As the third conductor, Prerauer was responsible for the chorus and for selecting the artists.[77]

A new phase in Kurt Prerauer's life began on 27 July 1934. On that day, he left England for Australia on the *Maloja*, which sailed between Europe and Australia for the Peninsula and Oriental Steam Navigation Company (P&O) using the Suez Canal, a faster connection than the route via Africa. The passenger list[78] shows which musicians sailed with Prerauer.

Thus the opera company consisted mainly of British citizens. The refugees from Germany, the conductor Maurice Abravanel and his wife Friedel, together with the musical assistant Kurt Prerauer, were the only foreigners who boarded in England. Under the heading 'Race', Prerauer entered 'Prussian, Germany' as it appeared in his passport. The last column on the passenger list was headed 'Country of intended Future Permanent Residence'. All the members of the opera troupe, even Prerauer, said they wanted to return to England when the tour was over.

Table 1: *Maloja* Passenger List, July 1934

Name	Occupation	Age	Country of Last Residence	Nationality	Race
Boarded in England					
Ainsworth, Robert	Musician	34	England	B.	British
Ainsworth, Muriel	Singer	34	England	B.	British
Allin, Norman	Singer	49	England	B.	British
Abravanel, Maurice	Conductor	31	France	A.	Portuguese
Abravanel, Friedel	Singer	29	France	A.	Portuguese
Fairnington, Gwyl.	Opera Singer	28	England	B.	England
Hitchen, Harry	Vocalist	44	England	B.	England
Hitchen, Ethel	Vocalist	40	England	B.	England
Moore, Samuel	Opera artist	50	England	B.	England
Mummery, Br.	Singer	43	England	B.	Australia
Pike, Jane	Singer	40	England	B.	England
Prerauer, Kurt	Musical Asst	33	England	A.	Prussian, Germany
Ross, Bernard	Opera artist	41	England	B.	England
Shepherd, Francesca	Singer	36	England	B.	England
Widdop, Walter	Vocalist	42	England	B.	England
Williams, Benjamin	Singer	41	England	B.	England
Boarded in Marseilles					
Dua, Octave Ed.	Opera singer	49	Belgium	A.	Belgium
Inches, Charles	Producer	59	England	B.	Switzerland

All the artists travelled first class. After passing through the Suez Canal, the ship docked at Colombo on 14 August and arrived in Fremantle, the first Australian port, on 28 August. Five days later, the company went ashore in Melbourne, where they were received by the Lord Mayor at the Town Hall. Their tour began with performances for the city's centenary celebrations in Melbourne's Apollo Theatre, and opened with Verdi's *Aida*, with Florence Austral in the title role. Like the rest of the operas on this tour, it was performed in English.

These guest performances brought to Australia a standard of opera that was hitherto unknown. Thus, in February 1935, an article in the *Sun* newspaper called for Abravanel and the Grand Opera Company to be kept in Australia. The composer Alfred Hill supported this idea, as it would raise the country's musical standards; the orchestra, previously conducted mainly by Joseph Post and Edgar Bainton, the Director of the Sydney Conservatorium, had improved enormously under Maurice Abravanel.[79] But Abravanel had made the mistake of criticising Bernard Heinze and his 'dictatorship', after which the Australian Broadcasting Commission (ABC) turned down his requests and rejected his suggestions.[80] The Grand Opera Company's guest season ended as planned in April 1935. Kurt Prerauer, who had conducted his own arrangement of Bizet's *The Pearl Fishers*[81] on 18 February, did not wish to return to England with the other members of the company, but now wanted to stay in Australia. In the meantime, he had made contact with the influential ABC and was to organise a series of operas to be broadcast by them in the 1935–1936 season. When Abravanel also came to the conclusion that, for the time being, he would have better performance opportunities in Australia than in Europe, he also extended his visit.

As a result of the collaboration between these two artists, Australia experienced an opera season such as never before. The series of concert opera performances, which were all broadcast, began on 5 November 1935 with the Australian premiere of Mussorgsky's *Boris Godunov*, conducted by Abravanel. Because of the opera's length, the ABC decided to divide it: the first half was transmitted from Sydney and the second half from Wilson Hall at Melbourne University. *Hansel and Gretel* followed on 25 December, and the Australian premiere of *Rosenkavalier* on 7 January 1936.

Arrival with the Royal Grand Opera Company 79

Puccini's *Manon Lescaut* was premiered on 5 March. *Parsifal* was prepared for Easter and presented in three parts. Other works from this season included *Fidelio*, *Die Meistersinger von Nürnberg* and *Das Rheingold*, some of which had considerable cuts for broadcasting purposes. Abravanel later summarised this tour as follows:

> During my stay of six months, the company presented the first Wagnerian opera in Australia in a quarter-century. We gave thirteen performances each of 'Tristan and Isolde', 'Walkure', 'Tannhauser', 'Lohengrin', and the regular French and Italian repertoire. We also introduced such operas as 'Rosenkavalier', 'Boris Godounoff', 'Prince Igor', 'Fidelio', 'Nozze di Figaro' and 'Don Pasquale' to the Australians for the first time.[82]

Ending with the Australian premiere of Borodin's *Prince Igor*, the season organised by Prerauer and conducted for the most part by Abravanel counts as one of the most outstanding events in the history of opera in Australia.[83]

CHAPTER 5

Mixed Feelings: Australian Reactions to German Racial Politics

The First World War damaged German–Australian relations enormously. A large military unit, the Australian and New Zealand Army Corps (ANZAC), was sent to Europe to fight on the side of the British against Germany and Austria-Hungary and suffered heavy losses, especially at the battle of Gallipoli on the Bosphorus. In addition, Australia sent a naval force to German New Guinea, seized the harbour, Rabaul, and the powerful radio station, occupied the Pacific island of Nauru (which also belonged to the German Empire) and sank German warships. To cheer themselves up, Australian soldiers sang satirical songs about Germany, 'Kaiser Bill' and his army, about marching on the enemy's capital ('Right on to Berlin we'll go!') and turning Germany into 'no man's land'.

Hate was also directed towards Germans on the 'home front'. Modelled on the British concentration camps[1] that had been set up for South African civilians during the Boer War (1899–1902), concentration camps for German-Australian and German citizens were now established in Australia. The largest, the German Concentration Camp (GCC) in Holsworthy near Liverpool, Sydney, could hold almost 6,000 detainees, among them Australians of German heritage who had long been naturalised, including honorary consuls, pastors and senior employees of German firms. Internment changed their attitude completely and led to a total break with Australian society; many of them were convinced they could never live there again.[2] This was clearly the intention of the authorities, who deported most of the internees after their discharge, even those that, despite their deep humiliation, wanted to remain in Australia.[3]

A further consequence of the war was South Australia's Nomenclature Act of 1917, which forbade the use of German names. The sixty-nine place names in South Australia were either renamed after British generals or battles, or given Aboriginal place names. For example, Bismarck became Weeroopa; Friedrichstadt, Tangari; Grünthal, Verdun; and Mount Kaiserstuhl, Mt Kitchener. The German *Liedertafeln*, traditional German male choirs, referring to King Arthur's round table, were now called Glee Clubs. Many of the remaining Australians of German descent tried even harder to adapt to their new surroundings; they often gave up their language and religion and married Australian partners.[4] On the other hand, other German-Australians developed a rather defiant, conservative attitude, which later led some to sympathise with the Nazi regime. After the First World War, Germans were no longer welcome and trade between the two countries was forbidden for several years; German immigration virtually ceased. After 1933, when the German Consul-General in Sydney tried to encourage immigration to Australia in order to strengthen the 'German element', he received little sympathy.

In those days, the Australian press reported in detail on all the ins and outs of British domestic and foreign policy, but seldom commented on developments in Germany. That said, in October 1933 one could read about the appeals by the League of Nations and Albert Einstein for the acceptance of Jewish refugees, and on 7 October the *Sydney Morning Herald* announced that 'German-Jews [sic] May Emigrate to Australia'. During a recent trip to Europe,[5] Hungarian-born Rabbi David Isaac Freedman, who was then living in Perth, had experienced the hopeless situation of German Jews and learnt that many of them wanted to escape to Australia; members of a German Jewish Aid Committee had asked him about employment opportunities for professors, teachers and doctors. To the Australians, however, such a message was alarming: up to then neither Germans nor Jews had been particularly welcome. Moreover, as a result of the Great Depression, the unemployment rate in Australia was extremely high (30 per cent). Even many of the British and Irish who had come to Australia to look for work were returning home. For the first time in the country's history, the number of emigrants exceeded the number of immigrants. Under these circumstances, Australians were, understandably, unprepared for the arrival of new workers from Germany. The news of Jewish persecution in Nazi Germany was met with mixed feelings. Even music journals reported it, for example in October 1933 in the *Australian Musical News* under the heading 'Of the Germans and Jews'. However, the minister for the interior, J.A. Perkins, had already confirmed in a memorandum in June that special measures to facilitate the immigration of German Jews were not envisaged.[6]

The *Australian Jewish Herald*, the official publication of the Australian Jews, also carried reports from Germany; for example, that German Jews could no longer enlist in the army.[7] According to an article written in July 1935, Hitler's cabinet would tolerate Jews, but would never allow them to regain their former status as citizens.[8] When, in the same month, the journal questioned Issy Spivakovsky about the situation in Germany, the violinist confirmed the bad news about the Nazi terror and showed his concern.[9] Readers were informed that this terror targeted mainly the regime's political opponents[10] and learnt about the Nuremberg Race Laws that further restricted the rights of Jews in Germany.[11]

The conductor Maurice Abravanel, often referred to in Australia as Maurice d'Abravanel, attracted a lot of attention when he visited the Jewish community in Melbourne at the end of his tour with the Grand Opera Company. After a Kadimah concert,[12] he talked about the persecution of Jews in Germany. He warned against the arrogance that arose from the Jews' perception of themselves as 'the chosen people':

> The Jews ask from the world nothing more than justice. We must not expect superlatives because we come of the Jewish race. I do not want to plead the cause of those who have persecuted us, but sometimes I think that Jews suffered because they expected things they did not deserve. We, Jews, ask for the same opportunity as other people, and if for whatever reason we are able to show that we have merit, then we have the right, as much as, but no more than other people, to expect recognition for our achievement.'[13]

According to the conductor, excessively vehement demands for the admission of Jewish refugees could have exactly the opposite effect.

Abravanel probably behaved so diplomatically because, at the time, he was interested in settling permanently in Australia. He was supported in this by Alfred Hill, who had played the violin under Arthur Nikisch in the Gewandhaus Orchestra during his student years in Leipzig. Hill had wanted to encourage such traditions in Australia and New Zealand, and had started several initiatives during his time as a conductor, composer and tenured professor at the Sydney Conservatorium.[14] In this sense, Hill saw Abravanel's arrival as a great opportunity. Abravanel's opponents, however, were of an entirely different opinion, among them the conductor Bernard Heinze, who sensed a dangerous rival, and Percy Grainger, who at that time was Australia's most prominent composer.

Grainger had studied from 1895–1901 in Frankfurt am Main and, swayed by the cultural-philosophical writings of Houston Stewart Chamberlain, had become an advocate of the 'Nordic' *Weltanschauung* [world view]. Whereas Chamberlain, who was originally British, had settled in Bayreuth during the First World War and married Richard Wagner's daughter Eva, Grainger distanced himself from Germany because its people did not seem 'Nordic enough'. He was greatly influenced by the North American racial theorists Madison Grant and Lothrop Stoddard, as were Hitler and his followers. Grant's *The Passing of the Great Race* (1916) and Stoddard's books *The Rising Tide of Color against White World-Supremacy* (1920) and *The Revolt against Civilization: The Menace of the Under-Man* (1925) were all in Grainger's possession. He had support from a student friend in Frankfurt, the English composer Henry Balfour Gardiner, who shared Grainger's own view of the special musical talent of blond, blue-eyed northern Europeans. For Grainger, this idea was closely associated with his conviction that British composers were superior to those from the European mainland. He was therefore very keen to propagate the Nordic–British musical tradition in Australia. Thus, on 24 August 1938, he wrote to Sir James Barrett:

> Continental Europe today has few composers who can be compared with such British geniuses as Elgar, Delius, Scott, Vaughan Williams, Roger Quilter, Arnold Bax, Holst, Balfour Gardiner and many others. I happened to be the close associate of these men just at the time when English music was resuming its old supremacy.

According to him, through the aforementioned composers, England was now the leader of the musical world. Since he thought this development was also of interest to Australians, Grainger had been collecting letters, concert programmes and other documents for decades. He wanted to put them at the disposal of the music museum that he was establishing at the University of Melbourne. Grainger's ideas on the supremacy of British music went hand in hand with antisemitic judgements, as when he dismissed the collaboration with Jews as an expression of 'bad taste'.[15] When asked whether he favoured the establishment of a permanent symphony orchestra in Melbourne, he explained: 'The arrant stupidity of the Continentals comes out in their lousy and filthy musicians.' This was clearly directed against foreigners, especially those from Germany and Austria. 'Is it likely that nations that cannot win wars, and who keep throwing the world into disorder, could do anything good in such a balanced art as music?' Grainger stated: 'Australians are more gifted than non-Australians.'[16] These utterances were sharply criticised and had the opposite effect, in that Abravanel was invited to give further concerts. Thus the *Australian Jewish Herald* reported in July 1935, under the heading 'M. d'Abravanel back in Melbourne':

> Accompanied by his charming wife [...] the noted conductor is back in Melbourne preparing for the two concerts in which he is to conduct the Melbourne Symphony Orchestra. The concerts have been guaranteed following the outburst of Mr Percy Grainger against Continental conductors and Continental music.[17]

In November 1935, when Abravanel was guest of honour at a banquet in Sydney, he devoted his speech to the problem of 'Jewish music'.[18] Once again, he warned against any exaggerated Jewish national pride, and reminded people that until fifty years earlier there had been no such thing as nationalism in music. One had simply considered the composers as individuals. In the case of Jewish music, he said, it was also particularly difficult to differentiate between Jewish, Russian and Spanish influences. As a child, he himself had heard 'Sephardic songs' from his Spanish mother, and had later found out that they were actually Spanish songs. Anyway, most music that was regarded as 'Jewish' actually came from non-Jews, for example Maurice Ravel. On the other hand, there was another type of Jewish music which was not part of any national tradition, but which was nevertheless Jewish in the truest sense. As an example, Abravanel mentioned Kurt Weill's music for the ballet *The Seven Deadly Sins*, the world premiere of which he had conducted in Paris; music whose strong melodic expression, free of any folklore, he perceived as Jewish.

The immigration of Jewish refugees had been announced in October 1933, but so far few had arrived. Of the 60,000 people who fled from

Germany in 1933, only fifty-two received visas for Australia. In 1934, a further forty-five refugees arrived, and in 1935 just eight.[19] The European Jews rightly believed that Australia could, and should, accept more refugees. In May 1936, on behalf of a Hamburg aid committee, one Hugo Hertz sent a written request to Bertram Stevens, the premier of New South Wales, asking whether it would not be possible to permit immigration on a larger scale for Jews who wanted to leave Germany.[20] These immigrants could prove themselves useful to Australia as workers in many areas. The experience of Palestine, he said, had shown that Jews could be successful not only in academic professions, but also in farming.

The Department of the Interior in Canberra heard about such advances from Australia House in London. Thereupon, on 6 August 1936, chief clerk Thomas Hugh Garrett drafted a memorandum concerning the admission of Jews to Australia. In it he repeated the warning he had already formulated in 1933 that this group of people did not assimilate well because they were so protective of their Jewish identity. The immigration of numerous Jews to the Commonwealth of Australia was therefore, in his view, not to be recommended.[21] In any case, the Australian Government was not interested in admitting people of other nationalities into the country. On 28 September 1937, Prime Minister Joseph Aloysius Lyons confirmed that the majority of inhabitants were British citizens and should remain so in the future. 'Our population is 99.1 per cent of British nationality and we wish to keep it so.'

Another of the hurdles relating to emigration to Australia was the demand that, on their arrival, every immigrant should produce the sum of £500, the so-called 'Landing Money'. Many of the refugees could not fulfil this request, as it was extremely difficult for them to take money out of Germany. A representative of the London Council for German Jewry referred to this problem in a letter to Australia House and asked the British authorities to cancel any request for monetary deposits if a committee of leading Jews in the relevant state could assume the necessary guarantees.[22] The Australian Jews, including the above-mentioned Rabbi David Isaac Freedman, tried to put together the money for exiled European Jews. In 1936, Sir Samuel Cohen, the doyen of the Jewish community in Sydney, convened a meeting expressly for this purpose. The considerable sum of £70,000 was put aside for a 'German Jewish Relief Fund'.[23] From then on, the refugees, for whom this new organisation now provided a guarantee, only had to produce £50 on their arrival; for immigrants without such surety, the Landing Money was reduced to £200. Woburn House in London, which co-ordinated refugee activities with financial support from a committee chaired by Lord Rothschild, was immediately informed. One of the most active helpers there was the young stockbroker Julian Layton, a descendant of the Löwenstein family, who had moved from Frankfurt am Main to London in 1893. In the meantime, the German Jewish Relief Fund in Sydney was up and running and helped to settle Jewish arrivals. The Committee sent part of the relevant money directly to the refugees in Britain and Germany. Dora Peyser was a particularly important member of this organisation, and co-ordinated the aid from her home. In 1936, another German Jewish Relief Fund was set up in Melbourne, where the work was also carried out in people's homes. In 1937, these two committees combined with other organisations to form the Australian Jewish Welfare Society,[24] and for the first time they acquired their own offices. Dora Peyser, the epitome of a committed social worker,[25] became the general secretary.

One of the first refugees to enter Australia with the support from this organisation was Fritz Coper, who on arrival presented himself as a baritone and pianist.[26] In a letter accompanying his application for citizenship in February 1942, he wrote: 'I was one of the first refugees brought to Australia by the Australian Jewish Welfare Committee and was guaranteed by its then president Sir Samuel Cohen.' Question 17 on the immigration form, 'Personal Statement and Declaration', asked how much money the refugee had. Those who had brought less than £50 were asked to name an Australian who would guarantee their living expenses. Coper entered the name of Sir Samuel Cohen. Soon after his arrival, he began to work as a singing teacher at Palings, a large music and instrument shop that also arranged music lessons. Here he quickly got to know the New Zealand-born sales assistant Mary Raine Stevens, whom he married in November 1937.

A little later, Karl Josef Berg also entered Australia with the help of the German Jewish Relief Fund and the Australian Jewish Welfare Society. Unable to obtain a permanent residence permit in Britain, he had wanted to go to Chile or South Africa.[27] In London, however, Berg found personal connections to Australia and subsequently made an effort to get there, even though he did not have a job offer. At the age of twenty, exactly one year after his arrival in England, he boarded the Orient Line ship *Ormonde* and arrived in Melbourne in September 1937. Intending to become a musician, he packed his violin. He sold it on arrival, however, and gave up the violin[28] as apparently there was no work for musicians in Australia. Berg had to put his passion for music to one side as there were more important things to take care of first: his younger sister Henriette followed him in September 1938, and soon afterwards, in February 1939, his mother Rosina. Thus, the immediate family was saved and reunited in Australia.

The Australian Jewish Welfare Society also helped Kurt Herweg-Hirsch to leave Britain. He was able to accompany the dancer Anny Fligg as pianist on her Australian tour. After an unusually stormy crossing on the *Orford*, he arrived in Sydney in April 1938, where he explained: 'Germans are too busy exercising as Storm Troopers to have any time for their musical exercises.' There were hardly any good musicians or music teachers left in Hitler's Germany, he said.[29] When they heard this, supporters of the Nazi regime were outraged and demanded that the new arrival present himself at the German Consulate. Herweg did comply. However, he published an explanation, in which he claimed to have been misunderstood during the interview. By July he was allowed to work as a conductor in Melbourne. In Sydney, he lived for a year in a hotel before finally moving into his own flat in Potts Point.

Walter Dullo, who arrived in Sydney with his wife Annemarie in September 1937, was not financially dependent on the support of the Welfare Society. In his arrival information, he declared a considerable cash sum of £300. Dullo did need help, however, in finding housing and employment, as well as in dealing with the necessary formalities. Luckily for him, he knew Dora Peyser, who was experienced in such matters. He had given her name in his arrival declaration, according to which the ex-Berliner lived in Edgecliff, one of Sydney's east coast suburbs. Not far from there, in New South Head Road, the Dullos found a small ground-floor flat, the front section of which became their confectionery shop. Here they set up the equipment they had brought with them and started manufacturing and selling chocolates, with only a curtain between production and sales. They were happy to be making a secure living, even if the focus of their new life had little in common with a career in music.

CHAPTER 6

'Muss i denn, muss i denn zum Städtele hinaus?':
Persecution and Flight

Berlin 1938

In 1938, as one of three Jews in a class of nineteen students, Klaus Loewald had completed his matriculation without any problems in Berlin, his home city.[1] In school he was treated fairly. 'Perhaps the Herder Gymnasium in Westend was an exception, but in my time no Jewish student was ever expelled – whether his father was a Frontkämpfer [Front Soldier] or not. My father did not serve at the front.' Loewald ascribed this tolerant atmosphere to the director who, like most of the teachers at the school, was a decent man. He remembered 'only one remark, made only once and with some justification by one teacher: "There is too much chatting in class, especially among the Jewish students." He was quite right. Otherwise there was never the slightest hint of any real discrimination.' The literary critic Marcel Reich-Ranicki's experience at the Fichte Gymnasium in Wilmersdorf was similar. Even classmates who belonged to the Hitler Youth did not express any antisemitism, but Reich-Ranicki put this down to their good, middle-class upbringing as well as to the unrealistic propaganda. 'The official propaganda against the Jews referred to an abstract concept (such as "World Jewry") and I presume that they [the fellow students] did not necessarily associate it with their classmates, whom they had known and respected for years.'[2] A large percentage of Jewish girls attended the Princess Bismarck School,[3] founded in 1857 as the first girls' secondary school in Charlottenburg. (Issy Spivakovsky taught music there until 1933.) As Inge Deutschkron remembered, on entering the classroom the teachers had to use the greeting 'Heil Hitler', but they did this 'with obvious distaste'. 'They made no distinction at all between us and the non-Jewish members of my class.'[4]

At other schools, by contrast, liberal teachers were pensioned off and replaced by bureaucrats loyal to the regime. Non-Aryans were increasingly forced into a ghetto. Georg Dreyfus, scion of an assimilated family, now attended the Zionist Theodor Herzl School at Adolf-Hitler-Platz (today Theodor-Heuss-Platz).

The Ghettoisation of Musicians

Initially, Jewish musicians had been allowed to join the Reichsmusikkammer, as officially confirmed in 1934: 'The Reichskulturkammer Act [Reich Chamber of Culture Act] does not contain any regulation corresponding to the Aryan paragraph in the Civil Service legislation and the Editor Act. Accordingly, non-Aryans, like foreigners, are not excluded from membership of the Reichskulturkammer.'[5] Therefore, about 8,000 Jewish musicians received a membership card entitling them to practise as professionals in Germany. Minister Goebbels, however, was indignant about this regulation: 'I am amazed to find that, owing to the lack of an Aryan paragraph, Jews who are gradually being forced out of other professions are now seeking new employment opportunities in cultural life.'[6] Since, according to the Minister, Jews were generally unsuitable for the administration of German culture, the 'Guidelines for the Acceptance of Non-Aryans into the Professional Associations of the Reichsmusikkammer' of April 1934 were adopted and sent to offices marked 'Highly Confidential!'. According to the Civil Service Restoration Act enacted the previous year, people with one non-Aryan parent or grandparent were classified as non-Aryan. The 'cleansing' of the Reichsmusikkammer was so slow and discrete, however, that at first it was hardly noticed.[7] The government used this to designate foreign 'horror propaganda' as completely overblown; the panic spreading among German Jews was, it said, totally unfounded. This counterpropaganda, together with the founding of the Jüdischer Kulturbund, led to a decrease in the number of refugees, and until mid-1935 many Jews who had already gone abroad even returned to Germany.

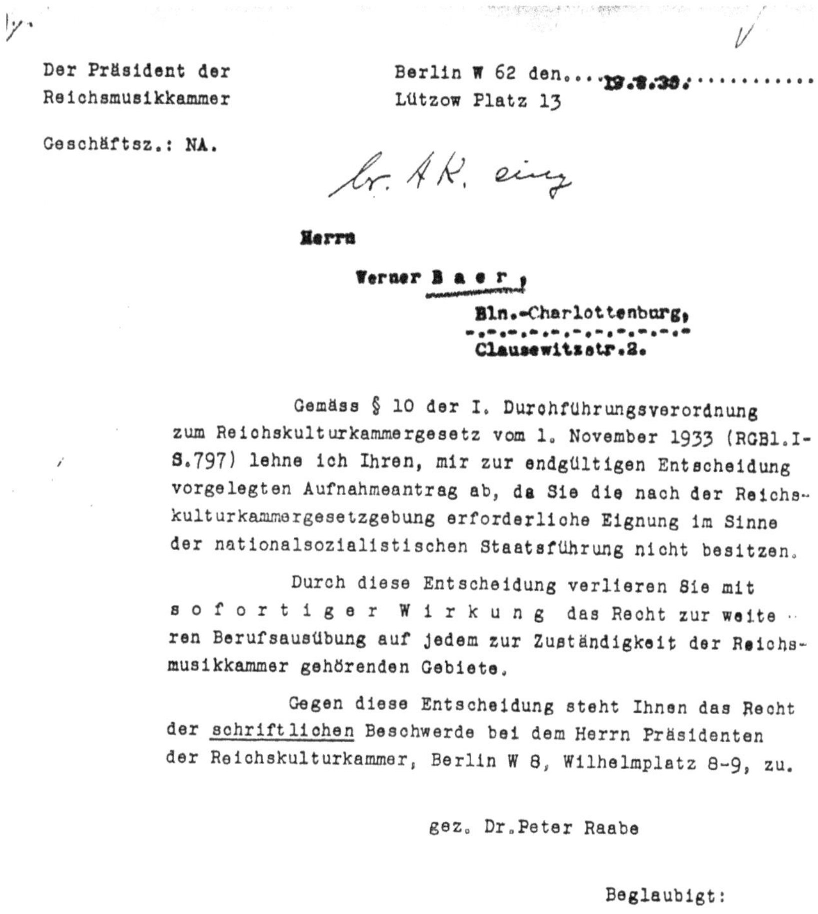

Der Präsident der　　　　　　　Berlin W 62 den... **19.8.38.**
Reichsmusikkammer　　　　　　Lützow Platz 13

Geschäftsz.: NA.

　　　　　　　　　　　Herrn

　　　　　　　　　　　　Werner B a e r ,
　　　　　　　　　　　　　Bln.-Charlottenburg,
　　　　　　　　　　　　　Clausewitzstr.2.

　　　　　Gemäss § 10 der I. Durchführungsverordnung
zum Reichskulturkammergesetz vom 1. November 1933 (RGBl.I-
S.797) lehne ich Ihren, mir zur endgültigen Entscheidung
vorgelegten Aufnahmeantrag ab, da Sie die nach der Reichs-
kulturkammergesetzgebung erforderliche Eignung im Sinne
der nationalsozialistischen Staatsführung nicht besitzen.

　　　　　Durch diese Entscheidung verlieren Sie mit
s o f o r t i g e r   W i r k u n g das Recht zur weite-
ren Berufsausübung auf jedem zur Zuständigkeit der Reichsmusikkammer gehörenden Gebiete.

　　　　　Gegen diese Entscheidung steht Ihnen das Recht
der schriftlichen Beschwerde bei dem Herrn Präsidenten
der Reichskulturkammer, Berlin W 8, Wilhelmplatz 8-9, zu.

　　　　　　　　　　　　gez. Dr. Peter Raabe

　　　　　　　　　　　　　　　　Beglaubigt:

Figure 6: The Reichsmusikkammer refuses Werner Baer's application for membership. (Bundesarchiv, former BDC, RK R 1, Picture 2754)

That said, from March 1935 an Aryan paragraph applied to the Reichsmusikkammer, which triggered numerous exclusions. In a standard letter dated 17 August, most musicians of Jewish descent were notified that they had been refused membership of the Reichsmusikkammer and that 'in accordance with the legislation for the Reichskulturkammer they did not possess the necessary qualification as defined by the National Socialist leadership'. It explained: 'Through this decision you lose your right to continue working professionally in all areas under the jurisdiction of the Reichsmusikkammer with immediate effect.' That August, such letters were sent to Werner Baer, Ellen Byk-Cohn, Willy Coper, Adolf Frischer, Majer Pietruschka, Hermann Schildberger, Theodor Schoenberger and others. Although Pietruschka was allowed to continue playing in the Kulturbund Orchestra – which was not under the purview of the Reichsmusikkammer – he saw little future for himself as a professional musician and, therefore, in December 1935 started an apprenticeship as a cutter of women's clothing, so he could find work in this sector as well.[8]

On the other hand, Ellen Byk took advantage of the possibility which the Reichsmusikkammer provided of making a written complaint.[9] Her complaint was promptly followed by a letter of rejection. But the violinist did not allow herself to be intimidated and submitted a second appeal that similarly was turned down on 11 July 1936. In conclusion, the letter stated: 'With regard to further professional employment, I refer you to the National Association of Jewish Culture Leagues.' It was not until October that Ellen Byk was required to hand in her teaching certificate forthwith: 'You are no longer authorised to engage in any teaching activity for Aryan youth.' By submitting her complaint, the violinist had nevertheless been able to slow the deterioration in her living conditions. However, as she stated herself, from 1933 onwards she had already lost all of her non-Jewish students, so her income was effectively halved.[10] Her older brother had supported her intermittently, but this was no longer possible after Walter Cohn Byk lost his position as a director of AEG in 1937.[11] She had therefore moved from her flat at 93 Paulsborner Straße into more modest accommodation at 10 Markgraf-Albrecht-Straße, right next door to the Friedenstempel synagogue. As she was no longer able to play in concerts or teach Aryans, in the Berlin address book her designation was changed from violinist to artist.

Similarly, as a result of the Nazi legislation, the Stern Conservatory was Aryanised on account of its Jewish owners. It reopened on 1 February 1936 as the Konservatorium der Reichshauptstadt Berlin with Bruno Kittel as director. Shortly before, Kittel had maintained in the *Völkische Beobachter* 'that, although it was founded by Jews and temporarily threatened to succumb to Jewish influence in its approach to culture, the German spirit and the German concept of art had finally triumphed in this institution'.[12] The Jewish teachers who were dismissed subsequently founded 'The Hollaender Jewish Private Music School' and hired rooms at 9 Sybelstraße, directly opposite the Spivakovskys' former home. Among the thirty-nine lecturers who taught the exclusively Jewish enrolment were the singer Paula Salomon-Lindberg, the musicologist Anneliese Landau, the choral conductor and music writer Dr Oskar Guttmann and the pianist Theodor Schoenberger. Schoenberger, who took only advanced students, had also filed a complaint against the Reichsmusikkammer's letter of 17 August 1935. Although he worked only in Jewish institutions from 1936 onwards – as choir conductor at the synagogue in Dresdener Straße, as music lecturer at the Jewish Teacher Training College in Lindenstraße and at the Hollaender Music School – he appealed against decisions of the Reichsmusikkammer several times, so the Kammer was still dealing with his case in February 1938.[13] For young Werner Baer, however, one complaint was enough, especially as he was working for the Jewish community and had a secure income. In addition, he also became a lecturer in organ and modern dance music at the Hollaender Music School.

'My nature is not to join in hate but to join in love'

Baer was also musical director of the Jewish Kulturbund Cabaret. At one of its performances, he got to know the attractive young Ilse Presch, whose father, like his own, was in men's clothing manufacturing. Nathan Presch and his brother Max ran the lucrative textile business Max Presch & Co., which gave the family a secure income. In 1914, the Presch family had moved into a large six-room flat at 68 Mommsenstraße in one of the most sought-after parts of Charlottenburg. The *Generalmusikdirektor* Leo Blech lived directly opposite at No. 6, and next to them in No. 5 was a star of the State Opera, the celebrated bass Michael Bohnen, who was renowned for his interpretations of Mozart, Wagner and Strauss.[14] Ilse Presch went to the nearby Princess Bismarck School, where she received a liberal education. The school's humanistic educational aims, rooted in Greek antiquity and the German Enlightenment, were depicted in its frescoes. Under the gable of the boys' wing, a frieze bore the Kant quotation 'Two things fill my mind with ever new and increasing admiration and awe: the starry heavens above me and the moral law within me'.[15] On the girls' wing, the saying 'My nature is not to join in hate but to join in love',[16] from Sophocles' *Antigone*, was written on the sandstone in the original Greek and in the German translation.[17] Even as a schoolgirl, Ilse Presch was very independent; she admired emancipated women like the writer Karin Michaelis and the actress Marlene Dietrich. At the age of twelve, she joined a socialist youth group, took part in demonstrations and distributed pamphlets against the Nazis:

> When Hitler arrived, I got another pile of leaflets which I was supposed to stick up all over the place. However, my brother saw them and threw them into the toilet. He said, 'They'll kill you if they find you doing that!' I had no idea; I was only fifteen at the time.[18]

Because of her good marks in German, the young girl had wanted to become a writer or journalist. After 1933, such goals were unthinkable, and against her will Presch had to begin an apprenticeship as a dressmaker.[19]

After Robert Baer's untimely death, his men's clothing business was run by his wife Lucie and their son Fritz. When the firm went bankrupt, the Presch brothers acquired it and retained Fritz Baer as an employee.[20] In the meantime, Fritz and Werner Baer had moved with their mother to Charlottenburg, not far from the Café Leon and Mommsenstraße. It is possible that even when he first met her at the Kulturbund Cabaret, Werner Baer had already known about Ilse Presch through his brother. She had been fascinated by the theatre from an early age and was now impressed by the tall pianist who accompanied Max Ehrlich so brilliantly in his performances. A close friendship developed, and they eventually became a couple.

Before he began working with Max Ehrlich, the multi-talented Werner Baer was already active as an assistant organist at various synagogues. While substituting for indisposed organists, Baer stumbled across the Walcker organ in the Fasanenstraße synagogue:

> My one and only Jewish organ teacher, the blind Richard Altmann, was the organist there under the direction of Theodor Schoenberger, choirmaster and outstanding piano teacher. Altmann was often absent on account of illness and I used to stand in as his deputy.[21]

As Baer proved successful with this kind of work, in 1934 he was offered the position of organist at the liberal synagogue on the Prinzregentenstraße in Wilmersdorf, the Berlin suburb with the highest percentage of Jews.[22] The synagogue had only opened in 1930 and staged concerts with well-known artists such as Joseph Schmidt, Alexander Kipnis, Carl Flesch and Paula Salomon-Lindberg. The Steinmeyer organ installed there was even more pleasing than the one in Fasanenstraße, and, along with the Walcker organ in the New Synagogue on Oranienburger Straße, was one of the city's best instruments.

'An infinitely tougher regime': Vienna after the Anschluss

Although at first Austria was a popular country of exile for refugees from Germany, it soon began to restrict political freedoms. In March 1933, Chancellor Engelbert Dollfuß closed down parliament and banned the Republikanische Schutzbund [Protection League], the Social Democrat paramilitary organisation; the following May, he also banned the Fatherland Front, the Communist Party and the National Socialist Party. The end of the Social Democratic Party and Austria's free trade unions finally came when the general strike of 12 February 1934 was bloodily suppressed. The Republic was replaced by a corporatist state led by Dollfuß, who forced his opponents into exile.[23] Although it modelled itself on fascist Italy, Austrofascism strictly distanced itself from Hitler's Germany; it strove for independence and, with support from the local press, refused to persecute the Jews. For the most part, therefore, Jews remained in Dollfuß's Austria, especially as prominent intellectuals like Karl Kraus, Ernst Krenek and Franz Werfel supported the regime. Austrian Jews like Adolf Brenner, who could no longer work in Germany, often returned to their homeland despite the political restrictions. In doing so, they usually found that their circumstances deteriorated. After finishing his studies in Berlin in 1933, the pianist Peter Stadlen went back to Vienna, where he made his name as an interpreter of contemporary music. Together with Ernst Krenek, Stadlen gave the first performance of Krenek's Bagatelles for piano four hands in a coffee house theatre.[24] In October 1936, Stadlen was a soloist in Stravinsky's *Concerto per due pianoforti soli* in the Mozartsaal of the Konzerthaus. A year later, he played the world premiere of Anton Webern's Piano Variations Op. 27.

The *Neues Wiener Tagblatt*, founded in 1867, was Vienna's best-selling newspaper. From 1889–1901, its arts section was headed by none other than Hermann Bahr. When the music critic Ernst Decsey assumed this role in 1924, he ensured that music received wider coverage. Maximilian Forst (*b.*1877, Vienna) was also on the newspaper's editorial board. Since 1935, musical criticism had appeared in the arts section of the *Neues Wiener Tagblatt* signed 'h.f.', the initials of Maximilian's son, Hans Forst. For example, on 2 February 1938 he discussed, in a single article, a piano recital by Robert Spitz, a recital by the Norwegian singer Frederica Anthonisen and an evening of compositions by Richard Stöhr.[25]

The *Neues Wiener Tagblatt* was subtitled 'An Organ of Democracy', and as such it frequently published reports critical of the racial politics in Germany. Thus on 9 January 1937, the title page carried a warning about the literary work of Houston Stewart Chamberlain: 'In contrast to the cosmopolitan and liberal thinking of those days, it propagates racial theory, antisemitism and the primacy of Teutonicism in human history.'[26] On 20 January 1937, the *Neues Wiener Abendblatt* (the evening edition) carried the headline 'Eden's Serious Words against Racial Politics', followed by an editorial under the heading 'A Ray of Hope': 'Yesterday's speech by the British Foreign Minister will doubtless have strong repercussions in Europe, perhaps strongest of all in Germany.' As the paper was to confirm two days later, the measures taken by the Nazi regime had a damaging effect on musical life in Austria as well. The Reichsmusikkammer now allowed very little foreign music to be imported; this was aimed directly at several Viennese music publishing houses. Germany already had huge debts with these publishers.[27]

Chancellor Dollfuß was murdered during an attempted Nazi coup in July 1934. Germany put its neighbour under increasing pressure; finally, on 9 March 1938, Dollfuß's successor, Kurt von Schuschnigg, made an impassioned speech pleading with the Austrians to unite; to this end, there would be a referendum on Sunday 13 March. On 10 March, the *Neues Wiener Tagblatt* had the news on its front page. An editorial headed 'Avowal for Austria' called for a million 'yes' votes in order to preserve the country's freedom. There was eager support from the Israelitische Kultusgemeinde [Vienna Israelite Community].[28] Hitler, who wanted to avoid the referendum at all costs, acted with lightning speed and sent German troops into Austria on 11 March. Under military duress, Schuschnigg resigned on the same day. On 12 March, a special edition of the *Neues Wiener Abendblatt* appeared with the huge heading 'Triumphant Reception for Führer in Linz'. The paper's subtitle was missing; the editorial staff had been dismissed and replaced by collaborators. On 14 March, they printed a huge swastika on the title page, together with the announcement 'The Führer Comes to Vienna Today'. With that, they said, the majority that had been repressed for so long would finally achieve justice. With his quick action, Hitler had secured peace. 'If Schuschnigg had gone ahead with the plebiscite, there would have been a bloody revolution. Austria could have perhaps become a second Spain.' The next day, 15 March, the Führer spoke at the Vienna Heldenplatz [Heroes' Square], greeted by a jubilant throng of cheering people. Dissenting opinions no longer had a chance; non-Aryans were now also persecuted in Austria.

Austria was 'cleansed' and 'brought into line' [*Gleichschaltung*] more quickly and more brutally than Germany had been. The first antisemitic riots took place on 11 March, immediately after Schuschnigg's resignation.[29] On 13 March, a Law for the Reunification of Austria with the German Reich was proclaimed, and the Rathausplatz was renamed Adolf-Hitler-Platz. On 19 March, the University of Vienna received a new acting administration. On 23 March, there was a propaganda march-past of 15,000 SA men along the Ringstraße, followed on 29 March by a speech by Goebbels in the huge, festively decorated hall of the Northwest station. On 31 March, Maximilian Forst was given notice by his newspaper, and on 30 April he was summarily dismissed. Other Jewish employees were in a similar situation.[30] On 1 April, colleagues who were categorised as dangerous had already been sent with the first Austrian transportation to the Dachau concentration camp. In the run-up to the vote on 'Greater Germany' and the election of the Greater German Reichstag on 10 April, there was a big concert by the German police on the Heldenplatz on 8 April and a speech by Hitler the next day, the 'Day of the Greater German Reich'.[31] On 24 April, a quota system was decreed for Jewish students at Austrian universities.

On 23 March, the *New York Times* reported:

> It is becoming clear that whereas in Germany the first victims were the Left political parties – Socialists and Communists – in Vienna it is the Jews who are to bear the brunt of the Nazis' revolutionary fire. Within fourteen days it has been possible to subject the Jews under an infinitely tougher regime than they achieved in Germany in a year.[32]

Hertha Langer, the wife of lawyer and pianist Peter Langer, wrote about this period of terror:

> This time taught me to see what no historical reports could ever have taught me. Everything that happened in Vienna in those days must have happened the same way in all times of revolution. It tore a veil from my eyes and showed me the people. If I had, like every young person sympathized with communist ideals, I now learnt something different. I believe that people in Vienna particularly had sunk down because of unemployment, hunger and hopelessness. However, many people who had not had these terrible experiences also behaved like pigs, and I have learnt to despise them. They rushed at the Jews, first a few and then more and more of them, circled around, plundered, did wrong and murdered. Like lazy dogs they made the worst noise where opposition was weakest. Everyone could demand money from Jews, or from the former supporters of the ruling party without impunity.[33]

Shops and businesses owned by Jews were spontaneously looted.[34] In their despair, many of those affected committed suicide. Special laws were soon introduced to regulate the forced takeover of Jewish firms by Aryans. Beforehand, according to a decree of 26 April, the Jews had to submit detailed lists of their assets to the authorities.[35] Dr Hans Spitzer, who was married to the cellist Therese Spitzer, also had to hand in such a declaration.

His wife had interrupted her studies at the Vienna Music Academy in 1921 and, after a long sojourn in the USA and Czechoslovakia, had given birth to two children. In his declaration of assets, Spitzer indicated that he was a Jew of German nationality – all Austrians were automatically given German citizenship after the Anschluss – and that, in addition to agricultural assets, he owned a share in the pharmacy 'At the Rotunda'. The name came from the famous round building that had been the main attraction at the Viennese World Exhibition of 1873, but had burnt down in 1937. He now had to hand over their pharmacy to an Aryan owner.[36] He gave the exact market value of this prime property close to the Prater.[37] At the time, around half of all Viennese pharmacies were similarly affected.

Lists of assets were also demanded from Hugo Holzbauer, owner of a grocery store, and from Julie Edelmann, the proprietor of a piano shop. With all these seizures, most of the affected families lost their livelihoods. When submitting his list of assets, Julie Edelmann's son Hans recorded that two months earlier he had lost his job as a bookshop employee; he was referring to the large bookshop of Alois Reichmann, which was very quickly Aryanised. Since then, he had been unemployed and had no assets at all. Only his wife was earning: forty RM a month.[38] As a Social Democrat, Edelmann had already been arrested on 14 April for 'defaming the Führer'. He was released from prison quickly only because the Gestapo [Secret State Police] officer-in-charge, a professional boxer, took a liking to him on account of his sporting knowledge.[39]

The new rulers showed a great interest in Vienna's Jewish music publishing houses, not least profitable organisations like the Josef Weinberger Verlag, which published the works of Johann Strauß, Carl Zeller, Franz von Suppé, Franz Lehár, Robert Stolz and Carl Ziehrer. Founded in 1885, the publishing house was located at 11 Mahlerstraße, right next to the State Opera, and was managed by the founder's nephew, Otto Blau. By 25 April, Dr Max Winkler, head of the notorious Cautio Treuhand GmbH [Trust Ltd], could report to his commissioning authority (the Reich Ministry for Public Enlightenment and Propaganda) that an agreement had been reached with Dr Otto Blau.[40] Since Blau had reckoned on a German invasion, he had already set up a publishing house in London and transferred the most important rights, thereby keeping his most significant source of income out of German hands. In order to secure his remaining assets in

Vienna, after Hitler's invasion Blau immediately began negotiations with a publisher in Leipzig, to whom he pretended to sell his Vienna business. But the Berlin publisher Dr Hans C. Sikorski, who on Winkler's behalf had already played a significant role in these Aryanisations,[41] forced Blau to sell not only his Weinberger publishing house, but also to retransfer the rights that had been transferred to London. In return, Blau received non-Aryan music rights, including those to the works of Leo Fall, Emmerich Kálmán, Gustav Mahler and Oscar Straus, in which Germany had no interest. In a contract signed on 20 June 1938, Dr Blau also undertook to help the Aryaniser Sikorski to realise the potential of the publishing firm through co-operation and propaganda.[42]

When Otto Blau filled out his 'list of assets' form on 14 July, he answered the question about his trade or profession: 'without profession (because the business has been Aryanised)'. He listed his personal assets, but added that the Reich Flight Tax was to be deducted from that amount. As a consequence, on 15 August the Vienna office of the Gestapo issued a seizure order, as a result of which 'for reasons of public safety and order, the entire assets and all rights and claims of Blau Otto Isr. [...] are to be seized, for later collection in favour of the German Reich'. Blau fled Vienna on 30 September and moved to London.[43] Not only was his former publishing house Aryanised, but also its address: Mahlerstraße, commemorating the great conductor and composer Gustav Mahler, was renamed Meistersingerstraße. The new rulers were thorough in erasing all traces of the Jews.

The music publisher Victor Alberti was more fortunate than Otto Blau. Alberti had fled from Berlin to Budapest and moved from there to Vienna in 1935. In that year, because of poor sales in Germany, Karczag Publishing had had to file for bankruptcy. Emmerich Kálmán, the composer of *Czárdásfürstin* and *Gräfin Mariza*, had subsequently transferred his rights from Karczag to Alberti. As Alberti had immediately transferred these valuable rights to Octava Ltd,[44] a firm that he had established in Zurich, he was able to keep them out of the hands of the Nazis. The fact that he was out of the country when Hitler marched into Austria also worked to his advantage. Alberti did not return to Vienna, but fled to Zurich where, in the meantime, Kálmán and his librettist Paul Knepler were also living.[45]

It was not easy for Austrians who were being politically and racially persecuted to leave the country, as the Hungarian and Czechoslovakian borders were closed to them. In addition, they had to get numerous papers together: a tax clearance certificate, emigration permit and passport as well as a medical certificate, a certificate of good conduct from the police and proof of accommodation. The Reich Flight Tax could amount to 30 per cent of their assets and the 'Atonement Tax' to 20 per cent.[46] Since the procurement of a German passport meant further delays, many Jews who wanted to escape tried to cross the borders illegally without this document to Czechoslovakia, Hungary, Yugoslavia, Italy or Switzerland. Hans Blau and his wife were spared these problems thanks to prominent intervention. Their mediator was none other than the Duke of Windsor, the former Prince of Wales, whom Blau had often entertained with his Viennese songs in the Rotter-Bar. Blau told the authorities South Africa was his new domicile but he actually settled in Switzerland, where he had an engagement at the Bellevue Palace in Bern. On 17 August 1938, the German Embassy in Bern provided him with a German passport that had to be extended every three months. In October, when Blau presented it to the German consul in Zurich, the latter made two significant additions: according to the new passport regulation of 5 October, he stamped a big, red 'J' (Jew) on the first page of the passport, and added 'Israel' as Blau's second name. The popular entertainer Hans Blau was now designated 'non-Aryan' and excluded from the *Volksgemeinschaft* [people's community].

Peter Stadlen, too, was spared serious difficulties as in March 1938 he was abroad. 'Because of the flu, which I caught while returning from a concert in London, I wasn't in Vienna for the Anschluss, but in bed in Amsterdam.' Stadlen, like Blau and Alberti, had also feared the German invasion. In October 1937, he was in Vienna preparing the premiere of Anton Webern's piano variations. During a walk with the composer in the Prater, he had broached the subject of the threat hanging over Austria. Would it not mean the end of the music of the Schönberg School? At the time, Webern had reassured him: 'If the Nazis come, I'll go to Goebbels and tell him that he is ill-advised, and that twelve-tone music is no cultural Bolshevism.' Stadlen had replied: 'Perhaps you will convince him of that, Doctor. But you will surely never convince him that Schönberg is not a Jew?' 'No', said Webern, 'but he is *nonetheless* a decent man.'[47] Stadlen was not as naïve as the composer. He knew that the Nazis were not susceptible to such moral arguments. When another member of the Webern circle had told him in Amsterdam about the parade of German troops on the Ringstraße, the pianist decided not to return to Vienna. Although Stadlen kept his flat in the Rechte Bahngasse until 1940,[48] he travelled from Amsterdam back to London. His exile had begun.

On the initiative of Adolf Eichmann, who was in charge of Jewish Affairs for the Gestapo in Vienna, a Central Agency for Jewish Emigration was established in the former Palais Rothschild, in Vienna's Fourth District.[49] The Israelitische Kultusgemeinde in Vienna advised emigrants in their own Department of Emigration. Adolf Brenner presented himself there on 20 May and filled out a questionnaire. He described himself as a conductor, pianist, and teacher of piano and theory who, 'after many years of professional activity at theatres in the heart of Germany' (he mentioned working sojourns in Sondershausen, Arnstadt and Regensburg), had finally become a music teacher in Vienna. Brenner knew that musicians were not wanted abroad, so he had taken courses in typewriting, stenography and English in order to pursue a commercial career if necessary. To be able to emigrate, he declared that he was prepared 'to undertake any kind of work, even outside of my profession'. He was still unable to answer the question 'Where do you want to emigrate to?' He was, as he stated, destitute and had no valid passport.

The singer Leonie Feigl was also desperate to leave, as her personal situation had continued to deteriorate ever since she left Russia. When her mother and her husband both died suddenly in the autumn of 1933, she had to give up her large flat in Hietzing. She moved into more modest accommodation in the Ninth District, an old house where a relative was living. But she was no longer able to invite people to her musical soirées as in the past. The terror that followed the German invasion shocked the singer so much that on 27 March she attempted suicide. Her daughter Julie succeeded in leaving Vienna with her husband in September, after they received a warning; the frightened mother stayed behind.

As sons of a Jewish father, Josef and Heinrich Krips were regarded by the regime as 'half Jews' and forbidden to work. Josef Krips had been employed as a conductor at the Vienna State Opera since 1934, and from 1935 his younger brother Henry had been musical director at the Vienna Volksoper as well as chief conductor for the Salzburg Municipal Theatre. Heinrich Krips was more partial to light music than his brother and also

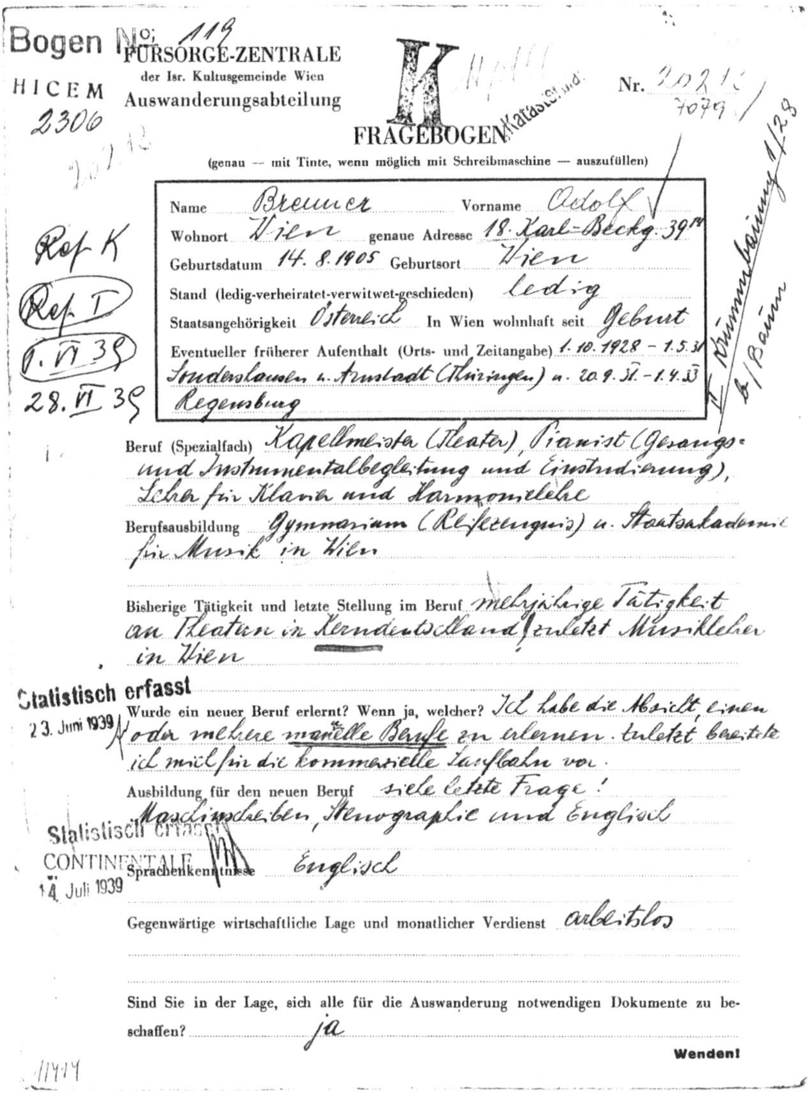

Bogen No: 119
HICEM
2306

FÜRSORGE-ZENTRALE
der Isr. Kultusgemeinde Wien
Auswanderungsabteilung

K

Nr. 20212 / 7079

FRAGEBOGEN

(genau — mit Tinte, wenn möglich mit Schreibmaschine — auszufüllen)

Name Brenner Vorname Adolf
Wohnort Wien genaue Adresse 18. Karl-Beckg. 39
Geburtsdatum 14. 8. 1905 Geburtsort Wien
Stand (ledig-verheiratet-verwitwet-geschieden) ledig
Staatsangehörigkeit Österreich In Wien wohnhaft seit Geburt
Eventueller früherer Aufenthalt (Orts- und Zeitangabe) 1. 10. 1928 – 1. 5. 31 Sondershausen u. Arnstadt (Thüringen) u. 20. 9. 31. – 1. 4. 33 Regensburg

Ref K
Ref. I
1. VI 39
28. VI 39

Beruf (Spezialfach) Kapellmeister (Theater), Pianist (Gesangs- und Instrumentalbegleitung und Einstudierung), Lehrer für Klavier und Harmonielehre

Berufsausbildung Gymnasium (Reifezeugnis) u. Staatsakademie für Musik in Wien

Bisherige Tätigkeit und letzte Stellung im Beruf mehrjährige Tätigkeit an Theatern in Norddeutschland, zuletzt Musiklehrer in Wien

Statistisch erfasst
23. Juni 1939

Wurde ein neuer Beruf erlernt? Wenn ja, welcher? Ich habe die Absicht, einen oder mehrere manuelle Berufe zu erlernen. Zuletzt bereitete ich mich für die kommerzielle Laufbahn vor.

Ausbildung für den neuen Beruf siehe letzte Frage! Maschinschreiben, Stenographie und Englisch

Statistisch erfasst
CONTINENTALE
14. Juli 1939

Sprachenkenntnisse Englisch

Gegenwärtige wirtschaftliche Lage und monatlicher Verdienst arbeitslos

Sind Sie in der Lage, sich alle für die Auswanderung notwendigen Dokumente zu beschaffen? ja

Wenden!

11414

Figure 7: Questionnaire of the Emigration Department of the Welfare Centre of the Viennese Kultusgemeinde, completed by Kapellmeister and pianist Adolf Brenner on 20 May 1938. He declares his willingness to learn a new profession for his emigration. At present he is unemployed. (CAHJP, A/W 2590, 28) made appearances as a composer; his operetta *Fiordaliso* was premiered in Milan in 1935. In the same year, the Berlin Komische Oper showed an interest in his operetta *Chrysanthemums*; but it was not performed as neither the authors nor the publisher belonged to German professional associations.[50]

After the German invasion, the New Viennese Conservatorium housed in the Musikverein building was disbanded. Its lecturers included the singer Anna Bahr-Mildenburg, the music critic Ernst Descey, the pianist Alfred Grünfeld, the composers Ernst Kanitz, Egon Wellesz and Eugen Zador and the violinist and violist Simon Pullman. Born in White Russia, he had studied in St Petersburg and with Martin Pierre Marsick at the Paris Conservatoire; he subsequently directed a chamber music series in Warsaw until 1921. He soon had an outstanding name as a teacher in Vienna. His pupil Richard Goldner remembered that Pullman paid particular attention to tone and quality of sound, and that he referred his students to new works by Schönberg, Krenek, Wellesz and Honegger.[51] The Pullman Chamber Orchestra that he established in 1931 caused a sensation when its seventeen string players performed works representing the pinnacle of chamber music – such as Beethoven's *Große Fuge* Op. 133, or the String Quartet Op. 131 – without a conductor.

Equally important for Richard Goldner was the Musica Viva Orchestra, founded by the musical pioneer Hermann Scherchen in late summer 1937, which consisted largely of unemployed Jewish musicians. At the time, Goldner wrote to Carl Flesch that 'for seven years not one single Jew has been employed by either of the great orchestras – the Philharmonic and the Symphony'.[52] As there were no longer any professional opportunities for Jewish musicians, Goldner sought to take refuge abroad. On 13 May 1938, in a questionnaire for the Emigration Department of the Kultusgemeinde, he nominated the United States of America as his destination. In answer to the question 'Have you learnt a new profession? If so, which one?' he wrote: 'Engraver and carver of all materials'. He mentioned his brother Gerhard, who was already working as a wood-carver. He said he wanted to travel with him to the USA in order to undertake 'the commercial production of carved and turned fashion accessories as well as arts and crafts items and artificial flowers'.[53] That said, he also hoped to continue practising his musical profession.

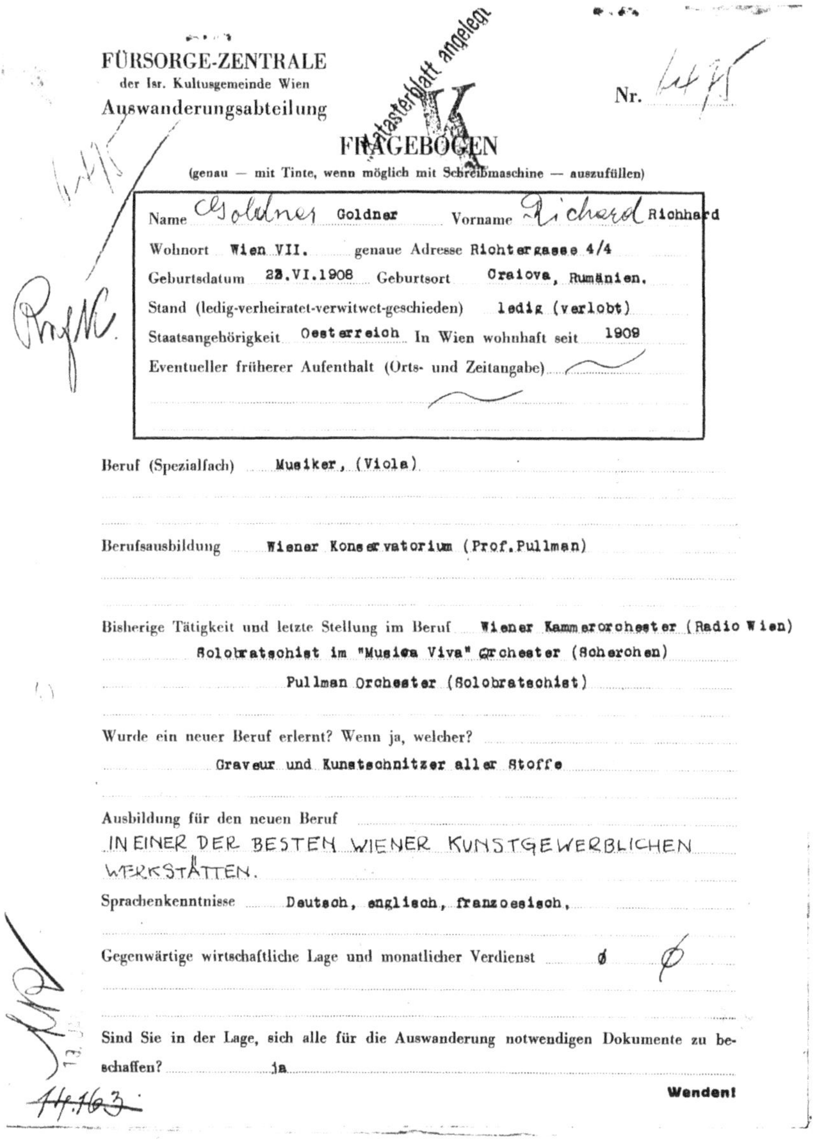

Vienna after the Anschluss

FÜRSORGE-ZENTRALE
der Isr. Kultusgemeinde Wien
Auswanderungsabteilung

Nr. 44/75

FRAGEBOGEN
(genau — mit Tinte, wenn möglich mit Schreibmaschine — auszufüllen)

Name Goldner Vorname Richard
Wohnort Wien VII. genaue Adresse Richtergasse 4/4
Geburtsdatum 22.VI.1908 Geburtsort Craiova, Rumänien.
Stand (ledig-verheiratet-verwitwet-geschieden) ledig (verlobt)
Staatsangehörigkeit Oesterreich In Wien wohnhaft seit 1909
Eventueller früherer Aufenthalt (Orts- und Zeitangabe)

Beruf (Spezialfach) Musiker, (Viola)

Berufsausbildung Wiener Konservatorium (Prof. Pullman)

Bisherige Tätigkeit und letzte Stellung im Beruf Wiener Kammerorchester (Radio Wien)
Solobratschist im "Musica Viva" Orchester (Scherchen)
Pullman Orchester (Solobratschist)

Wurde ein neuer Beruf erlernt? Wenn ja, welcher?
Graveur und Kunstschnitzer aller Stoffe

Ausbildung für den neuen Beruf
IN EINER DER BESTEN WIENER KUNSTGEWERBLICHEN
WERKSTÄTTEN.

Sprachenkenntnisse Deutsch, englisch, franzoesisch,

Gegenwärtige wirtschaftliche Lage und monatlicher Verdienst Ø   Ø

Sind Sie in der Lage, sich alle für die Auswanderung notwendigen Dokumente zu beschaffen? ja

Wenden!

Figure 8: Questionnaire of the Emigration Department of the Welfare Centre of the Viennese Kultusgemeinde for Richard Goldner. On 13 May 1938 he states that he learnt the profession of an engraver and carver. At present he has no income.
(CAHJP, A/W 2590, 74)

Prospects for emigration to North America appeared good, especially as a relative was already living in Pittsburgh. Surprisingly, Goldner received a letter from London advising him that Jewish musicians were being sought for a first-class chamber orchestra in New York. After some to-ing and fro-ing, he discovered the identity of the unknown writer: it was the violinist Fritz Rothschild, who mentioned that a huge sum of money had been made available by the banker Gerald Warburg for the establishment of a 'New Friends of Music' orchestra. In the light of such financial indemnity, Goldner's departure seemed imminent, so he married his girlfriend Marianne Reiss on 31 July. On 17 August, the Vienna branch of the Reichsmusikkammer confirmed that, as an emigrating professional musician, he was permitted to take his Italian viola with him. Thus his disappointment was all the more acute when he discovered that no more visas were available for the USA, because the quotas had already been filled.[54] Goldner now had to find a new country of refuge.

Political Refugees

Besides the racially persecuted, there were the political refugees. Among them was the family of landowner Moritz Ritter [Knight] von Bauer, originally from Brünn. Kaiser Franz Josef granted him the title Ritter von Chlumecky-Bauer. The name Chlumecky had a good ring to it: Johann Freiherr von Chlumecky had been the Leader of the House of Lords in Vienna until 1918. After the First World War, however, Moritz Chlumecky-Bauer lost his possessions in Moravia and his title and moved to Vienna, where he settled in the smart Nineteenth District. Although the Vienna Address Book still designated him as a landowner, he had to build a new life for himself. He invested a large sum of money in the book distributor Literaria Ltd, which, however, went bankrupt. The former landowner then changed to dealing in postage stamps. There were four children from his marriage to Margarethe von Remiz: Nikolaus (*b*.1919), Johannes (*b*.1920), then Anton and finally a daughter, Elisabeth. The sons Nikolaus and Johannes both took violin lessons with Professor Rudolf Fitzner, leader of the Fitzner String Quartet. In 1931, they transferred to Professor Julius Winkler, one of whose students was the famous Wolfgang Schneiderhan. Of the two brothers, Johannes had a greater talent for the violin, which is why Nikolaus finally decided to play the cello.

Gustav Edler von Remiz,[55] their mother's brother, owned Fuschl Castle near Salzburg. His wife Hedwig von Remiz was a granddaughter of August Thyssen, the founder of the eponymous steel concern. His son Fritz had financed the Nazi Party since 1923 in order to gain the Party's support in fighting the German Labour Movement; at the time, Thyssen had helped the then still stateless Adolf Hitler to address the Düsseldorf Industrial Club in 1932. But, as he disapproved the persecution of Jews, from 1935 onwards the industrialist increasingly dissociated himself from the Nazi regime.[56] In 1936, when Moritz Chlumecky-Bauer and his family visited their relatives at Fuschl Castle, Fritz Thyssen was also one of the guests.[57]

As a monarchist, Gustav Edler von Remiz was strongly opposed to National Socialism. After Dollfuß was murdered, von Remiz had identified several Nazis as the perpetrators. German Foreign Minister Ribbentrop knew this and had von Remiz imprisoned as 'an invidiously active enemy detrimental to the National Socialist movement' and deported to the Dachau concentration camp. He died there in 1939.[58] Fuschl Castle was forcibly sold and handed over to Ribbentrop, although Hedwig von Remiz had categorically rejected the idea. Given his wife's close relationship to the Dachau prisoner Gustav von Remiz, Moritz Chlumecky-Bauer felt that both he and his family were in danger, although as so-called 'one-eighth Jews' and as Roman Catholics who regularly visited the Carmelite Church in Döbling, they were not directly affected by Nazi racial politics. In view of his political opposition to the regime, Moritz thought it wise to flee with his family to Belgium in August 1938. This took place without the knowledge of the Viennese authorities, who only later noticed the Chlumeckys' absence. On 13 December 1939, the Viennese registration office registered for Johannes Chlumecky-Bauer: 'No longer resident at this house.' At that point, the family was already on its way from Belgium to Britain. By then, Fritz Thyssen no longer lived in the German Reich either – he had fled to Switzerland.

'Musicians Unsuitable': Immigration Policy in Britain and Australia

After the Austrian Anschluss, the number of refugees soared. Attention quickly turned to sparsely populated Australia. As early as 6 April 1938, the Australian Prime Minister received news that in just three weeks the British Embassy in Vienna (which represented Australian interests) had had more than 10,000 applications for emigration to Australia.[59] Whereas from the beginning of 1933 to September 1938 a total of 11,000 asylum seekers had gone to Britain, 35,000 now arrived in a single year from September 1938 to September 1939.[60] As neither the aid organisations nor the authorities could cope with this influx, on 27 April 1938 the Foreign Office introduced a visa requirement for refugees from Germany and Austria. Decisions relating to visa procurement lay with the British Passport Control Office. The most important criterion for the issuing of British visas was 'Suitability or Unsuitability of the Applicant for the United Kingdom'. As a rule, the United Kingdom was not interested in musicians. Accordingly, on the same day, the Foreign Office sent out standard letters with the information: 'Among those who must be regarded as *prima facie* unsuitable will be: [...] Minor musicians and commercial artists of all kinds.'[61] Immigration would only be considered in the case of high-ranking artists. In addition, it was now made even clearer to asylum seekers that Britain could only be regarded as a country of transit. As a rule, visa applicants had to state a destination for their onward journey. Visa procurement also became more difficult with the introduction of the mandatory financial guarantees in 1938.

Frank Foley, the British Passport Control Officer in Berlin, had problems with these new restrictions. He knew the German capital and spoke fluent German. Before the First World War, he had been a teacher in Hamburg and had come to Berlin in 1920 for a new job as a top spy with the British Secret Service, MI6. Alongside his activities as a secret agent, which mainly concerned the fight against communism, he was officially in charge of the Passport Control Office at 17 Tiergartenstraße. From Wilmersdorf, he moved to a large flat at 56 Lessingstraße. Many wealthy and well-educated Jews were living in this old Hansa district, not far from the Levetzowstraße synagogue. On 10 May 1935, Foley had already written in a memorandum:

> The position of the Jew in Germany, even if he [sic] possesses capital, is a desperate one: he is being ruined economically and at the same time he is unable to emigrate as he cannot obtain the release of even a moderate proportion of his capital sufficient to enable him to do so.[62]

Since the 1920s, Foley, a practising Catholic, had been a friend of the warehouse owner Wilfried Israel, who had been born in London and moved to Berlin as a child. In 1921, Israel joined the Nathan Israel department store managed by his father. This store, which had grown out of a second-hand clothing shop founded in 1815, was one of the oldest firms in Berlin. The Israels had come to this city as protected Jews in 1741, at the beginning of Frederick the Great's reign. After the death of his father, Wilfried Israel and his brother Herbert took over the management of this long-established family business. Wilfried founded the firm's own trade school, and he took an active interest in the social and educational care of his employees. Furthermore, in order to assist Jews over and above his work in the firm, from 1937 onwards he also joined the executive of the Hilfsverein der Juden in Deutschland [Aid Association of Jews in Germany]. Established in 1901 by, among others, the merchant James Simon, this organisation aimed to foster the social standing and education of Jews. In 1904, it amalgamated with the Central Office for Jewish Emigration which, despite its name, concerned itself primarily with Eastern European Jews who were aspiring immigrants, hence was, in effect, an office for immigration. Since Hitler's rise to power, the German Jews could no longer help those in other countries: instead they needed support themselves. Germany was no longer an immigration, but an emigration country, and the Hilfsverein now took on the task of helping Jews to leave. It took care of emigration to all countries except Palestine, for which the Palästina-Amt [Palestinian Office] on Meinekestraße was responsible. Although the Jewish community promoted emigration to Palestine 'in principle', many Jews recoiled from this desert-like and politically contested destination. As a voluntary worker in the Palestinian Office, Alfred Dreyfus could easily have obtained a visa for that country but, as his son George remembered, 'he didn't want one'.[63]

Thus the Palestinian Office was never a serious rival for the Hilfsverein. In its magazine, *Jüdische Auswanderung* [Jewish Emigration], the Hilfsverein published information about the entry requirements and living conditions in various countries. As one of its main collaborators, Wilfried Israel supported the emigration of thousands of Jews, whereby his friendship with Captain Foley proved beneficial.[64] The fact that one of Foley's colleagues, Hubert Pollack, had been a classmate of Israel's brother Herbert was also an advantage.[65] This was an excellent basis for close collaboration between the Hilfsverein and the British Passport Office, and British visas were generously issued. Many Jews were happy just to pay the visa fee of 8.30 RM and collect their entitlements, which gave them a feeling of security – even if they did not actually use them to emigrate.[66]

The more the pressure mounted in Germany and Austria, however, the more difficult it became to find countries willing to take in the refugees. In March 1938, US President Franklin D. Roosevelt had already called for the establishment of an international refugee committee to organise controlled emigration of German and Austrian Jews, and to this end he convened the Evian Conference of July 1938. It was originally to take place in Geneva at the Headquarters of the League of Nations, but the Swiss rejected this proposal, apparently through fear of Germany; and so the organisers relocated to Evian, a French health resort. To ensure that as many nations as possible would be willing to accept the refugees, delegates from thirty-two countries were invited. High expectations were focused on Australia, which was sparsely settled; but the Australian delegate, the Minister for Trade Colonel Thomas White, let them down terribly. Although shortly before in London, White had invited British emigrants to Australia, in Evian he explained that in the present circumstances his country could do nothing for the refugees. Without ever mentioning the native Aboriginal people, he delivered a plea for a continuation of the White Australia Policy:

> Under the circumstances Australia cannot do more, for it will be appreciated that in a young country manpower from the source from which most of its citizens have sprung is preferred, while undue privileges cannot be given to one particular class of non-British subjects without injustice to others. It will no doubt be appreciated also that as we have no real racial problem we are not desirous of importing one by encouraging any scheme of large-scale foreign migration.[67]

White's performance in Evian caused some bitterness, even among his compatriots.[68] One of the commentaries in the *Sydney Morning Herald* noted that he had even failed to mention the professed tolerance that was so eagerly expressed in Australia:

> It is a truism that the Commonwealth has no racial problem and has no desire to import one. On the other hand it prides itself on being a democracy with a strong tradition of tolerance, and any undue suggestion of racial intolerance constitutes a betrayal of our cherished traditions.[69]

Four weeks later, the paper stated that Australia had missed a great opportunity to gain some of the most talented minds in Europe.[70] On the other hand, White received support from Labor Party circles and from *The Truth*, a newspaper that called for Australia to protect itself from unwanted and non-assimilable Hebrews.[71] In Germany, Australia's insistence on racial purity had already been favourably compared with the racial mixture in the USA.[72] In his book *Australien. Der menschenscheue Kontinent* [Australia: The Unsociable Continent], published in Berlin in 1939, Heinrich Hauser discovered in the White Australia Policy 'an astounding affinity with the ideas of the new Germany'.[73]

'There's a ship, the black freighter': Ways of Escape, 1938

Direct Travellers to Australia

The Hilfsverein informed people about Australia's immigration policy and about the hostility of the trade unions there.[74] In spite of this warning, and although in 1937 barely 4 per cent of their assisted emigrants had gone to Australia,[75] one of their information brochures was emblazoned with a splendid photo of Sydney harbour and the great Sydney Harbour Bridge.[76] In May 1938, the *C.V.-Zeitung*, the newspaper of the Jewish Central-Verein, published a series on Australia in several parts that ended with the sceptical question: 'They [the European Jews] are waiting patiently for admission at the gates of a continent which, until now, has only presented a narrow opening for white immigrants. Will they wait in vain?'[77] By contrast, in September the paper carried the announcement by Australia's Minister for Internal Affairs that his country wanted to take in 5,000 Jews annually.[78] This news was immediately picked up by the Zionist *Jüdische Rundschau*,[79] with the qualification that the country needed tradespeople rather than artists or intellectuals.[80] In the light of difficulties with immigration in other countries and the limited quotas for the USA, problems in Australia were only relative.

In this situation, one of the refugees who chose Australia was Heinrich Adler. On completing his schooling, he had started an apprenticeship at the Nathan Israel department store, also doing casual piano work. He married at the beginning of March 1938. By then, at the latest, the young couple must have been giving some thought to the future. As an employee at the Israel department store, Heinrich would have heard about the Hilfsverein, and he might have even seen the front cover of the aforementioned emigration brochure. In any case, he was interested in this distant continent. On 18 July, he obtained an alien's passport, and the very next day he picked up a transit visa for Australia from the British Passport Control Office. Then the young couple departed, but not via the usual route. Vera and Heinrich Adler travelled west over the Atlantic, crossed Canada by rail, and in Vancouver boarded the ship *Aorangi*, which took them across the Pacific to Australia. On their arrival form, Heinrich gave 'Sales-manager' as his profession; he stated that he had enough money in cash and wanted to work in a textile shop in Australia.

Henry Adler, as he now called himself, was lucky. In April 1939, his daughter Joan was born. Around the same time he found employment – not, as was originally envisaged, selling textiles, but as a piano and accordion teacher at Nicholson's College for Modern Music. This music school was tied to a large music business in central George Street. In the multi-storied building where sheet music, records and musical instruments were sold, and which also housed the editorial staff of the *Australian Music Maker and Dance Band News*, Adler taught 'modern music', in other words, popular entertainment music. Although at first he had to familiarise himself with this repertoire, by December 1939 his accordion students were able to put on a recital.[81] Whereas Adler was unsuccessful in his attempts to bring his parents and parents-in-law to Australia, his siblings Siegbert ('Bob') and Lilli arrived in Sydney in September, on board the *Nestor*. During the crossing, Bob had helped out as the drummer in a band.[82] In Australia he could not earn his living with music, so he took a job in the textile industry.

A month after Henry Adler's arrival, another music lover landed in Sydney, aboard the *Romolo*: Ernst Norbert Kaufmann, a forty-six-year-old physician who had already composed several works and had them performed in Germany. He went to Australia with his wife Maria, although his medical qualifications were not recognised there. Also on the same ship was Mordchais Danemanis, a singer travelling on a Lithuanian passport who had adopted the stage name Mario Dane in Vienna. Dane disembarked in the fairly unattractive city of Fremantle, and for several months lived in Perth, Western Australia, where his mother Eta-Rose had been resident since 1935. From there, he organised his move to Melbourne where, prior to his arrival, the *Jewish Herald* had already advertised him as an operatic tenor from Vienna.[83] The singing teacher Adolf Spivakovsky had high praise for the mellifluous voice of this new arrival, who was engaged by the ABC for several appearances in 1940.[84]

Dane belonged to the earliest arrivals from Nazified Vienna. The threat and the pressure to leave were much greater after the Anschluss, and new arrivals were more frequent. Many even undertook the long journey without complete documentation, like the Viennese pianist Käthe Weiss. After matriculating, she took private lessons from Russian-born Professor Paul de Conne, a pupil of Rubinstein. In addition, as an external student at the Vienna Music Academy, Weiss had studied as minor subjects harmony (with Richard Stöhr), piano literature (Fischer) and organology (Mandyczewski). In 1922, she married the manufacturer Artur Neumann and had two sons; Käthe Neumann had, however, continued her career as a pianist. After the German invasion of Vienna, this Jewish family felt very threatened and made desperate attempts to emigrate. Although the Neumanns obtained only a tourist visa, on 23 August 1938 they deregistered at the Viennese Registration Office, giving Australia as their destination. Like the members of the Spivakovsky–Kurtz Trio, Artur Neumann, his wife Käthe and their sons Gerhard and Herbert travelled as tourists first class on the Orient Line's *Oronsay*. In October, when they arrived in Melbourne, they handed over to the immigration officer an arrival form clearly stamped, 'Tourist Visitor'. The head of the family stated explicitly that they were merely visiting, and that they wanted to remain in Australia for three to six months.[85] Apparently Artur Neumann produced return tickets and sufficient cash, because from the middle of 1937 foreign tourists were only allowed to enter the country under these circumstances.[86] But the family had no intention of returning to Vienna: these 'tourists' were actually refugees who wanted to settle permanently in Australia.

The lawyer and pianist Peter Langer and his wife Hertha left Vienna immediately after the German invasion. They arrived in Melbourne on 7 November together with other refugees on board the *Nieuw Zeeland*. Although they hoped to return to their homeland one day, they took as much as possible with them in their luggage, including furniture and even a bidet. According to Hertha Langer, the 'bidet was never installed, but sat for many years, a symbol of another life, in the garage'.[87]

The ship *Viminale* arrived in Sydney Harbour on 18 November. On board were the conductor Heinrich Krips and his wife, and the pharmacist Dr Hans Spitzer, his wife Therese and two children. Immediately prior to leaving, on 3 September, Krips had married his childhood friend Luise Deutsch but, because there was so little time, her name was missing on the German passport that he received on 8 September. The conductor had obtained a landing permit for Australia beforehand. The fact that his sister Maria had already emigrated to Australia probably also played a role in his choice of country; she and her husband Walter Leicht had arrived in Sydney on the *Marella*. On arrival, Krips gave 'Director Orchestra' as his profession; this was commensurate with the description 'Kapellmeister' in his passport, and he wanted to work as a conductor in the new country. He had bought cheap third-class tickets for himself and his family in order to save the considerable sum of £400 in cash for more important purchases.

Just two days later, the *Franken* docked in Sydney with Dr Martin Krutsch, and the *Niagara* from Canada with the music critic Dr Hans Forst on board. Forst later stated that the singer Alexander Kipnis, whom he had previously interviewed, had helped him to get a visa for Australia.

Perhaps at the time it took longer to get a British visa in Vienna than in Budapest. This might explain why he gave his destination as Hungary when he deregistered from his Vienna flat at 55 Untere Viaduktgasse on 9 September. He had lived together with his parents in this prestigious building, which was also the home of Sigmund Freud's brother, the privy councillor Professor Alexander Freud. From here, Forst travelled to the Hungarian capital, where he obtained a visa for Australia from the British Passport Control Office on 19 September. From Cherbourg, he took the western route to Canada, where he boarded the *Niagara*. On his arrival in Sydney, he indicated in his 'Personal Statement' that he was a journalist, but that he could also work in Australia as a teacher, musician or salesman. Forst was intending to demonstrate his flexibility and thus increase his chances. When asked about an acquaintance in his future homeland, he named a Mr Goldman in Brisbane, whose address he had been given by Kipnis. The said Mr Goldman had actually provided a guarantee for a Viennese man otherwise unknown to him,[88] which explains the swift visa allocation.

Via Britain

People who, unlike Heinrich Krips, lacked contacts in other countries or, unlike the Neumanns, were reluctant to take risks, often fled to Britain, where they would decide on a final destination. In July 1938, Rudolf Siegfried Laqueur initially travelled to Genoa with his parents, since his father had been threatened with expatriation on account of his membership of a Masonic lodge, the Lessing Lodge.[89] In his home town, Breslau, Rudolf Laqueur had attended the old Realgymnasium am Zwinger and also had piano lessons. He continued his education in Genoa. After three months in the Dutch city of Leiden, the Laqueurs finally went to London, where from 1939 Rudolf studied organ and piano at the Royal Academy of Music. Meanwhile, in Breslau, the Gestapo had issued expatriation orders for both Laqueur's wife Rosalie and son. In a letter to the Berlin Gestapo dated 2 May 1939, the Breslau State Police Office justified this 'kin liability' with a long list of assumptions:

> L. belongs to the Lessing Lodge in Breslau that has been declared subversive and disbanded. [...] On the grounds of L.'s Lodge membership and his racially conditioned opposition to National Socialism, it can be assumed that, while abroad, he will take every opportunity to act to the detriment of the German Reich. The wife condones his behaviour, since she shares his abode.[90]

Because the authorities presumed that the Laqueurs were still in Genoa, they made enquiries at the German Embassy in Rome and received a reply on 7 July that it had no concerns about the expatriation of the other family members.

Beta Mayer, from Schwäbisch-Gmünd, had fled to England from Stuttgart in 1938 with her two sons, Fritz and Heinz Sigmund. As they had to escape illegally, they travelled separately. Although Fritz, with financial support from an uncle in New York, was able to attend a boarding school in Bournemouth, Britain offered only a temporary transit stop. The small family urgently sought a country that would accept them for a longer period. Beta Mayer submitted applications for Canada, the USA, Australia, Uruguay, New Zealand and Argentina. Fritz Mayer finally received his German passport on 1 November in The Hague, and from there he travelled to Amsterdam where, two days later, the British Consulate issued visas for Australia. They were then certain of their destination. Beta and her two sons landed in Sydney on board the *Jervis Bay*; luckily they were able to stay with a relative there initially.

A great number of Viennese refugees had come to Britain immediately after the Anschluss. On hearing the bad news, the pianist Peter Stadlen returned to London from Amsterdam, where he had just been giving concerts. By contrast, Kurt Kohn was studying the violin at the Music Academy in Vienna and witnessed the invasion by the German troops in March 1938. On 21 May, he deregistered from his flat at 15A Eszterhazygasse and gave his destination as London. Kohn had a particular talent for modern, popular music. He was soon working in England under the name Ray Martin, making appearances as a solo violinist on a popular programme, the Carroll Levis Discoveries Vaudeville Show, and as a member of the stage and radio team 'Band Wagon' under the well-known band leader Jack Hylton. The violinist Fritz Kramer had also applied for a transit visa for Britain, which he received on 10 September 1938. Five days later, he left his flat and deregistered with the destination London.

Departure was relatively easy for Friedrich Klopfer, managing director of the Viennese branch of the record shop His Master's Voice, 30 Kärntner Straße. According to his daughter Evelyn, this centrally located store was known for its attractive range of recordings and for its pretty salesgirls. Klopfer liked one of them so much that he married her, even though he was Jewish and Leopoldine Gottwald was Catholic. Prominent recording stars like Franz Lehár, Jack Hylton and Richard Tauber were frequently guests in the shop. When the Weintraubs Syncopators played in Vienna in 1930, they visited the shop and presented the owner with a photo signed by Stefan Weintraub, Horst Graff, Kurt Kaiser, Baby Schulvater, Arno Olewski, Ansco Bruinier and Georg Haentzschel, and inscribed 'To our dear Mr Klopfer, the kind protector of our work in Vienna'.[91] As a 'full Jew', Friedrich Klopfer had to give up the shop in 1938. In the face of persecution, his non-Jewish wife (who had had a daughter in 1936) anxiously urged that they leave. Their departure for England was supported by the British recording firm but, since Britain was still only functioning as a country of transit, Klopfer had originally given Canada as their final destination. The decision to go to Australia was made in London. On 10 January, the family of three arrived in Sydney on the aforementioned *Jervis Bay*. The global recording company helped them to find employment and accommodation.

For Erwin Frenkel, the sixteen-year-old son of the principal cantor and rabbi at the synagogue in Leopoldsgasse, escape from Vienna turned out to be more difficult. This precocious musical talent[92] had gone to Bratislava as a Talmud scholar before continuing his education in Vienna in 1936. In view of his Orthodox Jewish upbringing, the journey to the Holy Land was natural for him, so when Frenkel deregistered from his flat on 18 August 1938, he named Palestine as his destination. To this end, he travelled to Trieste in Italy, where he stayed for five weeks. There he changed his plans and moved to Switzerland for several weeks; he then decided on Britain, where he arrived with only two suitcases. He earned his living illegally by working as a pianist in various London pubs.

The eighteen-year-old Viennese student Eduard Kassner was only a little older than Frenkel. When he went to the registration office to deregister from his flat near the West station, he gave Belgium as his destination. As Kassner later explained, he finally arrived in England only after a dangerous escape through Germany, Belgium and the Netherlands.[93] Hans Edelmann also reached Britain indirectly. As his non-Jewish wife was not in immediate danger, she had not obtained a visa. The couple had fled to Yugoslavia in October, but there was still no visa for Helene Edelmann. In this uncertain situation and with heavy hearts they decided to separate, in order at least to save the Jewish husband's life. Helene returned to her parents in Vienna, while Hans moved to Britain.

Via France

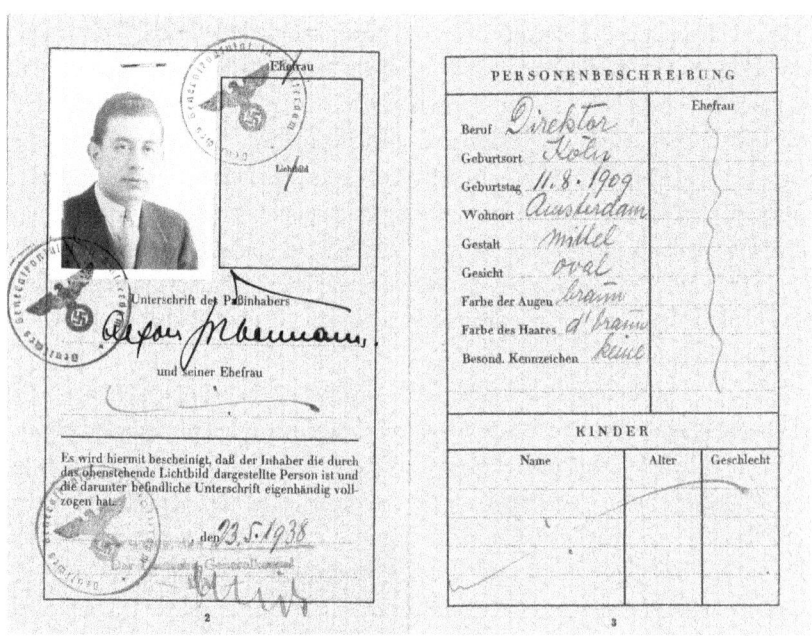

Figure 9: German Passport of Alphons Silbermann, issued on 23 May 1938 at the German General Consulate Amsterdam. Job description: 'Direktor'. The Passport was valid only until 22 November 1938. Just in time, on 13 October, Silbermann arrived in Sydney. (NAA: A435, 1947/4/4169)

Alphons Silbermann first fled from Cologne to the Netherlands, followed by his parents. In Amsterdam, they bought shares in a printing business, while their son worked in advertising. In 1937, against the will of his parents and therefore without their financial support, he decided to go to Paris, where he earned his living in restaurants, at first washing dishes and then as a waiter. At the beginning of 1938, his work and residence permit expired and he was forced to leave France. While visiting his parents in Amsterdam, he obtained a German passport in May 1938. Fluctuating between the despair and megalomania characteristic of exiles, he entered 'Director' as his profession in the document and Amsterdam as his place of residence. In reality, Silbermann wanted to plan his next journey from Paris, but there was the urgent question of 'where to?' Owing to insurmountable difficulties, neither Palestine nor the USA could be considered:

> It was a matter of choosing countries where immigration was not yet intentionally hindered by impenetrable red tape. That was one of the considerations that brought Silbermann – ridiculed by most of his friends who still believed in the American fairy tale – to decide on Australia as his next place of residence.[94]

At that stage, he knew nothing about Australia, or about its population, living conditions or employment opportunities. He did not even know that he needed a British visa to enter. He only learnt this as he was standing in front of the building that he had been told housed the office that represented Australia's interests.

> What was he looking at in astonishment? The Dominion of Australia is represented by the British Consulate, by the particularly narrow-minded motherland in matters of emigration, whereby, so the sign on the impressive building reads, the office hours for Australian affairs are from 8 o'clock to 10 o'clock in the morning.

As visa forms had to be collected, a passport lodged and photos delivered, and there was only one official responsible for Australia, the refugee had to join the queue at 6 a.m. in order to be admitted in time. An applicant needed a lot of patience. 'The amazingly self-righteous affectation of the English was simply unsurpassable, especially as it became apparent that the consulate queue was growing longer every day.'[95]

His parents rejected Australia as being too remote, so they asked their son to apply for a visa for Iceland. Thus Alphons Silbermann stood alternately in the queues at the British and Icelandic Consulates, 'and in addition at the Embassy for the Dominican Republic, where there were supposed to be passports for sale'.[96] Finally in August, just before his passport expired, he received a permit for Australia. The decision had been made. When Silbermann filled out his mandatory 'Personal Statement' in Paris on 18 August, the question about his occupation appeared again. He was indecisive. On the form he first wrote 'Restaurateur'. Then he crossed it out and replaced it with 'Hotel Manager'.[97] This was probably a better match for the ambiguous designation 'Director' in his passport.

Now he only had to pay for his passage. As luck would have it, just at that time his old car was stolen, and Silbermann was able to get the funds together by means of insurance fraud. Although there was only just enough money for a place in a six-bed cabin in the cheapest category, he was exhilarated as he boarded the *Stratheden* in Southampton. He wanted, finally, to put the succession of failures behind him. Despite his small cabin, limited cash and modest smattering of English, the refugee felt as free as a bird on the big cruise ship. At last he was neither supplicant, nor dishwasher, nor waiter, but a paying passenger who was himself being waited upon. 'Amidst the seasoned British' he felt 'like a tourist on a pleasure trip'. His sense of time altered during the six-week crossing, where he saw mostly water and the occasional port. After passing through the Suez Canal, the *Stratheden* stopped at Port Sudan, then Aden and finally Bombay. Here he had enough time to make a brief tour of the city, where, besides holy cows, he saw a lot of filth and still more poverty. The ship docked at Colombo on 25 September and reached Fremantle, the first Australian port, on 4 October. His arrival in Sydney on 13 October did not make a deep impression on Alphons Silbermann, especially as there was no Statue of Liberty to admire.

Rudolf Werther also obtained his Australian landing permit in Paris. The Berliner had lived in the French capital since 1930 and was involved in the export business. In 1933, he also helped his son, Frank, to move there. As Werther wanted to remain in France on a permanent basis, he applied for French citizenship in 1935, but was told he would have to wait a long time. After divorcing his first wife, Hertha, he remarried in January 1939. As apparently a longer stay in France was not possible, he decided to emigrate to Australia. Thanks to personal connections within the British Embassy, he quickly received the necessary visa. At the end of April, he boarded the *Oronsay* in Toulon with his wife and son and sailed to Australia. Rudolf Werther had taken a lot of luggage, including five boxes of music and a piano. In Paris, as in Berlin, he had been involved in music; his dream was to continue this to an even greater extent in Australia.

Via Luxembourg

Alongside France, Switzerland, Belgium and the Netherlands, tiny Luxembourg suddenly became interesting as another Western European country that was independent of the Nazi regime. At the age of thirty-seven, the violinist Paul Steiner found his opportunity in this small grand duchy, squeezed in between Germany, Belgium and France. In Vienna, he had grown up in the very same building where the pianist, Käthe Weiss was living. Whether the two musicians ever met in those days is uncertain, but cannot be ruled out. But even in their wildest dreams they could never have imagined that, independently, they would both later move to Australia. In 1919, he had returned to Vienna for a short time (he lived in the Leopoldsgasse, not far from Chief Rabbi Frenkel's Polish Schul), then to Krems and finally to Innsbruck, where he married the Catholic Emma Schlemmer in 1923. Paul Steiner toured Austria, Germany and Switzerland with his own ensemble; from 1936 onwards he lived in Salzburg. From there, in June 1938 he escaped to Luxembourg, where he had an engagement at the Bacara & Clou Bar, and in August the rest of the family joined him there. Since a longer stay in this country was unthinkable, Steiner applied at the German Embassy for a German passport, which he received in January 1939. Inside, on the first page was the red letter 'J', and it now identified the passport holder as 'Israel Paul Steiner'. He had given his vocation as 'Kapellmeister'. Steiner must have been inquiring about the possibilities of emigration for several months. In view of all the difficulties, he finally decided on the farthest place, Shanghai, which was not very attractive for musicians, but did not require a visa. In Marseilles, he and his family boarded a French ship that landed in Singapore on 12 July. They then determined to go ashore in the British colony.

The engineer Egon Stern and his twenty-six-year-old wife Dobra ('Dory') also found their way from Vienna to Luxembourg. In her youth, Dory Stern had taken piano lessons at the Conservatorium, but left at the age of seventeen. One explanation is that from 1925 her mother had to bring up her daughter on her own. Her husband had gone to the USA on a business trip and never returned. In 1934, the young pianist married Egon Stern from Breslau. Faced with the German invasion, the young couple had to leave Vienna and they moved to Luxembourg in July 1938. In search of a permanent solution, they both decided on Australia and applied at the German Embassy for a passport, which they received in April 1939. In it, 'Sara' had been added to Dobra Stern's first name, as well as the 'J' stamp. She had not given her occupation. A month later, once they had received the desired visas for Australia and transit visas for France, they travelled to Marseilles, where they boarded the *Strathallan* and sailed via the eastern route to Australia; they finally went ashore in Sydney.

Further Detours (India, Singapore)

Many of the refugees had not chosen Australia as their destination, but arrived there after considerable detours. In 1938, the Viennese choreographer Gertrud Bodenwieser first escaped to France with her husband, the director Friedrich Jacques Rosenthal. From 1920 onwards, she had taught at the Vienna Music Academy, and from 1926 had been a professor. Since 1925 Bodenwieser, a pioneer of modern expressive dance, had toured with her own dance group not only in Europe, but also performed in New York and Japan. For her, in contradistinction to her dance colleagues Mary Wigman and Rudolf von Laban, music played a central role. In 1920, Marcel Lorber had become her pianist at just twenty years of age. On account of his capabilities as a pianist, improviser and conductor, he took over the musical direction for most of the company's performances.[98] From improvisation he moved to composition; during one of the troupe's performances in the Vienna *Burggarten* [Castle Gardens], at which Lorber and Herbert Zipper conducted the Vienna Symphony Orchestra; Lorber's *Heroic March* and a tango parody were played. In 1936, he wrote the music for the dramatic dance sequence *Lucifer's Masks*, which could be understood as a protest against any form of dictatorship. As a Jew, Gertrud Bodenwieser was unwilling to take the oath to Hitler; she lost her chair in Vienna in 1938.

In Paris she was surprised to receive, through her pupil Magda Brunner-Hoyos, who had studied for a time in Santiago de Chile, the opportunity to tour in Colombia. In mid-1938, Marcel Lorber also travelled to Bogotá where, for example, the Bodenwieser Company appeared at a gala event for the investiture of the new president, Eduardo Santos. Although the hosts were expecting to hear rousing Viennese waltzes and Austrian folk dances, Gertrud Bodenwieser was not about to renounce the core of her work – thematically focused choreography. She succeeded in having her visa extended, so the company remained in Colombia for ten months. Then, following appearances in Wellington, New Zealand, the dancers arrived in Sydney on board the *Maunganui* on 23 August 1939. Lorber entered on an Austrian passport and indicated in his 'Personal Statement' that he would be pursuing an 'artistic engagement' as a 'composer' – presumably because he wanted to avoid any difficulties with the Musicians' Union. In answer to the question relating to the length of his stay, he deliberately wrote 'undecided'.[99]

The violinist Charles Reither was in Burma when he heard the startling news of the Anschluss. Shortly afterwards, he moved with his band to Colombo, where he promptly presented himself at the German Consulate on 12 April. In his Austrian passport, which he was allowed to keep on a temporary basis, they inscribed the words: 'Ballot paper for vote on 10 April 1938 granted'. Retroactively, the violinist could have taken part in the sham election to decide Austria's fate. He, too, was led to believe that it was a democratic election. Reither soon learnt the official result, according to which 99.73 per cent of Austrians and 99.01 per cent of Germans were reported to have voted for the Anschluss. Austria (as 'Ostmark') had now become part of the Greater German Reich, and Austrian travel documents lost their validity. But for the moment, because he was staying in Colombo as a member of Nick's Versatile Six and as conductor of his own group, Reither did not need a new passport. This only became necessary when, at the beginning of 1939, he was planning to move to British Singapore in the Straits Settlements. Despite the fact that his wife was British, all his efforts to obtain a British passport were in vain; so on 14 March he obtained a German passport from the German Consul in Colombo. With that, his Austrian passport became worthless.[100] The violinist arrived in Singapore on 5 May. He had secured an engagement at the exclusive Tanglin Club in Stevens Road, to which only Europeans were admitted.[101]

Eva Hitschmann, the Viennese singer, lived in India from the beginning of 1939. After her matriculation in 1932, she had studied voice at the New Vienna Conservatorium and taken extra private lessons from Professor Rosner. Every year she would audition for the *Kammersänger* [chamber singer] Hans Duhan, accompanied at the piano by Kapellmeister Carl Bamberger. At the beginning of 1936, a dream came true when, on the recommendation of Benjamino Gigli, she was awarded a scholarship to study in Rome. Originally intended for only six months, her stay was extended when she met a young German in a bookshop in the Italian capital. As a non-Aryan, he had had to leave the University in Bonn and was now continuing his medical studies in the city. Eva Hitschmann fell in love on the spot and decided to study medicine, too, concentrating on paediatrics and physiotherapy. Her partner had specialised in tropical medicine; he obtained his doctorate in Rome and immediately after the wedding in October 1938 moved to India. His young wife then deregistered in Vienna and followed him in January 1939. Together they found employment at a modern hospital built by the Maharaja of Bikaner, a friend of Churchill's, not far from what is now the Pakistani border. Eva Hitschmann-Mayer worked there as a doctor, but occasionally appeared as a singer on entertainment programmes.

Like Charles Reither, the Viennese Kapellmeister Mischa Stiwelband had already performed in India before 1938. When he travelled to Bombay at the beginning of 1937 with a contract to work at a luxury restaurant, he did not contemplate permanent residence. He wanted to return to his wife and their two sons in Vienna. The Austrian Anschluss changed all this as it was impossible for him, a Jew, to return. Instead, he now had to bring the rest of his family to Asia. In May 1938, after more than a year in British India, Stiwelband took an engagement as bandleader at the Hotel Runnymede in Penang, Malaya, where the British had built a settlement in 1786. Steeped in tradition, the hotel had been extended in the 1930s. It was now a large, three-storey building with its own telephone exchange and post office. There was a huge ballroom on the ground floor, where cocktail dances were held every Monday, Wednesday and Friday, and dinner dances every Thursday and Saturday night. Correct dress was observed at these dance evenings: dark suits for the men and evening gowns for the women. Mischa Stiwelband's band, which played in this festive setting, was also correctly attired. In Penang, the Viennese Kapellmeister learned of the difficulties that his family had been facing since the Anschluss. When he heard about the favourable employment and living conditions in nearby Singapore, he decided to move there. The plan succeeded: at the end of October 1938, his wife Margarete and younger son arrived in this colony to start a new life.

The Southeast Asian city-state of Singapore, covering several islands at the southern tip of the Malay Peninsula, dates back to the establishment of the British East India Company, which acquired these islands in 1824. Two years later, together with Malacca and Penang, they were merged into the Straits Settlements, which became a colony in 1867. The opening of the Suez Canal two years later increased Singapore's military and economic significance. After the First World War, the British converted the islands into a garrison, their most important military base east of India, a 'Gibraltar of the East'. Nonetheless, it remained a trading centre with a cosmopolitan presence, in which a predominantly Chinese population lived alongside Malays, Indians and Europeans. The Europeans, mostly British, enjoyed the greatest privileges: their luxuries included cheap local servants and comfortable hotels and clubs that also offered high-quality entertainment music. More than a few refugee musicians found attractive employment there.

The pianist Kurt Blach, from Rinteln in Westphalia, had moved to Singapore as early as the beginning of 1935. After his education at the Bückeburg Music School, he appeared as a musical entertainer in cafés and hotels in Cologne. From 1933, he continued his work for another twenty months in Amsterdam where, in the meantime, other members of his family had arrived. There he noticed an advertisement in the newspaper which read: 'Pianist for Salon Orchestra in Singapore sought. Jews preferred.'[102] Blach applied straight away, and made the long journey. He and his trio subsequently played regularly for afternoon tea in the elegant Raffles Hotel, named after the founder of this trading centre, Sir Stamford Raffles. He soon got to know the Indian-born, Jewish dressmaker Louisa Maisie Isaac, whom he married in April 1935.[103]

The multi-talented pianist Heinrich Portnoj had also heard of the favourable living conditions that existed in the British colony, despite its humid climate. In the summer of 1937, he was still being employed by Count Salm as an accompanist at the Salzburg Festival,[104] but after the Anschluss he soon had to find new ways to support himself and his wife. Portnoj had plenty of experience in entertainment music and was able to build on that when he received an offer from Penang in May 1938. At the invitation of the hotel director, Redway, he lived and worked for six months at the same Runnymede Hotel where Mischa Stiwelband was working. The two Viennese must have got to know each other here, if not before. When their contracts expired at the end of September, though, they had to look for new employment. They both came to the conclusion that Singapore offered a particularly good lifestyle. Like Stiwelband, Portnoj also moved to the colony, where on 24 October he was able to receive his wife Annie, who had just arrived from Europe.

Several other Viennese musicians fleeing persecution arrived in the city-state, apparently on Stiwelband's initiative. Among them was Hans Blau, with whom Mischa had played in Vienna, but who was unable to remain permanently in Switzerland. Mischa Stiwelband procured a Singapore visa for his colleague. Blau received the official stamp from the British vice-consul in Zurich on 16 November. Stiwelband provided further assistance, as is shown by a letter to Blau and his wife Helene ('Nelly'). In it he presented the tantalising prospect of life in Singapore:

Singapore, 18 November 1938

My dear Hans, dear Nelly,
 Since your first letter I have had no news until today, it was a real feat sending you the visa, every day immigration becomes more difficult.
 Now I can give you the following good news, my boss has had to guarantee you for two years, the conditions were recorded by the immigration officer, so listen to the good conditions: until the opening of the new premises (the opening is on 15 July 1939) we are playing in 'Coconut Grove', you'll have free accommodation in

the same Coconut House, food will be at cost price, and the salary will be about 200 dollars a month!!!! In the new premises you, and possibly Nelly, will have everything free of charge. We'll all live in the same house where the new premises will be, then AT LEAST 200 dollars salary!!!! These conditions were dictated by the authority and my sweet boss agreed.

[…] I advise you to sell all your winter things, furs, winter coats and buy for yourself or yourselves, respectively, light stuff, just for the journey, one at the most. Here everything is dirt cheap! India is an Eldorado, especially for women!!! Once again, sell everything!!!!! My dear wife is looking especially forward to dear Nelly, we live right next to the sea (a few metres away), it's a villa, the food is very good, the air is the same as in Europe, we can bathe in the sea, there's a big garden in front of the villa, it's a real Paradise!!! Your eyes will be out on stalks when you get here, the working hours are laughable, we're supposed to start at 7.45 p.m., most of the time it's 9 or 9.30, it finishes at 12 or 11.50 when the anthem is played!!!! The actual work is over two hours but don't ever think we play straight through, we play 'concert music' till 10 o'clock, then we start the dance music, we play three foxtrots, then our boss sings three numbers, his partner accompanies him on the guitar, our bosses are Cowan and Beily [corr. Bailey], they're well-known film comedians, two of the most popular artists from America. Mr Cowan is the real macher, he is half Jewish but better than the frummest Polish. We've all made a hit with these people, you'll be amazed that there are still real menschen in the world!! You know, dear Hans, your cousin has always had Mazel [luck]. And so on and so on. Now my dear, stay healthy. I wish you both all the best for the journey.

Hearty greetings from your Mischa.[105]

It sounded charming: easy work – about two hours' performing a day – for two pleasant American bosses was guaranteed for two years, and well paid; in addition, the accommodation was free. Convinced by this offer, Hans Blau deregistered himself with the Zurich Aliens' Police on 1 December, and gave Singapore as his destination. According to his passport, he arrived on 11 January in Colombo, and on 16 January in Singapore, where he was met by Stiwelband. As promised, Blau had accommodation right next to the Coconut Grove in Pasir Panjang Road, the club in which he took up his engagement together with Stiwelband and Heinrich Portnoj. In Vienna, Blau had appeared as Hans Balu-Blau in the Vienna Splendid Club Orchestra, as well as in other well-known Viennese bars, cabarets, dance halls and hotels. Even then, the musicians had advertised that they had a mastery of 'all styles'. One of Blau's specialties was to imitate

Maurice Chevalier, complete with straw hat and accordion. In Singapore, he extended his repertoire to include new English songs that also proved to be very popular. When his passport expired after three months, Blau went to the German Consulate General in Singapore and was granted a six-month extension. For the time being, he did not have to apply for further extensions because, on 26 July, the thirty-three-year-old musician received a brand new ID card from the Straits Settlements government, a 'Certificate of Admission' in a bright yellow envelope, that was valid for three years.[106]

A little later, another Viennese musical entertainer must have arrived in the city: the violinist Oskar Fleischer. By February 1938, he had already left Vienna, deregistered and gone to Czechoslovakia. It is still not known when he arrived in Singapore, but eventually this unmarried musician also joined the band that entertained visitors to the Coconut Grove (and later the Cathay Ballroom and Roof Garden) with their catchy tunes and captivating songs and rhythms.

CHAPTER 7

After Kristallnacht

Detour via Sachsenhausen

Compared with Vienna, things remained relatively quiet in Berlin in the spring of 1938. Non-Aryans were not excluded from professional and cultural life all at once, but on a step by step basis. Appointed choirmaster and organist for the liberal synagogue on Levetzowstraße in January, Werner Baer remained musical director of the Kulturbund's Cabaret until September; he was also teaching at the Hollaender Music School. The Nazi State might have prevented him from becoming an opera conductor, but it did not affect his activities in fields still open to Jews. Suspecting that things would get worse, the young man made enquiries about possibilities for emigration. With this in mind, he married his girlfriend Ilse Presch on 31 May; as he later indicated in a questionnaire, he wanted to go with her to the USA.

Then came the night of 9–10 November, which went down in history as Kristallnacht [the Night of Broken Glass]. With the exception of the New Synagogue on Oranienburger Straße, which was protected by the courageous police officer Wilhelm Krützfeld, almost all the Jewish places of worship in Berlin were destroyed, and businesses owned by Jews were ransacked. Captain Foley hid a few particularly endangered people in his flat, such as Leo Baeck, the President of the Reich Representation of German Jews.[1] On the other hand, thousands of Jews were arrested and taken to concentration camps 'for their own protection'. This was how the musical entertainer Willy Coper came to be in the Sachsenhausen camp; since 1935 he had only been able to play for Jews.[2] After his release, he obtained a German passport in February 1939, a visa for Australia in March, and in June he landed in Sydney, where he was met by his brother, Fritz.

The synagogue on Prinzregentenstraße was among the Berlin synagogues destroyed on Kristallnacht; its principal cantor, Dr Martin Krutsch, had already left the city at the end of September, bound for Australia. The synagogue organist, Werner Baer, was arrested in his flat at midnight.³ Although at first there was only talk of an interrogation, the musician and his brother were taken into police custody for one and a half days and then to Sachsenhausen. His young wife pulled out all the stops to have him released. Ilse Baer had experience in dealing with the Nazi authorities: in September, the police had arrested her father for not carrying a valid identification card but, through her stubborn persistence, she succeeded in having him released. She knew that the chances were good of getting those arrested out of prison, if they were able to leave Germany immediately. She had already discussed emigration with her husband but, for lack of a visa, their intended emigration to the USA via Cuba had fallen through.⁴ Before 10 November, Baer had declined an offer to travel to the East as a member of a band.⁵ Now, in dramatically worsened circumstances, his wife took up the idea again. The day after his arrest, she went to a travel agency and secured the last four tickets with Norddeutscher Lloyd for a ship to Bangkok: she wanted to facilitate an escape not only for herself and her husband, but also for his mother and brother. But Lucie Baer declined the offer. She was still of the opinion that her sons would merely be interrogated; besides, she had no interest in emigrating to Southeast Asia.

As Ilse Baer knew the perils of concentration camps, she ignored such considerations and took the tickets to the police headquarters in Alexanderplatz. As she later recounted, she herself did not feel in any danger. When she requested that her husband be released, the official even helped her. "'I'll fill out the form for you, and then you just have to sign it'. He asked me what Werner's names were. And then he said, "He'll come home tomorrow."' The promise was kept. Although her husband later said that he was released from Sachsenhausen in December, he was actually freed on 27 November, weeks before his brother Fritz. He could be recognised as a former inmate by his shaved head.

On 12 November, State Commissioner Hans Hinkel had already promised a Kulturbund delegation that their performances would begin again soon. When his visitors explained to him that 'technically we're not in a position to do so since a number of our most important musicians are in protective custody', he ensured that, 'wherever possible, the release of the Kulturbund's most important musicians should happen shortly'.⁶ In order to secure the work of this vital instrument of Nazi racial politics, approximately 120 people were freed quickly. On 22 November, a Kulturbund theatre performance took place; Max Ehrlich's cabaret performances also resumed. Herbert Freeden confirmed this: 'Even before the curtain went up again, all the members of the Kulturbund who had been arrested were freed from the concentration camps.'[7] Thus, as one of the most important musicians in this organisation, Baer would have presumably been set free, even without the tickets produced by his wife.

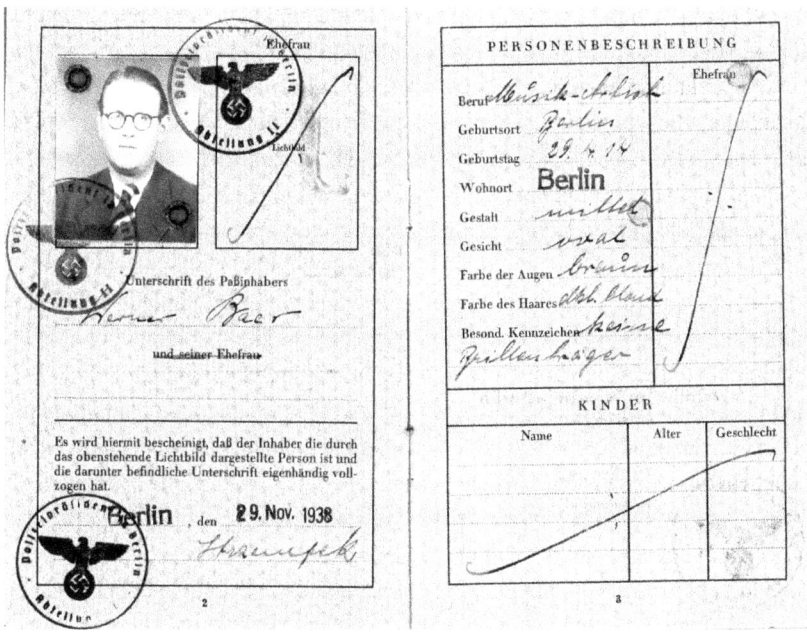

Figure 10: German Passport of Werner Baer, issued in Berlin on 29 November 1938, after his release from the Sachsenhausen concentration camp. Job description: 'Musik-Artist'. On 6 December he left Germany with his wife Ilse.
(NAA: A435, 1945/4/1221)

After signing a declaration that he would never return to Germany,[8] Baer received his German passport on Tuesday 29 November. The photo, taken earlier, shows him with the round glasses that he would wear for a long time and a parting, not a shaved head. He gave his hair colour as 'dark blond' and his occupation as 'Musical artist'. Under 'Name', he entered 'Werner Baer', without his middle name, Felix. Instead, someone else added 'Israel' on the first page of the passport. Together with the red 'J' stamp, this identified him as a non-Aryan. They needed to hurry, as the *Potsdam* was to leave Genoa on 7 December. The same day, the young couple obtained the currency needed for Italy.[9] In order to emigrate to Bangkok, they also required a British transit visa for Siam (Thailand) via Singapore. On Friday 2 December, Ilse and Werner went to the British Consulate, where they had to join the long queue. After waiting for ten hours, they were finally called, only to discover that such a visa could not be issued at such short notice. In despair, the young woman confronted the official: 'You can see that my husband has a shaved head. They'll take him to the concentration camp again. He is about to leave the country!' But in spite of her fervent pleas they had to go home empty-handed. The situation seemed hopeless, especially as on the next day, a Saturday, Jews were not allowed on the streets after 11 a.m. 'Then I said to Werner: you stay at home. I'm going to try again.'[10]

That Saturday, the brave woman went by herself, with both their passports, to the British Consulate. In the queue, she stood next to a non-Jewish German, to whom she described her desperate situation. 'Then he said: "Come with me". He came in with me and we got two transit visas.' This is confirmed by Werner Baer's passport: his emigration visa is dated 3 December. Since it was already after 11 o'clock and the Jewish curfew was in operation, her helper drove the young woman home in his car. More than seventy years later, in Melbourne, Baer's former wife remembered the spontaneous help that presumably saved their lives. 'So you see, there were also decent Germans.' That day, when Werner Baer received the urgently needed visa from his wife, he could only comprehend it as a miracle. Contrary to expectations, he was indeed a Werner *Felix*, a lucky Werner.

Now everything happened quickly. The most essential things for the journey had to be packed, including the work certificates necessary for their future employment, and references from various Jewish organisations that were provided just before their departure. A letter from the Jewish Winter Aid, dated 30 November, reads as follows:

> We have employed Herr Werner Baer often and gladly for our events. His all-round flexibility as an organist and pianist has made him especially valuable. Herr Baer has served as organ soloist and accompanist in a great many of our synagogue concerts. He is an exceptionally fine and sensitive player who has a mature mastery of technique on his instrument and, in spite of his youth, one of the leading Jewish organists in Germany. [...]
>
> In conclusion it must be emphasised that Herr Baer is also a high-ranking expert in the field of dance music. We have therefore asked him to lead the dance band for a number of our most important social events; he took part as a pianist and accordionist, and with his captivating playing was primarily responsible for their success.[11]

The Künstlerhilfe [Artists' Aid of the Jewish Community] confirmed:

> We have known Herr Werner Baer as a good musician for a long time. He received an excellent education, under, among others, Professors Massbach, Jenssen, Bertram, and Arnold Dreyer. He has mastered the following instruments: piano, organ, accordion and harmonium. After his studies he regularly worked in first class Berlin institutions such as the Barberina, Ambassador, and in the hotels Adlon, Eden and Bristol. After 1933 the Jewish Community employed Herr Baer as organist and choral conductor.
>
> He was the preferred performer of the Künstlerhilfe and other Jewish organisations, which engaged him as a concert organist and concert pianist for significant events. At the same time he worked as repetiteur and was repeatedly chosen as an accompanist by prominent singers. In addition, he was the Musical Director at the Jüdischer Kulturbund's Cabaret. Alongside his educational activities as teacher for organ and musical theory at the officially approved Jewish Music School in Berlin, he had engagements with almost all the Jewish congregations in Germany. Without doubt, Herr Werner Baer is among the best musicians in the Jewish Community.
>
> We regret that due to his emigration we are losing an outstanding musical colleague who, because of his versatility, is irreplaceable. We can recommend Herr Werner Baer to every Jewish organisation and every other employer abroad in the fields of serious and light music, especially as he also possesses outstanding human qualities.[12]

Similarly high appraisals were given by Hermann Schildberger for the Prussian Association of Jewish Congregations, and Hans Zander for the Kulturbund. On 2 December, Max Ehrlich also wrote a glowing reference for his former musical director:

> His strong musicality and his great pianistic facility, which give him virtuosic mastery over a wide range of music from classical, through modern, to jazz, have made him a darling of the public and the press.

> His energy, his devoted diligence, and his fine sensitivity for the actor's psyche have formed the basis for the success of the programmes. His polite behaviour, his integrity and his humour are invaluable characteristics of his innermost being.
> In Werner Baer I am losing my best and dearest colleague and comrade.[13]

Only a few months later, Max Ehrlich was also to leave Berlin. He followed his colleague Willy Rosen to the Netherlands, where he was arrested in 1943 and taken to the Westerbork concentration camp. From there he was transported to Auschwitz in 1944 and gassed on 1 October.

Werner Baer was spared this cruel fate. On 5 December, he collected more currency from the American Express office in Berlin and he and his wife departed the same day. She remembered the last S-Bahn ride in her home city, when she made up her mind: 'I do not want to see you again, never again!'[14] At the Anhalter Bahnhof, they boarded the train that took them to Italy. And so the young couple arrived at the port in Genoa in time to board the *Potsdam*, which sailed for Asia the next day. After passing through the Suez Canal, the ship docked in Colombo on 19 December, and arrived four days later in Singapore. En route, Baer had heard that the colony's Far Eastern Music School needed music teachers, so he immediately asked for further details. When the news was confirmed, he decided to stay, and on the same day a landing permit was stuck in his passport. In a letter, Baer later described it as follows: 'On board the ship I rebooked for Shanghai, and in Singapore I was taken from the ship by the Jewish Committee on account of my good command of English and my references [...]; within two hours I had a job at the so-called music academy there, and life in Singapore could begin!'[15]

Bach Fugues and the Volga Boat Song: Organist in Singapore

One day before Christmas, the Baers moved into a room at the simple Hackmeyer Boarding House. In the light of their hectic escape and all the necessary fees and other expenses, they had very little cash, but the Jewish Relief Committee in Singapore was able to offer support. Some of the city's roughly 1,500 Jews were wealthy, not least the late Sir Manasseh Meyer, who made his fortune in trade with India and in 1905 had his own synagogue built in the grounds of his palatial residence after a quarrel with the Jewish community. Soon the Baers were no longer dependent on financial assistance from the Relief Committee, as one of Ilse's uncles sent money from Stockholm. Furthermore, thanks to Werner's versatile musical talent, he soon found other jobs in addition to his teaching, even before the hair that was shaved off in Sachsenhausen grew back again:

> On 15 January I gave my first organ concert in the Town Hall there; it got rave reviews and unleashed a press campaign for a city organist in the two leading papers. On the basis of another fund-raising concert, in May I was appointed as City-Organist in Singapore, and had to give two organ concerts every month.[16]

His first concert, with organ works by Bach and Mendelssohn and songs by Schubert and Loewe, got a standing ovation; according to the newspaper report, it was greater than any other artist had ever experienced in that city.[17] The critic expressed the hope of hearing the neglected instrument regularly in the future. In the Victoria Memorial Hall (which, crowned by a fifty-four-metre-high bell tower and with 616 seats, was the largest concert hall in the city), the St Clair organ had been installed in 1932 and named after the founder of the Philharmonic Society; it was one of the best organs in Asia. Several readers were keen on the idea of using it for regular organ recitals.[18] In a long letter published in the *Straits Times* after one of Baer's sold-out organ concerts, one reader wrote: 'The public is here, the organ is here, the organist is here [...]. I would throw out a suggestion of half-hourly recitals every Wednesday at 1.30, with at least 2 full recitals on Sunday evenings every month.'[19] In the same issue, it was reported that the relevant committee recommended introducing such a concert series on a trial basis. On 7 May, the first city organ concert took place, with Werner Baer and a vocal soloist. It was enthusiastically received,[20] and from then on, city organ concerts with Baer and different soloists took place regularly in the Victoria Memorial Hall and were advertised in the *Straits Times*.[21] By August, one reviewer was writing that it had become good manners to go to organ concerts on a Sunday evening.[22] In addition, from the middle of August more 'popular' organ concerts were put on once a month on

Friday afternoons. The first concert of this kind drew a wide audience.[23] Even after Britain entered the war against Germany (on 4 September, the heading in the *Straits Times* read 'BRITAIN IS AT WAR/TO CRUSH THE NAZI REGIME') these concerts continued on a regular basis. On 14 September, the next programme was published, and it included one of the organist's own works:

> Prelude (Frescobaldi)
> Pavane (William Byrd)
> The Lost Chord (Sullivan)
> Songs with Edwin Brown
> Allegro maestoso and Fugue, from Sonata in C (Mendelssohn-Bartholdy)
> Fantasie Romantique (Hugh Blair)
> Paraphrase of the 'Volga Boat Song' (W. Baer)
> More Songs
> Prelude and Fugue in E minor (J.S. Bach)

As well as his own paraphrase on the 'Song of the Volga Boatmen', Werner Baer occasionally played other secular works on the organ, like the March from *Aida* or Dvořák's *Humoresque*.[24] He also put on concerts as fund-raisers for patriotic purposes. In particular, it was noted that at the concert on 4 February 1940 Baer, a German citizen, played the Allies' anthems followed by two German choral improvisations, 'O Haupt voll Blut und Wunden' ['O sacred Head, sore wounded'] and 'Dir, dir Jehovah will ich singen ['I will sing unto Thee, Jehovah'].[25] The paper described him erroneously as a Jewish refugee from Vienna; it is possible that, on account of the war, they wanted to hush up his Berlin origins. In the meantime, together with the music-lover and accountant Mark Gordon Van Hien, Baer established the city's first series of subscription concerts. He also taught at the Far Eastern Music School that had been opened by a young Filipino, Marcello R. Anciano. From the beginning, Anciano had organised his curriculum around the Trinity College London Examinations, which meant that the standard was very high.[26]

Werner Baer proved himself as a teacher and organist in Singapore, just as he had at the Hollaender Music School and the Prinzregentenstraße synagogue. He and his wife succeeded in helping their closest relatives to emigrate. While the Presch parents escaped to Brazil, Werner's mother and brother got away to Shanghai. For Lucie Baer, who in November had still refused to take the long trip by sea, the only remaining solution was a train journey to Vladivostok; but even she was finally safe when she arrived in Shanghai.

Ilse Baer contributed to their living expenses by working as a dressmaker and the young couple was able to move into a more comfortable flat. This was also important for another reason: Ilse was now pregnant. On 25 October she gave birth to a daughter. The socialist parents chose the Jewish name, Miriam Marjorie. Soon afterwards, Baer established a children's choir in Chesed El, Sir Manasseh Meyer's private synagogue at Oxley Rise. In spite of its completely different climate and diverse cultural context, Singapore had become a new home for this small family.

'Protective Custody' in Dachau

On the night of 9 November 1938, synagogues and temples went up in flames in Vienna, as in Berlin and other German cities. 6,547 Viennese Jews were arrested and 3,700 of them were taken to the concentration camp in Dachau.[27] These intensified antisemitic measures instilled fear and terror in the singer Leonie Feigl. Her daughter Julie had left Vienna with her husband in September. Her son Joseph, previously employed in Vienna's Intourist [Soviet travel] office, was able to open a snack bar in Paris and help his mother with the move. On 16 November, a week after the pogrom night, the singer arrived in Paris where she was safe, for the moment.

By contrast, the conductors Hans Bader and Adolf Brenner were arrested, along with the trainee lawyer Dr Arnold Hacker. Shortly after the German invasion on 15 April 1938, Hacker and his pianist wife Gertrud Hacker had moved from Ybbs-an-der-Donau to Vienna, where they lived with her mother, and where Gertrud Hacker was once again able to take piano students. Arnold Hacker had already applied for an Australian visa on 2 April; his half-brother Leo had lived there since 1928. When the lawyer announced his departure at the Emigration Department of the Israelitische Kultusgemeinde, he stated that in his future domicile he wanted to work in another field, for example as a chauffeur or knitter. His brother in Melbourne would look after him and his wife. Hacker wanted to leave first with his wife and then later bring over his mother-in-law and sister. Since he had had to leave his passport at the police station in Ybbs, the responsible official at the Emigration Department wrote a note describing their case as urgent; it said the applicants were 'without any income, willing to work and both highly qualified', therefore their support would be 'most warmly approved'. He requested the missing 1,200 RM for their travel expenses and landing fees, and organised reservations for a trip to Melbourne on the steamship *Baloeran*, departing on 23 November.

Initially, everything went according to plan. The money was approved and on 13 September Hacker received a new passport. However, the pogrom night upset all their plans, as he was arrested on 10 November for student political activities. That day, he was deregistered from 51 Stumpergasse with the note 'under arrest'. He had not been sent to Dachau, however, but 'only' taken into police custody. On his mother's intercession, he was released, and travelled immediately to the Netherlands with his wife. On 23 November, the couple obtained their Australian visa from the British Passport Control Office in The Hague. Having missed the *Baloeran*, they took another ship, the *Comorin*, and arrived in Melbourne at the beginning of January 1939, giving 'Solicitor' and 'Pianist' as their occupations. They had been able to take their household goods, including their Ehrbar baby grand piano.[28]

The November pogrom had worse consequences for the conductor Hans Bader, who had been debarred from the Reichsmusikkammer in October.[29] A family man with two children, he and many other Austrian Jews had been taken to Dachau on 12 November as so-called *Schutzhäftlinge* [protective custody prisoners]; he was given the number 25444 and regarded as incriminated both as Jew and as a Social Democrat. Four days later, having previously tried in vain to emigrate to the USA, his conductor colleague Adolf Brenner arrived at the same camp, where he was assigned the number 29140.

German Jews were also sent to Dachau after Kristallnacht. The Munich bank official Max Meyer had converted to Catholicism in 1935, and moved with his wife to a district near Oberammergau, the scene of the famous passion play; there he earned his living as a music teacher. This play, however, always emphasised the Jews' shared responsibility for the death of Christ, so some sections of the Oberammergau population might have regarded the re-enactment of Jewish persecution with some satisfaction. Anton Preisinger, who was later to play the part of Christ, was an active member of the Nazi Party;[30] he remembered the Jewish background of the diligent church-goer Max Meyer, and denounced him. Thereupon, Meyer was arrested and sent to Dachau on 11 November as *Schutzhäftling* No. 20344. In the concentration camp's entry book, Meyer was registered as a 'composer'. Alongside his work at the bank he had, in fact, also composed. After his conversion, he had written mainly church music. When he was released from Dachau three months later, he immediately moved to England, leaving his non-Jewish wife behind in Germany.

In May 1939, Werner Hans Katz, a composer, pianist and conductor from Berlin, was also sent to Dachau as a *Schutzhäftling* after being denounced by an informant.[31] After completing his studies at the Berlin Hochschule für Musik, Katz composed numerous works for opera, film and entertainment under the pseudonym Hans Werner, including the foxtrot hit 'Koketten Frauen soll man nicht trauen' ['Flirtatious women are not to be trusted'][32] for Luigi Bernauer in 1929. Katz also married a non-Jewish woman with whom he lived in Grätzwalde, near Berlin. After 9 November 1938, a 'race-conscious' neighbour apparently reported him on the grounds of his mixed marriage. After his release from Dachau, Katz fled to England; his wife and daughter remained in Germany.

Like Werner Baer's wife, Hans Bader's spouse had also discovered that her husband could be released from the concentration camp if there was any possibility of his emigration. She turned to the emigration department of the welfare centre of the Kultusgemeinde in Vienna and indicated in a questionnaire that her husband wanted to travel to Tientsin (Tianjin), a city in the north-east of China. He had musician friends in the orchestra there. Moreover, Bader had held a valid German passport since September 1938. On the basis of these facts, the responsible official proposed that the emigration department should finance the trip to China. Because Grete Bader urgently needed money in order to support herself and the children, she took in subtenants in her flat. She was lucky: her husband returned from Dachau on 20 December. On 28 December, he went in person to the emigration department, where he now stated that he wanted to go to Shanghai, where, however, he had no friends or relatives. Nonetheless, the official noted: 'The applicant makes a thoroughly favourable impression, so nothing [...] should stand in the way of an approval, all the more so because he must leave the Reich by 15.1. at the latest.'[33] The next day, the official applied for a grant of 300 RM for the trip from Vienna to Shanghai. This was one-third of the total price for the ship's passage from Trieste to Shanghai on board the *Verdi*, which at that time cost 868 RM.

At the same time, however, in Ipoh, Hans Blau had bought a ticket on the *Conte Biancamano* for his Viennese colleague. In a telegram to Bader he wrote:

BIANCAMANO TICKETS BOUGHT HERE WHEN YOU HAVE TICKETS LEAVE SAME DAY TRAVEL TO GENOA YOUR DISEMBARKATION SINGAPORE GUARANTEED – HANS[34]

Thus it can be assumed that Bader travelled to Singapore not on the *Verdi* but on the *Conte Biancamano*, a luxury ship built in Britain and first used on the Atlantic route. Bader arrived on 24 January, and just two days later he was able to take a short-term engagement at an establishment appropriately named the Vienna Café. After that, he received a new offer from the city of Ipoh on the west coast of the Malayan Peninsula, which had a predominantly Chinese population; there he was able to obtain the necessary emigration papers for his family. By May, he was able to embrace his wife and two children.

Adolf Brenner was less fortunate: he was released from Dachau only on 24 April 1939. On his release, like all the others, he had to swear to absolute silence concerning his detention. His mother was no longer living in the familiar two-and-a-half-room flat in Karl-Beck-Gasse. As Karl Isidor Beck, the author of the poetic line 'An der schönen blauen Donau'

['The Blue Danube'], was found to have been Jewish, the street had in the meantime been renamed Gustloffgasse in memory of a Nazi murdered in Switzerland. During Brenner's incarceration, his mother had had to move out of her lovely flat in Währing to a lodger's room in the Second District. She had sold all the house furnishings and linen in order to eke out a living. During her son's stay in the concentration camp, his unemployment benefits were cancelled, so she was now dependent on financial support from her daughter in Amsterdam and the Kultusgemeinde. After his release, Adolf Brenner moved in with his mother. While living in these extremely cramped conditions, he returned to the emigration department of the Kultusgemeinde on 26 May and applied for financial support for his trip to Shanghai on 14 June. The welfare centre recognised the precarious situation in which this musician found himself. In judging his case, they noted:

No. of Persons and destination	1 Person to Shanghai: Adolf Israel Brenner
Requirement:	1 × Vienna – Shanghai 850 RM
Provided:	Down payment 300 RM
Still available:	–
Living conditions:	Single, lives with his mother. Her flat: Formerly: 2½ rooms, kitchen, front room. Now: 1 room as lodger rent 27 RM; upkeep for mother and son (2 people)
Family circumstances:	Single. Mother formerly supported by Adolf Isr. Brenner. Sister housemaid in Amsterdam.
Economic situation:	Assessment 5 RM, waived. No household goods [...] Until 1933 conductor in the Old Reich, since then living from private tuition. Now little income. Until Nov. 1938 unemployment benefits approx. 7 RM

	Lives from support of sister and a friend, 10 RM per month and food from Kultusgemeinde. Household goods sold. Linen etc. pawned.
Connections abroad:	Only the sister in Amsterdam.
Imprisonment, expulsion:	10.XI. – 24.IV. Dachau. Expelled as of 31.V.
Summary:	Information is genuine. <u>It is possible that Brenner will be put in a camp.</u>[35]
Claim:	As much support as possible.[36]

The original travel schedule could no longer be kept. On 19 June, Brenner told the emigration department that he wanted to leave for Shanghai on 13 July, and the next day the sum of 400 RM was approved. Although his passage from Trieste to Shanghai was reserved on the *Victoria*, Brenner hesitated, because the British passport authorities had warned of the difficult living conditions in that Chinese city. As Captain Foley told his superiors in January 1939, such warnings were usually ignored by the applicants: 'They refuse to listen to us and say that Shanghai under any conditions is infinitely better than a Concentration Camp in Germany.' According to Foley, this view was to be respected: 'They would rather die as free men in Shanghai than as slaves in Dachau.'[37] But after his stay in Dachau, Brenner was horrified by the thought of possibly being put behind barbed wire again in Shanghai. In the end, therefore, he gave up the trip. On 27 June, he again appeared at the emigration department and said that he now wanted to go to Italy, and as soon as 7 July. The department adjusted to the new situation, and the very next day declared that it was prepared to finance his train trip to Milan. But again this deeply unsettled musician reversed his decision. On 12 July, he submitted another application – the fourth in just a few months – in which he announced that he wanted to move to London on 16 July. The emigration office accepted this decision too, cancelled the ticket to Milan on the same day and instead provided him with a trip to London, supplemented by an additional 50 RM. This decision was final: Brenner left Vienna on 16 July and moved to England.

Ultimate Destination Australia

Transit via Britain

Hermann Schildberger was among the many refugees to arrive in Britain looking for help in March 1939. Since 1934, when the Reichsmusikkammer had withdrawn his provisional membership, his musical activities had been limited to the Kulturbund and Reform Congregation. In January 1935, officials of the Reichsmusikkammer had informed him 'that according to the statutory provisions, employment in two professions is not permitted [...]. Therefore we cannot issue a membership card and cannot allow you to practise music'.[38] Schildberger did not accept this and argued that his musical activities were not merely a sideline. On 17 August 1935, his renewed application for acceptance into the Reichsmusikkammer was also rejected, but this time on grounds of his Jewishness.

In contrast to the Zionists, supporters of the Reform Congregation like Schildberger were not eager to get out quickly. Years ago, they had already crossed out passages in their prayer book that spoke of a 'return' to Palestine. Moreover, Schildberger was not under any pressure; as director of the Berlin Künstlerhilfe, he had a regular income. In 1937, he married Ilse Wolff and moved into a new flat in Charlottenburg. After Kristallnacht, however, when the Reform Congregation synagogue was completely destroyed, he, too, started to think about emigrating; in December 1938, he applied for a visa at the American Consulate General. In view of the slim chances for an immigration permit for the USA, he also applied for a visa for Britain, as after 9 November the British had relaxed their entry requirements. They were now accepting migrants in transit on condition that they promised to leave the country within two years. At the beginning of March 1939, Schildberger obtained a new German passport in which he gave his occupation as 'Music Lecturer and Musician', because he thought that he would have a better chance abroad as a musician than as a lawyer. On receipt of the visa, he disposed of his household assets and travelled to England with his wife on 21 March. The Certificate of Registration he received stipulated that he could not accept any work in the country, either paid or unpaid. This document gave his occupation as 'Refugee'.

All Schildberger's hopes were now focused on Australia. He owed this decision – and also the practical help with the move – to Hermann Sänger. Sänger had studied in Paris, Geneva and Cambridge and obtained a doctorate in Romance languages. In 1933, he had been appointed rabbi at the New Synagogue in Oranienburger Straße where, on account of his excellent linguistic skills, he functioned as a kind of foreign minister for the congregation. Once, when the body of a scientist who had died in Sachsenhausen was returned, he gave the last blessing with the words: 'Here lies German culture.'[39] At that time, to mourn the body of a tortured Jew as a part of German culture required audacity; it was a more significant expression of resistance to official racism than the singing of Jewish songs. A spy reported Sänger's remark to the Nazi authorities. One night in 1936, the rabbi received a call and was ordered to leave the country the next day. He complied.

In London, Sänger heard that a young congregation in Melbourne's St Kilda, Australia's first liberal Jewish community, was in severe crisis and in desperate need of a capable rabbi. Thanks to his excellent knowledge of languages, he immediately took on this task. He arrived in Melbourne on the *Viminale* in August 1936. In the same month, he acquired a block of land in Alma Road, St Kilda, and in July 1937, together with Sir Isaac Isaacs (the first Jewish Governor-General of Australia) he laid the foundation stone for a new synagogue, Temple Beth Israel. This synagogue had particularly close ties with Berlin, not only through Hermann Sänger himself, but also through three precious Torah scrolls that were sent to Melbourne from the Lindenstraße synagogue.[40]

From England, in mid-May 1939, Hermann Schildberger contracted a Berlin removal firm to ship his possessions, which were to leave for Melbourne on the German steamship *Lahn* on 21 July.[41] Meanwhile, his wife enquired about other contacts in Australia and received the following recommendation from Paris, where her sister-in-law, Lucie Schildberger, had been living since 1933:

> Should you ever meet Curt Prerauer when you are there (your husband knows him too, but I'm not sure if they like each other much), please give him my regards. He's already been there five years, is currently living in Sydney and seems to have made quite a name for himself in musical life.[42]

Indeed, Prerauer, the former State Opera repetiteur, had in the meantime become conductor of the Royal Philharmonic Society in Sydney and obtained Australian citizenship in August 1938. In her letter, Ilse Schildberger had written about their first disappointing experiences in exile, to which her correspondent in Paris, Alfred Alexander-Katz replied:

> It doesn't surprise me to hear what you say about your experiences with old friends, whose nature has changed since you have become a refugee. For non-Jews we are highly uninteresting, and for Jews highly embarrassing, because our influx could draw attention to their own situation and thereby make it worse. In an excellent French book I recently found the sentence that the Jew is never an individual. Everything he does is judged from the perspective of the community to which he belongs. He is never again anonymous, nor individual. C'est comme ça, il faut prendre l'habitude. [That's how it is. We have to get used to it.] But there again, one of the great experiences of emigration is to discover spontaneous friendships that one would never have expected and thereby to be spared from otherwise inevitable pessimism. My dear child, emigration is a big adventure and you have to try to be happy about every high, and with every low to hope for the next high.[43]

At the beginning of June, the anticipated letter from Hermann Sänger arrived, together with the permit for Australia. Schildberger received his permit because Sänger was offering him a position as organist and choirmaster at his new synagogue. The invitation was a privilege that distinguished Schildberger from the majority of musicians who had already gone to Australia. They did not tell the authorities that it was only a small congregation with scarcely a hundred members, or that the fine-sounding title 'Director of Music' came with a modest annual income of ninety pounds that would never cover the cost of living for a family. Nevertheless, Hermann and Ilse Schildberger set out on the long journey with their child. On 1 July 1939, they boarded the *Moreton Bay*, which brought them to Melbourne on 7 August. The next day, he was introduced by the press as one of the leading personalities in Jewish cultural life; in spite of an invitation to the USA, he had chosen Australia.[44] He could now begin his work as organist and choirmaster for Temple Beth Israel.

In the same year, another of Schildberger's colleagues from the Kulturbund, the administrative director Hans Zander, went to Britain, where he worked temporarily as a pianist for the Kurt Jooss Ballet.[45] But whereas Zander only arrived in Australia after the war, the pianist and long-term choral director at the Fasanenstraße synagogue, Theodor Schoenberger, moved there straight from Germany.[46] He had been one of the most experienced piano teachers at the Stern Conservatory and later at the private Jewish Hollaender Music School. His pupils there included Horst Prentki and Alfred Guttmann/Goodman, both of whom survived in exile. Even as late as 22 January 1939, the Music School had put on an event 'Celebrating the 65th birthdays of our Masters Theodor Schoenberger and retired *Generalmusikdirektor* Prof. Julius Prüwer'. The pianist had decided on Australia, as his daughter Eva and her husband had been living in Sydney since September 1938. With their help and sponsorship, Schoenberger obtained the necessary visa. Three days after a promotional concert at the music school, he and his wife left for England; they arrived in Sydney aboard the *Mooltan* early in July. Among the pianist's most important possessions were letters of recommendation from Artur Schnabel, Frederic Lamond, Bruno Walter and Otto Klemperer.[47] By August, he had a position as organist at Temple Emanuel, a liberal synagogue in east Sydney that had been opened the previous year, also on Hermann Sänger's initiative.

Not all the refugees had such useful contacts as Schildberger and Schoenberger. In April 1939, the Berlin violinist Majer Pietruschka was happy just to be able to leave Germany. This opportunity arose through the opening of a new internment camp, the Kitchener Camp in Richborough, near Sandwich (Kent). The London Council for German Jewry had taken over this neglected camp dating from the First World War and turned it into a transit camp as an emergency solution for the many German and Austrian Jews who, after the November pogroms, were only released from the concentration camps if they could prove they had an opportunity to emigrate.[48] The opening of the Kitchener Camp allowed officials like Captain Foley in Berlin to send more Jews to Britain at short notice. The British Home Office realised that those who were being persecuted could not organise their emigration quickly, and allowed them to remain on a temporary basis on condition that they made efforts to move elsewhere. Thus the visa stamp read 'For transit only: Richborough Camp, pending emigration'. Meanwhile, the Jewish Refugees Committee provided the necessary guarantees.[49]

In March 1939, the Kitchener Camp was renovated and every barrack (or hut) divided in two, each half accommodating thirty-five to forty people in double-decker bunks. The camp could take a total of 3,000 people. As in the army, there were communal bathrooms and a dining room. Classrooms for language courses were also set up. Every internee had to take two hours of English a day, one with a local teacher and the other with a qualified refugee. In addition, there were lectures and discussions, a library, and from March a monthly camp newsletter. By April, the second edition of the *Kitchener Camp Review* was already reporting on musical activities. Max Burwood, the leader of a string orchestra in the neighbouring town of Sandwich, invited musically talented refugees to join the ensemble and stated that once there were enough musicians in the camp, he wanted to visit them and start a separate Kitchener Camp Orchestra.[50]

As there were many musicians among the refugees – including the composer Werner Katz and the violinists Majer Pietruschka and Otmar Silberstein – the camp orchestra was established forthwith. Because they had been working outside until the last minute, the musicians gave their first performance wearing muddy gumboots. The concert in the makeshift hall opened with 'God Save the King' and continued with a Haydn symphony.[51] A Haydn string quartet opened the next concert on 22 April; this was followed by Edward Elgar's *Pomp and Circumstance*, Edward German's *Morris Dance*, Henry Purcell's *The Virtuous Wife* and *The Blue Danube* by Johann Strauß. In May, when a programme of artistic entertainment was organised for the English friends of the camp, the works by Elgar and Strauß were heard again.

The camp orchestra, which eventually consisted of about twenty musicians, was one of the camp's favourite institutions and was also sent as an 'ambassador' to the surrounding towns. In November, the *Kitchener Camp Review* reported on an atmospheric concert given by the orchestra in the church of St Clement's in Sandwich, and also on a performance for students at The King's School in Canterbury. Even the London *Times* mentioned the event at The King's School, at which Johann Sebastian Bach's Double Concerto was performed.[52] One of the two violin soloists was Majer Pietruschka, now a leading member of the camp orchestra.[53] Alongside the Bach concerto, the programme included Schubert's Rondo for violin and strings, *Liebestraum* by Max Reger and the Serenade in F major by Karl Goldmark. After the concert, the refugees were able to converse in English with students and teachers at the school.

Most of the internees had applied for visas to other countries. They longed for news from abroad and envied those who had already received their papers. A few of the first arrivals had been able to leave for Australia on 3 May. From the ship, they wrote about their journey for the camp newsletter, and their report was printed in July. Even the beginning must have unleashed dreams of longing for the readers:

> Life afloat. Impressions of a voyage to Australia.
> (from Nos. 6, 7, 8, who left the Camp for Australia on May 3rd)
>
> Suez Canal, on our way between Port Said and Suez
>
> Dear Mr Editor,
> Imagine lying in comfortable deck chairs on board our liner. Above we see a clear blue sky, beneath, the green coloured water ...[54]

Urgently Sought: Guarantors for Australia

It was more convenient to leave directly for the country of exile without waiting in England. As an employee of the Canadian Pacific Railway Company, the Vienna-born Pole Janusz Harband was particularly well-informed about all the latest travel possibilities. This Canadian company had its office on the Opernring in central Vienna. As Austrians were more interested in its ship passages than train journeys, it was listed in the Vienna Directory of 1939 as the Canadian Pacific Shipping Company. In January 1939, when Harband obtained an Australian visa in Vienna for himself and his Austrian wife Eva Susanne, they both travelled to England. About four weeks later, they boarded a ship for Canada before taking a Canadian Pacific train to the port at Vancouver. They arrived in Sydney aboard the *Aorangi* on 8 April. Janusz dropped his Polish first name and henceforth called himself John Edward Harband. According to the Registration Office, he only deregistered in Vienna on 20 July 1939, by which time he had been living in Sydney for four months.

Migration to Australia was considerably easier when relatives or friends who were living there provided the mandatory guarantees. Ernst Cohn, son of the violinist Lisbeth Cohn, had taken his medical exams in Germany in 1935 and then moved to Britain in order to complete a second doctorate in Edinburgh. On a friend's recommendation, he migrated to Australia, where he called himself Ernest Colin. His parents, Lisbeth and Willy (a medical doctor), wanted to follow him, so the passport that Lisbeth had obtained in September was stamped 'for emigration to Australia'. But then came the pogrom. Willy Cohn was transported to the Buchenwald concentration camp, where he died on 27 November – presumably as a result of maltreatment. On 7 December, Lisbeth Cohn received a visa ('Transmigrant to Australia, Landing Permit') from the British Consulate General in Frankfurt am Main. In order to get to England as quickly and safely as possible, she took a plane to London on 21 January 1939 and used her short stay there to learn English. Then, along with eighty-three other Jewish refugees, she boarded the *Ascanius* in Liverpool. During the stopover in Cape Town, she was invited by the Jewish Congregation to take part in the traditional Passover, which was being celebrated for the refugees by a rabbi who had fled from East Prussia; the Passover, of course, commemorates the passing-over of the Israelites in Egypt.[55] At the age of fifty-six, the violinist began a new career in Melbourne, under the name Elizabeth Colin.

Fritz Brandmann found a contact in Australia by chance. The son of a Polish father and Austrian mother, he had acquired German citizenship in Berlin in 1908. He changed his first name Salomon to Fritz in order to express his willingness to integrate. In 1913, he married Charlotte Schirmeister from Berlin and they had five children. They were all given typical German names: Fritz, Johanna Lotte Victoria, Hans-Joachim, Lieselotte and Eva. Fritz Brandmann ran a jewellery shop that an Australian customer entered during the 1936 Olympic Games: the Scottish-born William John MacKay, Sydney's Chief of Police. They started talking and the Australian noticed immediately how much the owner admired Britons. After the pogrom, Brandmann remembered this meeting and asked the Australian for assistance. MacKay was indeed prepared to help the Jewish family obtain permits. Brandmann's son Hans-Joachim received his visa in December 1938. On 31 December, he flew from Tempelhof airport to London, where he waited for the other family members, who arrived in February. They had booked a passage on the *Narkunda*, and all seven of them finally disembarked in Sydney on 13 April. Fritz changed his name to Frederick Brandman and found a job as an interpreter with the police. At first he worked in the area of Alien Control, as in the meantime his sponsor, the Scottish-born W. J. MacKay, had become Head of the Commonwealth Security Service, which also specialised in counterintelligence. MacKay also employed one of Brandman's sons in the Security Service and helped his father to become naturalised quickly. Additionally, Brandman was cantor at Temple Emanuel.

The piano teacher Emma Weiss also came to Australia through the good offices of an acquaintance. Weiss had studied at the Vienna Conservatorium under her maiden name, Emma Bondy. After 1913, she lived from time to time in Britain, where she taught music and German and acquired a good knowledge of English. After her marriage, Weiss was a piano teacher in Linz until the time of the annexation. In spite of her conversion to Protestantism, she was now considered a non-Aryan and could no longer teach. In this situation, an Australian woman, Dr Georgina Sweet, came to Weiss's rescue and applied for an entry permit for her. In 1916, Sweet, a zoologist and women's rights activist, became the first Australian woman to be appointed a university professor. In 1935, she was awarded an OBE (Officer of The Order of the British Empire) for her contribution to the women's movement. She was President of the Australian YWCA (Young Women's Christian Association) from 1927 until 1934, and after that Vice-President of the International YWCA. It is possible that she heard about Emma Weiss through this organisation and was able to arrange her immigration. In March 1939, the pianist arrived in Melbourne on the *Strathnaver* which, according to the ship's records, she had only boarded in Colombo. Emma Weiss stayed with the courageous and helpful zoologist in the Melbourne suburb of Glenferrie.

The violinist Ellen Byk had turned to Bernard Heinze in April 1938; she wrote to him from Berlin Zehlendorf asking if he could arrange a job for her in Melbourne:

Dear Professor Heinze!

Some days ago, I had a letter from my friend Professor Dr Marshall Allan from Melbourne. He was so very kind to give me your address and asked me to go in touch with you. – I am a violinist, always lived in Berlin, where I had a very good repute as a violin player and teacher. I used to give Concerts and to play also for the Broadcasting Station. —
 The way things are going now, it is quite impossible for me, to get on with my profession. So I would like to be able to come to Australia and I would be very grateful to you, if you would see any chance for me to come over. The Woburn House in London, where I called last summer, sent my papers and certificates to Australia, but they informed me, that it would be very difficult for me to get the 'permit'. I would be very much obliged, if you would try to give me a chance, I would be able to supply a position as violin teacher on a music-school or in the Broadcasting Station. – Professor Dr Allan informed me, that you are now in the U.S.A. and that you will come later on to London and perhaps to Berlin. May I ask you to write to me, at which point of time you will be in Europe? [...]

Yours sincerely
Ellen Cohn-Byk[56]

Although the violinist had attached concert reviews from the main Berlin papers, like the *Berliner Tageblatt*, *Vossische Zeitung* and *Börsencourier*, the conductor and conservatorium director replied on 8 May telling her that there was no position available:

> I regret to have to inform you that for the moment I could not possibly take the responsibility of encouraging you to migrate to Australia in a permanent capacity. Were you willing to go there and slowly work up a teaching connection, I feel your experience in Europe would stand you in good stead, but as far as offering you a position on the staff of the University Conservatorium is concerned, I'm afraid that this is quite impossible.

This rejection was confirmed by a resolution of the Music Faculty.[57] Nevertheless, the violinist endeavoured to migrate to Australia. She was supported by Professor Allan (mentioned in the first letter), who had instigated the first diploma examinations in gynaecology and obstetrics in Australia and was a staunch member of the Presbyterian Church. Allan had studied in Dublin and Edinburgh and had worked in obstetrics in Paris, Vienna and Berlin. Regardless of how he had made contact with Ellen Byk, in view of the antisemitic riots after the November pogrom, and despite her failed application for a position at the Conservatorium, the doctor was prepared to bring the violinist to Australia, now as his domestic servant. At the end of November 1938, he sent his government an 'Application for Admission of Relatives or Friends to Australia' in which he declared himself willing to invite the fifty-one-year-old woman to Australia. She was currently a violinist, he said, but wanted to work as a housemaid in Melbourne. He stated that as a university professor (Allan became Dean of the Medical Faculty in 1944[58]) he had sufficient funds. The application succeeded, and the violinist proceeded to organise a passport, which she received on 10 February. She then disposed of her household assets, completed the necessary formalities and travelled to England, where a week later she boarded the *Ormonde*. There were English courses for the more than 200 German and Austrian refugees on board.[59] In the passenger list, the violinist's occupation is given as 'Home Duties', commensurate with Marshall Allan's application. This is repeated in the 'Personal Statement' where, in answer to the question about friends in Australia, she wrote: 'Allan, Malvern, Victoria'. At first, Ellen Byk did indeed live in the professor's home in the Melbourne suburb of Malvern. From here, a few days after her arrival, she again asked Bernard Heinze for a music position, as she had never wanted a job as a domestic. Heinze invited the violinist to the Conservatorium on 18 May; again, however, he had nothing to offer. Ellen Byk now had to try and survive under extremely difficult circumstances, as can be seen from her frequent changes of address.

> During the first years that I was here, it was simply impossible (for immigrants) to eke out a living as a musician or music teacher and it was very hard for me. I was then already fifty-two years old, had no assets (I emigrated with 10 Marks) and was completely alone. To eke out an existence I had to work as a housemaid, then later in factories, etc.[60]

She left Allan's house after seven weeks, lived in Melbourne's city centre for two months, in St Kilda for a week, in South Yarra two years, in Toorak five months, in both Glen Iris and Camberwell a month, in Auburn four months and in Hawksburn eighteen months – a restless and unsettled life.[61] Ellen Byk was only rarely heard as a violinist in little concerts, accompanied by the pianist Mary Baillie.

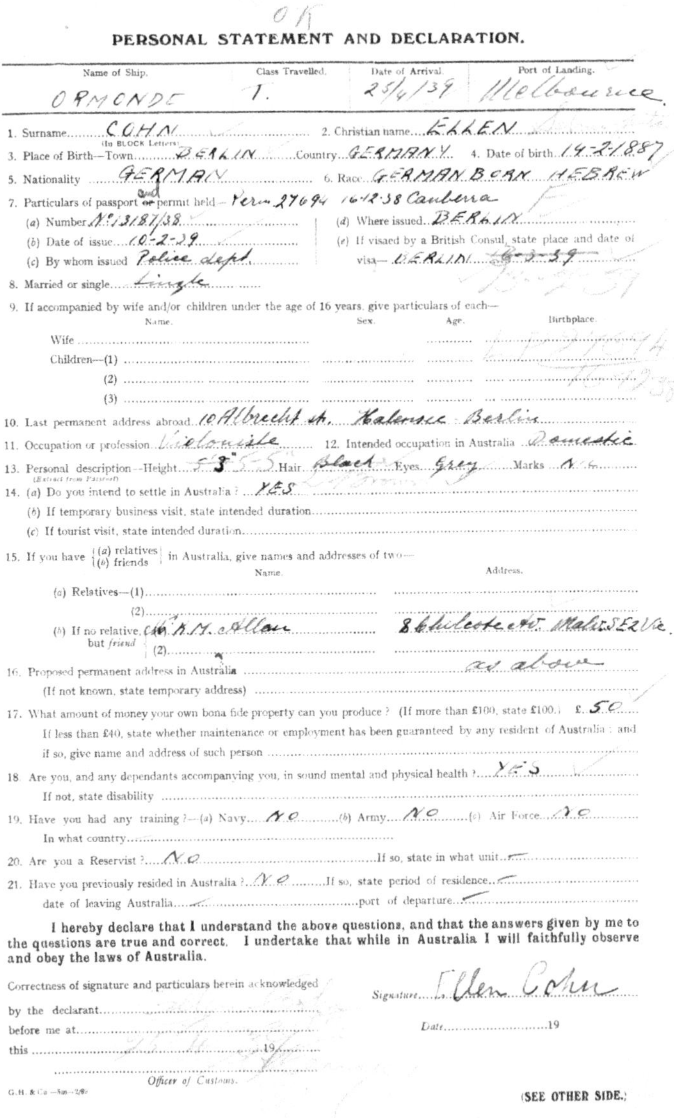
OK

PERSONAL STATEMENT AND DECLARATION.

Name of Ship.	Class Travelled.	Date of Arrival.	Port of Landing.
ORMONDE	T.	25/4/39	Melbourne.

1. Surname (In BLOCK Letters) COHN 2. Christian name ELLEN
3. Place of Birth—Town BERLIN Country GERMANY 4. Date of birth 14-2-1887
5. Nationality GERMAN 6. Race GERMAN BORN HEBREW
7. Particulars of passport and permit held — Perm 27694 16-12-38 Canberra
(*a*) Number No 13187/38 (*d*) Where issued BERLIN
(*b*) Date of issue 10-2-39 (*e*) If visaed by a British Consul, state place and date of
(*c*) By whom issued Police dept. visa— BERLIN ~~6-3-39~~
8. Married or single single
9. If accompanied by wife and/or children under the age of 16 years, give particulars of each—

	Name.	Sex.	Age.	Birthplace.
Wife				
Children—(1)				
(2)				
(3)				

10. Last permanent address abroad 10 Albrecht str. Halensee Berlin
11. Occupation or profession Violoniste 12. Intended occupation in Australia Domestic
13. Personal description (Extract from Passport)—Height 5' 5" Hair Black Eyes Grey Marks No
14. (*a*) Do you intend to settle in Australia? YES
(*b*) If temporary business visit, state intended duration
(*c*) If tourist visit, state intended duration
15. If you have (*a*) relatives (*b*) friends in Australia, give names and addresses of two—

	Name.	Address.
(*a*) Relatives—(1)		
(2)		
(*b*) If no relative, but *friend* (1)	Mr. R.M. Allan	8 Chilcote Av. Malvern S.E.2 Vic.
(2)		

16. Proposed permanent address in Australia as above
(If not known, state temporary address)
17. What amount of money your own bona fide property can you produce? (If more than £100, state £100.) £ 50
If less than £40, state whether maintenance or employment has been guaranteed by any resident of Australia; and if so, give name and address of such person
18. Are you, and any dependants accompanying you, in sound mental and physical health? YES
If not, state disability
19. Have you had any training?—(*a*) Navy NO (*b*) Army NO (*c*) Air Force NO
In what country
20. Are you a Reservist? NO If so, state in what unit —
21. Have you previously resided in Australia? NO If so, state period of residence —
date of leaving Australia — port of departure —

I hereby declare that I understand the above questions, and that the answers given by me to the questions are true and correct. I undertake that while in Australia I will faithfully observe and obey the laws of Australia.

Correctness of signature and particulars herein acknowledged by the declarant before me at this 19

Officer of Customs.

Signature Ellen Cohn

Date 19

G.H. & Co.

(SEE OTHER SIDE.)

Figure 11: 'Personal Statement and Declaration' for Ellen Byk-Cohn, completed on 25 April 1939. As her 'race' she states 'German born Hebrew', as former occupation 'violoniste', as future occupation 'domestic'. As contact she names R.M. Allan. (NAA: A12508, 21/741)

Among the many calls for help that Bernard Heinze received at that time was a letter from Curt Teichert, written on 21 August 1939. Teichert was working as a palaeontologist at the University of Western Australia. With reference to Artur Schnabel, he spoke up for the musician and music-writer Kurt Singer. The former President of the Kulturbund was then living in exile in Amsterdam. As he had no chance of getting a non-quota visa for the USA, Singer had asked Schnabel for references for a musical career in Australia. Teichert's letter contained written recommendations for Singer from Leo Blech, Ernst Kurth (Bern), Egon Wellesz, Wilhelm Furtwängler and Carl Flesch. Heinze had noted that the Singer case should be discussed, but no result is recorded. Kurt Singer was sent to Westerbork concentration camp in Holland in 1943 and died of exhaustion the following year in Theresienstadt.

'Larino, safe haven': The Kindertransports

After the 1938 November pogrom, Britain organised special Kindertransports in order to facilitate a quick and uncomplicated escape for Jewish children. Several aid organisations joined together in November to form the Refugee Children's Movement, a privately funded body that provided guarantees for 10,000 children, especially orphans and destitute children up to the age of sixteen. Until the beginning of the war, these transports brought children from Germany, Austria and Czechoslovakia to Britain, where many were taken in by families. They were allowed to stay in Britain until they had completed their education. The Quakers also helped to organise Kindertransports,[62] on one of which the young Leo Roth from Graz came to London in 1938.

A total of only seventeen children were sent from Germany directly to Australia.[63] Most of them came from Berlin, including the brothers Richard and Georg Dreyfus, who had noticed the official antisemitism even in this big city. For example, Georg discovered that certain shops now refused entry to Jews. The feeling of belonging to a persecuted minority made him a nervous and restless child. During Kristallnacht, his father only escaped arrest by staying away from home for several days, loitering instead in trains and railway stations. Only after that did Alfred Dreyfus – who loved Germany very much – think of emigrating. The USA was his dream destination but, as he could not get a visa for the States, he recalled Berlin friends who had gone to Australia. The lawyer Dr Wolfgang Matsdorf and his brother-in-law Ernst Buchhalter did indeed help him to emigrate. It was presumably through them that Alfred Dreyfus was able to secure places for his two sons on one of the Hilfsverein's Kindertransports, after he had transferred a large sum of money to Sydney.[64] The Landing Permit was issued in Canberra in April 1939. In June, the parents took their sons to the Zoo Station and, after a tearful farewell, the boys travelled together with other children to Bremerhaven, accompanied by the paediatrician Erna Falk. On 13 June, the seven boys and ten girls, aged between five and twelve years, boarded the *Europa* for Southampton. Many of these young travellers did not really understand what was happening to them. Rather, like Georg Dreyfus, they were living in a dream world, which gave them protection. When the visa for Australia arrived in London, the group put to sea on the *Orama* on 17 June. Five weeks later, the ship with its many refugees – and the conductor, Malcolm Sargent – docked in Port Melbourne. From there, the children were taken to a home in the suburb of Balwyn. This huge house, Larino, which had been rented by the Jewish Welfare Society, seemed to them like a palace. The *Jewish Herald* reported the arrival of these children who were now to begin a new life.[65]

The Dreyfus parents only left Germany seven weeks after their sons. Because they suspected that, in view of the long voyage, they would never see many of their relatives and friends again, they made a detour to Palestine, and from there flew via Karachi and Bombay to Australia. Their visit to their sons at the home caused great surprise, as until then the home manager had taken Georg and Richard Dreyfus to be particularly poor children. They had to leave Larino quickly and moved in with their parents. In their two-room flat in St Kilda, the family now lived much more modestly than in their villa in Dahlem, Berlin. But, unlike their relatives in Germany, they were spared deportation and death. They were also spared from the war, which had meanwhile begun in Europe. Much later, George Dreyfus dedicated his Variations for Wind, *Larino, safe haven*, to this children's home.

'Where everybody goes': New Attractions in Singapore

Direct emigration to Australia was the exception. Most of the refugees went to other countries first, for example Singapore, like the violinist Salo Max Tichauer. After experiencing difficulties in Breslau after the November pogroms, he had applied for a German passport, which he received on 20 December 1938. The first page was resplendent with the red Jewish stamp, and further on was his occupation, 'Musician'. With this passport, Tichauer fled Germany and arrived in Italy on 31 December. In Trieste, he went to the Chinese Consulate, where he obtained the necessary documents for China without any problems. Like others travelling to China, during the stopover in Singapore, Tichauer decided to stay. As an experienced bandleader in Germany and the USA, he was immediately offered an engagement at the Vienna Café in Orchard Road, for which he put together his own ensemble. When the Viennese pianist Hans Bader arrived a few days later, he included him in the band. The engagement at the Vienna Café was limited to two weeks, and after that both musicians began a new engagement at the Grand Hotel in Ipoh, a largely Chinese city on the west coast of the Malayan Peninsula. Bader remained for several months in Ipoh, where he appeared at the Chez Luty and Jubilee Cabaret clubs, and also taught piano and accordion. Tichauer, however, moved on. On 1 March, he was offered a job at the Easter Hotel in Kuala Lumpur, and was able to retain this position for a year. He only went back to Singapore in April 1940 in order to renew his passport at the Dutch Consulate General. The Vienna Café had been closed down shortly after the war began, an act that had been welcomed in a letter to the editor of the *Straits Times*, since the owners would now avoid the revenue going to Hitler's Germany. Tichauer received new offers in Singapore, first until the end of June at the Pavilion Theatre in Orchard Road, and then in July at the Arcade Restaurant on Collyer Quay. By 1 May, Hans Bader had also returned to Singapore. Like Tichauer, he appeared at the Pavilion Theatre and in the Arcade Restaurant – thus the 'old' team from the Vienna Café were reunited.

The band, comprising Mischa Stiwelband, Oskar Fleischer, Heinrich Portnoj and Hans Blau, appeared at the Coconut Grove Club in Pasir Panjang Road until December 1939. The club, with the advertising slogan

'Where everybody goes', had actually wanted to move in June,[66] but this had been delayed until a notice in the newspaper on 6 December referred to its 'temporary' closure. The notice stated: 'The New Cathay opens Sat. Dec. 9th.' Like Coconut Grove, the Cathay Ballroom and Roof Garden on Orchard Road would also be run by the two Americans, Cowan and Bailey.[67] The *Straits Times* reported on the well-attended opening of the Cathay and highlighted the captivating band: 'There is plenty of rhythm in Mischa's orchestra.' According to this article, Stiwelband was the bandleader, and it was soon to become one of the most popular night clubs in the city.[68] Attached to the club were a roof garden and a luxurious cinema with comfortable armchairs. The advertisements recommended visiting the club after the film: 'Patrons Purchasing Circle Seats Are Admitted Free to Cabaret and Roof Garden.' The musicians and their spouses were able to live at Coconut Grove until February 1940, but after that they had to find new accommodation.

By May 1939, the experienced traveller Carl/Charles Reither had already arrived in Singapore, where he accepted a position as bandleader at the exclusive Tanglin Club. Since he had recommendations from Radio Colombo, he and his band, 'Nick's BMBC [British Malay Broadcasting Corporation] Dance Six' also appeared regularly for this radio network. Among the new arrivals were the bandleader Paul Steiner, who had left Marseille with his wife Emma and their daughter in June 1939, bound for Shanghai. When the ship arrived in Singapore, however, like Werner Baer and Salo Max Tichauer he decided to stay. As Steiner later reported,[69] he received crucial assistance from his colleague Kurt Blach, who had already been there for four years. Steiner was soon offered an engagement for several months at The Majestic in Ipoh, a hotel rich in tradition that still stands today at the centrally located railway station. From November onwards, he was bandleader at the Singapore Swimming Club, the oldest in the colony. This club, which until 1952 restricted membership to Europeans, also provided musical entertainment.

After fleeing Frankfurt, the clarinettist and saxophonist Walter Würzburger worked as a jazz musician in France, Belgium, the Netherlands, Switzerland and Scandinavia. In Amsterdam, he heard about favourable employment possibilities in the colony, where he, too, lived from 1939 onwards. In January 1940, the GAP Road House was advertised as the city's newest attraction. Under the open sky, in large grounds, one could dance and dine in the moonlight; dance music was provided by the GAP Melodians on three evenings a week.[70] From February, Werner Baer gave a piano concert there every Monday. Apparently it appealed to the versatile musician to devote himself to light music again alongside all his organ recitals. In April, several advertisements again promoted 'something new' at the GAP Road House: 'WALTER with his accordion for your personal entertainment.' WALTER was Walter Würzburger, who in the meantime had put together a six-piece swing band, and in the breaks between dances he would play audience requests on his accordion. In order to educate himself, he took theory lessons with Werner Baer,[71] who was still teaching at the Far Eastern Music School and at Raffles College.

Like Baer, from May 1940, Heinrich Portnoj was also lecturing at the Far Eastern Music School during the day; he taught theory and practice at this school on Kirk Terrace, mainly piano but also other subjects: violin, jazz piano, Solfège and early music education ('Kindergarten'). In September 1940, the director gave him a glowing reference. The fact that all his students had passed their exams with scores of 100 per cent was evidence of his successful teaching: 'I cannot speak too highly of Mr H. Portnoj, for he has contributed much to the advancement of this school in general and to each of his pupils in particular.'[72] The virtuosity and versatility of these refugee musicians from Europe had significantly improved the standard of music education and performance in Singapore's musical life,[73] a fact that has since been acknowledged there.

With the exceptions of Oskar Fleischer and Walter Würzburger, all the refugee musicians in Singapore were married. Kurt Blach, who lived longest in the colony, had married a local woman in 1935. Werner Baer, Heinrich Portnoj, Carl Reither and Paul Steiner had all come with their wives. Hans Bader, Mischa Stiwelband and Salo Max Tichauer all succeeded in obtaining the necessary papers and bringing their wives to Singapore. Bader and Stiwelband were also able to save their children. Some of the wives also had jobs: Ilse Baer was a dressmaker and Paul Steiner's daughter Helga found an occupation as a saleswoman. The situation was more difficult for Hans Blau: after he discovered that his wife had found another partner in Vienna, he advised her to stay in Europe. But Nelly Blau still travelled to Singapore, which resulted in considerable tension. Hans and Nelly quickly recognised that their marriage was no longer viable. Even Ilse Baer noticed the unhappy Viennese musician. In front of the house in which she and her husband were living, there was a bus stop where Hans Blau regularly waited for public transport. Werner Baer's wife did not know him. She did not even suspect that he was a musician. But she noticed the sad expression on his face and began to develop an interest in him. They were to meet each other again in the internment camps in Singapore and Tatura.

'Song of the Moldau': Escape from Prague and Budapest

After 1933, quite a few persecuted German musicians escaped to Czechoslovakia, which was very cosmopolitan under its liberal President Tomáš Masaryk. The city of Prague developed into one of the most important centres for exiles at the time, for example, for Leo Kestenberg, a key figure in the musical life of the Weimar Republic, not least because of its influential German Jewish minority. When the Berlin music critic Hans Heinz Stuckenschmidt, who as a 'cultural Bolshevik' had become a figure of hate, accepted a job as critic with the *Prager Tagblatt* in 1935, he found a cheerful city with cosmopolitan, sophisticated musical life.[74] This all changed with the annexation of the Sudetenland in October 1938 and in particular after German troops entered Prague in March 1939. The cheerfulness of the metropolis and its surroundings faded. In the new, Nazi-run 'Protectorate of Bohemia and Moravia' political opponents and non-Aryans were henceforth as threatened as in Germany. Rudolf Thomas, head of the arts section of the *Prager Tagblatt*, subsequently committed suicide.

Until that time, German-speaking Jews in Prague formed a cultural and economic elite. Their numbers included the industrialist Emil Kolben, whom the famous American inventor Thomas Edison had once chosen as his chief engineer.[75] After his return to Prague, Kolben founded the Kolben Ltd engineering works that soon merged to become Bohemian-Moravian-Kolben-Daněk [Česko-moravská-Kolben-Daněk, abbreviated as ČKD]; it produced trains, power-plants, aeroplanes, cars and household appliances. Thanks to his excellent relationship with Edison, Kolben was able to use many parts from the USA, for example Chrysler motors for his 'Praga' brand of cars. Decorated with high honours under the Habsburg monarchy and the recipient of an honorary doctorate from the German Technical University in Prague in 1908, Emil Kolben also commanded great respect in the Czech Republic, for example as Vice President of the Prague Industrial Club. His daughter Greta married Ignaz Schück, who changed his name to Ignaz Schück-Kolben after the wedding – his father-in-law had made him the director of one of his companies.

This non-denominational family lived in a large villa in the Prague vineyards, where their son Robert Schück-Kolben grew up; he had been born in 1929 and immediately christened a Protestant. His father was a passionate amateur violinist who also played string quartets. After one of their joint visits to the cinema, to see an American aviation film, Schück-Kolben discovered his son's extraordinary musical talent when they returned home and heard the film's title theme being played on their Bösendorfer grand piano. It was not his wife playing as he had at first presumed, but five-year-old Robert, who until then had never touched the piano. The film music had made such an impression on him that he was picking out the melody by ear. It was clear that Robert should have piano lessons, and he made such enormous progress that, after just a few weeks, he was able to play in a school concert.

> I no longer know what I played. My father told me that someone sitting next to him said, 'I'm going to give that boy a contract!' It was some impresario. My father replied, 'You can certainly do that, but first he has to go to school.'[76]

After the German annexation of Austria, the Kolbens could no longer spend the summer holidays at their villas in Weißenbach on the Attersee, which they had bought after Kolben Ltd electrified the Salzkammergut district. Greta Kolben, Robert's mother, was very worried and convened a family meeting. In Robert Kolben's words:

> I still remember 1938: the whole family was sitting in our living room in Prague, my grandfather Emil Kolben, my grandmother, my aunt and my uncle and perhaps

their children too. My mother said, 'Now they've taken Austria, and we're next.' But my grandfather was adamant: 'Nothing will happen to us, I'm too famous for that.'

The old man's self-confidence reminded the musician of Joseph Haydn:

> Napoleon was bombarding Vienna, and he said 'Never fear, wherever Papa Haydn is, nothing will happen.' That was also my grandfather's attitude: 'I'm President of the German Electrotechnical University in Prague, Chairman of the German Electrotechnical Association and I'm in the SPD presidium (as if that had helped him!) and they won't do a thing to me.'

Even though the Pečeks, a powerful banking family, had already shifted their wealth out of the country (the Gestapo was later to use their palace as its official residence in Prague), the Kolben family had faith in their patriarch. Only his daughter Greta remained nervous. Fearing a German invasion of Prague, she recommended emigration to her husband. In December 1938, nine-year-old Robert acquired a Czech passport. Before the invasion of the Wehrmacht in March 1939, his father transferred a large sum of money (£4,000) to Britain and went to London. Since Ignaz knew that Britain could only be regarded as a transit country, while he was there, he filled out an application for himself and his family to emigrate to Australia.[77] In it, he stated that he wanted to establish a new company in Australia, for which he had the required capital. The first step was to bring the rest of the family to England. Once they had received their visas, Greta travelled to London with her two sons on 26 April. Looking back, Robert's father confessed that if it had not been for his wife's persistence he would have stayed in Prague – like the worldly wise Emil Kolben, whom the Germans carried off to Theresienstadt. His prominence had not protected him at all.

The outbreak of war prevented the Schück-Kolben family's anticipated journey to Australia. Although Ignaz had no work permit, after some delay and on account of his outstanding specialist knowledge, he got a poorly paid job as manager of a cable factory in Manchester. 'By his own account, he doubled their production in a few weeks by ignoring the English traditions, which of course was a mortal sin.'[78] Robert went to Manchester Grammar School and became used to regarding England as his new home.

His father found him an instrument and a piano teacher, so his talent was soon being noticed at school.

The German invasion of Prague in March 1939 shocked Wolfgang Wagner just as much as it did the opera and lieder singer Lily Kolos. Wolfgang Wagner, the son of a Jewish doctor from Teplitz-Schönau, was manager of Albert Hahn, a big tubular steel works that he first worked for in Berlin. After marrying his wife Charlotte there in 1927, he moved to Vienna. Because the Bohemian town of Teplitz now belonged to Czechoslovakia, Wagner had become a Czech citizen. In April 1935, he obtained a Czech passport and from 1937 the family lived in Ostrava, previously Mährisch Ostrau. Wagner's daughter Hannah was born there before they moved to Prague. After the German invasion, Wagner saw no future for himself in that city. Since his cousin Hellmuth Hendon was already living in Australia, he, too, wanted to move there with his family. While still in Prague, he obtained a visa for Britain and for subsequent travel to Australia. They managed to leave quickly, since the family of five landed in Sydney in May 1939. Wagner trained there as an accountant and worked for the Whitmont Shirts textile company for quite some time.

After her music studies in Vienna, Lily Kolos worked as a permanent concert singer at Radio-Journal in Slovakian Bratislava. From there, she contacted the Viennese concert agent Dr Hohenberg who organised a tour for her. However, after the Austrian annexation, it could not take place because the soprano was Jewish. Following Slovakia's declaration of independence, Lily Kolos moved to be with her sister, Olga, in Prague. From there, on the recommendation of their brother and cousin, both of whom were already living in Australia, she wrote to the ABC in June 1939 requesting a concert tour; in the letter, she listed her extensive opera, lied and operetta repertoire, and mentioned that she had the support of Bruno Walter.[79] The tour did not materialise, however, so the desired departure to Australia was delayed.

The Hungarians also felt threatened after the occupation of the neighbouring country. Alarmed, Béla Bartók had written to a friend in Switzerland in April 1938: 'The imminent danger is namely that Hungary will also succumb to this system of robbery and murder. The question is only when, how?' By that time, he already felt the need to emigrate, especially as his publisher, the Viennese Universal Edition, had been Aryanised, as had the Austrian Performing Rights Society, AKM, to which the composer belonged. When Hans Heinz Stuckenschmidt visited Bartók in Budapest in the autumn of 1938, the latter appeared nervous. He indicated that, because of the threat posed by the hated Nazis, he did not want to stay in Hungary much longer.[80] In February 1939, Bartók reported to a student that he had succeeded in transferring to the English Performing Rights Association. 'The fatal influence of the Germans is steadily increasing in Hungary. […] What I would like most is to turn my back on the whole of Europe. But where would I go?'[81] The violinist Endre Hoffmann was racked by the same questions. He had been brought up as a Protestant, but came from a Jewish family. In his home town, Budapest, he had studied with the legendary Jenő Hubay and then formed his own string quartet. Antal Dorati, who had been touring the distant continent since September 1938 as conductor of the de Basil Russian ballet company, suggested to him, and the publisher Victor Alberti, that they should emigrate to Australia. Thereupon Hoffmann applied for a permit on 26 April; just a few weeks after the Germans entered Prague.[82] In his application, he wrote that he wanted to work as a violinist and music teacher in his new homeland and was therefore already in contact with the Australian Broadcasting Commission. As contacts he named Pastor Bottomley in East Melbourne, and Antal Dorati. His application was successful, even though the war made the journey difficult. Finally, at the end of January 1940, Hoffmann boarded the *Viminale* in Genoa, the ship that also brought Lily Kolos and her sister to Sydney on 18 March. His life had been saved. That said, it was years before Endre Hoffmann was able to work again as a musician. Lily Kolos was luckier, both professionally and personally. She married soon after her arrival, having met her future husband on the ship during the voyage.

CHAPTER 8

The Refugee Problem from an Australian Perspective

Thorold Waters and the *Australian Musical News*

The Australian musical public was always interested to hear what was happening in Britain and on the European Continent, the models that they wished to emulate. London was regarded by them as the centre of the musical world, followed by Berlin, Leipzig, Vienna and Bayreuth. In response to this interest, by the summer of 1933 the monthly *Australian Musical News* (established in 1911) described the effects of Hitler's rise to power on German musical life. Apparently the great soloists Fritz Kreisler, Bronislaw Huberman and Pablo Casals were refusing to play with the Berlin Philharmonic in protest against the racial policies of the Nazi regime.

Thorold Waters, editor of the *Australian Musical News* since 1923, was born in London, where he was a young singer until the First World War ended his musical career.[1] He had already experienced the first wave of Zeppelin bombing in the British capital before he enlisted as a soldier. Despite a patriotic admiration for his countryman Edward Elgar, he had once regarded Arthur Nikisch as the greatest living conductor[2] (even above Beecham and Toscanini) and also revered Fritz Kreisler, Lotte Lehmann and Wilhelm Backhaus. The war, however, taught him to distance himself from Germany.[3] In 1916, London's Bechstein Hall was seized and closed, and reopened in 1917 as the Wigmore Hall. Some years after the war, Waters moved to Australia, where he became the first full-time professional music critic. In 1933, his wartime experiences led him to compare Hitler with Kaiser Wilhelm II. Waters reported that the conductors Bruno Walter and Otto Klemperer had been excluded from German musical life, and that further restrictions were now to be feared: 'Presumably the music of

Mendelssohn, Mahler and others who were Jews will also be banished by Herr Hitler.'[4] Meanwhile, besides Kreisler, Huberman and Casals, famous artists such as Wilhelm Furtwängler and Arturo Toscanini were said to have also protested against the persecution. Waters welcomed this and then made a suggestion:

> Since Germany has made herself an artistic outcast in the estimation of so many eminent musicians, this might be an opportune moment for enterprising Australian concert managements to negotiate for some of those who would otherwise have been busy in Berlin and the other German cities for several months of the year. What about that grand violinist Bronislaw Huberman for a tour?[5]

Jewish readers of the *Australian Musical News* would have followed such reports and comments particularly closely. The next edition reported that, as a result of Hitler's 'mean and cruel policy', the Australian pianist Nancy Weir had left Berlin with her teacher Artur Schnabel in order to continue her studies with him in Italy. She demanded a German boycott: 'Don't go to Germany while Hitler is running it.'[6] Then in February 1934 there was an article about Mary Baillie, another Australian Schnabel student who had followed her teacher to Italy. Herr Hitler, she said, had turned Schnabel into a musical nomad.[7]

In April 1938, the same publication ran a comprehensive 'Editorial of the Month' about the musical consequences of the Anschluss. Up to now, Hitler had been astoundingly successful by following the Bismarck model. If this success continued, the world would be faced with the difficult task of finding a home for the persecuted Jews. Under the heading 'Would Touch Australia', Thorold Waters suggested that Hitler's Jewish policies could also affect this country. Following the news that Wilhelm Backhaus had been ordered by the Reichsmusikkammer not to appear under a Jewish conductor in Antwerp, Waters posed the question: What would happen if this highly esteemed pianist were to give a concert in Melbourne with Bruno Walter? Could it reach the point where by raising an objection the Reichsmusikkammer in Berlin could control musical life in Australia? If one were forced to choose between German and Jewish artists, the author continued, Jews were preferable.[8]

While the editor of the *Australian Musical News* considered Hitler to be far more dangerous than Bismarck or Wilhelm II, other members of the Australian musical public regarded these views as exaggerated. At around the same time, in March 1938, the music theorist from Melbourne's Conservatorium, James Arthur Steele, found himself in Vienna just as the German troops invaded. In the *Australian Musical News*, Steele reported on the large squadrons of warplanes that he had already observed in Munich. In Vienna, he happened to be staying at the same hotel as the German High Command but, according to him, the German officers had behaved correctly and as gentlemen.[9] Steele had obviously not noticed any persecution of Jews, as he made no mention of it. Rather, he reported the deep musical impressions he experienced in Vienna, following those in Mozart's birthplace in Salzburg, the Bach House in Eisenach, the Leipzig Thomaskirche and the masterly performances at the Berlin State Opera.

'I'm absolutely plagued by refugees': Bernard Heinze and the ABC

Professor Bernard Heinze, a colleague of the pro-German James Steele at the University of Melbourne Conservatorium, took his time to form an opinion. He had connections to Germany through his ancestors: his father, a German watch maker, had emigrated to Australia and married a British woman. Although Heinze fought with the British during the First World War, he later studied violin with Willy Hess at the Berlin Hochschule für Musik. He was now Head of the University Conservatorium in Melbourne, an institution that also represented German traditions, since it was originally founded by George Marshall-Hall along the lines of Dr Hoch's Conservatory in Frankfurt am Main (hushed up after the war). Heinze had always been interested in radio as an educational tool. Established in 1932, the Australian Broadcasting Commission had been modelled on the BBC, so the British conductor Malcolm Sargent was intended to be its first music adviser. When Sargent cancelled at short notice, Heinze moved into this influential position, even though he was not of the same calibre.[10] Once in, with the support of ABC Chairman Charles Moses, he defended his leading role all the more doggedly.[11] Although in 1935 Heinze was of the opinion that foreign Jewish artists already exercised enough influence on Australian musical life,[12] he still invited star soloists like Yehudi Menuhin (1935), Bronislaw Huberman (1936) and Artur Schnabel (1938).[13] On the other hand, he was more touchy about conductors, whom he regarded as rivals. His relationship with Maurice Abravanel, who was a better conductor and very popular with the Australian public and press, was particularly tense. When one of the major newspapers, Sydney's *Daily Telegraph* proposed Abravanel as chief conductor of the Sydney Symphony Orchestra, Heinze defended himself vehemently.[14]

Heinze admired the Finnish conductor Georg Schnéevoigt, who had trained in Leipzig and Vienna and was for many years chief conductor of the Helsinki, Oslo and Malmö orchestras; he had toured Australia several times.[15] From January to November 1938, Heinze undertook an extensive concert tour of the USA and Europe in order to broaden his knowledge and make a name for himself as a conductor outside Australia. In Los Angeles he heard Otto Klemperer, but was unimpressed. In New York he went to a concert featuring Abravanel that only confirmed his negative opinion; he felt this colleague was 'a nuisance'.[16] In contrast, Heinze proudly reported the positive reaction to his own concerts in Europe, where he had clearly flaunted his British nationality: 'Every night, with my prayers, I repeat fervently, "Long Live England and God Save the King", and thank you for making me a Britisher.'[17]

In Europe, Heinze was exposed to political discussion, which kept returning to the threat of war. When they heard of his influential position in Australia, many Jewish musicians approached him, but he saw no way to help them. In June 1938, he wrote to his Conservatorium colleague Sutton Crow:

> I am being absolutely plagued by refugees from Germany and Central Europe, who think that I have unlimited positions to offer them in Australia. The enclosure is just another one of hundreds of applications. [...] Would you be so good as to place her application before the Faculty and write to her address a card explaining that there is not a vacancy at present.[18]

Time and again, he warned interested parties of the difficulties involved in emigrating to Australia. In June 1938, he told one prospective immigrant that if he did not bring enough money to last for a year, he should not even consider emigrating.[19] He was evidently unaware of how desperate the situation was for these applicants, for whom it was often a matter of life and death.

Earlier, Heinze had already established that Australia had no permanent positions on offer: 'Have your visiting conductors and artists by all means but let it be understood they are visitors.'[20] Otherwise Australia would quickly become a dumping ground for the unemployed from the Old World.[21] He cited the USA as a warning: there, the 'invasion' of European musicians had caused many complaints from local artists.[22] In another letter from Europe, Heinze mentioned a 'Jewish invasion in Australia', for which a solution was urgently needed. With the exception of Switzerland, he had experienced antisemitic campaigns all over Europe in response to this wave of refugees. As Britain and France could no longer take in any more Jews, hopes rested on the USA. Germany had unleashed eighty-two opera conductors and seventy-six concert conductors on the world, all of them experienced in their profession. As nowhere were there as many opera houses or symphony orchestras as in Germany, these Jewish conductors were now being 'poured over the face of the globe like treacle over a bread roll'.[23] It was particularly awkward that these Jews did not want to understand that there were not enough jobs in this field. An impresario in New York had shown him a list of twenty-eight qualified conductors, 'all of whom were willing to take the next boat for anywhere in Australia. They all appeared to have great credentials'. Some months previously, in an official letter to the head of the ABC, Heinze had already warned of 'the coming deluge of refugee conductors'.[24] As the very best artists had already found work, he said, many desperate provincial conductors were now crowding the market. Although they often had glowing references, one should be extremely careful. After all, the limited number of positions in Australia were already filled. Overseas guests could be unwelcome competition or even a threat – not least to Heinze himself.

In his official reports for the ABC, Heinze assumed that there would be hardly any first-rate musicians among the refugees by then entering into the country. In June 1938, however, in a letter to Percy Grainger, he mentioned that during his stay in England he had been approached by first-class conductors of top orchestras such as the Berlin Philharmonic, Vienna Philharmonic, Milan's La Scala and the Berlin State Opera. In September, he asked Bronislaw Huberman for advice as the enquiries were piling up. Huberman replied that there was no central register for musicians who were out of work. He recommended that Heinze travel to Vienna himself to contact former members of the Vienna Philharmonic who had lost their positions on account of being Jewish or married to a Jew and had to leave Vienna as a matter of urgency.[25] That said, Heinze's willingness to help was limited not only by the job situation. He also feared that the influx of Germans and Austrians would jeopardise the so far distinctly British character of Australian musical life. In the above-mentioned letter to Percy Grainger, of whose racist views he was well aware, he wrote: 'This exodus from Germany seems to me to indicate the replacement of British musicians by others throughout the world.'[26] At that time, even the otherwise tolerant composer Ralph Vaughan Williams warned of a 'Little Europe' in England, which he saw not as an opportunity, but as a threat.[27] From the point of view of cultural dominance, the 'infiltration' of outstanding musicians was regarded as even more dangerous than the influx of second-rate provincial conductors.

'The fickle nature of the Australian musical public': Handling the Immigrants

Heinze only gradually developed these reservations about Jewish musicians from Europe. At the beginning of 1933, when the members of the touring Spivakovsky–Kurtz Trio revealed their intentions to settle permanently in Australia, several musical institutions regarded this as a great opportunity and offered them positions. The fact that they decided on the Melbourne University Conservatorium was influenced by their personal relationship with Bernard Heinze, who soon became a friend of Jascha Spivakovsky. The Trio gave a series of four concerts at the Conservatorium as early as September 1934.[28]

In 1934, just two years after it was founded, the ABC started to put on concerts, which was viewed as serious competition by the commercial concert agencies that had dominated the scene for so long.[29] The powerful J. & N. Tait agency, already suffering from the Great Depression, lost its battle for supremacy. The national broadcasting body became the main concert agency and, as a monopoly, ABC Radio was probably unparalleled in any other country. The Spivakovsky brothers now had to accept that, for the next few years, or possibly even decades, the ABC would be their sole concert agent. The Australian Broadcasting Commission used the prominent artists available to them. In May 1936, together with the Melbourne Symphony Orchestra, the ABC launched its 'Celebrity Concerts' with the conductor Maurice Abravanel and the piano soloist Jascha Spivakovsky.[30] An Adelaide-based agency by this name had brought the Spivakovsky–Kurtz Trio to Australia, and the term 'celebrity' continued to refer to foreign guest artists.

When the Spivakovsky–Kurtz Trio arrived in 1933, they were promoted as a unique opportunity for Australia to hear 'Three World Stars in One Programme [...]. Time will permit only a very limited number of recitals in each city'. This changed when the artists settled in Australia; in principle they were now available all the time. What was limited, though, was the demand, especially for a specialist ensemble such as a piano trio. Moreover, Australia was not the ideal starting point for more extensive concert tours. Edmund Kurtz recognised this quickly and was the first to draw the consequences. On 10 July 1936, he wrote to the Chairman of the ABC:

> Dear Mr Moses,
> After much consideration about my future in Australia or America I have decided to leave here. I think America will offer bigger opportunities for my future. I have yet to arrange the necessary formalities, but I do not think there will be any difficulties and we shall probably leave by the 'Mariposa' on 15th August from Melbourne, or 19th August from Sydney. I will be very sorry to leave Australia because I have been so happy here [...].[31]

From the point of view of his career, this was a clever move, particularly as Kurtz could only receive citizenship in 1940 at the earliest. At first the cellist had lived in Melbourne's Menzies Hotel, but had to move out because of his copious practising. He found a new space in the Centenary Building in Exhibition Street, where the artist and cartoonist Noel Counihan visited and turned pages for him and also drew a portrait.[32] Kurtz formed other contacts among the locals, including the Australian Barbara Bellair, whom

172 CHAPTER 8: *The Refugee Problem from an Australian Perspective*

Figure 12: Programme for a Celebrity Concert of the Melbourne Symphony Orchestra in cooperation with the Australian Broadcasting Commission on 23 May 1936 at the Melbourne Town Hall. Guest stars were Jascha Spivakovsky and the conductor Maurice de Abravanel. Weber's *Oberon* Overture was followed by the Brahms Symphony No. 1, Beethoven's Piano Concerto No. 4 and his *Leonora* Overture No. 3. (Michael Spivakovsky, Melbourne)

he married in May 1936. In spite of his marriage and his lectureship at the University Conservatorium, he did not want to stay in Australia. In 1937, they moved to the USA where he was immediately engaged as principal cellist for the Chicago Symphony Orchestra, a prestigious position that Australia would never have been able to offer.

For Jascha and his brother Tossy, such a decision was impossible, as they had already encouraged other family members to come to their new country. Naturally they made an effort to arrange regular performances in Australia, which at the time was also in the ABC's interests. In August 1936, Charles Moses offered the members of the Trio a long-term arrangement in the form of weekly broadcasts. This deal formed the basis for Jascha's decision to stay permanently in Australia and, since it was to be a long-ranging contract, he accepted lower fees than usual. But evidently the Australian public was not yet ready for such a solution. In December 1936, in his capacity as Director of Music for the ABC, Heinze was already warning Charles Moses of the changed circumstances in a memorandum:

> There is no doubt about the fickle nature of the Australian musical public. When Jascha Spivakovsky came to Australia in his first solo tour his success was a furore. The press could not find sufficient superlatives to accommodate it in its approval of his work, and the public flocked to hear him. The moment he signified his intention to stay in Australia he was labelled 'local', a foul term guaranteed to sink even one of the heavenly muses in the fickle sea of public opinion.[33]

It is possible that, during his studies in Berlin, Heinze had come across the pianist who was now his friend and neighbour in Melbourne's illustrious Toorak. He knew only too well that the Australian public wanted something 'sensational'. The pianist himself was aware of this, which is why he tried hard to present a variety of programmes. From 1935 onwards, he and his brother Tossy gave a concert every Sunday evening on ABC radio, and in the process they performed almost their entire repertoire. Unfortunately, almost none of these recordings survive. Jascha then offered the ABC some interesting programmes intended to demonstrate the historical development of the piano concerto. However, the ABC had problems integrating such ideas into its programming.

Because of the public's attitude described by Heinze, it became increasingly difficult for the ABC to use the brothers' weekly recordings. In December 1937, Charles Moses wanted to change their contract. But in a letter that they both signed, Jascha and Tossy stressed

> that the conditions of this agreement are the basis of our living and, therefore, we came to the conclusion, after much consideration, that it is impossible for us to accept a change of the essential feature of our contract, viz. the regularity of our weekly engagements.

In February 1938, when the ABC informed the pianist that they would no longer pay his usual fee, he answered that under these conditions he was not prepared to make any appearances. As the ABC had a monopoly on orchestral concerts in Australia, Jascha Spivakovsky was not heard in a single orchestral concert for the next two years.

Although the brothers were allowed to play their weekly performances as per contract, other members of the broadcasting company now shared the reservations expressed by Heinze and Moses. In March 1938, Keith Barry wrote in a memorandum:

> Frankly, I am very concerned about this weekly appearance of a foreign violinist and pianist over such a very long period. No one questions the excellence of the work in particular of Tossy Spivakovsky, but one doubts whether from the point of view of the listeners he has not overstayed his welcome, especially in view of the large fee we are paying him.

In June 1938, Jascha Spivakovsky gained Australian citizenship and was no longer a foreigner. For him, this was not an entirely positive development, since he and his brother had been highly esteemed precisely on account of their European descent. When they became ordinary citizens, this attractiveness disappeared. Jascha was now forced to acknowledge that a much friendlier welcome was extended to guest soloists like Yehudi Menuhin or Artur Schnabel, whom he considered his equals. Schnabel was taken aback by the 'publicity madness […] surpassing everything managed elsewhere'. He explained it by the underdeveloped musical life in Australia. 'Until six years ago, they knew only "sensations" of the variety type: impresario-celebrities. Music, as a value of its own, begins only now to enter.'[34]

In February 1939, Jascha Spivakovsky sent a telegram to Charles Moses asking to speak with him personally. This put Moses in a difficult position because, although he greatly admired the pianist, he also had to take into account the opinion of his staff. In June 1939, Moses received a letter from Heinze in which he complained that in a recent concert, Tossy – contrary to their agreement – had played an encore. 'This is just another example of the arrogance of this family, and I only hope that the Commission will deal summarily with this misdemeanour.' Now Heinze described the two brothers as arrogant. Their 'arrogance' lay in their insistence that they were world class; also, they were regarded as being impertinent to artists who were not their equals. In personal discussions with Heinze, Jascha had often expressed the opinion that standards in Australia were well below those in Europe, especially in the field of piano playing. There had been quarrels about this as Heinze had not always given Spivakovsky the best students. Naturally, Tossy was also surprised and shocked when the ABC informed him that, before he could be engaged for any more recordings, he had to pass an audition.

Although both Spivakovsky brothers should have become legends in Australian musical life, they were criticised more and more. In July 1939, Moses received another memorandum from one of his colleagues:

> From the point of view of programme interests I do not think the Spivakovskys mean anything more than any other resident Australian artist. They undoubtedly do better work than practically any of the other artists but their prolonged series of appearances has quite taken the edge off the listener's appetite for them.[35]

Evidently artistic quality was less important than the principles of novelty and variety. Furthermore, their less capable colleagues were jealous and felt themselves at a disadvantage – a phenomenon known in Australia as 'tall poppy syndrome'.[36] Bernard Heinze might well have had the Spivakovsky brothers in mind when, in the summer of 1938, he reacted with such reservation to the immigration plans of other European musicians.

Final Negotiations: Official Immigration Policy

At the Evian conference in July 1938, very few countries had been willing to accept Jewish refugees. Switzerland reacted negatively: in August 1938, the president of the Swiss Centre for Refugee Aid asked 'whether it wouldn't be better to close the borders completely, because it would be much more difficult to remove refugees than to keep them away'.[37] Indeed, on 7 September the Swiss police actually ordered that 'German passport holders who were Jews or very probably Jews' be turned away. Today there is still speculation about whether the Jewish stamp put into German passports from autumn 1938 onwards was in fact introduced on the initiative of Switzerland. Hopes were focused on the Intergovernmental Committee on Refugees, which was founded at the end of the Evian conference to draw up and implement an aid programme. The director of this committee, lawyer George Rublee from Washington (a personal friend of President Roosevelt), negotiated with representatives from the German government. His first negotiating partner was the President of the Reichsbank, Hjalmar Schacht, who had developed a plan for the controlled emigration of 150,000 to 200,000 Jews following the excesses of Kristallnacht.[38] In January 1939, when Schacht was relieved of his position because of disagreements with Hitler, negotiations were continued by Ministerial Director Helmuth Wohlthat; this finance specialist from Göring's 'Office for the Four-Year Plan' [Amt für den Vierjahresplan] had lived for several years in New York and represented Germany in Evian.[39] In January 1939, a little-known deal was drawn up through correspondence, under which the German government agreed to the controlled emigration of 400,000 Jews.[40] In July 1939, at its meeting in London, the committee was satisfied that anti-Jewish restrictions in Germany had now been relaxed.[41] Although there was no doubt that the long-term intention was to expel Jews from Germany, there were still not enough countries prepared to take in these refugees. Therefore the German government supported the idea of their migration to British-mandated Palestine – to this end, Heydrich's Security Service worked together with the Zionist Mossad – and also discussed deportation to the island of Madagascar, a plan developed in the Foreign

Office.[42] The Intergovernmental Committee, on the other hand, favoured countries like Australia, Canada and the Dominican Republic.

After the Evian conference, Australia declared itself willing to accept a total of 15,000 refugees from Germany within a three-year period. Five hundred of these were to be chosen annually from Jewish welfare societies, which would then also provide financial guarantees. The majority, namely 300 people a month, could immigrate as long as they were able to provide the 'landing money' of £200. Finally, each year Australia would admit 1,000 people for whom relatives or friends in Australia could provide security.[43] Compared with the c.29,000 people who were admitted annually to the USA and the 50,000 immigrants Australia took in every year before the Great Depression, this offer appeared modest. That said, prior to this, markedly fewer Austrians and Germans had received landing permits for Australia. The numbers had risen from five Austrians and thirty Germans in 1933 to six and thirty-seven (1934), five and fifty-eight (1935), seventeen and 161 (1936), and by 1937 to forty-four Austrians and 543 Germans. According to the Australian department of the interior, probably 90 per cent of these immigrants were Jews.[44] By 1938, the numbers of refugees had grown enormously: by December 1938, 5,100 refugees had already arrived in the country.[45] Although the news of Kristallnacht aroused horror in Australia – according to the *Sydney Morning Herald*, Germany had regressed to the Dark Ages of Attila[46] – and although the High Commissioner had even suggested to the Prime Minister that 30,000 Jewish refugees be accepted, the number remained unchanged: 15,000 within a three-year period.[47] In view of concerns that the newcomers could take jobs away from the locals, it was requested that only 'suitable' persons be allowed to immigrate. This was also welcomed by the majority of Australian Jews, who did not want their secure social status to be threatened by any new antisemitic sentiment.[48] The government went along with these demands, and basically treated refugees as migrants.[49]

When John McEwen, the Australian Minister for the Interior, announced on 1 December that his government was prepared to accept 15,000 German refugees over the next three years, the response was predominantly positive. The High Commissioner in London criticised the issuing of landing permits in Canberra, however, as this usually took five months or more. In order to reduce these delays, he asked that the selection of acceptable refugees take place in Europe. Thus, on 25 January 1939, T.H. Garrett, Assistant Secretary to the Minister for the Interior, suggested in a memorandum that a central immigration office under the control of a Chief Migration Officer should be established in Australia House in London. He was to be assisted by two experienced officers from Australia, and if necessary by local support staff. In 1936, however, Garrett had still been very sceptical about accepting Jewish refugees:

> Jews as a class are not desirable immigrants for the reason that they don't assimilate; speaking generally, they preserve their identity as Jews. It would not be desirable that the Government should give its blessing to any scheme involving block nominations of Jews for admission into the Commonwealth.[50]

This scepticism also affected his new proposals: London could approve immigration for Jewish applicants with at least £3,000 and Aryans or non-Aryan Christians with at least £200, if 'there is no doubt that they can be absorbed in Australia without detriment to Australian workers or industry'.[51] All other cases, by far the largest proportion of applications, were to be sent to Canberra for further processing. This proposal, which substantially favoured non-Jews over Jews and left poorer applicants with almost no chance, was ratified by the cabinet within a month.

To test the plan's feasibility, Garrett travelled to London in April with Major R.H. Wheeler, who was responsible for immigration. On 11 July, the two Australians arrived in Berlin where they visited Captain Foley at the British Passport Control Office. They explained to him that the purpose of their visit was to select suitable refugees for Australia, and Foley was immediately prepared to co-operate. Although he had previously made efforts to accommodate Jews who wished to emigrate, he now expressed concerns to his visitors, and thereby confirmed their reservations:

> Captain Foley, who takes a leading part in interviews, stated that many Jewish refugees who had received landing permits for Australia had created an unfavourable impression when they called for visas. He expressed the view that quite a number of them were unsuitable.

The Australians spent the rest of the day in the interview room of the Passport Control Office. 'The alien applicants for visas, who were

Official Immigration Policy

virtually all Jews, presented an interesting study. There were some excellent types, but on the other hand many would not be considered suitable for Australia.'[52]

Three days later, Foley arranged a meeting with two representatives from the Hilfsverein, Julius L. Seligsohn and E. Cohn. The report that Garrett sent to Canberra includes the following:

> The Commonwealth's policy in regard to refugees was outlined to these gentlemen. Dr Seligsohn stated that he appreciated what the Commonwealth Government was prepared to do to alleviate the position of refugees, and that it was the desire of his organisation that only the best should be selected.[53]

> Dr Seligsohn stated that there were approximately 300,000 refugees in Germany and 200,000 in Austria, all of whom would like to go to Australia.

> Dr Seligsohn wanted to know what categories Australia wanted. In reply, he was informed that every case was dealt with on its merits and that categories could not be given. He was informed that people who could not follow their professions in Australia would not be acceptable, generally speaking, for the reason that in Australia they would be unskilled workers.

The next day, 15 July, Garrett – having had no discussions in Berlin with the relevant state authority, the Reich Centre for Jewish Emigration [Reichszentrale für jüdische Auswanderung] – met a Mr W. Creighton at the Passport Control Office in Nazi-occupied Prague. Creighton represented a London co-ordination bureau that had put aside £1,000,000 for refugees from Czechoslovakia. Although Creighton at first wanted to supervise the selection of these refugees himself, the job had meanwhile been taken over by the Czech Minister for Welfare. Nevertheless, Creighton confirmed that the Czech Jews were good people.

The two Australians' tour of inspection continued the following day in Vienna. Here they visited Mr Berry, the British Passport Control Officer, who right from the start was in enthusiastic agreement that at last a selection process should be introduced for refugees:

> Mr Berry expressed the view that the Jews in Berlin were a much better type than those in Vienna. He emphasised that the further east one went, the poorer was the type of Jews. He stated that most of the Jews in Vienna come from Hungary, Roumania and Poland.

> Mr Berry pointed out that, for the most part, the German Jews had been resident in Germany for many generations and had become civilised whereas the Jews in Austria had, for the most part, resided in Austria for one or two generations only. Mr Berry expressed the view that the main idea of the Kultusgemeinde was to get as many Jews out of Austria as possible and that there was a grave danger that, on compassionate grounds, as many applications as possible would be endorsed by this Organisation.

The Kultusgemeinde, however, along with the police and other Viennese authorities, was not to be trusted. 'He described the authorities and people in Vienna as the most corrupt in the world.' That was why, on principle, the Passport Control Office would never accept references from the police. The Briton reiterated his views on the limited suitability of Eastern European Jews in Vienna, thereby adopting the racial hierarchy of the Nazi regime: 'The Polish Jew is the worst, then come the Hungarian and Roumanian in that order.' Only at the end did he mention the terrible plight of many applicants:

> Mr Berry stated that if a refugee had some prospect of emigration, it may prevent him from being placed in a concentration camp. He suggested that it would possibly help the individual if he were to receive a communication to the effect that his application was under consideration.[54]

The next day, following their visit to the relevant British official, the two Australians interviewed representatives of the Israelitische Kultusgemeinde. They openly described the desperate situation of the Austrian Jews:

> They informed us that on 13th March, 1938, there were 180,000 Jews in Austria, of whom 165,000 were in Vienna. 15,000 Jews who were outside Vienna had since gone to Vienna. On 20.6.39, there were about 73,000 Jews left in Austria, all in Vienna.
>
> We were informed that of the 73,000, there were 40,000 being fed from soup kitchens conducted by the Organisation.
>
> Generally speaking Jews now remaining in Vienna have very little money left. None of them has been permitted to work for over a year and any money they had has been used in living etc.
>
> The big problem now confronting the organisation is to dispose of the 73,000 who are almost entirely without funds. The representatives of the organisation stated that it would be useless to expect that these people would have landing money.

> The conclusion reached was that the best types had already left Austria and that a very rigid selection would be necessary in respect of those who are left.

After this discussion, Garrett and Wheeler were convinced that the selection process of the Kultusgemeinde was driven not by 'objective' measures but above all by sympathy. This was confirmed when one representative suggested that Australia should take in 50,000 Jews per year instead of 5,000. It gave them pause for thought to hear that the German Jewish Aid Committee in London re-examined all refugees from Vienna. Nevertheless, so far only 1,600 Austrian Jews had moved to Australia. Far greater contingents had gone to the USA (21,100), South America (6,500), Africa (2,500) and Asia (17,100). These details provided by the Kultusgemeinde referred only to practising Jews. Right at the end, Garrett and Wheeler learned of approximately 100,000 more non-practising Mischlinge who were still living in Austria.

In Vienna, the two Australians checked out the Kultusgemeinde soup kitchen and also its main synagogue, which had been destroyed. They were shocked by the condition of the synagogue: 'One could not imagine that in a so-called civilised community such wanton havoc and destruction could have been wrought.'[55] Their tour of inspection then continued through Budapest, Bucharest, Warsaw, Geneva, Paris and Brussels before ending in London in August. Here Garrett and Wheeler met members of Jewish committees who made it clear during heated debates that they disagreed with the position taken by the Australian Jewish Welfare Society. Garrett reported to Canberra on August 24: 'The chief difficulty, however, is not ours, although we are definitely interested. It is the relationship between the Jewish Committee here and the A.J.W.S. [Australian Jewish Welfare Society] in Australia. The Committee here holds the purse and wants to call the tune.' Clashes like this had arisen earlier, for instance towards the end of 1936, when Otto Schiff, the chair of the Jewish Refugee Committee in London, inquired of Julian Layton:

> What I am desirous of knowing is whether you think there is a chance in Australia for selected Refugees. You want to be a bit careful whom you approach on the subject, as, unfortunately, many of our co-religionists, instead of helping, are only too anxious to keep out these unfortunate people.'[56]

At the time, Layton was travelling to Vienna and Berlin on behalf of the Home Office (Aliens Department) in order to seek out suitable candidates for the Kitchener Camp in Richborough.

Garrett summarised the results of his travels in a final report. He pointed out that the Berlin Hilfsverein was not to be trusted in the selection of refugees because of its dependence on the Gestapo. Representatives of the German Jewish Aid Committee in London, he said, had confirmed his opinion. And even less so could the Viennese Kultusgemeinde act as a selection committee. Polish Jews were not at all suitable for emigration to Australia, anyway, as his visits to several ghettos had shown. In view of these serious reservations, the Australian government official proposed that the selection be left to Australia House in London:

> As a result of further investigation of the question, it is considered that, from the point of view of Australia, the best results would be obtained if all cases submitted to Australia House by applicants and thought worthy of consideration were to be vetted by an official organisation.

With regard to the refugees, not humanitarian considerations, but his country's economic interests were the main consideration for this Australian official. That said, the number of refugees with sufficient funds and therefore of interest to his country as potential immigrants had, as Garrett observed, dwindled to almost nothing:

> Moreover, as time goes on, the refugees, especially in Germany, Austria and Czechoslovakia will deteriorate from the point of view of quality; speaking generally, the best have already left those countries. The number in Germany and Austria with sufficient capital (£200) to enable them to submit applications to Australia House is diminishing. It is understood that in a very short space of time this class will have virtually ceased to exist.

Garrett sent this devastating final report from London to the government in Canberra on 24 August. In an accompanying letter, he wrote: 'The international situation is anything but clear at the moment and, if war breaks out, the whole of my proposals for the time being at any rate would be skittled.' This warning was only too justified: just one week later, Hitler's Germany began the Second World War. As soon as Britain declared war on Germany, Australia stopped accepting further Jewish refugees.[57] The agreements reached with the Intergovernmental Committee in July 1939, on which so many hopes had been pinned, never came into effect. While the influx of refugees into China, that is Shanghai, continued to swell, including 17,500 Viennese Jews in 1940–1941 alone, in these two years only 1,701 Viennese Jews found refuge in Australia.[58] The promised number of 15,000 refugees was not nearly met. Nonetheless, 9,000 Jews came to Australia between 1933 and 1943,[59] a number that, when compared with the total number of inhabitants in that sparsely populated continent at the time, cannot be deemed low.

'You will be all right': Arrival in Australia

Prior to the war, which made immigration much more difficult, Jewish refugees from Germany had been arriving in Australia on a regular basis. Before disembarkation, they had to fill out a 'Personal Statement and Declaration' form in which, among other things, they were required to give details of their nationality and race. This irritated many refugees, as they hoped by now to have escaped from racial problems. Under 'Race', most of the Weintraubs Syncopators entered the word 'European'. Theodor Schoenberger decided on 'White', and Hermann Schildberger wrote 'German Jewish' – for him, the German was just as important as the Jewish. Further uncertainty was caused by the question about their intended occupation: the musicians knew that there were few opportunities for them in Australia. In 1935, when the Secretary of the Musicians' Union, Frank Kitson, warned the department of the interior of an influx of refugee musicians, he received the reply:

> Aliens desirous of entering the Commonwealth are always required to state the occupations they have followed and their intended occupations in Australia, and, under the existing rules, it would not be practicable for any influx of alien musicians to take place.[60]

As a result of this practice, Walter Dullo had immigrated as a masseur and confectioner. Heinrich Adler nominated 'Sales-manager' as his profession; he wanted to work in a fashion store in his new abode. In order to come to Australia, the violinist Ellen Cohn-Byk had written 'Home duties' on the form. Alphons Silbermann said that he wanted to work as a 'Caterer', and then replaced the word with 'Hotel Manager'. Some gave several occupations, especially if a musical profession was mentioned in their passport. The violist Richard Goldner named his intended occupations in Australia as 'Musician' and 'Carver'; the music critic Hans Forst wrote 'Teacher, musician or commercial', while the violinist Fritz Kramer preferred to immigrate as an 'Employee'.

Those who could show that they already had engagements as musicians were in a far better position. Kurt Herweg entered as an accompanist for the German dancer and Laban student Anny Fligg, who had been invited by the Women's League of Health and Beauty; immediately afterwards, he secured employment as a conductor at His Majesty's Theatre in Melbourne and as an organist on the grand cinema organ in Sydney's Prince Edward Theatre.[61] As pianist for the Bodenwieser Dance Company, Marcel Lorber was similarly privileged, although on the above-mentioned form he had written 'Composer'. With a contract for a position with the Beth Israel congregation in St Kilda, Hermann Schildberger was able to state 'Organist and choirmaster' as both his previous and future occupations. The self-confident Heinrich Krips had 'Conductor' in his passport and gave his preferred occupation in Australia as 'Director Orchestra', although he had no prospect of a position. Theodor Schoenberger called himself a 'Professor of Music', and stated that it was his desired occupation in Australia. At least he had relatives there. Gertrud Hacker from Vienna gave her profession as 'Pianist', although her prospects for future employment as a piano teacher were uncertain.

Most of the refugees settled in Melbourne and Sydney. Alphons Silbermann, who came to Sydney in October 1938, gave a graphic description of his arrival: 'Under the light of the roaring Australian sun', and 'drenched in sweat', he devoted his attention to 'answering endless questions from stocky customs officials in short pants'. He had to listen very carefully, as Australian English was markedly different in its pronunciation and vocabulary from the 'schoolboy' English with which he was familiar. When Silbermann's documents, landing permits and forms had been checked, he was met by representatives of the Australian Jewish Welfare Society, which then transported the refugees by bus directly to their community halls. They were urged to avoid any 'un-British' outbursts and not to speak German in public.[62] Fearful because of the widespread anti-Jewish and anti-German feeling, this organisation kept the arrivals as inconspicuous as possible, stipulating at the most six refugees per ship, always accompanied by an English teacher. A representative from the organisation then asked Silbermann to present himself for registration at their office in the Maccabean Hall in Darlinghurst:

> Apart from that, a meeting place was set up in a street called Pitt Street, where at lunchtime you could get a cup of tea and a buttered roll or something similar for three pence and good advice from volunteers from the Welfare Society.[63]

Silbermann did not find the recommendations very helpful: to adopt Australian manners and practices as quickly as possible, not to wear a long raincoat or carry a European leather briefcase, to Anglicise names and prepare for quick naturalisation.[64] Time and time again, the volunteers stressed how pleasant and liberal Australia was, and how generous it had shown itself to be by taking in the refugees. When it came to finding employment, however, the urgently hoped-for support did not materialise:

> The words 'You will be all right', accompanied by a jovial pat on the shoulder, still ring in his ears today as a motto for the Australian attitude to life in its entirety: everyone for themselves; beholden to none; see how you get on; it'll be OK; people don't perish in the land of pioneers – in reality that is the essence of this crash barrier erected in utter conviction.[65]

Besides the Australian Jewish Welfare Society,[66] which was judged more favourably by other refugees, there were other aid organisations such as the German Emergency Fellowship Committee (later renamed the European Emergency Committee) founded by the anthropologist Camilla Wedgewood in association with the German Jewish biochemist Max Rudolf Lemberg, the Victorian International Refugee Emergency Council, and the Inter-Church Committee for non-Aryan Christian Refugees. With the help of these organisations, the refugees were initially accommodated in boarding houses or furnished rooms. These were often located in busy neighbourhoods like Sydney's Kings Cross, especially Macleay Street and Challis Avenue, or in Melbourne's Carlton and St Kilda. In these suburbs, sometimes viewed with suspicion as Jewish enclaves,[67] the locals, who were accustomed to British food, were astonished to find a number of central-European delicatessens, cafés and restaurants. Sometimes weeks or months went by before the new arrivals had unpacked their luggage or containers.

Some of them succeeded in finding work relatively quickly. Palings, the large music house in George Street in the centre of Sydney, offered Fritz Coper work as a singing teacher. Emma Weiss was able to resume her profession as a piano teacher shortly after her arrival. The *Australian Musical News* had already referred to her in a short, illustrated article in May 1939.[68] Later it carried her advertisements offering tuition in piano, aural development, accompaniment and coaching for instrumentalists and singers. Coverage of the pianist Käthe Neumann, who had originally come on a tourist visa, was even more extensive. In March 1939, shortly after the young Viennese pianist had stepped in as soloist for a piano concerto by Eugen d'Albert, she gave a demanding piano recital that was generally well received,[69] followed by a radio performance on 23 June.[70] Until then, the pianist had given the impression that her residence in Australia was temporary. She only announced her intention to stay in the *Australian Musical News* of January 1940, when she offered to teach advanced students in the Rubinstein tradition of her own teacher, Paul de Conne.[71] By that time, Käthe Neumann knew that her parents were on their way to Australia, where they arrived in May.

The Viennese singer Emmy Kimmel, who came to Sydney with her husband and two children, faced huge difficulties. Her husband, the lawyer Dr Hans Kimmel,[72] had indicated on the application form that he had substantial capital and wanted to open a clothing factory in Australia, so he received a landing permit in 1938. Unfortunately, he then became ill, so initially his desperate wife wanted to emigrate without him in March 1939. The couple had already sold their flat in the Eighth District and had to vacate it. Emmy Kimmel and her children went to a boarding house while her husband was admitted to the Rothschild Hospital and then to the Kultusgemeinde Hospital. At the end of May, he was certified as healthy and discharged, whereupon they decided to travel together. There were further problems, however, as the Australian visa had been sent to their old address. On 3 June, the Kimmels finally checked out of the Pension Althan giving 'America' as their final destination, almost certainly in order to deceive the authorities. The family of four arrived in Sydney in mid-July, but Hans Kimmel soon fell ill again, and was admitted to a psychiatric clinic on account of his 'acute melancholy'. Under these circumstances, it was impossible to open a clothing factory. With the threat of deportation hanging over them, Emmy Kimmel earned their living by teaching voice and piano, and by making string shopping bags. In addition, she tried to bring her sick Catholic brother from Bolivia, yet, despite the intercession of Charles Pilcher, the Anglican Bishop of Sydney, her application was rejected. To improve her husband's nervous condition, the singer moved with him and the children from the city to the rural suburb of Pennant Hills in 1942. For 'security reasons', she was not permitted to give radio broadcasts during the war. She was, however, allowed to give recitals at the Conservatorium.

In rare cases, exile offered the refugees a chance to begin a new life in new surroundings, and to fulfil musical dreams that could never have been realised in their homeland. The economist Dr Rudolf Werther is one example. He had worked in the export business in Berlin and Paris and played music as a hobby. In May 1939, he arrived in Melbourne with numerous scores and a piano, where he quickly noted the city's well-developed musical life and the competition among the other refugees. He therefore decided to move to Tasmania and settle in the small city of Launceston, whose scenic beauty appealed to him. By August, he was giving lectures in music history, as well as piano tuition. Heinrich Adler, who had called himself a salesman on the application form, was also able to achieve his ambition to be a musician: he found work as a piano and accordion teacher at Nicholson's College for Modern Music.

Most exiled musicians, however, did not find work in their chosen profession but had to earn their living in other fields. Hence, outsiders would never know their real profession – as musicians they were neither seen nor heard. Peter Langer, for example, took up bookkeeping after his arrival in

Melbourne, which earned him a living. After that, he and a friend bought a sawmill with the money they had brought with them, which made substantial losses when petrol prices rose as a result of the war. The Viennese couple Arnold and Gertrud Hacker could only afford a small flat, so their Ehrbar baby grand remained in storage for a long time. Meanwhile, Gertrud Hacker worked in various jobs, including in a milk bar. The pianist Dory Stern also found no work in her profession at first; with her husband, she lived as the housekeeper for a language teacher, while her spouse, an electrician, tried to find a job. The violinist Ellen Cohn-Byk, who had started in Australia as a maid, later found only strenuous factory work. Endre Hoffmann, a violinist and Hubay student from Budapest, who had once played under Bruno Walter, had on arrival not hesitated to call himself a musician. Although the ABC invited him to make recordings, he tried in vain to become a member of the Musicians' Union and had to work in a shoe factory for three years. The violinist Fritz Kramer had entered as an 'employee', but hoped to continue his career as a musician. A few months after his arrival in Melbourne, an Australian woman recommended him to Bernard Heinze for an orchestral position. Kramer made an effort to obtain the required membership of the Musicians' Union, but this was denied as he was not yet naturalised. The violinist then reverted to his former occupation as a bookkeeper. The violist Richard Goldner found himself in a similar situation. Having at first intended to continue his musical career, he was also rejected by the Union; he and his brother then earned their living making brooches in a leather goods factory. The musical entertainer Willy Coper found casual work as a singer in a synagogue choir, and as a pedlar, but he also needed the support of his brother, Fritz. Cyril Schulvater, formerly a member of the Weintraubs Syncopators, was also initially unable to work as a musician in Australia. Together with his brother Ernest, a professional musician who had also come to Australia in 1939,[73] he ran a kosher meat business and later a hamburger shop. It was equally impossible for physicians to obtain work in their profession. Ernst Kaufmann's application to the NSW Medical Board was discussed in October 1939 and rejected on 7 August 1940.[74] Dr Martin Krutsch received similar news.

In the *Australian Musical News*, Thorold Waters suggested that a country as large as Australia should actually have been in a position to feed many more Jewish refugees. The problem was that there were so many intellectuals, lawyers and above all musicians among them. 'For every foreign barrister who slips through, there will be, in existing conditions, a round hundred or more musicians.'[75] It would be impossible to accommodate all of them in their previous professions. Just how difficult it was to find positions for the exiled musicians can be seen from a letter that Bernard Heinze wrote to Sir James William Barrett on 8 June 1939. This man, who rendered meritorious services to the university, had written in support of the violinist Lisbeth Caspary who, since her arrival, called herself Elizabeth Colin.

> Dear Sir James,
> [...] The whole matter of refugee musicians was discussed at length by Faculty this week. There were some ten applications for appointment to the staff of the Conservatorium. After serious deliberation it was decided to write to all of them stating that, while we were quite sympathetic with the desire to find employment for refugee musicians, unfortunately it would be wrong to encourage them to come to Australia on an appointment to the Conservatorium, which would carry no monetary advantages until such time as they were able to attract students [...].
>
> The position of the Spivakovskys was discussed, and it was pointed out that here the Conservatorium was actually engaging musicians of world repute, yet not enough students attended the classes of these teachers to warrant the appointment of still more foreign musicians to our staff. The case of Tossy Spivakovsky is lamentable: he has three students; this after being long with us and playing to Melbourne audiences for five years.
>
> I met Mrs. Colin. She was brought to the Conservatorium by Mrs. Kenny. I found her a charming, elderly woman, who apparently had been a student of Joachim. However, the Faculty felt that no good purpose would be served by appointing any of the applicants to the staff until we had reached a period in the development of music where we might reasonably expect that such teachers would be sought after by prospective students.
>
> With kindest regards,
> Bernard Heinze, Ormond Professor[76]

A year later, considering the under-developed musical life in Australia, Tossy Spivakovsky decided to leave the country and move to the USA, as had the cellist Edmund Kurtz before him. If such highly qualified musicians were giving up their lectureships and leaving Australia, it could hardly be expected that less eminent newcomers would find satisfactory jobs in this field.

CHAPTER 9

Under Union Scrutiny: The Weintraubs Syncopators

The Fight for Jobs

In Australia, there was strong resentment against German refugee musicians. Antisemitic and anti-German feelings were mixed with the anxiety that the new arrivals might take away jobs. In view of the economic crisis, the fear of even greater unemployment was prevalent among other professionals, including lawyers, doctors and dentists. The view was widespread that all unemployed Australians should have a job before allowing more foreigners into the country. The Labor Party warned that the influx of refugees would cause economic and social standards to fall. The Musicians' Union of Australia was particularly sensitive. It went beyond its traditional role of defending the workers' jobs by supporting the xenophobic and racist White Australia Policy, and by rejecting musicians from enemy countries; in April 1918, all Germans had been excluded from membership.[1] In 1929, the union's articles of association included the following aims:

- To promote industrial peace and efficiency in the workplace by all amicable means, such as conciliation, arbitration, or the establishment of a personal tribunal.
- To control the entry into the profession of any person who may desire to adopt same as a means of earning a living, and to make the profession as lucrative as to eliminate the necessity of any members having to resort to other employment outside the profession.
- To uphold and maintain the White Australia Policy, and prohibit the admission of colored races as members.

- To oppose, by all constitutional methods, the admission into Australia from overseas of professional orchestral musicians under contract or agreement to contract after arrival in Australia.
- To keep orchestras British.
- To insure that orchestras shall not include a greater percentage of foreigners than ten per cent.

Therefore, the members of the Musicians' Union were obliged

> to refuse to enter into employment in any orchestra where foreigners are employed in excess of the following proportion, that is: Orchestras of ten and under, 1 foreigner; of over ten and not more than 20, 2 foreigners; [...] and so in like proportion. [...] It shall not be deemed a breach of this rule if a member enters into employment in an orchestra with OVERSEAS VISITING MUSICIANS, in which the above proportions are exceeded, if the Federal Council shall approve. For the purpose of this rule foreigners shall mean all OVERSEAS MUSICIANS, other than natives of BRITISH (ENGLISH-SPEAKING) countries, who have joined the Union after Armistice Day (11th November 1927), and those who may hereafter join this Union.[2]

These rules were tightened in 1929 in reaction to the Great Depression and the introduction of sound film, which left three-quarters of the union members unemployed.[3] The union now stipulated a complete embargo on foreign musicians. At first this regulation applied only for one year, but was extended on an annual basis until 1935. In addition, the union was authorised to admit non-British applicants as members only after they had been resident in the country for five years and had obtained citizenship.[4]

On the other hand, the institution was also keen to foster any ideas for the employment of additional, home-grown musicians. Therefore, in 1935 it supported Maurice Abravanel's initiative for the establishment of a permanent symphony orchestra in Sydney. In interviews, the conductor had referred to musical life in Germany, where even the smaller cities funded their own orchestras, and he suggested that Australia should follow their example.[5] When Yehudi Menuhin supported the idea of a permanent orchestra and praised the qualifications of Australian musicians, the secretary of the Musicians' Union, Frank Kitson, issued a statement, emphasising that Australia had enough qualified workers.[6] However, as visiting conductors were often critical of the standards of Australian orchestras,

The Fight for Jobs

the ABC requested confidential reports from internationally renowned experts like Bronislaw Huberman and Georg Schnéevoigt. They agreed unanimously that there were weaknesses in certain sections, and declared the urgent need for overseas musicians and conductors to improve quality.[7] In this situation, applications from European refugee musicians must have seemed like a gift from heaven. On 5 December 1938, W.G. James, head of the ABC's Music Department, drafted a memorandum for Charles Moses entitled 'Refugee Musicians'. In it, he referred to the application from the Viennese conductor Heinrich Krips, who was said to be better in the field of opera than any conductor in Australia. Moreover, he explained, refugee musicians from Europe were arriving 'almost daily'. 'The work of some of them is of a high standard, so high that it is obvious that, if they are to be used on our programmes, they will, to a certain extent, displace Australian artists.' The ABC would therefore need to work out its own position regarding refugee musicians. He saw the following possibilities:

1. To replace a certain number of Australian artists by foreign artists whose work is possibly of a higher calibre;
2. To include foreign artists for our programmes on an equal footing with our own artists;
3. To pay to certain refugee artists a higher fee than that which is paid to the best Australian artists;
4. In regard to Orchestral Players, the possibility of certain members of our own Orchestras being thrown out of employment, as a result of an influx of middle-European artists of a possibly higher standard of work.[8]

As the overriding concern of the ABC's management was the musical quality of its broadcasts and concerts, in January, Charles Moses supported James's suggestion in a further memorandum:

> My own opinion is that if the Commonwealth Government is prepared to provide a home for some thousands of political refugees from Central Europe, it would not appear to be in keeping with Government policy were we to refuse opportunities to such of them who are sufficiently good to justify their inclusion in our programmes. Apart from the advisability of conforming to the policy of the Commonwealth Government, our duty to listeners is to provide them with the best radio entertainment it is within our power to give.

> [...] I would recommend that where a refugee artist is better than local artists of the same type, he should be given engagements at a fee at least equal to that paid to such Australian artists. It is unlikely that we will be swamped with an influx of artists of outstanding ability: in any case, our programmes are not so filled with first-class artists that we cannot give employment to a few more, better than those available to us at present.[9]

This was roughly the position taken by the BBC towards musicians in exile.[10] But when Charles Moses asked the secretary of the Musicians' Union for his opinion, he promptly replied: 'Preference of employment should be given to Britishers already resident in Australia. It seems abundantly clear that foreign musicians cannot be absorbed without injuring local players.'[11] He continued by saying that a single engagement for a foreigner was dangerous, because it would trigger a further influx of refugee musicians. Difficulties with the Musicians' Union had already surfaced in July 1938, when Malcolm Sargent asked the ABC to invite a few outstanding musicians from abroad in order to improve its orchestras. Moses had replied that he would gladly accept such a solution, as long as the union agreed.[12] The *Sydney Morning Herald* took this opportunity to promote a more generous approach to refugees and cited the architectural profession, which up to then had benefited from immigration. In this context, the paper mentioned the unsympathetic position taken by the Musicians' Union, whose secretary, Kitson, had explicitly spoken out against the immigration of foreign musicians from Hitler's Germany.[13] He could only support Sargent's suggestion if it involved British musicians who would remain in Australia for no longer than six months. The *Telegraph* reported Kitson's reservations about another group of people:

> We are clearly specifying Jews, because Dr Sargent may have some idea that his imported talent is coming from Palestine. He has been there, and he has talked so much about Palestine orchestras that we are wondering just what he has in mind.[14]

Moses was not intimidated by such objections, and asked for advice from the Postmaster-General, A.G. Cameron. But even Cameron sided with the union:

> I have no hesitation in saying that the Broadcasting Commission must give preference to Australian artists, and further, that no encouragement must be given to the

introduction of foreign artists for other than temporary engagements and on the understanding that they will depart from this country after the expiration of the term of their engagement. Refugee artists who desire to remain must take the same chances as refugee doctors, lawyers and other professionals.

Furthermore, Cameron went on:

Whilst the Commonwealth is endeavouring to attract population to this country, our main objectives are (and must remain) to attract persons who will be settlers, artisans, workers, or who would undertake the establishment of new industries. The capacity of this country to absorb musicians as such is strictly limited.[15]

When, despite this, Moses made further attempts to attract top-class musicians, including former section leaders from the Vienna Philharmonic, Kitson flatly denied that this was necessary. The local musicians, he argued, would meet all the requirements. Moses replied indignantly: 'In view of the Commission's endeavours to strengthen the weaker sections of the orchestras, and our undertaking that the imported players would not displace any of the existing players, the decision of your Union is disappointing, to say the least.'[16] Kitson's inflexible attitude was catastrophic for the ABC, for, indeed, there were not enough qualified musicians in Australia.

Needless to say, when migrant musicians applied for a work permit, the union was not obliging. For example, Richard Goldner tried in vain to join the Musicians' Union; even Tossy Spivakovsky and Bernard Heinze, whom he had asked to intercede on his behalf, were unable to help. Spivakovsky was outraged and wrote to Goldner: 'It is obvious that orchestras here are in dire need of a violist like you, – but what does ability count when nationality and "race" are the prerequisites for an existence even in this country!'[17] The violinist Fritz Kramer had also turned to Heinze on account of his problems with the union, whereupon the latter asked Jascha Spivakovsky, a union member since 1929, to mediate, but once again in vain. Kramer's violin colleague, Endre Hoffmann, was treated no better. In each case, the union sent the standard reply that Australian citizenship was a prerequisite for membership. And waiting time for that was five years.[18] The Conservatorium Director, Edgar Bainton, protested against this regulation, which one newspaper report declared downright crackpot:

A newcomer can join the union if he happened to be born in Britain, Ireland or Canada. But he can jump in the lake or work in a pickle factory if he happened to be born in Hungary or Austria. A fine advertisement for our liberalism and culture![19]

'Somewhere in the World': Jazz Stars on Tour

> Somewhere in the world
> There's a little bit of luck,
> And I dream of it every moment.
> Somewhere in the world,
> There's a little bit of bliss,
> And I've been dreaming of it for a long, long time. (Werner Richard Heymann and Robert Gilbert, 1932)[20]

The Musicians' Union's hostility to foreigners had a particularly disastrous effect on the fate of the Weintraubs Syncopators. 'Crazy People', 'New York – Berlin', 'Somewhere in the World' and 'Carnival' – these were the ominously suggestive titles of numbers from the jazz revue presented by the band in Berlin's Wintergarten in February 1933, before their performances were banned. In February 1935, the Weintraubs gave a farewell concert in Berlin, at the end of which, all that remained on stage were five empty chairs. The newspapers were not allowed to cover it. After that, the group went to Czechoslovakia in May, then to Switzerland and Sweden, and in September they began their highly successful tour of the Soviet Union. Following their spectacular concerts in Leningrad, there were appearances in Moscow and Tiflis in December and in Baku in January 1936. The tour was interrupted by guest performances in Hungary and Romania, and then continued in May with concerts in Soviet cities such as Stalingrad, Sochi, Smolensk, Vitebsk, Rostov and Odessa. In November 1936, the celebrated band arrived in Japan, where the unsuspecting promoters had decorated the venue with huge swastikas. By January 1937, they were making recordings in Tokyo and Kawasaki. The response was excellent, especially as the versatile Weintraubs used Japanese musical instruments in their programmes. But their manager, Heinz Barger, was looking around for new opportunities.

On 28 May 1937, Barger signed a contract in Sydney with Snider & Dean Theatres Ltd, one of the country's biggest cinema groups.[21] The Weintraubs troupe of twelve, consisting of seven performing artists, three of their partners, a lighting technician and a stage assistant, were to take their stage and vaudeville act on a sixteen-week tour, with the possibility of extensions. A flat fee of £225 per week was negotiated, as well as the travel costs from Kobe, Japan. Just a few days later, the Australian press reported on the engagement of 'about twelve instrumentalists' who played all kinds of music, 'ranging from jazz tunes to grand opera'.[22] After signing the contract, Barger travelled back to Japan, while Snider & Dean immediately approached the Australian department of the interior for an entry permit. On 3 June, a memorandum from the department described the agency as serious and financially sound. Since the tour would not threaten any Australian jobs, but rather create additional employment, it was considered favourably. This was by no means automatic: only a few months earlier, the union had protested against the entry of overseas bands.[23] The department now offered the Weintraubs a stay of twelve months, if the agency would undertake to guarantee them. Four days later, the minister signed the memorandum, and immediately a telegram was sent to the British Consul in Tokyo: 'Visit Australia approved Weintraubs theatrical troupe twelve persons. Interior 7.6.1937.' On the following day, the department sent a corresponding notification to the agency, which provided confirmation on 12 June:

> We ... herewith, as requested, undertake
> (a) the maintenance of these persons whilst in Australia,
> (b) that they will ultimately depart from this country,
> (c) that they will not become a charge upon any public or charitable institution whilst in the Commonwealth.

The above-mentioned telegram authorised the British Consulate in Kobe to issue a temporary visitor's visa for Australia for twelve months. Their passports in the Australian National Archives confirm that the respective visas were issued in Kobe on 11 June.[24] Apparently, that same day, the seven musicians and their entourage travelled by ship to Shanghai, whence they sailed south along the coast to Hong Kong, where they had to pick up an American transit visa, as the ship intended to sail for the US-controlled Philippines.²⁵ On 20 June, they arrived in Manila where they stayed for three days. Then the group – with its copious luggage, including a lot of instruments – transferred to the *Gorgon*, which docked in Fremantle on 14 July. The passenger list shows eleven members of the Weintraubs troupe with their profession, age, marital status and 'race':

Table 2: Weintraubs Syncopators according to the *Gorgon* Passenger List

Name	Profession	Age	Married/Single	Race
Mr Leo Weiss	Artist	29	M	German
Miss G. Bergmann	Dancer	23	S	Swedish
Mr J.K. Kaiser	Artist	30	S	Peruvian
Mr E. Frischer	Artist	24	S	Polish
Mr H. Graff	Artist	32	S	German
Mr S. Weintraub	Artist	39	S	German
Mr F. Goldner	Artist	23	S	Austrian
Mr C. Schulvater	Artist	29	S	S. African
Miss M. Graham	Dancer	23	S	English
Miss A. Paris	Dancer	20	S	Italian
Mr F.J. Wise	Artist	32	S	American

Under the heading 'Country of Last Permanent Residence', they had all entered 'Japan', whereas under 'Country of Intended Future Residence', they had all written 'Australia'. Personal Statement and Declaration forms had already been handed out during the trip; they had to give the name of the ship, travel class, date and place of arrival, as well as personal information including their nationality, and where their passports were issued. As their last permanent address, they gave their flats in Berlin.²⁶ With regard to the tricky questions about their former and future occupations, Weintraub, Graff and Weiss avoided the term 'Musician' and wrote 'Artist'. Unfavourable experiences with the American Musicians' Union may have played a part in this. Emanuel Frischer was even more cautious, and put

'Dentist' under both headings. The form also had questions about their funds, guarantors and whether they were tourists or planning to remain on a permanent basis. In view of the twelve-month temporary visa, Stefan Weintraub indicated that this was a year-long business trip.[27]

Once they reached Sydney on the *Manunda*, they began a four-week series of performances at the Mayfair Theatre. The combination of stage and screen had been announced as the latest trend in international cinema.[28] Twice daily, at 2 p.m. and 8 p.m., the musical troupe could be heard before a screening of the adventure film *Michael Strogoff* (after Jules Verne) at the film palace in elegant Castlereagh Street. The Weintraubs' live appearances brought enthusiastic reactions from the public and press alike. The critic for the *Sydney Morning Herald* described the musicians as 'particularly witty and adept exponents of their particular medium'. They brought much more to their programmes than just competent music-making; they were comedians and dancers who changed positions for new scenes with lightning speed, and masters of the art of suggestion. No matter how riotous the fun became, they maintained perfect timing and professionalism down to the smallest detail, and the time flew by. 'Although the entertainment actually lasted for 25 minutes, it seemed, in retrospect, to have occupied only half that period at most.'[29]

On 21 August, a short, three-minute Cinesound newsreel was issued, 'Weintraubs bring new musical act to Australia: Sydney'.[30] It showed the seven musicians in radiant white suits. A drum kit with the word 'Weintraubs' stood in front of a draped curtain rigged up with a giant saxophone, and in the centre was a white grand piano. While playing, the musicians would stand up and change places and instruments without interrupting the performance. Whoever was not sounding a wind instrument would also sing. The smooth transitions functioned with magical ease. At the end, Emanuel Frischer put two trumpets to his mouth and blew both at the same time. For the next number, the stage was in darkness with only one instrument in the spotlight: a violin. But there were no violin sounds, only that of a saxophone. After a few bars, a saxophone would enter with banjo sounds, or a piccolo in the bass register. Basically, you could not trust your eyes, because the sounds always contradicted the visual impression, creating an aural–optical illusion. John Kaiser performed an aria with all the dramatic gestures of an opera singer; he, however, moved just his lips, mouth, hands and shoulders, while the 'song' was produced by an invisible trombone using a wah-wah mute. Stefan Weintraub used drumsticks on his own head, increasing the volume by blowing out his cheeks as a resonating chamber. All these effects followed in rapid succession.

On 4 August, the day the Weintraubs began to perform in Sydney, an illustrated article in the *Sydney Mail* referred to a forthcoming tour of the Comedy Harmonists.[31] For each appearance, a large concert hall was booked for a whole evening; probably a source of some envy among the Weintraubs. Admittedly, their cinema appearances represented only part of their contract with Snider & Dean. The highlight was to be a spectacular revue, for which such well-known Australian entertainers as the comedian Roy Rene 'Mo', the Tivoli Ballet Girls and 'Australia's Queen of Song', Gladys Moncrieff, had been engaged.[32] This show fell through, however, as the rapid spread of a polio epidemic from Tasmania caused all schools and theatres in Melbourne to be closed. Hence, the Weintraubs' Melbourne performances planned for September were also cancelled. Instead, the musicians stayed in New South Wales, which was spared the epidemic, and toured smaller cities like Katoomba, Dubbo, Bathurst, Parkes and Orange. From there, they went north to Brisbane, Queensland, where they appeared twice daily in 'De-Luxe Sessions' at the St James Theatre, once again in association with a film screening. The advertisements said: 'Here's Hot Rhythm … Swing Music … Jazz and Comedy … Presented by world-famous Syncopators.' In October, they returned to Sydney to play at the Civic Theatre, again with the film *Michael Strogoff*, but the grand revue never took place. Polio prevented what was to be their most spectacular show.

From Concert Tour to Immigration

After fulfilling the Snider & Dean contract, the group signed an agreement with the ABC that expired in January 1938. What would happen after that? The Weintraubs had been almost constantly on the move for six years. Whereas previously they had proper homes in Berlin, they were now homeless. Moreover, their German passports were soon to expire.[33] Given the impossibility of returning to Germany, their Australian sojourn, which had begun as a business trip, was turning imperceptibly into immigration. The once-popular stars became applicants who now had to face the fact that a longer stay was not encouraged. Indeed, thanks to their popularity, these musicians were dangerous rivals for their Australian colleagues.

On 27 October 1937, Stefan Weintraub wrote to the department of the interior saying that he had fallen in love with Australia and wanted to stay permanently. Knowing that musicians were hardly ever given an open-ended residency permit, he signalled his willingness to change profession and work as a pharmacist again: 'I would like to work in my old business chemistry which I have carried on in Germany for many years before I became an artist.' He wanted to manufacture and sell a mouthwash for Australia modelled on a German product, and perhaps also a shoe polish. In view of the difficult circumstances, other members of the band were also prepared to change their professions. Leo Weiss stated that he wanted to open a concert agency. Emanuel Frischer had already discovered that his medical training was not recognised in Australia and that there was no chance of his settling there as a dentist without further tertiary education. While looking for another profession, he came up with the idea of opening a European-style café. He spoke six languages (English, German, Polish, Russian, Italian and French) and during his travels as an artist he had got to know so many cafés that he was confident of his ability to manage such an establishment successfully.[34] Frischer gave the same address for himself as Weintraub: 12 Roslyn Avenue, Darlinghurst, while Leo Weiss and John Kaiser lived at 51 Roslyn Gardens, Potts Point.

Inspector Mitchell, a member of the Investigation Branch, checked the applications on behalf of the department of the interior. He viewed Frischer's chances with scepticism: he thought that cafés in the style of Viennese coffee houses, where one mainly read the paper, would attract a kind of Bohemian society, but hardly a well-paying clientele. As a typical Polish Jew, Frischer himself was a sort of Bohemian – or so the Australian suspected – who would probably turn back to his music. The inspector judged the applications of Weiss and Weintraub more favourably. Weintraub had at least worked for six years in a large Berlin chemical firm, and had an Australian partner in this field willing to co-operate with him; the report sent to Canberra on 8 December assessed his chances as good.³⁵ After the department had made a positive decision on the Weiss application, similar news arrived for Weintraub in December; Frischer became the third member of the band to receive permission to reside permanently in Australia, on 21 January 1938.

Even if the Weintraubs now privately regarded their stay in Australia as immigration, they appeared publicly as travelling artists. The *Australian Music Maker and Dance Band News* had the Comedy Harmonists pictured on the front cover of their August edition; it only introduced the second Berlin group in November, when the Weintraubs' tour had already finished. Amazingly, there were only short notes on their appearances ('a programme of intelligent humour [...] probably the most original dance act yet to be seen in this country'), but more space was devoted to their world travels and the seven musicians, who were profiled one after the other.³⁶

According to the magazine, Stefan Weintraub was a German citizen, a drummer and the leader of the group. Horst Graff, originally a business economist, played all the instruments in the band and was also an arranger, like the thirty-year-old Peruvian 'John Kay', as Kurt Kaiser now called himself. At that time, his family name, Kaiser, was even more disadvantageous in Australia than in the Weimar Republic, so he changed it to the pseudonym from the Berlin jazz band Sid Kay's Fellows. Kay played trombone, saxophone, clarinet and accordion and was also well-versed in composition. The South African Cyril Schulvater said he had studied commercial art in Berlin and had performed as a cellist in public before he joined the Weintraubs. The American Freddie Wise, who joined the band in Paris, had previously belonged to Danny Polo's American College Band in Berlin and the Casa Loma Orchestra, while the pianist Leo Weiss acquired his first jazz experiences with Lud Gluskin's American College Band. The youngest member was the Polish trumpeter and violinist 'Manny Fisher' – the name under which Emanuel Frischer appeared in Australia.

The band was formed in August 1924 with the aim of making audiences laugh. They achieved great success in Max Reinhardt's theatres and also in films, not least in collaboration with Friedrich Hollaender and Marlene

Dietrich. Given that several of the musicians applied to immigrate at the same time, the assurance that there was no connection between the political situation in Germany and their trip to Australia is questionable. It is possible that the Weintraubs themselves suggested this in order not to appear as refugees, so the article mentioned other stops on their world tour: 'When they leave Australia, they are going to India and South Africa, and so, on and on in their never-ending quest to play new theatres in new places.'[37]

When Heinz Barger heard in Japan about the cancellation of their Melbourne performances, on 9 December he inquired about the fate of the group at the Australian Trade Commission in Tokyo. He had apparently heard conflicting reports. The Commissioner passed on his enquiry to the department of the interior on the same day. Horst Graff rejected any suggestions that the Weintraubs had by now become penniless and helpless as unfounded. After a regrettable argument about finances,[38] the band had stopped collaborating with the reliable Heinz (Henry) Barger and transferred the management to Graff. Meanwhile, Graff had in fact been able to negotiate a very attractive tour for the 'Weintraubs Comedy Melodians' with an agent in New Zealand. Although in their applications the Weintraubs had stated their willingness to change professions, they naturally wanted to work as musicians for as long as possible.

On 5 January 1938, Graff informed the department about their forthcoming tour of New Zealand and applied for a visa for eleven people to re-enter Australia. He attached letters from the Sydney radio station 2UW and from the large Sydney agency J.C. Williamson, both of whom had shown an interest in engaging the Weintraubs after their return from New Zealand. When the group originally landed in Fremantle, it also comprised eleven people. Graff used the same number but changed two of the names. Instead of Cyril Schulvater, who had now left, and the British dancer M. Graham who, in any case, did not need a visa, he added two German citizens: Kay's girlfriend Gerty Pfund and her father, Richard Pfund, who had arrived in Australia in October.[39]

As the group's business manager, Graff provided a written affidavit on 18 January waiving any claims against Snider & Dean. The band's future existence would be secured by a contract with New Zealand's Radio Features Corporation in Wellington, initially for the next four weeks. They also had options for the period after their return to Australia. For the four weeks in New Zealand, Graff had arranged a total fee of £720. In the report sent by the department of the interior to the department of trade on 1 February, this amount became the staggering fee of £720 per week.

The band that boarded the New Zealand-bound ship *Wanganella* on 28 January comprised only six members. Cyril Schulvater had left because of internal disagreements and was now earning a living from various business interests, for example a hamburger shop. Freddy Wise, who in the meantime had married the dancer Antoinette Paris, also announced that he wanted to leave the band so that the couple could return to the USA. Replacements were sought while they were in New Zealand. Manny Fisher suggested his brother Adolf, who meanwhile was still appearing in a French club in Beirut. The department agreed to this suggestion. On 7 April, it sent a communication to Horst Graff in Auckland:

> [...] to inform you that the Minister has approved of Mr Frischer and his wife being admitted to Australia for a period of twelve months to enable him to perform with the above-mentioned troupe. As requested by you, a cablegram was sent, on the 7th April, 1938, to the British Consul at Beirut, Syria, advising him of the authority granted in favour of Mr and Mrs Frischer.[40]

In New Zealand, the Weintraubs were once again centre stage, no longer having to share their evenings with film screenings. In Auckland, where they arrived on 1 February, they were announced as 'Comedy Harmony Syncopation: The Weintraubs'; apparently they had come directly from a triumphant European tour – the lie was necessary for advertising purposes – and were the most amusing and versatile vaudeville musicians New Zealand had ever seen. Performance venues included Auckland Town Hall and Wanganui Opera House. At last, they were no longer in the shadow of the Comedy Harmonists, but were receiving critiques of the same length. One review of their guest appearance in Christchurch read:

> To see and hear the Weintraubs is to understand why in cultured Europe, America, Australia, and New Zealand, not one dissentient voice has been raised against their performance. Musicianship of a quality as graceful as it was polished marked the concert given by the troupe at St James' Theatre last evening. The playing throughout was virile, but never showy, and led one on, enchanted, from mood to mood. No passion inserted into music that was without it; from good music the players drew

its essence, following it in all its excessive speeds, lingering with it when necessary, as in the Viennese melodies, and accompanying it to all its endings with the same good taste and finish.

Modern jazz and swing tunes made up most of the programmes. Considering the amazing talent displayed by each member of the Weintraubs party some music-lovers may have thought this a pity. Nevertheless, bright novelty items unexpectedly interspersed with exquisitely played quotations from the masters were not resented. The players could have found in the large audience no lack of warmth or encouragement to make them give of their best. Throughout the concert they played with fine vigour, losing nothing of musical substance. The whole performance was a joyous achievement.[41]

Once again, the enormous versatility of the musicians was emphasised, as well as their capacity to play well-known songs like 'Trees', or the French song 'Annabelle', in various historical styles, à la Bach, Mozart, Beethoven or Wagner. That was not merely original, but outstanding. In summary, they said: 'The Weintraubs carry delight in their hands.'[42]

The group was still playing in February, at His Majesty's Theatre in Dunedin and at the Municipal Theatre in Hastings, followed in March by standing ovations at the Mayfair Theatre in Palmerston and at His Majesty's Theatre in Auckland. As a result of the high demand, their tour was extended by two months. The press resorted to superlatives: 'The best of its class ever heard in Wellington', said the *Dominion*. And in the *Auckland Star*: 'Such excellent musical clowning was a revelation.'[43] Another paper summed things up: 'It is doubtful whether New Zealand has ever heard any other musical combination to compare with the Weintraubs. They are something refreshingly new and they have made a great impression.'[44]

After this triumphal tour, the Weintraubs returned to Sydney on 21 May as first-class passengers on the *Awatea*, but, as on their first arrival in Australia, they all had to fill out Personal Declaration forms. With the exception of Kaiser, they all gave Berlin as their last fixed address. In Australia, they were to be working as artists[45] for the next twelve months. They could declare this openly because the restrictions for a temporary visitor's permit for musicians were less onerous than an application for permanent residency. To the question 'Do you intend to settle in Australia?', Weintraub and Weiss answered that they had already 'settled' there. They were evidently referring to the fact that their permanent residency had already been granted.

Once again, they were all permitted to stay for another twelve months which, for the time being at least, saved them from having to change their occupations. Meanwhile, Adolf Frischer had arrived in Sydney and, under the name 'Adi Normand', replaced Cyril Schulvater as the bass player. Nevertheless, in spite of their brilliant success in New Zealand, and despite declarations of intent by the radio station 2UW and from the J.C. Williamson agency, for the next three months the band had no engagements at all. Radio appearances materialised only from October. On station 2KO, where they were heard up to four times a week, the Weintraubs dazzled their audiences both as an instrumental and a vocal ensemble.[46] In the same month, the *Australian Music Maker* announced more regular broadcasts by this internationally famous band, in which every performer played six or seven instruments, and whose microphone technique amazed even the radio experts. They were now also being heard on 2CH Sydney and broadcasting regularly over a further twenty-six stations throughout Australia. Listeners were very enthusiastic about these offerings: 'Ever since their first presentation by 2CH, the station has been inundated with letters of praise, and countless telephone messages are received after each broadcast by listeners asking for the repetition of special numbers.'[47] The *Radio Pictorial of Australia* announced that the impressive versatility of the Weintraubs had inspired some listeners to learn several instruments themselves.[48] Later editions of this magazine mentioned their 'Melody Riddles', which was broadcast regularly on Thursday night; every show contained five melodic riddles that were presented in the form of sketches. There were weekly prizes of ten pounds for each winner, and for everyone who sent in a new riddle.[49]

'My Melancholy Baby': Prince's Restaurant

After months of radio work, the Weintraubs were finally offered some stage performances at the end of 1938. The initiative came from the Danish-born James C. Bendrodt, who had come to Sydney as a nineteen-year-old and in 1923 founded his own firm, which ran a dance palace and night club. In

1938, when the luxury Italian restaurant 'Romano's' moved to new premises at Martin Place in Sydney's city centre, Bendrodt felt challenged to offer the city a second first-class restaurant – also in Martin Place. As 'Romano's' already had its own band, he wanted something similar for 'Prince's', and if possible better. To this end, he auditioned several bands in Melbourne and Sydney. Finally it came down to two: Craig Crawford's Melbourne ensemble, and the Weintraubs. When they played him a 'whispering' version of the well-known hit 'My Melancholy Baby' (Ernie Burnett/George Norton, 1912), the impresario decided on the latter. Manny Fisher had written the arrangement specifically for this purpose when he heard that it was Bendrodt's favourite tune.

Nevertheless, shortly before the opening of the restaurant, Bendrodt informed the editors of the *Australian Music Maker* that the decision had not yet been made. The magazine announced this in their December edition under the heading 'Weintraubs or Craig Crawford for Sydney "Prince's"', and at the same time they sided unmistakeably with the Australian band: 'The general consensus of opinion around Sydney is that Craig Crawford will be chosen for the job.'[50] Their rivals were certainly successful, but they had two shortcomings: 'The Weintraubs are non-unionists and only two of their number are naturalised Australians.' The New Zealand-born Crawford knew the regulations well: as recently as 1935, he himself had not been allowed to work in Sydney because neither he nor the other band members had joined the union.[51] In November 1938, the *Music Maker* had just supported the Musicians' Union in their fight against the influence of overseas musicians, and showed its approval by sending the following circular to all the relevant agents.

> Dear Sir,
> Owing to numerous inquiries relating to musical employment and membership of this organisation having been received from foreign musicians, both local and overseas (probably due to the exile of Jews from countries under Fascist control), we have deemed it advisable, in protection of Australian musicians to restrict further membership to Britishers. The vast number of capable, employed musicians in Australia renders such a course essential.
> There is no greater incentive to attain a high standard of musicianship than the prospect of employment and employers would be wise, therefore, in their own

interests, to foster local talent. Apart from our present unemployed the conservatoriums and other training grounds are turning out a number of proficient young Australians annually with little prospect of employment, after years of study and expense. The impossibility of absorbing new arrivals, except by inflicting gross injustice on our people is, therefore, apparent.

I trust you will agree with this organisation that any work available in Australia should be the prerogative of Australians.

Yours faithfully,
FRANK KITSON, Secretary.[52]

Thus, it was not an artistic ideal, but rather the labour market that drove the *Music Maker* to make its recommendations to Bendrodt. The only thing they had against the Weintraubs was that they were foreigners and, as usual, the union rules applied. As with earlier cases, the impresario now had to give in to union pressure and employ Crawford's band as well as the Weintraubs.[53] When the opening of the new restaurant took place in the art nouveau MLC building in Martin Place, the Australian band played for the dancing, while the foreigners were only allowed to follow later as a 'Specialty Act'.[54] Despite their Berlin heritage, the Weintraubs were announced as 'Prince's Imported Viennese Novelty Show Band'. As their theme song, rather than something from *The Blue Angel*, they chose Sigmund Romberg's schmaltzy 'You Will Remember Vienna'. Berlin's Comedy Harmonists were also presented on Australian radio with title themes such as Schubert's 'Heideröslein', or 'Vienna, City of My Dreams'.[55] At the time, one critic wrote about the group: 'All are Viennese'.[56] Bendrodt would also have preferred to be able to say that the Weintraubs all came from Vienna.

According to the menu, 'Prince's' specialised in French cuisine and was operating as 'Australia's Most Famous Restaurant'. Lunch was from 12.30 p.m. to 2.30 p.m., followed by afternoon tea from 3 p.m. until 5 p.m., and on Saturdays this included dancing. There was an early dinner at six o'clock. The socially attractive 'Dinner with Dancing' began every night at 8.30 p.m. and ended at 1 a.m. Craig Crawford's band carried the lion's share of the entertainment. The Weintraubs were only allowed to come on stage after midnight, when the union members had retired for their evening meal. Although their late performances were limited to one hour, they had much of the public on their side. Reading between the lines of the *Music Maker* magazine, one could sense that there was a fight going on behind the scenes. When the restaurant opened, it wrote: 'The Weintraubs, with their comedy and remarkable instrumental virtuosity, are meeting with the unanimous approval of the patrons.' Nevertheless, the magazine only supported the Crawford band. Whereas it profiled the Australians in several articles, after that first contribution in November 1937, their rivals were never given the same exposure. The only references to the Weintraubs' existence from December 1938 were in the form of advertisements. At the end of the year, they themselves placed a half-page advertisement in the *Music Maker*, in which they sent best wishes to their friends throughout Australia. The 1939 February edition included a two-page spread with photos of the band; this was also a paid advertisement. Once, the Weintraubs posed with a new drum from the firm Boosey & Hawkes, and then there was a two-page advertisement for the saxophone manufacturer Conn that showed the two bands side-by-side: on the left, one saw the Weintraubs, dressed in white and all playing saxophones, while on the right were the members of Craig Crawford's band, in black suits, smiling and simply holding their instruments in their hands. A huge heading, 'The Choice of the Artists', spanned the two pages. It could also have been taken to mean that the public had to decide between the two artistic groups engaged by 'Prince's' – between those who really played, and those who simply posed with their instruments. This advertisement was paid for by the two largest instrumental retailers in the country: Allan & Co. (Melbourne) and Nicholson's Pty Ltd (Sydney); in so doing, they defied union pressure.

In May 1939, with another paid advertisement, these two firms again forced the *Music Maker* to refer to the Weintraubs. The following text was printed above an enormous photograph of the group:

CONN
Congratulates
THE WEINTRAUBS
Who, already an unqualified success at Prince's, Sydney, have now captured the coveted 2CH 'Rinso' Programme Broadcast on a network of 27 stations.
Their 'all-Conn' Saxophone equipment was chosen by the Weintraubs because Conn instruments help musicians to get the most out of their ability.

Marketing for the instruments was cleverly combined with reference to the musicians. The commercial radio stations also withstood the union pressure and offered time slots to the popular band. In June 1939, when the *Radio Pictorial of Australia* introduced the group to its readers,[57] the first sentence of the three-page article stated that the name Weintraubs was a synonym for modern music: 'It is subtle, arresting, and pre-eminently continental.' The Weintraubs were one of the best orchestras ever to have visited Sydney, and their 2CH broadcasts were extremely popular. Stefan Weintraub told the reporter about his youth in Breslau, where he started piano lessons at the age of seven; but he had only become a professional musician after meeting Horst Graff and once their band was established. Blushing, he added that, to their own surprise, they had become increasingly well-known, and finally famous.

The tall and strongly built John Kay was quite a different personality. With his dark eyes sparkling behind tortoiseshell-rimmed glasses, according to the reporter he radiated self-confidence. Born in Peru, he had grown up in Germany, where he joined Weintraub and Graff's new band. His special talent was for arranging, but he was also an intelligent and well-read man with wide-ranging interests and with his own thought-provoking opinions on many different subjects. In complimenting the Australian women on their independence, he threw in the sentence: 'Yes, I would like to stay in Australia always.'

Adolf Frischer (now Adi Normand) had already joined the band for its farewell concert in Berlin in 1935. Since he had last been engaged at a French club in Beirut, he wanted to be introduced as a Frenchman, and he combined a few French words with his still broken English. Manny Fisher impressed the reporter both with his rimless glasses, which gave him the air of an intellectual, and with his perfect English. He was supposed to have come across the Weintraubs during his medical studies in Warsaw, although that was not quite accurate. The good-looking Horst Graff told how he had discovered the new music of jazz from the USA during his engineering studies at Berlin University. In spite of his purely classical music education, he had quickly become enthusiastic about this kind of music-making, and had then established the band with Stefan Weintraub. Finally, the dark-haired Leo Weiss had already undertaken international tours with several other bands before he joined the Weintraubs.

Waiting for Residence Permits

The Weintraubs, who radiated such good humour and were pictured with beaming faces in the *Radio Pictorial of Australia*, were at the peak of their artistic career. Countless listener requests confirmed that they were very popular with the Australian public. For their fifteenth anniversary, in 1939, they published an expensive brochure containing facsimiles of glowing press reviews, above all from New Zealand. On the back, there was a brief summary of their various programmes:

- World Famous Stage Show for Theatre, Music-Hall, Vaudeville or Movies (a 30 minute riot of Melody, Comedy, Burlesque and Laughter)
- Full Evening Concert (2 Hours of Musical Features ranging from Symphony to Hot Rhythm)
- Whispering Swing (an exclusive Novelty in Dance Time)
- Tea Concert (specially selected Programmes for Entertainment)[58]

They had offered the stage show at the beginning of their Australian sojourn and the full evening concert more recently in New Zealand, while at Prince's Restaurant they entertained the public with their 'Whispering Swing' in the late hours. In May and June 1939, they also presented startling stage shows in which they appeared once as Mexicans, and another time as convicts in clinking chains.[59]

The Weintraubs' popularity rested on their natural abilities and the skills they had developed in Germany. This connection had been an existential problem for them since 1933, both in Germany and abroad. Whereas the Hitler regime had long excluded them from German culture, in Australia they became increasingly identified with it. The Weintraubs, however, repeatedly made it clear that they no longer regarded Germany as their homeland. Since Kristallnacht, it had become obvious that Jews could no longer live there. All the band members tried, therefore, to help their nearest relatives to emigrate.

When Adolf Frischer arrived in Sydney in May 1938, he soon applied for his parents to move to Australia. On the basis of his standing as a member of the band, he undertook to guarantee their cost of living, and received the necessary permit. Salomon and Feigel Frischer left Germany just in time, arriving in Sydney on 4 October 1939. Leo Weiss managed to arrange his father's move to Australia, and Cyril Schulvater helped his brother Ernest and his wife to immigrate. Horst Graff, too, made the effort to bring his seventy-four-year-old father, his sixty-six-year-old mother and his brother Wilhelm to safety in Australia. He undertook the necessary guarantees for all three by citing his contract with Prince's, which ran until 30 June 1939 and paid £9 a week.[60] A similar income was anticipated from radio appearances. If necessary, he could also arrange work with the Weintraubs for his brother, a violinist.[61] Inspector Mitchell accepted Graff's application at his office in the vicinity of Prince's Restaurant. That said, at the end there was a handwritten note adding that the 'Weintraubs Orchestra' would not obtain permanent employment as its members were not in the Musicians' Union.

On 17 February, Horst Graff wrote to the union on behalf of the band: 'We all intend to stay in this country and to become loyal citizens. To safeguard ourselves, we would like to be under the wing of the Union and are only too willing to obey its rules.'[62] He was available for any further questions. Through personal discussion with Graff, Frank Kitson had obviously discovered that the band was appearing with the approval of the Commonwealth Government. The union secretary then turned directly to the Minister for the Interior, John McEwen:

> Dear Sir,
> I have been informed by the representative of the Winetraub Comedy Melodians, which comprise Messrs. Stefan Weintraub, John Kay, Leo Weiss, Manny Fisher, Adi Normand and Horst Graff, that they are accepting musical employment in Australia under some form of license issued by the Government. [...] Will you please inform me if that information is correct, and if so, what form the licenses take? [...] In view of our large list of unemployed and the meagre amount of musical work in this country, it appears unfair that foreigners should obtain the little available. Will you be good enough to supply me with a copy of the various types of license issued by your Department and inform me if it is contemplated that further licenses shall be issued to musicians? [...][63]

Kitson also referred to the conductors Heinrich Krips and Kurt Herweg, criticising the fact that foreigners were obtaining jobs while there were still so many Australian musicians unemployed. The department subsequently checked the entry procedures for the band. The Minister's secretary confirmed in a memorandum of 20 March that the Weintraubs had arrived in July 1937 for a contract with the firm Snider & Dean. Three of the band members, Leo Weiss, Stefan Weintraub and Manny Fisher, who wanted employment in other professions, had already received permanent residency permits. Meanwhile, there were applications from Sydney John Kay and Horst Graff, which, however, had not yet been decided.[64]

Before a written reply to this memorandum was sent to the union, there was a change of government. Kitson repeated his requests in a letter to McEwen's successor, H.S. Foll, on 18 May, when he presented the facts with even more urgency:

> Dear Sir,
> The question of musician migrants to this Country has occasioned great concern to members of this organisation because of the unemployment which exists in the profession. [...] Consequently each migrant musician admitted to Australia imposes an injustice, real or potential, to the Australian unemployed musician. On the 24th February last I wrote to your predecessor, the Hon. J. McEwen and pointed out that Messrs. Stephan Weintraub, John Kay, Leo Weiss, Manny Fisher, Adi Norman, Horst Graff and Heinrich Krips are accepting musical work here under some sort of permit issued by the Government. [...]
> I am inundated with inquiries from abroad and from musicians who have already arrived here as to the possibility of them securing employment and there is no doubt that the situation has become alarming. I earnestly request your co-operation in preventing an influx of foreign musicians, for however much our sympathies are aroused on their behalf, we can do nothing tangible for them without inflicting an injustice on our Australian players.

Since his predecessor had already prepared the relevant documents, Minister Foll's secretary, J.A. Carrodus was able to reply promptly. In a letter dated 22 May 1939, he informed Kitson: 'Messrs. Stefan Weintraub, Emanuel Frischer and Leo Weiss were granted permission to remain here permanently. Messrs. John Kay and Horst Graff are still under temporary permits, although they have made applications for permission to remain permanently.' It was a principle of the department, the letter went on, to judge the applications on an individual basis. That said, they had taken note of the union's view and would not admit applicants who were members of bands or orchestras in competition with unemployed Australians: 'In view of the representations made by your Union, special care will be exercised in dealing with any future applications for the admission of foreign musicians into Australia.'[65] Under pressure from the union, the department tightened its already restrictive attitude towards immigrant musicians. On 24 April, Frank Kitson informed Graff that his application for membership had been rejected: he did not give a reason.[66]

This was a cause for concern, as the twelve-month residency permit that the Weintraubs had obtained after their return from New Zealand was due to expire at the end of May 1939. Graff had therefore already written a letter to the department of the interior on 9 January, applying for permanent residency. On 5 February, John Kay also submitted a similar application.[67] In it, he gave a comprehensive account of his life history, his parents' ancestry, his early engineering studies and his collaboration with the Weintraubs Syncopators. Unlike Frischer, Weintraub and Weiss, however, he did not offer to change his profession. In a subsequent letter, Kay had added that he was financially independent and would not be a burden on the state; he still had a considerable sum of money in a Leipzig account as well as a share in the house owned by his family in Zwickau's famous central market square. Inspector Mitchell noted this information, together with more facts about Kay's earnings.

In contrast to the applications of his colleagues, Weiss, Weintraub and Emanuel Frischer, Kay's application for permanent residency was declined on 13 July. 'The matter has received careful consideration', wrote the department, 'but it is regretted that your application has not been approved for the present.'[68] Five days later, Horst Graff received similar news, which now called into question not only his own future, but that of his parents, as well as the band that he managed. One may assume that Graff and Kaiser did not receive further residency permits because they were not prepared to renounce their music profession, and it could not be ruled out that they would continue to play in the 'Weintraubs Orchestra'. Thus the union's demands had been met.

Meanwhile, as the Weintraubs' business manager, Horst Graff had got to know prominent personalities who were interested in the band remaining in Australia. They included the New Zealand-born journalist and writer Frederick Ehrenfried Baume, a descendant of German Jews. Since 1931, he had been chief editor of the *Sunday Sun and Guardian* in Sydney, as well as a novelist and radio commentator.[69] Baume took such a stand against Hitler's Germany in his commentaries for the radio station 2GB that, in response to strong protests from the German Consul-General, Dr Rudolf Asmis, the broadcasts were taken away from him. This eminent journalist kept up an elegant lifestyle and entertained artists such as Gladys Moncrieff and the Ballets Russes de Monte Carlo on a regular basis in his villa. When he heard about Graff's fate, he turned indignantly to the Minister for the Interior:

> The Sun 28th July, 1939   Private & Confidential
> The Hon. H.S. Foll
> Parliament House
> Canberra
>
> My dear Senator,
> I have marked this letter 'private and confidential' because, for the first time, I am asking you a very personal favour.
>   Mr Horst Graff, whose number with the Department of the Interior is 39/3082, is a most successful leader of the Weintraub Band. He has been in this country 18 months, but has not been given a permit to remain. He is earning £20 a week, his wife is British[70], and in addition he is a very fine type of fellow.
>   As well as his own permit being refused, permission to bring his parents to this country, their number being 39/458, has also been refused.
>   I do think that this is a particular case. Were I not to think so I would not raise my voice about it, but it seems extraordinary, where perhaps some types might not suit you or your Department, that a man of his calibre should be debarred.
>
> Yours sincerely,
> F.E. Baume, Editor [71]

In August, Baume took a new position in Europe and moved from Sydney to London, which delayed the minister's reply. In September 1939, before Horst Graff's case could be re-opened, a completely new situation developed, whereby the chances of permanent residency slipped into the realm of the unreachable.

CHAPTER 10

'Down with the fifth column!': Britain during the War

When Britain entered the war, the situation of German and Austrian refugees in the British Isles deteriorated overnight. With the declaration of war, recently issued visas lost their validity and no more refugees were accepted after 3 September 1939.[1] In spite of their opposition to Hitler, refugees already in the country were now treated as enemy aliens and were directly affected by the anti-German mood fomented by the xenophobic campaigns in sections of the press.[2] The German Jewish Aid Committee reacted against this xenophobia, which, surprisingly, was most widespread among the educated circles of the middle- and upper-classes,[3] by publishing a brochure: 'While you are in England: Helpful Information and Guidance for Every Refugee'.[4] Eight rules of behaviour recommended that the refugees should conduct themselves quietly and inconspicuously: 'Refrain from speaking German in the streets and in public conveyances and in public places such as restaurants. Talk halting English rather than fluent German.' On no account were they to criticise any measures being taken by the government.

From October onwards, all foreigners living in Britain, including Jews who had fled from Hitler, were brought before closed tribunals so that their political views could be checked. Previously, during the First World War, male enemy nationals had been imprisoned in Britain, just as they were in Germany. Edgar Bainton found himself in the internment camp at Ruhleben, Berlin, simply because he happened to be visiting Germany at the time. Here, together with Ernest MacMillan, he organised choral and orchestral concerts that were actually reviewed in the camp's newspaper.[5] However, the blanket arrest of foreigners during the war years also led to many injustices, so in 1939, Britain wanted to draw a clear distinction between refugees from Germany and Austria and enemy aliens. One hundred and twenty tribunals set up throughout the country were to divide all foreigners into three categories:

A: absolutely unreliable persons, who were to be interned immediately,
B: persons who could remain free, but were subject to certain restrictions under the Aliens Order of 1920;
C: reliable persons, so-called 'friendly aliens'.

A memorandum gave the chairpersons of these tribunals advice on categorisation. Refugees who had left their homeland on account of racial or political suppression were assigned to Category C. 'They will be hostile to the Nazi regime and ready to assist this country rather than to assist the enemy.'[6] Foreigners who had been living in Britain for longer were also to be designated as 'friendly aliens', as long as their loyalty could be clearly identified. Caution was to be exercised, however, as even Germans and Austrians of strong character were liable to experience conflicting loyalties.

During the first weeks, the tribunals were still uncertain and assigned many of the refugees to Category B; sometimes it was enough if they answered the question 'Are you German?' with a 'Yes'. Over time, the B portion began to decline.[7] A total of 73,400 of the 74,200 enemy aliens were heard and about 64,000 – by far the greatest percentage of them – were considered to be reliable persons, or Category C. Most of the Kitchener Camp internees were in this group. In all, 55,500 people were judged to be 'refugees from Nazi-oppression'.[8] As Francois Lafitte wrote in a study published in 1940, after these hearings the British authorities were better informed about the refugees than about most of the population.[9]

Six thousand and eight hundred foreigners were assigned to Category B and 568 to Category A. Erwin Frenkel was put into that small group of people who were supposed to be absolutely unreliable. The twenty-year-old son of a Viennese synagogue cantor, Frenkel had been earning his living as a bar pianist in the London suburb of Finsbury Park. During the hearing, the chair assumed that he could not really make a living from these appearances, and that he was being kept by a woman friend. The young man took this as an insult and described his opponent as a 'dirty old man'. Even though Frenkel had brought recommendations from London rabbis and cantors, he was assigned to Category A and immediately arrested.[10] Two hours after his arrival at the police station in Piccadilly Circus, he was taken to Chelsea and from there, together with other prisoners, to a former holiday camp in Seaton, Devon, which had been transformed into an internment camp. There he was allowed to earn pocket money by making fishing nets. At first, there were only Jews and communists in the Seaton camp, until finally some sailors were brought in from a hijacked German ship, among them apparently some Nazis.[11]

'Collar the lot!' The Internment of 'Enemy Aliens'

When German troops occupied the neutral Netherlands on 10 May 1940, fear of invasion increased in Britain. Prime Minister Neville Chamberlain, who had attempted to reach a settlement with Germany, resigned. His successor, Winston Churchill, formed a committee of national defence, chaired by Lord Swinton, which was given almost unlimited powers and was not answerable to either Parliament or the Cabinet. This committee attributed the surprisingly rapid German advance in the Netherlands and Norway to support from local sympathisers, describing them as the Nazis' 'Fifth Column',[12] a term borrowed from the Spanish Civil War.[13] The subsequent press campaign against Jewish refugees resulted in growing antisemitism in the population.[14] On 12 May, after an internal dispute and contrary to the earlier decisions, Churchill ordered the temporary internment of all male Germans and Austrians between the ages of sixteen and sixty who lived near the coast. In consequence, 2,000 men were taken into custody, including Rudolf Laqueur, Leo Roth and Eduard Kassner on 16 May.[15] The violinist Max Pietruschka had already been arrested at the Kitchener Camp on 12 May. The composer Hans Werner Katz and the violinist Otmar Silberstein were also detained there on 26 May. Members of other nations had to present themselves on a daily basis at the nearest police station; they were not allowed to use cars or bicycles, and had to observe evening curfews.

By late May, British intelligence agencies concluded that, under favourable conditions and with a well-developed plan, a German invasion could take place at any time. Indeed, as late as 1939, Hitler had discussed with SS brigade leader Walter Schellenberg that Germany and the British, whom he still saw as a 'Nordic people', should exercise joint power over Europe. Without Hitler's knowledge, tentative plans were drawn up. In late June 1940, Schellenberg was ordered to produce a secret Gestapo handbook; that summer, he completed his *Information Booklet on Great Britain*. It also contained concise information about the refugee organisations and the tribunals that had assigned most of the German refugees to Category C, 'Victims of Nazi Oppression'. It was assumed that the British aimed to integrate them into the national defence system.[16]

The refugees themselves, however, did not have the impression that they were integrated into British society at all. Rather, their interment felt like ostracism. The fact that they were now regarded as potential spies came as a real shock to those who had fled Hitler's Germany. Many of them felt like the young Harry Seidler from Vienna (later a prominent architect in Australia), who wrote in his diary on 12 May: 'Us! – – – – – Spies! It's laughable! We – driven out of Germany – are now suspected of being spies for our deadliest enemy! And in spite of this, they seem to be serious!'[17] Despite opposition from the Home Secretary, Sir John Anderson, and from MI5 Intelligence, Churchill and the War Office went ahead with these mass internments.[18] The slogan was 'Collar the Lot!' In late May, they ordered the immediate internment of all male and female refugees in Category B. In the last week of June, all men from enemy countries between the ages of sixteen and sixty were rounded up for internment, which Churchill explained as a prerequisite for the country's security, as well as for the safety of the refugees themselves: 'Internment would probably be much safer for all German-speaking persons themselves since, when air attacks develop, public temper in this country would be such that such persons would in a greater danger if at liberty.'[19] All the refugees from Germany and Austria previously assigned to Category C were now also affected by these measures.

The new wave of arrests began on 25 June. That morning, Chief Constable Dewsbury arrived at the House of the Resurrection in Mirfield, West Yorkshire, an estate where priests of the Church of England were trained. The lawyer Dr Ehrenfeld, having fled from Vienna and subsequently joined the Church of England, was in residence. The policeman arrested him on account of his German citizenship; Ehrenfeld had to pack a few of his personal belongings quickly and go with him. Felix Werder, who had already been studying in England for six years, was also startled by an unannounced visit that day:

> Suddenly overnight two pathetic little men marched in and arrested me as a German spy. The two of them searched my room. Naturally I had a lot of German books, and with each book they said, 'Now we've got him. Where did you get this book from?' I tried to explain that I was a refugee. They didn't understand this, and didn't want to know about it. Then they dragged me off.[20]

The following morning, Werder's father, Boas Bischofswerder, was also arrested; he had found a second home in England, and was stunned. Twenty-year-old Günter Hirschberg, who was studying music and theology at university, was also interned on 25 June along with Klaus Loewald and Erich Liffmann. The next day, the same fate befell Peter Stadlen and Adolf Brenner, followed by Kurt Behrens and Max Meyer on 27 June. Sometimes these arrests took place at night,[21] but they were usually carried out early in the morning, after six o'clock. On the other hand, owing to the German submarine attacks, the refugees were not permitted to leave Britain. By mid-July, approximately 20,000 men from Germany and Austria had been interned.[22] Those arrested in London were usually taken to the provisional internment camp at the Kempton Park racecourse to the west of the city. The simple accommodation consisted of thin mattresses on a stone floor. Often a hundred people had to share one room, which lacked chairs and cupboards.[23] Many families suffered without their breadwinners.[24] Like Cantor Bischofswerder's family, the Chlumecky-Bauer family was torn apart by the internment of the father and both sons, Nikolaus and Johannes. The Viennese commercial artist and musician Alfred Landauer also had to leave his wife behind.

The internees were taken from Kempton Park and other smaller camps either to the Isle of Man or to Huyton, near Liverpool, where large crowds met them at the station. As the new arrivals walked through the city in a column three-abreast, with their luggage, they were abused with cries like 'Down with the fifth column' and 'Down with the spies'. The British soldiers used bayonets to drive them at a faster pace on this hour-long walk; for many, it was a painful reminder of the behaviour of the SA and

SS in Germany.[25] The Huyton internment camp had been set up hastily on a council estate that had barely been completed.[26] Instead of socially deprived families, twelve men now moved into each one-family house. In the absence of furniture, some of the internees had to sleep on straw sacks on the floor; others slept in tents. Food was inadequate and of poor quality,[27] and the health care was miserable,[28] although this improved as the internees' self-administration took effect. To prevent the inmates from escaping, the camp was surrounded by barbed wire, patrolled by armed soldiers and floodlit at night.

The Kaiser's grandson, who called himself Count Lingen, was among the approximately 6,000 refugees, as were the heir to the Austrian throne, Archduke Otto,[29] visual artists like John Heartfield and Kurt Schwitters, and several musicians, including the well-known composers Hans Gál and Egon Wellesz and the pianist Peter Stadlen. Living conditions were far better in the five camps on the Isle of Man.[30] There the internees had furnished houses in which, among others, Eduard Kassner, Kurt Kohn (Ray Martin), Leo Roth and Hans Zander were all accommodated.

'My luggage went into the ocean': The *Arandora Star* and *Dunera*

As Churchill was of the opinion that interned enemy aliens still represented a security risk, he ordered their deportation. On 3 June, he suggested that 20,000 internees be taken to Newfoundland or St Helena, and on 7 June, a request was sent to the Canadian High Commissioner in London. Canada agreed, and by 20 June the first ships were loaded with people considered dangerous. The *Duchess of York*, with 2,602 passengers, was followed on 30 June by the requisitioned luxury liner *Arandora Star* with 1,213 passengers. Erwin Frenkel was among the 473 Category A people who were sent to Canada on this ship, along with 717 Italian internees. Frenkel did not really regret this, because he had relatives there, and life aboard the *Arandora Star* was luxury compared to the preceding weeks of internment. However, no safety precautions were taken and all the life-boats were in a state of disrepair. When the ship was struck by a German torpedo two days later, panic erupted.³¹ The *Arandora Star* sank and 800 people drowned. Frenkel, a good swimmer, managed to save himself, but lost all his personal possessions. Dressed in a cast-off British uniform, he arrived back at Huyton a few days later, with all the other survivors of the catastrophe. News of the sinking of the *Arandora Star* aroused horror in the camp, as internees now feared that future transport ships could meet a similar fate.³²

A few days later, the survivors of the *Arandora Star* were put on another ship, the *Dunera*, which supposedly was also taking them to Canada. Other internees on board included Klaus Loewald and Leo Roth, who volunteered for fear of a German invasion. Moritz Chlumecky and his son Johannes were resolved to get to Canada by hook or by crook as Nikolaus had already been deported there; but even the internees who wished to remain in England were picked up in Huyton and put on this ship.³³ Peter Stadlen and his brother ended up on board as a result of unlucky circumstances. On the initiative of Thomas Mann, Yehudi Menuhin and Eleanor Roosevelt, the pianist was due to be released from internment, but the news did not arrive in time. 'We were picked up by the Sergeant Major at random', he reported later, 'without any regard to our age, fitness or professional qualifications. It was pure chance that my brother and I stood in the same file and were therefore shipped together.'³⁴ On boarding the ship, they all noticed straight away that it would be no pleasure cruise: they were treated by the guards as dangerous persons, as criminals, and searched. Their luggage was taken from them, sometimes ripped open with bayonets and thrown overboard. Money and valuables disappeared into a big pile. 'The English soldiers took whatever they liked. They were just poor fellows with absolutely no idea who we were.'³⁵ Soon word got around about the 'Pick-pocket Battleship Dunera', a play on words based on the English term for armed warship ('pocket battleship'). When Moritz Chlumecky explained that the violin case he had brought with him contained an instrument belonging to his son, it was confiscated and thrown into the sea.³⁶ Because so much of the internees' luggage kept going overboard like this, someone changed the lyrics of 'My Bonnie lies over the ocean' to 'My luggage went into the ocean'; the new refrain was 'bring back, bring back, oh bring back my luggage to me'.

Everything had to be done hastily, as the *Dunera* was due to cast off on 10 July. When the ship left Liverpool early that morning with 2,542 German, Austrian and Italian internees on board, many of them were convinced they were destined for Canada. The Captain steered at first towards Scotland and the north coast of Ireland. When he then turned south instead of west, they assumed that their destination was South Africa. After stopovers in Freetown (Sierra Leone) and the Gold Coast, the ship docked in Cape Town. Meanwhile, the men on board were informed that their final destination was Australia; like Canada, it had also declared itself willing to accept internees and prisoners of war from Britain. Further shocks included a German submarine attack, and abuse from the security guards on board. In the middle of the night, one of the soldiers demanded that young Leo Roth give him his golden signet ring. When he refused, the British soldier dragged him to the bathroom and took the ring by force. Antisemitic utterances were heard not only from the Nazis on board, but also from the soldiers. In an official report, their Commandant, Lieutenant Colonel W.P. Scott, described the Jewish refugees as 'subversive liars', who were not to be trusted.

Deportees were housed below deck in cramped quarters, with closed hatches and no daylight. Barbed wire barred the exits from the dormitories. Since there were not enough hammocks, some of the men had to sleep on the floor; others on benches and tables. Faced with the poor sanitary conditions, many of them became ill, whereupon it was decided that individual groups be allowed ten minutes each day on deck, where they were guarded by soldiers with machine guns.

In spite of all this, the unfortunate travellers tried to spend their time as sensibly as possible. They organised lectures (for example, on the traditions of the Vienna Boys' Choir, or the history of Australia), a discussion club, musical performances and even a cabaret. Occasionally, when men in the hold leaned against the railing and, to the throbbing of the ship's engine, listened to jolly songs like 'South of the Border' or 'When I ride along', some of them were reminded of scenes from an Eisenstein film.[37] One crewman noted in his diary:

> A number of small choirs which sprang up among the prisoners have been turned into a cabaret. They give a first-class show to an audience of about 1500 which usually

ends in community singing. Most of the songs are in English (almost every German on the ship seems to be able to speak some English), but occasionally an entertainer breaks into guttural German. The bright spark and instigator of the cabaret is Kurt who was very well-known in England under an English name. He studied for years at the Vienna Academy of Music and in England linked up with the popular stage and radio team known as 'Band Wagon'. Several of his compositions have been published.[38]

The 'Kurt' mentioned was Kurt Kohn, who appeared in Britain as Ray Martin. He had evidently been allowed to keep his guitar, and he performed current hits as well as brand new songs of his own.

Among the numerous versatile and educated men on board the *Dunera* was Gustav Clusmann, a sculptor from Hamburg who had moved in surrealist circles in New York, Italy and France. During a visit to London in 1939, he was called up for German military service. To avoid this, he applied for British citizenship; but before it was granted war broke out, followed by the internment of enemy aliens. Clusmann sang unaccompanied Negro spirituals, the blues 'Careless Love', and excerpts from Gershwin's opera *Porgy and Bess*, which he knew from New York. Someone they called 'Boxer' chimed in with Broadway hits like 'Begin the Beguine', 'In My Solitude' and 'Ride, Tenderfoot, Ride'.[39] During the trip, the men also liked to strike up the well-known song 'Ich bin nur ein armer Wandergesell' ['I'm just a poor wandering fellow'] from the Künnecke operetta *Der Vetter aus Dingsda* [*The Cousin from Nowhere*], which they associated with their own situation, especially the lines 'And if I have to leave again tomorrow morning, I'll take my memories as my only luggage'. Boas Bischofswerder embodied a different musical tradition: on the long voyage, he led a small Jewish choir and composed a *Phantasia Judaica* for four tenor voices. Given the dearth of musical instruments, the men were dependent on their voices or on whistling. Thus, as Klaus Loewald remembers, two music enthusiasts sat by the air duct in the summer heat and whistled, softly and precisely, the solo parts from the slow movement of Bach's Concerto for Two Violins.

Musical Example 1: J.S. Bach, *Largo* from Concerto in D minor, for 2 violins and orchestra, BWV 1043 (Helmut Kickton)

Such activities helped to make the long, fifty-seven-day voyage more bearable. The refugees had only been able to bring a few cases and utensils, most of which they had had to surrender when they boarded. But they carried important parts of their cultural identity in their memory, which accompanied them on the long journey. Indeed, for many, their memories were often the only luggage they had left.

CHAPTER 11

Interned and Defamed in Australia

The Hour of Denunciation

Britain's declaration of war on Germany on 3 September 1939 triggered a similar statement by Prime Minister Robert Menzies that evening: Australia was now also at war with the German Empire, and police began to arrest suspicious persons the very next night.¹ The Commonwealth Investigation Branch (CIB) had been preparing lists of relevant names since 1938 so, during the first weeks of the war, 343 Germans were apprehended as enemy aliens and taken to internment camps.² One of them was a German engineer, Dr Mathias Schönzeler, an opponent of Hitler who had fled to Australia just one year earlier and was arrested at his home in Sydney's Rose Bay on 4 September. To enable his musically gifted son Hans-Hubert to escape the influence of the Hitler Youth, he had sent him to the German school in Brussels in 1936. At the time of Schönzeler's arrest, fourteen-year-old Hans-Hubert and his mother were on their way to Australia aboard the *Remo*; surprised by news of the outbreak of war, however, the Italian ship put all its British passengers ashore in Colombo. When mother and son arrived in Sydney on 29 September, they discovered to their horror that the head of the family had already been taken to a camp. As a rule, the victims' homes were searched and all letters and documents confiscated.³ Separately, all foreigners had to undergo a security check, as the German government was suspected of smuggling in secret agents amongst the refugees.⁴ To prevent enemy aliens from exchanging information with their homeland, their mail was checked, which further delayed letters. They had to surrender their cameras and radios – a particularly painful restriction for musicians – and were only able to leave their residential area in exceptional circumstances.

The Weintraubs, too, were now mistrusted, even though they promptly declared their willingness to support the British Empire in the war against Germany and entered their names on relevant lists. On 4 September, their employer, J.C. Bendrodt, testified to the department of the interior: 'I am able to say that they [the Weintraubs] have expressed to me on many occasions, strong anti-Nazi political beliefs, and are, as I am aware, eager to become loyal naturalised Australians.'[5] The department thanked Bendrodt for his letter but pointed out that, since the outbreak of war, control of aliens was now under the jurisdiction of the department of defence.

A few days later, the Paddington police station received information that contradicted the positive testimony of Bendrodt and Baume. A resident in Potts Point, where almost all the Weintraubs lived, had reported the group's suspicious wheeling and dealing. This William Buchan informed the police that he had already come into contact with the musicians in Leningrad in 1937. According to him, the Russian secret police had detained two of the band members for spying and found a complete plan of the Kronstadt naval fortress on them. He stated that, at the ensuing trial, a woman – apparently the mother of one of the band members, Jenny Schulvater – shouldered the blame; she was sentenced to twenty years in prison, while the rest of the Weintraubs were banned from Russia. The light sentence was only due, Buchan believed, to the active intercession of the German Consul. The band then travelled on to Japan, where they stayed for about six months until they received the Snider & Dean contract. The informant had allegedly seen with his own eyes how the Weintraubs had played in front of 'a number of young Germans who have extreme Nazi tendencies', including employees from a German wool-trading company known for its Nazi sympathies. According to Buchan, all the members of the band were living with women to whom they were not married, so they were not only politically dangerous, but also immoral.[6] They were German citizens with additional passports for other countries, and presumably working as spies in Australia. This assumption was unfortunately reinforced by the fact that the musicians' lawyer had already been arrested. Finally, Buchan advised the authorities to always interrogate Graff on his own, and not in the presence of his English wife, 'as she is known to be a very shrewd and cunning woman'.[7]

Where had Buchan gathered this strange mixture of true and false information, and why had he collected it? Was he motivated purely by patriotism? By his own account, he had served with the Royal Air Force during the First World War and then worked as a salesman for the Burckhardt & Buchan trading company in Shanghai. On a business trip to Leningrad, he had heard of the court case against the Weintraubs from an acquaintance, a high-ranking employee of the Soviet government. It is doubtful whether this statement was true. That said, the passenger list of the *Gorgon* confirms that a businessman named Buchan living in China (albeit with different initials) had travelled with the Weintraubs from Singapore to Australia. Although he had travelled first class (unlike the Weintraubs), he might well have become acquainted with the musicians during the voyage, as there were only thirty-nine passengers on board and he would have had ample opportunity to observe the artists and their partners over several days.

The police investigated these serious allegations, as they had heard only good things about the Scottish-born Buchan. First, they went with him to the houses of Weintraub and Graff and made discreet inquiries as to whether these persons actually lived there. Next, they searched the offices of the said wool-trading company[8] and conducted further interrogations.[9] The authorities visited Emanuel Frischer at his flat, where they also met his brother Adolf, his brother's wife Hildegard and two German visitors. They confirmed the Frischer brothers' personal details and learnt that they were both members of the 'Weintraubs Orchestra'. When asked why the band left Russia before the end of their contract, Emanuel Frischer answered that, in the meantime, they had obtained an engagement in Manchuria. He then informed them of his marriage in Moscow,[10] and gave details of his Russian wife Lidia's subsequent arrest and his unsuccessful attempts to trace her whereabouts.

The officer on duty noted all this in the dossier, adding, though, that Emanuel Frischer had not answered with the same honesty as his brother. 'Adolf Frischer and his wife appear to be quite good types of citizens, but Emanuel seemed to resent our questioning him as to his private life whilst in the U.S.S.R.'[11] The police also interrogated Cyril Schulvater's brother Ernest, who was married to a Russian dancer. He stated that he had known Frischer's Russian wife before they were married. At that time, she had been better dressed than most Russian women. After the Weintraubs' departure from Russia, she had been arrested and sentenced to five years in prison. Neither Schulvater nor Frischer was able to give any reason for her arrest. On 10 October, the information collected so far was summarised under the heading 'Six members of the Weintraubs Band – aliens – employed at Prince's Restaurant, Pty Ltd' and forwarded to Inspector Keefe of the Military Police Investigation (MPI) section at police headquarters.

On the same day, the intelligence department received an anonymous letter from an informant who signed himself 'Loyalist'. He had noticed suspicious movements at 51 Roslyn Gardens where, according to him, an older and a younger man had been living on the first floor for some fifteen months with a strikingly pretty, blond woman. It struck the informant as strange that these men were always at home during the evening, although they were supposedly working in the theatre. Finally, he reported: 'The last three months the young man has appeared to be very busy, last Friday and Saturday a number of Germans went up to the flat with heavy suitcases and came away with them empty.' This neighbour must have been observing the enemy aliens' home in great detail in order to have seen the visitors leaving and been able to estimate the weight of their suitcases, but it was war-time and the informant, who wished to remain anonymous, thought he was doing his country a service: 'I pass this information on purely as a precaution and definitely in the interest of my country who is at war.'[12] The designated address was known to the police: another member of the Weintraubs was living on the first floor, and had likewise been denounced as a potential public enemy. The three people observed by the informant were John Kaiser, his wife Gerty (the Weintraubs' stage manager, whom he had married on 4 September), and her father, Richard Pfund.

The war flushed out all the old anti-German prejudice again. But when it came to calls to boycott German music, Thorold Waters issued a warning in the *Australian Musical News*: 'Bach, Beethoven, Mozart, Schubert, Schumann, Weber and even Wagner of the heroes and mythigods, are not our enemies but our friends.'[13] On the other hand, works of living German composers on which royalties were still being paid were no longer performed. As early as October 1939, Bernard Heinze had used this argument to remove a piece by Richard Strauss from his programme.[14] Six months later, in a confidential document, the BBC ordered a 'Ban on alien composers' that prohibited the broadcasting of works by living foreign composers, including refugee musicians from Germany.[15] The ABC followed this programming decision and, in addition, required singers to perform German Lieder only in English translation.[16] To Thorold Waters' regret, the upshot of this was that the culture suddenly became politicised and provincial.[17] He also criticised the fact that the main theme of Beethoven's Fifth Symphony, which was displayed as a victory symbol on a giant banner in Melbourne's Town Hall, was incorrectly notated. From 1941, he illustrated his editorials with this theme, correctly notated and with the sub-text 'Hitler is doomed! Hitler is doomed!' Meanwhile, although even he believed that by now German music had lost its innocence,[18] Waters continued to defend Richard Wagner.[19]

Strong xenophobic tendencies were rife within the Sydney police force and held not least by W.J. Mackay, the New South Wales Chief of Police. Although he had helped the Berlin Jew Fritz Brandmann to immigrate, Mackay was notorious for his mistrust of foreigners; at times he is said to have regarded them as criminals, and as a danger to the local women.[20] Given this mood, it is no wonder that the above-mentioned denunciations provoked the Director of Military Operations and Intelligence in the Ministry for the Army, Major W.J.R. Scott, to take immediate action against the suspects. One of his colleagues, Inspector Keefe, warned him against acting too hastily, on the grounds that they did not yet have enough evidence to justify any 'drastic measures'; but he thought it sensible to open a dossier on the relevant persons and compare it with other documents.[21]

On 15 September, Frank Kitson made a pointed enquiry on behalf of the Musicians' Union at the department of the interior regarding the nationality of the band members. His discovery that Graff, Weintraub and Weiss were German citizens was welcome ammunition for his struggle against them. In Kitson's view, the Weintraubs represented such dangerous competition that even the help of the secret service was needed. It was probably not coincidental that he chose as his contact person the zealous Major Scott. (It is now known that Scott was chief of staff for the fascist Old Guard and a right-wing radical, who at times spied for Japan.)[22] It was to this dubious officer of all people that Kitson wrote on 29 November:

> CONFIDENTIAL
>
> Dear Sir,
> Enclosed please find a copy of a further application by the combination known as the Winetraubs, which has been rejected by the Union.
>   It would appear from same that the activities over the air of the Winetraubs are likely to increase rather than decrease. I am aware of your difficulties in the matter, but am sending along a copy of the application in the hope that it may be of assistance to you in curtailing their employment whilst we have competent Britishers capable of carrying out the same work.
>
> Yours faithfully,
> F. Kitson
> Secretary[23]

In view of the war, Kitson – who himself was working as a musician – exploited the general fear of underground activities by enemy aliens. As if it were a matter of national security, he asked the officer in the army ministry to help him to eliminate this unwelcome competition. Kitson might have marked it confidential because he was conscious that his request lay outside the officer's normal area of responsibility, and possibly the law. Although he suspected there would be problems, he believed that with Scott he would find a sympathetic ear. After all, he invoked patriotic interest: from his point of view, the preferential employment of local musicians. The enclosed copy of Horst Graff's letter of 23 November – under the letterhead 'The WINETRAUBS Comedy Melodians' – contained an impressive list of the cities in which they had appeared ('Performed and Broadcast in Amsterdam, Antwerp, Auckland, Berlin, Brussels, Budapest, Bucharest, Copenhagen, Geneva, Milan, Moscow, Mukden, Munich, Oslo, Paris, Prague, Rome, Shanghai, Sydney, Tokyo, Vienna, Wellington, Yokohama, Zurich and 200 other Cities') and read as follows:

Dear Sir,
Now that nearly a year has passed since our last conversation, I hereby apply again on behalf of the Weintraubs for membership to the Musicians' Union of Australia. The Weintraubs have been in Australia now for nearly three years and intend to make this country their home. As you are probably aware, two of our members are Poles, one is a Peruvian and three arrived here as Non-Aryan Germans, but their passports have become invalid.

You will find that during our stay here, we have never broken any of the Union's rules, but would feel much happier if we had your support and guidance. We pledge ourselves never to work individually but only as in our present combination. As we anticipate in the near future, bigger radio performances with eventually additional musicians, it appears rather a pity that we should select these men from the ranks of the non-unionists, when we know that unionists would be more entitled to this work.

If your present rules forbid you to accept alien members, we would be very glad to become associate members until such time as our status allows us to achieve full membership.

Looking forward to a favourable reply

Yours very truly,
Horst Graff
Business Manager

Leo Weiss, John Kay, Manny Fisher, Horst Graff, Stefan Weintraub, Ady Normand[24]

With this letter, Graff clearly signalled that the Weintraubs wanted a good relationship with the powerful Musicians' Union. The group's expanding activities could also provide new jobs for Union members.

Graff's information was correct, as the department of the interior well knew. This is evident from a letter that the minister's secretary, J.A. Carrodus, sent to Kitson on 28 December. Once again, Kitson had protested against the continued presence of Stefan Weintraub, whom he called the 'conductor' of the band. In his reply, Carrodus, who was usually conservative in refugee matters, pointed out that the employment of the Weintraubs Band at Prince's Restaurant did not endanger any Australian jobs but, on the contrary, resulted in new work. He noted that, in the meantime, Craig Crawford's band had added four Australian musicians. Therefore, one had to admit that the Weintraubs' engagement had in no way harmed the aims of the union.[25]

A ministerial memorandum of 19 October specifically mentioned the positive testimony that a personality like F.E. Baume had provided for Horst Graff. The department noted with unease that the union opposed issuing permanent residency permits:

> Mr Graff and Mr Kay are both men of superior class in their profession, and the only difficulty standing in the way of granting permanent admission is the objection raised by the Musicians' Union of Australia to the permanent admission of alien musicians who are likely to play in dance bands or orchestras.

The department was shrewd: in the case of the Weintraubs, it said, acceding to the Union's demands would result in the band splitting up:

> Several members of the 'Weintraubs' were granted permission to remain permanently before the protest came in from the Union and it would be unsatisfactory to break up the combination by not allowing Messrs Graff and Kay to continue with the troupe.

Although this was the obvious consequence, and both men were known to hold resolutely anti-Nazi views, the department still did not dare to make a decision against the stubborn union. And so the memorandum pleaded for an adjournment. 'It is suggested that authority to remain permanently be deferred for the present, the matter to be further reviewed in, say, six months' time.'[26] Minister Foll agreed with this suggestion: the applications from Graff and Kay were to be considered again at the end of May 1940. Thus Frank Kitson had won another battle in his fight against foreigners. He was determined not to give an inch.

The influx of Jewish refugees had subsided since the outbreak of war. On T.H. Garret's recommendation, they were now permitted to enter only if they had relatives living in Australia, or were special cases.[27] The London-based cellist Otti Veit was able to immigrate in January 1940 only because her husband, the mining engineer Kurt Eisner, had been living in Kalgoorlie, Western Australia, since February 1939. To avoid submarine attacks, the newspapers no longer reported ships' arrivals and departures. Thus the steamship *Reno* docked in Melbourne unannounced in February 1940. On board were the music publisher Victor Alberti, whose daughter Emilie had been living in Australia since 1939, as well as the fifteen-year-old Adolf Faktor, who had recently trained as a musician in Paris and changed his first name to Adrian. Every morning, the travellers had had to put on their life-jackets. 'In the Mediterranean, as we came down we actually saw the British submarines on one side and the German ones on the other', Factor remembered. 'And they were signalling to one another, just waiting for something to happen.'[28] In spite of this threat, the *Remo* arrived unscathed in Australia.

Only with the greatest difficulty did the singer Leonie Feigl find a passage to Australia at this late stage. Her daughter, Julia, and her husband, Viktor Kerner, arrived in Sydney in January 1939, followed by her brother Ernst in August. Only in May 1940, with the help of the Quakers in Paris, had Leonie Feigl obtained a passport and visa for Australia. In Marseilles, she caught the last ship travelling to Australia, the *Commissaire Ramel*, which was already on the high seas when German troops entered Paris on 14 June. This led to a conflict of loyalties for the French crew, especially as the authorities in Noumea, New Caledonia, sympathised with the Vichy regime. For over two months, the *Commissaire Ramel* roamed around, until on 18 July, during a stopover in Suva (Fiji), the governor requisitioned the ship in the name of the British government. Five days later, armed personnel of the New Zealand *Achilles* came aboard and took the ship via the New Hebrides to Sydney, where it arrived with its remaining sixteen passengers on 5 August 1940. Leonie Feigl was overjoyed to be finally safe with her relatives in Australia, after such a long and arduous journey. On the other hand, the *Commissaire Ramel*, which was henceforth used as a British ship, was sunk by a German auxiliary cruiser in September.

Ousted by Competitors: The Fate of the Weintraubs

Meanwhile, the Weintraubs were facing other problems. Whereas the band had been presented on its arrival as a 'musical League of Nations'[29] and a 'continental combination', to many Australians it was now just a German group, a mouthpiece for the enemy. Thus, in late 1939, they had to prematurely end their lucrative participation in the radio programme 'Rinso

Melody Riddles'.[30] In early 1940, however, they were still playing every night at Prince's Restaurant, and with great success. The guests included Prime Minister Menzies, who was seen in press photos with the German refugee band. He had expressly warned against the dangers of precipitous boycott actions and declared that it would be a disaster if enlightened countries, in defending freedom, were to put their own freedom at risk.[31] On 17 November 1939, the Weintraubs appeared with their rivals, the Comedy Harmonists, at a Red Cross fund-raising concert in Sydney Town Hall – probably for the first time in their history, both Berlin groups stood on stage together, and in Sydney of all places. The motto for the evening was 'We'll Hang Our Washing on the Siegfried Line',[32] and the patrons were the British Governor-General and his wife, Lord and Lady Gowrie, and the Governor of New South Wales, Lord Wakehurst. In March the following year, the Weintraubs learned from Bendrodt that they were to play at other fund-raising functions, namely at a garden party at Government House in Canberra, where Lady Gowrie would be the host, and at a ball in the Canberra Hotel under the patronage of Mrs C.A. Carrodus, wife of the secretary of the department of the interior.[33] That enemy aliens, of all people, had been chosen for such exposed, patriotic occasions must have seriously alienated men like Kitson and Scott. It was probably owing to them and their pressure that the band was experiencing the increasing problems that eventually led them to break up.

Horst Graff had no idea of the dark clouds gathering when, on 15 April 1940, he applied to the police for the necessary permit for the band to travel to Canberra. After all, enemy aliens were subjected to travel restrictions during the war. The officer on duty was surprised by the self-assured presence of the tall, well-dressed German who arrived at the Darlinghurst police station at 2.40 p.m., made his request in a loud voice, and evidently expected to receive the permits immediately. Much to his annoyance, Graff was told that written applications were necessary. The police officer found Graff's behaviour provocative and asked for his file, where he read that his visitor had a German passport. On 22 November, the censors had intercepted a letter to Graff in which his brother (who was living in Honduras) asked for support for their parents, who had remained in Berlin. The police officer had no idea of the brothers' solicitousness about their Jewish parents

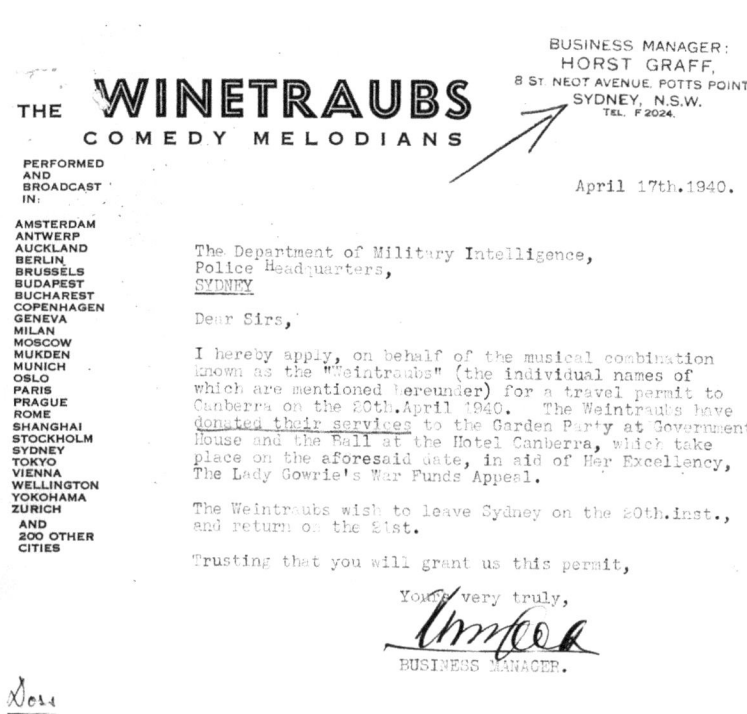

Figure 13: On 17 April 1940, as Business Manager of the 'Winetraubs Comedy Melodians' Horst Graff, applied for permission to travel to Canberra for a charity concert. The printed stationery lists places where the group had performed. (NAA: C123, 1213)

in Germany; in view of the war, it was enough for him to know that an enemy alien was in contact with Berlin. That same day, he drafted a memorandum to the security service, in which he warned against issuing a travel permit. 'In the circumstances the desirability of this man and his Band playing at what is probably a patriotic function seems very much open to question.' Affixed to his letter was a note written on 16 April, possibly by Major Powell, confirming this recommendation under the heading 'Horst Graff with Weintraubs': 'It is strongly recommended that this application be refused. It is highly improbable that Lady Gowrie can know what sort of people these are, and there is no justification for them being allowed to play at a patriotic function.'[34]

Horst Graff, however, still felt very confident, especially as the invitation had come from a high-ranking official. Two days after his visit to the police station, and only three days before the performance, he submitted the required written application to the Military Intelligence department at police headquarters. He did, in fact, receive the required permit. It was therefore with some pride that, on the morning of 20 April – while Hitler's birthday was being celebrated in Germany – the six musicians travelled to Canberra, where they were once again the main musical attraction. After the garden party, some of the guests moved to the Canberra Hotel, where the Weintraubs performed the music for the ball. The *Canberra Times* announced this as the highlight, for they were Sydney's best-known dance band.[35] According to another newspaper report, the hall was decorated with gladioli, chrysanthemums, dahlias and palms, and the numerous guests included both the British and the Canadian High Commissioners and their wives. When the musicians did not immediately stop playing at midnight, as stated in their agreement, a police warning followed, and was promptly recorded in the musicians' dossier in Sydney. Nevertheless, even after that, Graff succeeded in securing another important live appearance. As reported in the *Music Maker* on 30 April, the Weintraubs' 'Crazy Show' would soon be playing at the Tivoli Circuit, Sydney's leading variety theatre.[36] But this never took place.

Once again, Frank Kitson did everything in his power to prevent further activities of this jazz band that enjoyed such eminent patronage. On 3 May, he wrote to Lady Gowrie and pointed out that inviting an overseas band to Canberra had created a very awkward situation. In his reply, the Governor-General's private secretary vigorously defended the invitation that had been extended to the Weintraubs; Lady Gowrie had wanted to help these Jewish victims of Nazi tyranny. Kitson was not satisfied with this; rather, in a further communication, he made it clear to Lady Gowrie in no uncertain terms that these successful musicians were by no means in need of help.[37]

In light of the German army's rapid advances and the danger of invasion in Britain, many Australians now felt stronger ties to the United Kingdom than ever before. The wave of solidarity with the empire led to a blanket distrust of members of enemy nations.[38] As in Britain, there were warnings in Australia about a fifth column, and it was feared that docks and harbours could be threatened. Just at this time, the six-month period expired, after which the department of the interior was to review the permanent residency permits for Graff and Kay. On 19 May, Kay reminded the department that a decision was due.[39] Being aware of the Musicians' Union's opposition, he did not mention his membership of the Weintraubs band. Instead, he argued solely from the point of view of a music publisher; on Microphone Music Publishers letterhead, Kay explained that with a permanent residency permit he could make the case for Australian artists much more effectively than had been possible hitherto.

In this critical situation, however, the department of the interior was unable to issue any new residency permits, since this responsibility now lay with the department of defence.[40] New regulations facilitated the internment of refugees who still had relatives in Germany and therefore appeared to be susceptible to blackmail. In this matter, the authorities worked on the assumption that many of the refugees emigrated with the permission of the Gestapo.[41] Such warnings fell on fertile ground at the New South Wales Security Service. On 6 June, hundreds of foreigners were detained in Sydney, including some who had already been imprisoned on 4 September and subsequently released. In the early hours of the morning, police officers in groups of three went to the homes of the persons sought, most of whom were still asleep. They had to dress quickly and were then taken to city prisons. Among them were three of the Weintraubs Syncopators: Horst Graff, Sydney John Kay and Stefan Weintraub. On the other hand,

Leo Weiss, who had also arrived with a German passport, and the Frischer and Schulvater brothers were spared.

A newspaper article that day reported that these arrests were based on comprehensive police research carried out during the previous nine months. Most of the victims were Germans who lived in the eastern suburbs close to the harbour, and therefore near sensitive military installations. The newspaper failed to mention that the majority of these refugees had chosen Potts Point and Bellevue Hill not for spying, but for practical and financial reasons.[42] Walter and Annemarie Dullo, for example, were located on New South Head Road in Double Bay. Ernst Kaufmann, the physician who was passionate about music, also resided near the harbour in Potts Point, in the very same house as Graff (8 St Neot Avenue). On 25 September, he had to submit a written Form of Parole confirming that during the war he would undertake no action, either directly or indirectly, that could harm the security of the British Empire.[43] After that, he was left in peace.

Those arrested were only allowed to take a few personal belongings with them.[44] Stefan Weintraub was put in a cell with all the others at the nearest police station, then taken to Darlinghurst Prison, and finally in a barred van to Long Bay Gaol, where he was treated as a criminal.[45] On 10 June, along with 112 other Long Bay prisoners, Graff and Weintraub were transferred to a transit camp in Orange, 260km away, where 580 provisional flatbeds stood on a clay floor in a barn-like hall.[46] There was very little seating, and hardly any room for their luggage.[47] Orange had been chosen because of its distance from the coast; here it was impossible for suspected spies to gather information about port facilities. The camp was surrounded by a double barbed wire fence and guarded by soldiers from the 54th Garrison Battalion.[48]

Weintraub was outraged at his imprisonment, which was apparently triggered solely by his German passport. He felt it was a deep injustice – after all, he was no Nazi, but rather a victim of the regime. A few days after his committal, he wrote a letter to the camp commandant.[49]

17 June, 1940

Dear Sir,
I hereby obediently apply for release from internment for the following reasons:
I am of full Jewish origin and therefore naturally opposed to the Nazi regime.

> I have proved my loyalty to the British Empire on many occasions and I am prepared to assist the Commonwealth of Australia in any capacity required.
> An investigation will immediately establish the above mentioned facts. Hoping that my request will be dealt with favourably, I am yours obediently
>
> Stefan Weintraub

His appeal was to no avail. Rather, Weintraub learned that while searching his flat, the police had seized his wife's Swedish passport, which put her in a precarious situation. Irene Weintraub turned to the Swedish Consulate-General, which urgently requested the police to return the passport.

Her husband made further desperate attempts to leave the internment camp. In another letter to the camp commandant, he provided further information in proof of his loyalty to the British Empire. He stated that he had already applied for Australian citizenship one and a half years before the war began. In September 1939, he had offered his active support to the king and his dominion; this offer lay, in writing, before the Jewish committee in the Maccabean Hall. He and his colleagues in the band had stood up in various ways for the patriotic cause: 'Amongst many appearances a number of performances were given before and on behalf of their excellencies Lord and Lady Gowrie, the Red Cross, the Lord Mayor's Fund, before soldiers in camps, and on many other occasions.' Irene Weintraub visited her husband in the camp on 21 July. Since they both believed he had been arrested by mistake, they thought it appropriate to provide more detailed information. The next day Stefan Weintraub drafted a type-written declaration in which he mentioned his grandfather, the principal cantor at the Great Synagogue in Königsberg, and sketched a history of the band.[50] Once again, he referred to their patriotic performances and emphasised that he did not know the reason for his internment. Presumably jealous rivals had spread false rumours about him. Indeed, the fact that Horst Graff, Sydney John Kay and Stefan Weintraub were so relentlessly pursued was probably caused by the fatal combination of colleagues' envy, the Musicians' Union xenophobia and suspicion of espionage.

As a rule, most of the other refugees who had landed in Australia signed a declaration of loyalty to the British Empire (Form of Parole) in September 1939. Despite this, there were repeated expressions of mistrust.

For instance, in November 1940, one of Walter Dullo's neighbours complained that people conversed in a foreign language (presumably German) in his chocolate shop. The conductor Kurt Herweg also came under suspicion, because neighbours reported on parties at his flat where a German victory had supposedly been celebrated with calls of 'Heil Hitler' and 'Down with the English'. When it was discovered that Herweg had been a sergeant in the German army during the First World War and that both his parents were still living in Germany, he was also arrested and taken to the Tatura camp in October 1940.[51]

In Stefan Weintraub's file, there are two curious documents dated 9 August 1940. One states that the contents of his home, including new furniture, an electric vibraphone and other musical instruments[52] had been sold, and that the proceeds were to provide a regular income for his wife for the next eleven months.[53] The second is a declaration by Cyril Schulvater that he wished to employ Stefan Weintraub at his café in Ashfield.[54] It is possible that Weintraub's release was conditional upon his having a secure income. Until then, the band members had never had any financial problems. Around 1930, the group was said to have been the most expensive jazz orchestra in Germany, earning at least 1,000 to 1,200 RM a night.[55] Evidently, further performances were in doubt, so they had to find other ways to earn money. The internment of its leading members had become a question of survival for the band. Initially, the Frischer brothers and Leo Weiss continued to appear as a trio at Prince's, but without Horst Graff, Sydney John Kay and Stefan Weintraub there was no Weintraubs Syncopators. Stefan Weintraub's own energetic efforts to secure his release were motivated not just by his own fate, but also that of his colleagues. Although in August he wrote yet another letter requesting his release and offering additional fund-raising concerts for patriotic purposes, he remained in detention.

In September, Graff and Weintraub were transferred to the large camp at Tatura in northern Victoria, which was also intended for those enemy aliens considered the most dangerous. The conditions in Tatura at that time are described in a chronicle compiled by German prisoners:

> The corrugated iron huts were hot in summer and cold in winter, and draughty in all seasons, in short: always uncomfortable. In summer it was 109° Fahrenheit

[43° Celsius] and in winter it often went down to freezing point. Instead of windows there were metal flaps. There was nothing other than a miserable straw sack and the usual blankets. There were no beds, tables or chairs at all.[56]

Stefan Weintraub was housed in this camp, along with open supporters of Hitler and Mussolini, so he fought all the harder for his own release. When he wrote again to the camp commandant on 14 September, three months after his arrest, he again stressed his complete loyalty; as he had no other explanation for his detention, he again assumed that he was the victim of denunciation by other musicians.

> As I am a Jew and therefore have in no way any possibility to go back to Germany or any other country of this kind, I considered Australia as my new homeland since I arrived in this country 3¼ years ago, and, after having got the permission to stay here indefinitely (in 1937) I learned to adopt an enthusiastic patriotism for the Commonwealth, as every Australian who is acquainted with me, knows. I tried to be naturalised nine months before the outbreak of war and I did everything in my power to prove my loyalty [...].
>
> I could not possibly think of doing anything harmful to an Empire, at war with a country which expelled me only because I am of Jewish race and which robbed me and my relatives of all that we had and deprived me of all rights. No-one in Australia could despise such a country and his inhabitants more than I.
>
> I am interned now for more than three months. The reason for it is absolutely unknown to me, I can only presume that untrue denunciations of jealous competitors – because I had some success with my work – could have been the motive for my internment. What have I done that I have had to go through all this and that I cannot find a corner in the world where I am welcome? I never had anything to do with politics, I never did anything against the laws of any country where I have been, and I endeavoured especially to become an honest and useful Australian citizen. I am sure that the Intelligence service must have found out that all my correspondence, my personal contacts and behaviour showed my loyalty to this country and I only wished to prove that any suspicion against me is groundless and therefore I am compelled to think that my internment is unjustified.[57]

Stefan Weintraub had doubtless heard that by no means all the Jewish refugees with German passports had been interned. Henry Adler, who also came from Berlin, was still giving his accordion class at Nicholson's College for Modern Music. Weintraub knew from one of his wife's letters that the band members who were still free had established a new ensemble: Fisher's

Sextet, together with Henry Adler and Samuel Lee. But residence in the vicinity of the harbour had not led automatically to detention. Walter and Annemarie Dullo continued to manufacture and distribute pralines, even though suspicion was aroused when their chocolates reached the Governor-General's office. Because Stefan Weintraub was not implicated by William Buchan's accusation of espionage, it can safely be assumed that the main reason for his arrest was his leading role in the band. Furthermore, Buchan's allegations against the group's 'immoral' lifestyle no longer applied to him, since he had married his Swedish partner, Gertrud Irene Bergmann, in September 1939.

Figure 14: From the Peruvian Passport of John Kurt Kaiser, issued on 28 March 1934 in Zurich. (NAA: A435, 1946/4/1792)

John Kay also felt that he had been treated unjustly. Immediately after he was apprehended, Kay had informed the Military Investigation Department of his Peruvian citizenship in a letter written from Long Bay Gaol:

> Dear Sirs,
> I, John Kurt Kaiser have been arrested as enemy alien, but I am of Peruvian Nationality – my grandfather Jacob Kaiser lived in Peru, my father Morris Kaiser was born in Canao (Peru) – unfortunately he went back to the Continent and so I was born in Leipzig. But I was never recognised as German by the German authorities. I was duly registered as a Peruvian national at the Peruvian consulate in Berlin, 28th March 1925. [...]
>
> I would like to mention that I was driven from Germany – not being allowed to work on account of being a Jew – I have given many times proof of my loyalty in playing as a musician for Red-Cross-Concerts, the Patriotic Fund and Lady Gowrie's Red Cross Ball. I declare again that I feel 100% pro-British and Anti-German.[58]

In this letter, Kay (Kaiser) gave further reasons for his opposition to the Nazis. After all, they had stolen all his assets. His Berlin-born wife and her father – both of whose immigration to Australia he had organised – had also lost all their possessions in Germany. Incited by these experiences, he had composed and conducted the music for the Australian animated cartoon *Adolf in Plunderland* that was produced by Eric Porter.[59]

On 10 June, Kay was also taken from the prison to the internment camp in Orange but, unlike Graff and Weintraub, he was not transferred from there to Tatura. Several weeks later, when he had still not been released from Orange, on 25 September his wife Gerty turned to Major Powell, to whom she gave her utmost assurance that her husband had never sympathised with the Nazis. A month later, there was still no satisfactory outcome, so on 16 October Kay sent a plea for release directly to the Prime Minister; he knew that Robert Menzies had been outspoken about cautious internment, and that he knew and appreciated the Weintraubs. The musician reminded him of the band's contribution to the war effort and described his situation of being locked up with Nazis as desperate. Kay was appealing to the well-known British sense of justice. Like Stefan Weintraub, he was unable to explain his internment any other way than through malicious slander. He urgently requested a hearing in order to prove his innocence. Having already told the camp commandant in several letters that he was not a German citizen, on 18 October he again requested a hearing before the Appeals Board.[60] Since he had, in fact, immigrated with a Peruvian passport, he was released from the Orange camp after six months, on 19 November.

Kay and Weintraub's assumption that they were the victims of incrimination triggered by rivals is supported by documents in Weintraub's file. Evidently rumours about the Russian espionage case had leaked out and been used for further defamation. The file contains a letter, dated 26 October and headed 'Jewish Refugees', which mentions the suspicion of espionage and repeats the allegation that the band had performed for Nazis. In conclusion, it says of Stefan Weintraub: 'He is an enemy alien and his release from internment is not recommended.'[61]

And so Graff and Weintraub remained in detention with Nazi supporters and other Nazi opponents in Tatura. The Hitler opponents included the conductor Kurt Herweg and the auditor Max Joseph, who had once advised emigrants in Berlin.[62] (In Sydney, Joseph opened a laundry, which was such a success that it provoked jealousy among his competitors.) On 3 December, Graff, Herweg, Joseph and Weintraub all signed a letter to Percy Spender, the Minister for the Army, requesting that they be heard before a tribunal.[63] It was unbearable for them as Jews, they said, to be interned with Nazi supporters. On 30 January, they had had to witness how these people celebrated the anniversary of Hitler's rise to power, and how they blamed the Jews for Germany's defeat in the First World War. A complaint was filed on 4 February. A few days later, these internees discussed the question as to whether they should adopt the definition of Jews as set out in the Nuremberg Race Laws. As to who, exactly, should be considered as a Jew, three points were to be debated:

a) All those who were Jewish as set out in the Nuremberg laws, plus all those who described themselves as refugees.
b) All those who were 100% Jewish according to race.
c) Only those of Jewish faith.

They adopted suggestion C. Max Joseph, whom the Jews in Tatura had elected spokesman, approached the camp commandant on 27 February;

he recounted these events, including the celebrations of 30 January – involving not physical, but emotional distress – and requested separate accommodation.[64] In response, the 'Aryan' Germans declared that in future they would no longer insult the Jewish refugees.[65]

When the Aliens Tribunals were established in March 1941, there was finally a chance for release. Tribunal No. 1 heard Horst Graff's appeal on 21 March. Graff had already emphasised his absolute loyalty in a letter to the camp commandant; since his marriage to a British woman, he had tried to erase his German characteristics and had avoided using the German language.[66] First, the claimant's representative confirmed Graff's Jewish heritage and his continuous activity with the Weintraubs Syncopators since 1924. Graff was also sworn in and heard by the Tribunal. He added that, until 1914, his father had owned a chain of department stores, before switching to other commercial enterprises. His brother, formerly a lawyer, lived in Honduras. His British wife, who was not Jewish, was the daughter of Sir William Graeme, a member of the Prince of Wales' staff. At the beginning of the war, Graff had offered his service to the country in Sydney's Maccabean Hall. When the committee wanted to know whether the Weintraubs had played any anti-Hitler songs, Graff gave an example:

> Mr Menzies was at one of our performances and applauded very heartily. You may remember there was a song called 'Little Sir Echo';[67] we took the music of it and as far as I can reconstruct it, it was as follows: 'Little Sir Hitler, where can he be, I ask, I ask … He is a cruel little wretch, I do not like his moustache.'

The Tribunal also considered a letter from the well-known journalist and radio author Alexander Macdonald, who had known Graff for four years as a decided opponent of the Hitler regime:

> To me, who have worked with Mr Graff almost constantly up to the time of his arrest, it appears incredible that anyone could conceive him as an 'enemy alien'. I can assure you that he has nothing but gratitude and love towards this country.[68]

Finally, the Aliens Tribunal recommended Graff's release from internment. However, it took the relevant security authority until 25 August to take up the case. It summarised, once again, that it was a case of an enemy alien of suitable age for military service, whose mother and father were still living in

Berlin. In spite of considerable security concerns, which above all stemmed from the Weintraubs' alleged involvement in the unexplained matter of espionage in Russia,[69] the authority finally took notice of the Tribunal's recommendation. Before Graff's release from Tatura on 4 September, he had to sign a declaration of loyalty:

> I, Horst Graff, hereby solemnly promise and undertake that I will not do any act whatsoever or be guilty of any omission whatsoever which may directly or indirectly be or tend to be hostile or unfriendly or detrimental to the interests or the defence of Great Britain and/or the Commonwealth of Australia in the present war or which may directly or indirectly assist any enemy of Great Britain and/or the Commonwealth of Australia in the present war.
>
> Dated at Tatura, Victoria, this 4th day of September 1941.
> Horst Graff

The long internment and the protracted disputes with the Musicians' Union had frustrated Graff to such an extent that he no longer saw any possibility of working as a musician in Australia.

A few days later, Stefan Weintraub was also heard before the Tribunal.[70] Mr D. Menzies represented the Minister for the Army, and Mr A. Masel appeared on behalf of the claimant. In his opening speech, Masel pointed to the similarities with the Graff case. Like Graff, Weintraub was Jewish, and special emphasis was placed on his grandfather's work as a cantor.[71] Once again, a detailed history was given, then Weintraub was sworn in and questioned by his lawyer. He stated that he had last performed in Germany as long ago as February 1928, and that he had never returned because of the Nazis. He could not answer any questions relating to the alleged espionage. That said, it was clear that he held Cyril Schulvater in less esteem than other members of the band. After almost one and a half years of pointless detention, Weintraub was finally released at the same time as Herweg and Graff on 4 September 1941.

It was a difficult new beginning, as in the meantime Weintraub's furniture had been sold. Instead of the band named after him, Fisher's Sextet was now playing at Prince's Restaurant. Why, after the return of the three internees, was there no revival of the earlier ensemble? Did the members of Fisher's Sextet regard their former colleagues as rivals, or were they bound by contracts? One thing is certain: Craig Crawford and his men did everything they could to prevent a revival of the competition. They had warmly welcomed the arrest of Graff and Weintraub, and advocated longer detention. According to a police report of 12 September, 'Members of Craig CRAWFORD'S band (Australians) have expressed amazement at the release of GRAFF and WEINTRAUB since, they say, both are "Nazis of the Nazi-ist", particularly GRAFF'. Strangely, the police report ruled out fear of competition or envy as motives for such statements, as the Australian band had long received preferential treatment anyway.

> It has not been lost sight of that jealousy of the other Band (WEINTRAUB'S) may be a factor. This seems unlikely, however, since WEINTRAUB'S Band acted merely as a stop-gap, playing for about half an hour while the members of CRAWFORD's Band were having supper round about midnight. WEINTRAUB'S Band does not appear, therefore, to have jepordised the prospects of CRAWFORD'S Band in any way.[72]

The fact that they were not a stopgap, but a serious rival in terms of quality and public appeal remained undocumented by the police, who were thereby suggesting that the infamous allegations against the Weintraubs were possibly justified. The report emphasised that all the members of Crawford's band shared these views.[73] In March 1935, this New Zealand band had come to Australia in the face of strong opposition from the Musicians' Union.[74] Six years later, the former foreigners were in the driving seat: they themselves were furiously persecuting 'foreign' rivals.

Stefan Weintraub was disappointed that his former employer, Bendrodt, did not make him any satisfactory offer after his release. While the impresario was allowing Fisher's Sextet to appear afternoons and evenings under better conditions, he offered Weintraub only a one-hour slot per day. Was Bendrodt also pressured by the war? Annoyed, Weintraub began negotiations with Bendrodt's competitor. Romano's Restaurant, on the corner of Elizabeth Street and Martin Place, was interested in a small four-piece band made up of Weintraub, Graff, Karoly Szenassy[75] and Henry Adler, and offered them £40 per week. Weintraub accepted this offer, although Graff declined at first for fear of another internment. When Bendrodt heard about these negotiations, he called the musicians into his office where, according to Weintraub, the following conversation took place:

> 'Well, Mr Weintraub, I have heard you are going to play at Romano's. Do you know that the Musicians' Union will make some trouble? How would you like that the papers write about you – "Former German soldier plays in leading Restaurant"? Of course I cannot blame you for being a German soldier, you know how people are when they read something in the papers. Then they will make trouble.'
>
> I said to him, 'Well Mr Bendrodt, I know that in your Band there is a German too, a Mr Weiss.'
>
> He said, 'Yes, but that is different. He was not a soldier and his parents are Polish.'
>
> I said, 'Well Mr Bendrodt, I worked with Mr Weiss for nine years, and I never knew before that his parents were Polish.'
>
> He said, 'Yes, that is different. You were a soldier and people will be against you.'[76]

Weintraub took this as a threat, so ten days later he went to the police, who questioned Graff, Kitson and Bendrodt about the allegations; but Bendrodt denied having threatened Weintraub. In any case, he could not offer him any work.

> He pointed out that he could not again employ Weintraub or Graff seeing that they were of German nationality and had been interned, as he had a duty to perform to his patrons, although he would like to do so as he had no personal grievance against them and that they were first class artists.[77]

Because of the war, not even this formerly brave entrepreneur dared to revive the Weintraubs band. Bendrodt bowed to the pressure of public opinion, which in this case was again essentially controlled by the Musicians' Union.

According to the police report, Kitson had also put Romano's under pressure by goading a friend, the Secretary of the Returned Sailors' and Soldiers' Imperial League of Australia (RSSIL),[78] to join him in protest against the employment of foreign musicians. This man – or so he admitted to the police – did not even know the Weintraubs. When Kitson was asked whether he could accuse the Weintraubs of anything negative, he had

The Fate of the Weintraubs

to deny it. It is remarkable that, during this police hearing, Kitson justified his reservations against the foreigners on the grounds of public opinion: 'He contends that Romano might be well advised not to employ Aliens in the Band at his Restaurant seeing that he was dependant on the Australian public for his livelihood.' In the light of such a statement, one can assume that Kitson also threatened Bendrodt with this argument, which was vague but at the same time effective.

As Romano's Restaurant continued to employ Stefan Weintraub and his four-piece band, the union secretary launched an all-out attack in an interview with the *Truth* newspaper.[79] Under the heading '"Society Folk Prefer Alien Musicians". Union Secretary in Spirited Protest', one read about his outrage that the Weintraubs were apparently getting preferential treatment in jobs. They had even been allowed to appear at a garden party at Government House in Canberra, against which he (Kitson) had already taken a stand in a letter to Her Excellency Lady Gowrie. It was strange, he said, that they were appearing in the most elegant night clubs, where they were in contact with rich people and leading personnel from the navy, army and air force. Since he had written to Lady Gowrie, several members of the group had been interned, but they had now been released. He complained that these musicians were appearing in public again, some of them in Romano's Restaurant. In the familiar style of an informant, Kitson then gave the full Italian name of the proprietor: Orlando Azalin Romano. Three other Weintraubs were to be heard at lunch and dinner in Prince's Restaurant, and a fourth in the Café La Palette in Double Bay.[80] The leader of the group was the German Jew Weintraub. 'Stefan Weintraub is said to be the proud possessor of a high military decoration from the last war, given to him by Kaiser Wilhelm.' Here it was, the denunciation that Bendrodt had warned about. Weintraub continued to play with his four-piece band at Romano's but, from then on, he was tarred with the brush of Prussian militarism and received no further engagements.

This negative image was conjured up quite consciously. A telltale sign was an anonymous letter sent to the police in February 1942:

> Looking for spies? Try the Weintraubs, a dance band of 6 Germans. Three are playing at Romano's and three at Princes Restaurant. Have a look at Mr Graf (the name

speaks for itself) and see if you can see a German officer in mufti looking at you. If there is any 'benefit of the doubt', it should be on our side.[81]

Although the Weintraubs had split into two bands as a result of the internment, and although their members were of different nationalities, they continued to be stereotyped as German spies. Given the preceding events, one can speculate about the statement quoted in the police report of 12 September ('both are "Nazis of the Nazi-ist", particularly GRAFF'). By then, what had formerly been the most famous German dance and jazz band no longer existed. From 1942 onwards, its founding members, Horst Graff and Stefan Weintraub, had to earn a living outside the world of music, as mechanics. Graff took a job with a wire company in Annandale[82] and moved to a new flat that Bishop Pilcher arranged for him.[83] The bad luck continued for Stefan Weintraub, whose wife left him. During her husband's internment, she was able to have her Swedish citizenship reinstated, having lost it after the marriage, and was now working as a mannequin and beautician. On the other hand, Weintraub still had the impression 'that I can't find a corner in the world where I am welcome'. Sadly for him, it seemed that the consolatory message in the 1932 hit – that 'somewhere in the world' there must be 'a little bit of luck' – would never be realised.

CHAPTER 12

'In corrugated iron huts': Deported to Hay and Tatura

'I came here a stranger': Arrival at the Camp

Following in Britain's footsteps, from June 1940 Australia interned many enemy aliens for reasons of national security. It was Prime Minister Menzies' wish that this should affect only single persons who were regarded as dangerous, for example communists, Jehovah's Witnesses or people who were considered to be spies. A little later, when Britain asked Canberra for direct support, Australia signalled its willingness to accept 6,000 internees and prisoners of war from the United Kingdom.[1] The Ministry for the Army suggested that 2,000 men should be accommodated in the desert-like town of Hay, NSW; 3,000 men, women and children should go to Tatura, Victoria, and 1,000 to a place in South Australia yet to be determined. Whereas at first the detainees were housed in prisons and temporary camps, the agreement to assist Britain led to the construction of special facilities. Australia set up a total of nineteen internment camps that were guarded by veterans of the First World War: among them were Camps 1, 2, 3 and 4 in Tatura and Camps 6, 7, and 8 in Hay. About 7,000 of the internees had been living in Australia and a further 8,000 came from overseas. Some of these people were interned for up to seven years.[2]

The *Dunera* left Liverpool on 10 July, a week after Australia agreed to help, and arrived in Melbourne on 3 September. There, the first group to disembark included Dr Adolf Ehrenfeld and the brothers Leonhard and Manfred Adam, but also the approximately 460 German and Italian survivors of the *Arandora Star*, including Erwin Frenkel; all dressed in old British uniforms. They boarded a train to the northern town of Rushworth, whence they were taken in lorries to Camp No. 2. The remaining *Dunera* passengers went on to Sydney, where they went ashore in Darling Harbour on 6 September. After fifty-seven terrible days at sea, these 1,984 refugees were exhausted, hungry and unkempt, but happy at last to have their feet on firm ground. Many of them, like Otmar Silberstein, had been ill and were taken straight to hospital. They were used to being hurried along by the British soldiers and thought the Australians would expect the same; thus it was that they ran as fast as they could with their few possessions from the ship to the trains with barred windows waiting at the pier. But 'the moment we were in the train, everything changed. Everything was more leisurely. A few armed soldiers were sitting in the train, and we began to make friends with them'.[3] The Australians in their strange uniforms had heard horror stories about the new arrivals, but their mistrust soon disappeared when they discovered that they were not guarding former soldiers from Hitler's army, but Jews, Catholics, Protestants, communists or union members who had been racially or politically persecuted.

Once again, the new arrivals were not told where they were going. They only knew that the train had left Sydney and was chugging through a wide plain with bare trees and dusty scrub, a scene that hardly changed until dusk. The monotonous clattering continued through the night. In the morning light, the country looked even more bleak and uniform. Now and then, they saw a few kangaroos and gum trees. After an eighteen-hour journey, the train finally reached its destination. The sign at the little station read 'Hay'. This isolated location 720km south-west of Sydney was meant to prevent enemy aliens from becoming involved in any espionage or other dangerous activities, or attempting to escape. Just on 2,000 men left the trains, which had pulled up one after another. In the searing heat, surrounded by a cloud of dust and guarded by soldiers on horseback, they marched in columns onto the bare, brown plains. Camps 7 and 8 were each surrounded by barbed wire and had four watch-towers manned by soldiers carrying machine guns.[4] The men marched through three gates and then assembled on a big parade ground where they were counted, and the camp rules read out. By this time, some of the music lovers among the refugees might well have felt truly isolated, like the wanderer in Schubert's *Winterreise*.

The two camps were only 200 meters apart, but a partition erected between them blocked the view and prevented any communication. Each camp consisted of thirty-six hastily built corrugated iron barracks on wooden posts, each of which housed twenty-eight men. Camp 7 held predominantly Jews and Camp 8 more political prisoners and Catholics.[5] The camp rules followed British practice. Each barrack elected a speaker. The detainees from every six huts selected a captain, from whose ranks a camp supervisor was chosen to help the guards maintain order and discipline. All the internees had to follow the guards' orders. Anyone who tried to escape would be fired at after one warning. The possession of any sort of weapon was strictly forbidden, as were conversations with anyone outside the camp. Each prisoner was allowed to write at most two letters per week, clearly legible and if possible in block letters. Parcels with books and sheet-music could be received, but they would be checked first. There was a strict daily routine: 6.30 a.m. reveille; 7.00 a.m. bedding made up; 7.30 a.m. breakfast; 10.00 a.m. first roll call; 10.45 a.m. camp inspection; 12.30 p.m. dinner; 4.00 p.m. evening roll call; 4.30 p.m. tea, followed by supper and lights out at 10.15 p.m.[6]

'Hay Days': Music behind Barbed Wire

Two months after the *Dunera* deportees arrived at the camps in Hay, they were visited by Major Julian Layton, the British Government envoy.[7] In his report, he stated:

> Hay is situated in one of the most inhospitable parts of the State, the surrounding country for hundreds of miles being virtually desert for the greater part of the year. […] It seems that this uninviting district must have been chosen for the reason that should any internee manage to escape, his only means of survival would be to keep to the river.[8]

Attempts at escape would necessarily end at the Murrumbidgee River, and therefore in the immediate vicinity. But Layton also mentioned the beginning of a cultural life in both internment camps:

> There is a Musical Union which organises plays, literary evenings – including readings by Shakespeare and Chaucer –, musical comedy, vaudeville etc. I was sent a special invitation to be present at a Vaudeville entertainment on Saturday night 2nd inst. It may not be out of place to mention that the invitation bore a monogram of

the Musical Union and the title of the Show was 'Hay Days Are Happy Days'. The monogram and title had been made by a stamp artistically carved from a potato, but the only paper available was a piece torn from a perforated roll!!

The stage had been improvised from tables and boards, army blankets were used as curtains, and spotlights were made from jam jars and kerosene containers. After the very entertaining performance, everyone had sung 'God Save the King', which one would not have expected from enemy aliens. Afterwards, he, the commandant and the officers were entertained over a cup of tea with violin and piano solos and songs.[9] Since the show was for the detainees and their guards, it was performed in English.[10] According to Layton, about 120 people took part, more than 10 per cent of the internees in one of the camps.

Under the heading 'Personal Problems', he added how the men were suffering from being designated as 'dangerous enemy aliens'.

> Between 700 and 800 internees have visas, or permits to enter other countries, e.g. countries in North or South America, Palestine etc. but especially U.S.A. Their papers are, however, in England, and they are worried whether they will be able to get them.

Already outraged over their deportation to Australia, the refugees were now deeply disillusioned; protesting against their recurring accommodation behind barbed wire and the separation from their wives,[11] the primitive living conditions and the hot desert climate. At first, they contemplated boycotts; but gradually the idea prevailed that their difficult situation could and should be improved by their own cultural programme.[12] After all, in both camps there were many well-educated and artistically talented people. They could tie their experiences of British internment to new cultural activities, including language courses and lectures.[13]

Professional musicians in Camp 7 included the composer Hans Werner Katz, the pianist Peter Stadlen, the violinist Majer Pietruschka and the music student Werner Baerwald and, in Camp 8, the conductor Kurt Behrens, the composers Ray Martin, Eddy Kassner and Max Meyer and the music students Johannes Chlumecky and Otmar Silberstein (violin) and Rudi Laqueur (piano). The title of the programme mentioned by Layton, 'Hay Days are Happy Days', referred to an ironic song that two musicians in Camp 8 had written about their accommodation.[14] Ray Martin and Eddy

Kassner[15] were even able to extract something positive from the brutal desert heat: in Hay, nobody needed to complain about rain or storms.

Hay Days
Hay Days, Hay Days,
Make your Hay days your play days,
Sing on everyday Doo-de-loode-a.
Smile with never a care.

Hay Days, Hay Days,
Make your Hay days your gay days,
Yours is all the fun, yours is all the sun,
For it shines everywhere.

Long as we're all palls and we're together,
Never mind the rain and stormy weather

I know, you know,
Troubles come, but they do go.
Doors will be opened up
You'll be right on top
Live your life your own way
Calling every day: Hay day.

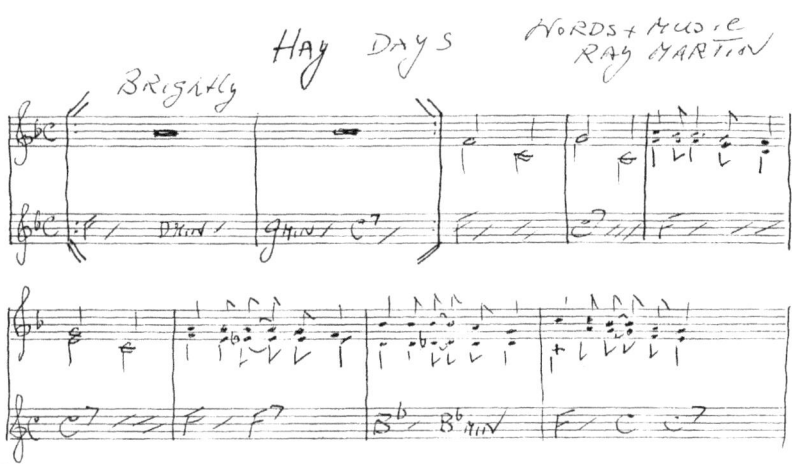

Musical Example 2: Ray Martin, *Hay Days* (Lippmann Archives, Sydney).

In another song, Martin and Kassner encouraged the detainees to associate the word 'Hay' with 'happy'. Then you would not want to die. 'Blow all your troubles/Away like bubbles!' Internment had one more advantage: Since there were no women, the men could get up earlier every morning – hurrah!

Say Hay For Happy
Say Hay for happy
And you feel snappy
And you won't want to cry
Say Hay for happy
And you feel snappy
And you won't want to die
Though you even sell your overcoat
For just the sight
Of one more bite
Of tasty butterbrot
Blow all your troubles
Away like bubbles
And start a little game
Without your girlie
You get up early
Oh what an awful shame!
So you say: R for Rosenthal
B: for Blumenduft
And S for snappy
So say Hay for happy

Later, Ray Martin wrote more 'Broadhay songs', including a satirical one about the hated Lieutenant O'Neill from the *Dunera*.[16] The refrain was:

Oh, Oh, O'Neill, My dear O'Neill
I wish you'd only know just how we feel
You don't know how much we love you
For the kindness we got of you
Man of steel; Oh, Oh, O'Neill.

Some of these songs were accompanied by vocal 'jazz bands', in which the men imitated various instruments with their voices.

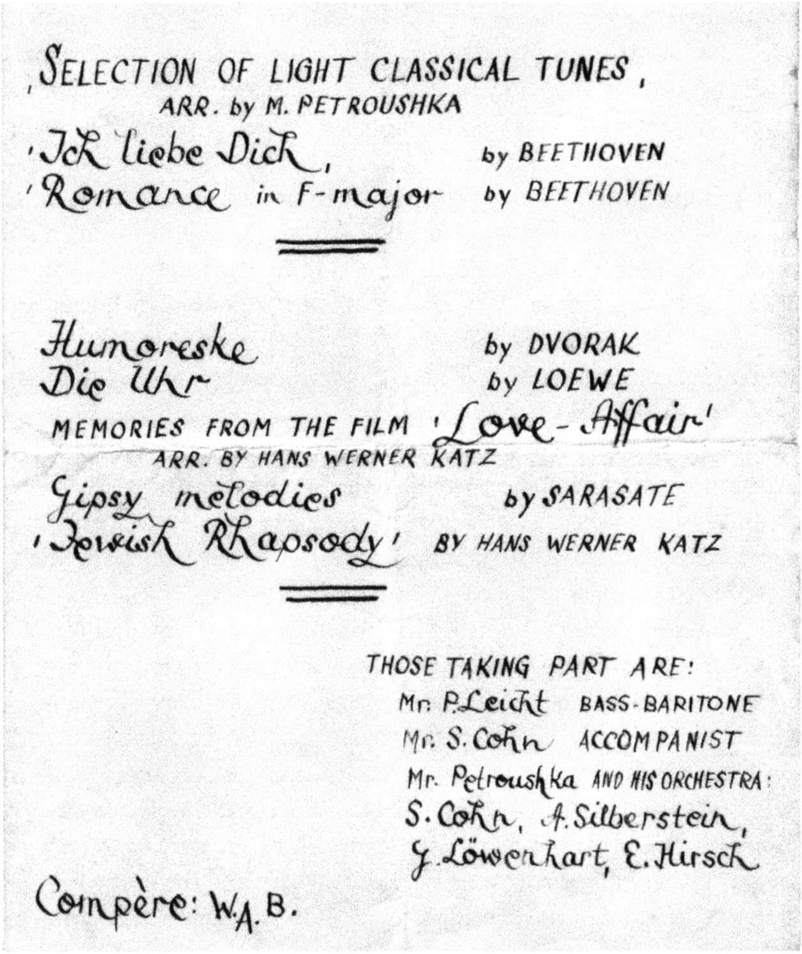

> SELECTION OF LIGHT CLASSICAL TUNES,
> ARR. by M. PETROUSHKA
>
> Ich liebe Dich,   by BEETHOVEN
> Romance in F-major   by BEETHOVEN
>
> ———
>
> Humoreske   by DVORAK
> Die Uhr   by LOEWE
> MEMORIES FROM THE FILM 'Love-Affair'
> ARR. BY HANS WERNER KATZ
> Gipsy melodies   by SARASATE
> 'Jewish Rhapsody'   BY HANS WERNER KATZ
>
> ———
>
> THOSE TAKING PART ARE:
> Mr. P. Leicht   BASS-BARITONE
> Mr. S. Cohn   ACCOMPANIST
> Mr. Petroushka AND HIS ORCHESTRA:
> S. Cohn, A. Silberstein,
> J. Löwenhart, E. Hirsch
>
> Compère: W. A. B.

Figure 15: Handwritten programme for a concert with light classical tunes on 12 December 1940 at the Hay internment camp, arranged by Majer Pietruschka, performed by men who had been deported aboard the *Dunera* to Australia. (Tanya Makin, Melbourne).

Camp 7 also offered a concert on 10 December for the army chaplain, Rabbi L.A. Falk, the envoy of the Jewish Welfare Society. The four-piece 'Petrushka Orchestra' played pieces by Beethoven, Dvořák and Sarasate as well as a *Jüdische Rhapsodie* by Hans Katz, supplemented by songs and ballads by the bass baritone Peter Leicht.[17] The rabbi was moved by this show of talent and afterwards campaigned for the construction of a recreational barrack and for more musical instruments.[18] Whereas Camp 7 was supported by Jewish patrons and the Quakers (Society of Friends), Camp 8 received a harmonium, a piano and a violin from the Catholic community in Hay.[19] Besides Ray Martin and Eddy Kassner, Camp 8 also included former members of the London Kleine Bühne [Little Theatre], where exiles like the actors Josef Almas,[20] Leo Bieber[21] and Hugo Schuster had performed. They lived in the same barrack as the painter Hans Abarbanell and the communist poet Max Zimmering. At the end of the year, they presented a twelve-part revue, *Erinnerung an Europa* [Remembering Europe]. According to Zimmering, it was a resounding success: '1,500 spectators out of a camp population of 1,000 attended the four performances.' There was a wall newspaper, the *Camp News*, which reviewed the performance and observed that '"Remembering Europe" approached the very best traditions of pre-Hitler German and Austrian cabaret'.[22]

The *Camp News* was usually in the refugees' mother tongue. This was compatible with the predominantly socialist orientation of Camp 8, and the belief in an internal German resistance, in 'the other Germany'. In December, Goethe's *Faust* was performed here in its original version, with music arranged by Max Meyer,[23] who also composed a 'Dunera Mass'.[24] In contrast, racially persecuted Jews tended to dissociate themselves from their former homeland. They openly demonstrated their loyalty to the British cause by giving preference to the English language and the host country's lifestyle. One leading article entitled 'Our Future' that appeared in Camp 7's weekly newspaper, *The Boomerang*, stated: 'In order to succeed against tremendous odds, we shall have to break away from our German-trained mentality, pare off all that is too ostensibly "continental" in our behaviour and adopt the English or American outlook on life.'[25]

Camp 7 had a Recreation Department with a camp theatre led by the journalist Simon Hochberger.[26] Two months after the refugees' arrival in Australia, they presented a play with music called *Hay-Fever*, its title referring ironically to the locality. Sigi Cohn and Hans Katz were responsible for the music and the stage construction was organised by the architect

Emil Wittenberg, who mentioned in the camp newspaper that communal enthusiasm overcame all their difficulties.[27] The stage curtain was designed by Hein Heckroth,[28] a specialist who, prior to 1933, had been Head of Stage Equipment at the Municipal Theatre in Essen, and had taught stage design at the Folkwang Academy. In 1932, he had built the prize-winning sets for the anti-war ballet *Der grüne Tisch* [The Green Table] by Kurt Jooss and, like Jooss and his dancers, had fled to Britain. While Sigi Cohn played the piano and accordion as a hobby, Katz was an experienced composer. At the time, there was still no piano available for *Hay-Fever*, but they apparently had a few violins and accordions and evidently a saxophone. Hochberger's programme was handwritten on a piece of coloured paper:[29]

> Ouverture
> Four Funny Fellows On Accordeon (Gross, Löwenhaard,[30] Wurmser, Altmann)
> The Vagabond Snipers (Federn, Wurmser)
> MAN and Cigarettes (K. Levy)
> Optimist and Pessimist. Scetch by Maas (Komorner, Maas)
> Some Music on an Accordeon (S. Cohn)
> Entre'Acte Tango (Pietruschka, Silberstein, Löwenhaard, Cohn, Gross)
> The Illustrated Phrase-Book (Komorner, Siho)
> Three Niggersongs (Clusmann, Cohn, Saxophon: Adler)
> Csardas by Monti (Pietruschka, Cohn)
> Selected Melodies (Pietruschka and his Band)

Music and sketches in English followed each other in seamless succession. The musical climax and finale was a potpourri led by the violinist Majer Pietruschka. Given the lack of sheet music in the camp, the famous Csárdás by Vittorio Monti and other works must have been played from memory or improvised. That same month, there was another programme of entertainment with the clowns 'Ric and Rac', the Parisienne singer 'Lia Montez' played by a man, and *The Naughty Nineties*, a composition by Hans Katz, once again performed by Pietruschka and his band.

According to an article in *The Boomerang*, Camp 7's Recreation Department was one of the controversial aspects of its self-governance. Unlike in Camp 8, there was criticism of the low percentage of professional artists, which left the impression that the standard of European theatre seemed unattainable.[31] The author of the article therefore recommended that they give up classical theatre for the time being and concentrate on entertaining revues. Correspondingly, in February, there was a revue titled *Trips and Onions*; in March, a *Show without a name* (with Tartini's Devil's Trill Sonata played by Pietruschka and folksongs with Clusmann); in April, an evening of entertainment and, to conclude, another revue, *Wir reisen um die Welt* [We travel round the world] with music by Katz performed by a nine-piece orchestra.[32] Georg Rapp – a former Oxford student and a member of Erich Fried's London poetry circle – had written suitable lyrics for the nine revue scenes, including 'Soon the day will break away' (Hawaii), 'You are in the pink, sir' (New York) and 'Je t'embrasserai' (Paris). According to Klaus Loewald, some of these tunes could have become hits, had they been circulated outside the camp.[33]

The Recreation Department in Camp 8 was led by the film producer Max Kurt Sternberg. Following the revue *Ernst-heitere Weltumsegelung* [Serious-light-hearted Circumnavigation] by Max Zimmering, which reminded the internees of the *Dunera* odyssey with songs like 'Eine Seefahrt die ist lustig' ['A cruise is fun'] and 'It's a long way to Tipperary', on 27 December he presented another programme entitled *Snow White – S3828*.[34] In the title, a mysterious number was added to the fairy-tale character of Snow White; no programme note or any other documents have survived. There was a repeat performance on New Year's Day, and on 22 February a gala premiere entitled *Snow White and the Seven Hay Days*, with highlights from earlier shows.[35]

The young Camp 8 pianist Rudi Laqueur was equally passionate about classical music and jazz – he participated successfully in a jazz competition and on 2 February he also accompanied the violinist Johannes v. Chlumecky (who had evidently obtained another instrument) in works by Schumann, Tchaikovsky and Chopin. By contrast, in Camp 7, Peter Stadlen concentrated solely on 'serious' music. Since there was no piano, at first he had to look for other possibilities to practise. The commandant actually allowed him to leave the camp regularly, albeit accompanied by a guard, in order to play on a church organ.[36]

In the absence of a piano, Peter Stadlen established a choir that rehearsed Austrian folksongs and hand-written compositions. As soloists for the Christmas concerts on 25 and 26 December, he chose the bass baritone Günter Hirschberg and the Viennese tenor Hans Edelmann. The programme included a choral work by Orlando di Lasso, three Christmas songs arranged by Stadlen, arias from Mendelssohn's oratorio *St Paul*, and excerpts from the C major Mass attributed to Mozart (K. App. 232). Beginning in the cool of the evening at 9.00 p.m., this concert evoked a real Christmas mood in the desolate environment: both singers and audience were transported to a 'better world', one that was reflected in the watercolour on the programme, which depicted a filled choir loft with organ next to the figure of Christ. The Mozart Mass excerpts were so successful that they were repeated at another concert by the Stadlen choir on 18 February 1941. Majer Pietruschka and Otmar Silberstein played Bach's D minor Concerto for two violins in the first half of the programme, and Günter Hirschberg sang the Schubert lieder 'In die Ferne', 'Du bist die Ruh' and 'Aufenthalt'. Then they found a piano score of Handel's oratorio *Israel in Egypt*, whose subject could be compared with the plight of the German Jewish refugees in the Australian desert.[37] On 14 May, this symbolic work was performed in an arrangement for choir, violins, one viola, a cello and piano with Edelmann and Hirschberg as the vocal soloists.[38] Apparently, among the approximately seventy choristers there were some Orthodox Jews who, on the advice of their rabbi, just sang meaningless syllables when the words 'God' or 'Jesus' appeared in the text.[39]

Meanwhile, in accordance with a rental agreement dated 4 January 1941, a Thürmer piano arrived in Camp 7, but it proved to be out of tune.[40] Among the small amount of sheet music available was one score of Beethoven's Fourth Symphony from Klaus Loewald's hand luggage. On hearing of Loewald's arrival,[41] Walter Dullo sent him the early Beethoven piano trios from Sydney. Adolf Brenner wrote to Bernard Heinze, who forwarded piano arrangements of symphonies for two and four hands.[42] Mary Baillie also offered to help. Soon after her arrival in Melbourne in 1939, she had met Schnabel, who was then undertaking a tour of Australia, and had fulfilled one of his heart's desires by showing him a platypus, known in German as *Schnabeltier*. On his departure, Schnabel had given her a framed portrait with a raised forefinger, inscribed with the words 'Always Courage First!'.[43] Mary Baillie may well have had this exhortation in mind when, together with her sister and another friend, she established

Figure 16: Handwritten programme for Christmas concerts of the Stadlen Choir on 25 and 26 December 1940 at the Hay internment camp.
(Felix Edelmann, Vienna)

a Refugee Internees' Assistance Committee with her own funds, a relief organisation that, among other things, provided support for Peter Stadlen, whom she had heard in a concert. Stadlen thanked Baillie in a letter of 1 February, in which he mentioned the 'strange experience' of not having touched a piano since July:

> Do you think you could possibly interest musical circles sufficiently to make representations on my behalf? I feel I could do my best by playing for benevolent purposes as I did prior to my internment in England and at the same time make some contribution to the musical life here.

He then reminded her that, after his last concert in London in May 1940, the Australian politician (and later Prime Minister) Harold Holt wanted to invite him to Australia. He explained that he had last met Schnabel at the beginning of 1939.[44]

In his next letter to Baillie of 29 March, Stadlen mentioned the efforts made by Thomas Mann and Artur Schnabel to secure his release. At the beginning of the month, a miserable rental piano had arrived at the camp, which was only suitable for light music. That said, he was able to use it for an hour now and then. Soon there would arguably be better practice facilities in the new devotional hut, where the piano was to be installed. However, he did not give up hope that, with Mary Baillie's help, he would one day have a more suitable instrument. He preferred a piano with a light and even touch; one that he would look after well and return once the camp was disbanded.[45] Because he had set his hopes on this instrument, Stadlen made no mention of the piano recital he had given that month with Schubert's B flat major Sonata, Beethoven's E major Sonata Op. 109 and a Mozart Sonata in C, probably still on the aforementioned rented instrument.[46] On 13 April, he gave another piano recital. Klaus Loewald called these concerts 'necessary, important, yes, overwhelming contributions to the cultural life of the internees';[47] he was passionate about the pianist's activities. The young man had caught Stadlen's attention when he was whistling the theme of the third movement from Beethoven's Fourth Symphony in the next-door shower cabin. Stadlen questioned him about it and subsequently allowed Loewald to listen while he was practising.

The Jewish cantor Boas Bischofswerder also withdrew from popular entertainment programmes. In his luggage, he had saved a miniature edition of Goethe's *Faust* and a tuning fork; he had directed a choir on the *Dunera*, and continued to do so in Hay. Scores were provided by his son Felix, who had a great gift for retaining music in his head and would write out classical works from memory. This reconstruction of the past gradually transformed itself effortlessly into the construction of original works in the style of Rameau, Handel and Mozart, so that in the Hay camp, Felix Bischofswerder the art student became Felix Werder the composer. Owing to the lack of manuscript paper, he notated his first works on toilet paper.[48]

In March, the choir from neighbouring Camp 8, directed by the Hamburg conductor Kurt Behrens, took part in a 'confessional' Beethoven programme. The Prisoner's Chorus from *Fidelio* made a particularly strong impression: 'O what delight, to breath freely in fresh air. Up here alone is life!'[49] As could be read in the review in the German-language *Camp News*: 'The resounding cry of the prisoners' call to freedom from the impotent apathy of degrading imprisonment was a twofold experience for us, the cry of a fear-filled question.' Their personal situation had rendered their singing all the more intense: 'Particularly poignant was the faithful devotion of the choir, a body of sound conjured up from nothing that in such a short span of time moved beyond the usual black-and-white technique of *forte* and *piano* to achieve ever more delicately nuanced tones.' The reviewer's description of the effect on the listeners was not without pathos: 'A ray of light came over their faces – the light of Beethoven. This solitary source outshines the darkness of the age, which grows deeper and denser the more it is illuminated by the blazing cities of Europe.' In the minds of the audience, he wrote, the little hut in which the concert took place expanded into an imaginary space 'that no longer consists of austere walls and wooden benches, where a clapped out honky-tonk piano no longer clinks and the glimmer of dim ceiling lights fed by an over-worked power plant gives way to a blaze of light that emanates directly from the genius of Beethoven'.

Dresden-born Franz Feuerstein completed the programme with the Sonatas Op. 26 (with funeral march) and Op. 27 No. 2 ('Moonlight'), which were 'technically and emotionally at a very high level', in so far as this was possible on such an instrument. 'In spite of everything, Herr Feuerstein did his name (= Firestone) proud in that he managed to strike so much fire from such a rocky instrument'.⁵⁰

In Camp 8, even the canteen contributed to the musical culture. The chef, Erwin Kallir, was responsible for the delivery of goods, so on 30 January 1941 he inquired about renting a piano from the firm G.H. Harrison & Son in Hay. One of his orders for sheet music fell into the hands of Victor Alberti who, with the help of his son-in-law Rudolph Baré, had found a job with the music business Allans and Co. in Melbourne. On 6 March, Baré advised the camp canteen in writing that the vocal scores they had ordered for the *Flying Dutchman*, *Parsifal* and *Rigoletto* were being sent immediately to Hay, along with volumes of arias for tenor and bass.⁵¹ However, the planned recital apparently never took place.

To some extent, these cultural activities helped the internees to forget the dark side of camp life, the extremes between the hot days and cold nights, and the storms which blew dust right into the huts. On 8 May, the Berliner Dr Arthur Urbach, now working again as a dentist in Hay, wrote to Hermann Schildberger in Melbourne:

> On the whole we're managing here. The food is good. Our intellectual life too, in so far as that is possible. Stadlen is trying hard and making good music here. The composer Katz has written some nice things, and sends his greetings. Lectures, languages, courses are all taking some of the pressure off our internment.⁵²

The detainees were also glad that their mistreatment on board the *Dunera* had led to a decision by the British Parliament to pay compensation. In addition, Major Layton had been able to organise their transfer to another camp with more favourable climatic conditions, so something resembling a farewell mood developed. Some of those who had been most involved in the musical life of the camp received letters of thanks from the camp administration. The letter to Stadlen included the following statement:

> For a long time without instruments and with practically no music, you created with unflinching determination a choir which was the kernel of the musical activities of the past nine months. It has been a matter of admiration to see how much you achieved with only amateurs. We realise the magnitude of your efforts in setting for male choir, four violins, piano and harmonium parts of Mozart's Masses, and Handel's oratorio 'The Children of Israel in Egypt', of which you had at your disposal merely the piano

scores for mixed choir. All the same, more impressive still was your piano recital on the obsolete upright. Let us conclude by saying that your great art has been a source of inspiration and that thanks to your energy, artistic and intellectual values were upheld under adverse circumstances.[53]

Another summary stated: 'What is the Spirit of Camp 7? Put briefly, it is a combination between Oi-Wie-Bitter-ism and So-What-ism. Or, in plain language: Realisation of our helpless situation, and defiance in the face of the unalterable.'[54]

Before all the internees were transferred to Tatura, some of the 'Dunera boys' went temporarily to a provisional camp in Orange, NSW, where the climate was more pleasant and they experienced a different landscape; where fresh green replaced the brown, red and yellow-grey colours they had encountered hitherto. Although there was no piano in the Orange camp, Peter Stadlen thanked Mary Baillie for sending him the score of the *Well-Tempered Clavier*. He said he was even grateful for the Shostakovich piano music, which usually did not interest him.

> So, with my choir split up [...] there is complete absence of music and I spend my time partly with reading Shakespeare and Goethe, but mainly by trying to make out whether there is still a chance of getting to the States or whither [sic] I should catch the next bus back to England.[55]

In late June, when Mary Baillie offered to have an instrument transported to Orange, Stadlen assured her that he would soon be taken to Tatura.

> I live in one hut together with 22 men (most of them artists or scientists and all of them very nice) and when some of them were ordered to go to Orange we others volunteered to go with them in order to avoid splitting up our community which means quite a lot to us. So I hope it won't be necessary for me to choose between my friends and a good piano. The prospect to be able to work again is a great consolation to me – it has been just in these last weeks that I felt how the lack of one year's regular practice began to tell on me. And to play chamber-music would be too good – I longed for that all the time in Hay, even while I performed my arrangement of 'Israel in Egypt'.

A month later, he was able to tell her that their departure for Tatura was imminent. Recently, a mediocre piano had arrived, on which he was practising. Stadlen did not mention that he had just given a private concert with a Schubert Sonata in A minor and the very demanding *Trois Mouvements de Petrouschka* by Igor Stravinsky for the inhabitants of Hut 14 on 14 July.[56] Instead, he told her that he was pinning all his hopes on Tatura, and added: 'I must confess the prospect of indefinitely prolonged internment is terrifying.'

In London, too, people were anxious about relatives and friends still living behind barbed wire. In May 1941, the *Zeitspiegel*, published by the Austrian Centre London, reminded its readers that the internments had begun exactly a year earlier and printed a poem by a young Viennese emigrant, Erich Fried.[57] Only twenty at the time, he later became one of the best-known German-language lyricists of the twentieth century. The same edition of the *Zeitspiegel* carried a belated report on Christmas in the camp at Hay. In late June, there was even better news: 'Sixty-two internees from Australia and 300 from Canada are on their way back to England. The Australians are mostly married men whose wives live in England.'[58] In August, this emigrants' publication printed the first report on the voyage of the *Dunera* and the internment in Hay.[59] This camp, it said, had now been dismantled.

'It is hope that keeps us going': Meeting Place Tatura

The largest group of Australian internment camps was located ten miles west of Tatura, a small town in northern Victoria, 167km north of the state capital, Melbourne, and eighteen kilometres west of the regional centre of Shepparton. Camps 1 and 2 accommodated only male detainees, both local and from overseas: In Camp 1, Compound A there were Germans and Italians from abroad (including Horst Graff, Kurt Herweg and Stefan Weintraub) and in Compound B German and Italian citizens who had lived in Australia for a while. In Camp 2, there were local Germans, Jews and Italians (Compound A) as well as Germans and Jews from overseas (Compound B). Camp 3 was a family camp comprising four compounds, while Camp 4, also divided into four compounds, housed various groups:

Japanese (A), Nazis and communists (B), Jews and anti-Nazis (C) and political refugees from Europe (D). While blackouts were ordered in the rest of the country, these four camps were brightly illuminated by searchlights. The lights went out at 10.00 p.m. and the day's activities in Tatura were tightly structured, just as they were in Hay.

In Camp 1, Hitler supporters were placed together with anti-Nazis who had been arrested in Australia, which caused considerable conflict. The Hitler supporters defiantly held to their convictions, and bellowed the 'Tatura Lied' with the refrain 'Patience, comrades, be of good cheer/ once Germany's won/all will be well again'.[60] The director of the Vienna Mozart Boys' Choir, Dr Georg Gruber, was also put into this camp in March 1941. On a world tour in early June 1939, he had arrived in Australia, where the choir's appearances caused a greater sensation than the guest performances of Artur Schnabel, who was also touring at the time.[61] When war broke out, the choir was appearing in Perth, but, since they were now regarded as enemy aliens, no further concerts could take place. A return journey was impossible, so the young singers stayed with their director in Melbourne, where the Catholic Archbishop, Daniel Mannix, offered them a new home in St Patrick's Cathedral. Gruber took over the direction of the cathedral choir, which Gerhard von Keußler had conducted years before. Amid the war hysteria, one of the local choristers denounced Gruber as a Nazi (without any proof), and thus he was taken to Tatura, where he established and conducted an orchestra. When he escaped from internment at the beginning of 1947, he was arrested and deported back to his homeland, although the young singers from his Vienna choir were allowed to remain in Australia. One of them, Stefan Haag, later became a significant innovator on the Australian operatic scene.[62]

The survivors from the *Arandora Star* were at first taken to Camp 2, early in September 1940. At the end of the month, after a violent dispute between the Nazis and anti-Nazis that culminated in arson, the two groups were separated and the anti-Nazis transferred to a separate division of Camp 3, the family camp.[63] This meant a considerable improvement for these men, as they now had two-bed rooms and their own vegetable garden. They could even see women, if only from a distance. It was here that Adolf Ehrenfeld (who now preferred his third name, Alfred) practised folk songs with his choir, but he declined the suggestion of adding a new verse to the song 'Horch, was kommt von draußen rein' ['Hark! What is that sound I hear?'], which used the words 'Love is an Omnibus, holeidi, holeida/that one has to wait a long time for'.[64] Erwin Frenkel received a visit from a student and friend of his father, the Reverend Joseph Kalb, who had meanwhile become a cantor at the synagogue in Toorak Road, Melbourne. Frenkel himself was chosen as the camp cantor, and opened a 'Viennese Coffee House' to earn some money; he also continued his musical education by studying jazz orchestration.[65]

In September, Tatura saw the arrival of another large group of 272 refugees from Singapore, where enemy aliens had also been interned. They were transported to Australia on the *Queen Mary* under the supervision of forty-two soldiers. With only these few passengers on board, including women and children, this huge ship left Singapore on 18 September and arrived in Sydney a week later. From there, they were taken by train to Shepparton and then by bus to Tatura, where the family camp, Camp 3, had been set up for them. The families of the musicians Hans Bader, Werner Baer, Kurt Blach, Hans Blau, Heinrich Portnoj, Karl Reither, Paul Steiner and Mischa Stiwelband were all housed in Compound D. As for the 'Dunera boys', it was a shock for these people to have to live behind barbed wire. Just two days after their arrival, they spoke to the camp commandant, urgently requesting their release.[66] When their appeal had no effect, they began to adjust to the situation, and even to organise cultural events. With his vast experience in Viennese clubs and cabarets, Hans Blau produced a programme entitled *Tatura Melody 1940*, which was shown on 3 November. As director, he chose Heinrich Portnoj, whose wife Annie made all the costumes. The show offered classical music (Reither and Blach), Russian melodies (Stiwelband and Blau) and 'Camp Swing'. Paul Steiner appeared as 'A Man with Six Instruments', accompanied by Hans Bader at the piano. To conclude, Hans Blau (with his accordion) sang entertaining songs like 'Malayan Moon' and 'Wien, Wien, nur du allein' ['Vienna, City of my dreams'] before the evening ended with the anthem 'God Save the King'.

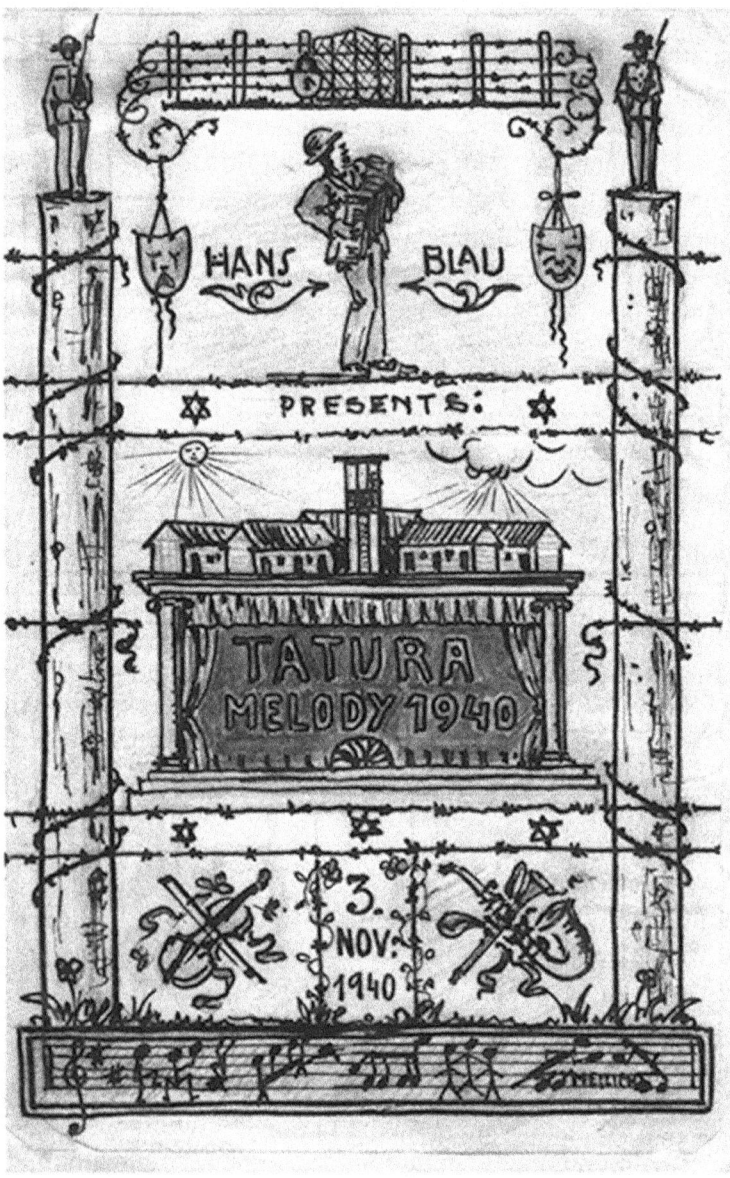

Figure 17: Invitation to the programme *Tatura Melody 1940*, presented by Hans Blau on 3 November 1940. The performers had been deported in September 1940 from Singapore to Australia. (Ilse Blair, Melbourne)

Oskar Fleischer, Hans Holzbauer and Walter Würzburger, all single, were also housed in Camp 3, but separated from the family quarters by a wire-mesh fence. There they met the anti-Nazi faction of the survivors from the *Arandora Star*. At the end of the year, one of them, Uwe Radok, wrote in his diary of his co-inhabitants: 'There are a few nice people among them; for example, we now have a jazz band, an organist and a violinist, in all 15 musicians [...]. We are already expecting our first tea dance.' A bad piano had arrived before Christmas. He wrote about Fleischer, Holzbauer and Würzburger: 'All original, and just like musicians.'[67] Radok was soon to befriend Würzburger in particular. Despite their separate quarters, the division between the unmarried men and families was not insurmountable, as was evident from the entertainment programme *Laugh and Forget*, in which musicians from both parts of the camp participated. Once again, Hans Blau was responsible for the organisation. The programme cover depicted a huge whale superimposed on the outline of Australia and – possibly a reference to the Old Testament Book of Jonah – spitting out a clown behind barbed wire. The programme consisted of twenty-two numbers, where sketches like 'Mathematics, the Gate to Science', 'Reality and Dream', 'How They Got to Bed' and 'Strength through Joy' alternated with a fashion show and musical interludes provided by Reither, Bader, Steiner and Blau. The three unmarried men, Fleischer, Holzbauer and Würzburger, appeared as 'Three Lonely Musicians'.

Werner Baer used his unwelcome internment to further his musical education. Unlike the *Dunera* refugees, he had been able to bring specialist literature from Singapore to Tatura: two German histories of music, three musical biographies, the *Oxford Companion to Music* and several books on harmony and counterpoint. He resumed his contact with Martin Krutsch and Hermann Schildberger, two old friends from Berlin. Baer hoped to receive new music literature from Schildberger:

> For example, an interesting book on harmony by P. Hindemith has come out; I think it was published in London, and other modernists have also published their ideas in book form. I have got harmony books by H. Riemann and by G. Bumcke, dry books that can't tell me anything, books on counterpoint and form that are fifty or more years old, so I would really like to keep up with the times, especially as here we are cut off from the outside world. In Singapore I already found no stimulus any more; on the contrary, I had to give people things from my tiny treasure, which, indeed,

was regarded there as sensational, but unfortunately I know only too well how much I know, and how much I don't know! Hence my despair about being completely isolated and not getting back into in my profession here, where only light music is recognised because people simply can't concentrate on good music.[68]

All the same, in the camp Baer managed to establish a mixed choir of twenty-five singers, who brought some distraction into the grey monotony of everyday life. In response, Baer did receive several parcels of books from Hermann Schildberger, including writings by Nietzsche and Pfitzner and a two-volume history of music by Otto Keller.

The letter that Baer wrote to Schildberger on 16 April sounded even more negative. He had had to give up the choir, and he did not feel well: 'Living together in such a cramped space is not always very fruitful, and it is not easy to put one's ideas into practice. It's probably called barbed-wire-psychosis!' Early in the year, he had still been able to set some optimistic lyrics by Hans Blau to music:

> Hans Blau: It's Hope That Keeps Us Going
>
> It's hope that keeps us going in our longing
> For some happiness or luck.
> So what if Destiny's opposed – we see it
> Coming back.
> A little spark concealed within the heart
> Keeps courage safe, to burn anew,
> And suddenly you stumble on a path –
> Life smiles on you.
> Things always change, so why should we complain?
> Later there'll be time for sorrow.
> Don't despair – what's there to gain?
> Remember there is always a tomorrow.
>
> Nowadays great optimism seems
> Completely out of place, a thing of dreams.
> But pessimism's altogether worse,
> So keep you head when things are in reverse:
>
> It's hope that keeps us going ...
>
> Watches, rings and even rhinestone fancies,
> All the presents from your ancient aunties,

Can be returned to you if ever lost,
But one thing disappears at great cost:

It's hope that keeps us going ...[69]

Several months later, in June, Baer composed another song (also to Blau's lyrics) that was much more pessimistic and sarcastic. 'The Ballad of the "Un"-forgotten Israelites' began as follows:

Here in corrugated-iron huts
A hundred Israelites are bravely living.
Men and women – children not forgetting,
Who in course of time are going nuts.
Why we're here is something no one knows.
The hope of freedom dwindles day by day,
And each commission tells us at the close
'We can be sure we'll soon be on our way'.

Musical Example 3: Werner Baer/Hans Blau, 'The Ballad of the "Un"-forgotten Israelites' (Author's Archive)

Another verse looks back at the carefree times in Singapore; what once seemed like paradise is now in the past:

> That dream is over, past and gone.
> We've turned ourselves to more delightful things,
> To argument and fighting on and on.
> Whose fault is this, to whom our thanks are owed?
> Barbed wire all around, no onward road –
> An all-the-same where none of us belong.[70]

The bitter irony with which Hans Blau mentions the vague promises of help from various politicians at the end of the ballad also finds its way into Werner Baer's music for these verses. In the piano introduction, there is a quotation from the evangelical chorale 'Praise the Lord, the mighty King of Glory', and then he adopts the ballad style of the *Threepenny Opera*, whereby there is a striking melodic resemblance to Brecht–Weill's 'Ballad of the Pleasant Life'. Between verses, the piano quotes a minor version of the famous drinking song from *Fledermaus* [*The Bat*] by Johann Strauß, for which the words are: 'Happy is he who forgets what can't be altered anyway!' As the hopes triggered by pledges of help were deceptive, apparently all that remained was a fatalistic acquiescence to the status quo.

When Major Layton visited the camp in June, he was appalled by the low morale, which he reported back to London:

> I returned rather perturbed about the whole position, as I found many of the middle-aged men in despair, and the younger internees in a very depressed state, in fact, there is no doubt that the morale of the camp is deteriorating.[71]

In mid-1941, all the single men had to leave Camp 3, because evidently their twin-bed rooms were needed for new couples and families. The news of their impending transfer to the men's Camp 4 caused indignation among those affected. Oswald Volkmann captured this mood in a poem, 'Farewell to Camp 3': 'Uns're Wut ist unbeschreiblich/Denn wir gehn nach Lager vier,/Uns're Nachbarinnen, weiblich,/Bleiben leider alle hier' ['Our anger is indescribable/for we're going to Camp 4,/Our female neighbours/are unfortunately all staying here'].[72] Those affected by the transfer to Camp 4D included Oskar Fleischer, Hans Holzbauer and Walter Würzburger.

In the new camp, Fleischer taught the violin, so he asked A. Constance Duncan from the Victorian International Refugee Emergency Council for some etudes and solo pieces. He wrote to her saying that, in the meantime, there was a piano in Camp 4, and that the pianist Arthur Fuhrmann would like some music, for example the 'Pathétique' and 'Moonlight' Sonatas of Beethoven, as well as Chopin's Polonaise in A major. Fuhrmann was a businessman from Vienna who had lived in Singapore since 1927 and had shown himself in internment to be a skilful amateur pianist. 'It is our intention to provide our fellow-internees with as much benefit from good music, as we have the possibility to do.'[73] Duncan passed the request on to Mary Baillie, who promptly sent Schubert string quartets and some piano music by Brahms and Chopin to the camp. Later these were followed by some Beethoven string quartets and Bach's E major violin concerto.[74] Fleischer reported that, with the help of the music, concerts could be organised in Camp 4D. According to Klaus Loewald, Margaret Holmes, who worked on behalf of the World Student Christian Movement, also made a significant contribution with books, musical instruments and sheet music.[75]

In Camp 4D, Walter Würzburger moved into a communal hut with the photographer Helmut Neustädter, who had also been deported from Singapore. The latter, who later became world famous as Helmut Newton, fondly remembered his clarinet-playing friend 'Wally':

> He was a very gifted musician and possessed a fabulous sense of humor. We decided to set up house together. We were very happy. We used to sit outside our front door, on the steps. Wally composed music. He used to compose it in his head while he was doing camp jobs.[76]

In the 'Camp University', the so-called *Collegium Taturense*, Würzburger gave courses in counterpoint, jazz and arranging, while Dr Ehrenfeld taught music history and theory, and Neustädter introduced photography. In his diary, Radok wrote of Würzburger: 'Discussion about music, especially atonal. Harmonic possibilities exhausted, therefore back to polyphony that consciously avoids vertical connections, groups of harmonically related voices on various planes (Hindemith).'[77] Radok was fascinated that Würzburger could even perform two-part melodies by whistling and humming at the same time. He was interested when his friend mentioned music courses with his father, his early compositions and his life as an exiled jazz musician in Paris.[78]

The Camp 3C internees had a thirst for knowledge, so Mary Baillie sent them books, including literature on the Aboriginal people.[79] The latter greatly interested Leonhard Adam who, as an ethnologist with the German army during the First World War, had interviewed an indigenous Australian soldier. In August, he informed Baillie about an ethnological seminar that he was organising at the *Collegium Taturense*. She promptly sent him a *churinga* (the Aboriginal word for a ceremonial wooden plate), and a boomerang. On 26 October, at a celebratory event marking the first anniversary of the Camp University, a performance of Mozart's *Così fan tutte* overture was followed by Adam giving the keynote lecture.[80] Gradually, he found he had more and more interests in common with Mary Baillie; this resulted in an extensive correspondence and, in 1943, the German scientist and the Australian pianist married. Later, in Australia, they actually managed to identify the Aboriginal person who had long before triggered Leonhard Adam's interest in this distant continent.[81]

On 26 May 1941, most of the 'Dunera Boys' from Hay arrived in Tatura, where they were housed in Camp 2B for the most part; Boas Bischofswerder and his son Felix were accommodated in the family camp. Just six weeks later, the internees enjoyed a programme of light music, arranged and directed by Majer Pietruschka. A small orchestra consisting of four violins, guitar and flute played a colourful selection of works by Delibes, Rimsky-Korsakov, Dvořák, Boccherini, Gounod, Paganini and Johann Strauß ('The Blue Danube') and ballads sung by Anton Ehrenzweig, a judge from Vienna. Hans-Heinrich Gurland had brought his C recorder from London, the only flute in the camp; Landauer's guitar had been crafted by the sculptor Alfred Huttenbach in Hay.[82] In September, when they presented Jaroslav Hašek's *The Good Soldier Švejk* in the camp theatre, the Pietruschka orchestra performed a supporting arrangement of the music, provided by Hans Katz. Peter Stadlen gave his first piano recital in Tatura on 17 September, beginning with Schubert's Sonata in A minor D784 Op. 143, followed by the Beethoven Sonata *Quasi una fantasia* Op. 27 No. 1, Chopin's 24 Preludes and the three movements from Stravinsky's *Petrouchka*.[83] Two days later, Mary Baillie was finally able to visit the pianist in person, and to announce that a good Zimmermann piano would soon be delivered. She also brought the music for the Mozart string quartets, a Schumann piano trio, manuscript paper and a viola. That same day, a string quartet was formed, in which Stefan Pető played the viola.

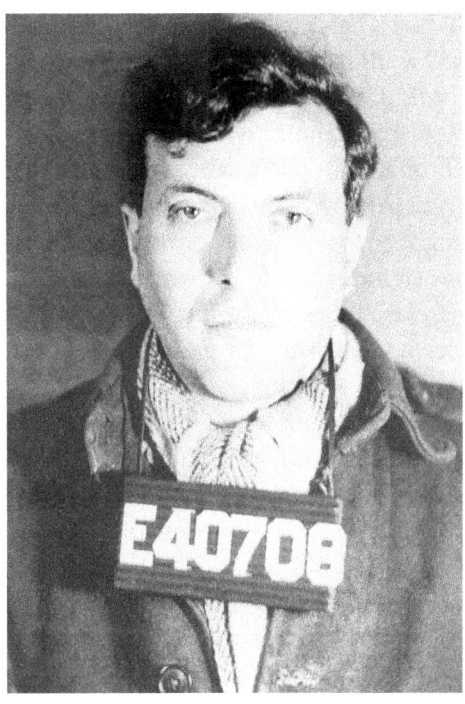

Figure 18: The concert pianist Peter Stadlen applied for registration in Tatura on 16 September 1941, confirming it by his fingerprints.
(NAA: B6531, AUSTRIAN/STADLEN PETER)

Pető, a mathematician and amateur musician, lived in Hut 4, the so-called 'musicians' hut'. Some of the musical enthusiasts (who had lived mostly under the same roof in Hay and Orange) clustered around Peter Stadlen, whom they all recognised as the superior musical authority. Other members of this circle included his brother Erich Stadlen, who was a radio technician, the Berlin writer Ulrich Alexander Boschwitz, the amateur pianists

Gerhard Hamburger, Felix Behrend, Klaus Loewald and Harry Nagler, and the chemist Cornel Polatschek, the only cellist in the camp. They put on private musical evenings in their hut during which, at Pető's instigation, they sight-read string quartets. On 27 September, Stadlen wrote to Baillie: 'A volume containing thirteen string quartets has appeared in camp and these, like the Mozart ones, have all been played through at least once during this week.'[84] Stadlen was also grateful to Mary Baillie for lending him her Schnabel edition of the Beethoven 'Hammerklavier' Sonata.[85] The promised Zimmermann piano arrived, but the pianist did not give any more recitals in Tatura, as he was finally offered the chance to return to Europe. Before his departure, Stadlen conducted Handel's *Israel in Egypt* again, this time arranged for small orchestra and an eight-part male choir. For many, this was an unforgettable experience, 'in which the choir and orchestra sang and played their hearts out'.[86]

Gustav Heinrich Clusmann, the Gershwin interpreter, had already been allowed to return to England on 4 June. In August, Leo Roth, who was cherished in Hay as a chorister and footballer, received an opportunity to reunite with his family in Shanghai. On 13 October, Stadlen, Kurt Behrens, Eddy Kassner and Ray Martin all received their discharge papers. A ship named *H.M.T.D3* – possibly the *Stirling Castle* – headed towards Liverpool via the Pacific route, past New Zealand and through the Panama Canal, in order to avoid German submarines. Whereas, on their journey to Australia on the *Dunera*, the four men had been housed below deck in primitive conditions, this time they were regular passengers. On 1 November, they helped to put on a concert entitled *V for Victory – Variety* in the ship's first class lounge; Ray Martin arranged the music. Eleven days later, two performances of *We're in Love!!* were presented by 'The Stirling Singers. Conducted by Kurt Behrens'. Once again, the music was written and arranged by Ray Martin, with help from Eddy Kassner.[87] These men, who just a year earlier had been regarded as dangerous enemies and were now turning their back on Australia, had in the meantime become a popular attraction.

Although the musicians' hut lost its focal point with the departure of Peter Stadlen, musical life continued in Camp 2. Adolf Brenner made himself available as a choir director, and in October he asked Bernard Heinze for some suitable music. The amateur musician Gerhard Hamburger, who had not dared to play the piano in Stadlen's presence, now overcame his inhibitions and played chamber music with Pietruschka, Johannes von Chlumecky and Cornel Polatschek. In November, he accompanied the promising bass baritone Günter Hirschberg in an aria recital. The Zimmermann piano also came into its own in a programme of Schubert piano duets. Hans Katz used it in November for the revue *Journey Round the World*, an extended English-language version of *Wir reisen um die Welt* that had been performed in Hay and now comprised twelve scenes.[88] In the Russian and Italian scenes, Hans Edelmann shone with his tenor voice, while the orchestra, led by Pietruschka, boasted a xylophone built by the Bauhaus artist Ludwig Hirschfeld-Mack, who had once taught instrument-making in Berlin.

For Christmas and New Year, the Snow White programme was also revived, this time under the double title *Snowhite – Snowhite Joins Up*.[89] Ray Martin's music, based in part on well-known melodies, was heard in a new piano arrangement played by 'Jonny Flynn' (possibly Hans Fichmann from Vienna), Rudolf Laqueur and the amateur pianist Herbert Voss from Berlin. No fewer than eleven musicians took part in a grand entertainment concert on 20 January, once more under Pietruschka's direction, with compositions by Fritz Kreisler, Franz Lehár, Jacques Offenbach, Emmerich Kálmán, Paul Lincke and, last but not least, Hans Werner Katz. His works included an overture and entr'actes from *The Naughty Nineties*, the tango 'I hob' a G'spus' ['I have a girlfriend'] and the English waltz 'Pour t'embrasser je donnerais ma vie' ['I would give my life to embrace you'] from the revue *Journey Round the World*, a Hawaiian song, and a medley entitled 'From Heidelberg to Richborough'.[90] For a musical and literary evening on 1 May 1942, at which there was a mandolin orchestra, the versatile Katz contributed a medley of Russian folksongs and battle songs.[91] Katz, whose non-Jewish wife had remained in Berlin, was free to return home in August. He boarded the Dutch freighter *Westerland* in Sydney, together with forty-two other internees. On 8 October, he transferred in Cape Town to the motor ship *Abosso* which, in spite of warnings, set off for Liverpool without an escort. On 29 October, the ship was hit and sunk by German torpedoes near the Azores. Hans Werner Katz was one of the 362 people who drowned when the ship went down. The return to Europe was his undoing.

New Perspectives

Complaints by British citizens about their internment had to be brought before an advisory committee independent of the military, whereas the Aliens Tribunals were introduced in 1941 to allow internees to appeal against their detention. These Tribunals could only recommend release from internment when there was no threat to public security. In cases of doubt, security interests took precedence.[92] Horst Graff's and Stefan Weintraub's appeals were finally considered in August 1941, and a month later they were allowed to leave Tatura. The conductor Kurt Herweg had applied for a tribunal hearing on 3 December 1940, together with Graff and Weintraub. This took place on 31 March 1941, and Herweg made a good impression. When his release was delayed, he requested a lawyer and was eventually released on 4 September, but he had to pledge in writing that he would not meet with any enemy aliens other than members of his own family, and that he would present himself to the police on a weekly basis.

On 7 October 1941, there was a change of government, and under John Curtin the opportunities for the detainees improved still further. Most importantly, after the Japanese attack on Pearl Harbor in December and the capture of the fortress of Singapore by the Japanese on 15 February 1942 – according to Churchill the most serious defeat in British military history – Curtin took the initiative in order to protect the country from the threat of a Japanese invasion. The working potential of the internees was now utilised, for example for the fruit harvest around Tatura. Top priority was soon given to strengthening the Australian army. The offers of many internees to contribute in some way towards the country's defence were finally heard, which in turn led to the establishment of unarmed military units. In February 1942, when Mary Baillie wrote to the camp commandant enquiring as to the whereabouts of several musicians, she received the news that they had been moved to Camp 2. At the moment, he said, they were picking fruit, and soon after that they would probably be transferred to an Army Labour Corps.[93]

CHAPTER 13

Snow White in Uniform: The Music Revue *Sergeant Snow White*

'A funny looking crowd': The Eighth Australian Employment Company

Owing to the threat posed by Japanese and German warships, which sank the *Orama* in June 1940, for example, transports from Australia to Europe were first restricted, then discontinued. This radically changed the perspective for those internees still in Tatura. They now faced a lengthy stay in Australia and were, therefore, particularly interested to hear that, on 4 February, the Australian Parliament approved the establishment of Army Labour Corps to enable foreigners to participate in the country's defence. The Eighth Labour Company was set up especially for these people and was soon operating as The Eighth Australian Employment Company. Walter Würzburger and Erich Liffmann enlisted in this unarmed military unit very early. On 8 April, more musicians followed: Werner Baer, Kurt Blach, Oskar Fleischer, Günter Hirschberg, Hans Holzbauer, Rudolf Laqueur and Otmar Silberstein, and just a few days later Paul Steiner and Salo Tichauer. New members in May included Erwin Frenkel, Heinrich Portnoj, Majer Pietruschka and Herbert Voss; Mischa Stiwelband joined up in June. Hans Blau, Adolf Brenner, Johannes and Moritz Chlumecky and Karl Reither enlisted in the unit only in September, followed by Otto Blau, Alfred Landauer and Klaus Loewald in October. Hans Blau was released from detention quite late because his wife Nelly's brother was deemed to be a Nazi.[1] As one of the last, Felix Werder only joined in May 1943 as his father was ill and he hoped that, as a member of the military, he could get him better care. This company, totalling 600 men overall, included an unusually high number of musicians.

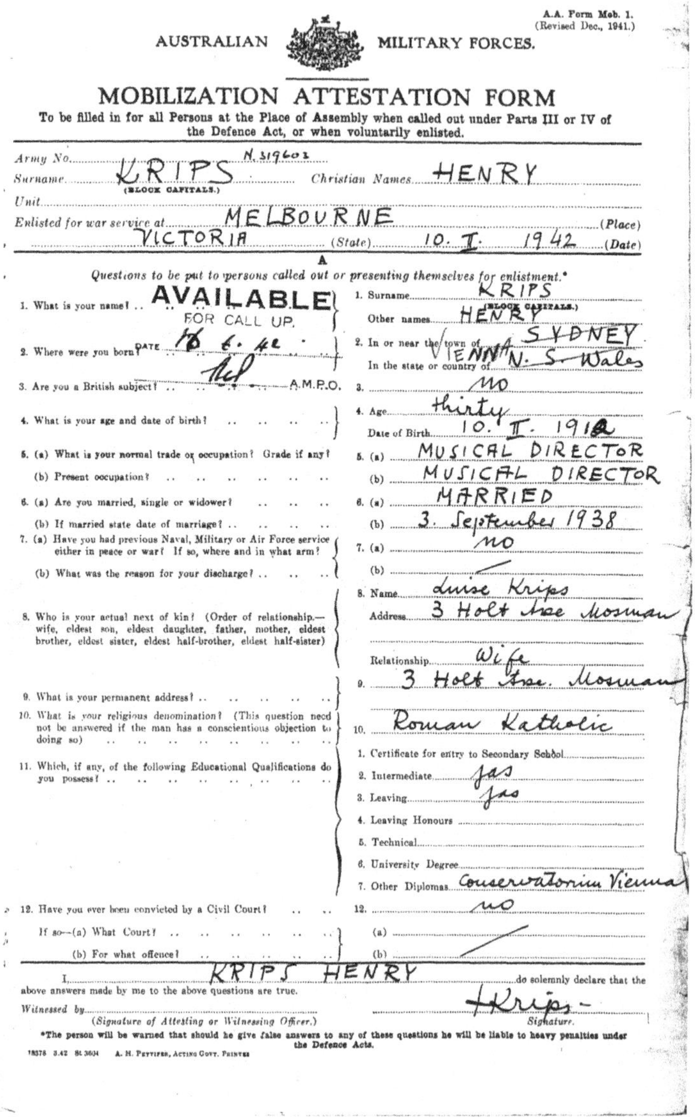

A.A. Form Mob. 1.
(Revised Dec., 1941.)

AUSTRALIAN MILITARY FORCES.

MOBILIZATION ATTESTATION FORM

To be filled in for all Persons at the Place of Assembly when called out under Parts III or IV of the Defence Act, or when voluntarily enlisted.

Army No. N.319603
Surname KRIPS (BLOCK CAPITALS.) *Christian Names* HENRY
Unit
Enlisted for war service at MELBOURNE *(Place)*
VICTORIA *(State)* 10. II. 1942 *(Date)*

A

*Questions to be put to persons called out or presenting themselves for enlistment.**

1. What is your name? .. AVAILABLE FOR CALL UP.	1. Surname KRIPS (BLOCK CAPITALS.) Other names HENRY
2. Where were you born? DATE 16. 6. 42.	2. In or near the town of VIENNA SYDNEY In the state or country of N. S. Wales
3. Are you a British subject? .. A.M.P.O.	3. no
4. What is your age and date of birth?	4. Age thirty Date of Birth 10. II. 1912
5. (a) What is your normal trade or occupation? Grade if any?	5. (a) MUSICAL DIRECTOR
(b) Present occupation?	(b) MUSICAL DIRECTOR
6. (a) Are you married, single or widower?	6. (a) MARRIED
(b) If married state date of marriage?	(b) 3. September 1938
7. (a) Have you had previous Naval, Military or Air Force service either in peace or war? If so, where and in what arm?	7. (a) no
(b) What was the reason for your discharge?	(b) —
8. Who is your actual next of kin? (Order of relationship.—wife, eldest son, eldest daughter, father, mother, eldest brother, eldest sister, eldest half-brother, eldest half-sister)	8. Name Luise Krips Address 3 Holt Ave Mosman Relationship Wife
9. What is your permanent address?	9. 3 Holt Ave. Mosman
10. What is your religious denomination? (This question need not be answered if the man has a conscientious objection to doing so)	10. Roman Katholic
11. Which, if any, of the following Educational Qualifications do you possess?	1. Certificate for entry to Secondary School 2. Intermediate jas 3. Leaving jas 4. Leaving Honours 5. Technical 6. University Degree 7. Other Diplomas Conservatorium Vienna
12. Have you ever been convicted by a Civil Court?	12. no
If so—(a) What Court?	(a)
(b) For what offence?	(b) —

I, KRIPS HENRY do solemnly declare that the above answers made by me to the above questions are true.

Witnessed by .... *(Signature of Attesting or Witnessing Officer.)* H Krips *Signature.*

*The person will be warned that should he give false answers to any of these questions he will be liable to heavy penalties under the Defence Acts.

18378 3.42 St. 3604 A. H. Pettifer, Acting Govt. Printer

Figure 19: Like many other refugees the conductor Henry Krips joined the Australian army. (NAA: B884, N319603)

No less than 44 per cent of the 1,200 male refugees volunteered for army service – a much higher proportion than the percentage of Australian conscripts – and more than a quarter of them of them were accepted.[2] Those who had been in Australia longer, like Henry Adler, Willy Coper, Hans Forst, Adolf and Emanuel Frischer, Heinrich Krips and Curt Prerauer, also joined the army. Since music was allowed in the Second Australian Employment Company, Emanuel Frischer founded his own band, which performed once a week. When Prerauer wanted to establish a soldiers' choir, however, his supervisor regarded it as a waste of time.[3] By contrast, in the Sixth Employment Company, where the young Adrian Faktor began his military service in March 1942, it was the company commander who suggested the establishment of an orchestra.[4] He also sanctioned a string quartet, in which Faktor played the violin.

Walter Dullo was recognised as a refugee alien in July 1940 and put to work with the Allied Works Council from 1943 to 1944; together with Stefan Haag, he worked on building military facilities in Alice Springs, a town in the hot, dry centre of Australia. From November 1942 until his release in September 1943 on account of back and stomach problems, Kurt Herweg was employed as a charcoal worker. Horst Graff applied for military service in March 1942 but was not considered because of the unresolved allegations of espionage. Nor was Stefan Weintraub able to enlist, as he was also regarded by the authorities as a security risk.

The majority of these European refugees came together in the aforementioned Eighth Australian Employment Company, which included volunteers between eighteen and sixty years of age. The oldest was Moritz Chlumecky (*b*.1882), who died in 1945. The company was stationed in Camp Pell, a well-appointed US army camp in Royal Park, Melbourne, just north of the university. For these men, who until now had only known Australia from behind barbed wire, this meant the beginning of a more liberated lifestyle. Many of them were very proud to wear the Australian uniform, including the wide-brimmed slouch or 'Digger' hat, a hallmark of the Australian army since the nineteenth century. Because many members of the company received forage caps at first, they were taken to be Americans. As common soldiers, they were put to various tasks in Melbourne and other towns in Victoria, often loading and unloading ships and trains.

The commander of this unit, Captain Edward R. Broughton,[5] a Maori from New Zealand, treated his subordinates with unusual generosity. He memorised their first names and birthdays, spoke some broken German and provided them with a 'Leave Pass' so that they could leave the camp in uniform in the late afternoon. Many enjoyed the hospitality of Australian families, moved into a room in the city and attended university courses and various events. However, they had to be back in Camp Pell for the morning roll call.

Except for the families who had come from Singapore, single men and those whose wives had remained in Europe had been living only with other men in Hay and Tatura. Their free time now gave them an opportunity for contact with the opposite sex. Friendships developed, then engagements and marriages. During his time with the military, Curt Prerauer married the twenty-year-old Marea Wolkowsky. When Erwin Frenkel played the piano for a celebration at the Melbourne Hebrew Congregation (known as the Toorak Shule) in 1942, he met sixteen-year-old Frankfurt-born Ellen Lubasch, who had been living in Australia since 1939; two years later, they were married while he was on leave. Oskar Fleischer married a German woman, Margarete Friedlich, soon after meeting her in 1943, and in November 1944 Felix Bischofswerder tied the marital knot with Mena Waten from Jaffa, Palestine. On the other hand, married men like Kurt Blach, Heinrich Portnoj, Mischa Stiwelband and Salo Tichauer used their free time to visit their families, who by now had been released from Tatura.

There were probably very few army units in the world with such a high proportion of Jews. This unusual company, which referred to itself as 'a funny looking crowd',[6] or as 'a gentlemen's unit', soon became well-known and popular in Melbourne. The attacks against those in uniform that Werner Baer recalled[7] were the exception rather than the rule, even though people who did not speak fluent English were often met with mistrust. Members of this company were frequently seen at concerts and theatres; after all, there was a great need to catch up in this area after their long months of internment. These men soon represented a particularly attentive section of public audiences and were one reason for the increase in the number of performances. They listened to artists like Peter Dawson,

Jeanne Gautier, Raymond Lambert and Jascha Spivakovsky and smiled when Australian radio announcers ascribed 'The Blue Danube' to a 'Johann Sebastian Strauss'.[8]

But they themselves also contributed to Australian musical life by appearing with their own programmes in Melbourne, or in country towns like Albury, Finley and Tocumwal. A 'Viennese Orchestra' made up of Werner Baer (piano), Charles Reither (violin), Hans Blau (accordion and drums), Kurt Blach (accordion), Oskar Fleischer (trumpet and violin), Walter Würzburger (saxophone and clarinet) and Rudolf Laqueur (piano), would play works of Johann Strauß, Stolz, Lehár, Brahms, Puccini or Mascagni in front of an illuminated backdrop depicting the city of Vienna, to the delight of both the public and the press. An army magazine reported that some of these men would have become world famous in better times.[9] In 1943, when the company was put to work on the railway in Tocumwal, on the border between Victoria and New South Wales, Hans Blau dedicated a song to this small rural town in which he paraphrases the famous 'Vienna, City of my dreams':

> Tocumwal, Tocumwal, city of my dreams,
> Lovely in the sunshine
> And when moonlight beams
> Kindly the people, the girls,
> And so the boys
> Lovely the surroundings and painted like toys.

Probably the high point of these men's artistic activity was Kurt Sternberg's thoroughly revised production of their Snow White revue, *Sergeant Snow White*.[10] The first three performances at the University of Melbourne's Union Theatre in April 1943 were so successful that three more evenings followed in May. Even though the show was not broadcast, the radio paper, the *Listener In*, published an enthusiastic review.[11] It said that the revue told the Grimm brothers' fairy tale in a new way, supported by the personal experiences of the participants, refugees from Germany and Austria who were now members of the Eighth Australian Employment Company. The review concluded that here was the core of a team that could open up new pathways: 'Novel Show Pointer to [Australia's] Theatrical Future'.

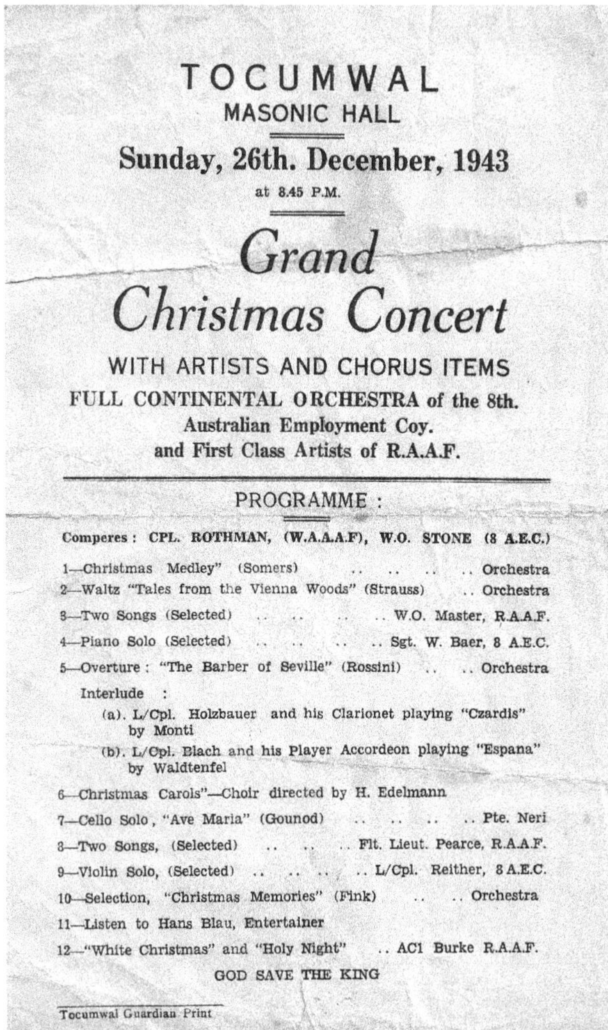

TOCUMWAL
MASONIC HALL

Sunday, 26th. December, 1943
at 8.45 P.M.

Grand
Christmas Concert

WITH ARTISTS AND CHORUS ITEMS
FULL CONTINENTAL ORCHESTRA of the 8th.
Australian Employment Coy.
and First Class Artists of R.A.A.F.

PROGRAMME :

Comperes : CPL. ROTHMAN, (W.A.A.A.F), W.O. STONE (8 A.E.C.)

1—Christmas Medley" (Somers) .. .. Orchestra
2—Waltz "Tales from the Vienna Woods" (Strauss) .. Orchestra
3—Two Songs (Selected) .. .. W.O. Master, R.A.A.F.
4—Piano Solo (Selected) .. .. .. Sgt. W. Baer, 8 A.E.C.
5—Overture : "The Barber of Seville" (Rossini) .. .. Orchestra

Interlude :
   (a). L/Cpl. Holzbauer and his Clarionet playing "Czardis"
      by Monti
   (b). L/Cpl. Blach and his Player Accordeon playing "Espana"
      by Waldtenfel

6—Christmas Carols"—Choir directed by H. Edelmann
7—Cello Solo, "Ave Maria" (Gounod) .. .. Pte. Neri
8—Two Songs, (Selected) .. .. .. Flt. Lieut. Pearce, R.A.A.F.
9—Violin Solo, (Selected) .. .. .. L/Cpl. Reither, 8 A.E.C.
10—Selection, "Christmas Memories" (Fink) .. .. Orchestra
11—Listen to Hans Blau, Entertainer
12—"White Christmas" and "Holy Night" .. AC1 Burke R.A.A.F.

GOD SAVE THE KING

Tocumwal Guardian Print

Figure 20: Programme for the Christmas Concert on 26 December 1943 at the Masonic Hall in Tocumwal (Victoria). The 'Full Continental Orchestra' consisted exclusively of members of the 8th Australian Employment Company. Soloists were Werner Baer (piano), Hans Holzbauer (clarinet), Kurt Blach (accordion), Charles Reither (violin) and Hans Blau (entertainer). (Felix Edelmann, Vienna)

```
To-morrow  Night   ::   To-morrow  Night
        (TUESDAY) AND AGAIN THURSDAY, JULY 3 AND 5
            At the ROYAL PALAIS at 8 p.m.
            THE VIENNESE ORCHESTRA
         MAKING THEIR FIRST PUBLIC APPEARANCE IN ALBURY
    Happy Troubadours. Bringing Music for Everybody. .... From Grand Opera to Swing
                  SOME OF THEIR ITEMS WILL INCLUDE:—
  "The Blue Danube," Waltz ......,.  Orchestra.      "White Horse Inn," Selection ...... Orchestra
  "Madame Butterfly," Selection ...... Orchestra     "Orpheus in the Underworld," overture
  3 Accordeons : KURT, HANS, SIG                         Orchestra.
      (a) "La Cumparsita"; (b) "Spanish Valse."     Piano Solo : "Warsaw Concerto."    WARNER
  "Desert Song," Selection ......... Orchestra      Swing of Yesterday and To-day ... Orchestra
  Cello Solo, "Ave Maria" ......... E. NERI         Clarinet Solo, "Rumanian Dance" .. JOHNNIE
  4 Wizards : WARNER, HANS, OSSI, JOHNNIE           "Tales of the Vienna Woods," waltz . Orchestra
      "Russian Impromptu."                          HANS will entertain you now!
  Violin Solo, "The Canary" ......... CHARLIE       "There'll Always Be An England" . Orchestra
              PROCEEDS A.C.F. QUEEN OF SERVICES GROUP
      ADMISSION 4/, 3/ and 2/.  Booking at Mac's Store for Men, opposite Globe Hotel, Dean St.
```

Figure 21: All members of the 'Viennese Orchestra' that played in July 1945 in the small town of Albury belonged to the 8th Australian Employment Company. Soloists were Werner Baer (Warner), Hans Blau (Hans), Oskar Fleischer (Ossi), Hans Holzbauer (Johnnie) and Charles Reither (Charlie). (Charles Reither, Jr, Melbourne)

'Some Day My Prince Will Come': Walt Disney's Snow White Film

Public interest in the fairy tale of Snow White had been heightened by the world-wide release of the Disney film *Snow White and the Seven Dwarfs* for Christmas 1937. The first feature-length animated cartoon in colour – and with a sound track – was a sensation, a pioneering achievement; it was in production for almost four years and cost the enormous sum of

1.7 million dollars. Walt Disney, whose mother was of German extraction, had already used the story in 1933 as a model for the five-minute animated cartoon strip *Snow White*. In the new film, the love between Snow White and the Prince was given more substance. At the beginning, the princess, in her degraded position as a maid, dreams of her Prince Charming. While Walt Disney is still thanking his staff personally on screen, one can hear the film's musical leitmotiv in the background, the sentimental waltz melody 'Some Day My Prince Will Come', composed by Frank E. Churchill to lyrics by Larry Morrey.

Other songs from the film also became popular. In June 1938, Australia's leading music publisher, Allans, brought out sheet-music arrangements of 'One Song', 'Heigh Ho! The Dwarfs' Marching Song', 'Some Day My Prince Will Come', 'With A Smile And A Song' and 'Whistle While You Work'.[12] At the time, with reference to the film hits, Nicholson's – Sydney's biggest music house, with sheet music and instruments as well as its own music school – decorated a whole store window with fairy-tale woods, dwarves and the figure of Snow White. Their in-house newspaper, the *Australian Music Maker and Dance Band News* depicted this display, and a complementary article emphasised the musical significance of the Disney film: 'If ever a motion picture sang – literally and figuratively – it is "Snow White and the Seven Dwarfs", Walt Disney's feature-length animated musical fantasy made from the famous Grimm fairy tale.'[13] With few exceptions, all the characters sang, either individually or in an ensemble. The dwarves vocalised 'Heigh Ho!' in chorus on their way to work, or warbled 'Buddle Uddle' while they were doing the washing. Snow White had three songs: 'Some Day My Prince Will Come', 'Wishing Well Song' and 'Whistle While You Work'. The prince, who sometimes partnered Snow White, was characterised by his own romantic 'One Song'. The birds played an important role by imitating the songs, as did an invisible choir, which underlined meaningful moments; and finally, the orchestra illustrated every detail of the action with a perfection never seen before. 'Even the sound effects are given musical interpretation. If a door closes, a floor board squeaks, or if someone brushes against a branch, the music tells that.'[14] Disney's Snow White film defined and altered the reception of the Grimm fairy tale. Although hardly ever screened today, it is one of the most frequently screened productions in the history of film and an acknowledged classic of the genre.[15]

Disney's *Snow White and the Seven Dwarfs* was certainly not conceived as an anti-fascist manifesto. In fact, Walt Disney had at first observed the rise of the Nazi regime with some respect. Hitler and Goebbels also admired the work of the Disney studio, something which was taken into consideration by the Propaganda Minister when he did his Christmas shopping. On 22 December 1937, he noted in his diary: 'For Christmas I'm giving the Führer 32 classic films from the last 4 years and 12 Mickey Mouse films with a wonderful art album! He's very happy about it. Absolutely delighted with this treasure.'[16]

Germans had to travel abroad to see *Snow White*, for example to Venice, where it was shown at the 1938 Biennale; at the time, however, Leni Riefenstahl's Olympic films won the Golden Lion, the festival's highest accolade. The competitors respected one another: when Riefenstahl toured the USA and went to Los Angeles in December, she was met by Disney and shown around his studios. In spite of Germany's massive foreign currency deficit, Goebbels was still trying to acquire the film right up until January 1939. After the November pogrom, however, German–American relations deteriorated to such an extent that such a deal was no longer possible. Nevertheless, the fascination remained. On 12 February 1940, Goebbels noted in his diary: 'We're seeing the American Disnay-Film "Snow White", a great work of art. A fairy-tale for adults, thought through in detail, and made with a great love of people and nature. A real artistic pleasure!'[17] When Hitler saw the film in his own private theatre at the Obersalzberg mountain retreat, even he praised it as one of the greatest works in the history of film.[18]

The refined animation technique developed in *Snow White and the Seven Dwarfs* stimulated Goebbels to promote the production of German cartoon films and then actively encourage it when the USA entered the war in 1941, since the screening of Disney films was banned in Germany – not because of the content or for artistic reasons, but because the films originated in the USA. Walt Disney, who had used Goethe's ballad of the Sorcerer's Apprentice for his film *Fantasia* as late as 1940, now explicitly distanced himself from the Nazi regime and began to create Hitler caricatures at the demand of a government contract.

The fairy-tale world of the Disney film stood in stark contrast to the situation in the Australian internment camps. In Hay, however, a programme entitled *Snowhite – S3828* had premiered on 27 December 1940; it was developed further in Tatura and performed at Christmas 1941 as *Snowhite Joins Up. A merry Xmas – New Year Revue*.[19] Snow White was represented as a soldier, so by then the production already reflected the internees' new perspectives on life. The names of some of the participants were recorded, for example Doc K. Sternberg (author, producer and director), Ray Martin (composer) and Jonny Flynn, Rudolf Laqueur and Herbert Voss (musical arrangers). The forty-two-year-old producer Manfred Kurt Sternberg had reportedly been employed by the UFA in Berlin but, after his escape to Britain, he transferred to the film company RKO Radio Pictures, which was also renting the Disney film.[20] Sternberg had been head of the entertainment department in Camp 8,[21] and it is probable that the Snow White revue was his idea. Among the songs that Ray Martin and Eddy Kassner composed were the aforementioned 'Hay Days' and the songs 'Say Hay for Happy', 'Don't release me, Mr Layton!' and 'Good-bye to you, Australia'. The piano, played by Rudolf Laqueur, was apparently the only instrument available. Meanwhile, Hein Heckroth had returned to England, so Emil Wittenberg was now in charge of the sets.[22]

The Revue *Snowhite Joins Up* shown in the Tatura internment camp at Christmas 1941 originated just as the former association between Disney and Hitler's Germany was coming to an end, and provided an opportunity to transform the world-famous film into an anti-fascist story. This had already happened, perhaps for the first time, in the short propaganda film strip *Seven Wise Dwarfs* that was released by Disney Studios in mid-December 1941. In it, after their work in the diamond mine, the seven dwarves did not return to Snow White; instead, singing 'Heigh Ho!' they marched into the city in order to exchange their jewels for war bonds.[23] It is, however, highly unlikely that the German detainees ever saw this brand new film clip in the camp.

Jew-ropeans in Australia: The Revue Text

Few documents of the revue presented in Tatura have survived. There is, however, a stage manuscript[24] for the later programme, with the following title page:

> Sgt. Snowhite[25]
> A Doc K. Sternberg Production
> Presented at the Union Theatre, University Grounds
> Melbourne, Victoria, Australia
> on
> April 15th, 17th and 19th 1943

This is the manuscript for the revue shown in Melbourne in April 1943. According to the script, it consisted of three acts, 'Fairy Wood', 'Europe Calling' and 'Sergeant Snow White', each of which was subdivided into individual scenes. The third act was at first planned differently, as revealed by slight differences between some scenes in an attached overview (here denoted as 'sketch') and the manuscript version.

Part I: FAIRY WOOD
1. Ouverture
2. Grandma Prologue
3. The Mirror Scene
4. Fairy Wood
5. The Banquet

Part II: EUROPE CALLING
1. Ouverture
2. Prologue
3. Europe Calling
4. Journeys End
5. France
6. Russia: Melodies of Russia
7. Austria: Prater Dream
8. Czechoslovakia: Schweyk
9. Entre Act: The Witch at Work

10. Germany: Gestapo Office
11. Poland
12. Sounds of Europe
13. Ghosts of Europe

Part III: SERGEANT SNOW WHITE

(Sketch)	(Realised Version)
Ouverture	Ouverture
Prologue	Prologue
1. The Dwarfs at the Wharves	The Dwarfs at the Wharves
2. Music on Parade	Music on Parade
3. The Sergeant Major	
4. On arguing the Point	On arguing the Point
5. The Tent	The Tent
6. Orderly Room	Orderly Room
7. Happy Birthday to You	Happy Birthday to You
8. Finale	Finale
9. Speech	
10. The King	

Many authors have been inspired for various reasons to make their own adaptations of the Grimm fairy tale.[26] What attracted the internees of Hay and Tatura about the fairy-tale figure lay probably not so much in her beauty or her love for the prince as in her banishment from home and country, an innocent 'refugee'. Erwin Fabian's woodcut engraving depicted on the programme (Figure 22) shows the title figure as a curious cross between an Australian soldier and an elegant female dancer. The mirror, which replaces the head, is a reminder of the magic mirror in the fairy tale. From the right, various masks framed by a wolf and a witch look into the picture. While the figure holds up a streamer with the title of the show in her elegant left hand, the male right hand carries an army hat. On the invitation itself (Figure 23), which was also created by Fabian, the Digger-hat plays an even more prominent role: all the figures of the play issue from it as if from a magic bottle.

The revue is presented as an old story that a grandmother is telling a child. Hundreds of years ago, according to the prologue, Snow White was wandering lost through a dark wood, persecuted because of her beauty, 'a

Jew-ropeans in Australia: The Revue Text 295

Figure 22: For the programme of the revue Erwin Fabian depicted Snow White as a combination of man and woman, soldier and dancer. (Ilse Blair, Melbourne)

Figure 23: Invitation to the 'Sergeant Snowwhite' revue with a woodcarving by Erwin Fabian. (Ilse Blair, Melbourne)

refugee from the Queen's oppression'. In the following castle scene, the chamberlain gives the queen a news bulletin instead of a mirror. The monarch's vanity no longer refers to her external beauty, but to her representation in the press – her public image. From her name, Columina the Fifth, and the following scenes, we gather that the queen represents public opinion. In the next scene in the woods ('Fairy Wood'), Snow White is sought not only by the prince, but also by a witch, and by a new character, Wolf

Long-Nose. Whereas the film included many different woodland animals, the wolf is the only animal character in the revue.

The following scene, a banquet at the queen's court, deviates from the Grimm model. The French and Russian ambassadors, together with Hitler, dressed in an animal skin as 'His Beastliness, Wolf von Braunau', are given a friendly welcome by the queen. When the witch appears, the queen at first turns away in horror, until she notices that the witch is wearing a padlock. This, she discovers, is because the Employment Company is in the city: 'Since the boys from the 8th are in Melbourne!!' Then 'His Royal Shyness, Prince Charming' pays his respects to the queen and charms her with a song by Franz Lehár. The seven dwarves finally appear when the banquet is opened up to a wider audience.

But where is the lead character, Snow White? The valet discovers a picture of her as the winner of a bathing suit contest in an Australian illustrated magazine. The action becomes more and more grotesque because now Hitler, dressed as a wolf, asks the queen to join his 'Axis'. When the monarch steadfastly refuses, he threatens to take 'protective measures'. Soldiers appear at his command and arrest all the guests at the banquet. They are slowly led away to the strains of Chopin's funeral march,[27] followed by a heavily armed official who holds the key to the padlock in his hand.

The revue combines fairy-tale make-believe with the reality of the Second World War. At the beginning of the second act ('Europe Calling'), the grandmother tells the child that the witch and the bad wolf have arrested all the good fairies. Snow White and the seven dwarves will all be freed in the end. But first the action must move to Europe, where the witch and the wolf have started a war. In this second act, the wolf and the witch are seen together building a giant barbed wire network. When an illuminated picture of Hitler appears, the witch laughs out loud, while the wolf calls out to his own likeness: 'Heil! Myself!'

Snow White, the prince and the seven dwarves remain invisible in this act. In an eerie scene the lawyer, Dr Blizzard von Oz, complains to the Gestapo about the arrest of Snow White, the most beautiful girl in the world. The lawyer evades the Gestapo official's question about whether the offender is Aryan. He causes even more confusion by indicating that the girl has two fathers, namely the brothers Grimm, and that she is also living together with seven men, the seven dwarves. Thus from the Gestapo's point of view, Snow White is an abnormal, immoral being who must be taken to a concentration camp. This scene, which mocks Hitler and his regime, must have seemed ambiguous to the initiated: those who were racially and politically persecuted by the Nazi regime, and who were hidden behind the fairy-tale characters, had been not in German concentration camps, but in British internment camps. Both internment and the murder of the Jews[28] were omitted, as this would have gone too far for a light-hearted fairy-tale revue. Instead, scenes were inserted from the drama *Journey's End* by R.C. Sherriff, and from Jaroslav Hašek's *Schwejk*.

The third act is set in a camp, though neither Hay nor Tatura, but Camp Pell, not far from the Union Theatre.[29] In the prologue, the child asks the grandmother how the story continues. He learns that the war instigated by the witch and the wolf has now spread throughout the world and that Snow White, like many beautiful girls, has enlisted in the army and quickly risen to the rank of sergeant. The seven dwarves, the prince and even the queen have also volunteered. 'Oh, I know', the child adds: 'They joined the Eighth *Enjoyment* Company.' But the grandmother corrects him: '*Employment* Company!!' 'Couldn't they get a discharge?' asks the child. 'Oh no', the grandmother replies, 'they hadn't reached the age limit of a hundred and twenty years.' Here again there was a background reference to the all-too-long internment. But a happy ending was promised.

In this third act, the seven dwarves are simple soldiers who sing the mining song from the Disney film while they are at work. Deviating from the Grimm fairy tale, there is a surprising love affair between the prince and the queen. In the scene 'Music on Parade', the dwarves are commanded by a sergeant major modelled on Captain Edward Broughton. When he asks to see their sergeant, they reply that she, Snow White, is a woman and is still asleep. The sergeant major is astonished. Nonetheless, he asks his troops who would like kosher meals. All seven of them raise their hands – another reference to the predominantly Jewish heritage of the participants.

The printed programme carefully noted the actors' military status. Only a few of the participants had risen above the original rank of private, but it was probably no coincidence that those who were promoted were also the artistically outstanding members of the company: the dancer and choreographer Peter Schmitz from Berlin and the stage designer Emil Wittenberg were corporals; the producer Kurt Sternberg, the actor Sigurd Lohde and the pianist Werner Baer were all sergeants. The core of the company consisted of former internees from Camp 8 in Hay, including the amateur tenor Eric Liffmann, who had been discovered by Sternberg and featured as a sensation on Australian radio from 1942.[30] Several professional actors had already returned to London, but not Sigurd Lohde, who had previously worked at the Berlin Volksbühne and become well known through several films;[31] until his internment he had appeared in the London emigrant cabaret, 'Laterndl'. He had written a text and melody for the new company's own marching song. Since detainees from Camp 3 also belonged to the Employment Company, the *Sergeant Snow White* artists included some who had come to Australia from Singapore, professional musicians like the pianist and organist Werner Baer, the Viennese entertainer Hans Blau, as well as Kurt Blach, Heinrich Portnoj and Walter Würzburger. On the other hand, Bader, Pietruschka and Steiner were missing, as they had been discharged from military service early on account of illness.

In its first versions, the revue was intended not for an urban audience, but for internment and military camps, so it contained insider jokes like the roll call scene. Since both the internees and the participants were all bilingual, there was ample opportunity for clever puns and subtle witticisms – for instance, when the lawyer in the Gestapo scene introduces himself as 'Dr Blizzard von Oz, solicitor of Potsdamer Plotz'. The scene with the mellifluous title 'The Dwarfs at the Wharves' contains dialogue with jokes that can often only be understood by Germans. When the chamberlain (who is also assigned to the army) asks the dwarves about their equipment, each one names seven little plates, knives, forks and spoons in German. When he pleads with them to speak English, they promptly transfer the German diminutive form to the English words, and call out: 'Seven Plate-*chens*, seven Knife-*chens*, seven Fork-*chens*' etc. The queen praises the members of the company as good dancers: 'They are mostly Jew-ropeans! Many of them from Austria. We call them "Austri-Aliens"!!!' These witty formulations actually masked a more serious concern, since the racial persecution that lay behind the newly coined 'Jew-ropeans' persisted in Australia for some time as a defence against aliens.

300　　　　　　　　　　　　　　　　　　CHAPTER 13: *Snow White in Uniform*

Figure 24: Men and 'women', led by Hans Blau (centre) as Maurice Chevalier, join for the Can-Can. (Ilse Blair, Melbourne)

Blue Danube, Brown Spree: Viennese Melodies instead of German Music

Understandably, the German language remained largely taboo in Australia during the war. When German was occasionally used in conversation, it was explained to outsiders as the language of neutral Switzerland. Germany, Adolf Hitler's Reich, was the enemy, so German music was generally missing in the *Snow White* revue. Other countries were characterised by attractive musical examples: France by the *Marseillaise* as well as 'Je cherche après Titine' ['I'm looking for Titine'] and 'Paris, je t'aime', the song made famous by Maurice Chevalier; Poland was represented by a Chopin Nocturne, Czechoslovakia by the music of Smetana, and Russia by a medley of folk-songs performed by six accordionists. Only the 'Potsdam Glockenspiel' melody stood for Germany – 'Üb immer Treu und Redlichkeit' ['Forever true and honest be'] – a tune that was used from March 1933 to signify pauses on the German radio station *Deutschlandsender*. The fairy tale's German origin was only mentioned in the Gestapo scene that referred to the brothers Grimm as Snow White's fathers. Otherwise, the show's point of departure was the Disney adaptation, from which three songs were borrowed: 'Some Day My Prince Will Come', the Prince's 'One Song' and the dwarves' 'Heigh Ho!'.[32] Immediately after this work song, there was an instrumental version of Paul Lincke's 'Glühwürmchen' ['The Glow Worm'], of whose German origins the Australian public was presumably ignorant.

If, due to the current political climate, the German language and German music were by and large downplayed, Austrian music was all the more present. Whereas German exiles abroad largely failed in their efforts to promote a more nuanced or subtly differentiated picture of Germany, many Austrians were successful in representing their homeland as the victim of fascist aggression. Berlin was perceived one-sidedly as the city of offenders and Vienna just as one-sidedly as the city of victims. This practice had started in London and continued seamlessly in other parts of the British Empire. Hence in this revue, Austrian music was heard alongside the Disney film songs. It was fortunate that in Hans Blau they had an authentic interpreter of Viennese songs. In the Prater scene, introduced by a Shrammel quartet, he first sang Eysler's 'Fein, fein schmeckt uns der Wein' ['Fine, fine is the taste of the wine'] in German. Here the script included a heckler in the audience who complained about the incomprehensible language. When asked whether the Austrians did not speak English, the singer replied: 'They do, Sir, they do!' – whereupon he sang the second verse in English. After that there were apparently no problems when this was followed by Ralph Benatzky's 'Ich möchte mal wieder in Grinzing sein' ['I want to be in Grinzing again'], sung in German, and the Strauß waltz, 'The Blue Danube'. After the film's 'One Song', Prince Charming (played by Eric Liffmann), too, sang two Austrian operetta songs by Franz Lehár, albeit in English translation: 'O Mädchen, mein Mädchen' ['O Maiden, My Maiden'] and 'Dein ist mein ganzes Herz' ['You Are my Heart's Delight'].

Apart from this residual sympathy for Viennese songs and operetta, the show was decidedly British in flavour. The participants presented themselves as proud Australian soldiers celebrating the first anniversary of their company. That said, they did not forget that just a few years earlier they had been internees. They reworked one of their earliest songs, 'Say Hay for Happy', written in 1940 to refer to the company: 'Say Eight's for 'Appy':

> When you are feeling low down
> And when you've had a blow down
> Take it easy as it comes and goes
> Then you're feeling chilly
> And everything looks silly
> Show that you can be right on your toes:
> Say Eight's for 'appy
> When you feel snappy
> And you don't want to cry
> Say Eight's for 'appy
> Then you feel snappy
> And you don't want to die
> So you'd even give your ration card
> For just the sight of Sergeant Snowwhite
> Don't take it to your heart
> Blow all your troubles
> Away like bubbles
> And start a little game.
> Without your girlie
> You get up early
> O what an awful shame.
> You're saying R for Rosenthal
> B for Blumenduft and S for snappy
> Now Say Eight's for 'APPY!

This song can really only be understood by someone who knows both versions and is aware of its genesis. The song 'Pay Days', which is mentioned in the manuscript, is also presumably a new version of the earlier internment song, 'Hay Days'.

Like the Disney film, the *Snow White* revue has a happy ending with the announcement of Sergeant Snow White's marriage to Prince Charming. Both are evidently Jewish, since the wedding is supposed to take place in the St Kilda synagogue.[33] The bride is still unseen; we are told that she is on holiday for ten days in Sydney. Equally unseen is the second, political, happy ending, which the grandmother announces to the public. She simply reports that the bad wolf and the witch were both caught, and that Snow White served the army until the day of victory was nigh.

'Sounds of Europe'

All the performances took place in Melbourne's Union Theatre, a recently renovated university theatre seating 500. After the programme on 15 April, there was a dinner dance in nearby Melba Hall.[34] Two days later, there was a 'gala performance' – 'starring the well-known Tenor Pte E. Liffman'[35] and augmented with new swing arrangements by Private Fraenkel (Frenkel) – and the money raised was to be used to rescue Jewish children from enemy-occupied regions.[36] This series was so successful that three repeat performances were given in the same theatre in May, when the revue was advertised as 'Sergeant Snow White. A Happy-go-lucky musical revue of bad old and good new times'. The lower half of the programme sheet shows the production's musical set-up. There must have been several pianos, since it mentions Lance-Corporal Portnoj and Privates E. Fraenkel, H. Fichman, H. Voss, S. Cohn and R. Laqueur 'at the pianos'. Apart from a vocal swing sextet, six accordionists and a Shrammel quartet are listed. The programme also acknowledges three musical arrangers, S. Cohn, H. Fichman and Ray Martin, but unfortunately the music for the performance has never been found.

The numbers shown on this printed programme differ slightly from the manuscript for the April performances. In the second act, a scene entitled 'The Cosmopolitan' was added, played by young Lincoln Oppenheimer from Frankfurt, who also acted as the child in the story's prologue. The aforementioned write-up referred to a vivid scene with this actor: 'Private L. Oppenheimer tells the poignant story of a boy who wanted to travel the world. As a refugee – driven from country to country – he cries: "This world bores me to tears. I've known this world already – twenty years".'[37] While there is no corresponding scene in the stage manuscript for the first series, the programme does mention chansons by E. Lehrburger, F. Gottfurcht, R. Popper, A. Gray and F. Hollaender that are not specifically identified. With the help of the authors' names, one song was found, with words by Fritz Gottfurcht and Egon Larsen (pseudonym for Egon Lehrburger), which is similar in content to the scene described in the review. The music was written by a student of Arnold Schönberg, Josef Szmigrod, who later composed successful film music under the name Allan Gray.

The Twenty-year-old

Je ne connais tout le quartier
Et au Montmartre les cabarets
Paris est belle quand on est riche
*Mais comme une refugiée – je m'en fiche.**

In Cuba we were not allowed
To land. In Spain I felt at home.
A kindly sailor, when the mine
Exploded, fished me out the foam.

I've seen the world, and it's a cage,
And I am all of twenty years of age.

Shanghai was raided by the Japs.
I saw our boarding-house collapse.
In Hollywood, without a cent,
I could not even pay the rent. *

A Rio gent was keen on me,
Even as his wife, I guess.
I thought of Hans in Germany
And whether he'd escaped the mess.

I have seen the world. It leaves me cold.
I'm already a whole twenty years old.

I dreamed of journeys as a child,
Adventures in the wind and wild.
Now to a house in dreams I roam,
And to a town that once was home.

> I'd like to see that town at last,
> And hear the German of my past.
> I'd understand, and then I'd know
> That all of this is over now.
>
> I've seen the world – it's just a cage,
> And I am all of twenty years of age.[38]
> * Original French/English

This song was written for *Was bringt die Zeitung?* [What's in the News?], a revue staged by the exiles' cabaret Kleine Bühne in London from the middle of May 1940. Whereas in that production the lament was sung by Agnes Bernell, who played the homeless young exile driven from one country to the next, in Melbourne it was presented by a young man. In the title, he was called a 'Cosmopolitan', which meant virtually the same thing as exile. This bitter complaint was set against the poem 'Listen brother – listen sister' by Simon Hochberger, a passionate appeal for opposition against Hitler, formerly entitled 'Sounds of Europe' and now called 'The European'. The first three stanzas describe the destruction of Europe by barbaric armies, but this last verse deals with the victims' rebellion, an uprising by the peoples of Europe against their executioners:

> Listen brother – listen sister:
> From far comes the rhythmic sound of a drum
> Listen lady – listen mister
> The sound enters palace and slum
> The conquered are stirring, they pull at their chain
> A glint of new hope in their eyes –
> They listen and find all their courage again
> The peoples of Europe will rise ...
> Listen brother – listen sister:
> The armies of freedom are on their way
> Forward worker – forward soldier!
> The hangmen of Europe will PAY!!!!!

Sigurd Lohde's presentation of this militant poem made a strong impression on the audience. According to the review previously mentioned, it was one of the most impressive acting highlights of the evening.

Fairy tales had been used before for political satires and allegories. Prior to 1933, Friedrich Hollaender had drafted a topical revue entitled *Once upon a time ... a Christmas Tale for Adults*, on which authors like Bertolt Brecht, Ernst Toller, Erich Weinert and Erich Kästner were to have collaborated.[39] One of the most successful numbers of the Free German Cultural League revue *Going, Going – Gong!*, which premiered at the London Arts Centre on 21 July 1939, was a new version of the Andersen story 'The Emperor's New Clothes', with Hitler and Mussolini as 'heroes', namely as naked emperors.[40] In February 1943, just two months before the two runs of *Sergeant Snow White*, the bilingual revue *Mr. Gulliver Goes to School* had its premiere in London, and this became the most successful production staged by the Free German Cultural League. In one school scene, this revue also used fairy-tale characters, including Snow White and the seven dwarves. Here the situation was reversed. Snow White, living in British exile, acted on stage while the numerous dwarves remained invisible: they were still in Hitler's Germany, where they were active in the underground. In the Australian exile revue, there was no talk of resistance activities inside Germany. Snow White and the seven dwarves had all joined the Australian army in order to conquer Hitler's Germany in partnership with other countries.[41] Nevertheless, the show was still the work of exiles, even though they were wearing Australian uniforms and were celebrated by the press as the creators of a new Australian theatre. At this time, they could not foresee that almost half the *Dunera* passengers (including many of the participants in the *Snow White* revue) would stay in Australia after Germany's defeat, or that they would have such an influence on Australia's cultural development.[42]

A few months later, when the ABC organised a composing competition for members of the military, Simon Hochberger remembered his poem 'Sounds of Europe' and asked Werner Baer if he would write a melody for it. Baer immediately agreed; he composed the song in just ten minutes, and the jury chose it as the winner from 167 anonymous entries. They were surprised to learn that 'Sounds of Europe' was the work, not of Australian soldiers, but of two aliens. The ABC broadcast the song nationwide, but decided not to publish it.[43]

CHAPTER 14

The Year 1945: Lost and Found

Remigration or Naturalisation?

By the end of the war, at the latest, the refugee musicians had to decide whether to return to Europe or stay in Australia. Would their earlier domicile be home again after the fall of Hitler? Or should they take the chance and start anew? Many who still had close relatives in Europe were eager to return; Max Meyer had already left Tatura in November 1943 to return to Britain. Immediately following his discharge from the army in 1946, Hans Edelmann went back to his wife in Vienna, where he was once again able to work as a bookseller in his old firm. Hans Blau, too, would have returned to Vienna, the city to which he had dedicated most of his songs, but as his new life partner, Ilse Baer, had decided on Australia, he stayed.

The cantor Boas Bischofswerder longed to see his wife, who had remained in London, but by July 1941 he was already quite ill and was transferred from Tatura to the Waranga Hospital. As an orthodox Jew, however, he required kosher food; since this was not available, he refused to take any nourishment. He was only discharged from Waranga in July 1943, when his medical care was guaranteed by his son Felix. But Boas Bischofswerder was by then so weak that he never regained his strength, and in 1946 he died in a private clinic in Melbourne, aged fifty-one. He never saw his wife Helene again.

The young music publisher Otto Blau wanted to return to London for professional rather than personal reasons. Even in Australia, he had cultivated his publishing contacts. In Melbourne, he had visited his colleague Victor Alberti, who unfortunately succumbed to cancer in July 1942. Blau negotiated with overseas contacts by telegraph, for example about an arrangement of *Fledermaus* by Max Reinhardt and Erich Wolfgang Korngold that was published in New York in 1942 under the title *Rosalinda*.[1] In March 1943, Blau ended his military service with the Eighth Employment Company prematurely, at the age of forty-nine, on account of ill health. Apparently at that stage he was still contemplating a longer stay in Australia for, in the same year, he contacted the British firm Novello and offered to represent the company in Australia, but Novello declined. This may have prompted Blau's decision to return to London, where his uncle Hugo Golwig was in charge of what remained of the Weinberger publishing house after its Aryanisation. In December 1944, Blau boarded the *Glenstrae* in Sydney and set out for New York.[2] From there, he continued to England, where he put his energy into rebuilding his publishing empire. One of his new tasks was the management of Victor Alberti's Octava music publishing house, which had retained the operetta composer Emmerich Kálmán as its most important author.

Günter Hirschberg had left the army even before Blau, at the urging of the Jewish congregation. At the beginning of 1941, when Rabbi Falk visited Hay and heard about Hirschberg's theological background, he had already taken an interest in the young Berliner with the beautiful bass voice. After joining the Eighth Employment Company, Hirschberg turned to the rabbi at the liberal Temple Emanuel in Sydney, Max Schenk, who then organised his release. Hirschberg describes this in a letter to his aunt, who was meanwhile living in Ankara:

> In January 1942 I was released from internment because I volunteered to join the Australian army [...]. We were given the opportunity to prove our loyalty and – for the first time – to do something against the people we hate so much. Besides, it was the only way of getting out from behind the barbed wire, where I had been for 18 months for no reason at all. [...] I also thought of my parents, then I thought I was doing it for them too, that their future now depended on mine.

Then a contact from the liberal congregation in Sydney appeared:

> One day I received a telephone call from the Rabbi of that congregation telling me that he was in Melbourne and would like to see me. We had a talk and I sang to him and (to make it short) he secured my discharge from the army to be his Assistant.[3]

This quick decision was due to the fact that, after Pearl Harbor, numerous US soldiers, including Jews, had come to the country as allies. Rabbi Schenk, an American citizen, had been appointed as the Australian Director

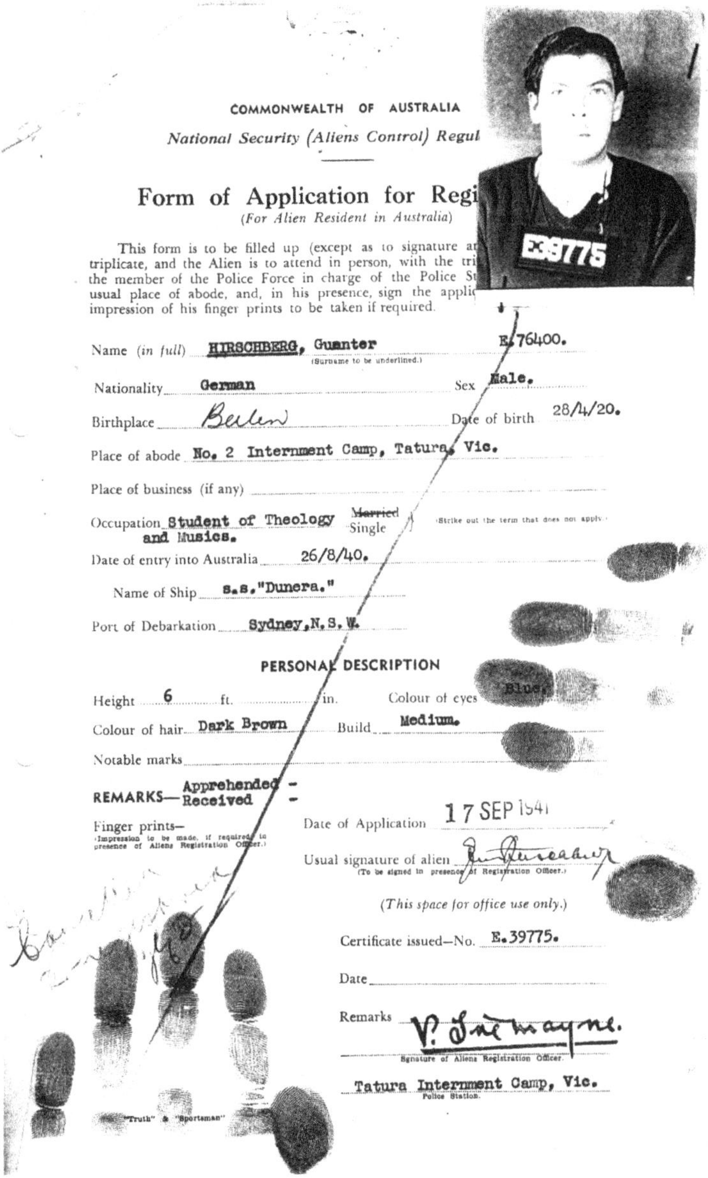

COMMONWEALTH OF AUSTRALIA

National Security (Aliens Control) Regul

Form of Application for Regi

(For Alien Resident in Australia)

This form is to be filled up (except as to signature a[...] triplicate, and the Alien is to attend in person, with the tri[...] the member of the Police Force in charge of the Police St[...] usual place of abode, and, in his presence, sign the applic[...] impression of his finger prints to be taken if required.

E39775

Name (*in full*) HIRSCHBERG, Guenter (Surname to be underlined.) E. 76400.

Nationality German Sex Male.

Birthplace Berlin Date of birth 28/4/20.

Place of abode No. 2 Internment Camp, Tatura, Vic.

Place of business (if any)

Occupation Student of Theology and Musics. ~~Married~~ Single (Strike out the term that does not apply.)

Date of entry into Australia 26/8/40.

Name of Ship S.S. "Dunera."

Port of Debarkation Sydney, N.S.W.

PERSONAL DESCRIPTION

Height 6 ft. in. Colour of eyes Blue.

Colour of hair Dark Brown Build Medium.

Notable marks

REMARKS—Apprehended - Received -

Finger prints— (Impression to be made, if required, in presence of Aliens Registration Officer.)

Date of Application 17 SEP 1941

Usual signature of alien G. Hirschberg (To be signed in presence of Registration Officer.)

(This space for office use only.)

Certificate issued—No. E. 39775.

Date

Remarks

V. Tremayne. Signature of Aliens Registration Officer.

Tatura Internment Camp, Vic. Police Station.

"Truth" & "Sportsman"

Figure 25: Günter Hirschberg, a student of theology and music, who was interned in Tatura, was forced by National Security Regulations to register in September 1941. (NAA: ST1233/1, N32842) of the Jewish Welfare Board of America; owing to the demands of his job, he needed someone who could step in for him;[4] Hirschberg subsequently became the assistant minister at Temple Emanuel. Since he lived right on the coast in Bellevue Hill, as an alien he had to report to the police every week and eventually give up his flat. The substantial correspondence in which the congregation protested against this chicanery, and the record of a police interrogation at the beginning of March 1943, have survived. The authorities finally gave in, and at the end of the year Hirschberg was even given permission to go to Melbourne.

Many members of the Australian congregations were distrustful of the Jews arriving from Europe. According to Alphons Silbermann, they were often third generation Polish emigrants who 'had the same extravagantly distanced attitude as the assimilated Jews in Austria and Germany had towards emigrants from Eastern Europe during the time of Kaiser Franz Joseph and Weimar'.[5] These prejudices increased during the war, and it certainly did not help that many of the refugees were working as doctors, lawyers, architects, journalists and musicians when there were restrictions on admission to these professions in Australia. Since even Australian Jews expressed criticism,[6] eventually, in November 1943, the refugees decided to establish their own organisation, the Association of Jewish Refugees,[7] as had existed in Britain since 1941.[8] Dr Max Joseph became the General Secretary and Günter Hirschberg Honorary Secretary.[9] Joseph did not let his own set-backs and difficulties discourage him – he lost his laundry business to arson, and after it was rebuilt it was confiscated. Under his leadership, the Association of Jewish Refugees sought a more relaxed relationship with the local community. It was thanks to this independent self-help organisation that victims of Nazi persecution were now officially recognised as 'friendly aliens' instead of 'enemy' aliens.[10]

'Deported to Poland': Bad News from Europe

During the police interrogation of 3 March 1943, Günter Hirschberg was asked about his parents. He said that when he was in England he had visited them twice in Berlin, but that he had not seen them since

March 1938. 'I received a letter two days ago through an Aunt of mine informing me that my parents had been deported to Poland. With the current stories about what is going on in Poland, I have not any hopes left that they are still alive.'[11] In November 1942, Walter and Edith Hirschberg were taken from Berlin to Theresienstadt and from there to Auschwitz.[12] Günter Hirschberg said later that the Jewish persecution in Europe only served to strengthen his Jewish faith. Other refugees also received bad news from Europe. In December 1940, Cyril and Ernest Schulvater received a written cry for help from their mother in Lublin via the Polish Red Cross, but they never heard from her again.[13] In February 1942, when Hans Bader had to fill out a form in Tatura that asked for his parents' current address, he wrote 'Vienna, but believed to be deported to Poland'.[14] Hans Holzbauer's father was taken in October 1941 to the Łódź Ghetto (Litzmannstadt), where he died six months later.[15] Erwin Frenkel's father had been shot in Latvia. It must have been a terrible shock for Adolf Brenner to discover that his mother had been deported to Riga in January 1942; only a few months later, his father was taken to Auschwitz.[16] Rudolf Werther's parents were also transported to Riga. In December 1945, Kurt Blach heard from a friend of the family that his brother and sister-in-law, who were in hiding in Amsterdam, had been betrayed to the Nazis; the traitor was the very same man who had taken money to provide security for the refugees.[17] Eric Liffmann travelled to West Germany towards the end of 1946 to search for his family; he learned that his sister had survived Dachau, whereas his parents had died in Auschwitz.[18] From 1940 onwards, Adolf Eichmann, who had already organised the deportation of the Jews of Vienna, was in charge of the deportation of all Jews in areas under Nazi control. His Berlin office was, of all things, in the Jewish Fraternity Building in which the Weintraubs Syncopaters experienced their first great success.

For many, such shocking news dispelled any dreams they had about returning to their homeland. On the contrary, they were glad to have left this horror scenario in time. Before the war, Emanuel Frischer had been able to save his family by bringing first his brother Adolf, and then his sister Charlotte and parents to Australia in 1939. Leo Weiss's father made it to Australia in October 1939. The continent that was once unloved now proved to be their saving grace. For Werner Baer, it was comforting that his mother and brother were relatively safe in Shanghai. While Alphons Silbermann was also successful in helping his parents to immigrate in July 1939, Horst Graff applied in vain to bring his father and brother Wilhelm to Australia, and attracted suspicion by retaining contact with relatives in Germany during the war.

Those deported from Singapore were never offered the chance to return to that colony;[19] but they were interested in at least being released from internment. Those who did not enlist had to fill out a comprehensive questionnaire to prove their suitability for life outside the camp. They had to provide their personal details, information about their parents, partners, children and other relatives and, finally, their occupation. They also had to give details about their various places of residence and the date of their final departure from Germany or region occupied by Germany. In addition, they were to give reasons for their departure, as well as the conditions under which they were allowed to leave their homeland. Then came details of later addresses, date and place of internment, followed by the date of the transport to Australia. Under the heading 'Means', they had to list what belongings they had brought with them. Then: 'If released, would you be in receipt of any income? If so, give details including the source of the income.' Because so few had any income, the next question was: 'Is there any refugee or similar organisation here or abroad, interested in your case?' After being asked about their health, the final question was about their future employment: 'Do you wish to follow any occupation or occupations if released? If so, give particulars.' The entries in this questionnaire gave authorities a comprehensive picture of this group of people, and today it is a good source material for the fate of, for example, Hans Bader, Werner Baer, Heinrich Portnoj and Paul Steiner. Portnoj answered the question about his future employment as follows: 'Any occupation which will help the Austr. War Effort, or in my own profession (Musician and -teacher).'[20]

Hans Bader was not accepted by the army because of his walking disability, so he continued to live in the Tatura camp with his wife Margarethe and their small daughter. In February 1942, he answered the question about future employment with 'Musician and Music teacher',[21] which possibly delayed his release. Camp internees could only be discharged if they could prove they could earn a secure living. As a result, in September Margarethe Bader wrote to Major Layton requesting his help in looking for work. She mentioned the heavy kitchen duties that her husband carried out despite his affliction, as well as his capabilities as a carpenter and shoemaker:

> He also could be lift attendant, janitor, storkeeper, ammunition worker or could fulfil other defence jobs, the importance of which is so vital at present. The fact that he is a pianist does not necessarily imply that he is a musician only.

She, too, could contribute to their living expenses: 'I am a well trained Milliner and Dressmaker, and could also be employed as a machinist in a defence clothing factory.'[22] In November, Hans Bader did indeed get a job in a pipe factory, so he and his family were able to leave Tatura. Their school-age son had already been taken to the children's home, Larino, in Melbourne.

The above-mentioned 'Application for Release from Detention' forms distributed in Tatura in February 1942 had no questions about long-term plans. Whether the internees would return to their homeland or stay in Australia was left open. When questioned about the conditions under which they had left Germany, most said they had had to leave all their assets behind and promise never to return. In fact, the majority of applicants decided to stay in Australia. Hans Bader found a suitable flat in Melbourne and submitted an 'Application for Permit to Enter Australia' in January 1944. In February he was acknowledged as a 'refugee alien'; thus one more hurdle was overcome. When questioned later by security officers regarding his application, he gave detailed information about his income, and about furniture that he had bought. As a result, in March the authorities advised the Commonwealth Investigation Branch that there were no grounds on which to preclude Hans Bader and his family from residing permanently in Australia.[23] Two years would pass before he received official notification of his naturalisation, on 6 June 1946. Like all new citizens, he handed in his former papers, renounced his former citizenship, and swore the oath: 'I, Hans Bader, swear by Almighty God that I will be faithful and bear true allegiance to His Majesty King George the Sixth, his heirs and successors, according to law.'

Figure 26: The Kapellmeister, pianist and arranger Hans Bader.
(Lisa Vinnic, Melbourne)

Stages of Integration

An 'Application for Certificate of Naturalisation' was only considered after a minimum stay of five years; it then had to be supported and signed by a British citizen with official standing, such as a teacher or member of the police force. Previously, the public had to be informed of these applications through announcements in two daily newspapers. Jascha Spivakovsky obtained his citizenship this way in 1938, as did his brother Adolf the following year. When Curt Prerauer was naturalised in 1938, his previous stay in Britain was taken into consideration. The fact that Emanuel Frischer had entered Australia on a Polish passport helped him gain citizenship in April 1942, in the middle of the war years. On the other hand, German citizens who had arrived at the same time had to wait until they were recognised as 'refugee' rather than 'enemy' aliens.[24] Stefan Weintraub's application in April 1942 was therefore declined, and his second application in February 1944 was not approved until October 1945. Horst Graff's experience was similar. Although Fritz Coper and Walter Dullo had been living in Australia since 1937, they waited until 1944 for their citizenship, as did all the 1938–39 arrivals: Heinrich (Henry) Adler, Hans Forst, Heinrich Krips, Martin Krutsch, Ellen Cohn, Willy Coper, Richard Goldner, Gertrud Hacker and Wolfgang Wagner. When it was discovered that Henry Adler[25] and Otti Veit's husband had some contact with communist circles there were delays: leftist sympathies, once quite natural for many refugees in their home country, were no longer considered opportune. In the light of this situation, quite a few decided to return to Europe, where some found a new home in the German Democratic Republic (GDR).

Rudolf Werther's naturalisation was delayed when an informant accused him of an immoral lifestyle. Furthermore, it was thought doubtful the woman with whom he was living was actually his wife. A security official regarded Werther as 'very Jewish'. The Honorary Justices' Association of Tasmania warned that he had been a German officer in the last war and apparently did not appreciate Australia as a country of exile as he had been seen hurrying out of a picture theatre before the national anthem was played. The Launceston Chief of Police confirmed that Werther was lawfully married and that there had never been any complaints about him from the Tasmanian Musical Festival Society. Further clarification was needed as to whether the musician had consciously avoided the national anthem. On 30 April 1945, Werther stated for the record that, until now, he had conducted and sung the national anthem seventy-five times at concerts and opera performances; that said, he sometimes left the theatre early to catch the last tram. As there were still some concerns, he was notified in July 1945 that his naturalisation was not possible at the moment. The musician was appalled, as was the Tasmanian Musical Festival Society. Luckily, that same month it was announced that the person responsible for citizenship was no longer the Minister for the Interior, but the new Minister for Immigration, Arthur Calwell. In early August, the Tasmanian Treasurer, Edmund Dwyer-Gray, sent Calwell a comprehensive letter pleading Werther's case, with the support of twelve others, including the mayor of Launceston. This letter represented a breakthrough and his citizenship was finally granted in September 1945.[26]

Naturalisation also took unusually long for those deported from Singapore, even though the crown colony was in the Commonwealth. The delay is explained by the fact that after the war it often took months for the necessary certificates of good conduct and other documents to arrive from Singapore. Werner Baer was given refugee status in 1944 and received his permanent residency permit in February 1945, while he was still serving in the army. He immediately applied for citizenship, but no decision could be made since the documents from Singapore were missing. There was still no decision in November, when he was discharged from the army. On 8 March 1946, the Australian Jewish Welfare Society informed the department of the interior that, as a musician, Baer needed to join the Musicians' Union, but that he could only become a member once he had been naturalised.[27] This finally happened in May, and soon after that all the other musicians deported from Singapore received their certificates of citizenship: Hans Bader, Kurt Blach, Heinrich Portnoj, Paul Steiner, Mischa Stiwelband and Salo Tichauer.

For the refugees, however, the end of the war did not automatically mean the end of their military service. Even married men were, as a rule, only discharged at the end of 1945, while most unmarried men returned to civilian life only in mid-1946. Felix Bischofswerder stayed in the army until 26 June 1946, two days before his father died. He had been seen as an outsider, and had provoked his superiors because he preferred to speak German despite his excellent knowledge of English. With his father's death, the purpose of his army service came to an end. Now he was free to make a decision about his future. He had applied for a residency permit five years after his arrival on the *Dunera*, when he had specified interior design as his profession; a year after his father's death, Felix Bischofswerder applied for citizenship. On account of his military service, he was naturalised more easily and, moreover, free of charge. In addition, the army's repatriation scheme helped with his reintegration into professional life. He subsequently decided to become a teacher, and shortened his surname to 'Werder'. Oskar Fleischer changed his surname to Fletcher, while from January 1945 Hans Holzbauer was known as John Wood. From 1946, the repatriation scheme also allowed Henry Adler to further his education at the Sydney Conservatorium after he was discharged from the army. Walter Würzburger had already begun studies at the University of Melbourne's Music Faculty during his military service. In December 1944, he had taken exams in form and analysis, orchestration, history and aesthetics, harmony and counterpoint. After two years of theoretical studies, he was allowed to transfer to the instrumental programme in June 1946.[28]

Ironing or Music? Deciding on a Vocation

Professional musicians in particular urgently required citizenship in order to join the Musicians' Union. Mischa Stiwelband and Adolf Brenner both had the same problem as Werner Baer. Adolf Brenner, now known as Dolf, wrote to the department of immigration on 4 June 1946:

> Ever since I was discharged from the army after the well over three years of uninterrupted service, I have been experiencing nothing but difficulties on account of my not being naturalised yet. Whether it is the Austr. Broadcasting Commission, the Musicians' Union, or many schools I applied to, they all insist on my being naturalised. I am an operatic conductor, chorus master, and musical coach. May I appeal to you to speed up my naturalisation without which I am debarred from every professional activity.[29]

The matter was indeed quickly dealt with and Brenner was finally able to resume work as a professional musician.

Leonie Feigl was just as concerned about the long waiting period. In December 1945, she wrote to the department of immigration saying how important citizenship was to her, since without it she could not obtain a position as a music teacher. In January 1946, the Minister's private secretary intervened personally on the singer's behalf, but it was another six months before she had the desired certificate in her hand.³⁰ As citizens since 1945, Ellen Cohn-Byk and Heinrich Portnoj were able to advertise as music teachers. Similarly, Erwin Frenkel, Marcel Lorber and Curt Prerauer all began to work officially as private piano teachers.

In contrast to their Australian colleagues, recently naturalised musicians had to pass an audition in order to join the Musicians' Union.³¹ Although this represented further discrimination against the 'new Australians', after the test they were usually accepted without any problems. When the violinist Fritz Kramer was naturalised in 1944 and subsequently joined the union, he no longer eked out an existence as an accountant, but as a professional musician – from 1945 as a member of the Melbourne Symphony Orchestra (MSO). Peter Langer gave up his unprofitable sawmill business; after naturalisation, he became a member of the union and then a cellist with the MSO. Walter Lemberg from Breslau, who had arrived in 1939, was also now recognised by the Musicians' Union of New South Wales as a professional violinist and violist.³²

Sydney John Kay, the trombonist and arranger from the Weintraubs Syncopators, caused a stir by taking the powerful union to court. When his first application for membership was declined in 1939, he submitted another in March 1944, pointing out that he had already been in Australia for nearly seven years. He requested admission as a trombonist, saxophonist and clarinettist as well as a conductor, arranger and composer, and mentioned his present employment with the G. Patterson (or Colgate-Palmolive) Radio Unit.³³ When this second application was rejected, he complained to the State Industrial Commission. At the hearing, a union representative maintained that Kay had not disproved the allegation that he was an enemy alien. The judge, however, found in favour of the plaintiff, who again emphasised his Peruvian citizenship; the grounds on which the union had withheld his membership were deemed invalid.³⁴ After the hearing, Kitson defended his union's position in the press, saying that foreigners like Kay were well off. Kay had indicated a considerable income of twenty-five pounds a week, but Kitson interpreted this as exaggerated generosity on the part of the Australians: 'I am sure that an Australian in Germany would not be getting £25 a week.' He then suggested that Kay was

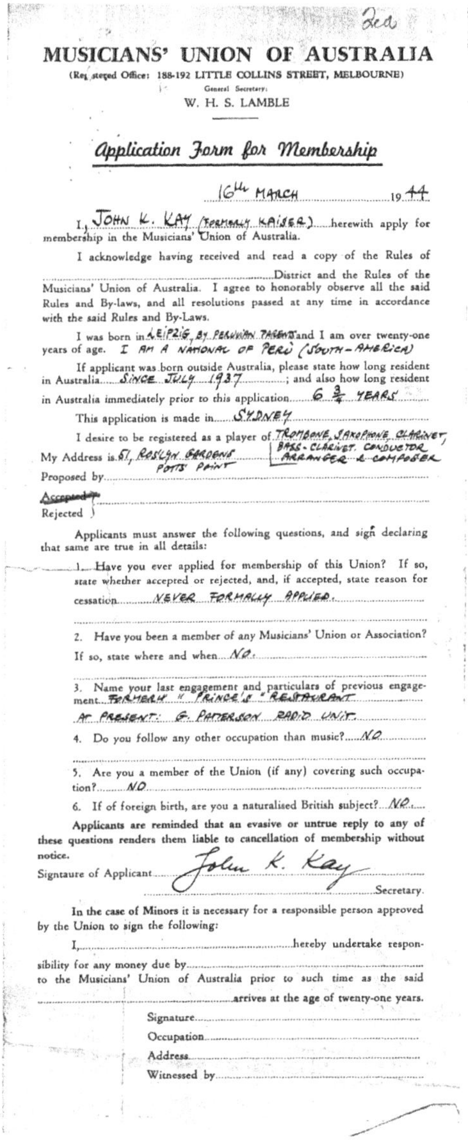

2nd

MUSICIANS' UNION OF AUSTRALIA

(Registered Office: 188-192 LITTLE COLLINS STREET, MELBOURNE)

General Secretary:

W. H. S. LAMBLE

Application Form for Membership

16th MARCH 1944

I, JOHN K. KAY (FORMALLY KAISER) herewith apply for membership in the Musicians' Union of Australia.

I acknowledge having received and read a copy of the Rules of .... District and the Rules of the Musicians' Union of Australia. I agree to honorably observe all the said Rules and By-laws, and all resolutions passed at any time in accordance with the said Rules and By-Laws.

I was born in LEIPZIG, BY PERUVIAN PARENTS and I am over twenty-one years of age. I AM A NATIONAL OF PERÙ (SOUTH-AMERICA)

If applicant was born outside Australia, please state how long resident in Australia SINCE JULY 1937; and also how long resident in Australia immediately prior to this application 6 ¾ YEARS

This application is made in SYDNEY

I desire to be registered as a player of TROMBONE, SAXOPHONE, CLARINET, BASS-CLARINET, CONDUCTOR ARRANGER & COMPOSER

My Address is 51, ROSLYN GARDENS POTTS' POINT

Proposed by ....

~~Accepted~~ } ....
Rejected }

Applicants must answer the following questions, and sign declaring that same are true in all details:

1. Have you ever applied for membership of this Union? If so, state whether accepted or rejected, and, if accepted, state reason for cessation NEVER FORMALLY APPLIED.

2. Have you been a member of any Musicians' Union or Association? If so, state where and when NO.

3. Name your last engagement and particulars of previous engagement FORMERLY "PRINCE'S" RESTAURANT AT PRESENT: G. PATTERSON RADIO UNIT.

4. Do you follow any other occupation than music? NO

5. Are you a member of the Union (if any) covering such occupation? NO

6. If of foreign birth, are you a naturalised British subject? NO.

Applicants are reminded that an evasive or untrue reply to any of these questions renders them liable to cancellation of membership without notice.

Signtaure of Applicant John K. Kay

.... Secretary.

In the case of Minors it is necessary for a responsible person approved by the Union to sign the following:

I, ... hereby undertake responsibility for any money due by .... to the Musicians' Union of Australia prior to such time as the said .... arrives at the age of twenty-one years.

Signature ....

Occupation ....

Address ....

Witnessed by ....

Figure 27: Application Form for Membership for the Musicians' Union of Australia, completed by John K. Kay on 16 March 1944. (Noel Butlin Archives Centre, Australian National University: Musicians' Union of Australia, E156-2-3) living at the expense of musicians who had made sacrifices to serve their country.

> My union wants to preserve as many jobs as it can for members when they are released from the Army and the munition factories. Our membership is 958. Of these 258 of them are in uniform. Many of these men would like to be released so that they could take a £25 a week position like that of Mr Kay.[35]

He failed to mention that there was hardly anyone else in his union capable of taking on Kay's highly qualified work as an arranger and conductor. Although at this time Kay did not really depend on membership of the union, to him, the win signified a triumph, and a belated revenge against the Weintraubs Syncopators' gravedigger, Frank Kitson.

Although this jazz band broke up during the war years, several members continued to play in other groups. Emanuel Frischer, now known as Manny Fisher, was accepted by the union, as were his brother Adolf ('Addy') and Leo Weiss (Leo White). The fact that Jenny Schulvater caused them all such difficulties with her black market activities in Russia was probably the reason why her son Cyril had already left the band in 1938. After that, he and his brother Ernest opened a hamburger shop in Ashfield and a second one in Bondi in 1941; in 1942, he became a turner in a factory. When the war ended, Cyril had approval from the union to resume work as a musician, from 1946 as a cellist in the Sydney Symphony Orchestra (SSO). For the band's founders, Horst Graff and Stefan Weintraub, though, after the dissolution of the Weintraubs Syncopators and the failure of their new venture at Romano's Restaurant, an existence as professional musicians was inconceivable. Their musical careers were over. Whether they ever applied for union membership is doubtful.

Paul Steiner, a versatile instrumentalist in Singapore and in the camp at Tatura, was at least able to use his various skills in an associated area: Allans Music in Melbourne gave him a permanent position as an instrument repairer. Many of the refugee musicians, however, did not succeed in returning to their profession. For many, it was already too late as they were past their prime, while some had already died, including the piano teacher Emma Weiss, the music publisher Victor Alberti, the pianist Theodor

Schoenberger and the cantor Boas Bischofswerder. They were denied a career in their later years through persecution, flight and war.

Shortly after his arrival in Australia, Karl Berg decided against a musical career and worked as an accountant. After the war, Walter Dullo, too, decided not to change his profession. Instead, he continued to make chocolates, but intensified his part-time commitment to musical life. As a chorister at the synagogue, Willy Coper did not make enough money to make music his main career, but earned his living in a jewellery business. Mario Dane was not able to survive as an opera and operetta tenor, so he worked mainly as a photographer. The Viennese opera singer Olga Hajek-Bodan, having come to Australia from Shanghai, eked out a living initially as a tobacco saleswoman and her actor husband as a barber. In 1945, the pianist Gertrud Hacker also had priorities other than a return to her career. Her husband was not recognised as a lawyer in Australia, so they both ran a milk bar before he retrained as an accountant. After their daughter was born in 1946, she could only begin to think about teaching piano again in 1949. Majer Pietruschka, so active as a violinist and leader of the orchestras in Hay and Tatura, suffered from diabetes and was therefore discharged from the army in August 1942. On account of the union's xenophobia, he could not obtain work as a musician, but had to earn a meagre living ironing clothes in a dry cleaning business. When he finally applied for permanent residency, he gave his occupation as 'Ironer', which matched his 'proposed occupation in Australia'. He was only able to return to the music profession after his naturalisation in 1946, by which time he had already married an Australian. In 1947, he gave one of his instruments, an old bassoon, to the young George Dreyfus, who later wrote about this present that 'it saved my life' – he was finally able to begin studying the bassoon.[36]

In order to flee Europe and enter Australia, Alphons Silbermann had chosen the vocation of chef. He opened a sandwich shop, and it was so successful that, with help from his parents, he built a whole chain of 'Silvers Food Bars'. In March 1944, when his application for citizenship was rejected, he instructed the law firm Abram Landa, Barton & Co. to assist with his appeal. The proprietor of the firm was also a member of parliament, and he argued that Silbermann's business had an annual turnover of over

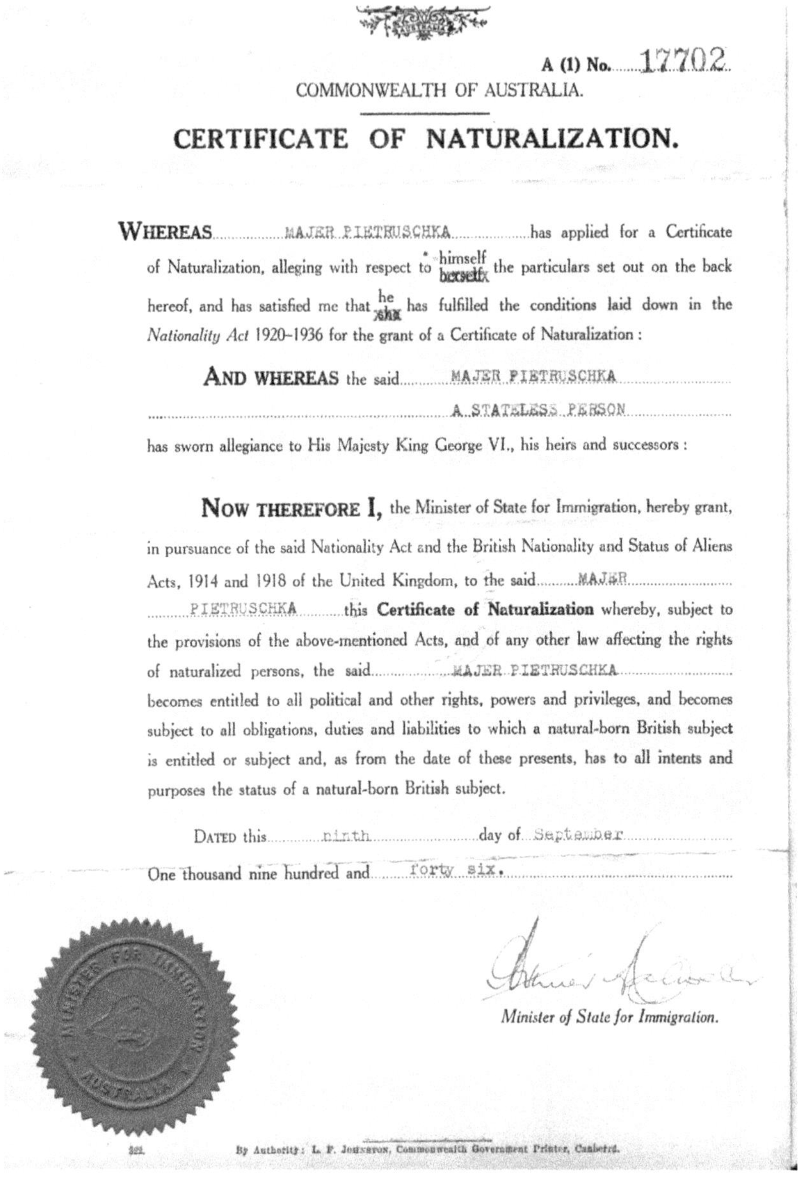

A (1) No. 17702

COMMONWEALTH OF AUSTRALIA.

CERTIFICATE OF NATURALIZATION.

WHEREAS MAJER PIETRUSCHKA has applied for a Certificate of Naturalization, alleging with respect to himself ~~herself~~ the particulars set out on the back hereof, and has satisfied me that he ~~she~~ has fulfilled the conditions laid down in the *Nationality Act* 1920–1936 for the grant of a Certificate of Naturalization :

AND WHEREAS the said MAJER PIETRUSCHKA A STATELESS PERSON has sworn allegiance to His Majesty King George VI., his heirs and successors :

NOW THEREFORE I, the Minister of State for Immigration, hereby grant, in pursuance of the said Nationality Act and the British Nationality and Status of Aliens Acts, 1914 and 1918 of the United Kingdom, to the said MAJER PIETRUSCHKA this **Certificate of Naturalization** whereby, subject to the provisions of the above-mentioned Acts, and of any other law affecting the rights of naturalized persons, the said MAJER PIETRUSCHKA becomes entitled to all political and other rights, powers and privileges, and becomes subject to all obligations, duties and liabilities to which a natural-born British subject is entitled or subject and, as from the date of these presents, has to all intents and purposes the status of a natural-born British subject.

DATED this ninth day of September One thousand nine hundred and forty six.

MINISTER FOR IMMIGRATION AUSTRALIA

Minister of State for Immigration.

322. By Authority: L. F. Johnston, Commonwealth Government Printer, Canberra.

Figure 28: Certificate of Naturalization for Majer Pietruschka. (Tanya Makin, Melbourne)

£100,000 and had 160 employees. The firm sold two million meals a year to people from all walks of life, including members of the army. In addition, Silbermann was a member of numerous charitable organisations and had influential friends. The department of the interior based its case on the fact that the applicant had bribed officials in order to avoid military service.[37] Moreover, on several occasions his firm had not observed the blackout orders, supposedly through some arrangement with the union, and he was said to keep company with persons of dubious moral character; this barely disguised the allegation of homosexuality, which in those days was severely frowned upon. After several tussles with government agencies, and although Silbermann was not particularly interested in adapting to his new surroundings, he nevertheless applied for citizenship again in 1945. In June of that year, after further legal help, it was approved. In the meantime, he had taken piano lessons at the Sydney Conservatorium, but was not anxious to make music his main profession, as he did not want to leave his thriving business in the lurch. When he flew to the USA with his new passport in 1946, he did so primarily to learn about a new product for the Silvers Food Bars, one that he had heard about from the American soldiers. He subsequently marketed the first doughnuts in Australia.[38]

CHAPTER 15

'The cultivated enthusiasm of a handful of missionaries': The Genesis of Musica Viva Australia

Over the centuries, Europe had gradually developed a concert life that sought neither to entertain nor to provide religious edification, but to communicate artistic values. The bourgeoisie had taken over these ideals from the nobility and brought them to a high point. By contrast, in Australia, utility was the order of the day; there had never been a tradition of nobility and that of the bourgeoisie developed very late. Therefore, material gains were of greater importance than intellectual or spiritual values, which were seen as either nebulous, or sentimental and effete. Accordingly, the arts, or what was called high culture, attracted less attention than sport, whose role in physical training was obvious. Concerts were only regarded as useful or worthwhile if they served as entertainment, which is why, to this day, Australian newspapers review them under the heading 'Entertainment'. In those days, the word 'music' had a more limited meaning than the German word 'Musik'. Around 1945, the most important cultural activities were the cinema, dancing, ballet and choral societies, as they were all associated with social gatherings. Opera performances by guest companies and ABC symphony concerts were most popular when famous celebrities performed. In such cases, however, free tickets are said to have been regularly distributed in order to spare guest artists the embarrassment of half-empty halls. Under these circumstances, an art form as quiet and unspectacular as chamber music must have seemed altogether exotic; it demanded concentrated listening and was meant for connoisseurs, of which at the time there were very few in Australia.

German settlers in South Australia nurtured their 'Hausmusik' but, in view of anti-German feeling, it was hardly heard in public after 1918. Having taken up residence at the newly founded Sydney Conservatorium in 1916, the Scottish Verbrugghen Quartet had already disbanded by

1922. Later initiatives like the Melbourne Beck Quartet, the NSW State Conservatorium Quartet and the Sydney String Quartet had only a limited impact. Overseas chamber ensembles rarely came to Australia, so tours by the Spivakovsky–Kurtz Trio (1933) and the Budapest String Quartet (1935 and 1937) remained notable exceptions. Yehudi Menuhin was a special case. He first visited Australia in 1935 and later returned because, in London in 1938, Bernard Heinze had introduced him to the Australian heiress Nola Nicholas with spectacular success: the violinist married Nola, and his sister, the pianist Hephzibah Menuhin, married Nola's brother, Lindsay Nicholas.[1] This explains why Yehudi and Hephzibah gave several concerts in Australia, including chamber music recitals. That said, while staying at her husband's property west of Melbourne, Hephzibah devoted most of her time to the sheep and philanthropic ideas. The German-trained cellist Carl Gotsch even performed and broadcast Hindemith and Milhaud with his Collegium Musicum in Sydney, but he was seen by some as rather eccentric.[2] At that time, chamber music was regarded as elitist; few saw it as a necessity.

By 1940, however, changes in Australia's concert life were becoming more apparent as Jewish refugees from Europe flocked to the concert halls. Their great love of the 'sacred art' of music meant higher standards. In her biography of Bernard Heinze, the distinguished Melbourne musicologist Thérèse Radic observes:

> Today we credit post-war migration with the cultural advances that are the basis of what we see as national maturation. But in fact the forced migration of the pre-war years, nurturing and sustaining our small cultural life during the isolation of wartime, is the primary source of what came after, at least as far as music is concerned. If Heinze could not find a place for the too-many conductors from Dresden, the country found a place for those who used to listen to such conductors.[3]

The critic Lindsey Browne was also struck by the change:

> The pre-war audiences were socialites for the most part, doing the right thing by being at a concert. They were not really responsive, and this only changed with the arrival of European refugees in the Town Hall audience. They were used to really listening to a performance, and that helped bring about a change in audience behaviour, and indeed, in the make-up of the audiences.[4]

It was probably thanks to this new section of the public that the proportion of classical music broadcast by the ABC grew from 5.99 per cent in 1939 to 6.73 per cent at the end of the war.[5] From 1942, refugees who had joined the army also came in uniform to the concerts, where seats were reserved for them in the front rows. They were conspicuous in the predominantly female audiences and important as a contribution to socio-cultural change in macho Australian society: making music acceptable for males. For them, music was not a luxury, but the essential ingredient representing a 'better world', the elixir of life. These cultured, critical listeners often had a good knowledge of repertoire and compared what was offered in Australia to what they had once experienced in Vienna or Berlin.

Among these musical enthusiasts was the violist Richard Goldner. There had been three orchestras on the luxury Dutch ship *Marnix van Sint Aldegonde* that had taken him to Colombo. Goldner had played the Brahms sextets with some of the musicians on board and, at the same time, he dreamed of being able to establish an ensemble in his new country like the one led by his teacher, Simon Pullman, in Vienna. Pullman had written to him from Paris in October 1938, saying that one could achieve great things in many areas in Australia, 'and perhaps especially in music'.[6] When Goldner arrived in Sydney, he introduced himself to the Sydney Symphony Orchestra. Although very impressed by his musicality, they could not accept him because the Musicians' Union refused membership to foreigners. The union's vigilance regarding citizenship contradicted the leniency with which it defined the concept of a musician.

> In Vienna, only a full-time professional was called 'Musician'. It was one of my greatest surprises that no distinction was made in Australia at that time between a professional and an amateur. [...] I had the impression that the average Australian did not consider music as something that could provide a living.[7]

As Goldner could not be accepted into the orchestra, he took up the substitute occupation given on his entry form: the manufacturing of jewellery. Together with his brother, he joined the small jewellery and leather goods firm, Natty Novelties, run by some friends from Vienna. The 'Bluebird of Happiness' brooch that he designed was so successful that within three months the firm had more than fifty employees. Several newspaper articles and two newsreels were devoted to this expanding business. Good revenue enabled Goldner and his brother not only to pay back the money they had borrowed for the landing fees, but also to bring their parents to Australia; they arrived in Sydney on the Italian *Esquilino* in April 1940, just before Italy joined the war. By then, however, Goldner missed his music so much that in 1941 he and three other enthusiasts established the 'Monomeeth String Quartet', 'monomeeth' being the Aboriginal term for 'welcome'. His colleagues were two Australians and Endre Hoffmann from Budapest, a student of Hubay. With Antal Dorati's assistance, Hoffmann had arrived in March 1940 but, being unable to join the Union, he took work in a shoe factory, where he remained for three years.

The products of Goldner's jewellery and leather goods factory were not considered important for the war effort, so the firm was to be closed down. At the same time, however, the government was on the lookout for imaginative minds in more relevant industries. It was known that Goldner had invented a special mute in Vienna so, one day in 1942, Squadron-Leader Russell Robinson appeared at the factory and asked to speak with him. Goldner regarded the uniformed visitor with suspicion, fearing some kind of inspection, but Robinson explained to him that it was a matter of national importance. In view of the war, and the loss of Britain as protective power, Australia now had to strengthen its own capacity for self-defence. New ideas were being sought and Robinson, himself an inventor, had been appointed by the government as a talent scout. He made it clear to Goldner right from the start that they needed a three-dimensional zipper for military purposes, one that was not affected by mud. Goldner said that he did not even know how an ordinary zip functioned; nevertheless, Robinson asked him to think about it and then left the office.[8]

Goldner was puzzled by this strange commission but, when he awoke as usual at 3 a.m. the next morning after just four hours' sleep, he already had an idea for a three-dimensional zipper. He made a model from soft copper wire, and tried it out. To his surprise, this new version worked. He immediately contacted his client, who could hardly believe that he already had a result. He tested Goldner's invention, and a few days later informed him that the jewellery and leather goods factory would not be closed: instead they were to receive new machinery and a government contract to

CHAPTER 15: *The Genesis of Musica Viva Australia*

manufacture zips. The new firm, Triflex Pty Ltd, was even more successful than the previous one and produced thousands of these special zippers for the navy and air force during the war years.

In January 1944, when Goldner went to the doctor, he found a journal, the *Jewish Forum*, in the waiting room. While leafing through it, he suddenly caught sight of an article that said:

> In the Warsaw Ghetto an orchestra under the able leadership of Simon Pullman was active. Whenever the opportunity presented itself, concerts of beautiful orchestral and chamber music provided moments of rest and escape. Pullman and all the members of the orchestra, including the violinist Ludwig Holzman, were killed in Treblinka.[9]

In summer 1939, Pullman, who lived in Paris, was visiting Warsaw when war broke out. After reading of Pullman's death, part of Goldner's world collapsed; he was devastated since, until then, he had been hoping that his teacher could come from Paris to Australia in order to continue their previous work with a new ensemble. Of course, they would have needed a lot of money and some outstanding musicians to make this idea a reality.

Goldner had only entrusted one of his closest friends with this dream of an Australian Pullman ensemble: Walter Dullo. Dullo had come into the factory one day offering his chocolates for sale. Richard Goldner was enthusiastic, but regretted that he could not afford such delicacies. 'We had already cut out the luxury of an occasional milkshake which we all adored.' Although Goldner was not one of Dullo's customers, they began to converse. Thus the chocolate salesman and the jewellery manufacturer discovered, to their surprise, that they both shared a passion for music. As Goldner writes, Dullo then came in almost every day; they did not talk about chocolates or brooches, but about chamber music and a future Pullman ensemble. 'It did not take long before he got "infected" with my dream. From then on we dreamed together. He certainly was no more realistic than I was.'[10]

When Simon Pullman was arrested in the Warsaw ghetto, he had been playing one of his favourite works with his orchestra: Beethoven's *Great Fugue* (*Große Fuge*) Op. 133. In memory of his teacher, Goldner and his Monomeeth Quartet had already studied this work, often regarded as Beethoven's most daring composition on account of its uncompromisingly radical approach.[11] The news of Pullman's murder now gave him an extra incentive for establishing the ensemble of his dreams. He discussed the idea with Dullo but, because of the war, it was at first only possible at house concerts. This exchange of ideas was temporarily interrupted when Dullo was sent to work for the Allied Works Council in Alice Springs in 1943–1944. But by August 1945, after Germany and Japan had surrendered, it was finally time to air their plans in public. Goldner decided to found a permanent string ensemble comprising several independent string quartets, like the Pullman Orchestra in Vienna. He used the earnings from his zipper production to engage seventeen musicians, namely four string quartets and a bass player, and arranged a lot of rehearsals. He worked as though possessed every day for three months with each of the four ensembles, supported by Dullo, who came regularly and encouraged the musicians. Beethoven's *Große Fuge*, which actually consists of several fugues and was described by the composer as 'just as free as it is artistic', demands the utmost concentration from each musician, indeed almost overtaxes them in its density of themes and contrasting dynamics. To complement this unwieldy masterpiece, Dullo arranged Mozart's *Fantasia* in F minor for a Mechanical Organ, K. 608, for strings.[12] Once each of the four string quartets had studied these two works, together with other compositions by Purcell and Handel, they were finally brought together as an ensemble: 'Richard Goldner's Sydney Musica Viva'.

Richard Goldner's Sydney Musica Viva

This name refers to Goldner's second great role model: the conductor Hermann Scherchen. A pioneer of new music since the Weimar Republic, Scherchen had premiered numerous important works in Europe and also carried out electro-acoustic experiments. Regarded by the Nazis as a 'cultural Bolshevik', he had left Germany for Switzerland in 1933. In 1935, he established the 'Ars Viva' publishing house for old and new music in Brussels and a year later the quadrilingual magazine *Musica Viva*. In Vienna, he regularly conducted the Vienna Concert Orchestra, in which Richard Goldner was principal violist and, in the late summer of 1937, with great hopes for the future, he brought in particular young Jewish players together in a Musica Viva Orchestra, in which Goldner again played first viola. Goldner was fascinated by Scherchen's dedication in daily rehearsals, and by his art of verbalising musical phrases; a close relationship developed between the conductor and the musicians. Goldner also admired Scherchen's perfectionism, his enormous energy and his ability to make do with only a few hours' sleep. Goldner attended Scherchen's conducting course and later acknowledged in his memoirs that this teacher had comprehensively broadened his musical horizon. In winter 1937–1938 the Musica Viva Orchestra performed a major Mahler cycle. The composer's widow, Alma Mahler-Werfel, praised the interpretation of the Fifth Symphony in particular as 'indescribably splendid': 'Scherchen did the work perfect justice.'[13] After that, in February 1938, they began a six-part series in the Great Hall of the Musikverein of compositions by Johann Sebastian Bach, which ended abruptly, after the German invasion. At the end of March, Scherchen wrote to Goldner from Switzerland: 'You can imagine how much I worry about the MV Orchestra and how much I wish that we could continue the work we began there. How this will be possible, I can't quite say yet; only time will tell.'[14] In order to promote his violist, Scherchen provided him with a glowing reference: 'Mr Richard Goldner, Principal Viola with the Musica Viva Orchestra, Vienna, is one of the most intelligent and artistically refined violists alive today. I would always use him as the principal.'[15]

According to Scherchen, true artists were recognised by the degree to which they envisaged and championed a society of the future. He acknowledged the pioneering features of Bach's *Art of Fugue* and Beethoven's *Große Fuge*, which he thought was created 'against the rejection of his contemporaries and of today's listeners'.[16] Contemporary music played a central role in Scherchen's concept of Musica Viva. In this sense, it was carried on by his student Karl Amadeus Hartmann, who in 1945 established the Musica Viva concert series in Munich that still exists today. Hans-Joachim Koellreutter, another Scherchen student, brought the Musica Viva movement to Brazil; its founding manifesto described it as 'a type of gate which is open to contemporary music and also plays an active part in intellectual development'. Like Scherchen, Koellreutter understood musical composition as 'the highest form of human thought and feeling and the most sublime embodiment of life itself'. He and his Brazilian colleagues fixed their eyes on the present: 'Musica Viva wants to show that in our era music, too, is an expression of the times and of a new intelligence, by disseminating modern compositions of all styles, especially from the American continents, through concerts, broadcasts, lectures and publications.'[17] The Brazilian Música Viva movement indeed succeeded in considerably influencing musical life there.

Like Scherchen and Pullman, Goldner had also taken part in numerous performances of contemporary music in Vienna; for example, in October 1937, together with Peter Stadlen and Erich Simon, he had performed works by Schönberg and Webern at the Society for New Music. Although he remained committed to contemporary music until he died, it was not one of the main objectives of his Australian Musica Viva. In the invitation to the ensemble's first dress rehearsal (what was called an 'audition performance') in December 1945 that he and Dullo formulated, Goldner wrote:

> In forming the Sydney Musica Viva my aim was to create a repertoire ensemble, destined to perform well-rehearsed music, and to do experimental work in methods of rehearsing with a view to achieving greater precision and better quality, volume and balance of sound; and to carry out any other experiments, the results of which might be beneficial to the interpretation of the masters in concert performances, recordings and broadcasts.
> The first result of such experimental work is the S.M.V. Orchestra, whose string chorus will be introduced at the audition performance. This string chorus consists of a number of string quartets, as germ cells. In rehearsing, all works are being studied separately with each individual quartet, so that, when combined as a chorus, each player retains the mentality, responsibility and initiative of a solo quartet player.[18]

Accordingly, the Australian Musica Viva focused not on new repertoire, but on the exemplary performance of masterpieces in the true spirit of chamber music. The frequently used concept of experimentation probably came from Scherchen, although Goldner left this unmentioned. On the other hand, he referred quite clearly to his other mentor:

> The principles of my work are based on the original ideas of my great teacher and friend, the late Simon Pullman, who established a similar ensemble in Vienna in

1931, and directed it till 1938. Sydney Musica Viva is meant to be a continuation and development of the work started by him. It is also proposed to use the string chorus as he did, for performing a selected number of string quartets, the interpretation of which is either beyond the scope of a solo string quartet, or would at least gain, by a chorus performance; for example, Beethoven, Op. 130, with its original finale, *The Great Fugue*; Beethoven, Op. 131; Schubert, G major; Schoenberg, D minor; Elgar, Piano Quintet; Korngold, String Quartet & Piano Quintet etc. Most of these works were successfully performed by The Pullman Orchestra in Vienna. Schoenberg, Elgar, Korngold and several other contemporary composers expressly approved of these performances of their works.

With the name Musica Viva, Goldner was referring to lively music, but above all to making Pullman's ideas 'come alive' again. For this a permanent ensemble was needed:

> The existence of a trained group of instrumentalists kept in permanent co-operation on the principles described, naturally opens yet another field; i.e. the use of the players for chamber music works of any conceivable combination. The respective literature for the various instrumental combinations in chamber music, except Sonatas, String Quartets and Piano Trios, is not sufficiently large to justify the formation of special ensembles (Quintets, Sextets, Septets, Octets, etc. – String and Wind Combinations). Therefore, a great number of master works for such combinations have to remain stepchildren of the rostrum. The Sydney Musica Viva intends to make it one of their tasks to keep such works permanently in their repertoire.

Even before the first appearance of Goldner's Sydney Musica Viva, the press announced that no performance in Australia had ever been so well rehearsed.[19] Their first concert, on 8 December 1945, almost had to be cancelled because of a power failure, but the ABC quickly supplied an army generator so that Sydney Conservatorium's Verbrugghen Hall could be adequately lit. Probably out of curiosity, and because of the free tickets, the public arrived in such large numbers that there were not enough seats. Even Goldner, who was in the audience, was surprised by the evening's high artistic standard. 'It is quite amazing how special inspiring circumstances can elevate a performance to undreamt-of heights! [...]. The *Great Fugue* came off in a way that moved even the least experienced listeners.'

Remarkably, the reaction from the press was not entirely enthusiastic. In the *Sydney Morning Herald*, Neville Cardus found fault with the intonation, and the *Australian Musical News*, which translated the concept of

Musica Viva as 'Live-Music', criticised the fact that the performances were not as 'lively' as they could have been. 'Rhythms were rather too square and dogged, and tone often steely in climaxes.'[20] Other papers, in contrast, spoke of encouraging results that had led to the founding of a non-commercial organisation, one which, it was said, would finance the chamber orchestra, which wanted to give ten concerts each season.

> All profits from concerts will be used to further the objects of the society, which include meetings, lectures, publication of a monthly leaflet and the assistance and encouragement of young musicians. A music library and clubrooms will also be established. Next year it is also hoped to give concerts in country districts.[21]

In the first edition of the Association of Refugees' new monthly newspaper, the *New Citizen*, Walter Dullo acknowledged the work of Musica Viva as an important contribution to Sydney's musical life.[22] In the June edition, he introduced his friend Richard Goldner as a musician and inventor. At the beginning of the war, when a security official had asked him about his occupation, Goldner had replied: 'My former profession is now my hobby and my former hobby is now going to be my job.' Goldner had indeed made his music profession a hobby in Australia, and jewellery production, which had previously been incidental, had become his main occupation. But music was his passion. Dullo described Goldner's unforgettable, sparkling eyes: 'They radiate his obsession, they are the eyes of a man who is well aware for what he is striving.' This obsession was for his 'hobby', Musica Viva, in which he invested a huge amount of time and money. In conclusion, Dullo revealed that Goldner was preparing another surprise for Sydney's music lovers: 'He has secured for his orchestra an outstanding violinist of world fame whose name cannot be disclosed yet.'[23]

This was presumably Szymon Goldberg, concertmaster of the Berlin Philharmonic until 1934, whom the Japanese had interned in Java in 1942 while he was on a concert tour with his associate artist, Lili Kraus. After his release, Goldberg came to Australia, where he conducted Hindemith's *Trauermusik* for viola and string orchestra at a Musica Viva concert. He himself did not play in Goldner's ensemble, but instead recommended Robert Pikler, another Hubay pupil who had also been interned in Java. Pikler had already arrived in April, after Goldner had provided him with the necessary financial support. He soon became one of the pillars of Musica Viva. While seeking more first-class musicians for his ensemble, Goldner remembered Theo Salzmann who, during his own student years in Vienna, had been principal cellist of the university orchestra and later the Vienna Symphony. From 1938, Salzmann held the same position with the Palestine Orchestra.[24] Since he was unhappy there, Goldner invited him to Australia and the cellist actually accepted the invitation in 1947.

According to Eva Wagner, in December 1946, the future of Musica Viva seemed uncertain, but the public voted for its continuation. Unfortunately, important documents have disappeared, so those years can no longer be accurately reconstructed. About this time, however, Goldner must have decided to replace the string ensemble with a permanent string quartet. As he wrote in his memoirs, it was to be a quartet of international standing. At first, he only wanted to direct the rehearsals as he felt that, technically, he could no longer satisfy his own high standards. It was only when the others pleaded with him that Goldner consented to play. Thus, he once again made music his profession. While his brother Gerhard took over the main responsibility for the firm, Richard (viola) became a founding member of the Musica Viva String Quartet, with Robert Pikler and Edward Cockman (violins) and Theo Salzmann (violoncello). In 1948, when the addition of the pianist Maureen Jones created a quintet, the ensemble was renamed the Musica Viva Players. In this formation, it toured Australia and New Zealand and gave no fewer than 200 concerts a year.

The first Sydney Musica Viva concert in December 1945 was financed solely by Goldner, but it was clear to everybody that this had to be an exception. As it was planned to charge admission for future concerts, Walter Dullo and Friedrich Klopfer, later proprietor of The Music Lounge record store at 563 George Street, suggested a subscription. They immediately attracted 807 subscribers, most of them refugees from Europe, and the first subscription concert took place in March 1946. The series would not have survived, however, without generous sponsors and hosts like Mella Selby in Sydney, her brother Fritz Mandel, the Wenkart family,[25] Dr Steven Kinston (Siegfried Kinsbrunner) in Brisbane and Edith Dubsky[26] in Adelaide. The ensemble and its soloists frequently stayed in their private homes, which were also used for rehearsals and performances. The atmosphere was similar to that of a Viennese salon, as Eva Wagner confirmed:

> It was all very nice when we first went to the Selbys. They had a wonderful house and the old lady always opened the door. Then the Wenkarts took over, and it was just the same. There was a big swimming pool, and French doors that were opened up in the summer heat. The living room with the piano was only dimly lit, since light came from outside, sometimes moonlight. By European standards it was simple, but here it was fantastic.[27]

By far the greatest section of the public consisted of European exiles, who identified with chamber music. 'When we came out here', said Charles Berg, 'we missed that, although at the beginning we could scarcely afford it. We looked for opportunities to be involved in it, particularly after the war, when the restrictions of the war were lifted.'[28] According to Goldner, the search for a familiar community also played a role:

> I venture to speculate that it was a time when most of us migrants felt something like an intangible danger of possible rejection of the European 'transplant' into the indigenous Australian 'body'. Therefore, it probably was not chamber music per se which attracted most of them, but something that offered an opportunity to join together to form a non-political, innocuous unity to confront the Australian community as a 'benevolent cultural power'.[29]

The refugees spoke mainly English in their everyday life. Even at home, Goldner had given up using German immediately after his arrival in order to adjust completely to his new surroundings. Chamber music, however, remained a sort of secret code that united the former refugees. The music student Sibilla Lighezollo, who had come to Australia from Italy with her anti-fascist parents shortly before the war, also made contact with this circle:

> By going to these places, I met so many of these newcomers, who happened to be Jewish. It was an at-home-thing. Then I'd go there again and got involved in various locations. The conversation was great. After all I was a country-girl coming to Sydney. But it didn't take me very long to learn that these people had the same principles and the same feeling of family as my own.[30]

The immaculately dressed Walter Dullo, who usually remained modestly in the background, was an indispensable advisor to Musica Viva. He prepared arrangements, gave advice on musicological questions and wrote the programme notes. Goldner remembers how on numerous occasions 'when I needed some musical data, [...] it was much quicker and more reliable, rather than go to the library, just to ring Mr Dullo and, as a rule, get the required information from him on the spot'. If sheet music was needed, Dullo ordered it immediately. 'At times when this was impossible he would write out scores and parts for me with his meticulous beautiful manuscript writing, always in soft black pencil, protected against smudging by a coat of fixative.'[31] After Dullos's death, Goldner praised his friend as a man of boundless humanity, completely free of vanity. Without him as co-founder, Musica Viva would never have existed.

In January 1948, the *New Citizen* declared: 'Schubert's 150th birthday would have passed unnoticed in our now so music-conscious city, had not the Musica Viva Society devoted the last concert of the 1947 season to celebrate the occasion.' For people like Walter Dullo, chamber music was a heartfelt need; it provided access to a 'better world'. Thus, in March the paper wrote: 'After two full months of complete musical starvation, the 1948 season opened with a concert of the Musica Viva Society, which augured well for the future.' It was with some pride that former refugees regarded classical music, and above all chamber music, as their gift to their new country. In a review of twelve years in Australia Karl Bittman wrote in 1950:

> In the cultural field, the predominant interest of the new citizen is music. Their devotion to music is very intense and it is only fitting to remind ourselves that in this field, the newcomers have probably made the greatest contribution to development of cultural life in Australia, not only by patronising concerts, but also through the creation of the Musica Viva, and while this is the work of a few able people, and we do not want to take credit for their work as a group, I believe we can justly say that this has been a definite recognised contribution.[32]

That said, the concept of Musica Viva would only have a long-term future if it did not limit itself to nostalgic reminiscences about an idealised past, so their concerts included contemporary as well as classical works. On 19 March 1949, Felix Werder's compositions were performed in Melbourne's Assembly Hall: his Violin Sonata No. 4; the Trio Op. 24; the Cello Sonata Op. 22 and his third String Quartet. In 1950, there was another Werder evening in the Union Hall at the University of Melbourne featuring his 'Reineke Fuchs' String Quartet, a violin sonata and another string quartet. Almost all the Musica Viva concerts were broadcast. By this time, the chair of the ABC, Charles Moses, had sensibly given Musica Viva sole responsibility for chamber music. There were advantages on both sides: it was a relief for the radio network, which had a very high profile in Australia, and the chamber music concerts reached a much wider audience. Charles Berg, Musica Viva's honorary secretary since 1946, wanted to avoid a situation where the organisation was seen as an institution simply of and for migrants. Not least on his initiative, in 1950, the Australian-born Regina Rich and Kenneth Tribe were engaged as professional managers.

In spite of capable management, a large circle of friends and the idealism of the musicians themselves, it proved impossible to finance the Musica Viva Players' concerts on a permanent basis without public support so, in January 1951, the *New Citizen* asked its readers for help. It was remarkable that the Musica Viva Players had been able to dedicate themselves solely to chamber music for several years, but pride in this joint achievement of 'old' Australians and new citizens was not enough:

> If Musica Viva is to go on through the coming years, it must have the continuous support of everyone interested in serious music. 1951 will be hard owing to the rising costs on all sides. Every New Citizen who joins Musica Viva Society as a member will have the satisfaction of contributing to one of the finest causes propagated from our midst.[33]

This appeal could not prevent the Musica Viva Players from disbanding in November 1951, after more than 600 concerts. The members of the Musica Viva Society were told that, from the end of the year, all musical activities had to be abandoned:

> The reason for this decision is the inability to maintain the Society's income on the present membership basis at a level which can guarantee to members of its permanent ensemble sufficient salaries to enable them to devote their time exclusively to the performance of chamber music.[34]

With public support, or with just another 1,000 members, continuation of the work would have been possible. But the reasons for its demise were not only financial. More to the point, it had eventually become too stressful for the musicians to give approximately 200 concerts a year in Sydney, Melbourne and Adelaide. The large number of appearances brought with it the danger of routine, something which Goldner, a self-critical perfectionist, feared most because it threatened their artistic standard. Robert Pikler had already resigned in September. Once the ensemble was disbanded, there was no longer any reason for Theo Salzmann to stay in Australia; he moved to the USA, where he became principal cellist with the Pittsburgh Symphony Orchestra. In spite of this sad ending, the fact that a professional ensemble could exist for years without any subsidy remains a remarkable pioneering achievement. With its equally high standards, it played a fundamental role in educating an audience for chamber music in Australia.

The Rebirth

There would be no Musica Viva in Australia today had help not arrived from New Zealand. In January 1940, Frederick Turnovsky had arrived in Wellington as a Jewish refugee from Prague and was soon earning a fortune manufacturing watch-bands. A passionate music lover, Turnovsky established the Wellington Chamber Music Society in 1950 and, on several occasions, invited the Musica Viva Players. In addition, he encouraged chamber music societies in other New Zealand cities, and brought them together as the New Zealand Federation of Chamber Music Societies, which he directed for years.[35] On his numerous business trips, he met other chamber ensembles and invited them to tour New Zealand, and it was this successful model that Turnovsky now proposed for Australia. Charmian Gadd, Goldner's second wife, thinks that Turnovsky's admiration for Hephzibah Menuhin also played a role.[36] As early as August 1953, an article by Wolfgang Wagner in the *Canon* hinted that ideas to revive Musica Viva had been broached in New Zealand.[37] In October 1954, under the heading 'Musica Viva Re-birth', the *Australian Musical News* revealed that invitations to guest ensembles were planned. Nonetheless, it took until the spring of 1955 for this plan to be realised.[38] The first foreign ensemble to arrive was the French Pascal Quartet, whose viola player had once played in Scherchen's Musica Viva Orchestra. Their programmes included the F minor Piano Quintet of Brahms, in which Hephzibah Menuhin played the piano.

Paul Morawetz, another businessman from Prague, was also an admirer of this attractive pianist and, as a consequence, also became a patron of chamber music. Morawetz had arrived in Australia as a refugee at the beginning of 1940 and, like Turnovsky, became a successful entrepreneur.[39] In 1947, Morawetz organised a concert for Hephzibah Menuhin at the Prague Spring Festival, after which they visited Theresienstadt together. She was deeply moved and, as a result of this trip, a romantic liaison developed. In 1954, having meanwhile separated from her husband, Hephzibah Menuhin moved to Sydney, where she gave concerts and continued her philanthropic activities.[40] It is highly likely that she encouraged Morawetz to support Musica Viva financially. In the first season after its rebirth, the pianist appeared not only with the Pascal Quartet, but also in an evening recital duo.

Richard Goldner observed the revival of Musica Viva with mixed feelings. On the one hand, he was pleased that the society's financial situation had stabilised and that it was once again presenting high quality chamber music concerts. On the other, he deplored its commercialisation and the lack of a permanent ensemble, as this had been at the core of his idea for the institution. In his concept, guest appearances were to merely supplement and finance the permanent ensemble, so he was deeply disappointed that this was not re-formed. Still, remnants of the ideals he had picked up from Scherchen and Pullman were realised at the Chamber Music Camps founded in 1958 that took place regularly at Easter in rural Mittagong, south-west of Sydney, at which family members of former emigrants could meet in a relaxed atmosphere for workshops, discussions and concerts.[41] At the 1964 Easter Festival, after an introduction by Goldner, the Austral String Quartet performed Felix Werder's String Quartet No. 6. By contrast, overseas ensembles like the Amadeus, Koeckert and Smetana Quartets mostly offered the usual classical and romantic repertoire. They could hardly ever be moved to include contemporary – let alone

Australian – music in the programmes for their Australian tours. With ticket sales in mind, Ken Tribe and Charles Berg favoured proven classics; something that eventually made Musica Viva a rather conservative institution. At the time, Felix Werder said bitterly that the society should call itself 'Musica Morta'. Richard Goldner was seen less and less frequently, and finally left on bad terms in 1969. However, he had long kept silent about the fact that the name 'Musica Viva' came from Hermann Scherchen and originally signified an orientation towards works that pointed to the future.[42]

The cautious programming policy, however, was financially responsible and often in the public interest. New audiences, who did not yet even know the Beethoven quartets, had to be gradually initiated into the chamber music repertoire, while the former refugees' desire for familiar works also increased as they grew older. Today, Musica Viva Australia is no longer just the small association of a few idealists, but the biggest chamber music organisation in the world. Early members like Eva Wagner would never have thought that it could have flourished so spectacularly: 'I think that in Australia and New Zealand more people per capita listen to chamber music than anywhere else in the world. We have a lot of professional quartets or trios.'[43] Roger Covell suspects that, for many Australians, a certain snobbishness might initially have played a role: the desire to join an elitist organisation. In this, Australia is repeating what happened in Europe where, from 1800, the bourgeoisie began imitating the practices that until then had been reserved for the nobility. For a long time, chamber music was heard in large halls such as the Sydney Town Hall or other big, general purpose halls that were acoustically unsuitable but, in the meantime, many smaller, more appropriate venues and recital halls have been established throughout the country.

Although today the descendants of former refugees are only a minority of the organisation's members, they still feel a special responsibility for it. Charles Berg's son Anthony assumed management functions. However, he did not support the publication of Richard Goldner's memoirs, which the latter had sent him in 1989. At least excerpts were printed in the brochure published for the fiftieth anniversary of Musica Viva Australia in 1996.[44] Goldner complained in his manuscript that the organisation had come to value glamour and power more than the original idea of music education. The organisation had lost its soul and was now ruled by managers, not musicians. That was why, in an interview in 1989, he advised Musica Viva to take another name.[45] He was also embittered that his pioneering role in its foundation was often overlooked or downplayed.

In the meantime, no one doubts that, had it not been for Richard Goldner and his circle of friends, chamber music in Australia would never have flourished as it has. In this field, Goldner played a similar role in Australia as the patroness Elizabeth Sprague Coolidge in the USA. Although Scherchen's ideas have still not received recognition, Musica Viva has for some time attached greater importance to new music. A short history written to celebrate the society's fiftieth anniversary in 1995 listed commissions for new works and first performances, including the sixth String Quartet by Felix Werder and the *Sextet for Didjeridu and Wind Quintet* by George Dreyfus.[46] Besides, Musica Viva today no longer limits itself to inviting prestigious overseas ensembles, but also promotes Australian chamber music groups, such as the University of Adelaide Wind Quintet or the Goldner Quartet, named after its founder. Meanwhile, Goldner's idea for a string orchestra has been developed independently by the Australian Chamber Orchestra (ACO) under the capable direction of Richard Tognetti.

For Eva Wagner, one of Musica Viva's special features is that chamber music is not just listened to, but lived. As Roger Covell explained, the transfer of the 'informed enthusiasm' of a European audience to Australia, with its completely different traditions, required 'not merely a handful of missionaries, but a significant supporting community equally possessed of an ingrained belief in the primary function of chamber music as an index of musical cultivation'. Men like Richard Goldner and Walter Dullo were such missionaries, men who, like other founders and supporters of Musica Viva, came to Australia as a result of Hitler's racial politics. Covell also added:

> [...] the successful implantation of belief in the paramount status of chamber music among an influential stratum of Australian society may represent one of the most striking consequences of that dispersal to be found anywhere. And this is despite the obvious circumstance that the number of these refugees was far smaller in Australia than in North America.[47]

Musica Viva Australia found a permanent place in Australian society, just like the refugees themselves. It differs considerably from other commercial agencies in that it is still a not-for-profit organisation that essentially depends on donations and voluntary work. Since 1981, when the state-sponsored 'Musica Viva in Schools' programme was established, the society has played a crucial role in musical education and the preparation of future audiences.

CHAPTER 16

Between Adjustment and Self-Assertion: Refugee Contributions to Australian Musical Life

Expulsion, flight and war triggered a setback in the careers of all refugee musicians, at least a break and in some cases sadly the end. Even if they succeeded in obtaining citizenship, Australia's music industry was smaller and less developed than those of Germany or Austria, so it proved much more difficult to survive as a professional musician. Many artists were forced to accept music as a second job or a hobby, and earned their living in another profession. The clarinettist and saxophonist Hans Holzbauer (John Wood) had worked as a professional musician in Singapore and always given 'musician' as his occupation in Australia. 'Sergeant Beethoven', as he was known in the army, could not earn sufficient income performing in Melbourne cabarets and became a clerk of the court. The musical careers of Horst Graff and Stefan Weintraub essentially ended with their internment. Their colleague Manny Fisher also decided to change his occupation. Although he had no problems working or appearing as a musician, his experience was similar to that of Maurice Abravanel, who declared in December 1946: 'It is impossible for a good musician really to earn a fine living in Australia today.'[1]

Conductors

Guest conductors from Germany and Austria were very highly regarded in Australia, but hardly welcome as applicants for permanent positions, as both Abravanel and Curt Prerauer learnt in 1935 when they wanted to stay in the country at the end of their successful opera tour. By working with the ABC, they succeeded in organising yet another opera season that was very positively received by both the public and the press. But the outlook for them was not good. Whereas Abravanel departed when he saw no opportunities for himself in Australia, Prerauer stayed, as he assumed that his abilities might be needed in a country where as yet there was no professional training for conductors. At first Prerauer pinned his hopes on the ABC, where he already had good contacts. But in March 1937, W.G. James, the Federal Controller of Music, informed him that the planning for the next season was already complete. 'We are not entering, at present, into further negotiations in respect of orchestral conductors.'[2]

As Prerauer was well versed in choral music, the Royal Philharmonic Society appointed him as their conductor in May 1938. Founded in 1885, this amateur organisation had been responsible for significant premieres of large-scale choral works and oratorios, so Prerauer decided to risk presenting concert versions of opera with them. His preparation of Verdi's *Il Trovatore* was highly praised; the society that had recently been in crisis now actually excelled itself. 'The Choir, which has always sung well, can do extremely good work whenever it is highly disciplined. And the Society's amateur orchestra, chastened and purged of its major offences, proved that it can preserve a musicianly relation with the score.' This improvement was thanks to the new conductor. 'Evidently, he has exercised both patience and authority; and the latter quality is essential in dealings with any group of Australian amateur performers, to whom the national watchword "It's near enough" is good enough.' This particular concert in Sydney Town Hall on 10 August 1938 drew a much larger audience than usual; they experienced a considerably higher musical standard, especially in the orchestra. 'Judged by ordinary criteria, the playing was very fair; by recent Philharmonic standards, quite brilliant.' And evidently the choir, which was in any case the stronger section, never lost its sense of tone and balance even in the massive *tutti* effects.[3] Curt Prerauer had been naturalised on 9 August, the day before the concert, but if he hoped that he could make a new start as a conductor in his new country, he was disappointed. Not all the members of the Royal Philharmonic Society were willing to bow to his strict authority, and eventually a dispute about his 'dictatorial' style of leadership led to his resignation the following February.

Prerauer subsequently became a music critic for the *ABC Weekly* and a teacher at the Alfred Hill Academy of Music, but he still wanted work as a conductor. To this end, he presented the ABC with the excellent references from Wilhelm Furtwängler and Leo Blech. When he referred to his collaboration with Sir Adrian Boult in London, the latter was also asked to provide a reference. The chief conductor of the BBC Symphony Orchestra wrote of Prerauer:

> I can say with absolute conviction that I know of no one who would be more conscientious in undertaking any kind of coaching and preparatory work of any kind. [...] This naturally does not enable me to speak with conviction about the possibility of Mr Prerauer's taking over a directional post. He has, I should say, all the qualities for this, though if I were to look for a fault I should say that he might be a bit unwilling to suffer fools gladly and might also be impatient and perhaps tactless with second-rate work.[4]

This reference arrived at ABC headquarters in April 1940. Keith Barry, the Controller of Music, supplemented it with his own reservations in a letter to the general manager:

> If one can judge Mr Prerauer from his writings, he belongs to a type of musician commonly found in Middle Europe. One who is devoted to the Three B's (Brahms, Beethoven and Bach) and is very intolerant of other types of music.

This was said to be typically German: 'No-one, in point of fact, is so musically intolerant as the typical academic German.' And there was something else to consider:

> We must not forget in this time of War that Mr Prerauer has only recently received naturalisation and one wonders whether in the event of the present regime being destroyed and the position of the Jew being made as secure as it was some years ago, he and other recent arrivals would not be amongst the first to return to the country of their birth and – despite Hitler – the country of their fathers; the country, in point of fact, that sang its hymn of hate (Jews and Aryans alike) against England and everything British in 1914 to 1918.[5]

In this opinion, because of his past and his musical preferences, the German Jewish refugee was deemed to be a typical German. W.G. James also objected that, despite his prominent referees, Prerauer had not yet proved that his practical musical abilities surpassed those of many Australians. Thus, ultimately political and nationalist interests prevented Prerauer from receiving any more opportunities as a conductor. Maria Prerauer, his future wife, surmised that Bernard Heinze was unwilling to tolerate working alongside a possibly superior rival.[6] Maurice Abravanel, Jascha Horenstein and Antal Dorati were also interested in conducting positions in Australia and presumably gave up any hopes for similar reasons.

Adolf Brenner could not present such glowing German references as Curt Prerauer and had come to Australia under much more difficult circumstances. But, after a good training, he had also gained valuable experience as a conductor. After the war, when he married Herta Jotkowitz from Hamburg, he first found work as a music editor and repetiteur with the producer Hector Crawford who, since 1938, had organised 'Music for the People', a successful series of free, open-air concerts that were regularly broadcast by Radio 3DB. In addition to this, Brenner directed amateur choirs in various Melbourne suburbs, namely the St Kilda Philharmonic Society and, from 1948, the Sandringham Choral Society. That said, this commendable range of activities did not bring him to the attention of the music public. As a lecturer at the old Melbourne Conservatorium of Music, the so-called Albert Street Conservatorium in East Melbourne, he was able to devote himself to opera, his true field. In May 1947, he conducted two performances of Smetana's *The Bartered Bride*, the first time it was heard in Melbourne. The review included the following: 'Mr Dolf Brenner and Mr Hyman Lenzer [leader] are to be complimented on the smoothness of the continuity which, even with student singers as soloists, helped to lift the whole cast into a semblance of operatic motion.'[7] In March 1950, Brenner appeared for the first time with a symphony orchestra in a concert in the neo-Gothic Assembly Hall in Collins Street. At this, his debut in Melbourne City, he came across as an 'unspectacular but quietly determined personality' who 'imprinted cultured and thoughtful musicianship and a sense of authentic style upon a group of Melbourne musicians', as one critic wrote. Brenner conducted the first Australian performances of Haydn's Sinfonia Concertante and Mozart's Adagio and Fugue in C minor, K. 546 'with precision and definition'. The highlight of the evening, Mozart's Symphony in E flat major, K. 543, demonstrated his control:

> In the direction of all these works M. Brenner kept his own and his orchestra's resources well controlled; always holding in reserve these collective powers to effect an artistic balance of nuance and phrasing. [...] This was, altogether, an unusually interesting concert, not only for its introduction to us of Mr Brenner as a musician and conductor of gentle but convincing authority, but, also, for its air of veracity, a quality only achieved when conductor and musicians are in artistic unity, and holding an intelligent audience attentive to their music.[8]

After this successful evening, the *Australian Musical* News introduced the conductor in a comprehensive article that mentioned his musical training with renowned Viennese teachers like Eusebius Mandyczewski, Hugo Reichenberger, Joseph Marx and Guido Adler.[9]

At last, there seemed to be a chance for Brenner to continue his career in opera, as in February 1951, the same magazine ran an illustrated article that presented him as the musical director of Otto Nicolai's *The Merry Wives of Windsor*, another work that was as yet completely unknown in Melbourne, and for which the music could only be procured with great difficulty.[10] By now, Brenner was already known in Melbourne as a competent musician, so this student performance promised to be one of the highlights of the forthcoming Commonwealth Jubilee. Indeed, the participants were invited to perform for two weeks in June at the prestigious Princess Theatre but, when the season opened, amazingly it was not Brenner who stood on the rostrum, but the Australian organist and choral conductor Herbert Davis.[11] Brenner the artist must have been deeply hurt that, after such a long interruption to his career, he was still not able to adequately realise his musical potential. In 1951, he gave up any thoughts of being a professional musician, and instead became an employee at the Immigration Office. Even the ABC, who engaged him for a concert the following year, could no longer reverse his decision. After that, Dolf Brenner and his wife Herta lived a secluded life in St Kilda, and later Camberwell, for almost four decades. For a while, he led a Jewish male choir, where his successor Felix Werder knew him as an unhappy man who considered himself a complete failure.

Figure 29: The conductor Kurt Herweg (centre) prepares a recording for the animated cartoon 'Christmas Bells'. (NAA: SP1426/4, 1)

Kurt Herweg and Heinrich Krips had better opportunities, as they both started out in areas of music for which Bernard Heinze showed little or no interest. After his release from internment in 1943, Herweg found work as a composer and conductor with various dance groups, as well as for private firms, Radio 2CH and George Patterson Productions. In this field, away from classical concert life, he was able to blossom and, in 1957, the ABC appointed him Director of Light Music. Heinrich Krips had openly declared himself to be a conductor in his immigration papers. In a portrait of Krips published in the *New Citizen* in 1948, Walter Dullo wrote:

> He was allowed to enter Australia as a musician, but although this was clearly stated in his landing permit, he had to wait from 1939 until 1944 when he was naturalised, to be admitted to the Musicians' Union. Unfortunately, those four years were practically wasted.[12]

In November 1938, immediately after his arrival, Krips had applied to the ABC for a conducting position. They were very interested, but the negative attitudes of the union and the Postmaster-General prevented his engagement. Apparently it was unclear to what extent the union was actually responsible for conductors. In a letter to the department of the interior of 24 February 1939, its secretary, Kitson, even described the conductor as a pianist. Krips found his way into the film industry and in 1939 he was appointed musical director for Cinesound Productions. He composed and arranged film music, including the soundtrack for *Ants in his Pants*, a comedy which had an Irish operatic tenor as its central character. From 1940, Krips became musical director for the Kirsova Ballet, where, apart from an interruption for military service in 1942, he also composed. In 1943, he obtained a position as an arranger with the George Patterson Advertising Radio Unit in Sydney. In the light of these professional opportunities, Krips wanted to remain in Australia, so he made the appropriate application and became a citizen in July 1944.

Hermann Schildberger, who had entered as organist and choirmaster for the St Kilda synagogue, also entertained conducting ambitions. After all, as musical director for the Jewish Reform Congregation in Berlin, he had led an important recording project and often conducted the Künstlerhilfe orchestra. In 1941, he established the New Melbourne String Orchestra, with which he performed mainly Baroque music. Two years later, he was pictured on the front cover of the *Australian Musical News* with the descriptive caption: 'Dr Hermann Schildberger, Conductor of the New Melbourne String Orchestra, which has Given a Number of Successful Concerts, and Director of Music of Temple Beth Israel, St Kilda, also Organist and Choirmaster of the Methodist Church, Brighton.' A long article in the magazine was dedicated to his various musical activities in Germany, although it falsely called him a 'Doctor of Music'.[13] (Like Rudolf Werther before him, Schildberger hardly ever corrected this misunderstanding, one that could advance his career.) An ambitious and experienced organiser, he founded the Brighton Philharmonic Society in 1943 and a similar one in Camberwell the following year.

Figure 30: The conductor Hermann Schildberger (centre) with his Camberwell Philharmonic Society. In uniform, the tenor soloist Hans Edelmann.
(Felix Edelmann, Vienna)

His favourite oratorios included Handel's *Israel in Egypt* and Mendelssohn's *St Paul*. In 1951, he also became director of the Victorian Public Service Concert Orchestra. But Schildberger's real interest lay in the field of opera. In this, he was like Rudolf Werther, who was able to realise ambitions as an opera conductor in Australia that he could hardly have contemplated in his homeland, on account of the daunting competition.

Henry Krips, whose rapid advance began after the war, was the only conductor to have a long-lasting effect. Although in 1946 he had undiplomatically called Australian orchestral musicians 'craftsmen rather than artists',[14] two years later, he became chief conductor of the ABC Orchestra in Perth. At the time, Walter Dullo wrote that, for the thirty-four-year-old conductor, this new position meant 'but one step on his path towards ultimate unambiguous recognition as an outstanding musician'. For, thorny though this path may have been, 'Krips is bound to win through, not only by virtue of his talent, but also by his conquering personality, his energy and industry, his obsession with a mission bestowed on him and his irrepressible will to succeed.' According to Dullo, in spite of his loyalty to his new homeland, Krips was actually a European, or – to be precise – Viennese from head to toe:

> His charming slovenliness in using both English and German with a typical nasal twang, his natural hilarity and sarcastic sense of humour, all those important little faculties that have brought Austrians into favour with the rest of the world, make him what he is, – an awfully amiable fellow who with an artist's sensuality adores life, eats, drinks and dresses with gusto and hates frustrating arguments.[15]

Meanwhile, he added, Henry Krips had become a valuable part of Australian musical life. He was particularly successful in performing the works of the Australian composer Alfred Hill.

At the beginning of 1949, there were sixty applicants from all over the world for the position of chief conductor of the ABC's Adelaide Symphony Orchestra. Krips was chosen and, in September, he assumed the chief conductorship of the South Australian orchestra in addition to his position in Perth. The *Australian Musical News* subsequently named him as the model 'new Australian' and, in the face of the usual British conservatism, celebrated his appointment as a sensation: 'Congratulations and good wishes go naturally to conductor and orchestra – but, most of all, to the authorities who have recognised a true, though comparatively New, Australian.'[16] In Perth, with his combination of temperament, artistic perfection, and wealth of nuance, Krips kindled an enthusiasm among both audiences and critics such as the local musical public had never shown before.[17] Connoisseurs even saw in him a rival for Eugene Goossens, the new conductor and beacon of hope for the Sydney Symphony Orchestra. When Henry Krips conducted the Victorian Symphony Orchestra[18] for the first time in Melbourne in 1950, to the critics' amazement he achieved 'a miracle of transformed tone and quickened artistic response' in just four rehearsals; under his direction, Bruckner's Seventh became 'a magnificent spiritual experience.'[19] On a visit to Australia, Otto Klemperer also confirmed the leap in quality made by these orchestras.[20] Krips, the tall and athletic conductor, his wife Luise and their small son Henry became the darlings of the public, and in June 1950, the happy family was pictured on the front cover of the *Australian Musical News*.

Figure 31: Henry Krips with his family on the cover of the *Australian Musical News*. (Author's Archive)

Apart from his one general rebuke of Australian orchestral musicians, this artist had done everything correctly. Besides works from his Austrian homeland, not least Bruckner and Mahler, whom he introduced to Australia, he continued to conduct British and Australian works. In 1951, when a competition was held to find a new national anthem for the Commonwealth Jubilee, he took part with one of his own compositions, the song 'Land of Mine', and won first prize. The text was composed by John Wheeler:

> Land of freedom, land we cherish,
> Wearing beauty like a crown:
> Where in heaven brightly shining
> All the stars of God look down;
> Like a vision they abide,
> Symbol of our hope and pride;
> Send our song to heaven above:
> Land of mine! Freedom's shrine –
> God be with you, dear land we love!

Like 'God Save the Queen', this is no aggressive marching tune, but a melodic and dignified, almost chorale-like lied in three parts. Whereas, at the beginning, the melody gradually descends, at the end, it gradually ascends, thereby exhibiting a certain similarity to Haydn's Emperor's Hymn. Although the conductor had thereby clearly identified with his new homeland, his guest tours abroad always raised anxious questions. 'Adelaide is asking ... Will Henry Krips Return?' was the headline in 1953.[21] But, on his return in July 1954, the reception was all the warmer. Krips was faithful to Australia. He remained chief conductor in Perth until 1971 and in Adelaide until 1972, longer than any of his successors. He then moved to London, although he died in Australia in 1987, in Adelaide.

Two conductors had come to Australia as refugee children. Hans-Hubert Schönzeler was thirteen years old when he arrived with his mother in Sydney in September 1939. At the time, his father was already interned as an enemy alien. Hans-Hubert went to Sydney High School until 1942, when he and his mother were also arrested and taken to Tatura. As his father had worked for a large German steel company and applied to return to Germany in 1944, his son was only allowed to leave the camp in 1946, after four years behind barbed wire. By then, he was twenty-one years old. Both his parents had to wait another month before they finally gained their freedom. Hans-Hubert had begun violin lessons at the age of five, and continued with his music in Tatura. His music teacher in the camp was Dr Georg Gruber, the former director of the Vienna Mozart Boys Choir. After his release in 1946, Schönzeler enrolled at the Sydney Conservatorium. Apart from Eugene Goossens, another conducting teacher was Rafael Kubelik, who encouraged him to move to London. There he worked for the Jewish-owned Eulenburg publishing house, which had moved to England after being expelled from Leipzig. He also composed, wrote books about Bruckner and Furtwängler, and directed a chamber orchestra. In 1967, his activities as an international guest conductor led Schönzeler back to Australia for a season with the West Australian Symphony Orchestra; it was the beginning of a long association. He made a name for himself, not least with his interpretations of Dvořák and Bruckner.

The conductor Gerald Krug had come to Australia with his Jewish parents as a five-year-old in 1937. His father was interested in music, and one day received tickets for a concert by the SSO under Bernard Heinze. 'I remember my father insisting that I go', said Krug later, 'although I didn't want to, but when we got there I was completely swept off my feet [...]. At the end of that concert, I knew I wanted to be a conductor and nothing else.' During his military service, Gerald's father met Curt Prerauer and Henry Krips and learned about their work as conductors. He therefore asked them to advise his ten-year-old son on his desired career. 'Curt and Henry both told me that it was best to start as an opera repetiteur, accompanying singers in rehearsal.' Gerald Krug took bassoon lessons during his school years, and continued with tertiary music studies at the Sydney Conservatorium. From 1953, he studied for two years at the Paris Conservatoire, and then at the Salzburg Mozarteum with Igor Markevitch. Krug said later that it was only through this teacher that he finally understood what conducting really meant.[22] As advised, he began as an opera repetiteur and conductor, and in the early 1960s returned to Australia where he made a name for himself as a conductor of, among others, the West Australian Opera Company.

Orchestral Musicians

Permanent symphony orchestras could not be taken for granted in Australia. Without the ABC's financial protection, driven mainly by Bernard Heinze, they would hardly have existed. Heinze had recommended the British BBC model to Charles Moses, the chair of the ABC, and from 1936 small groups of professional musicians were organised in the capital cities of the six Australian states. These eventually developed into permanent institutions and, during the war, Heinze took leave from his position as Head of the Conservatorium at the University of Melbourne in order to devote himself completely to these ABC orchestras. There was a qualitative advance when Eugene Ormandy came to Australia in 1944 to conduct an orchestra that had been put together especially for him. At the ABC's request, he wrote a report in which he advised that musicians who had just arrived from Europe should also be allowed to apply for orchestral positions. Such openings, however, only arose at the end of the war, provided that the musicians had been naturalised and accepted into the Musicians' Union. In 1945, Fritz Kramer took advantage of this opportunity. Until 1952, he was in the second violin section of the MSO, which had meanwhile been renamed the Victorian Symphony Orchestra (VSO); he then transferred to the SSO. His Hungarian colleague Endre Hoffmann applied for naturalisation and joined the union in March 1945; in 1946, he secured a position as a first violinist with the SSO. Nonetheless, at first the union only allowed him to perform in New South Wales. Cyril Schulvater also played in the SSO from the beginning of 1946. Like Kramer and Hoffmann, this former member of the Weintraubs Syncopators had had to work in other professions during the war, as a café proprietor and machinist.

The Musicians' Union strongly opposed the recommendations of the conductors Ormandy and Goossens to invite overseas orchestral musicians to Australia. Whereas the British Union (the Incorporated Society of Musicians) modified its defensive position after the war, and even admitted mistakes,[23] the Musicians' Union of Australia did not correct its restrictive attitude. In November 1948, it imposed a freeze on admissions for all musicians who had been in the country for less than ten years. Its aim was to preclude interested parties from overseas (refugees) who were 'lured by good conditions, including food and other considerations'.[24] The union also pushed through a rule that no more than 10 per cent of the members of any orchestra could be born overseas. Accordingly, new arrivals had only a slim chance. Because of this ruling, Frank Kitson was celebrated by his colleagues,[25] whereas the ABC and friends of music like the Conservatorium Director Edgar Bainton, or the parliamentarian Abram Landa, complained about such narrow-minded protectionism.[26]

Eugene Goossens argued strongly against Kitson's claim that there were enough qualified musicians in Australia. He mentioned the Polish violinist Samuel Helfgott, who had arrived in 1948 and was the only applicant to show the abilities required by the SSO; they therefore accepted him for the position, despite his poor English.[27] But Helfgott was rejected by the union, whereupon he asked Werner Baer for advice. Baer referred him to Henry Krips, who remembered the case of Sydney John Kay: he had become a union member after a successful appeal in 1944. Kay advised Helfgott to apply again, explicitly requesting membership in New South Wales. The union tried to talk him out of this idea by saying that he would then be allowed to play only in that state; but Helfgott was undeterred, and was accepted by both the union and the SSO in the same year.[28]

The policy that, from now on, native-born Australians were to make up 90 per cent of all orchestras resulted in many dismissals. Werner Baer, who by this time had risen in the ABC hierarchy, also had to enforce this rule, which was not easy for him; besides which, it made him many enemies.[29] Those affected included the violinist Fritz Kramer and the cellist Cyril Schulvater, both of whom played in a gala performance for the new queen, Elizabeth II, before leaving the orchestra in November 1954. Prior to this, in a letter to the ABC, Kramer had complained that he was still considered an alien by the union, sixteen years after his arrival and ten years after his naturalisation.[30] With that, Kramer and Schulvater disappeared from the scene once more. After his dismissal, Schulvater first ran his own delicatessen, and then a picture-framing business. Kramer married a doctor and helped her in her medical practice.

Having unsuccessfully run a saw mill during the war, Peter Langer joined the MSO as a cellist in 1946. Because he thought chamber music was the epitome of music, he was shocked to learn that the leader of the orchestra, Bertha Jorgensen, had no experience in this field. His critical comments and occasional nervousness made him so unpopular with his colleagues that he was gradually moved from the front to the back desks of the cello section, until he eventually had to leave the orchestra. After re-auditioning in April 1954, he was rejected on account of the ruling mentioned above.[31] Langer's dismissal meant that he had to sell his house. To improve his chances as a cello teacher, he undertook several months of study with Pablo Casals in Prades before moving to New Zealand in 1956, where he obtained a position as a cellist with the New Zealand Symphony Orchestra. His nervousness in performances increased, however, so his professional future was also threatened there. Peter Langer died in a mountaineering accident in 1964.

Georg Dreyfus was eleven when he came to Australia. Although his father experienced the move as a culture shock, his love of music was an important incentive for the young boy, and fortunately Melbourne High School had a creditable music programme. George, as he was called, took clarinet lessons in order to join the school orchestra; at the same time, he directed a choir and was soon known at the school as 'Mr Music'. Attending a concert by the VSO in St Kilda Town Hall one Sunday afternoon, he made a decision: to play with them one day! During his last year at secondary school, the young man was already taking clarinet lessons at the Conservatorium; however, he was not very successful, especially as he had to help his father with his carpet-cleaning business. He switched to the bassoon, but again he did not fulfil expectations and had to leave the Conservatorium. When the ABC Youth Orchestra needed a bassoonist in 1947, George was interested, and a year later J.C. Williamson's Italian Opera Company offered the enthusiastic young musician a position as a bassoonist. In order to prepare, Dreyfus turned to the bassoonist with the VSO, Fred Morgan, and learnt that he was also self-taught on the instrument. After one and a half years with the opera company and performances throughout Australia, his mother bought him a better instrument – a genuine Heckel bassoon – with restitution money that she had received from West Germany. When Fred Morgan died in 1953, Dreyfus was offered his position: thus his dream had become a reality.

Aware of his technical weaknesses, in 1954, Dreyfus travelled to Europe to take lessons from Prof Karl Öhlberger (later principal bassoonist with the Vienna Philharmonic) at the Vienna Music Academy. These three hours each week were immensely important to Dreyfus, who greedily soaked up the European culture that he had heard about from his parents, but only partly experienced as a child. On his return from Europe, he was offered a position as principal bassoonist in Perth, where he sought the friendship of another emigrant musician, Karl Berent. As he was unhappy in Western Australia, Dreyfus resigned from his job with the orchestra and returned to Melbourne. There he was appointed second bassoon in the VSO, which was now conducted by the Austrian Kurt Wöss. George Dreyfus was a member of this orchestra until 1964, when he gave up his career as an orchestral musician to become one of Australia's first freelance composers.

Around 1949, the violist Otmar Silberstein also played briefly with the VSO before moving to the USA, where his father and an aunt were living. Another 'Dunera Boy', Majer Pietruschka would play in this orchestra even longer than George Dreyfus. Among the German-speaking refugees, Pietruschka was one of the musicians with the longest orchestral experience. After his discharge from military service, he had to eke out a living ironing clothes before he was able to become a violin teacher. Finally, in 1949, he obtained a position in the Radio 3DB Concert Orchestra, directed by Verdon Williams. An article about this orchestra informed its readers that in his youth Pietruschka had played in symphony orchestras in Warsaw and Łódź and, until 1938, in the Kulturbund orchestra in Berlin. In recent years, he had taught music and played chamber music.[32] Majer Pietruschka left the 3DB Concert Orchestra in 1951 and joined the second violin section of the VSO, where he remained until he reached pension age in 1967.

The violinist Carl (Charles) Reither was deported from Singapore as an enemy alien in 1940; he was one of the leading soloists both in Tatura and in the Eighth Australian Employment Company concerts. After an ABC audition in July 1946, he was selected as a casual for orchestral concerts and, in 1949, joined the ABC Variety Orchestra. In view of his vast musical experience, including as a member of the Victorian String Quartet, he finally obtained a position with the VSO in 1961, just in time to become eligible for a pension. He continued to play with the MSO (the former

VSO) even after his retirement, until his work with the Melbourne Show Band under Brian May became his most important activity. There he played alongside Andy Factor, who had previously belonged to several other state orchestras and ensembles, including the Victorian Chamber Players.

Figure 32: The violinist Charles Reither, here with his saxophone. (Charles Reither, Jr, Melbourne)

Choirs

The rich British choral tradition fell on fertile ground in Australia during the nineteenth century. The German *Liedertafeln*, which relied on works for German male choirs, enjoyed great popularity in Adelaide, Melbourne and Sydney until the First World War, when they were either disbanded or dropped their German names.[33] In nineteenth-century Australia, choral societies were the leading concert promoters; a role they relinquished only gradually. Some of the refugee musicians from Germany and Austria were glad of a job in this field, and most of them had the chance to develop over a longer period of time than Curt Prerauer did with the Sydney Royal Philharmonic Society. From 1943, Hermann Schildberger directed a Methodist church choir in the Melbourne suburb of Brighton, where he found further interest in choral work and opera. After conducting a major choral concert of spiritual music in the town hall, the spontaneous idea of founding a City of Brighton Philharmonic Society took hold.[34] By the following year, it already had 130 members and, in May 1944, the response to a concert of opera choruses was so positive that two extra performances were given.[35] The programme now included the rarely performed Schumann cantata, *The Pilgrimage of the Rose*, and excerpts from Smetana's *The Bartered Bride*, supplemented by ballet scenes with professional dancers.[36] At the beginning of 1945, in view of public demand and the limited seating available in Brighton Town Hall, the Philharmonic Society transferred its next appearance (with Mendelssohn's oratorio *St Paul*) to the larger St Kilda Town Hall. Soon after this, Schildberger established the Camberwell Philharmonic Society and again he applied this successful concept. In March, he hired the tenor Hans Edelmann in order to strengthen the choir. In an abridged version of Offenbach's *Tales of Hoffmann* presented in July 1945, Mario Dane sang the demanding title role with vocal lustre in what was otherwise judged to be a patchy performance.[37]

The lawyer Dr Alfred Ehrenfeld was even more involved in choral work than Dolf Brenner, who took over the direction of the Sandringham Choral Society in 1948. Soon after his release from Tatura, Ehrenfeld, a devout Catholic, had obtained a position as director of music at the Collins Street Independent Church. He was then elected conductor of the Victorian Railways Institute Choir, established in 1935. In December 1945, this large, mixed choir joined the Mitcham Choral Society for a prestigious performance in Melbourne Town Hall. The commemoration of World War II and its victims with Elgar's choruses *To Women* and *For the Fallen* was very well received. 'The dignity and heartfelt emotion which a man such as Elgar could scarcely fail to express in association with Lawrence Binyon's inspiring poems were realised under the strongly sympathetic guidance of Dr Ehrenfeld.'[38] Unlike Schildberger, the Viennese conductor preferred British composers. For instance, the 1946 Christmas concert in the Assembly Hall had *St John's Eve* by Sir Frederic Cowen as its central work.[39] The critics emphasised the choir's control of *pianissimo* and *crescendo* passages; overall the artistic level was felt to have clearly improved under Ehrenfeld's direction.[40] In 1947, the programme of a concert by the Railways choir presented the choral ode *Sun Worshippers* by Arthur Goring Thomas and Elgar's *Banner of St George*. Ehrenfeld also sought out new works for the Kew Philharmonic Society,[41] which he founded as a choir in 1946 and then expanded to include an orchestra. At a celebrity concert in Hawthorn Town Hall in June 1948, he conducted the Kew Philharmonic Society in performances of *The Soldier* by the Australian composer Margaret Sutherland and an arrangement of *Waltzing Matilda*, the unofficial national anthem; the guest soloists included Henry Portnoj (piano), Charles Reither (violin) and Kurt Blach with his Hotel Australia Trio. After Ehrenfeld was appointed conductor of the Melbourne University Choral Society in 1950, he occasionally organised joint concerts with the Kew Philharmonic Society. In February 1953, as he was preparing an all-Schubert programme for Kew, he became ill and in November of the same year died of cancer. Melbourne music lovers mourned the loss of this popular personality.[42] The Kew Philharmonic Society's twenty-first subscription concert became a memorial concert for Ehrenfeld, who had devoted so much love and energy to this society.

Soloists

Unlike his trio partners Edmund Kurtz and Tossy Spivakovsky, who left the country in 1936 and 1940 respectively, Jascha Spivakovsky stayed in Australia. Neither Bernard Heinze nor the General Manager of the ABC, Charles Moses, despite being well-disposed towards him, could offer him the number of concerts and broadcasts or the fees to which he had previously been accustomed. Nevertheless, Jascha Spivakovsky also engaged in charitable work. For example, on 18 March 1939, he and his brother Tossy

ASSEMBLY HALL
Direction: AUSTRALIAN BROADCASTING COMMISSION

FREE CONCERTS FOR THE FORCES
Open to Members of the Fighting Services

FORTY-SECOND OF 1944 SERIES
FRIDAY, 1st DECEMBER, 1944, at 8.15 p.m.

JASCHA SPIVAKOVSKY
(Pianist)

PROGRAMME

GOD SAVE THE KING.

Variations on a Theme of Bach —
"Weinen"; "Klagen"; "Sorgen"; "Zagen" .... Bach/Liszt
Arabesque, Op. 18 .... Schumann
Carnaval, Op. 9 .... Schumann
    Preamble; Pierrot; Arlequin; Valse Noble; Eusebius;
    Florestan; Coquette; Replique — Sphinxes; Papillons;
    A.S.C.H. — S.C.H.A. (Lettres dansantes); Chiarina; Chopin; Estrella;
    Reconnaisance — Pantalon et Colombine; Valse allemande — Paganini;
    Aveu; Promenade; Pause; Marche des Davidsbundler.

INTERVAL

Rondo Capriccioso, Op. 17 .... Mendelssohn
Ballade Op. 38 in F .... Chopin
Two Mazurkas — Op. 6, No. 1 .... Chopin
              Op. 7, No. 1 .... Chopin
Arabesques on the "Blue Danube" Valse ...... J. Strauss/Schulz/Evler

FORTY-THIRD OF 1944 SERIES
FRIDAY, 8th DECEMBER, 1944, at 8.15 p.m.

MARGARET SUTHERLAND — Pianoforte
PAUL McDERMOTT — Violin
THOMAS WHITE — Clarinet
LESLIE BARKLAMB — Flute
EDGAR RICHMOND — Oboe
ROY WHITE — Horn
FREDERICK MORGAN — Bassoon

Figure 33: Programme for a free concert for the military. After the usual National Anthem Jascha Spivakovsky played works by Bach/Liszt, Schumann, Mendelssohn, Chopin and Johann Strauß. (Michael Spivakovsky, Melbourne)

gave a benefit concert for the European refugees in Melbourne Town Hall,[43] and on 1 December 1944, he presented a free recital for army personnel in the Assembly Hall.

His 'Farewell Concert Tour of Australia' in March and April 1947, prior to his departure for a tour of the USA, received greater attention. The fear that they were perhaps indeed losing a great artist drew audiences and critics to the concert halls again; they were very enthusiastic, as if they had not heard the pianist for a long time. The *Australian Musical News* counted the Sydney concerts, in which he played Max Reger's powerful *Variations on a Bach Theme*, among the best that Spivakovsky had ever given in that city.[44] In Melbourne and Adelaide, however, despite all the admiration for the great virtuoso, his mannerisms in tempo and expression were criticised.

Even at his belated USA debut in New York's Carnegie Hall on 24 January 1948, audiences were not prepared for Spivakovsky's expressive playing. His concerts were more successful in Europe, where people had not been able to hear him for almost twenty years. Although the publicity for his October 1949 concerts with the VSO under Heinze referred to his European tours, the Australian public was no longer so fascinated with the pianist. His recital of works by Johann Sebastian Bach in the large Melbourne Town Hall on 10 July 1950 was poorly attended; one critic therefore described Spivakovsky as 'both the finest and the most shamefully neglected pianist in Australia today'.[45] He did not limit his repertoire to popular works; for example, in October 1951, he played the *Concerto Symphonique* by Ernest Bloch with the VSO. A year later, he gave the first Australian performance of Benjamin Britten's *Concerto in D*. A three-month world tour followed but, in 1960, severe illness forced Jascha Spivakovsky to withdraw from the concert stage. Unfortunately, only a few recordings testify to his outstanding piano playing, which already pointed the way to Sviatoslav Richter.[46] Colleagues like Artur Rubinstein, Claudio Arrau, Daniel Barenboim, Vladimir Ashkenazy and Igor Oistrakh all visited him when they came to Melbourne. His exile in Australia had saved his life, no small thing, but he never enjoyed the high-profile artistic career that, under very different circumstances, he might have had in Europe.

Figure 34: Jascha Spivakovsky with his powerful hands at the concert grand. (Michael Spivakovsky, Melbourne)

Among the refugees, there was perhaps only one other pianist comparable to Jascha Spivakovsky: Ignaz Friedman. A Polish student of Leschetizky and renowned for his interpretation of Chopin, he had come to Australia for a concert tour in June 1940 and then travelled to New Zealand. In Java, where the outbreak of war took him by surprise, he decided to move to Australia, where he gave concerts until 1943, but rheumatism then forced him to limit himself to teaching. Neville Cardus and Curt Prerauer belonged to his inner circle of friends in Sydney. He was deeply disappointed that the Sydney Conservatorium did not offer him a teaching position and wrote to a friend in 1946: 'I would like to leave this first-class Siberia for Europe as soon as possible. A European should be buried there.'[47] Accordingly, when Ignaz Friedman died two years later, his wife had his ashes laid to rest in Switzerland.

Two other pianists, Käthe Neumann and Robert Kolben, attracted public attention, at least for a short period. A few months after her arrival,

Käthe Neumann played a demanding concerto by Eugen d'Albert with one of the ABC orchestras. Considering the short preparation time, Bernard Heinze regarded this as a significant achievement but, in his view, she did not play as brilliantly as Raymond Lambert,[48] who had been living in Melbourne for years. Her next concert, in the Music Teachers' Association's Kelvin Hall on 22 March 1939, included Beethoven's 32 Variations in C minor, Schumann's *Carnaval*, the *Bolero-Fantasie* by Chopin, various works by Liszt and a virtuosic paraphrase on *Fledermaus* by Leopold Godowsky. The critics emphasised the pianist's virtuosic talent, her precision in the Beethoven Variations, and her attractive Schumann interpretation, but there was some criticism of her choice of programme: 'The last group, mainly paraphrases, was not of a kind regarded affectionately by Melbourne connoisseurs; they prefer healthy modern music.'[49] In 1940, the *Australian Musical News* ran advertisements for her piano tuition. In May 1945, 'Kathe Newman' appeared with the cellist W.J. Magg in Kelvin Hall, and in March 1948, she played the Mozart Concerto in D major, K. 537 in the Town Hall. After that, her name hardly ever appeared in the newspapers.

In June 1949, a twenty-year-old engineering student from Sydney named Robert Kolben reached the finals of the ABC's Concerto and Vocal Competition. As a child, Kolben had fled from Prague to London with his parents. When his father lost his job as an operations manager in Manchester, he made an effort to organise the family's planned emigration to Australia – something which was easily accomplished since he had enough capital – and in February 1941, they boarded the freighter *Canadian Star* in Liverpool. They occupied two comfortable double cabins, and there was even a small grand piano on board that twelve-year-old Robert was allowed to play. The crossing took two months, as the ship made extensive detours to avoid German submarines. In order to remain independent, Robert's father bought a thriving dry-cleaning business in Sydney. As a Czech, he was not affected during the war by the measures taken against enemy aliens. He sent his son to the renowned Sydney Grammar School, although it hardly taught music. Hence, private piano lessons were all the more important. To start him with the best teacher, the father took his son to Ignaz Friedman. 'I played him the first movement of the *Moonlight Sonata*. He was very impressed, but said that I was still too young for him.'[50] Friedman recommended the Leschetizky pupil

Laurence Godfrey Smith – 'He is the best teacher at the Conservatorium' – and Kolben stayed with him for eight years. Then he had lessons from Alexander Hmelnitsky, who had lived in Australia since 1925 and taught according to the strict methods of the Moscow school. At that stage, it was not out of the question that the Kolbens would eventually return to Prague, where they had owned a factory and a villa. This probably explains why, despite his musical talent, Robert had to begin studying engineering, which he continued, even though in 1947, in view of the political developments in Czechoslovakia, where the Communist regime had nationalised all private firms, his father had decided to remain in Australia.

Robert Kolben continued to devote himself to music with increasing seriousness and intensity. He established a University Orchestral Society and took conducting lessons from Scherchen's student, Tibor Paul. In 1949, he was a finalist at the Sydney Eisteddfod, along with Richard Bonynge and Rachel Valler. That year, when he played the Brahms Piano Concerto No. 2 for the ABC competition, Dr Alfred Floyd, one of the judges, approached him and asked about his nationality. Kolben mentioned that he came from Prague, whereupon Floyd replied: 'I knew it, no Australian could play it like that.'[51] In those days, Dr Floyd presented a well-known weekly radio programme, the 'Music Lovers' Hour', in which he once introduced a Brahms Symphony with the words: 'This is the Vienna Philharmonic Orchestra under the direction of Bruno Walter.' Kolben doubted this. In a comprehensive letter to Floyd, he pointed out that it was actually a recording made with Leopold Stokowski. Floyd was impressed, and wrote back saying that he had never come across such an acute musical ear. Now, this same Brahms listener appeared before him as an equally precise Brahms interpreter. As the prize winner, Kolben was able to perform the first movement of the same concerto with the SSO under Eugene Goossens. The critic for the *Sunday Sun* described the young pianist's playing as 'vigorous and colourful'. The *Australian Musical News* was amazed that an engineering student had reached such a high standard, and reported on his plans for the future: 'Eventually this young pianist hopes to go to Europe for further experience, but feels that there is much that he can learn here.'[52] In 1951, Kolben took part in the ABC competition again, this time with the Brahms D minor Concerto but, 'although he brought plenty of power and a dramatic interpretation,'[53] on this occasion both the first prizes went to other artists.

Figure 35: The pianist Robert Kolben, publicity picture for the ABC. (NAA, SP1011/1, 2810)

On 13 May 1953, Kolben was a soloist at the competition's final concert. He played Rachmaninoff's Rhapsody on a Theme of Paganini and the *Sydney Morning Herald* wrote: 'Crisp and lucid playing, wide ranging in sentiment, resourceful in technique, often lacking high nervous tension, sometimes over-deliberate with spontaneity as the casualty.'[54] In view of his overall convincing achievement, Eugene Goossens invited the young man to give a repeat performance. At around the same time, Kolben appeared in the suburb of Epping as conductor and piano soloist with the Eastwood–Ryde Municipal Orchestra. A solo recital at the end of 1954 contained demanding works by Goossens (*Bacchanale*) and Ravel (*Scarbo* from *Gaspard de la Nuit*), although the critics especially liked his interpretation of Schubert's great Sonata in A minor, D784.[55] Meanwhile, Kolben had taken further lessons from Alexander Sverjensky, but eventually decided to finish his training in Europe. He played an ambitious farewell concert at the Sydney Conservatorium on 13 May 1955, in which he began with a Bach toccata and then went on to play Beethoven's Sonata Op. 111, the *Estampes* by

Debussy, *Quizzie/Procrastination* by the Australian Raymond Hanson (from whom he had taken a few hours of tuition in composition) and two pieces by Chopin. Two days later, he played Camille Saint-Saëns' Second Piano Concerto with the SSO, another work which in those days lay outside the standard repertoire. After this performance, he received a call from Hephzibah Menuhin, who invited him to her city office. There she admonished her young colleague: 'So, now you're leaving too. But make sure that you come back, or eventually we won't have any musicians left.' As Kolben later remembered, he swore on oath 'without the slightest intention of keeping it'. Two years later, when Hephzibah Menuhin and her brother Yehudi gave a recital in Frankfurt am Main, Kolben visited her in the green room and asked, ironically: 'Well, are we going to travel back to Australia together now?' She simply answered: 'Don't make me laugh!'[56] At the time, she was preparing to move to London. Robert Kolben never returned to Australia either. Although his family had once been driven abroad by the Germans, he eventually settled in West Germany – but as an Australian citizen. There he devoted himself to composers who had been interned in Theresienstadt and murdered in Auschwitz; he subsequently became one of the most important advisers on this subject to the Berlin friends' association, *musica reanimata*.

Violinist Tossy Spivakovsky was just as outstanding as his brother Jascha, the pianist but, in view of the limited opportunities, he left Australia for the USA in 1940. In contrast, the cellist Otti Veit stayed in the country. Following her arrival in 1940, she lived with her husband, a mining engineer, in Kalgoorlie, a desert town in Western Australia. At a concert there, she was very surprised to meet Dorcas McLean, a violinist with whom she had studied at the Royal College of Music in London, and the next day she accompanied her to the station. On the train back to Perth, McLean happened to meet W.G. James, Federal Director of Music for the ABC, so she mentioned Otti Veit: here was an outstanding cellist, hidden away in this isolated gold-mining town. James was interested, and the next day he sent Veit a telegram inviting her to audition in the tiny ABC studio in Kalgoorlie. When James and the conductor George Schnéevoigt listened to her performance in Perth, they both decided then and there that she should lead the cello section of the Perth Symphony Orchestra for the celebrity concerts.[57]

Surprisingly, the Musicians' Union declared itself willing to accept this artist, although she was not a British citizen. However, she had to pay the considerable membership fee of twenty guineas. As Otti Veit did not have the money, the ABC then offered her a generous fee for twenty fortnightly broadcasts, so she was soon able to pay and, as a member of the union, ready to perform under conductors such as Heinze, Dorati, Beecham and Schnéevoigt. She regularly travelled 600km by train for each of these orchestral concerts, until she and her husband finally moved to Perth in 1943.

Figure 36: The cellist Otti Veit. (Kurt R. Eisner, Melbourne)

Otti Veit and her husband were both naturalised in 1944, and in 1948 they moved to the livelier cultural city of Melbourne, where he had been offered a position. Her preferential treatment by the ABC there caused some envy among the local musicians, so she did not apply for an orchestral position. In 1951, she founded a string quartet with the violinist Paul

McDermott, who had just arrived from London, and they gave six subscription concerts a year. Other chamber music partners included Hephzibah Menuhin and Walter Susskind. When Otti Veit played all five Beethoven Cello Sonatas in five radio broadcasts, the press mentioned the beautiful old instrument she had bought in Germany when she began her studies with Nicolai Graudan.[58] However, when she returned to Europe in 1955 to meet members of her family, she looked for an even better instrument and managed to acquire a wonderful Hendrik Jacobs cello made in 1696. Otti Veit gave up her public quartet playing in 1956, in order to spend more time with her children, but she continued to give regular concerts, including new works by Felix Werder. Diagnosed with cancer in 1989, she continued to play in house concerts until 1995, for instance at Jascha Spivakovsky's mansion. After her death in 2000, her husband sold the valuable cello and put $250,000 from the proceeds towards an Otti Veit scholarship for gifted young cellists at the University of Melbourne.

For various reasons, the singers among the German-speaking refugees made little impression on the Australian concert scene. Marianne Mathy first presented herself to the public in 1939, but after that, she was mainly active as a highly respected singing teacher. Leonie Feigl, an experienced concert singer, had already passed her peak when she arrived in Australia at the age of sixty. In 1941, she auditioned for the ABC; yet, despite her wide-ranging repertoire she was not engaged.[59] On 3 July 1943, a lieder recital at the Sydney Conservatorium with works by Beethoven, Brahms, Liadov, Tchaikovsky and Wolf, organised by the Women's International Zionist Organisation (WIZO), was apparently her last public appearance as a mezzo-soprano. The soprano Lily Kolos from Prague had a better reception. Between 1942 and 1946, she presented several recitals of lieder by Mozart, Schubert, Schumann, Weber, Dvořák, Wolf, Strauss, Joseph Marx and Alban Berg accompanied by Marcel Lorber and Henry Krips at the Sydney Conservatorium. Neville Cardus called her 'the finest and most cultivated lieder singer at present resident in Australia'. Her appearance in November 1943 was said to have been one of those rare moments when a concert was transformed into a spiritual experience.[60]

Soloists 373

Figure 37: The singer Lily Kolos, photographed by Margaret Michaelis. (Karla Sperling, Sydney)

Shortly after her arrival, Emmy Kimmel had been introduced by the *Sydney Morning Herald* as a coloratura soprano.[61] After one of her early recitals, Cardus wrote that this artist knew the secret to singing lieder, something 'which apparently evades all vocalists not cultivated in Central Europe'; the *Australian Musical News* regarded her as one of the few artists who could serve the poet with unusual sensitivity without neglecting the work's musical integrity, a comment reproduced on the poster advertising her lieder recital at the Sydney Conservatorium on 29 July 1944. The programme included works by Brahms, Blech, Jensen, Pergolesi, Pfitzner, Schubert and Wolf, and the accompanist was Henry Krips.⁶² After the war, when Emmy Kimmel was finally able to give an ABC broadcast, there was already criticism of her intonation.⁶³ In 1946, the bass baritone Günter Hirschberg won a singing competition, and the following December, accompanied by Werner Baer, he performed Schubert's *Winterreise*; in the musical narrative about a homeless, wandering protagonist, both artists were able to refer to their own fates. A year later, Hirschberg moved to New York, where he wanted to train as an opera singer under Alexander Kipnis.⁶⁴ Eric Liffmann, whose tenor voice had charmed his comrades in the internment camp and in the Eighth Australian Employment Company, left more traces in Australia.⁶⁵ In 1942, the Allans Publishing Company put his portrait on its edition of the song 'Grisel' by the Argentinean composer Mariano Mores. He continued to work as a professional singer and appeared regularly in schools, nightclubs and Masonic Lodges.

Opera

The refugees made a more significant contribution in the field of opera, even though they also experienced considerable frustration. For decades, opera in Australia had been limited to guest performances by overseas companies, although time and again there had been attempts to found Australian ensembles. Refugees from Europe brought new inspiration.

> They were accustomed to going to opera in a number of different European countries and took it for granted that a town, no matter how small, would have its own opera house and, certainly, that there'd be a big one in a capital city. How wrong they were in Australia!⁶⁶

Whereas Curt Prerauer had no further offers after the opera season that he organised in 1935–36, at least after several years Henry Krips was able to use his experience as a former musical director at the Vienna Volksoper. With the Dutch baritone Sydney de Vries, he founded the Krips-de Vries Opera Company in 1944. '"Cavalleria", "Bajazzo", "Faust" and other famous operas were performed with the ABC Symphony Orchestra and an All Australian Cast', wrote the *New Citizen*. 'It was a successful attempt and a clear proof that things of that kind can be done in Australia, after all.'[67] Although in July 1944, one of the *Faust* performances at the Sydney Conservatorium was attended by Lady Gowrie,[68] this opera company only existed for one season. After that, Krips turned to other fields of music. Dolf Brenner, another conductor with experience of opera, was not willing to make such a change. Although he was responsible for the successful premiere of *The Bartered Bride*, after his negative experiences with Otto Nicolai's *The Merry Wives of Windsor* he withdrew from conducting altogether.

In 1940, the island of Tasmania was anything but one of Australia's musical centres. But it was there that Rudolf Werther wanted to develop musical life, including opera. As he wrote in his curriculum vitae in 1945, he had at first made other plans: 'After failure of different business propositions in Melbourne decided to earn living by music, my hobby all through life.'[69] His opportunities in the small city of Launceston were considerably better than in Melbourne, where he was competing with professional musicians. Shortly after his arrival, Werther proposed founding a Tasmanian Conservatorium.[70] By December 1939, he had already put together a chamber orchestra that performed Mozart's youthful opera *Bastien and Bastienne* and his Piano Concerto in B flat major, K. 595 to a packed house at the National Theatre. The premiere of *Hansel and Gretel* planned for May 1940 had to be cancelled at short notice, as Werther was now considered an enemy alien. For two years, he could no longer perform in public, but he was finally able to stage Humperdinck's fairy-tale opera in December 1943. The production with ballet, choir, soloists and thirty-three-piece orchestra was celebrated as 'the beginning of a new era for Tasmania'; the balance between orchestra and chorus, action and decorations were all praised.[71] The income from the production, which enjoyed several repeat performances in Launceston and Hobart, went to various charitable causes. Werther's operatic and concert activities, for which he received only a small fee, were only possible because he had brought money with him, taught piano privately and his wife Anna ran a fashion store. Werther founded the Tasmanian Musical Festival Society and the Hobart Operatic Society, and in July 1944, he conducted Mozart's *Abduction from the Seraglio*. His performance of Carl Maria von Weber's *Der Freischütz* was also celebrated as a 'Triumph for City'.[72] These successes generated envy, however, and the musician was reproached for being over-confident. Edmund Dwyer-Gray defended this attitude in a letter to Minister Calwell:

> [Werther] is somewhat assertive in his manner in the sense of wanting to get his own way quickly. This merely arises, in my opinion, from his physical and mental alertness and desire to get something done that should be done. Perhaps I could put it humorously by saying that a conductor of concerts and operas is naturally used to a certain amount of authoritative control.[73]

In October 1945, before he was naturalised, Werther organised an Opera and Ballet Festival in Hobart, in which he conducted excerpts from Gounod's *Faust* and Verdi's *Aida*.[74] Following a controversy with the Musicians' Union over their decision not to allow members to donate their fees to the United Nations, he then left Tasmania, where he had had so much success.[75] He moved to Melbourne, where the *Australian Musical News* referred to his remarkable pioneering work.[76] Unable to gain a foothold in the big city, however, he moved again in 1949, this time to the smaller city of Cairns in northern Queensland. There he conducted an orchestra and again successfully staged *Hansel and Gretel* before moving to Perth in 1950, where the German emigrant Dr Hans Briner had founded the West Australian Opera Society and already staged several operas, including *Figaro*, *Hansel and Gretel* and *La Traviata*.[77] There, Werther worked chiefly as a chorus master and musical educator, but was also able to conduct the occasional opera – Gluck's *Orpheus* (1952) and Mozart's *Abduction* (1953) – before compiling a brochure on *Opera in Australia*.[78] Meanwhile, his legacy in Hobart was taken up by Walter Stiasny, who had escaped from Vienna and, after several years in England, become the new conductor of opera and operetta at the Theatre Royal in 1951. The Tasmanian Musical Festival Society, which existed until 1962, regarded the Werther years as its heyday.[79]

Hermann Schildberger, who also worked intensively in the field of opera in Australia, had more perseverance than Werther. In August 1947, he conducted *Der Freischütz* with the Brighton Philharmonic Society, wherein choir and soloists (among them the young Stefan Haag) were accompanied by two concert grand pianos. One of the pianists was Hans Zander, who had just arrived in Australia. Among all German immigrants, Zander had without doubt the best knowledge of opera. As conductor of the Berlin Municipal Opera, he had made his debut with *Fidelio* before being appointed assistant to *Generalintendant* Tietjen. After his dismissal, he became the administrative director of the Berlin Kulturbund, before escaping to Britain in 1939. On his arrival in Australia, the press immediately referred to his qualifications and to his collaboration with singers like Lotte Lehmann, Richard Tauber, Alexander Kipnis, Emanuel List and Lauritz Melchior.[80] Zander's piano playing was one of the highlights of Schildberger's *Freischütz*, which was so successful that it was repeated in October.

Opportunities for a permanent opera in Melbourne were offered by the National Theatre Movement, established as an opera school in 1935 by the soprano Gertrude Johnson. Schildberger met the singer in 1947 and they planned future collaborations. Indeed, in 1948 he conducted performances of *Carmen*, *Faust*, *Figaro* and *Rigoletto* at the Princess Theatre, alternating with Joseph Post. Zander was given his own conducting engagements in the second half of the year. The review of his *Bartered Bride* read: 'Mr Zander took in his resources at a glance and concentrated on the music with such expertness that one forgot the players' shortcomings.'[81] In 1949, he conducted *Fidelio*,[82] *Martha*, *Eugen Onegin* and *Tannhäuser* in Melbourne, before transferring the following year to Sydney, where he became Executive Director and Chief Conductor of the New South Wales National Opera, a rival institution inspired by Marianne Mathy and founded the previous year by Clarice Lorenz.[83] Here he was responsible for both the administration and the artistic direction; Zander developed grand plans:

> The executive of the Opera is keen to bring back to Australia successful local artists who can return to their own country with some confidence for the future's stability – a stability which has been sadly lacking in the past. It is also the desire of the company to steadily increase the number of companies and seasons from city to country towns and then to other cities. The plan is an extensive and long-sighted one and, in carrying it out, the executive believes that it will remove the stigma of ignorance so often imposed on Australians and reveal and encourage our natural discrimination.[84]

When this company launched its first season at the Tivoli Theatre on 7 March 1951, he proudly told a reporter: 'We built it from nothing! The professionals said we would fail. But we succeed!' The same article said of Zander: 'He is developing a national opera for New South Wales with the same kind of long-range faith that mediaeval men used to build cathedrals.'[85] Although Zander was more qualified than most for such a demanding job, and although he had support from Eugene Goossens and even from Rudolf Bing in New York, he encountered considerable hostility in his own house. Deeply disappointed, he informed Schildberger in May that his one-year contract had not been renewed. The various difficulties had ruined his health. Six months later, he died of cancer. His colleague Eric Clapham, who visited him in hospital, regretted that Australia had not given him a greater chance. 'Hans Zander was a really brilliant man.'[86]

Hermann Schildberger, in contrast, had the opportunity to rehearse at the National Theatre Opera School and to direct performances at the National Opera in Melbourne. In 1969, five years before his death, he was still conducting *La Bohème* and *Rigoletto*. Henry Portnoj and his wife Annie also wanted to contribute to the further development of Australian opera: in 1947, they participated in an opera school that was established by the J.C. Williamson agency in conjunction with Thea Philips, a soprano who once worked at Covent Garden and had come to Australia with the Fuller Company in 1934.[87] At the time, Annie Portnoj recalled her pre-war experience of opera in Salzburg, and outlined her vision for an Australian Salzburg in Ballarat.[88]

Charles Berg and Stefan Haag exerted much greater influence on the opera scene by combining artistic enthusiasm with sober financial calculation. Having come to Australia as a member of the Vienna Mozart Boys Choir, Haag studied singing with Adolf Spivakovsky and was assistant conductor to Schildberger. In 1949, when Haag took over the direction of a performance of *Martha* conducted by Zander, he demonstrated the versatility of his talent. However, seeing no opportunity for permanent opera in Australia, in 1954 Haag travelled to Europe, where he announced that he would only return to Australia if conditions improved. Haag's departure caused a real stir, for at the time he was considered to be 'the most important figure in Australian opera production'.[89] He did return. In

1956, he became Head of Production and in 1960, Artistic Director of the Elizabethan Theatre Trust Opera Company, for which he even organised overseas tours; he became Executive Director of the Elizabethan Theatre Trust in 1962, a position he held until 1968. When Stefan Haag died in Sydney in 1986, the Australian press called him a 'theatre and opera giant'.[90]

In 1970, in order to stabilise its ongoing financial problems, the Elizabethan Theatre Trust Opera Company was reorganised as The Australian Opera (now Opera Australia): the country finally had a Sydney-based company that operated all year round. Charles Berg, chair of the board from 1974 to 1986, was known for years in Australia as 'Mr Opera'. One of his main achievements was to win significant sponsorship for the company, something he could only do by combining a great love of music with his experience in the business world and his perseverance. After the Nazi persecution had scuppered his planned career as a musician, Charles Berg the administrator made a significant contribution to musical life in Australia. In 1968, Stefan Haag was awarded the Order of the British Empire (OBE) for 'development of the arts';[91] Berg was appointed OBE in 1972 in recognition of his 'service to music and the theatre'[92] and received the Order of Australia (AM) in 1986, two years before his death.[93]

Synagogues

Most of the Berlin Jews who came to Australia during the Nazi era held liberal religious views. Those in the Hay internment camp tended to view with incomprehension the Zionist military chaplain, Falk, with his staunchly patriotic speeches. On the other hand, Rabbi Hermann Sänger was highly respected among the refugees. From 1936, he breathed new life into Melbourne's Beth Israel Congregation in the southern suburb of St Kilda; Schildberger owed him his position as organist and choirmaster there. Dr Martin Krutsch had arrived some months before Schildberger and been installed as cantor at this liberal synagogue in February 1939; the *Australian Jewish Herald* reported that, prior to this, Krutsch had been principal cantor at Synagogue Prinzregentenstraße in Berlin.[94] His mellifluous incantation, which from 1939 was broadcast several times, made him known beyond the congregation. In 1941, the Yom Kippur celebrations were described as follows: 'The Cantor, Dr Krutsch, interpreted with his beautiful voice the well-known traditional melodies for the High Holidays and the enlarged choir under Dr Schildberger seconded most effectively.'[95] With such a capable cantor, Schildberger could also venture to perform new works by the Mannheim composer Hugo Adler:

> His music is written in the modern style of Temple Music, and the new harmonies and melodies may sound a bit strange at first; but we are confident that, supported by the excellent interpretation and singing of our Cantor, Dr Krutsch, this attractive and original modern work will find the understanding and appreciation of all those who are so fond of the old tunes.[96]

Only a few months later, the fifty-one-year-old cantor suddenly collapsed in the middle of the Friday service and later died of a heart attack at home. A large crowd attended his burial service at the Melbourne General Cemetery in Carlton.

In a detailed article published in 1946, Schildberger called for a renewal of synagogue music. The classic Lewandowski works had to be gradually supplemented and replaced by newer compositions by Jacob Weinberg, Hans Schalit and Ernest Bloch.[97] Temple Beth Israel, however, only had a modest Hammond organ at its disposal, which was replaced at the initiative of the young Rabbi John Levi by a small pipe organ shortly before Schildberger's retirement. In order to improve the standard of the choir, Schildberger invited collaboration with the members of the Methodist choir that he also conducted. 'He used the church singers as part of his choir for the Temple. Some of them stayed with him for twenty years.'[98]

Rabbi Sänger was also responsible for the liberal Temple Emanuel in Sydney. The founding committee, which included the two former Berliners, Dora Peyser and Fritz Coper, met on 5 April 1938. The first service took place the following month in the Maccabean Hall and Coper (who was to be the future choirmaster) played on a borrowed Hammond organ. In the weeks that followed, he and his wife Mary, a talented singer, set about creating a choir. The volunteer cantor was Fritz (Frederick) Brandmann, who had arrived in Sydney at the beginning of 1939. In August, the congregation received as organist the highly qualified Theodor Schoenberger, who was also from Berlin. The *Sydney Jewish News* proudly announced the appointment of this 'world famous' artist, who had recommendations from personalities like Bruno Walter and Otto Klemperer and was a friend of Artur Schnabel. 'In the hands of such a Master as Mr Schoenberger, Temple Emanuel's modern electric organ will add infinite beauty to the services and sanctity to the proceedings.'[99]

In September, a new rabbi was introduced, the Swiss-born Max Schenk, who had been educated in the USA. On 10 November, he spoke at a service in memory of the victims of Kristallnacht. The financing of an organist and choirmaster were a cause of concern for the congregation, which by December had grown to 252 members. Although the 'Women's Guild and other ladies' in the congregation agreed to pay the costs of the choir, its performance, as Schoenberger complained to Schildberger in April 1940, was 'worse than amateurish'. The new organist was also annoyed that he could not get his way because of his poor English:

> The gentlemen certainly sense my superiority. Apparently the standard of performances offered does not disappoint them. The public is delighted, it hears some lovely voices. The wife of the conductor (Coper) sings the solos quite nicely. The low standard is only noticed by a few educated refugees. The others, like the conductor, are satisfied if they pull it off.

Schoenberger did not like working with such a second-rate choral conductor. It irked him 'that – although they are well aware of my reputation as a musician and piano teacher – no-one is helping me to achieve a modest standard of living by giving me references or recommending me as a teacher'.[100] He had a better relationship with Cantor Brandmann than with Coper, because he had already known the former in Berlin. 'He is grateful for every suggestion and I like helping him. Nevertheless, I have to transpose all his songs and during my absence that has caused some problems for the deputies.'[101]

Meanwhile, Rabbi Schenk had learnt that there was a talented cantor by the name of Günter Hirschberg in the internment camp at Tatura. In August 1942, Schenk and the president chair of the congregation, Cecil

Luber, reported on their meeting with the twenty-two-year-old Berliner, whose musical capabilities had impressed them. They reported that he had a beautiful, deep baritone voice, could play the piano, transpose and even compose. The congregation decided to apply for his release from the army.[102] When Günter Hirschberg became the full-time cantor at Temple Emanuel in 1943, Schoenberger had finally found a serious partner, and therefore was happy to accompany him in aria competitions and radio broadcasts. He was still dissatisfied, however, with the choir's achievements. Fritz Coper did not appreciate the way Schoenberger meddled in his affairs and recommended that the choir perform his own compositions. In order to clarify the situation, Luber eventually named the latter musical director, while reducing the responsibilities of the choirmaster. In 1944, as the quality of the choir was still a subject of discussion, Coper was asked to organise more regular rehearsals, attract new singers and produce five complete choral programmes. The competencies of the cantors Brandmann and Hirschberg also had to be clarified.

Such confrontations took their toll on Schoenberger's health, which had already suffered under the nervous strain of the years in Berlin, the stress of his escape and his struggle to survive in Sydney. He was diagnosed with stomach cancer and died on 10 February 1945 at the age of seventy-six. At his funeral on 16 February, some of his own compositions were performed, and Günter Hirschberg gave a moving eulogy. He recalled the discussions he had recently had with his older colleague about music, Judaism and humanity:

> Theodor Schoenberger was a great musician. He had accomplished much; he had every reason to be proud of himself and yet his music was not a means of an end unto itself. It was but a means of expression, it was the manner in which he expressed himself and I say that he was a great musician, because right through life he prayed that what he tried to express might be acceptable in the sight of God, might serve the cause of love and goodness, might open the eyes of man to things of beauty and culture, might make him forget injustice and cruelty, violence and strife, things which he abhorred from the very depths of his being.[103]

Werner Baer had an even more exalted view of music, as he once explained in an interview: 'Music is a religion in itself. It does not need any ministerial intervention whatsoever. Musicians speak to God directly.'[104]

The congregation was very pleased with Günter Hirschberg, but in April 1947 he left permanently. In December, he left Australia and flew to New York to continue his studies in singing. In the following year, Rabbi Schenk also said goodbye. Although Eric Smith was officially appointed as successor to Schoenberger, Werner Baer made himself available as deputy organist. He apparently had no difficulties working with Fritz Coper, who had meanwhile been appointed musical director. Having been choirmaster at the Great Synagogue in the inner city from 1946 to 1950, Baer became organist and choirmaster at the second Temple Emanuel in Chatswood on Sydney's North Shore, which was opened on Max Joseph's initiative in September 1961. Only a few days later, Temple Emanuel in Woollahra lost its long-standing choirmaster, when Fritz Coper died in a car accident. Georg Pikler succeeded him as musical director. From 1964, when Werner Baer started to share this position with him, and the synagogue also acquired a new organ, there was marked improvement in the quality of the music. The president of the congregation summed it up as follows: 'We had the benefit of musical services that were more magnificent than ever before [...] and music is the core of every Liberal Service.'[105] He was particularly happy about Baer's permanent participation. 'It is an established fact that as an organist he is one of our leading artists and especially in the field of liturgical music he has no equal in this country.'[106] Werner Baer gave up this poorly paid job only in 1980, after thirty-two years, when a new rabbi showed less appreciation for the significance of music and musical traditions.[107]

Whereas the German-speaking refugees played a key role in liberal Jewish congregations in Australia, they apparently had less influence in orthodox communities. Apart from Werner Baer and Henry Adler, who both served as choirmasters at the Great Synagogue in Sydney,[108] mention should be made of Joseph Kalb, who was appointed cantor of the Melbourne Hebrew Congregation in 1939. There he founded the Hazomir Choir, which was led first by Henry Portnoj, and then by Dolf Brenner and Felix Werder.[109] Besides his chief activities as composer and critic, Felix Werder was choirmaster at this Toorak Road Synagogue for almost four decades.

Ballet and Dance Theatre

Dance and ballet had a following in Australia quite early. Colonel de Basil's Ballets Russes de Monte Carlo, a successor company to the famous Diaghilev troupe that dispersed in 1929, made three very successful tours between 1936 and 1940. In 1938, one member of the company, Eduard Borovansky, decided to remain in Australia after hearing that the Germans had occupied his homeland, Czechoslovakia. He and his wife set up a ballet school in Melbourne and eventually founded the Borovansky Ballet, with which he performed well-known works such as *Giselle* and *Swan Lake* as well as his own choreographies, including *Terra Australis*. With support from the J.C. Williamson agency, the company performed in large theatres with orchestras. Sydney John Kay wrote the music for Borovansky's ballet *Lot's Wife*, which was broadcast in March 1944. Dr Floyd wrote a glowing review; he said that the composer, Kay, had something to say and knew how to express it.[110] Nevertheless, it is questionable whether Kay's music was actually used for the ballet. His music for *Romeo and Juliet*, written for Borovansky in 1947, was not.[111] Kurt Herweg, who had come to Australia as an accompanist for the dancer Anny Fligg, had more success in this sector. Despite frequent differences of opinion with Eduard Borovansky, he remained musical director of his ballet company for eleven years, from 1945 until 1956. The Danish dancer Hélène Kirsova, who was celebrated in Australia as a member of the Russian Ballet in the 1930s, also founded a ballet school in Sydney, which became the Kirsova Ballet. She engaged Henry Krips as musical director, and he created extensive two-piano scores for *Faust* (after Heine), which premiered to standing ovations on 22 November 1941,[112] and *The Revolution of the Umbrellas* (9 February 1943),[113] before the company disbanded in 1944.

European dancers who portrayed social conflicts in dance left a lasting influence on Australian dance culture. Gertrud Bodenwieser played a significant part in the transformation of ballet into dance theatre; her dance drama *Demon Machine* had already caused a stir in Vienna in 1924. After her arrival in Australia in August 1939, she immediately embarked on an extensive tour. Since her Viennese troupe consisted almost exclusively of women, it was not affected by internment during the war. Marcel Lorber, their long-standing pianist, was also able to continue working. To accompany their performances, he either used music that was already available, or created new compositions, as for the dance drama *Cain and Abel* that premiered at the Sydney Conservatorium on 25 October 1941. Gertrud Bodenwieser wrote in the programme notes:

> The dance drama sets out to stage this biblical drama of human relationships, the first known episode of social conflict. The subject is by no means only a tale of by-gone times: the problem is to become – in the perspective of the choreography – one of great topical significance. Cain and Abel are meant to be symbols of our present-day struggle. [...] The drama ends as present war is eventually bound to end: the true ideals reign supreme, while the principle of force is overthrown, according to the spirit which the whole creation demands. Life has to be preserved and positive values arise again in the miraculous course of nature. The seeming triumphs of destructive power never shake our firm belief in the good. Even if Abel falls as the victim of his brother's ruthlessness, Cain can never be victorious. It is the spirit of Abel that survives unharmed, which is re-born as long as mankind survives.[114]

This text combines visionary engagement with a theatrical thinking probably influenced by the choreographer's husband, the director Friedrich Rosenthal. Gertrud Bodenwieser did not understand dance as a luxury of the privileged class, but as a medium for social experience: in Vienna, she had performed in workers' cultural centres and clubs. Lorber's relatively demanding score for *Cain and Abel*, for piano, drums, violins and women's chorus, survives in the Bodenwieser archives.[115] The piece opens with an idyllic scene of heavenly peace in C major, after which, according to the score, Cain appears, played by Shona Dunlop, a New Zealand dancer, who joined the Bodenwieser company in Vienna in 1936. A vision of demons is followed by Cain's 'barbaric and resolute' solo, with powerful octave passages and numerous changes of rhythm. The second half begins with the 'Sacrificial Dance and Thunderstorm', composed as a fugue. After Abel's murder, the conscience stirs (Conscience Dance) and, departing from the biblical text, a mother and two angels appear. The work ends with a women's choir invoking the spirit of humanity in the radiant key of G major.

Lorber created and performed other musical works for the Bodenwieser Company, mostly for solo piano, such as *Form Emerging from Chaos* (1943) and *The Wheel of Life* (1944). In 1945, Lorber composed the music for Shona Dunlop's solo dance, *Trilogy of Joan of Arc*, after which the dancer and her husband travelled to revolutionary China. In December 1946, Lorber himself left with the Bodenwieser dancers Bettina Vernon and Evelyn Ippen on a tour of Japan lasting several months to entertain the occupying troops. Little did he suspect that the twenty-two-year-old British officer Bernard Keeffe, who accompanied them on the trip as a guide and interpreter, was there to monitor them. The paranoid US Counter Intelligence Corps had learnt that the three artists had once been enemy aliens. Keeffe spoke Japanese: during the war, he had decoded secret Japanese codes at Bletchley Park. It was a surreal situation: the intelligence corps of a nation that had triggered a massacre in Japan by dropping two atom bombs was still looking for 'suspicious persons', even after the country's capitulation, and their suspicion fell on three Jews who had fled from Hitler's Reich, which had also long since surrendered. 'So we set off in two jeeps with drivers on their tour of the camps', Bernard Keeffe recalled later.

> After a few days I told them of my interest in music, and that I had been studying singing as a baritone. Marcel at once suggested that we should make music together, for he had been accompanist to leading singers such as Leo Slezak in Vienna. He offered to teach me Schubert songs, and so we studied *Die Winterreise*.

Lorber's tuition was a revelation for Keeffe:

> I have never forgotten how he told me to colour the vowels and also to use the consonants as part of the poetic expression in words such as *Fruehling* [Spring] and *Der Winter kalt und wild* [The cold and wild winter]. We worked so well that we finally gave a performance of *Winterreise* in a hospital in Hiroshima that was run by German monks for victims of the nuclear bomb.[116]

This Schubert performance, interrupted only by the groaning of the wounded in the ruins of a devastated city, was a deeply moving, unforgettable experience for everyone. The German monks, who also had to undergo a security check, would never have expected to hear *Die Winterreise* in such an environment in their mother tongue. The Japanese also expressed their lively approval, although they did not understand a single word.

This tour of Japan was a turning point for the dancers as well as for Lorber. He rediscovered his old love of *netsuke* miniature sculptures and Bettina Vernon met her future husband, a highly decorated British fighter pilot. The latter event gave the impetus for the dancers and Lorber to move to Britain, and Bettina soon married her pilot. Gertrud Bodenwieser was not at all happy about this development, as she now had to do without two important dancers and, above all, Marcel Lorber.[117] In his place, she engaged the pianist Dory Stern, also from Vienna, who had already accompanied the troupe on a tour of New Zealand in April 1947. As composers, Bodenwieser acquired Werner Baer, Horst Graff[118] and Kurt Herweg.

After being discharged from military service in 1943, Werner Baer became the pianist for the Studio of the Creative Dance that the Bodenwieser dancers Hanny Kolm and Daisy Pirnitzer founded in Collins Street, Melbourne in 1939. In 1944, he handed the job over to Henry Portnoj, whose music for the ballet *A Fairytale* received high praise in August 1945.[119] He in turn was followed by Rudi Laqueur in 1947. Werner Baer, who, together with Lorber, had already played the piano for a Bodenwieser performance in December 1943,[120] also composed for her company: *The One and the Many* (1946), *The Life of the Insects* (1949, after Karel Čapek), *The Weaker and the Stronger* and *Test of Strength* (both 1953), *Waltzing Matilda* (1954) and *Dance Israeli* (1958). The choreography for the short film *Dance Israeli* was one of the last works by Gertrud Bodenwieser, who died in Sydney in 1959. Unlike her husband, who was murdered in Auschwitz in 1942, she not only survived in Australia, but had a lasting effect as a pioneer of modern dance.[121]

Popular Music

The Weintraubs Syncopators had introduced Australia to the lively entertainment culture of the Weimar Republic. When the war began, however, this famous band had to gradually disguise its Berlin origins until its sad end with the internment of its German members. After that, the brothers

Manny and Addy Fisher (Emanuel and Adolf Frischer), both Polish citizens, formed a group with Leo Weiss, Henry Adler and two Australians; they appeared as Fisher's Sextet at Prince's Restaurant, the Weintraubs' former venue. The group disbanded when Manny Fisher changed to a more lucrative profession: in 1949 he and a friend opened a meat-packaging factory that proved to be a huge commercial success. Henry Adler had already been appearing with his own band at the exclusive Gleneagles Restaurant since 1945; around 1951, he founded the Henry Adler Trio with Addy Fisher (bass) and Don Andrews (guitar), which regularly broadcast light music in both the classical and modern styles. Once Fisher's Sextet had disbanded, Leo Weiss, the last of the Weintraubs' pianists, changed his name to Leo White and began to perform on his own. He composed songs such as 'I Shall Never Forgive You', 'I'll Always See You', 'Sleep Baby Sleep' and 'A-Mooning in the Moonlight', and founded his own band, Leo White and his Orchestra, which could still be heard in Prince's Restaurant as late as 1955. In 1949, when South American samba rhythms became popular in Australia, White bought extra percussion instruments like rattles and claves for his eight-piece band.[122] He was often seen with his wife, Betty, a former Miss Victoria. On the other hand, Horst Graff and Stefan Weintraub, who continued to live in Sydney, only appeared as amateur musicians in German-speaking performances at the Kleines Wiener Theater [Little Viennese Theatre],[123] where productions like *The Threepenny Opera* recalled the European culture they had left behind. After separating from his first wife, Margo, Graff married a pianist whose white grand piano stood in their home, a reminder of his past as a professional musician. Sydney John Kay, a member of the Musicians' Union since 1944, worked as a film composer and arranger for the Colgate-Palmolive Radio Unit's Dennis Collinson Orchestra.

Many of the refugee light entertainment musicians settled in Melbourne, where they performed in hotels, restaurants, night clubs and cafés. Virtually none of them achieved the status they had once enjoyed in Europe or Asia. One episode reported by Andy Factor illustrates the attitude of the Musicians' Union. His repertoire included the Mendelssohn, Bruch and Brahms violin concertos but, when he applied for union membership and wished to perform a movement from a Mozart Sonata, he was immediately interrupted and asked: 'How about playing some *real* music?' The union members present had expected a popular song. Shortly afterwards, they informed the young violinist that they had found a job for him: the most horrible *glissandi* possible were required for a cat food commercial. 'The more rubbish music they wanted me to play, the better I was paid. Imagine, we used to play the Brahms clarinet quintet in recital at what they called the British Music Society. They would clap: Very nice! And we got a free cup of tea and a bit of cake. There was no money.'[124] Andy Factor almost always had to perform the music that meant most to him without a fee. He earned his living playing lighter fare for the Victorian Ballet Company or the ABC Melbourne Show Band.

At that time, Australia exerted a certain attraction for artists from the devastated cities of Europe. Having survived both Theresienstadt and Auschwitz, the jazz guitarist Coco Schumann came to Melbourne in 1950. There he met old acquaintances like the Polish accordionist Leo Rosner, who owed his life to the industrialist Oskar Schindler, and André Schuster, the former bass player in Teddy Stauffer's jazz band, whose playing in Berlin Schumann had never forgotten.[125] Although Coco Schumann had a lot of engagements, he did not feel right in Melbourne.

> I was not satisfied. For, Australian clocks run differently. When we hit the streets after we finished playing, there was a deathly quiet. For us it was really just 'high afternoon', but here the clock had already struck midnight, and no-one was around. Meanwhile my friends in distant Berlin were just starting their pub-crawl![126]

In comparison with Berlin and Vienna, the music scene in Melbourne was asleep. Together with Günther Becker, the former drummer with Walter Dobschinski, Schumann decided to return to West Germany.

Hans Bader could never work again as a bandleader; instead he was an arranger for Hector Crawford for many years and also wrote all the scores for Crawford's television productions, even for operas. Hans Holzbauer (John Wood) appeared in Maas' Restaurant & Cabaret in St Kilda, but his main work was as an administrator. Trained as a pianist, Rudi Laqueur played in the Moulin Rouge night club in Elwood, but gave it up because of the cigarette smoke; he changed his occupation and became a podiatrist. After Laqueur's departure, the owner of the Moulin Rouge, Leo Rosner, engaged Erwin Frenkel as a pianist. When Frenkel realised that such performances could not guarantee a living, he moved into the construction industry and played music as a hobby. Although he had trained at the Vienna Music Academy, Mischa Stiwelband ended up playing the violin 'like a Klezmer'.[127] According to his death certificate, Salo ('Solomon') Max Tichauer, who had led his own bands in Europe and Asia, remained a musician until the end, but little is known about his activities. He is another musician who disappeared 'down under'.

Hans Blau did not return to Europe, because his wife Ilse wanted to remain in Melbourne and, as an entertainer, he eventually regained some of the popularity that he had previously enjoyed in Vienna. The owner of Claridge's night club had seen him in the performance of *Sgt Snow White* and had immediately engaged him and the violinist Oskar Fleischer. For his performances at Claridge's and at the Hotel Australia, he was advertised as 'Hans, the former entertainer of The Duke of Windsor'. He loved singing emotional songs like 'Wien, Wien, nur Du allein' ['Vienna, City of my dreams'] and 'Wien wird bei Nacht erst schön' ['Lovely Vienna at night'] and accompanying himself on an accordion with the name HANS in glittering letters on its side. He was still performing these songs in his old age, as they cheered him up when he was in a bad mood.[128]

Like Hans Blau, Kurt Blach (now 'Black') also supported himself with the treasury of music that he had brought with him: two big boxes of 'coffee house music', charming salon melodies that had once been popular in the big cafés of Vienna and Berlin. He played them with his piano trio for twenty years (1955–1975) at the fashionable Hotel Australia (later Australia on Collins, now St Collins Lane), and subsequently at dinners and family celebrations. Regular broadcasts made these 'Continental sounds' popular in Australia too. John Harband concentrated predominantly on operetta melodies by Franz Lehár, Emmerich Kálmán and Robert Stolz; he performed as a soloist and with his own band in various Melbourne hotels such as the Oriental, Federal, Menzies' and Riverside Inn.[129]

Blau's colleague Oskar Fleischer, who changed his name to 'Fletcher' at the end of the war, played the trumpet, cornet and trombone as well as the violin. In 1943, he married a German, who already had two children.

Margarete Friedlich was bipolar and later committed suicide. For her sake, Fletcher bought a farm in the country. Initially, he regularly drove to Melbourne for his performances. The commuting soon became too onerous, however, and he gave up music as a profession.[130] Oscar Fletcher died in 1958 at the age of forty-seven.

Music Education

Music education is one of the fundamentals of musical life. In Australia, Germans played a substantial role in this field until 1918, for example at the University of Melbourne Conservatorium. Several Jewish refugees continued this tradition by teaching music, mostly in their own homes, where they were not subject to union control. In this situation, women were preferred, as they were deemed to be 'morally safer'.[131] Jascha Spivakovsky was one of the few refugees who had a permanent teaching position. From 1935, he gave group tuition (a method new to Australia) in Room 1 of Melbourne's University Conservatorium. Finding the level of performance to be well below European standards, he made high demands on his students and was considered a very strict teacher. Sometimes he continued his tuition in the enormous music room of his private home; one of his students, the music writer June Epstein, was even married there. Whereas Jascha Spivakovsky taught almost until the end of his life, most of the other pianists who immigrated from Germany and Austria – including Gertrud Hacker, Marcel Lorber, Käthe Neumann, Curt Prerauer, Theodor Schoenberger, Dory Stern, Emma Weiss and Rudolf Werther – soon gave up this activity. Schoenberger and Weiss died young, and Hacker suffered a hand injury. Lorber, who amazed his students with his quick intelligence and his capacity to transpose at sight,[132] left Australia at the end of 1946. It is puzzling that, in spite of her early concerts and her offer to teach advanced pianists in the Rubinstein tradition,[133] hardly anything more was heard of Käthe Neumann. She died in Melbourne at the age of seventy-two. In the Death Register, her occupation was given as 'Home Duties'.

Ernest Schulvater continued to practise the violin every day, even as a shop owner, and began teaching in 1947.[134] However, little is known about his violin tuition, or that of Ellen Cohn-Byk, Elizabeth Colin and Majer (Max) Pietruschka. It is verified that both Issy Spivakovsky and Otti Veit, who taught for almost three decades at Melbourne's University Conservatorium, were successful cello teachers.[135] Apart from Fritz Coper, Leonie Feigl and Emmy Kimmel (author of 'The Art of Perfect Voice Production', Sydney 1947), Marianne Mathy, Adolf Spivakovsky and Henry and Annie Portnoj must be mentioned as singing teachers. Henry Portnoj 'had a light Viennese accent and an easy charm that made his pupils feel comfortable from the start. He had an enormous influence in developing some of Australia's finest singers'.[136] Well-known students of his include John Shaw, Clifford Grant, Neil Warren-Smith, Jenifer Eddy, Neil Williams, Robert Simmons and Gregory Dempsey. Like Curt Prerauer and Werner Baer, Portnoj placed great importance on the art of lieder accompaniment,[137] and like Baer he was also an influential juror at singing competitions. After twelve years of private tuition with the 'wise and understanding' Adolf Spivakovsky, Sylvia Fisher became a star at London's Covent Garden. 'Perfection was his goal, and hers, constant study, humility to the great composers and to the pursuit of vocal beauty.'[138] The singer was indebted to him for her intimate knowledge of the German repertoire. In 1948, she made her debut in London as Leonore in Beethoven's *Fidelio*, and later was also an acclaimed Wagnerian singer. Alan Light, June Bronhill, Joan Sutherland and Lyndon Terracini were among Marianne Mathy's students. One of Hermann Schildberger's claims to fame was his discovery of the opera singer Marie Collier, who successfully stood in for Maria Callas in London in 1965.

When Maurice Abravanel visited Australia again in 1946, he mentioned the progress that had been made in musical life there:

> But the most interesting development was the formation of an organisation called Singers of Australia, Inc., composed of professional singers who act without managerial aid or interference, and act as a clearing house for their own talents. Eventually they hope to found a national opera company.[139]

This self-help organisation, which called itself 'A National Society for the Encouragement of Singers and the Advancement of the Art of Singing', was inaugurated in Sydney Town Hall on 6 March 1946. Its aims included the promotion of talented young singers, training for grand opera and the dissemination of Australian vocal works. Henry Krips was the first musical director[140] and Sibilla Lighezollo, one of Sydney de Vries' voice students at the Conservatorium, the secretary. Under Henry Krips' guidance, the young singers performed great works like Bach's *St John Passion*, Mozart's *Requiem* and Benjamin Britten's *Rape of Lucretia*. 'In the course of that venture Krips has been able to discover a new generation of Australian singers.'[141] One of them was the bass baritone Günter Hirschberg, whom Werner Baer accompanied in several performances. When Hirschberg took part in a singing competition, Baer was sure that he would win; however, the prize went to the Australian Joan Sutherland, also one of the 'Singers of Australia', whose London debut opened up an international career. Sibilla Lighezollo's work with Singers of Australia also had another consequence. In 1946, she had to turn the pages for Werner Baer when he was accompanying Joan Sutherland; it was the first time she had encountered this versatile musician. Two years later, Baer succeeded Krips as director of Singers of Australia[142] and, in 1950, Sibilla and Werner married.

Music Critics

Many of the refugees were familiar with the *Feuilletons*, or arts sections of the newspapers in Berlin and Vienna, which evaluated and compared concerts and opera performances according to recognised criteria. In the Australian press, where classical music had a much lower status, music critics played a modest role in terms of both space and significance. In a 1941 appraisal of Australian musical life, the London conductor Thomas Beecham called for a complete change of attitude: 'How is this to be brought about? Only by enlightening the public through the medium of the press.' That said, the prerequisites for this were lacking in Australia. 'I must confess that, with a few notable exceptions, I found the Australian papers to be without exaggeration the worst I have yet read in any so-called civilised country.' He continued by saying that one of the country's shortcomings was not to allow even the slightest criticism of its institutions:

> But until Australians are made acquainted with the deficiencies in their national way of life, how is it possible for them to realise that they have a long way yet to go before they can claim an intellectual and cultural equality with other nations?[143]

Beecham already had one author in mind whom he thought could contribute to this change of mentality. Born in Manchester in 1888, Neville Cardus had begun as a cricket commentator and then, without ever having studied music, became the music critic for the *Manchester Guardian*. Cardus had first visited Australia as a sports reporter in 1936, but accompanied Beecham on his 1940 Australian tour as a music critic. Cardus stayed in Australia until 1949 and became a national institution as a writer for the *Sydney Morning Herald*, and as the presenter of the radio programme 'The Enjoyment of Music'. Although Australia's first professional music critic, Thorold Waters, made fun of his English colleague's lack of specialist knowledge and his flowery language,[144] it was probably the very fact of Cardus's cricket connection that helped to raise the appreciation of music by bringing it closer to the sport the public worshipped.

Cardus also wrote for the *ABC Weekly*, a radio magazine with a wide circulation that was the Australian counterpart of the BBC's *Radio Times*. Since December 1939, Curt Prerauer had been in charge of a double-sided 'Music Page' for the *ABC Weekly*; in his first article, 'How Music Has Progressed in Australia', he had praised local developments.[145] He emphasised the country's many talented artists, adding that radio was making a significant contribution to their promotion. In straightforward language, illustrated with anecdotes, Prerauer covered basic questions such as the difference between absolute music and programme music, 'What is Meant by Interpretation in Music?', 'Should Opera and Lied Be Translated?', and 'The Difference Between Serious, Light and Entertainment Music'. Prerauer also called for radio broadcasts of opera. However, after the arrival of Cardus, he was given less and less space for his Music Page until it disappeared altogether. Under pressure from the rest of the press, advertisers boycotted the magazine and it was temporarily suspended on financial grounds in June

1941.¹⁴⁶ After the war, Prerauer published in other magazines such as the *Wireless Weekly* and *Tempo*.

The argument between Thorold Waters and Neville Cardus is typical of the development of Australian music criticism, in which amateurs were just as involved as specialists. Wolfgang Wagner, who in his youth had earned pocket money as a sports reporter, ran into Cardus at concerts in Sydney. When they discovered that they both shared a love of music and sport, Cardus encouraged Wagner to write music reviews as well. From 1946, reviews by Wagner appeared in the *New Citizen* and from 1947, in the *ABC Weekly*. After the death of his wife Charlotte, Wagner married the trained singer Eva Mayer, who had moved to Sydney when she separated from her husband. By coincidence, she lived in the same block of flats as Cardus. One of the early highlights of Wagner's career as a critic was the ambitious special issue that he published as co-editor of the *Canon* on the occasion of Arnold Schönberg's seventy-fifth birthday in 1949, after devouring Dika Newlin's book *Bruckner, Mahler, Schoenberg*. With contributions from prominent authors like René Leibowitz, Fritz Stiedry, Otto Klemperer, Eduard Steuermann and Rudolf Kolisch, this publication opened up new perspectives for Australian musical life.¹⁴⁷ Roger Covell called it 'a document of historical significance at a time when Schoenberg's work was hardly known in this country'. Wolfgang Wagner, who died in 1969, had also written for the *Australian*, and was the Australian correspondent for *Musical America* and *Opera* (London). An influential critic in his own right, Covell paid tribute to his colleague: 'Affable, informed and kindly, bringing with him to his adopted Australia the best elements of his Viennese background, he was the valued friend of a large number of resident and overseas musicians and music-lovers.'¹⁴⁸ And Bernard Heinze noted: 'Australia has lost one of the finest intellectuals of music the country has ever possessed.'¹⁴⁹

Aside from Wagner, Walter Dullo and Alphons Silbermann also wrote about music in the *New Citizen*. Hans Forst, who had formerly penned music reviews for the *Neues Wiener Tagblatt*, continued this practice for the *Sydney Morning Herald* and the *Australian* in his new homeland. He put his greatest effort, however, into building up a music archive for the *Sydney Morning Herald*, which today counts as one of the best in the world. Shortly before his death, he brought out a little book in which he gave political interpretations of the operas of Mozart, Beethoven, Wagner and Bizet. The *Sydney Morning Herald*'s obituary included the following: 'Forst identified with Australia from the outset and never revisited Europe. He never underrated Australian music and culture, and in recent years regarded Australia's contemporary composers as the equal of any.'[150]

Although during the war he had still been regarded as a 'typical German', Curt Prerauer, like Forst, continually wrote in defence of Australian musical life. In the 1950s, when he accompanied his wife, the singer Maria Wolkonsky-Prerauer, on her European concert tours, he often gave lectures on the state of music in Australia. In his articles for *Nation* and the *Sun* newspaper, he supported Richard Meale and Peter Sculthorpe and was thus partly responsible for their international recognition. Much of his writing was done in collaboration with his wife and published under the name 'C.M. Prerauer'. When he died in 1967, his colleague Kenneth Hince wrote the following tribute:

> It stands to his credit and his sense of responsibility that his own strongly-held views were generally applied to really constructive work – not the sort of tame politeness which performers call constructive criticism, but the kind of positive comment that advances the practice of music in a community and provokes intelligent discussion of its issues.[151]

Maria Prerauer continued her own work as a music critic with the *Australian* and later the *Bulletin*, until her death in 2006.

In 1949, at Wolfgang Wagner's invitation, the twenty-four-year-old Fred Blanks had reviewed a Youth Concert for *Canon*. Blanks had just finished his chemistry studies and had also been studying singing. When Blanks spent two years as an industrial chemist in London from 1952, he discovered that very little was known about musical life in Australia. Accordingly, in 1955, he became the Australian correspondent for the *Musical Times* and, until 1992, regularly wrote three or four articles a year for this important specialist journal. By so doing, he learned to concentrate on essentials. In 1963, the *Sydney Morning Herald* invited him to join their staff, as he was a regular concert-goer with special interests in young musicians and the social history of music. He had emphasised these objectives in keynote articles a number of times.¹⁵² In 1988, after writing for the *Sydney Morning Herald* for twenty-five years, he was awarded the Order of Australia for his services to music. Even after retiring from the paper in 1996, he continued his musical activity by writing for the *Northern Herald*, *Quadrant*, *Soundscapes* and the *Northshore Times*. Having attended around 9,000 concerts since 1944, he had actually created his own valuable databank. This continuity was only possible because Blanks' profession as a chemist gave him financial security.

Melbourne was once the cultural capital of Australia, until it had to compete head-to-head with Sydney in the twentieth century. By 1890, the *Age* (founded in Melbourne in 1854) already had a circulation of 100,000 and was one of the world's most successful newspapers. Felix Werder was its music critic for seventeen years. 'My literary career was thrust on me by economics', he maintained, while explaining his sometimes unusual grammar and syntax: 'I do the same thing with music. It's not dependent on style, but on content. You must have something to say, and people will listen to you.'¹⁵³ His predecessor as music critic for the *Age*, the composer Dorian Le Gallienne, had recommended Werder as his deputy in 1960;¹⁵⁴ as a consequence, Werder became the chief music critic after Le Gallienne's death in 1963. Like his predecessor, Werder was also an advocate of contemporary music. Although readers of the *Age* were accustomed to the fact that Werder was both a composer and a critic, his trenchantly formulated views were more radical than those of Le Gallienne, and even more orientated towards European standards, particularly those of the Continental mainland. He advocated performing early music with period instruments.

> In those days there was no Hogwood or Harnoncourt, only Sir Malcolm Sargent, Henry Wood and Beecham, who played Haydn symphonies with 100-piece orchestras. I once blasted Malcolm Sargent: 'That's not Bach that you're playing there. That's Malcolm Sargent, but not Bach! You need 12 or 16 and a completely different Baroque style!' We had a huge argument. But Sargent wrote me a letter and thanked me. We didn't agree, but he understood.¹⁵⁵

Werder received support from Bernard Heinze, who performed several of his orchestral works in Melbourne and Sydney, including *Brand: Symphonic Fragments*, *The Cranes of Ibicus* and *Tristrophe*. Werder became a part-time lecturer in musical aesthetics at the Conservatorium in 1966. In 1973, when he applied for a lectureship in composition, Heinze wrote a recommendation:

> I have been in close contact with Mr Werder since his arrival in Australia some thirty years ago. Since then he has earned for himself international recognition and approval as a composer, critic and author. His personal influence on public taste and understanding of music, particularly may I say contemporary music, has been of the highest importance to our musical development. As a lecturer he possesses a rare intellectual and imaginative approach to music which is the outcome of a cultivated, informed and disciplined mind. [...] He is utterly fearless in the expression of his beliefs and opinions.[156]

As with Brand, the character from the eponymous Ibsen drama, there were no compromises for Werder, only one thing or the other, black or white.

In spite of Heinze's support, Werder did not secure the position that he wanted. Instead of that – and once again on Heinze's recommendation – he was appointed a Member of the Order of Australia in 1976, only a year after the Order had been introduced. Only one other Australian musician had received this award: Heinze himself.[157] But Felix Werder's position with the *Age* was no longer secure. In 1977, he was dismissed after seventeen years on account of numerous complaints from the readers. 'In the end I had to lose. There were so many letters: "Werder has to go! He should go back to Germany, we don't need that here." So I just left.' Overnight, the number of performances of his works also declined. His successor at the *Age*, the music librarian Kenneth Hince, represented more conservative views. 'It was my mistake', said Werder on reflection, 'I tried to force a foreign culture on the people. [...] If you ask me now what's wrong with Australia, I would say: it's a country where people are perfectly happy with what they've got.'[158] Unfortunately, few readers are aware of Felix Werder's volumes of thoughtful essays discussing music in its political, philosophical and artistic context.

Music critics like Curt Prerauer, Felix Werder and Fred Blanks did not just mention symphony concerts in short paragraphs, but discussed them in comprehensive reviews. By treating music as an essential expression of culture, they were promoting the change of attitude that Thomas Beecham had called for. At the same time, concert and radio programmes broadened to include new features from other countries. The conductor Walter Susskind from Prague was already astounded in 1954: 'When I was in Australia eight years ago music in this country was a thing of the future; today it is very much a thing of the present. The development of music consciousness in Australia has been quicker and more intense than anywhere else in the world.'[159] Like the other musicians who had come to the country as refugees, the critics also participated in this qualitative leap by adopting standards that promoted a greater understanding of music and musical thought.

CHAPTER 17

'Land of Mine': New Compositions for a New Australia

In the 1930s and 1940s, Australian musical life still looked towards British models, whereby a combination of distance and conservative tendencies meant that developments in the United Kingdom were often adopted somewhat later. After the fall of Singapore in 1942, Britain's influence declined sharply. The loss of its largest naval base in the Asiatic region meant that Britain could no longer guarantee military security for the Commonwealth of Australia, so what until then had been unswerving trust in the motherland was now in crisis. In view of the Japanese threat, Australia chose the USA as its new protector. The stationing of American soldiers in Australia gradually changed its lifestyle: many old, familiar ways now appeared backward and provincial.

From 1945 onwards, the conductor Eugene Goossens was one of the key figures who helped the country to tap into the international repertoire and modern trends in music. Born in London, he had worked since 1931 in the USA, where he conducted the Cincinnati Symphony Orchestra for fifteen years. He was appointed as head of both the Sydney Symphony Orchestra and the Sydney University Conservatorium in 1946, which raised the status of contemporary music. At the time, many of the works he conducted, such as Stravinsky's *Rite of Spring*, Schönberg's *Verklärte Nacht* [*Transfigured Night*] and Prokofiev's Fifth Symphony had never been played by the orchestra before. Goossens' concerts were a huge success, particularly as audiences had gradually been transformed by the arrival of more European migrants after the war.

Refugee musicians who had arrived before 1945 also helped to open up Australia's musical life. Whereas from 1939 until 1945 they were forced to remain in the background, once the war was over, they could even contribute their own compositions, at first mainly in the areas of ballet and film. At that time, Australian films and film music were rare, as cinemas showed imported films from Europe or the USA almost exclusively. Of the few motion pictures that were made in Australia, most used music that already existed; and, as a rule, when international firms produced their films there, they brought their own composers with them. Thus, in 1946, it created quite a sensation when the major American company Columbia Pictures produced a film in Australia about the pioneer aviator Charles Kingsford Smith, and commissioned the music from a local composer: Henry Krips. The Americans entrusted the shooting of the film to the Australian company Cinesound, who may well have recommended this versatile musician, since he had already composed the music for their films *Gone to the Dogs* (1939), *Come up Smiling* (1939), *Dad Rudd, M.P.* (1940) and *The Power and the Glory* (1941). Krips created a big orchestral score for the new film; for instance, he underscored the daring Pacific crossing in a single-engine plane with triumphant brass fanfares. The commercial success of the film (entitled *Smithy* in Australia, and *Pacific Adventure* in the USA) was probably a factor in Krips receiving an even larger commission two years later: the music for *Sons of Matthew*, which was also set in Australia and became a popular success.

'The Back of Beyond': Film Music Pioneers

Sydney John Kay was even more significant for the development of Australian film music. He had already worked as a musician and arranger for several important film productions in Germany, not least *The Blue Angel* with Marlene Dietrich. In 1946, his music for the film *A Son is Born*, with Peter Finch in the main role, made people sit up and take notice. For instance, in a factory scene there are rhythmical machine sounds with xylophones and brass, reminiscent of Hanns Eisler's music for *Kuhle Wampe* [*Kuhle Wampe or Who Owns the World?*]. A year later, the Arthur Rank film company entrusted him with the music for *A Bush Christmas*, an adventure film with children in the main roles. 'In method, mood and idiom, it is more thoroughly and more delightfully Australian than any other full-length Australian fiction film that we have yet seen here', wrote the critic for the *Sydney Morning Herald*. 'John Kay's musical score is pertinent and observant, gently touching in little spots of comedy and tension in the right places.'[1] Another paper mentioned the perfect synchronisation:

> After the film was completed, Kay composed the score, timing each bar to the split-second. The MS was airmailed to London and recorded on the soundtrack by a 23-piece-orchestra conducted by John Reynders. So perfect was Kay's timing that most of the music was recorded with conductor Reynders merely checking his stopwatch and not seeing the actual image on the screen.[2]

A Bush Christmas was a great success, particularly with children – in London, Copenhagen and New York as well, and was chosen by the *Sydney Telegraph* as the best film of 1947. The screenplay was published in several languages in children's magazines and books,[3] and Chappell & Co. published a volume of musical excerpts from the film score.[4]

Kay particularly liked working with the director and producer John Heyer, today considered the father of the Australian documentary.[5] Their collaboration began in 1946 with *Native Earth*, a film about Australia's involvement in Papua New Guinea, and continued in further productions by the Australian National Film Board: *Journey of a Nation* (1947), a plea for the standardisation of the railways; *The Cane Cutters* (1948), a portrait of the sugarcane workers in Queensland; and *The Valley is Ours* (1948), a study of the Murray river. Once these films had brought him international recognition, Kay moved from the Film Board to the commercial Shell Film Unit, which offered him greater scope.

For this company, he made the legendary film *The Back of Beyond* (1954), which depicts the hard life of a mailman on the remote Birdsville Track and portrays the wide, almost totally unpopulated outback as a habitat for people of diverse cultures. On his long journey through the uninhabited land, also known as 'the Never Never', John Kruse meets a Muslim who uses camels as pack animals, and an Aboriginal Australian who takes him to the grave of a German Lutheran missionary. Kay's stylistically versatile music is suited to every moment of the action; for example, he introduces high strings when a flight of birds takes to the skies, woodwind tremolos are used to suggest animals that have died of thirst and a calling motif is repeated when two small girls are trying in vain to find their way in the desert. That year, *The Back of Beyond* became the first Australian film to receive the Grand Prix at the Biennale in Venice.

In those days, Australia did not have a film industry as such. There were more opportunities for local composers in television, which was launched in 1956, based on American and British models.[6] The composer Dorian Le Gallienne was engaged for the TV series *The Adventures of Sebastian the Fox* but, early in 1963, just as work started, he became seriously ill and had to look for a replacement. He remembered George Dreyfus, whose 1958 wind trio had struck him as being both intelligent and witty. Without further ado, he recommended the young musician to the director, Tim Burstall. Dreyfus later summarised Burstall's telephone call: 'I'd never thought of taking an interest in film music but an hour later Tim was on the doorstep and by one o'clock in the morning I was a film composer.'[7] The trust placed in him by Le Gallienne, who was also a critic, did as much to convince Dreyfus as the attractive fee, and he immediately set to work. He soon became used to timing himself with a stopwatch and, in the following year, he provided scores for no fewer than eight documentary films. As he found it easy to convert visual images into sound, Dreyfus regularly received commissions and eventually became one of the most sought-after film composers in Australia.[8] In 1964, he was able to give up his position as an orchestral musician and devote himself completely to composing.

George Dreyfus achieved real fame, however, with his music for the 1974 television series *Rush*. When Cliff Green, the author of the screenplay, suggested that these episodes from the nineteenth-century gold rush should be accompanied by contemporary folk songs, the composer bought the *Penguin Australian Song Book* published by John Manifold. One of the songs printed there, the 'Old Palmer Song', provided the inspiration for the title theme, which he played to the cast before the shooting started. In spite of its wide range, the melody, beginning with a double fanfare, caught on immediately. A recording of this work by the Melbourne Showband made the Australian Hit Parade, the first time a 'serious' composer had achieved this. Dreyfus, who scored his *Rush* theme for many different instruments, including a version for the flautist James Galway and an arrangement for the twelve cellists of the Berlin Philharmonic Orchestra, later maintained that he was inspired less by the 'Old Palmer Song' than by Siegfried's sword motif from Wagner's *Götterdämmerung*.[9]

Musical Example 4: George Dreyfus, *Theme from Rush*

'Vereinsamt' ['Loneliness']: Composing in Secret

In contrast to this success, whereby a short orchestral piece made the hit parade, other refugee composers from Germany and Austria had to wait for years before receiving any significant recognition. In late 1937, shortly after his arrival in Australia, John Kurt Kaiser did not anticipate the difficulties that awaited him when he submitted an article about the musical life in Japan and one of his own jazz compositions to the *Australian Music Maker and Dance Band News*. To hide his German origins, he dropped his surname, Kaiser. This was probably the first time that he used 'John Kay', which he adopted as his official name after the war. Based on his seven-month stay in Japan, his essay 'Music Life in Japan' described the playing of traditional instruments, the *samisan, koto, shakuhachi* and *taiko*. He then referred to the growing popularity of western jazz and dance music, and said that classical music, played by touring European artists or in the form of recordings, was also very sought after.[10] The same edition of the journal contained his score of 'Jammin' Dem Keys' in two versions: as a piano solo, and as an arrangement for piano, tenor saxophone, alto saxophone, trumpet, trombone, bass and percussion. The piece is in common time and in fast 'Jig Tempo'; its chromatic harmonies and effective piano voicing reveal an intimate knowledge of the works of George Gershwin. The arrangement, with a different piano part, shows Kay as an experienced arranger, which was exactly what he wanted the publication to demonstrate.[11] The two accordion arrangements that Henry Adler published in the same journal two years later,[12] 'Dark Eyes' and 'Lullaby', seemed less demanding than

Kay's compositions; however, they were not intended for professionals, but for the next generation of musicians at Nicholson's Piano Accordion Club.

In 1939, Henry Krips set 'A Waltz Refrain' to music, with lyrics by Harry Allen; the text expressed nostalgia for the old Danube metropolis, the city of music and love that was now just a distant memory.[13] In the following year, Hans Forst wrote a similarly nostalgic song: 'The Last Song of Vienna' called to mind his home city, one that was full of happy waltzes from morning to night ('The trees waved in waltzes/The birds twittered Strauss'). This happiness had now disappeared:

> What could your spell and your glamour enhance
> When you were asking the world for a dance?
> But by a fiend's hand your beauty was cleft
> Smashed your charm, ruins are left.

In 1940, Forst also submitted the song 'Goodbye, Johnny' for copyright, this time under the name 'Richard John'. A hit of the same name (lyrics: Hans Fritz Beckmann, music: Peter Kreuder) had been sung by Hans Albers in the 1939 UFA film *Wasser für Canitoga* [Water for Canitoga]. In this adventure film, the singer was thinking of a dead comrade whom he wanted to see again in the after-life:

> Goodbye Johnny, Goodbye Johnny, you were my best friend.
> One day, one day we'll be united again.

It can hardly be expected that Forst, who had come to Australia in 1938, knew the UFA film that premiered in Berlin in March 1939; he had probably chosen the same title by coincidence. Unlike the hit song from the German film, his own composition referred to the war: a woman takes leave of her partner, but tries to remain brave and not to cry. The text, written in fluent English, gives no reason for her departure. Only the music, an effective marching song, hints at the war. Like Krips, Forst also waited in vain for his work to be published. The manuscript has survived only in the National Archives of Australia.

Ray Martin had written popular songs like 'Hay Days' exclusively for his comrades in the desert camp at Hay; his works were intended to cheer up the internees. Cantor Boas Bischofswerder, however, had no time for this sort of fun. He regarded his internment as a deep injustice that robbed him of any cheerfulness. Guards on the *Dunera* had destroyed the golden pocket watch that had been given to him as a wedding present by his parents-in-law in 1920. Bischofswerder processed his own terrible experiences and those of his fellow believers by writing poetry in Hebrew. People, he felt, were treated like animals:

> We refugees were pushed to the lower part of the ship deck with sadistic brutality, like sheep before the herdsman's dog. They clubbed with their rifles like professional bandits. When one slipped over and fell, the ones that followed fell over him. When one cannot move further he has to fall. Right down the stairs soldiers stood with their rifles, the Sergeant with a big stick in his hands, ready to kill an ox.[14]

The fact that the sun still shone in the sky was regarded by Bischofswerder simply as bitter irony.

Musical Example 5: Boas Bischofswerder, *Phantasia Judaica*. Bars 9–11
(Archive of Australian Judaica Sydney)

He composed a *Phantasia Judaica* while he was still on board the *Dunera*. As no other instrument was available, he arranged the work without text for four high male voices. The leading role went to the man with the highest voice. The original is no longer extant; instead, there is an arrangement for violin and piano prepared by the composer in Hay in January 1941, in which presumably more ornamentation has been added to the solo parts. The piece begins with an eight-bar introduction in C minor, and in the following section the calm 4/4 rhythm changes to 3/4 time. In the lowest voice, there is a two-bar accompanying figure in floating, syncopated rhythm with the interval of a tritone in the middle. The other two accompanying voices take up this figure, but starting on different beats. Thus a pulsing, contrapuntal texture is created, outlining the C minor chord over eighteen bars. Above this, in the violin part, a broad melodic line unfolds that finally takes up the accompanying formula. In the second section, the violin part has a stronger rhythmic structure and is more highly decorated, and after a solo cadenza returns to 4/4 time. Nine bars later, there is a faster section in C major in compound duple (six-eight) time, but the bright key of C major soon changes to A minor, until finally the opening accompanying motif returns in the main key of C minor. This short composition shows that Boas Bischofswerder understood his musical craft and was able to create an attractive piece from simple elements like the two-bar accompanying motif.[15] One could regard the melismatic solo part as specifically Jewish, in that it resembles the synagogue chants. It is not known whether this version of the *Phantasia Judaica* was ever performed in Hay or Tatura. Bischofswerder's last compositions, seven rabbinic blessings for the wedding service for solo voice with piano or organ accompaniment, date from August 1944.

Prior to 1940, Walter Würzburger had performed exclusively as a jazz musician and popular entertainer. Helmut Newton, his room-mate in Tatura, characterised him as humorous and sociable. But internment changed the young musician, making him more serious. Würzburger might have been thinking about his parents, who had remained in Germany; he had not heard from them for a long time. He opened up this melancholy side to his friend Uwe Radok, and also told him about his early compositions; for example, he had once set a poem to music: 'Es war ein Kind, das wollte nicht zur Schule sich begeben' ['There was a child who would never/ agree to go to school'].[16] Radok encouraged him to start composing again and handed him the Nietzsche poem 'Vereinsamt' ['Loneliness'], which seemed appropriate for the internees' situation:[17]

> The crows cry
> And fly to the city
> Soon it will snow –
> Comfort to the one – who still has a home!
>
> Now I see you stand there rigidly,
> Looking back! For how long already!
> What a fool you are
> To flee before winter comes in the world?

The world – a folly,
Like a thousand deserts still and cold!
Who that loses,
What you have lost will stop nowhere.

Now you stand there
Cursed to winter wandering,
Like the smoke,
Searching for the cold skies.

Fly bird, sing your song
Like the Desert-Bird-Tone
Hide, you fool, your
Bleeding heart in ice and scorn!

Die Krähen schrein
Und ziehen schwirren Flugs zur Stadt;
Bald wird es schnein, –
Weh dem, der keine Heimat hat![18]

The six verses of this poem speak of the irreversible loss of one's *Heimat*. The monologue of the lyrical 'I' in the middle verses is framed by two almost identical outer verses: the first is directed at people who still have a country to call their home, while the last pities those who have lost their *Heimat*. Whoever suffers this fate is condemned to eternal wandering, indeed cursed. Walter Würzburger set this sombre poem to music in Tatura in 1941. According to Radok, this marks the beginning of his mature phase as a composer, marked in particular by chamber music (a string trio and two string quartets). The Nietzsche setting starts in C minor and then wanders restlessly through many different keys. Thus, for example, the second verse begins in G minor and ends in D major; from there it progresses chromatically to E flat major, and with the words 'cursed to winter wandering' it quickly lands in the distant key of B minor in order to get to F sharp major in the fifth verse ('Fly bird, sing your song'). The dynamic climax is reached with the words 'Hide, you fool, your bleeding heart in ice and scorn!' Then the melody descends, slows down and flows back again to the opening key of C minor for the last verse. The closing sigh, 'Weh dem, der keine Heimat hat' ['Woe unto him, who has no home'] was especially significant for the composer, as he repeats it.

This lament for the loss of *Heimat* is like a premonition of the news that Walter Würzburger was to receive a few months later: an article in the New York publication *Aufbau* informed him about the death of his father in Poland.[19] Siegfried Würzburger died in the Łódź Ghetto on 12 February and his mother on 3 May 1942. News of the death of his father, an organist who had immersed himself in the works of Johann Sebastian Bach, might have strengthened the son's resolve to devote himself to his father's field of interest, classical music, more intensely than before. He had already taken theory lessons with Werner Baer in Singapore. Now, during his military service, he began to study music part-time at the Melbourne University Conservatorium. When he met Uwe Radok again in December, he was in a bad mood; but discussions about music and improvisation were able to distract him. Radok noted in his diary at the time: 'For him the company of real musicians is alone important.'[20] Only in such company did Würzburger's loneliness disappear; in serious music alone did he find his *Heimat*.

During the war years, Sydney John Kay also turned from popular to serious music. When the Weintraubs Syncopators disbanded, he took a job as an arranger with the Colgate-Palmolive Radio Unit but, in 1944, in addition to the ballet music for *Lot's Wife*, Kay also wrote a *Fantasy* in D minor for large orchestra. His own company, Microphone Music Publishers, published a facsimile of the score. The scoring was for two flutes, two oboes, two clarinets, bass clarinet and cor anglais, four horns, two trumpets, three trombones and strings. The composition, marked *molto marcato*, begins like a Bach organ work, with woodwind and strings playing the main theme in unison, at first fast and then slower. After a few bars, this Baroque discipline gives way to whole-tone chords and a more gentle texture, with the performance instruction *espressivo, dolce*. The theme appears in a variety of tone colours, as in a series of variations, and stylistically it approaches impressionism and Richard Strauss. Larger sections are limited to core themes until, towards the end, a true *fugato* in B flat minor (reminiscent of Max Reger) returns to the serious mood of the opening. What motivated Kay to write this eleven-minute-long orchestral work which, in spite of its secure artisanship, often sounds like film music? Had he been inspired by the Leopold Stokowski Bach arrangements for the Disney film *Fantasia*

(1940)? Or had the Royal Air Force air-raids on his home city of Leipzig caused him to pay homage to Johann Sebastian Bach? The work's sad, faded conclusion might suggest this. It is also possible that Dr Floyd's praise for a broadcast of his ballet music *Lot's Wife* motivated this free composition. Sydney John Kay was again flexing his muscles and showing his capabilities; one simply wonders when and where he learned his compositional craft. Frequent use of the performance instruction *incalzando* [pressing forward] may be regarded as typical of him. Kay's *Fantasy* in D minor was recorded by the Sydney Symphony Orchestra under the direction of Percy Code at the end of 1944, but it has since been forgotten.[21] Both the score and a recording of the work are in the National Library in Canberra.

'Dear land we love': New Beginnings

In Australia, a period of cultural awakening began with the end of the war as the Labor government encouraged large-scale immigration. In 1945, Arthur Calwell, Australia's first Minister for Immigraton, declared that, within the next two years, Australia would take in 2,000 Holocaust survivors. Although Jewish passengers were not to exceed 25 per cent of the total per ship, the *Johan de Witt* was an exception: it arrived in Sydney in March 1947 with around 600 Jewish passengers on board, including the conductor Hans Zander. In spite of the restrictions, by the end of 1948, approximately 5,700 European Jews were able to migrate to Australia.

The refugees who had decided to stay, most of whom had been naturalised, no longer yearned wistfully for Europe, but committed themselves to their new country. Kurt Herweg, for example, obtained his citizenship in March 1946 and felt like a 'proper Australian'. In the same year, he wrote the music for two short films for the department of immigration in which the government actively campaigned for new immigrants by referring to the predominantly sunny weather and good sporting conditions in Australia. The films, entitled *Australia and your future*, were directed by Catherine

Duncan, who had once been so enthusiastic about the *Sergeant Snow White* revue. In 1948, Herweg also wrote the 'Australian Surf Life Savers' March' (lyrics: Ken Taylor) for the sport-loving country, and it was published in the same year. As these life savers were regarded as heroes or even gods (*Sun Gods of the Surf* was another film made at the time), the composer chose the 'heroic' key of E flat major for his marching song, which began with drum rolls.

After Werner Baer had won ABC's 1943 composing competition with his song 'Sounds of Europe' (lyrics: Simon Hochberger), in 1951 he was also successful in the competition for a new national anthem on the occasion of the jubilee of the Federation of Australia, when a replacement was sought for 'God Save the King'. In 1860, Carl Linger of Adelaide had already provided an effective alternative with his 'Song of Australia', which was again recommended to the Prime Minister in 1929, without success. Was this because Linger was German-born? The ABC ran further anthem competitions in 1943 and 1945. In the 1951 contest, Werner Baer won second prize for his 'Salute to Australia' to words by John Wheeler, a solemn marching song that ended with 'Australia, I love you!'.[22] The first prize was won by Henry Krips for his 'Land of Mine', also to words by John Wheeler, which ended with the words: 'Land of Mine! Freedom's shrine –/God be with you, dear land we love!'[23] Despite its success in the competition, 'Land of Mine' did not replace 'God Save the King'. Australians were notoriously reluctant to change their national anthem: after several unsuccessful attempts to do so, 'Advance Australia Fair' did not replace 'God Save the Queen' until April 1984.

The refugee composers from Europe wanted to contribute to the development of Australia's musical life with new works. Given the limited opportunities for performance in such a sparsely populated country, even Australian composers were only able to survive if they had some other main profession, for example, as an employee of the ABC. One of them was John Antill, composer of the ballet music *Corroboree*. Werner Baer, who succeeded him as the NSW Supervisor of Music in 1951, had his musical roots in the late nineteenth and early twentieth centuries. He wrote effective songs, ballads and film music, without providing any new stylistic impulses. The works of the composer and physician Ernst

Figure 38: A versatile radio-man: Werner Baer composing in his office. (NAA: SP1011/1, 952)

Kaufmann were also conventional. In 1944, the ABC broadcast one of his symphonic movements and in 1948, his Piano Concerto in E minor with Marjorie Hesse as soloist, which the conductor Joseph Post pronounced to be 'in a rather outmoded style'.[24] When John Antill judged Kaufmann's String Quartet Op. 9 and his Second Piano Concerto Op. 10 in similar terms, there were no further performances, and his works were eventually forgotten.[25] Rudolf Werther's comprehensive song-writing met with the same fate: specialists like Post and Antill described it as imaginative ('some excellent ideas') and well-crafted ('fairly well designed [...] good standard') but also as illogical in parts.[26] By contrast, new impetus was provided by a younger generation of composers, who came into the limelight around 1960 and received significant support from some receptive critics.

Moses Mendelssohn's Legacy: Felix Werder

Born in Berlin in 1922, Felix Werder was one of the younger generation. As a child, he had helped his father by copying scores, but it was his Australian internment that turned him into a composer. Encouraged by discussions with Walter Würzburger and Erwin Frenkel,[27] he made the gradual transition from imitative composition to his own, independent style of writing. He owed to his father, his first and only composition teacher, his understanding of synagogue music, of Carl Philipp Emanuel Bach and of the writings of Moses Mendelssohn – a monument to this great German Jewish philosopher stood in front of the school that Felix had once attended in Berlin. After the war, Schönberg and Bartók (whose music he already knew from Europe) also became his models. When he applied for permanent residency in Australia in autumn 1945, he described himself as an interior designer (he had begun to study architecture in London, because his father dismissed music as a profession). However, when Boas Bischofswerder died in 1946, his son applied for citizenship and called himself a musician. In spite of his earlier training as a violist, Werder's real strength was in music copying and composing. Henry Krips invited the young man to move from Melbourne to Sydney, in order to work for Radio 2GB as an arranger for Clive Amadio and his quintet. He accepted this invitation and was soon also assisting Werner Baer as a repetiteur for the 'Singers of Australia'. Baer arranged more radio contracts for him, and Sydney John Kay, who was always on the go, engaged him as a bass player for the Stork Club – Werder later admitted that he had learned a lot from this jazz experience.

Through his wife Mena, whom he had married late in 1944, Werder had access to a Melbourne circle of communist sympathisers that included Mena's brother, the writer Judah Waten, and the painter Noel Counihan. In Sydney, too, he associated with socio-critical writers and painters. He became acquainted with the violinist Szymon Goldberg at the Studio of Realist Art (SORA), where Goldberg (the former concertmaster of the Berlin Philharmonic) was exhibiting his collection of paintings by Emil Nolde and Käthe Kollwitz. Werder told him that he had sent some new compositions to the ABC, but that they had been returned as supposedly unplayable. Goldberg looked at the music and forwarded it, together with a letter of recommendation, to Eugene Goossens. When the conductor premiered his *Balletomania*[28] with the SSO in October 1948, it encouraged Werder to continue composing.

As he could not live from composing and arranging, in 1947, Werder started training as a music teacher in Melbourne. After that, he taught at various schools for several years, but with limited success owing to his unconventional style. He was much more interested in writing his own works, in which, apart from Goossens, he was also supported by Musica Viva. Following a Werder Portrait Concert in Melbourne's Assembly Hall in March 1949, the Musica Viva Players performed string quartets and a violin sonata by the young composer in Union Hall in November the following year. The Paul McDermott Ensemble, which included Otti Veit, also played some of his works. In 1954, Werder completed his First Piano Quartet, which was performed by members of the Melbourne String Quartet with the highly capable Walter Susskind, who was at that time chief conductor of the VSO.

Compositionally, however, Felix Werder felt himself to be at a dead end, so he immersed himself once more in the works of Bartók. His *Three-part Fantasias for String Trio* and the String Quartets Nos 4, 5 and 6 are among the fruits of this new orientation. A performance of the Fourth String Quartet by the Pascal Quartet in Paris was the first overseas performance of one of his works and encouraged him considerably. The Sixth String Quartet, composed at the invitation of Musica Viva, brought him even greater recognition when it was premiered by the Austral String Quartet at the Adelaide Arts Festival in 1964. In his introductory text, the composer wrote that this music expressed the spiritual disillusionment of the time. 'The work has five parts in which all run into each other. These parts are like acts in a play and indeed the thematic materials are the actors which unfold the story.' Since the actual theme is only recognisable at the end, Werder compared the work with the development section of a sonata whose exposition was missing. He outlined the five sections of the quartet as a dramatic narrative:

First Part – Allegretto
Unsentimental harsh statements. The tragedy of a theme that can't make up its mind.

Second Part – Lento – molto adagio
Climbing fugatos, puritanical in their emotions, but full of humanity.

Third Part – Allegro precipitato, sempre pizzicato
The theme struts like Oedipus, defiant, cool and unaware of fate.

Fourth Part – Adagio
The hopelessness and the collapse under the weight of enemies, perhaps the end.

Fifth Part – Allegro molto
Death, where is thy sting! With almost Handelian bravado the spirit of the new Promethean theme leaves the stage. Curtain.[29]

The critic Roger Covell described the Sixth String Quartet as a 'brilliant and masterly piece which has some claims to be Werder's most completely satisfying achievement'. He felt it was just as dense as his earlier compositions, but had more rhythmic variety and a more highly developed sense of time and space. There was also greater economy and conciseness in the thematic invention. 'The opening theme of the first movement is of structural as well as intrinsic melodic importance.' He noted that this revealed the influence of Ravel and Britten, while echoes of Bartók were to be heard in the *pizzicato* Scherzo and in the finale.[30] In retrospect, Werder himself said he had to write this quartet in order to free himself from Bartók's overpowering influence. But only in orchestral works such as *Brand*, *Laocoon* and *Monostrophe* did he find his own voice.[31]

Here, literary impressions took the place of musical influences: *Brand* refers to Ibsen, and *Laocoon* to Lessing. *Monostrophe* was played by the VSO and a year later by the SSO, and 'immediately established itself as the first large-scale orchestral work written in Australia to come within touching distance of the musical manners of the middle of the century'. According to Covell, the composition represented 'the impulses of a powerful and agile intellect, quick in perception, impatient of repetition, mercurial in mood, rapidly moving from momentary tenderness to perhaps defensive parody'.[32] In 1963, Werder's *Elegy for Strings* (together with several other Australian works) was performed by the VSO under Bernard Heinze in the presence of Queen Elizabeth II and Prince Philip at the Sidney Myer Music Bowl. *Laocoon* was heard even beyond Australia, when Walter Susskind conducted it at the Aspen Festival in America.[33]

This composer's growing influence was partly due to the fact that from 1960, he had established himself as 'possibly the most reviled and feared critic in Australia.'[34] Felix Werder attributed his critical artistic standards to thinkers and artists like Aristotle, Herder, Descartes, Spinoza, Moses Mendelssohn, Rousseau, Lessing, Carl Philipp Emanuel Bach, Schönberg and Kandinsky, but many of his Australian readers regarded this as presumptuous and arrogant. Nevertheless, he reached a relatively wide public. 'Everyone reads him.'[35] With his trenchant views, Werder was also the most important catalyst at the 1963 Composers' Seminar in Hobart, Tasmania. Twenty-two Australian composers and several music critics took part in this seminar, which has since been recognised by some as the birth of the musical avant-garde in Australia. Here, composers who until then had worked in isolation in different parts of the country had the opportunity to get to know each other and to hear some of their works for the first time. Roger Covell was also present and experienced Werder as a radical spokesman for the young composers. Through his often provocative comments, Werder questioned conventions and challenged his colleagues, including Peter Scultl horpe and Larry Sitsky, to show more artistic courage.[36] Years after this historic meeting, Werder's house in Melbourne remained an important meeting place for young composers. In ABC broadcasts, he and Keith Humble, a Leibowitz student who had returned from Paris, articulated their criticism of Australian musical life. 'Liked or disliked, charmed or not by him, the fact remains that Werder *cares* about music and the state of music in Australia, and he is prepared to crusade for causes in which he believes.'[37]

The Art of Adaptation: George Dreyfus

Six years younger than Werder, George Dreyfus was one of the composers whom he encouraged to explore new paths. Like Arnold Schönberg, Dreyfus had never had any academic training in composition, but had taught himself to be a creative musician by imitating his favourite composers. After his first woodwind quartet in 1948, he soon wrote more neo-classical chamber music. Although Dreyfus found Australia artistically uninspiring,[38] he rejected his father's wish to return to Europe, because he thought it would be easier for him to get a position as a bassoonist in Australia. Even when, around 1958, with the support of Kurt Wöss, then chief conductor of the VSO, he began to turn away from models like Hindemith, Britten and Shostakovich and move closer to the avant-garde, he still sought his musical mentors in Europe. This was the start of one of the transformations in style that are characteristic of George Dreyfus. He always created what was required, which is why he compared himself in his chameleon-like art of adaptation with Hanns Eisler, Erich Wolfgang Korngold, Stefan Wolpe and Kurt Weill – and with Zelig, the character from the eponymous Woody Allen film.[39]

In 1961, in order to perform the new works that he was getting to know through imported records and the German music magazine *Melos*, Dreyfus founded a New Music Ensemble in Melbourne. He was strongly impressed by an LP record of the chamber cantata *Le Marteau sans Maître* by Pierre Boulez and *Zeitmasse* for woodwind by Karlheinz Stockhausen. As he acknowledges, meeting these avant-garde works made him a modern composer 'overnight'.[40] They inspired him to write his twelve-tone *Music in the Air* (1961) and *From Within Looking Out* (1962) for the unusual combination of soprano, flute, viola, celeste and vibraphone. On hearing *Music in the Air*, Curt Prerauer saw in Dreyfus an Australian composer who, like Richard Meale, was seriously looking for a contemporary idiom.[41] In 1966, in an article for *Melos* on the promising beginnings of contemporary music in Australia, Prerauer wrote that the ABC's new head of music, John Hopkins, was partly responsible for this turnaround, and mentioned as composers Richard Meale, Nigel Butterley and Ross Edwards, as well as George Dreyfus.[42]

Dreyfus was convinced that Australian composers needed a greater effort to establish international contacts, so he welcomed it when, in 1960, Professor Donald Peart of the University of Sydney reactivated the Australian arm of the International Society for Contemporary Music (ISCM). Together with James Murdoch, Dreyfus started a branch in Melbourne, which presented its own new music concerts from 1965. Shortly before, he had given up his orchestral job and decided, with his mother's encouragement, to earn his living as a composer. A UNESCO scholarship enabled him to travel to Europe for six months in 1966. His original plan, to study with Karlheinz Stockhausen, became an extended educational tour that included numerous contemporary music concerts and no less than eighty-one operas.[43] To his amazement, however, Dreyfus discovered that the West German public showed little interest in new music. He was hardly back in Australia when he was able to take up another scholarship in 1967, one that allowed him to spend eighteen months at the National University in Canberra and devote himself exclusively to composition, which was an enormous encouragement and confirmation for him. 'It was the first time in Australia's cultural history that an artist was practically "nourished" by a public institution, i.e. solely to create art.'[44] For Dreyfus, it was not the money that was most important, but the feeling that he was needed. His major project in Canberra was to write his first big orchestral work, a symphony. Even before he left for the capital, the ABC promised to open its 1968 season with this new work. Before the premiere, however, the composer revealed in a press release that he had used the melody from a cigarette advertisement as the main theme. In his review, Felix Werder described this as tasteless. Dreyfus had lost a valuable supporter; yet, out of sheer delight in provocation, he titled his next orchestral work *Jingles*, although it made absolutely no reference to advertising music at all.

Musical Example 6: George Dreyfus, Symphony No. 1 (Allans Music Melbourne)

Together with his contemporaries Peter Sculthorpe, Nigel Butterley and Richard Meale, by 1970, George Dreyfus was one of the Australian composers of whom great things were expected. They received support from the critics Covell (who promoted Sculthorpe and Dreyfus in the *Sydney Morning Herald*) and Prerauer (who referred to Richard Meale and Dreyfus in the *Nation*). Unlike Werder, who continued to look primarily to European models, Dreyfus, Meale and Sculthorpe were prepared to deal with genuine Australian themes and materials. In this sense, the *Sextet for Didjeridu and Wind Quintet* by George Dreyfus was one of the key works in contemporary Australian composition.

In October 1970, David Cubbin, the flautist from the Adelaide Wind Quintet, advised the composer that they planned to commission a piece for didjeridu and wind quintet. The idea had occurred to them while performing a concert for Aboriginal people. Until then, such concerts were unknown but, when the government gave the indigenous people equal rights in 1967,[45] a programme was organised in which the Adelaide Wind Quintet alternated with various Aboriginal groups from the Northern Territory. The experiment was successful, and after the event the organisers asked themselves why white and Aboriginal musicians could not perform together and whether a suitable work could be written for this purpose. The commission went to George Dreyfus, whom the members of the Adelaide Wind Quintet knew was an experienced wind player.

But the composer was perplexed: 'The project was a new world to me. I had had no interest in Aboriginal or any other ethnic music.'[46] But, since the piece was to be premiered at the 1971 Musica Viva Spring Festival in Canberra, he set to work immediately. He sought advice from experts on Aboriginal music, who thought the idea of whites and blacks making music together was utopian: their styles of music were so different as to be incompatible. Nevertheless, Dreyfus travelled to Maningrida in the Northern Territory, where the didjeridu player George Winunguj introduced him to the traditional instrument. It has a very peculiar sound: over a long, deep bass note the performer blows higher overtones that can be varied both rhythmically and in terms of tonal colour. After returning to Melbourne, the composer sent a letter to the didjeridu player outlining the basic idea for his piece. His intention was to insert the player's own

George Dreyfus

material into a three-part structure. His only constraint was the duration, not what he played in this time. What was sought was not an adaptation to a western scheme; rather, in the spirit of peaceful co-existence, the two musical worlds were to run parallel, side by side. As the composer put it:

> You might ask, why should the black be the slave and have to follow the whites? And I would answer and say that the whites are the slaves, tied down, as it is in the European music tradition, by the composer's notated instructions, whereas the didjeridu player is unfettered, free to give full expression of his feelings through music.[47]

The whites play contemporary music with the distinctive sound textures then characteristic of compositions by Ligeti and Penderecki. By contrast, the Aboriginal musician, coming from a different musical tradition, retains their freedom of expression, and is able to react at will. As distinct from the five woodwind parts, which are precisely notated, the didjeridu part is merely scored with a thick band of black:

Musical Example 7: George Dreyfus, *Sextet for Didjeridu and Wind Quintet* (Dobson 1978, p. 132)

The *Sextet for Didjeridu and Wind Quintet* was performed as planned at the 1971 Musica Viva Spring Festival, and introduced by the composer. When the CD was launched, Roger Covell wrote that, already at the premiere, he was relieved to hear that Dreyfus had not understood his commission merely as a joke or harmed the integrity and dignity of either style of music:

Contrary to some people's thinking on the subject, I do not believe that this work represents the beginning of a slow but steady integration of traditions. I think that it is probably the first and final step of this particular kind.[48]

In fact, the composition embodied a cultural-political concept, namely the idea of multiculturalism based on mutual respect. Prime Minister Gough Whitlam was in office when the work was conceived; it was Whitlam who finally abolished the White Australia Policy in 1973. In keeping with this respect for 'others', George Dreyfus had the didjeridu part played only by Aboriginal people. As a statement about tolerance and respect for an indigenous cultural tradition, the *Sextet for Didjeridu and Wind Quintet* gains symbolic weight and credibility in that it was written by a composer who had to leave his own homeland because of racial persecution. The adaptation to Australian conditions that he himself had undergone was not something that he automatically demanded of others.

Figure 39: The composer George Dreyfus in October 2009 with the author in Berlin. (Author's Archive)

Two Diametrically Opposed Concepts of Music

In Australia, George Dreyfus and Felix Werder both lived and worked in the same city (Melbourne), not far from one another; but they represented different, even opposing types of composer. Werder – like Mozart and Schönberg – denied every external influence on his artistic creation. He kept his personal fate quite separate from his music which, thanks to his father, he saw essentially as rooted in philosophy and aesthetics. The close link to European traditions is clearly evident in the titles of his works, which relate to Greek antiquity (*Agamemnon, Electra's Strophe, Bruchstücke, Dionysos, Dionysos Dithyramben*), to European painting (*La Primavera after Botticelli, Cranach's Hunt, Dürer, After Watteau, Der Blaue Reiter*), architecture (*Dom zu Speyer, Sans Souci*) and literature (*Wessobrunner Gebet, Dramaturgie, The Cranes of Ibicus, Hölderlin Songs, Belsazer, Nietzsche Poems*). These titles verify the high educational standards, derived from Lessing and Schiller, that Werder associated with his music. In the light of this intellectual orientation, he felt he was better understood in Europe than in Australia. 'It was easy for Bartók to write Hungarian music – he had an 800-year-old tradition of Hungarian music behind him. It is just as easy for me to write Jewish music – I have 3,000 years behind me. But how can an Australian write Australian music? Australian music doesn't exist, because there is no Australian folk music.'[49] He was deeply disappointed that modern (colonial) Australia was giving up its former European orientation in favour of a stronger connection with Asia. Although, in the final analysis, Peter Sculthorpe was responsible for this paradigm shift, Werder considered him to be 'the best and most intelligent of the Australian composers'.[50] Although he initially praised Dreyfus as 'brilliantly witty', after the premiere of his Symphony No. 1, Werder expressed mostly contempt: Dreyfus, he believed, was driven not by any inner creative urge, but by a need for success, for public acclaim.

Werder will not have been left unaffected that, in 1963, Curt Prerauer wrote about one of his most important compositions that '"Monostrophe" might once have had claims to be Australia's most modern work, but not any more in the era of Sculthorpe and Meale and others.'[51] A year later, in a lengthy article headed 'New Stature in Creating', Roger Covell referred to Werder's String Quartet No. 6 and *Monostrophe* before adding: 'But the compositions that seem to represent, or at least promise, developments of a truly distinctive kind belong to Werder's immediate juniors: Meale's "Las Alboradas", Butterley's "Laudes" and Sculthorpe's "Irkanda IV" are notable examples of these.'[52] For this leading critic, Felix Werder was no longer a pioneering composer. After the publication of his *Fantasias for String Trio*, he was regarded almost as an old, academic master – in his review, Prerauer called him 'Dr Felix Werder'.[53] Werder's colleague Kenneth Hince wrote: 'The publication of this trio should help to establish Werder's reputation where it belongs. His mastery of his craft and the degree of his learning put him quite certainly in the front rank of Australian composers.'[54] But this bitter-sweet praise indirectly suggested that others provided more important impetus. In March 1966, the Australian Composers' Guild presented 'A Panorama of Australian Composers' in Melbourne's Assembly Hall in the order of traditional, moderately modern and avant-garde composers: George Marshall-Hall, Fritz Hart, Alfred Hill and Percy Grainger were regarded as traditionalists; Helen Gifford, George Dreyfus, Richard Meale and Larry Sitsky counted as avant-garde, whereas Werder, together with Arthur Benjamin, John Gilfedder, Dorian Le Gallienne and Margaret Sutherland were considered to be moderately modern.

Dreyfus, who at the time was still regarded as avant-garde, did not adhere to this progressive ideal for very long. His extensive European tour of 1966 led him to question whether the avant-garde circle was not an isolated, ivory-tower elite. Written after his return, his Symphony No. 1 manifested his new orientation, in which communication with the public was more important than the use of new or experimental sounds. Dreyfus wanted to be understood by his audience and therefore used familiar musical elements. The juxtaposition of various styles in this symphony – the slow movement cites Mahler's *Song of the Earth* – which irritated not only Felix Werder, can be regarded as a forerunner of polystylistic postmodernism. In contrast to Werder, Dreyfus considered his own orientation towards the listeners' expectations as an obvious necessity. He passionately espoused Australian topics such as Captain Cook, the convicts and the gold rush. He needed to be needed, so he was also prepared to write utility music for amateur groups such as wind or mandolin orchestras. Whereas Felix Werder spoke very seriously about the educational function of music, Dreyfus also wanted, not least, to entertain. He noted his life's motto, which he took from Oscar Wilde, above the second movement of his Second Symphony: 'Life is too serious to be taken seriously.'

However, there are points of contact between Werder and Dreyfus in the field of opera, which both men regarded as the core of their work. Werder disclosed to the musicologist Thérèse Radic that he would like to have written more operas, but that lack of opportunity had led him to use the corresponding ideas for 'instrumental dramas'.[55] Nevertheless, some of his operas were performed: the one-act *Kisses for a Quid* (1960, libretto: Alan Marshall) at the Q Theatre, Melbourne and *Private* (1970, libretto: Peter Rorke), commissioned by the ABC for television. For *Banker – A Music-Theatre*, for four solo voices and organ, he used an astonishingly contemporary text by Aeschylus (from *Agamemnon*):

> For War's a banker, flesh his gold,
> There by the furnace of Troy's field,
> Where thrust meets thrust, he sits to hold
> His scale, and watch the spear-point sway.

Musical Example 8: Felix Werder, *Banker – A Music-Theatre* (Author's Archive)

Commissioned by the Australian Opera, Werder's one-act opera *The Affair* (libretto: Leonard Radic) had its premiere, together with Larry Sitsky's

Lenz, on 14 March 1974. It was the first Australian opera staged at the Sydney Opera House, which had opened just a few months earlier. The composer had especially asked the librettist to provide a contemporary topic. The action took place in an Australian embassy. At the centre was a play within a play, whereby onstage a portrait of the queen changed into a portrait of Prime Minister Whitlam. On the first night, people laughed because Whitlam was in the audience. Werder had made reference to the operatic traditions of Gluck and Mozart, and characterised his music as a consciously deceptive Rococo of the twentieth century.[56] However, the consistent lack of melodic arias annoyed the public and, on account of their differences of opinion, Leonard Radic did not write any more libretti for him.[57] Moreover, the number of Werder's public performances declined abruptly when the *Age* ended his critic's contract in 1977. It made little difference that, in the previous year, the composer had received the coveted Order of Australia on the recommendation of Bernard Heinze. From that point on, Australian presenters rarely included Werder's compositions on their programmes, and Allans Music, his Melbourne publisher, did not print any more of his new works; this was their reaction to the loss of power by a man whose criticism they had once feared.

George Dreyfus, whose works continued to be published by Allans,[58] also turned to opera around the same time as Werder. While an earlier Casanova project stalled in its initial stages, and hopes of a collaboration with Patrick White were scuppered, in 1966 Dreyfus completed his two-act opera *Garni Sands* (libretto: Frank Kellaway), for which Hans Werner Henze's *Elegy for Young Lovers* served as a model. But before it could be premiered, the composer received a commission from the Australian Opera Company for a one-act opera. He accepted and, at the end of 1970, had completed *The Gilt-Edged Kid* (libretto: Lynne Strahan). When, by the end of 1971, there was still no production in sight for this commissioned work, Dreyfus protested loudly. Only later did he realise that his hot-headed appeals were hindering, rather than promoting, any opportunities for performance. *Garni Sands* was eventually performed in front of university audiences in Sydney and Melbourne in 1972, and was even invited to New York,[59] but the rejection of *The Gilt-Edged Kid* was a wound that did not heal quickly. Faced with this 'new Dreyfus affair', he defiantly wrote a chamber version of the opera for his own ensemble.⁶⁰ In his 1984 volume of memoirs, he called the idea of an Australian opera 'impossible nonsense' and swore, in future, only to visit opera houses outside Australia.⁶¹

After his deep disappointment over *The Gilt-Edged Kid*, George Dreyfus turned to his German Jewish roots which, until then, as he admitted in his memoirs, had hardly interested him. In the 1980s, while reading an essay on the former German Foreign Minister Walter Rathenau, he suddenly discovered in the combination of Judaism and German patriotism similarities to his own father, who had died in 1951 at the age of fifty. Like Werder, this loss at an early age now haunted him. In 1991–1992, funded by an Australian scholarship, he wrote his opera *Rathenau* which, in its form and dramaturgy, combines elements of film and oratorio. Based on a German text by Volker Pilgrim, the work premiered on 19 June 1993 at the State Theatre in Kassel, Germany, and was highly acclaimed by both the public and the press. For the first time since Marshall-Hall's *Stella* in London in 1914, an Australian opera was performed outside Australia. At the reception on the first night, the Australian ambassador read out a greeting from Prime Minister Keating: 'I hope that the opera enjoys a successful season there, and that Australian opera lovers will soon have the opportunity to enjoy the opera in their own country.'⁶² To this day, the wish remains unfulfilled. It was probably realised that a reaction anything like the one in Germany⁶³ was unlikely in Australia.

Before this, Felix Werder had already travelled regularly to West Germany. In 1974, in ironic reference to the well-known saying 'Bella gerant alii, tu felix Austria nube' ['Others might wage wars, but you, lucky Austria, marry!'], once coined for the imperial marriage policy of the Habsburgs, he founded the Australia Felix Ensemble, with whom he toured Europe (mainly West Germany) in order to present the works of Australian composers. In this way, some of his own works were still performed, albeit overseas. In hindsight, the composer regarded these tours, which he organised for about twenty years, as the best time of his life. 'So I now transferred my whole intellectual life back to Germany.'⁶⁴ Several of these tours were financed by the West German Goethe Institute, so in exchange, the ensemble, which consisted partly of jazz musicians, also presented new German music in Australia. Like George Dreyfus, who toured Germany and Australia in the 1990s with a *Surviving* Show and presented works by other persecuted composers such as Günter Raphael and Hans-Ulrich Engelmann, Felix Werder also became an engine of German–Australian cultural exchange and was now able to interest German publishers in his works. The Australia Felix tours ended around 1994, but Werder was still invited to give lectures, for example at the German–Australian Music Conference in Dresden in May 1996. At this conference, tribute concerts were dedicated to the two composers, George Dreyfus and Felix Werder. Memories of exile now united these otherwise so very different musicians.

Figure 40: The composer Felix Werder in 2008 in his flat in Camberwell/Melbourne. (Author's Archive)

CHAPTER 18

'Happily ever after': Hidden Contributions to Cultural Diversity

It is widely recognised and appreciated that composers, critics, musicologists and performers fleeing Central Europe as refugees contributed significantly to musical life and standards in the United States. The British, too, have for some years now acknowledged the contributions of 'Continental Britons' such as Hans Gál, Berthold Goldschmidt, Hans Keller, Karl Rankl, Franz Reizenstein, Mátyás Seiber, Peter Stadlen and Egon Wellesz.[1] As Daniel Snowman has observed, 'Britain's musical life was possibly the greatest single beneficiary of the Hitler exiles who settled there'.[2] Of the German-speaking refugees who arrived in Australia between 1933 and 1945, the 'Dunera Boys' became the most widely known, although so far, music has received little attention. When the music sociologist Alphons Silbermann spoke on this topic in Dresden in 1996, he expressed the sceptical view that Australian musical life had followed the English model too closely to admit any German influence at all. He felt that only in the area of chamber music had Musica Viva brought about a noticeable improvement.[3] Silbermann had voiced similar disappointment in Sydney as early as 1953. He and other German Jewish refugees had learnt the bitter lesson 'that we were only allowed to participate in a non-creative way, as onlookers, as paying guests'. Only a few persons in this group had obtained minor university appointments here and there. 'But never were they called upon to participate in a way commensurate with their established position and reputation in Europe.' According to Silbermann, in those days leading positions in Australia, unlike in the USA, were given only to people from Britain. 'We from the Continent are as little in demand as are the Australians themselves. Irrespective of our degrees, our experience, our diplomas or our international reputations, we are kept away.'[4]

The fate of the Weintraubs Syncopators or of the conductor Adolf Brenner seem to confirm this negative view. It is probable that other artists mentioned in the preceding chapters, such as Werner Baer, Hans Blau, or Jascha Spivakovsky, might well have had far better careers in Europe. Edmund Kurtz, Tossy Spivakovsky and Peter Stadlen were therefore acting on good advice when they left Australia so early. For a long time, many of the new Australians were treated as second-class citizens. Even before he was naturalised, Werner Baer discovered that he could only become a 'proper' Australian by being a hard drinker and familiar with horse-racing,[5] which he was not. In other parts of the world, hardly anyone remembered the musicians who had emigrated to Australia. When the violinist Ellen Byk visited Otto Klemperer in the green room after one of his concerts at Melbourne Town Hall, she introduced herself with a big smile: 'I'm Ellen Byk.' But the puzzled conductor only answered: 'And I am Otto Klemperer.'[6]

The obvious influence of German-speaking exiled musicians on chamber music and on the development of Australian opera are the exceptions. As a rule, the effect of the migrants was less visible and affected Australian musical life only in conjunction with other influences. For instance, the opening up of the concert repertoire was due not only to the high proportion of immigrants among concertgoers, but also to the diminishing influence of Britain after the fall of Singapore. Although the British national anthem was played at the beginning of all concerts until 1974, by then a more multicultural Australia had already developed. Alphons Silbermann could not experience this, however, as he had left Sydney in 1957. On the other hand, those who remained in the country noted a growing appreciation of music and an astonishing improvement in musical standards.[7] More recently, there are even Australian musicians, like Brett Dean, who have returned voluntarily to their homeland after success in Europe.

The refugees who entered between 1933 and 1941, mostly under difficult circumstances, paved the way for a more liberal immigration policy. The many Holocaust survivors who came to Australia after 1945 benefited from this. Eventually, air travel replaced the long voyages by ship. Whereas in 1945 there were fewer than 15,000 people in Australia who had been born in Germany, by 1954 there were over 65,000 and by 1961 just on 110,000, or about 1 per cent of the total population. All in all, around 135,000 Germans migrated to Australia between 1945 and 1975. In the 1991 census, 112,000 people gave Germany as their country of birth. By the end of the 1980s, it

CHAPTER 18: *Hidden Contributions to Cultural Diversity*   431

was said that over 1.3 million Australians had at least one German ancestor; in fact, the demographic influence of the immigrants from Germany is greater than any other non-British or non-Irish group.[8]

The influx of Germans after 1945, followed later by many Asians, caused the less than spectacular achievements of the previous German Jewish refugees to fade still further. Their contributions were often made under the most difficult conditions, as the case of Sydney John Kay demonstrates. Encountering strong opposition in the field of music, this energetic and imaginative musician moved into other areas after 1945. He used the revenue from his films to finance the Mercury Theatre, which he founded in Sydney in 1946, together with the then unknown actor Peter Finch, the theatre critic Allan Ashbolt, radio producer John Wiltshire and commercial radio manager Colin Scrimgeour. The visionary Kay, to whom the security authorities once attributed an 'abundance of confidence',[9] was the driving force.[10] 'He infected me with his burning passion for drama', Finch later reported, 'his titanic energy was a contagion. We were wild-eyed with fanaticism, desperate that something be done to drag the Australian theatre from the doldrums it had been wallowing in.'[11] Already, in 1944–1945, Kay had managed a children's theatre that he headed and financed with Rosemarie Benjamin.[12] This project used dance arrangements by Gertrud Bodenwieser and, although it had to be closed down after an epidemic, this in no way diminished Kay's passion for the theatre. Like the Mercury Theatre that Orson Welles and John Houseman started in New York, like the Old Vic and the American Repertory Company, the Australian Mercury Theatre wanted to present world theatre on a professional repertory stage. Kay made his debut with Peter Finch in July 1946 in three one-act plays by Gogol, Lope de Vega and Kleist (*The Broken Jug*). The performances took place at the Sydney Conservatorium, where Goldner's Musica Viva had given its first public performance the year before. Both the press and the public reacted with enthusiasm. In addition, the two artists founded a Mercury Club and a theatre school, where Finch taught the Stanislavski method, which he had learned at the Habimah Theatre during his time in the army in Tel Aviv. Kay was not naturalised until the end of September, and it was January the following year before he finally received his citizenship papers. The following commentary appeared in the *ABC Weekly* of 22 March 1947:

> Let it Rip-ley
> Congratulations to composer and arranger John Kay, ex-Peruvian, who received his Australian naturalisation papers a fortnight ago. John claims that, having been naturalised for only two weeks, he holds the record as the youngest 'Australian' musician the Commonwealth has ever known: even Mozart was seven years of age before he possessed perfect pitch! John showed me a letter he wrote to his brother in South America informing him of his change of nationality. He finished it thus ... 'Good-bye, and Peru to you.'[13]

As they were unable to find a suitable venue for the Mercury Theatre, the actors organised themselves as the 'Mercury Mobile Players'. Kay designed a portable stage for them that would fit into a truck. The *New Citizen* wrote about the artists:

> Under the enthusiastic guidance of their manager, producer, costume-designer and composer Sydney John Kay, they are meant to be 'mobile' which is indicated in their name. They carry their sceneries, stage accessories and talents out to the factories and schools where, under some scheme of the Education Department they perform to workers or students. It's all still in its infancy but it is a promising beginning which, in the long run, may carry them to what they feel should be their ultimate goal – the foundation in Sydney of a 'People's Theatre' of the kind that was known in Central Europe as 'Volksbuhne'.[14]

In another article, a month later, Walter Dullo introduced Kay as a pioneer of Australian theatre.[15]

On 11 August, the Mercury Mobile Players put on Molière's *The Imaginary Invalid* with Finch in the title role; Kay directed the whole production and also provided the stage music. Always self-assured, he invited Sir Laurence Olivier, who happened to be in Sydney on an acclaimed tour with the Old Vic Company. Olivier accepted, and on 18 August came with his wife to a performance for about 400 workers in a glass factory during their lunch break. He was deeply moved by this experience. The press reported:

> Sir Laurence Olivier said that in congratulating the Mercury Mobile Players he was breaking his rule not to comment on the work of professional colleagues. He said he was so impressed that he would do all he could to help them to establish a permanent theatre.[16]

However, the Mercury Mobile Players lost one of its greatest assets in November when, at Sir Laurence Olivier's invitation, Peter Finch travelled to London, where he launched an international career.

In spite of this setback, and although the Mobile Players only lasted until 1950, Kay did not give up, as he regarded his theatre as part of a long-range strategy: 'Only a good professional theatre will form a basis for the development of a future indigenous Australian playwright and maybe a typical Australian acting style, and eventually an artistic expression of Australian nationhood.'[17] In February 1952, he hired a proper home for his theatre in downtown Sydney, the old St James Hall that belonged to the Workers' Educational Association. A telegram arrived promptly from New York: 'Good Luck your enterprise regards + Vivien and Lawrence Olivier'.[18] The new Mercury Theatre was a co-operative: all the actors got a share of the profits, which was a sensation.[19] Nonetheless, Kay did not by any means limit himself to proven crowd-pullers. For the opening of the freshly renovated auditorium, he chose a work by the Roman author of comedies, Titus Maccius Plautus. He gave the role of a courtesan to the young Ruth Cracknell who, like Finch, later became a star. He himself provided the costumes and the music for this production.

The press described the Mercury Theatre as 'a kind of miracle'. Kurt Sternberg, the former director of *Sergeant Snow White*, wanted to support the project with a film, *Theatre in Australia*.[20] But it soon became clear that the theatre would not survive without public funding. In spite of mounting financial problems, in July 1953, when Kay put on the comedy *The Happy Time* by Samuel A. Taylor, the *New Citizen* wrote:

> The indefatigable Sydney John Kay has produced yet another play … under circumstances which would have been more than ample justification to any other theatrical manager to 'throw in the sponge'. It is common knowledge that the Mercury Theatre is on the verge of locking up and that desperate efforts are being made to avoid its going out of business. This paper said once before, and is repeating it now, that we new citizens have, as it were, a moral obligation to do everything in our power to support Mr Kay's theatre, if for no other reason than to put to the practical test our continuous complaints of a 'theatrical drought' in this city.[21]

But even this appeal could not prevent closure, in the absence of public funding. Kay made efforts right to the end to save it by investing all his own money, to the extent that his family could not even afford decent meals and his wife Lois had to take a job as a secretary.[22] At the end of 1953, he had to bury his theatre dream and close the Mercury Theatre. In the space of two years, it had presented 305 performances of twenty-nine plays by authors such as Shakespeare, Dickens, Strindberg, Chekov, Schnitzler, Wedekind, Shaw, Maxwell Anderson, Kästner, Anouilh, Franz Molnar, Jean Cocteau and Christopher Fry.[23] The repertoire also included the 'Informal Musical Topicality', *Happily Ever After*, for which Kay himself had written the music and the text, and in which the title song contained the significant lines:

> In the trot of daily strife
> Ev'ryone has ambitions,
> But our modern conditions
> Make it hard enough to survive – so
>
> In our struggle through the day
> Let us keep our illusions
> Let's keep out all intrusions
> Of reality on our way.

After the closure of the Mercury Theatre, Kay concentrated more than ever on film music for his livelihood. In 1952, he had written the music for the film *Broken Barrier*, which dealt with racism in New Zealand. In 1954, he devoted himself to the afore-mentioned documentary film, *The Back of Beyond*, the feature film *Long John Silver* (dir. Byron Haskin) and to the animated cartoon *Bimbo's Auto* (Eric Porter). The following year, he completed the music for the adventure film *Captain Thunderbolt* (Cecil Holmes) before he left Australia for England in June, where he had been promised contracts by Louis Levy, Alfred Hitchcock's film composer. During the stopover in Los Angeles, Kay stayed for a few days with Franz Waxman, an old colleague from the Weintraubs Syncopators, who had become a successful Hollywood composer. The two of them had orchestrated Friedrich Hollaender's music for *The Blue Angel*. In London, Kay discovered that Levy was ill; he died in 1957. But Ralph Smart, the director of *Bush Christmas*, helped Kay to obtain television contracts, so he decided to stay in Britain and sent for his wife and their son Anthony, who arrived in London in 1957. Kay had great success with his music for

CHAPTER 18: *Hidden Contributions to Cultural Diversity*   435

the twenty-six-part science fiction television series *The Invisible Man* (Dir. Ralph Smart, based on the novel by H.G. Wells).

I only heard about the diverse activities of this musician relatively late. At the end of 2003, I learnt through the German Society for musical performing and mechanical reproduction rights (GEMA) that a son of Sydney John Kay's was still living in Sydney, so I contacted him straight away. Anthony Kay, who was born in Sydney but grew up in London, was surprised and delighted that someone was interested in his father. In February 2004, he visited me in the National Library in Canberra, and brought all his father's manuscripts and tapes in his little car as a present for me. (This material was subsequently handed over to the National Library.[24]) In return, I was able to tell him many new things about Kay's early years. He shook his head in disbelief when he heard that his father had described the Weintraubs Syncopators as the Beatles of the interwar

Figure 41: Sydney John Kay around 1960 with his tape-recorder in London. (Anthony Kay, Sydney)

years. On one of the tapes, one can hear his father's voice: in a broadcast for Radio Zurich arranged by Henry Barger, the band's former manager, Kay talks about the group's beginnings in Berlin in German with a Saxon accent. In the National Film and Sound Archive, we watched several films for which Kay had written the music. Tony told me that he and his father had been to concerts and visited museums in Europe. Later, when Tony went on a world trip, his father warned him against visiting Australia, where he might be threatened with conscription and possibly action in Vietnam.

Sydney John Kay never returned to Australia. After several operations and a heart attack, he died in London in 1970. His death went almost unnoticed in Australia. But Sybil Baer, Werner Baer's wife, received the sad news from Stefan Weintraub. In a letter to Kay's widow she wrote: 'Our grief is real and our hearts heavy [...]. How can that huge, ebullient man, with his star just around the corner, be gone? That gentle, loving, kind, hard-working, idea-laden man? It's true.'[25] Encouraged by Sybil Baer, Lois Kay returned to Sydney with her son, where only a few people were still aware of her husband's achievements. Lois Kay was not present when the former members of the band, Adolf Fisher, Emanuel Fisher, Stefan Weintraub, Horst Graff and Cyril Schulvater, met in Sydney in 1976. Leo Weiss died that year, and Schulvater three years later. A year after Stefan Weintraub's death in 1981, Werner Baer reminisced about the famous band in a radio broadcast.[26] In 1986, he recorded for the ABC, with precise, 'swing' piano playing, internment songs like 'Hay Days' and 'Say Hay for Happy', as well as his own compositions, 'It's hope that keeps us going' and 'In corrugated iron huts'. He engaged the seventy-three-year-old Manny Fisher as the violin soloist for 'It's hope…'. When I visited Fisher in August 2000, he was eighty-seven years old and marked by illness. From 2004, I was able to continue my voyage of discovery with Tony Kay. We met Addy Fisher in his furniture shop in Oxford Street; he still lived in the flat that he had once shared with his brother. They were the last living members of the Weintraubs Syncopators. Manny Fisher died in 2006, and his brother a year later.

The trumpeter Ady Rosner, who once played with the Weintraubs, had survived by the skin of his teeth in the Soviet Union. In autumn 1973, he tried to evoke the vanished musicians by forming a group called the 'Weintraubs Sons' that performed on Berlin's Kurfürstendamm, but without lasting success. Seven years after the film by Klaus Sander and Jörg

CHAPTER 18: *Hidden Contributions to Cultural Diversity*   437

Süßenbach, I made a new attempt by informing the venturesome Berlin ensemble, the Neuköllner Oper,[27] about the fate of these musicians. The upshot was a revue titled 'Weintraubs Jazz Odyssey' in November 2007; Tony Kay travelled from Sydney to see it and, surprisingly, so did Manny Fisher's son Michael, who now lives in Zurich. Both children were from Sydney, but had never met. Michael Fisher had his father's trumpet with him, which the young actor who played Manny Fisher brought to life again. The meeting was very moving.

Figure 42: The second generation of the Weintraubs Syncopators: Tony Kay (right), son of Sydney John Kay, and Michael Fisher, son of Manny Fisher, in December 2007 on the occasion of the Weintraubs Revue in Berlin. (Author's Archive)

It is to be hoped that more steps will be taken to rediscover the musicians who were once exiled from Germany or Austria and then vanished in foreign countries. In Australia they contributed, in some cases significantly, to the cultural diversity of the country where they all lived happily ever after, at least some of them. Even Dullo chocolate is still available.

Notes

Chapter 1: Australia: So Far, and Yet so Near

1. Stadlen 1990, 128.
2. *Weintraubs Syncopators: Bis ans andere Ende der Welt* [Right to the Other End of the World]. A film by Klaus Sander and Jörg Süßenbach (WDR/Westdeutscher Rundfunk 2000).
3. Dümling 1995.
4. This opera was performed in 1870 by members of the Adelaide Liedertafel in a concert given for the German Imperial Franco-Prussian War Relief Fund. McCredie 1988, 254f.
5. Dümling 2000.
6. A large number of files at the National Archives of Australia have been opened and digitised at the author's initiative and can be accessed online (see italicised NAA files in Short Biographies).
7. Benz 1991.

Chapter 2: 'Oh sacred Art': On the Status of Music

1. Tr Walter Meyer; quoted in Julian Johnson, *Out of Time: Music and the Making of Modernity* (Oxford: Oxford University Press, 2015), 171.
2. Dullo diary, 23 May 1923.
3. ibid, 15 July 1923.
4. ibid, 28 March 1926.
5. Kampe 1992, 18.
6. In November 1931, of the *c.*1,700 professional musicians who made up the Bavarian Music Association, well over 1,000 were unemployed. Polster 1989, 10.
7. Silbermann 1989, 32.
8. ibid, 52.

9. ibid, 60.
10. Schildberger 1925.
11. Rürup 1995, 193.
12. ibid, 220.
13. Kampe 1992, 13.
14. Rürup 1995, 211.
15. ibid, 256.
16. ibid, 158.
17. Statistics on religion and nationality as well as on student hardship are from Rürup 1995, 160ff.
18. According to Baer this was an eight-room flat. 'Berlin revisited' 1959.
19. Together with a partner, he founded the fur business Baer & Salomon, and owned several houses. Communication from Sybil Baer, Sydney.
20. At the time, the family is said to have possessed two grand pianos. Werner played on the second one, imitating what Fritz played on the first. Trevor 1950.
21. 'Berlin revisited' 1959.
22. Baer 1983, 195.
23. Brooks 1956, 15.
24. Smith 1992, 22.
25. Baer 1983, 195.
26. Brooks 1956, 15.
27. According to the testimonial of the Künstlerhilfe [Artists' Assistance] of the Jewish Community, on 1 December 1938 (Sybil Baer).
28. Rave and Wirth 1961, 652.
29. Ansco Bruinier was the brother of Franz Servatius Bruinier, Bertolt Brecht's first composer.
30. Dümling 2004.
31. The story of Addy Fisher 2003.
32. Shabtai Petrushka (Siegmund Friedmann). Geisel/Broder 1992, 184ff.
33. Spivakovsky 1985a.
34. Interview with Felix Werder 11 October 1995, Berlin. The recordings were re-issued. Bergmeier 2001, 129ff.
35. Botstein 2003, 46.
36. Rabinovici 2000, 39.
37. Botstein 2003, 49.
38. Franz Mittler (1893–1970), composer, musician and lyricist, published *Zwei lustige Klavierstücke* Op. 2, *Kleine Walzer* Op. 4 and *Phantasiestück* Op. 5 with Universal Edition. Information from his daughter, Diana Mittler-Battipaglia.
39. Fritz Lunzer wrote the libretti for operettas like *Leute von Heute* and *Das Strumpfband der Pompadour*.

40. 'Endlich ein Kapellmeistergesetz!', *Österreichisches Kapellmeister-Journal*. Official publication of the Conductors' Union, Austria. vol 5, series 1, June 1934.
41. They had also given French names to both Marcel's older brothers, Oscar (*b*.1892) and Jacques (*b*.1894).
42. Genée 1992, 69.

Chapter 3: Failed Integration: Getting out of Germany, 1933–1937

1. Dullo diary, 12 April 1933. This meant that the family could no longer afford domestic servants.
2. Silbermann 1989, 108.
3. Bair 1984, 83.
4. Heyworth 1988, 462.
5. Berthold Goldschmidt in Traber/Weingarten 1987, 61.
6. Prieberg 1982, 44f.
7. For an English translation of this reference see Prerauer's ABC personnel file, NAA: SP173/1, PRERAUER, CURT.
8. Dümling 1994, 90.
9. See Berlin Address Book for 1932/33, and the entry under 'Address of last Residence' in Prerauer's Certificate of Registration.
10. Prerauer's documents accompanying his application for Australian citizenship include his German passport, issued in Charlottenburg on 5 June 1931, and his British Certificate of Registration, issued on 19 June 1933. NAA: A446, 1958/44648, 75.
11. Heer 2008, 102.
12. Zander cites excerpts from the references of Bruno Walter ('I have known Mr Hans Zander for years and it gives me great pleasure to testify to the value his co-operation has meant to me. As Opera Conductor, as a musician of great abilities, I remember his activity with gratitude') and Furtwängler ('I can warmly recommend Mr Zander as an artist of the first rank with a great mastery of his work') in an advertisement in *AMN*, 1 July 1947, 12.
13. Charles Berg's father, Richard Berg (*d*.1929) had also been a repetiteur at the Berlin Municipal Opera.
14. Questionnaire for Röder/Strauss 1983, p 2, in ZA.
15. 'Berlin revisited' 1959, 7.

16. Brooks 1956, 15.
17. Questionnaire for Röder/Strauss 1983, 2, in ZA.
18. Baer 1983, 194.
19. Dates taken from questionnaire for Fürsorge-Zentrale no 20212 of 20 May 1938. CAHJP, A/W 2590, 28.
20. Nagel 2001, 135.
21. *Regensburger Anzeiger* no 98, 1931/32. City Archives, Regensburg, Plank Collection.
22. *Regensburger Anzeiger* no 107.
23. See Cast Lists of the City Theatre, Regensburg. City Archives, Regensburg, Plank Collection.
24. The uncle, Franz Arnold, was born in Znin.
25. Brockhaus Encyclopedia of 1898.
26. See Herweg's declaration before the Aliens' Tribunal. NAA: ST1233/1 (Kurt Herweg), N33902.
27. Oral history interview with Charles Berg, March 1986. State Library NSW, Sydney, CY MLOH 437/109. Style and orthography follow original sources, even where this might be grammatically incorrect.
28. Questionnaire, Charles Berg for Röder/Strauss 1983. In ZA.
29. Galliner 2004, 129.
30. Dümling 1994, 91.
31. Kater 1998, 49; Martin/Alonzo 2004.
32. Kater 1998, 28.
33. Luise Rainer, who was later successful in Hollywood, led a competitive, all-female band in this film. Hans Albers would win the competition and finally marry the beautiful rival.
34. Kater 1998, 55.
35. Hans Blüthner in Polster 1989, 31. Also Kater 1998, 87.
36. Fetthauer 2004, 115.
37. According to his daughter, a warrant issued for his arrest had nothing to do with racial persecution, but rather with the jealousy of a rival. Interview with Susanne Gabor, 4 March 2004, Melbourne.
38. Kater 1998, 87.
39. 'Buhu, es ist zum Weinen', *Das Schwarze Korps* (25 November 1937), 12. Polster 1989, 66.
40. Communication from his brother Kenneth Ward (originally Karlrobert Würzburger), 16 March 2001.
41. Wolfssohn 2004.
42. Silbermann 1989, 29.

Notes: Chapter 3

43. See Adolf Brenner, Faktor, Frischer und Adolf Spivakovsky. Heinrich Adler's father was also called Adolf.
44. Salomon Brandmann also called himself Fritz Brandmann after becoming a German citizen in 1908.
45. See Hans Bader, Hans Blau, Hans Edelmann.
46. See Heinrich Max Adler and Heinrich Krips, Heinrich Portnoj.
47. See Kurt Herweg and Kurt Kaiser; Kurt Prerauer.
48. See Richard Forst and Richard Goldner.
49. See Werner Baer and Werner Katz.
50. Silbermann 1989, 33.
51. Interview with Ilse Blair, 20 July 2000, Melbourne.
52. Interview with Adrian Factor, 11 March 2004, Melbourne.
53. Strauss 1980, 317.
54. Büttner 1988, 14.
55. See the reconstructed membership list in Galliner 2004, 288–310.
56. Dreyfus 1984, 8.
57. Letter from Isabella Colin to the author, 19 March 2001.
58. Büttner 1988, 14.
59. Shapiro 2000.
60. Silbermann 1989, 92.
61. ibid, 93.
62. Blanks 1997.
63. Geisel/Broder 1992, 196.
64. Dreyfus 1984, 11.
65. Silbermann 1989, 15
66. Akademie 1992, 219.
67. 'Berlin revisited' 1959.
68. Statute of the Cultural League of German Jews, in Akademie 1992, 221.
69. Kampe 1992, 24.
70. Letter from the President of the Kammergericht [Court of Appeal] to Schildberger on 13 June 1933. Schildberger Papers, Box 3.
71. Galliner 2004, 150f.
72. *The complete poems of Heinrich Heine: A modern English version by Hal Draper* (Frankfurt/Main: Suhrkamp Insel, 1982), 66.
73. Mosse 1999, 23f.
74. *Berliner Tageblatt* (15 June 1929).
75. Hirsch 2010, 10.
76. This company owned what was then the biggest ship in the world, the *Leviathan*, which had been launched as the *Vaterland* in Hamburg in 1913.

77. Akademie 1992, 387.
78. Geisel/Broder 1992, 227.
79. Volker Kühn, 'Zores haben wir genug ... Gelächter am Abgrund', in Akademie 1992, 107.
80. 'Berlin revisited' 1959.
81. See List of Orchestral Members in Bergmeier 2001, 400.
82. S. Petrushka in Geisel/Broder 1992, 186f.
83. Testimonial for Chief Cantor Boas Bischofswerder. Archive of Australian Judaica, University of Sydney.
84. Report of the Jewish Refugees Committee of 28 June 1941. NAA: A367 (Bojas Bischofswerder), C75808.
85. Aldermann 1987.
86. Now Greatorex Road.

Chapter 4: On the Other Side of the World

1. See Jeannie Gunn's novel *We of the Never Never*, translated into German in 1927.
2. Voigt 2000, 15.
3. The death of the Australian explorer was also the subject of a novel, *Voss* (1957), by the Nobel Prize winner Patrick White, as well as of an opera of the same name (1986) by Richard Meale.
4. Covell 1967, 11.
5. Kisch 1937.
6. 'Australien' 1937, 28.
7. ibid, 43.
8. Jurgensen 1992, 11–110.
9. See 'Going Overseas' in Whiteoak 2003, 302–4.
10. O'Neill 1974.
11. Waters 1951, 116.
12. Alomes 1999.
13. 'Madame Orff-Solscher. Life in Germany', *Argus* (15 November 1930).
14. Whiteoak 2003, 475.
15. 'Dr von Keussler as Conductor', *Argus* (17 August 1933); 'Keussler. Broadcast concert next week', *Argus* (16 September 1933).
16. 'Appointment to St Patrick's', *Argus* (15 December 1933).
17. Information from Manuel Krönung.

18. His composition *Xenion*. A Symphonic Scene for large Children's Choir and large Orchestra, dedicated to Australian Youth, has as yet not been performed. Thanks to Manuel Krönung for this information.
19. 'Dr von Keussler. Gift from St Patrick's Choir', *Argus* (28 June 1935).
20. Gerhard von Keussler, Autobiographie. Keussler estate. Goethe- und Schiller-Archiv Weimar.
21. S.M. Normann, 'Gerhard von Keussler in Australien', *Zeitschrift für Musik* (August 1935).
22. Okrassa 2004, 192f.
23. Prieberg 1982, 263; Okrassa 2004, 323.
24. Krönung 2003, 67.
25. Bücken 1940, 218.
26. Tait concert agency's promotional material. Prompt Collection, National Library of Australia (ID 3531277).
27. *Table Talk* (Melbourne), quoted in Spivakovsky 1985a, 11.
28. Spivakovsky 1985a, 10.
29. *AMN* (21 January 1933).
30. 'Spivakovsky's Return', *AMN* (April 1933), 16.
31. Spivakovsky 1985b, 9.
32. Tregear 1997.
33. Radic 1986, 25.
34. NAA: A433 (Kurtz, E.; Spivakovsky, Jascha and others – Admission), 1943/2/1139.
35. See Max Hesse's Music Calendar for 1928.
36. Statutory Declaration by Adolf Spivakovsky. NAA: A659 (A. Spivak), 1939/1/9329.
37. 'M.I. Spivakovsky Interviewed', *AJH* (13 June 1935), 8.
38. 'Spivakovsky–Kurtz Trio: to settle in Melbourne', *AMN* (August 1934), 18.
39. In 1982, Michael Spivakovsky, the pianist's son, dedicated a written paper on the building to the Faculty of Architecture, Building and Planning at the University of Melbourne.
40. 'From Germany. Social Student Dr Dora Peyser', *SMH* (5 December 1934).
41. Dullo diary, 6 May 1935.
42. The Reich Citizenship Law: First Regulation (14 November, 1935). Alice Dullo's version differs slightly.
43. Dullo Diary, November 1935. Law for the Protection of German Blood and German Honour of 15 September, 1935. Again Alice Dullo's version differs slightly.
44. Dullo diary, 24 November 1936. In 1934, at an international conference for Jewish women, Dora Peyser had already referred to the persecution of Jews in Germany and suggested emigration to Australia. Fishburn 2005.
45. Peyser 1951. See also Regan 2005.

46. Dullo diary, 24 March 1937.
47. ibid, 31 March 1937.
48. ibid, 9 June 1937.
49. Emphasis in the original.
50. Emphasis in the original.
51. See the passports of Walter and Annemarie Dullo. NAA: A435 (Dullo, Walter), 1944/4/3968.
52. Fahrmeir 2003, 50.
53. Louise London, 'Britain and Refugees from Nazism: Policies, Constraints and Choices', in Steinert 2003, 75.
54. Fahrmeir 2003, 50.
55. Sherman 1994, 29.
56. Wasserstein 1999, 8.
57. Snowman 2002, 87.
58. Wasserstein 1983, 51.
59. ibid, 46.
60. Report by Berthold Goldschmidt, in Traber/Weingarten 1987, 57. For details of the arrival procedure, see Malet/Grenville 2002, 45–89.
61. See stamp from Harwich in Prerauer's passport. NAA: A446 (Curt Prerauer), 1958/44648.
62. Certificate of Registration dated 19 June 1933. ibid.
63. Goldschmidt in Traber/Weingarten 1987, 58.
64. Gerigk/Stengel 1940, 50.
65. NAA: C123 (Coper, Fritz), 6658.
66. NAA: A435 (Coper, Fritz), 1944/4/1616.
67. Flesch 2001, 7.
68. Aster 2007, 102.
69. NAA: A435 (Herweg-Hirsch, Kurt), 1946/4/586, 3.
70. Raab Hansen 1996, 200–22.
71. ibid, 74.
72. Flesch 2001, 53ff; Berghahn 1988, 141.
73. Elphinstone/Hancock 2005, 422.
74. ibid, 368f and 568f.
75. In the meantime, Abravanel had been living in Paris, where he had directed the world premiere of the Brecht–Weill ballet *The Seven Deadly Sins* in July 1933.
76. Gyger 1990, 303f.
77. Elphinstone/Hancock 2005, 437.
78. NAA: A907, 1934/9/43.
79. 'To Stay? Grand Opera Coy.', *Sun* (1 February 1935). Newspaper Clippings: Z401 Box 13. Noel Butlin Archives Canberra.

80. Buzacott 2007, 57f; Sametz 2001, 40f. See also 'Why De Abravanel Leaves', *Daily Telegraph* (19 June 1936).
81. *The Pearl Fishers* [*Les Pêcheurs de Perles*]. Freely adapted from Carré-Cormon by G. Bibo. Musical Arrangement C. Prerauer. Pno Arr Paris Choudens (VN 16726) © 1926.
82. Quoted from 'Maurice Abravanel Likes Australia', *AMN* (December 1946), 13. See also Durham 1989, 15–19.
83. Gyger 1990, 331.

Chapter 5: Mixed Feelings: Australian Reactions to German Racial Politics

1. Fischer 1989, 303f.
2. ibid, 320.
3. Corkhill 1992, 101f.
4. Konrad Kwiet, 'Inter-War German Community Life', in Jupp 1988, 490f.
5. The rabbi had founded one of the earliest Zionist societies in Australia, and in 1914 he had accompanied troops to Europe as a field chaplain.
6. Blakeney 1984, 106.
7. 'Hitler Bars Jews in Army', *AJH* (23 May 1935), 3.
8. 'Forced Emigration', *AJH* (6 June 1935), 11.
9. 'He confirmed first-hand all that I had read of the Nazi terror, and in his face I read something of what the sensitive artist had suffered.' 'M.I. Spivakovsky Interviewed', *AJH* (13 June 1935), 8.
10. 'In Hitler's Germany. The Brown Terror Rides On', *AJH* (1 August 1935), 6.
11. 'What Is A Non-Aryan', *AJH* (25 July 1935), 4.
12. The Kadimah is a Jewish cultural centre in Melbourne, founded in 1911.
13. 'Jewish Conductor in Melbourne. M. d'Abravanel receives welcome – and says something', *AJH* (20 June 1935), 10.
14. 'Hill came back to Australia and New Zealand to be one of the principal sources of German teaching practice in its first-hand form and not in its more familiar dilute form among English-trained musicians.' Covell 1967, 24f.
15. Pear 2001, 42.
16. 'Hits Symphony Orchestras. Grainger's Attack', *News* (Adelaide; 17 June 1935).
17. 'M. d'Abravanel back in Melbourne', *AJH* (4 July 1935), 5.
18. 'Address by d'Abravanel', *AJH* (7 November 1935), 9.

19. Blakeney 1985, 11.
20. Hugo Hertz, on 11 May 1936 to Premier of NSW. NAA: A434 (Admission of German Jews), 1949/3/7043, 15.
21. ibid, 7. Bartrop 1994, 31. The Canadian Immigration Officer Frederick C. Blair expressed similar opinions at the time.
22. Norman Bentwich (Council for German Jewry) to Dr Earle Page, Australia House, Aldwych W.C.1, 22 May 1936. NAA: A434 (Admission of German Jews), 1949/3/7043, 23.
23. Cullen 1981.
24. Rutland 1988, 174f.
25. 'Dora was the personification of the dedicated Social Worker.' Cullen 1981.
26. 'Personal', SMH (21 May 1937), 10.
27. Questionnaire Charles Berg for Röder/Strauss 1983. In ZA.
28. Letter from Anthony Berg to the author, 30 September 1996.
29. 'Music in Germany. Effects of Nazi Regime', *SMH* (8 April 1938), 13.

Chapter 6: 'Muss i denn, muss i denn zum Städtele hinaus?': Persecution and Flight

1. Loewald 1996, 72.
2. Quoted in Christoffel 1987, 210.
3. Today the Sophie Charlotte Secondary School.
4. Quoted in Christoffel, 211. At his school in Berlin, the son of the violinist Carl Flesch did not have any problems either and was all the more surprised about the antisemitism in Britain. Flesch 1990, 44 and 53f.
5. Schrieber 1934, 29.
6. Gerhard Splitt, 'Die "Säuberung" der Reichsmusikkammer', in Weber 1994, 43.
7. In February 1938, Goebbels complained that the 'de-judification' of the Reichsmusikkammer was progressing far too slowly. He was still finding 'opposition' in May 1938.
8. Testimony from the Josef Kumpan Private Cutting School dated 21 January 1936 (Tanya Makin, Melbourne).
9. Reichsmusikkammer file on Ellen Cohn. Bundesarchiv, formerly BDC, RK5, picture 1408–22.
10. Correspondence between Ellen Cohn-Byk and the Berlin Compensation Office. Register no 56322.

Notes: Chapter 6

11. Information by Rosemary Pattenden, Cambridge.
12. Fischer-Defoy 2008, 1.
13. Reichsmusikkammer file on Theodor Schoenberger. Bundesarchiv, formerly BDC, RK R24, picture 474.
14. In 1932, Bohnen moved to a flat at 50 Kurfürstendamm, where today there is a memorial plaque.
15. Quoted in Paul Guyer, *The Cambridge Companion to Kant* (Cambridge: Cambridge University Press, 1992), 1.
16. Sophocles, *Antigone*. Tr Reginald Gibbons and Charles Segal (Oxford: Oxford University Press, 2003), 76.
17. In March 2001, Eleonore Hertzberger, a former student who had to leave Berlin in 1933, called for the restoration of the gable in order to retain this important message for today's students.
18. Interview with Ilse Blair, 20 July 2000, Melbourne.
19. More information in her Application for Release from Detention. NAA: A367 (Ilse Baer), C81233.
20. Information from Ilse Blair, Melbourne.
21. Baer 1983, 194.
22. The population of Wilmersdorf was 13 per cent Jewish, whereas in Charlottenburg the proportion was 7 per cent.
23. Scheit 1993.
24. Krenek 1998, 915.
25. Donner 1951.
26. 'Houston Stewart Chamberlain. Zum zehnten Todestag', *NWT* (9 January 1937), 1.
27. 'Die Einschränkung ausländischer Musik in Deutschland. Wiener Musik schwer gefährdet', *NWT* (22 January 1938).
28. Moser 1988, 297.
29. ibid, 287f.
30. Decsey 1962, 148f.
31. Schrage 1938, 101f.
32. Quoted in Rabinovici 2000, 58.
33. Diary of Hertha Langer of 11 December 1939 (Susan Course, Melbourne).
34. Walzer 2001, 27.
35. *Reichsgesetzblatt* [Reich Gazette] I, 414.
36. Walzer 2001, 113.
37. Register of the State of Jewish Assets after 27 April 1938: Dr Hans Spitzer. VVSt 42 023 Va. Austrian State Archives.
38. Asset List. VVSt 11 443. Austrian State Archives.
39. Reichmann-Stieglitz, 12.

40. Fetthauer 2004, 146.
41. Dümling 2003, 218f.
42. ibid, 234.
43. Registration Office, Vienna.
44. Fetthauer 2004, 301 and 131.
45. Frey 2003, 251.
46. Rabinovici 2000, 109.
47. Stadlen 1988, 195.
48. Information from Registration Office.
49. Anderl 2004.
50. Prieberg 2005, 8631.
51. Goldner, 42.
52. Cited in Lühe 1998, 96.
53. Questionnaire for Central Welfare no 6475. CAHJP, A/W 2590, 74.
54. Goldner, 111.
55. von Stratowa 1937, 147f.
56. Fritz Thyssen escaped from Germany in 1939 and publicly opposed Hitler's war politics. He was expatriated, arrested in Vichy France, and taken to a concentration camp.
57. Information from Nicholas Chlumecky, Boston, 7 July 2001.
58. Hangler 2002.
59. Blakeney 1984, 109. According to Rabinovici 2000, 80, up to 1 April 1938 there were 6,000 applications for emigration to Australia.
60. Raab Hansen 1996, 29.
61. Cited in Wasserstein 1983, 54.
62. Sherman 1994, 57.
63. Dreyfus 1998, 72.
64. Shepherd 1985.
65. Smith 1999, 64.
66. Sherman 1994, 227 and Berghahn 1998, 76.
67. NAA: A434 (Refugees from Austria), 1950/3/41837, 133.
68. Blakeney 1985, 132.
69. *SMH*, 9 July 1938, quoted in Blakeney 1985, 133.
70. *SMH*, 8 August 1938, quoted in ibid.
71. *Truth* (16 August 1938), quoted in ibid, 134.
72. Stölting 1930, 82.
73. Quoted in Jurgensen 1992, 93.
74. 'Australien' 1937, 28.
75. Statistics of the Hilfsverein in *C.V.-Zeitung* (19 May 1938), 5.
76. Bergmeier 2001, 86.
77. Fritz Friedlaender, 'Australien – Bildnis eines Erdteils', *C.V.-Zeitung* (23 June 1938), 4.

78. 'Hoffnung auf Einwanderung in die Dominions', *C.V.-Zeitung* (22 September 1938), 2.
79. Trost 1938 and '5000 Juden nach Australien', *Jüdische Rundschau* (16 September 1938).
80. Wolfgang Matzdorff, 'Bericht aus Australien', *C.V.-Zeitung* (6 October 1938), 2.
81. 'Students Show Their Prowess', *AMM* (1 January 1940), 27.
82. Interview with Bob Adler, 18 April 2003, Sydney.
83. 'Tenor Here from Vienna', AJH (19 January 1939), 10. See also documents about his achievements as a singer. NAA: SP173/1, DANE, MARIO.
84. Picture in *ABC Weekly* (1 June 1940), 22.
85. Personal Statement and Declaration. NAA: A12508 (Neumann, Artur), 21/3178.
86. Blakeney 1984, 119.
87. Recorded in the diary of Hertha Langer (Susan Course, Melbourne).
88. NAA: A261 (Goldman, Harry), 1938/845.
89. Expatriation of Franz Laqueur. *Reichsanzeiger* no 211, 11 September 1939.
90. Gestapo Breslau on 2 May 1939 to Gestapo II B 3 in Berlin SW11, Archives of the Foreign Office, Berlin.
91. Title picture, provided by Evelyn Klopfer, Sydney.
92. Patkin 1979, 18–22.
93. Obituary, *Dunera News* 1997.
94. Silbermann 1989, 146.
95. ibid, 147.
96. ibid, 148.
97. NAA: A12508 (Silbermann, Alphons), 21/4019.
98. At one of the ensemble's performances in Schloss Laxenburg on 23 June 1928, the guest conductors, fellow-students Herbert Zipper and Herbert von Karajan, stood on the rostrum. Zipper, who later composed the *Dachau Song* in the Dachau concentration camp, conducted a masque with the fifteen-year-old Trudl Dubsky, his later wife, in the role of Amor. Karajan was assigned to the Strauß waltz *Morgenblätter* [*Morning Leaves*]. Bodenwieser Collection, Canberra. See Cummins 1993, 52f. Trudl Dubsky's father, Chairman of the Anker Insurance Company, emigrated with his whole family to Australia, where he opened a factory with his son. Embacher/Staubmann 1996, 32.
99. NAA: A12508 (Marcel Lorber), 5/219.
100. See the entry 'invalid'. In 1936, the Austrian passport was extended in Calcutta until 18 April 1939 and would have expired anyway.
101. Walsh 1991.
102. Information from Kurt Collinet, Cologne, 26 July 2002.
103. Statutory Declaration. NAA: A435 (Kurt Blach) 1945/4/2906, 28.
104. Annie Portnoj 1947.
105. Letter in possession of Ilse Blair, Melbourne.
106. NAA: A435 (Blau, Hans), 1945/4/1233, 14–16.

Chapter 7: After Kristallnacht

1. Smith 1999, 126.
2. Reichsmusikkammer file on Willy Coper. Bundesarchiv, previously BDC, RK R 5, Picture nos 2056–64 and 2540–2.
3. Information from Sybil Baer, Sydney.
4. Werner Baer's questionnaire for Röder and Strauss 1983, in ZA.
5. ibid.
6. Akademie 1992, 322.
7. Herbert Freeden in Geisel and Broder 1992, 268.
8. Application for Release from Detention. NAA: A367 (Ilse Baer), C81233.
9. Passport of Werner Baer. NAA: A435 (Baer, Werner), 1945/4/1221.
10. Interview with Ilse Blair, 20 July 2000, Melbourne.
11. Reference from the Jewish Winter Aid of 30 November 1938 (Sybil Baer, Sydney).
12. Reference from the Artists' Aid of the Jewish Community of 1 December 1938 (Sybil Baer, Sydney).
13. Reference from Max Ehrlich (Sybil Baer, Sydney).
14. Interview with Ilse Blair, 20 July 2000, Melbourne.
15. Baer to Hermann Schildberger. Schildberger Papers, Box 7.
16. ibid.
17. 'Jewish Organist Impresses At Singapore Recital', *ST* (16 January 1939), 12.
18. 'Singapore's Organ. Scope For A City Organist', *ST* (17 January 1939); 'More Werner Baer Recitals?', *ST* (19 January 1939); 'Singapore's Organ', *ST* (20 January 1939), 10; 'Regular organ recitals? (recommended by the Board of Control of the Victoria Theatre and Memorial Hall)', *ST* (16 March 1939), 13.
19. '"House full" Notice in Memorial Hall. Afterthoughts On A Record Singapore Concert', *ST* (16 March 1939), 15.
20. 'First Municipal Organ Recital Warmly Received', *ST* (8 May 1939).
21. 'Victoria Memorial Hall. Sun, June 4th, at 9.30 p.m./Organ Recital/Werner Baer – Aga Lahowska', *ST* (2 June 1939), 8: advertisement.
22. 'Big Audience at Municipal Organ Recital', *ST* (14 August 1939), 12. At this concert Baer played organ works by Brahms, Handel and Widor.
23. 'Packed House for Organ Recital', *ST* (19 August 1939), 12.
24. *ST* (18 November 1939), 10.
25. 'German Plays the Allies' Anthems', *ST* (5 February 1940), 10.
26. Abisheganaden 2005, 43f.
27. Rabinovici 2000, 126.
28. Phone interview with daughter Dr Sandra Hacker, 15 March 2008, Melbourne.
29. *Amtliche Mitteilungen der Reichsmusikkammer*, 15 October 1938, 69.

Notes: Chapter 7

30. Shapiro 2000.
31. Information from Brigitte Goldstein, Albuquerque (USA), the composer's daughter.
32. Version for Salon Orchestra published by Rondo, Berlin.
33. Questionnaire Fürsorge-Zentrale [welfare centre] no 20212 of 20 May 1938 (CAHJP, A/W 2590).
34. Copy received from Lisa Vinnic, Melbourne, Bader's daughter.
35. Emphasis in the original.
36. Questionnaire Fürsorge-Zentrale (CAHJP, A/W 2590, 28).
37. Foley to Ogilvie-Forbes, 17 January 1939. Quoted in Sherman 1994, 210.
38. Landesmusikerschaft Brandenburg on 7 January 1935 to Schildberger. Reichsmusikkammer file Hermann Schildberger. Bundesarchiv, formerly BDC, RK R 23, picture 922.
39. Interview with Rabbi John Levi, 24 July 2000, Melbourne. Also Levi 2009, 21.
40. Levi 2009, 43.
41. Letter of removal firm Silberstein & Co Berlin of 22 May 1939. Schildberger Papers, Box 5.
42. Alfred Alexander-Katz to Ilse Schildberger on 28 May 1939 from Paris. Schildberger Papers.
43. ibid.
44. 'Jewish Musical Personality', *Mercury* (Hobart; 8 August 1939), 3.
45. Röder and Strauss 1983, vol II, part 2, 1274.
46. Jacobsen and Segall 1926, 293; Hesse's Musiker-Kalender 1928, 24.
47. Schoenberger mentioned these recommendations when he was looking for piano pupils. See his newspaper advertisements in *SMH* (14 October 1939 and 14 February 1942).
48. Smith 1999, 154.
49. Freeden 1955.
50. 'Sandwich String Orchestra', *KCR* (April 1939), 3.
51. 'Classical Concert', *KCR* (May 1939), 11.
52. 'Entertainments: Concert by Refugee Orchestra', *The Times* (2 November 1939).
53. Raab Hansen 1996, 259. At the time, the author assumed 'M. Pietroushka' to be a woman from Austria.
54. *KCR* (July 1939), 9.
55. 'Expelled Rabbi Here', *Argus* (14 April 1939), 11.
56. Heinze Collection, Box 1.
57. Minutes, Faculty of Music: Byk, Ellen Cohn, 107: 1938 'Meeting No. 2. 20th July 1938: An application was received from Miss Ellen Cohn for appointment to the staff as a teacher of violin. The application was not recommended.'
58. Forster 1979.

59. 'Hundreds of Refugees', *Argus* (2 May 1939), 9.
60. CV, Melbourne 10 May 1952. Entschädigungsakte [compensation file] Ellen Byk, no 56322.
61. Statutory Declaration, 4 May 1944. NAA: A435 (Byk, Ellen), 1944/4/4170.
62. Göpfert 1999, 141.
63. Palmer 1997; Benz 2003.
64. Dreyfus 1984, 13.
65. 'Refugee children Begin New Lives', *AJH* (3 August 1939), 6.
66. Letter of Mischa Stiwelband to Hans Blau of 18 November 1938 (Ilse Blair, Melbourne).
67. According to Ilse Blair, Bailey hailed from the Barnum & Bailey circus family.
68. 'Big Attendance at Opening of Cathay Café', *ST* (11 December 1939), 10.
69. Questionnaire in Tatura. NAA: A367 (Steiner, Paul), C57693.
70. *ST* (20 January 1940), 7.
71. Information from Ilse Blair, Melbourne.
72. Testimony in NAA: A367 (Portnoj, Heinrich), C80891, 38.
73. Abisheganaden 2005, 72ff.
74. Stuckenschmidt 1982, 152.
75. Kolben 1985.
76. Interview with Robert Kolben, 4 October 2003, Munich.
77. Application for Permit to Enter Australia. NAA: A997 (Schuck-Kolben), 1939/192.
78. Interview with Robert Kolben.
79. Lily Kolos to the ABC on 15 June 1939. NAA: SP368/1, 7/34/5, Box 15, 1–3.
80. Stuckenschmidt 1982, 155.
81. Quoted in Helm 1965, 118, 120.
82. 26 April 1939: Application for Permit to Enter Australia. NAA: A997 (Hoffmann, Andrew), 1939/100.

Chapter 8: The Refugee Problem from an Australian Perspective

1. Waters 1951, 105.
2. ibid, 108.
3. ibid, 209f.

Notes: Chapter 8

4. 'Editor Says: A Hit Back at Hitler', *AMN* (September 1933), 3.
5. ibid, 4.
6. 'Of the Germans and Jews', *AMN* (October 1933), 3.
7. 'Nazis make musical nomads. Mary Baillie's experiences', *AMN* (February 1934), 12. See Mary Baillie, 'In Memoriam: Artur Schnabel', ABC Broadcast 31 August 1976 (Adam–Baillie collection L-2000/522/148).
8. 'Yet Germany marches behind. Sad effects of Hitlerism on music', *AMN* (April 1938), 2f.
9. James Steele, 'On the Fringe of History. There was also Music in Austria', *AMN* (June 1938), 23.
10. Radic 1986, 59.
11. ibid, 62.
12. Quoted in Sametz 2001, 43.
13. Radic 1986, 63.
14. ibid, 64.
15. ibid, 66. Thorold Waters also valued Schnéevoigt as an orchestral teacher. Waters 1951, 219.
16. Radic 1986, 75.
17. ibid, 88f.
18. ibid, 91. The accompanying letter was possibly the application from Ellen Byk, which was turned down by the Conservatorium on 20 July.
19. Heinze to Dr H.E. Heller, 28 June 1938 (Heinze Collection, Box 44). Radic 1986, 93.
20. Radic 1986, 60.
21. ibid.
22. ibid, 91f.
23. Heinze to Leo Doyle on 26 August 1938. ibid, 92.
24. Heinze to Charles Moses on 11 May 1938. ibid, 94f.
25. Huberman to Heinze on 11 September 1938. ibid, 93.
26. Radic 1986, 92f.
27. Raab Hansen 1996, 92f.
28. Souvenir Programme, original in NLA Prompt Collection, Spivakovsky–Kurtz Trio.
29. Inglis 1983, 51.
30. Programme for Celebrity Concert with MSO under Abravanel (Beethoven Piano Concerto No. 4), 23 March 1936. Author's Archive.
31. NAA: SP1558/2 (Jascha Spivakovsky), 166.
32. Smith 1993, 112f.
33. NAA: SP1558/2 (Jascha Spivakovsky), 166.
34. Schnabel 2014, 125f.

35. NAA: SP1558/2 (Jascha Spivakovsky), 166.
36. 'The mere fact of a musician of quality living in Australia for any length of time is very deflationary.' Waters 1951, 121.
37. Vogel 1977, 53; Kieffer 2002, 320f.
38. 'Problem of Jews. British Banker's Mission. Talks With Dr Schacht', *SMH* (4 January 1939), 14.
39. The British negotiating partners expressed themselves positively about Wohlthat ('easy to deal with [...] clearly Germany's No. 1 economist today'). NAA: A434 (Refugees from Austria – Special Committee Proposed by United States of America Government – Evian Conference), 1950/3/41837, 7f. See also Vogel 1977, 82–5.
40. Vogel 1977, 246–51. The Reich Central Office for Jewish Emigration had been led by Reinhard Heydrich since February 1939, and applied the practice of the Vienna Central Office to the Old Reich; its work now contradicted this long-term agreement.
41. NAA: A434 (Refugees from Austria), 1950/3/41837, 7f. The British press also reported this, see 'Relief of Refugees. Evian Policy to be reviewed', *The Times* (20 July 1939); 'Talks with Nazi Representatives', *Daily Telegraph* (20 July 1939).
42. The Madagascar plan is documented in Vogel 1977, 312–36.
43. Kieffer 2002, 265.
44. NAA: A434 (Refugees from Austria), 1950/3/41837, 149.
45. Turnbull 1999, 20.
46. Blakeney 1984, 119.
47. ibid, 121.
48. Rutland 1985, 37f. Sir Samuel Cohen, the founding president of the Jewish Welfare Society, had only wanted to admit young refugees, because only they would succeed in long-term social integration.
49. Bartrop 1994, XII.
50. ibid, 31.
51. Department of Immigration, 'Report and Proposals by Mr T H Garrett. Refugees from Europe – Selections of etc. (1939)'. NAA: A659, 1947/1/2109.
52. ibid.
53. In April 1939, the Reichsvereinigung [German Central Organisation of Jews] had referred to the strict moral standards that the Australians expected from the immigrants. Reichsvereinigung der Juden in Deutschland 1939, 17.
54. Department of Immigration, 'Report and Proposals by Mr T H Garrett. Refugees from Europe – Selections of etc. (1939)'. NAA: A659, 1947/1/2109.

55. ibid.
56. Otto Schiff to Julian Layton, 24 December 1936. Julian Layton Papers 1205/2/1–100. Wiener Library London.
57. Bartrop 1994, 215f.
58. '"Auswande[rung]" Statistische Erfassung der Auswanderung der österreichischen Juden und der Exilorte. Wien 1940–42', JMW, inv no 4452. Quoted in Hanak 1998, 137.
59. Rubinstein 1988, 179.
60. Carrodus to Kitson, 10 April 1935. NAA: A444 (Musicians Union of Australia), 1952/16/2762.
61. *Argus* (27 July 1938); see also 'Cinema organs', in Whiteoak 2003, 146f.
62. Interview with John Levi, 24 July 2000, Melbourne.
63. Silbermann 1989, 154.
64. Blakeney 1984, 109.
65. Silbermann 1989, 156.
66. Trost 1938.
67. In January 1939, a leading article in the Sydney *Sun* bemoaned the high concentration of refugees in Potts Point: 'Refugees from foreign persecution have taken it over like Grant took Richmond'. Quoted in Rutland 1985, 41.
68. 'Taught in Austria and England. Emma Bondy Weiss A Newcomer', *AMN* (1 May 1939), 19.
69. 'Her talent is of brilliant bravura type, fully expressed in the last group of solos.' Linda Phillips in *AJH* (30 March 1939), 8. See also the review in *AMN* (April 1939), 13.
70. *AJH* (15 June 1939), 10.
71. Kathe Neumann 1940, 9.
72. In 1931, he had changed his first name Jona to Hans.
73. On his arrival in Melbourne, Ernest Schulvater alleged that it was only his British passport that had saved him from the concentration camp. See 'Saved by Passport', *Argus* (8 August 1939), 4. His wife Antonia was pictured in the same edition, while three days later he was featured as a European band leader in the *SMH*, also with a photo.
74. Minutes of the Medical Board NSW. NSW Records Office, Microfilm 2658. Kaufmann received a fine when he continued to practise. *SMH* (26 September 1940), 3.
75. Waters 1939.
76. Heinze Collection, Box 44.

Chapter 9: Under Union Scrutiny: The Weintraubs Syncopators

1. Dreyfus, K. 2009, 3.
2. Musicians' Union of Australia, Rules. Melbourne 1929. Author's Archive.
3. 'Industrial Relations', Whiteoak 2003, 348.
4. Dreyfus K. 2009, 1.
5. 'Abravanel Points The Way To Permanent Orchestras In Australia', *Daily Telegraph* (28 June 1935).
6. 'Our Music In Ears Of Others', *Daily Telegraph* (28 June 1935). Noel Butlin Archives Centre. Z401 Box 13.
7. NAA: SP1588/2 (ABC File – Employment of foreign musicians – importation of key instrumentalists [Box 46]), 741.
8. Refugee Musicians. Memorandum by W.G. James to The General Manager, 5 December 1938. NAA: SP1588 (Employment of foreign musicians), 741.
9. Refugee Musicians. Memorandum by Charles Moses on 18 January 1939. ibid.
10. Raab Hansen 1996, 136–99.
11. Kitson to Moses on 6 February 1939. NAA: SP1588, 741.
12. 'Advice To Union on Music', *Sun* (27 July 1938). Also: 'Unions and Music. Progress Retarded, Dr Sargent Says', *SMH* (28 July 1938).
13. 'Refugees. Professions' Attitude', *SMH* (29 July 1938).
14. 'Will Welcome Only British Players. Musicians Would Object To Jews Or Foreigners', *Daily Telegraph* (29 July 1938).
15. Cameron to Moses on 18 February 1939. NAA: SP 1588/2, 741.
16. Moses to Kitson on 13 July 1939. ibid.
17. Tossy Spivakovsky to Richard Goldner on 20 April 1939, quoted in Goldner, 143. Erich Leinsdorf had already warned Goldner earlier about the American Musicians' Union.
18. The violinist Max Starkmann, a long-standing member of the Vienna Philharmonic, had been informed by Heinze on 23 May 1939 that, for an orchestral position, the Musicians' Union required a minimum of three years' residence in Australia (Heinze Collection, Box 44). Three years later, Starkmann was no longer alive; he was killed in a concentration camp.
19. 'Crazy', *Daily Telegraph* (1 August 1944). See also 'Alien Musicians Banned By Union', *Daily Telegraph* (30 July 1944). cf similar discussions in Britain, Raab Hansen, 96–116, and Levi 2004.

Notes: Chapter 9

20. Translation by Lilian Harvey, taken from <http://lyricstranslate.com/en/irgendwo-auf-der-welt-somewhere-world.html#ixzz3ZBBMsSJN> (accessed 15 November 2015).
21. NAA: A434 (Snider and Dean Theatres Limited – Admission of Artists), 1944/3/690.
22. 'Snider and Dean's Plans', *SMH* (2 June 1937), 21.
23. 'Musicians From Overseas. Objection to Bands. Minister Asked to Act', *Argus* (31 March 1937), 4. See further documents in NAA: A444 (Musicians Union of Australia), 1952/16/2762.
24. Stefan Weintraub's passport. NAA: A435 (Stefan Weintraub), 1946/4/988.
25. In Weintraub's passport, the transit visa is on page 16, dated 18 June.
26. By contrast, Kaiser gave the 'Imperial Hotel, Tokyo' as his last permanent address.
27. Leo Weiss's entry was '48 weeks', whereas Kaiser wrote '16–48 weeks'.
28. 'Film and Stage Attractions', *SMH* (3 August 1937), 9.
29. 'The Weintraubs. Clever, Witty Entertainment', *SMH* (5 August 1937), 4.
30. Title no 70618. National Film and Sound Archive, Canberra.
31. 'The Comedy Harmonists', *Sydney Mail* (4 August 1937), 31.
32. 'Life story of Manny Fisher.'
33. Leo Weiss's passport became invalid in 1939, and that of Weintraub in August 1940.
34. Emanuel Frischer to dept of interior on 21 December 1937. NAA: A434 (Snider and Dean), 1944/3/690.
35. Inspector Mitchell to the Commonwealth Investigation Branch on 8 December 1937. ibid.
36. Lucas 1937, 19–20.
37. ibid.
38. Letters of Henry Barger to Stefan Weintraub. Weintraubs Syncopators Archive, Item 83.
39. Gerty Pfund was the troupe's stage manager. List of Weintraubs' members. NAA: A6126 (John Kurt Kaiser), 197, 192.
40. NAA: A434 (Snider and Dean), 1944/3/690.
41. Unknown newspaper from New Zealand. Facsimile in Weintraubs promotional material. NAA: A434 (Snider and Dean), 1944/3/690.
42. ibid.
43. ibid.
44. ibid.
45. Kaiser even added here 'artist and composer'.
46. *Radio Pictorial of Australia* (October 1938) with photographs. See also the illustrated article 'Weintraubs Comedy Melodians'. *Wireless Weekly* (15 July 1938). Weintraubs Syncopators Archive, Item 61.

47. 'The Weintraubs Broadcast from Station 2CH', *AMM* (1 October 1938), 52.
48. 'Ambitious Lew Myers', *Radio Pictorial of Australia* (1 November 1938), 23.
49. 'Cash Prizes for "Melody Riddles"', *Radio Pictorial of Australia* (1 July 1939), 46.
50. 'Weintraubs or Craig Crawford for Sydney "Prince's"', *AMM* (1 December 1938), 4.
51. Memorandum of 2 May 1935. NAA: A444 (Musicians Union of Australia), 1952/16/2762.
52. 'Musicians' Union Takes Commendable Stand on Alien Musicians Question', *AMM* (1 November 1938), 4.
53. His plans to employ foreign musicians had already failed because of the union in 1923. NAA: A1 (J.C. Bendroth Admission. Coloured Musicians), 1923/2723.
54. '"Prince's" Open to Capacity Business', *AMM* (1 January 1939), 5.
55. The American tenor Richard Crooks had made this Rudolf Sieczynski song well known in Australia.
56. Vincent A. White, 'Meeting the "Comedy Harmonists"', *Sydney Mail* (11 August 1937), 18.
57. 'The Weintraubs. Their Private Life and Musical Careers', *Radio Pictorial of Australia* (1 June 1939), 26–7, 58.
58. NAA: A434 (Snider and Dean Theatres Limited – Admission of Artists), 1944/3/690.
59. See reports in *SMH* (29 May 1939, 4, and 10 June 1939, 11).
60. Weintraubs Syncopators Archive, item no 221.
61. Report on Application for Admission of Friends or Relatives into Australia. NAA A261 (Horst Graff), 790 1256.
62. Weintraubs Syncopators Archive no 103.
63. Frank Kitson to McEwen, 24 February 1939. Minutes of the Musicians' Union of Australia. Noel Butlin Archives E111/1/2–3.
64. Memorandum of the department for the interior (Horgan) of 20 March 1939. NAA: A444 (Musicians Union of Australia); 1952/16/2762.
65. J.A. Carrodus to Frank Kitson on 22 May 1939. ibid.
66. Correspondence Horst Graff–Musicians' Union. Weintraubs Syncopators Archive, item 103.
67. NAA: A434 (Snider and Dean), 1944/3/690.
68. ibid.
69. Manning 1967; Lawson 1993.
70. Graff had married the British Margery ('Margo') Minna Graham in Moscow in November 1936.
71. F.E. Baume to H.S. Foll on 28 July 1939. NAA: A434 (Snider and Dean), 1944/3/690.

Chapter 10: 'Down with the fifth column!': Britain during the War

1. Wasserstein 1983, 58.
2. This campaign was led mainly by the *Sunday Express* and *Daily Sketch*. Lafitte 1980, 67f.
3. Dokumentationsarchiv 1992, 54.
4. Berghahn 1988, 141f.
5. Stibbe 2008.
6. Gillman 1980, 43.
7. ibid, 45. See also the schedule in Lafitte 1980, 63.
8. Lafitte 1980, 37.
9. ibid, 41.
10. Margis 2001.
11. Patkin 1979, 12.
12. The 'fifth column' was first mentioned in connection with the siege of Madrid. Ernest Hemingway wrote his play, *The Fifth Column*, about this in 1939.
13. Gillman 1980, 69–80.
14. Seyfert 1983, 160.
15. Kassner gave 'Composer' as his profession in his military papers. NAA: MP1103, E39887. See also Bevege 1995, 52.
16. Schellenberg 2000, 83.
17. Seidler 1986, 34.
18. Gillman 1980, 145.
19. Quoted in Michael Glover, *Invasion Scare 1940* (London: Leo Cooper, 1990), 46.
20. Quoted in Rössel 1996.
21. See chapter 'Round-up Methods', in Lafitte 1980, 75f.
22. ibid, 74.
23. ibid, 102.
24. Flesch 2001, 112.
25. Seidler 1986, 40.
26. See pictures in Gillman 1980. A map of the camp is found in Seidler 1986, 46, and a detailed report in Lafitte 1980, 105–13.
27. Seidler 1986, 41–9.
28. There was one doctor to every 3,000 persons. Lafitte 1980, 107.
29. Bindemann 2000, 28.
30. Lafitte 1980, 113f.

31. Patkin 1979, 20.
32. As a consequence, the suicide rate rose. Lafitte 1980, 113.
33. For the origin of the *Dunera* passengers, see Bartrop 1990, 151.
34. Stent 1980, 115f.
35. Loewald 1996, 75.
36. Bartrop 1990, 152, confirmed by Nicholas Chlumecky, USA, 2 July 2001.
37. Fabian 2000, 124f.
38. Papers of Herbert Goldsmith, London. Wiener Library London, Documents 141, 741/2. Printed in Bartrop 1990, 196.
39. Information from Bern Brent, Canberra, 24 December 2008.

Chapter 11: Interned and Defamed in Australia

1. Bevege 1993, 1.
2. Internment camps for the State of New South Wales were in Liverpool, near Sydney, and in Bathurst.
3. 'Internment of Aliens. Swift Police Work', *SMH* (7 June 1946), 9.
4. Bevege 1993, 6.
5. NAA: ST1233/1, N19220, 68.
6. ibid, 144, 162.
7. ibid, 178.
8. Handwritten note on the report of 11 September.
9. The relevant records are dated 29 September 1939.
10. Recte Rostov-on-Don.
11. NAA: C123 (Emanuel Frischer), 1211, 78.
12. NAA: A6126 (John Kurt Kaiser), 197, 16–18. Gerty and Richard Pfund had arrived in Sydney on the *Maloja*, with the Weintraubs, on 5 October 1937; see files on Gerty and Richard Pfund in NAA: A12508, 21/3289.
13. 'We are at War: Is Music at War Too?', *AMN* (October 1939), 3.
14. Radic 1986, 111.
15. Raab Hansen 1996, 181–99.
16. Sametz 2001, 75.
17. 2 June 1941: 'Speaking Editorially ... A Half-Year of Musical Malnutrition. Strange Avoidable Hiatus in Australia's Efforts'; 1 September 1942: 'Speaking Editorially ... War and Our Need of Great Artists. Policy of Exclusion Is Much Too Extreme. Cultural Suggestion to the Federal Government'.

18. 'The Fall of Germany, France and Italy. Music is One of War's Outcasts', *AMN* (July 1940), 3.
19. 'The Real Richard Wagner Would Never Have Been a Nazi. Composer's Views on Militarism', *AMN* (October 1940), 3.
20. Bevege 1993, 68.
21. Inspector W.J. Keefe to Major Scott on 4 October 1939. NAA: ST1233/1 (Weintraub, Stefan), N19220, 160.
22. Cottle 2002 and Moore 1988. Also *New Citizen* (April 2004), 6.
23. Kitson to Major Scott on 29 November 1939. NAA: ST1233/1 (Weintraub, Stefan), N19220, 154.
24. ibid, 155.
25. Carrodus to Kitson on 28 December 1939. NAA: A444 (Musicians Union), 1952/16/2762.
26. NAA: A434 (Snider and Dean Theatres Limited – Admission of Artists), 1944/3/690.
27. Bartrop 1994, 167.
28. Interview with Andy Factor, 11 March 2004, Melbourne.
29. 'These musicians are themselves a "League of Nations", as their act is composed of a Canadian, an African, an Austrian, a Pole, a German, an Englishman, and a Frenchman.' *SMH* (3 August 1937), 9.
30. See correspondence in Weintraubs Syncopators Archive, no 138.
31. Bevege 1993, 25f.
32. The term 'Siegfried line' refers to the 'Westwall', a German defensive line.
33. 'Weintraubs' Ball', *Canberra Times* (22 April 1940).
34. Communication from Police Station to Major Powell on 15 April 1940, Ib Subsection I. NAA: C123/1 (Horst Graff), 1213.
35. *Canberra Times* (20 April 1940), 3.
36. 'Weintraubs for Tivoli', *AMM* (30 April 1940), 4.
37. Kartomi et al. 2004, 28f.
38. Bevege 1993, 70.
39. Sydney John Kay to the department of the interior, 19 May 1940. NAA: A434 (Snider and Dean Theatres Limited – Admission of Artists), 1944/3/690.
40. Bevege 1993, 54.
41. Military Security – Refugees: Internment: Fifth Columnists. 31 October 1940. NAA: MP1103/1 (Klaphake, Wolf), PWN1275, 1.
42. Bevege 1993, 55.
43. NAA SP11/2 (Ernst Kaufmann), GERMAN/KAUFMANN E.
44. According to the list signed by Stefan Weintraub and two police officers, he took one hand towel, one robe, one pullover, one pair of slippers, one pair of sandals, five pairs of socks, one cravat, two pairs of pyjamas, two shirts, two handkerchiefs,

one shoehorn, soap, one set of toiletries, one leather suitcase, one briefcase, one pipe cleaner, a notebook, two keys and one wristwatch, worth a total of one pound and one shilling.

45. Bevege 1993, 34, 56.
46. 'Chronik der deutschen Internierungslager'.
47. Bevege 1993, 57.
48. ibid, 68f.
49. NAA: ST1233/1 (Stefan Weintraub), N1922, 139.
50. Irene Weintraub sent a similar letter to Major Powell on 11 October.
51. NAA: ST1233/1 (Kurt Herweg), N33902.
52. List of his possessions in NAA: MP1103/2 (Stefan Weintraub), PWN1297, 4.
53. Horst Graff's possessions, including numerous musical instruments, were also seized. NAA: MP1103/2 (Prisoner of War/Internee: Horst Graff), PWN1261.
54. NAA: ST1233/1 (Stefan Weintraub), N1922, 127.
55. *Musik und Gesellschaft* 1 (1930/31), 32. Cited in Schröder 1990, 310.
56. 'Kurze Chronik der deutschen Internierungslager in Australien'. See also Bevege 1993, 47f.
57. NAA: ST1233/1 (Stefan Weintraub), N19220, 121.
58. NAA: A6126/16 (John Kurt Kaiser), 197, 32.
59. It was the first coloured animated cartoon to be released in Australia. 'Special music for the picture was written by Mr John Kay.' *SMH* (27 June 1940), 19; *West Australian* (5 July 1940). In December 1939, the *ABC Weekly* mentioned a radio play, 'Adolf in Blunderland': 'The play is a perfect parody of Lewis Carroll's classic'.
60. See extensive correspondence in the personal files of Sydney John Kay/Kurt Kaiser NAA: A6126 as well as NAA: SP1048/7, S56/1/1041.
61. NAA: ST1233/1 (Stefan Weintraub), N19220, 116.
62. See documents in the Max Joseph Collection, Archive of Australian Judaica, Sydney.
63. The Army's jurisdiction was justified by the fact that they were prisoners of war.
64. Max Joseph Collection, Archive of Australian Judaica Sydney, Box 3.
65. Wilhelm Alexander von Keudell, who was also interned in Tatura, took part in this resolution; he had married a Hungarian Jew and thus risked breaking with his family. NAA: ST1233/1 (Wilhelm A. von Keudell), N38602. Regarding Keudell's fate, see Bevege 1993, 124.
66. H. Graff to the camp commandant, 12 November 1940. NAA: C123/1 (Horst Graff), 1213.
67. Children's song written in 1917 by Laura R. Smith and J.S. Fearis.
68. Letter from Alexander Macdonald to Alien Tribunal Court, 25 February 1941. NAA: C123/1 (Horst Graff, Security Service NSW), 1213.
69. A report dated 7 September 1944 says of Horst Graff: 'His release from internment was strongly opposed by I.b. Eastern Command.' NAA: C123/1, 1213.

Notes: Chapter 12

70. NAA: C329 (Stefan Weintraub, Objection 1941), 997.
71. Zevi Hirsch Alter Weintraub (1811–1882), son of the well-known cantor Salomon Weintraub (1781–1829), was from 1838 to 1880 principal cantor in Königsberg.
72. NAA: ST1233/1 (Stefan Weintraub), N19220, 84.
73. 'Steps were taken to find out which member of CRAWFORD'S Band had talked most, with a view of questioning. Contact's report upon this enquiry was that any member would be as good as another, since all said the same thing.'
74. NAA: SP1588/2 (Employment of foreign Musicians), 741, and Memorandum of 2 April 1935 in A444 (Musicians Union of Australia), 1952/16/2762.
75. This Yugoslavian violinist, who also appeared with Werner Baer, had landed in Melbourne in 1938.
76. Police Report no 1212 of 12 November 1941. NAA: ST1233/1 (Stefan Weintraub), N19220, 61. For more information, see Kay Dreyfus, *Silences and Secrets: The Australian Experience of the Weintraubs Syncopators* (Melbourne: Monash University Publishing, 2013).
77. ibid, 62.
78. This organisation had already come to the fore in the 1920s with vehement protests against immigrants from Southern Europe. Bartrop 1994, 9f.
79. '"Society Folk Prefer Alien Musicians". Union Secretary in Spirited Protest', *Truth* (16 November 1941).
80. This café, opened by the German emigrant Walter Magnus in 1940, had become an important meeting place, and was even visited occasionally by Prince Philip. Cunneen 2000.
81. NAA: ST1233/1 (Stefan Weintraub), N19220, 54.
82. Wire Products Pty Ltd, Johnston Street, Annandale.
83. Although Pilcher had repeatedly intervened on behalf of refugees during the war, he might have been especially sympathetic towards Graff because he was a music lover; years ago he himself had worked as a bass clarinettist in the Toronto Symphony Orchestra. See 'Australian Portraits. Bishop Charles V. Pilcher', *New Citizen* (15 February 1948), 7.

Chapter 12: 'In corrugated iron huts': Deported to Hay and Tatura

1. Bartrop 1990, 33.
2. Hammond 1990, 9; Neumann 2006, 7–19.
3. Klaus Loewald in Rössel 1996, 13f.

4. Bartrop 1990, 235.
5. Bartrop 1994, 224. Similarly Paul König in Bartrop 1990, 236.
6. Hay Internment Camp. Standing Orders 7 September 1940 (Australian War Memorial 54,709/25/3).
7. The statement that Layton first visited Hay on 10 April 1941 (Bartrop 1990, 269) is therefore incorrect.
8. Report on Visit to the Internment Camp, Hay, NSW, Julian Layton Papers, 1205/1/26-84. Wiener Library London.
9. ibid.
10. Interview with Klaus Wilczynski, 27 January 2005, Berlin.
11. According to the Camp statistics, over a third of the Camp 7 internees were married. Bartrop 1990, 255.
12. Loewald 2000, 66-71.
13. Seyfert 1984 and Raab Hansen 1996, 258-68.
14. The text is reproduced in Bartrop 1990, 376.
15. On the other hand, in the 'Songs from Hay and Tatura' left by Henry Lippmann (Henry Lippmann – Dunera Archive, State Library of NSW, Sydney, ML MSS 5896), Ray Martin is named as the sole author of both the text and the music.
16. The song lyrics are reproduced in Bartrop 1990, 376.
17. Two originals of the programme, with different watercolour title pages (Biedermeier motifs), are in the Hay Internment Records, NLA MS 5392 and in the Deutsches Exilarchiv 1933-1945 in Frankfurt/Main.
18. Bartrop 1990, 240f. Falk, a fanatical Zionist, was not much liked, however, among the internees; see Silbermann 1989, 211, and Rutland 1981, 464.
19. Bartrop 1990, 254.
20. Previously at the Berlin Volksbühne.
21. Bieber was later one of the cast of Carol Reed's film *The Third Man*.
22. Zimmering 1969, 63. He was later awarded the National Prize of East Germany. Zimmering also described his Australian experiences in his children's book *Die unfreiwillige Weltreise* [The involuntary world trip] (1956).
23. The review in *Camp News* no 50 (11 February 1940) praised the choral singing on Easter morning, and above all the 'Dies irae' of the cathedral scene, as 'extraordinarily impressive'. It was incorrectly claimed that Ernst Hermann Meyer sent the music from England (Clarke 1989, 217).
24. Bartrop 1990, 236.
25. 'Our Future', *Boomerang* (2 March 1941). Cited in Bartrop 1990, 249.
26. For further information on the organisation of education and entertainment in Camp 7, see Bartrop 1990, 253.
27. Emil Wittenberg, 'Stage Work in No. 7 Camp', *Boomerang* no 12 (16 May 1941). Deutsches Exilarchiv 1933-1945, Frankfurt/Main: EB Kb 972.

Notes: Chapter 12 467

28. Programme in Deutsches Exilarchiv 1933–1945, Frankfurt/Main (Camp Hay-Material. EB autogr. IV. A 707).
29. Names are written as in ibid.
30. Gustav Löwenhart, *b.*1917 in Vienna. Employee.
31. Günter Heilbut, 'About the Recreation Department', *Boomerang* (14 April 1941), 9.
32. Programme in Dunera Archive Melbourne, 4023–2.
33. Loewald 2000, 66.
34. Diary of Kurt Lewinski in Archive of Australian Judaica, University of Sydney (Shelf List 17). Copy in Henry Lippmann – Dunera Archive, State Library of NSW (MLMSS 5896).
35. ibid.
36. Perhaps this was the one-manual Walcker organ built in Ludwigsburg in 1887, shipped to Sydney in 1900, taken by paddle steamer to Hay and installed there in St Paul's Anglican Church in 1927. The organ, which has since been restored, is still in the same place today. <http://www.gewalcker.de/gewalcker.de/0487.pdf> (accessed 13 November 2015).
37. Handel's Old Testament oratorios were also understood as a symbol of Jewish identity in concerts of the Kulturbund.
38. Programme. Dunera Archive Melbourne, 3155.
39. Stent 1980, 234.
40. Dunera Archive Melbourne, 4128–2.
41. Loewald 1996, 78.
42. Heinze Collection, Box 5.
43. Photo of Artur Schnabel, Sydney August 1939 (Adam–Baillie collection L-2000/522/149).
44. P. Stadlen to Mary Baillie, 1 February 1941 (ibid L-2000/522/136).
45. P. Stadlen to Mary Baillie, 29 March 1941 (ibid L-2000/522/137).
46. Programme. Dunera Archive Melbourne, 3129p.
47. Loewald 2000, 66.
48. Patkin 1979, 58–60.
49. 'Copy of Music Performed in Hay Camp'. Dunera Archive Melbourne, 3523 S.
50. 'Ein Beethoven-Abend', *Camp News*, No. 131 (18 March 1941), 6.
51. Papers of Herbert Goldsmith, London. Wiener Library Documents 141.
52. Schildberger Papers, State Library of Victoria, Melbourne.
53. Letter from Camp Spokesman and Group Captain to Peter Stadlen, 19 May 1941. Dunera Archive Melbourne, 3155.
54. Bartrop 1990, 280.
55. Peter Stadlen to Mary Baillie, 4 June 1941 (Adam–Baillie collection L-2000/522/138).

56. Dunera Archive Melbourne, 3541 P. Erwin Fabian also mentions a Stadlen Beethoven programme in Orange, to which the audience listened very attentively. Fabian 2000, 126.
57. Erich Fried, 'Ein Jahr Internierung', *Zeitspiegel* (11 May 1941), 6.
58. 'Rund um die Flüchtlingsfrage', *Zeitspiegel* (29 June 1941), 5.
59. 'Ein Heimkehrer aus Australien erzählt', *Zeitspiegel* (17 August 1941), 7. See also 'Als Internierter in Australien. Der erste Bericht eines Heimgekehrten', *Aufbau* (New York; 26 December 1941), 3.
60. Further documentation in the Australian War Memorial, Canberra.
61. 'Brilliance of Viennese Boys. Their Musicianship is Amazing', *AMN* (1 July 1939), 17.
62. More detailed information about the Vienna Mozart Boys' Choir can be found in Gill 2004.
63. Bern Brent, *Dunera News* 74 (October 2008), 11.
64. Information from Bern Brent, Canberra.
65. Patkin 1979, 113f.
66. Bartrop 1993, Part I, 153.
67. Dunera Archive Melbourne, 30001.
68. Baer in an undated letter to Schildberger. Schildberger Papers, State Library of Victoria, Melbourne.
69. Translation by Michael Turnbull.
70. Translation by Michael Turnbull.
71. Major Layton to F.A. Newman, Deputy Permanent Secretary of the Home Office, White Hall, London, 25 June 1941. TNA HO 215/26.
72. Reproduced in *Dunera News* 74 (October 2008), 13.
73. Fleischer to Duncan, 16 December 1941 (Adam–Baillie collection L-2000/522/121).
74. Fleischer to Baillie, 20 January 1942 (ibid L-2000/522/144).
75. Loewald 1985, 84; Cavanagh 2006.
76. Newton 2003, 101.
77. Diary entry of December 1942, quoted in Uwe Radok's letter to Hannah Wurzburger, 6 January 2000. Author's Archive.
78. Walter Würzburger remembered by Uwe Radok, 13 June 1995. Ms in author's archive.
79. Dr F. Eichenberg to M. Baillie, 8 July 1941 (Adam–Baillie collection L-2000/522/142).
80. Collegium Taturensis. Anniversary 1940–1941 (ibid L-2000/522/96).
81. Information from Mary-Clare Adam, Tel Aviv.
82. Programme in Adam–Baillie collection L-2000/522/99.
83. Programme in the possession of Felix Edelmann, Vienna.
84. Adam–Baillie collection L-2000/522/141.

85. ibid.
86. Loewald 2000, 67.
87. Programme in Dunera Archive Melbourne, 3372–3.
88. Programme in ibid, 3577P.
89. ibid, 3439–1. *Songs the People Love*, 8of.
90. The Kitchener Camp was located in Richborough.
91. Programme in Dunera Archive Melbourne, 3577P.
92. Neumann 2006, 17; Bevege 1993, 120.
93. Major Scurry to M. Baillie, 6 February 1942 (Adam–Baillie collection L–2000/522/119).

Chapter 13: Snow White in Uniform: The Music Revue *Sergeant Snow White*

1. Interview with Ilse Blair, 20 July 2000, Melbourne.
2. Krieger 1955.
3. Information from Dr June Factor, Melbourne.
4. Routine Order, 22 August 1942 (Australian War Memorial 22/1/15 6 Empl. Co. March–Aug 1942); information from June Factor.
5. Loewald 1993, 270–1.
6. Sigurd Lohde, '8 Aust Employment Company March'. Text printed in Bartrop 1990, 382.
7. Werner Baer, oral history in Mitchell Library Sydney (MLOH 437/107).
8. Loewald 1985, 84.
9. Bartrop 1990, 367.
10. On 22 April 1943, he applied for the copyright to the script, but it was not granted. NAA: A1336 (Manfred Kurt Sternberg), 38549.
11. Duncan 1943. The Melbourne *Argus* (13 May 1943) also praised this 'clever revue'.
12. Advertisement, 'Allan's Hit Releases', *AMM* (1 June 1938), 16.
13. 'Song is the Keynote of Disney's "Snow White and the Seven Dwarfs"', *AMM* (1 July 1938), 45.
14. Zipes 1994 and 1997.
15. 'Some Day My Prince Will Come' is classified as a jazz standard and is ranked no 19 in the American Film Institute's list of the most popular film songs.
16. Fröhlich 2000, 64.
17. Fröhlich 1998, 306.
18. Filmmuseum Potsdam 1991, 110.

19. Programme in Archive of Australian Judaica, University of Sydney, Cyril Pearl Collection (Shelf List 18).
20. Sternberg had already arrived in Britain in 1934 and co-produced the RKO films *Shadowed Eyes* and *Tilly of Bloomsbury*.
21. Patkin 1979, 73.
22. After the war, E. Wittenberg, an architect who designed the sets for *Snowhite Joins Up* and *Sergeant Snow White*, ran a furniture business in Chapel Street, Melbourne under the name of Emil Witten. He also worked as a set designer for the Kleines Wiener Theater in Sydney. *Dunera News* no 38 (February 1997), 12f.
23. Laqua 1992, 167.
24. Cyril Pearl Collection (Shelf List 18), Archive of Australian Judaica, University of Sydney.
25. The April productions were announced as 'Sergeant Snowwhite' (see illustration).
26. Gay men, for example, understood the seven dwarves as a symbol for male bonding. There was rarely any interest in the phenomenon of small size, as in a 2003 production at the Melbourne Comedy Theatre by an organisation called Short Statured People of Australia (SSPA).
27. 'Marche funèbre' from Chopin's Piano Sonata No. 2 in B flat minor Op. 35.
28. Bartrop 1990, 354.
29. The camp was named after Major Pell, a US parachutist who died in Australia's Northern Territory. The expression 'the boys from Camp Spell', in the scene 'The Dwarfs at the Wharfs', alludes to this.
30. 'He is Sgt. S - - -'s discovery. Those who know say he has a voice of world quality. He spends his spare time singing for soldiers in six languages.' Quoted in Bartrop 1990, 367. See *Songs the People Love*, 99–108.
31. Lohde had played alongside Hans Albers in the film *Draufgänger* (1931). He also took part in *Tannenberg* (1932), *Peter* (1934) and *Unerwünschtes Kino* (Vienna 1937). After his return to Europe, he again acted in films, among others in *Madeleine und der Legionär* (1957) and *Scotland Yard jagt Dr. Mabuse* (1963).
32. On the other hand, the song 'Whistle while you work', which British soldiers changed during the war to 'Whistle while you work, Hitler is a jerk', was not included.
33. In 1943, the first weddings took place here between members of the company and women whom they had often met at Jewish community social evenings. Bartrop 1990, 351.
34. Snowwhite invitation for 15 April 1943 (Dunera Archive Melbourne, 3683–4).
35. *Songs the People Love*, 113.
36. Invitation for Charity Gala Performance of 'Sergeant Snow White' (Dunera Archive Melbourne, 3683–5).
37. Duncan 1943.

Notes: Chapter 14

38. Hippen 1986, 120. Translation by Michael Turnbull.
39. Dümling 1985, 339.
40. Naumann 1983, 178.
41. The Snow White revue is also mentioned in 'Germans Who Help to Fight Hitler', *Argus* (18 May 1943), 2.
42. Catherine Duncan, who reviewed the show so enthusiastically, was a successful actor, author and filmmaker. After the war, she directed the Workers Theatre Group and collaborated on film projects for the department of immigration with Sydney John Kay and Kurt Herweg, before leaving Australia for Europe in 1948.
43. 'Soldier Musicians Win Award', *Advertiser* (Adelaide; 10 August 1943); Irma Schnierer, 'Preisgekrönte Europäer in Australien', *Aufbau* (New York; 21 January 1944), 10. Hochberger also wrote a poem about the Warsaw Ghetto and died in 1947 at the age of 41.

Chapter 14: The Year 1945: Lost and Found

1. Fetthauer 2004, 306.
2. Information from Richard Toeman, London.
3. Letter to Ilse Winkler. NAA: ST1233/1 (Gunter Hirschberg), N32842.
4. Telegram of 4 September 1942 to the Minister of the Army. NAA: A367 (Hirschberg, Gunter – Reverend), C56411, 17.
5. Silbermann 1989, 210.
6. Rutland 1988, 184.
7. S.D. Rutland, 'Jewish Refugee and Post-War Immigration' in Jupp 1988, 647.
8. Berghahn 1988, 156.
9. Max Joseph Collection. Archive of Australian Judaica Sydney. Box 7.
10. Krieger 1955, 27.
11. Report of hearing of 3 March 1943. NAA: ST1233/1(Gunter Hirschberg), N32842.
12. *Gedenkbuch* 1995, 517.
13. NAA: C123/1 (Emanuel Frischer), 1211, 1.
14. NAA: A367 (Bader Hans), C54505, 35.
15. Information from DÖW.
16. ibid.
17. F. Paradies, Amsterdam, 8 December 1945 to Kurt Blach, Melbourne (author's archive).
18. *Songs the People Love*, 165–74.

19. Bartrop 1993, 164.
20. Application for Release from Detention. NAA: A367, C80891, 37.
21. NAA: A367, C54505, 48.
22. Margarethe Bader to Major Layton, 17 September 1942. ibid, 23.
23. Inspector Brown, 21 March 1944. ibid, 15.
24. Irma Schmierer and Mark Siegelberg, 'Fünf Jahre Emigration in Australien', *Aufbau* (28 January 1944), 7.
25. Memorandum of Department of the Interior no 44/4/953. NAA: A435 (Adler, Henry Max), 1944/4/953.
26. All documents in NAA: A435 (Werther, Rudolf Theodor), 1946/4/381.
27. NAA: A435 (Werner Baer), 194574/1221, 13.
28. Minutes of 20 July 1946, Faculty of Music, Melbourne.
29. NAA: A446 (Brenner, Adolf), 1954/1826.
30. NAA: A435 (Feigl, Leonie), 1945/4/6246. She had, however, already advertised as a voice teacher in the *SMH* (13 January 1945).
31. Interview with Erwin Frenkel, 22 July 2000, Melbourne.
32. Membership list of Musicians' Union NSW Branch, 1947. Noel Butlin Archives Centre, Australian National University.
33. Noel Butlin Archives Centre, Australian National University, E156-2-3 (see Figure 27).
34. 'Union Ordered to Admit Alien', *Daily Telegraph* (10 August 1944). See also 'Musician Opposes Union's Alien Ban', *Daily Telegraph* (9 August 1944). 'Enemy Alien Musician Granted Right to Join Union', *SMH* (10 August 1944).
35. 'Enemy Alien Admitted to Musicians' Union', *Truth* (13 August 1944).
36. Dreyfus 1984, 30.
37. Silbermann has not denied this charge. Silbermann 1989, 196.
38. ibid, 223.

Chapter 15: 'The cultivated enthusiasm of a handful of missionaries': The Genesis of Musica Viva Australia

1. Menuhin 1979, 162.
2. 'Rare flavor in Sydney Labor of Musical Love', *AMN* (April 1941), 19. In his memoirs, Richard Goldner called him 'a strange figure, [...] like an actor playing the role of a cellist'.

Notes: Chapter 15

3. Radic 1986, 110.
4. Quoted in Sametz 2001, 128.
5. Radic 1986, 114.
6. Facsimile in Goldner n.d., 109.
7. ibid, 139.
8. Baker 2008, 250.
9. In his memoirs *Mein Leben* (1999), Marcel Reich-Ranicki mentioned Pullman as the most important musician of the Warsaw Ghetto.
10. Goldner n.d., 144.
11. Neville Cardus, 'Fine Chamber Playing', *SMH* (5 April 1943), 2.
12. A recording of this arrangement is in NAA: C100, 1594904.
13. Mahler-Werfel 1963, 226.
14. Facsimile of Scherchen letter in Goldner n.d., 75. See also Lühe 1991.
15. Facsimile in Goldner n.d., 77.
16. Scherchen 1991, 143.
17. From the Música Viva Manifesto, 1 May 1944. <http://www.latinoamerica-musica.net/historia/manifestos/1-de.html> (accessed 2 January 2016).
18. Quoted in Shmith and Colville, eds, 1996, 7.
19. 'Chorus of String Quartets', *SMH* (8 December 1945), 7.
20. Neville Cardus, 'New String Ensemble Disappoints', *SMH* (10 December 1945), 5; 'Sydney Musica Viva', *AMN* (January 1946), 21.
21. 'New Note in Music', *Daily Mirror* (10 April 1946).
22. Dullo 1946, 3.
23. Walter Dullo, 'Richard Goldner. Musician and Inventor', *New Citizen* (15 June 1946), 7.
24. Lühe 1998, 206.
25. Their hospitable home was at 2 Grosvenor Street, Wahroonga, NSW.
26. Pollnitz 2006.
27. Interview with Eva Wagner, 28 August 2000, Sydney.
28. Oral history, Charles Berg. Mitchell Library Sydney, MLOH 437/109.
29. Goldner n.d., 6.
30. Interview with Sybil Baer, 31 August 2000, Sydney.
31. Goldner n.d., 145.
32. Karl Bittman, 'Twelve Years in Australia', *New Citizen* (15 October 1950), 3.
33. 'Musica Viva Earns New Citizens' Support', *New Citizen* (15 January 1951), 4.
34. 'Musica Viva or Re-Viva?' *New Citizen* (15 December 1951), 7.
35. Renwick 2007.
36. Interview with Charmian Gadd, 25 August 2000, Sydney. Goldner remarried in 1970 after the suicide of his first wife (1969).
37. W.W. [Wolfgang Wagner] 1953–4, 35f.

38. 'Musica Viva Society', *AMN* (March 1955), 2.
39. Frydman 1995.
40. Menuhin 1979, 295.
41. Norst 1988, 136.
42. Scherchen had tried in vain to get an invitation to Australia. See his letter of 19 May 1938 in Heinze Collection, Box 1.
43. Interview with Eva Wagner, 28 August 2000, Sydney.
44. Shmith and Colville, eds, 1996, 4f. More passages are quoted in Baker 2010.
45. Amanda Lynch, 'A Giant Among Musical Pioneers', *Canberra Times* (28 May 1989), 28.
46. Shmith and Colville, eds, 1996, 37.
47. Covell 1996, 30.

Chapter 16: Between Adjustment and Self-Assertion: Refugee Contributions to Australian Musical Life

1. 'Maurice Abravanel Likes Australia', *AMN* (December 1946), 13.
2. W.G. James to Prerauer, 12 March 1937. NAA: SP173/1, PRERAUER, CURT.
3. 'Music in Sydney', *AMN* (September 1938), 7.
4. ABC Inter-Office Memo, 17 April 1940. NAA: SP173/1, PRERAUER, CURT.
5. ABC Memorandum of 22 April 1940. ibid.
6. Author's discussion with Maria Prerauer, Sydney.
7. 'Bartered Bride', *AMN* (July 1947), 23; *Argus* (27 May 1947), 10.
8. *AMN* (May 1950), 20; see also *Canon*, vol 3 (1949–50), 591.
9. 'Dolf Brenner Leaves Hector Crawford Productions', *AMN* (June 1950), 7.
10. 'New Opera for Melbourne', *AMN* (February 1951), 10.
11. '"Shakesperian" Opera for Melbourne', *AMN* (June 1951), 9; *Argus* (8 February 1951), 6.
12. Dullo, May 1948, 7.
13. 'Prodigious Service for Sacred Music. Dr Schildberger's All-Round Musicianship', *AMN* (February 1943), 12.
14. *AMN* (September 1946), 5.
15. Dullo, May 1948, 7.
16. 'ANDANTE – the new Australian!' *AMN* (October 1949), 2.

17. *AMN* (December 1949), 14.
18. Founded in 1934, the Melbourne Symphony Orchestra played under the title Victorian Symphony Orchestra from 1949 until 1965.
19. *AMN* (June 1950), 22.
20. *AMN* (November 1950), 11.
21. *AMN* (November 1953), 7.
22. 'Krug: a tough musician prepared for anything', *Australian* (3 November 1987), 2.
23. Levi 2004, 84.
24. Buzacott 2007, 227f.
25. 'Mr Frank Kitson. Australia's Petrillo. He fights for musicians', *Tempo* (June 1947).
26. 'Music: The big clean-up', *Daily Telegraph* (22 January 1949); 'Musicians' Ban', *SMH* (15 January 1949); 'New Discrimination by Musicians' Union', *New Citizen* (15 March 1950).
27. Goossens 1949.
28. Information from Eddy Helfgott, Sydney, 16 August 2000; P.R. Meyer-Thoene, 'Is the Musicians' Ban Legally Valid?' *New Citizen* (15 February 1949), 6.
29. Interview with Sybil Baer, 31 August 2000, Sydney.
30. Kramer to the ABC, 12 October 1954. NAA: SP613/1 (Sydney Symphony Orchestra – personnel), 6/1/7 Part II. Prior to this, Schulvater had already been temporarily dismissed several times.
31. Information from Sue Course, Melbourne, daughter of the musician.
32. 'The Band of the Month – Verdon Williams and his 3DB (Melbourne) Concert Orchestra', *Tempo* (September 1949), 7.
33. Tiemeyer-Schütte 2000.
34. 'Brighton Philharmonic Society', *AMN* (June 1947).
35. *AMN* (June 1944), 15.
36. 'Cantata and Ballet. City of Brighton Philharmonic', *AMN* (July 1944), 8.
37. 'Night of Opera. City of Camberwell Philharmonic'. *AMN* (August 1945), 27.
38. 'Twin Souls of Choralism'. *AMN* (December 1945), 17.
39. *AMN* (December 1946, 4 and January 1947, 18).
40. *Argus* (9 December 1946), 19.
41. 'Kew Philharmonic Society: Works by Australian Composers', *AMN* (May 1948).
42. *AMN* (December 1953), 15.
43. *AJH* (9 March 1939), 11.
44. 'Spivakovsky at his best', *AMN* (May 1947), 18.
45. 'Spivakovsky excels', *AMN* (August 1950), 20.

46. Excerpts are available at <http://jascha.com> (accessed 4 October 2015).
47. Evans 2009, 210.
48. Note in Heinze Collection, Box 12.
49. 'Pianist from Vienna', *AMN* (April 1939), 13; *Argus* (23 March 1939), 19; *AJH* (9 March 1939, 11 and 30 March 1939, 8).
50. Interview with Robert Kolben, 4 October 2003, Munich.
51. This and the following quotes are from ibid.
52. 'Bachelor of Engineering Wins Piano Championship', *AMN* (November 1950), 8.
53. 'ABC Concerto/Vocal Competition, NSW', *AMN* (June 1951), 17.
54. 'Winners Of ABC Competition', *SMH* (14 May 1953), 2.
55. *AMN* (December 1954), 25.
56. Interview with Robert Kolben, 4 October 2003, Munich.
57. Kurt Robert Eisner, in Foster 1986, 128.
58. 'Cellist and Pianist Present Second Beethoven Sonata', *AMN* (April 1951), 9.
59. NAA: SP173/1 (Feigl, Leonie – Soprano), FEIGL, LEONIE.
60. Neville Cardus, 'Splendid Lieder Singing. Lily Kolos's Concert', *SMH* (20 November 1943), 11. In 1944 the critic lauded her 'memorable interpretations of unusual beauty'. *SMH* (14 August 1944), 4.
61. 'Interesting visitors. Varied Array of Talent', *SMH* (21 October 1939), 10.
62. See poster and comprehensive programme, NAA: C123 (Kimmel, Emmy), 9021; Neville Cardus, 'Grand Lieder Singing', *SMH* (30 July 1943).
63. NAA: ST1607/2, KIMMEL EMMY; N. Cardus, *SMH* (27 June 1945), 4.
64. Neville Cardus felt that Hirschberg's Schubert interpretation was too operatic. *SMH* (25 November 1946), 5.
65. 'Eric Liffman's Singing', *AMN* (July 1944), 25; *AMN* (September 1949), 6; *Songs the People Love*, 121–31.
66. Warren-Smith 1983, 24.
67. *New Citizen* (15 May 1948), 7; 'New Opera Venture', *Argus* (4 April 1944), 6; 'Australian Talent in Grand Opera', *SMH* (1 June 1944), 4.
68. *Canberra Times* (8 July 1944), 2.
69. Curriculum Vitae, NAA: A435 (Werther, Rudolf), 1946/4/381.
70. *Mercury* (Hobart; 12 August 1939), 5; Daley 2003, 21.
71. 'First Grand Opera Well Received', *Examiner* (Launceston; 6 December 1943).
72. Webb 2003, 10.
73. Dwyer-Gray to Calwell, 9 August 1945. NAA: A435 (Werther, R), 1946/4/381.
74. 'Opera and Ballet Festival for International Week', *Mercury* (Hobart; 11 October 1945).

75. 'I feel so disgusted with this action of the Musicians' Union, which is killing generosity and enthusiasm, that I shall produce no more music in Hobart.' Rudolf Werther, 'Musicians' Union', *Mercury* (6 November 1945), 3.
76. '"Tassy" Yields to Melbourne', *AMN* (February 1946), 13.
77. The papers of Hans Briner/Brinnitzer (1901–73) are held in the State Library of Western Australia.
78. Werther 1957. See Daley 2003, 26.
79. Webb 2003.
80. 'German Musician Arrives', *SMH* (17 March 1947), 3; 'Berlin Pianist in Melbourne', *AMN* (June 1947), 7.
81. 'The Bartered Bride', *AMN* (January 1949), 25.
82. 'Revival of Opera Masterpiece', *Argus* (28 May 1949; Weekend Magazine).
83. *AMN* (January 1950), 11; Wagner 1950.
84. 'Further News of Sydney's Opera', *AMN* (June 1950), 11. Strangely Zander's name is not mentioned in the entry for the National Opera of NSW in Whiteoak 2003, 476.
85. 'The Man Behind the Coming Opera', *Sunday Herald* (4 March 1951), 8; 'Opera Director's Doubts Are Gone', *SMH* (7 March 1951), 6.
86. Telephone conversation with the author. See also the obituary in *SMH* (24 December 1951), 6.
87. *AMN* (April 1947), 10.
88. Annie Portnoj 1947.
89. *AMN* (June 1954), 7.
90. *Age* (27 December 1986), 4.
91. <www.itsanhonour.gov.au/honours/honour_roll/search.cfm?breif=false&page=1&search_view=~all~&view=10&search_type=simple> (accessed 4 January 2016).
92. <https://www.itsanhonour.gov.au/honours/honour_roll/search.cfm?aus_award_id=1107740&search_type=quick&showInd=true> (accessed 4 January 2016).
93. Tribe 2007, 89.
94. 'New Cantor at Liberal Synagogue', *AJH* (9 February 1939), 5.
95. *Australian Jewish News* (10 October 1941); Graff and Turnbull 2005, 37, 41.
96. *AJR* (September 1945), 9.
97. Schildberger 1946.
98. Interview with Rabbi John Levi, 24 July 2000, Melbourne.
99. *Sydney Jewish News* (18 August 1939).
100. Schoenberger to Schildberger, 29 April 1940. Schildberger Papers.

101. Schoenberger to Schildberger, 18 October 1941. ibid.
102. Simmons 2003, 100.
103. Günter Hirschberg, Obituary for T. Schoenberger. *Hebrew Standard* (22 February 1945). Quoted in Simmons 2003, 152.
104. Oral History of Werner Baer, 1984. Mitchell Library, Sydney, MLOH 437/106.
105. Simmons 2003, 221.
106. ibid, 224.
107. Information from Sybil Baer, 27 March 2004.
108. Solomon 1993, 908f.
109. Segaloff 1993, 24.
110. 'Dr Floyd's Column', *Radio Times* (25 March 1944).
111. Sydney John Kay, *Romeo and Juliet*. Piano edition, NLA MUS N m 786.2 R721.
112. *SMH* (24 November 1941), 4.
113. *Faust* (October 1941, Hélène Kirsova, two pianos), NLA, Symphony Australia A/C KRI 05 (digital online at NLA); *Revolution of the Umbrellas* (1943, Hélène Kirsova, two pianos), NLA Symphony Australia A/C KRI 16; Orchestral Suite 1949.
114. Crotty 1999, 65.
115. Papers of Gertrud Bodenwieser. NLA, MS 9263, Series 4, Piece 3.
116. Communication to the author from conductor and broadcaster Bernard Keeffe, London.
117. Vernon-Warren 1999, 106.
118. In 1946, Graff wrote the music *The Moving Finger* for Shona Dunlop's School of Dance. Crotty 1999, 67.
119. 'Impressive Modern Ballet', *Argus* (20 August 1945), 7.
120. Crotty 1999, 70.
121. Bodenwieser 1946, 5.
122. 'Hot Rhythm in the Samba', *Sunday Herald* (20 March 1949), 2.
123. The Kleines Wiener Theater gave guest performances first at the Independent Theatre in North Sydney and later in St James Hall and Anzac House.
124. Interview with Andy Factor, 11 March 2004, Melbourne.
125. Schuster had moved with his Australian wife to Australia, where he gradually adopted the 'gypsy' style of playing that he knew from his native Transylvania.
126. Schumann 1997, 145.
127. Interview with Erwin Frenkel, 22 July 2000, Melbourne.
128. Interview with Ilse Blair, 20 July 2000, Melbourne.
129. Telephone conversation with John Harband, 22 March 2003, Melbourne.
130. Information from Ilse Blair, Melbourne.

131. Radic 1986, 29.
132. Information from Harry Rich, Sydney.
133. Kathe Neumann 1940, 9.
134. See advertisement he and his brother Cyril placed, *SMH* (19 February 1947), 12.
135. Sela Trau (1898–1991), who escaped to London with her husband, Max Rostal, in 1934, was also an influential cello teacher. She came to Australia in 1961.
136. Warren-Smith 1983, 35.
137. Henry Portnoj 1949.
138. Linda Phillips, 'Sylvia Fisher', *AMN* (April 1955), 9–10.
139. *AMN* (December 1946), 13.
140. 'Singers of Australia', *Canon* 1/5 (1947–48), 20.
141. Walter Dullo, 'Portrait of a Promising Young Talent: Henry Krips', *New Citizen* (15 May 1948), 7.
142. 'Baer: New Musical Director of Singers of Australia', *AMN* (June 1948), 11.
143. Report by Sir Thomas Beecham, 10 January 1941. NAA: SP1588/2 (Employment of foreign musicians), 741.
144. '"Professional" Critics', *AMN* (January 1943), 13; 'Music Criticism as She is Wrote. An Effort in the Manner of Nervewill Discardus', *AMN* (June 1944), 5.
145. Prerauer 1939.
146. Inglis 1983, 93.
147. Shaw 2003.
148. Roger Covell, *SMH* (30 July 1969).
149. Wolfgang Wagner Papers, State Library of NSW (MLMSS 6621).
150. Obituary 'Dr Hans Forst 1911–1997', *SMH* (date unknown). Found in biographical cuttings at NLA (Bib Id 360846).
151. Kenneth Hince, 'A Critic Dies', *Australian* (16 December 1967), 13.
152. Blanks 1982; Blanks 1992, 34–5, 53.
153. Greer Fay Cashman, 'Father said: "Music alright as a hobby"', *Australian Jewish News* (23 July 1965).
154. Thomas 1997.
155. Interview with Felix Werder, 24 July 1995, Melbourne.
156. B. Heinze to the Registrar A.T.J. Bell, 10 January 1973. Heinze Collection, Box 34.
157. Radic 1986, 94.
158. Interview with Felix Werder, 11 October 1995, Berlin.
159. *AMN* (February 1954), 9.

Chapter 17: 'Land of Mine': New Compositions for a New Australia

1. *SMH* (22 December 1947), 10.
2. *Sun* (12 December 1947).
3. Pike and Cooper 1998, 205.
4. *A Selection of the Tunes of Bush Christmas. Film Music composed and arranged for piano by Sydney John Kay* (Sydney: Chappell & Co, 1948).
5. Joris Ivens also had a marked influence. He came to Australia in 1945 and worked with Heyer and Catherine Duncan.
6. Whiteoak 2003, 645f.
7. Dreyfus 1984, 57.
8. Dümling 2001.
9. Dreyfus 1984, 96 and Dreyfus 1998, 105.
10. John Kay, 'Music Life in Japan', *AMM* (1 January 1938), 25–6.
11. John K. Kay, 'Jammin' Dem Keys', ibid., 40–9.
12. Henry Adler, 'Dark Eyes', arranged for Accordeon. 'Lullaby' (Brahms), arranged for 3 Accordeons, *AMM* (1 January 1940), 68–9.
13. The music publisher Boosey & Hawkes acquired the rights to this song at the time, but it was not published as sheet music until 1945; it was only then that Krips' chances as a refugee musician improved.
14. Bischofswerder, n.d.. See also Patkin 1979, 46–50.
15. The Archive of Australian Judaica brought out a sheet music version of the *Phantasia Judaica* in 1996, supplemented by an expanded version with additional flute parts, which Felix Werder produced especially for the occasion.
16. Uwe Radok, 'Walter Würzburger remembered' (13 June 1995). The text is possibly a parody of Goethe's poem 'Die wandelnde Glocke' ['The Wandering Bell'], which begins with the lines 'Es war ein Kind, das wollte nie/zur Kirche sich bequemen [...]' ['There was a child who would never/agree to go to church.' Tr Chris Ackerly and Lawrence J. Clipper, *A Companion to Under the Volcano* (Vancouver: University of British Columbia Press, 1984), 113.]
17. The composer's daughter suspects, however, that the song had already been sketched during the voyage on the *Queen Mary*, Wurzburger 1996, 6f.
18. Tr James Luchte, quoted in James Luchte, *Out of Time: Music and the Making of Modernity* (Oxford: Oxford University Press, 2015), 171.
19. Arthur Holde, 'Siegfried Würzburger', *Aufbau* (25 September 1942), 10. 'A circle of friends and pupils informs that the singing teacher and organist of the Königsteinerstraße Synagogue in Frankfurt, Siegfried Würzburger had died in Poland

[...]. Restricted by a severe eye disorder, he had had to make the effort to persevere in Germany. He has become one of the innocent victims for whose fate his torturers will one day be held accountable.'
20. Diary entry of December 1942, quoted in Uwe Radok's letter to Hannah Wurzburger, 6 January 2000 Author's archive.
21. There was only one more performance, under the direction of Max Schönherr, on Viennese Radio ORF on 21 April 1961.
22. *Salute to Australia*. Words by John Wheeler, music by Werner Baer (Sydney: W.H. Paling & Co, c1951).
23. *Land of Mine*. Words by John Wheeler, music by Henry Krips (Sydney: Chappell & Co, c1951).
24. 'Ernest Kaufmann: A Talented Artist', *New Citizen* (15 July 1948), 4.
25. See Kaufmann's extensive correspondence with the ABC. NAA: SP827/2 (Australian Composers: Dr Ernst Kaufmann), KAUFMANN.
26. NAA: SP827/2 (Australian Composers: Dr Rudolf T Werther), WERTHER. Selected works are analysed in Daley 2003, 81–113.
27. Interview with Erwin Frenkel, 22 July 2000, Melbourne.
28. Werder later destroyed this early composition.
29. Felix Werder, *String Quartet No. 6* (Melbourne: Australian Music Fund, c1968).
30. Covell 1967, 185.
31. Warren Burt, 'Australia's Felix', *ABC Radio 24 Hours* (February 1992), 54f.
32. Covell 1967, 186.
33. Murdoch 1975, 194.
34. ibid, 191.
35. ibid.
36. Covell 1967, 186–9.
37. Murdoch 1975, 191.
38. 'Australia was disastrous for me in my formative years.' Dreyfus 1984, 28.
39. Dreyfus 1998, 7.
40. Dreyfus 1984, 57.
41. Curt Prerauer, *Nation* (20 October 1962), 18.
42. Prerauer 1966, 428.
43. See the detailed list of performances visited by Dreyfus; Papers of Kenneth Hince, NLA, series III, item 629 (Box 2), Diary of a Fellowship. Also in Dreyfus 2011, 4–7.
44. Dreyfus 1998, 81.
45. Jenny Isaacs in Dreyfus 2009, 63; Joel Crotty in Dreyfus 1998, 27.
46. Dreyfus 1984, 79f.
47. ibid, 82; Dümling 2000, 89–91.

48. Roger Covell, 'Didjeridu coexists in Dreyfus work', *SMH* (1 August 1972), quoted in Dreyfus 1998, 40.
49. Interview with Felix Werder, 24 July 1995, Melbourne.
50. Interview with Felix Werder, 11 October 1995, Berlin.
51. C.M. Prerauer, *Nation* (10 August 1963).
52. Roger Covell, 'New Stature in Creating', *SMH* (12 July 1964).
53. C.M. Prerauer, 'Scores in print', *Nation* (23 January 1965).
54. Kenneth Hince, 'Elegant score, sir', *Australian* (13 February 1965).
55. Radic 1978, 91.
56. Helen Frizell, 'Music with laughter', *SMH* (5 May 1973), 23; Felix Werder, '20th Century Rococo', *Opera Australia* (January 1974), 20–1.
57. Interview with Leonard Radic, 26 July 2000, Melbourne.
58. Richard Meale had signed a contract with Boosey & Hawkes in 1964. 'More Australian Music Published', *SMH* (28 December 1964).
59. Lucas 1973 and Dreyfus 2011.
60. Maria Prerauer, 'The Gilt-Edged Kid', *Australian* (12 December 1975).
61. Dreyfus 1984, 89.
62. Dreyfus 1998, 23.
63. See list of German reviews in ibid, 13.
64. Interview with Felix Werder, 24 July 1995, Melbourne.

Chapter 18: 'Happily ever after': Hidden Contributions to Cultural Diversity

1. Berghahn 1988, 103.
2. Snowman 2002, 321. 'Continental Britons' exhibitions were shown at the Jewish Museums in London (2002) and Vienna (2004).
3. Silbermann 2000, 116f.
4. Silbermann 1953, 12.
5. Information from Sybil Baer, Sydney.
6. Information from Mary-Clare Adam, Tel Aviv, 8 May 2004.
7. Kurt Eisner, husband of Otti Veit, letter to the author, 11 March 2001.
8. Information from the Australian Embassy, Berlin.
9. 'Other distinguished peculiarities: Dark and swarthy with an abundance of confidence.' NAA: A6126/16 (John Kurt Kaiser), 197, 248.
10. Faulkner 1979, 120f.

11. Dundy 1981, 118.
12. Robert Record, 'Eager Audience', *Sydney Morning Herald Magazine* (16 April 1946). See also Rosemarie Benjamin, *The Story of the Theatre for Children* (Sydney: Film Strip, *c*1949).
13. Kay was referring to his younger brother Peter, who had moved to Peru.
14. Walter Dullo, 'Metropolitan Mobile Players', *New Citizen* (15 July 1948), 7.
15. Walter Dullo, 'Sydney John Kay. An Australian Theatre Pioneer', *New Citizen* (15 August 1948), 7.
16. 'Oliviers See Play in Factory', *SMH* (19 August 1948), 3. A few days later Olivier appealed to the people of Sydney: 'They're lucky to have such a lovely city and such a beautiful climate. All they need to complete the picture is a good legitimate theatre.' *Daily Telegraph* (23 August 1948).
17. Sydney John Kay, 'Criticism – or Action?' *New Citizen* (15 March 1949), 4.
18. Information from Anthony Kay, Sydney.
19. Cracknell 1999, 79.
20. The script of March 1952 for this never realised film, proposing an Australian National Theatre, is preserved at the National Archives (NAA: A1336, 51672).
21. 'Mercury Theatre', *New Citizen* (July 1953), 6.
22. He had married the Australian in 1946. Meanwhile his first wife, Gerty, continued to run the Stork Club, from 1950 with radio entertainer Jack Davey. See Vagg 2007, and information from Anthony Kay, Sydney.
23. Programmes of the Mercury Mobile Players are collected in the National Library of Australia (Bib ID 3529623); reviews of the Mercury Theatre plus several issues of the *Sydney Mercury Theatre Magazine* are in the State Library of NSW (MLMSS 7164X).
24. Papers of Sydney John Kay. NLA Bib ID 3356648.
25. Sybil Baer to Lois Kay, 8 June 1970 (Anthony Kay, Sydney).
26. Baer 1982. Baer states incorrectly that the band stopped playing after the war because its music was no longer in fashion.
27. Neukölln is a working-class district of Berlin, far from the fashionable Kurfürstendamm.

Short Biographies

1. Italicised items have been digitised and are online.

Short Biographies

ADAM, MANFRED: *b*.31 March 1894, Berlin. Son of Meinhardt Adam (Jewish) and Katharina Ruth, née Schmidt (non-Jewish). Address: 6 Ansbacher Str., Schöneberg. Studied art history and music history at Berlin University, and Gregorian chant at the Maria Laach monastery, where he played the piano daily. Influenced by Wanda Landowska. Repertoire included Scarlatti, Couperin and Rameau; he also wrote compositions in this style. Escaped to Britain in 1939. Proofreader for Oxford University Press. Interned in 1940 and deported to Australia aboard *Dunera*. Interned in Tatura (Camp 3) where he taught Italian and Arabic. Released from Tatura in 1944; resumed work as proofreader. Lived with his brother Leonhard, Professor of Anthropology at the University of Melbourne. Died 1967, Melbourne. Sources: Dening 1993; NAA *A367, MP1103*;[1] Mary-Clare Adam, Tel Aviv.

ADLER, HEINRICH (HENRY) MAX: *b*.17 January 1914, Berlin. Son of Adolf Adler (Polish) and Anna, née Lauber (German). Jewish. He learned piano from the age of six and worked as a silk fabric buyer for the Israel department store. Married Vera Fanny Vogel, 1938. Last Berlin address: 43 Möllendorffstr., Lichtenberg. Arrived in Sydney 26 August 1938 aboard *Aorangi*. From 1939 piano and accordion teacher at Nicholson's College for Modern Music. From 1940 member of Fisher's Sextet with Emanuel and Adolf Fisher. Military service (2 Aust Empl Coy), 1942–1945. Naturalised 1944. From 1946 further education at Sydney Conservatorium (A. Mus. A). Pianist in Henry Adler Trio with Don Andrews (guitar) and Adolf Fisher (bass). Pianist, teacher, arranger and publisher. Choirmaster at Great Synagogue, Sydney, 1952–1955. Assisted J. Albert & Son in publishing international hits. Two children: Joan and Ronald. Died 28 May 2002, Sydney. Sources: *AMM*; NAA *A12508*; Henri Aram, Sydney.

ALBERTI, VICTOR GUSTAV: *b*.14 December 1884, Miskolc, Hungary. Son of Salomon Altstätter and Eva, née Roth. Jewish. Married Margit

Horvath *c*.1911. After military service in Hungary he opened a music and record shop in Berlin and established several publishing companies for light music, including Alrobi, Ufaton. Resigned as deputy treasurer of the Federation of German Music Publishers in April 1933. Relocated to Budapest and Vienna, where he directed Octava Publishing. Absent during German invasion into Austria; escaped to Zurich. Founded Octava Music Co. in London. Emigration to Australia recommended by Antal Dorati; permit received in Geneva. Arrived with his wife in Melbourne 11 February 1940 aboard *Remo*. Daughter Emilie and her husband, music publisher Rudolph E. Baré (*b*.1 October 1907, Budapest), already in Australia. Baré procured work for him in Allans Music store. Later suffered from cancer; wife earned their living by taking factory jobs. Daughter worked as a nurse for Hephzibah Menuhin. Died 25 July 1942, Melbourne. Sources: Brückner and Rock 1936; Fetthauer 2004; LexM; NAA A12508, C123; Susan Gabor (daughter).

BADER, HANS: *b*.29 November 1906, Pohrlitz, Bohemia. Son of cattle trader Maximilian Bader and Bertha, née Winkler. Jewish. Moved to Vienna in 1908. Studied violin at Academy of Music (without degree) 1920–1921, then completed eight years at Vienna Conservatory, and two years' study in conducting. From 1929 bandleader in Sils-Maria and Bucharest. Married Margarethe Löwy, milliner. Address: 19 Ausstellungsstr., Vienna II. Two children: Harry (*b*.1931) and Lieselotte (*b*.1936). Received notification from City of Vienna to vacate residence in August 1938. Expelled from Reichsmusikkammer in October and detained in Dachau, 12 November–20 December 1938. Departed for Shanghai in January 1939. Left *Conte Biancamano* in Singapore, where he secured engagements as a musician in light entertainment. Deported to Australia with wife and children in September 1940 aboard *Queen Mary*. Interned in Tatura, where he participated in several shows. Worked in a pipe factory after release. Recognised as refugee alien in February 1944, and worked as music programme arranger at Broadcasting Exchange, Melbourne. Naturalised 5 June 1946. Succeeded Dolf Brenner as arranger at Hector Crawford Productions, and worked as a piano teacher. Died 22 April 1964, Melbourne. Sources: Gerigk and Stengel 1942; NAA *A367, MP1103–2*; Lisa Vinnic (daughter).

BAER, WERNER FELIX: *b*.29 April 1914, Berlin. Son of Robert Baer and Lucie, née Bendix. Jewish. From 1929 organist at Sophien-Gymnasium. From 1931 studied at Stern Conservatory with Georg Bertram and Fritz Masbach (piano), Arnold Dreyer (organ, conducting), Gustav Bumcke (theory, composition). Organist and choirmaster at Synagogue Prinzregentenstraße, 1935–1938; also music director of Jüdischer Kulturbund cabaret. Taught organ and dance music at private Jewish Hollaender Music School. Married Ilse Presch, 1938. Last Berlin address: 2 Clausewitzstr., Charlottenburg. After November pogrom imprisoned for three weeks in Sachsenhausen. Departed 7 December 1938 aboard *Potsdam* for Singapore, where he was city organist and teacher at Far Eastern Music School. Deported to Australia in September 1940 with wife and baby Miriam aboard *Queen Mary*. Interned in Tatura, where he conducted a choir. Military service (8 Aust Empl Coy), 1942–1945. Directed an army entertainment unit; also pianist for Studio of the Creative Dance, 1943–1944. Won ABC competition with song 'Sounds of Europe', 1943. Naturalised 1946. Choirmaster at Great Synagogue, Sydney, 1946–1950. Divorced Ilse in 1950 and married Sibilla Lighezzolo. Worked as pianist, lied accompanist (for Rudolf Schock, Tito Schipa et al.), organist and choral conductor. Compositions for ballet, film and theatre. ABC manager, and finally Assistant Director of Music, 1951–1979. Awarded Member of the Order of the British Empire (MBE) for contribution to musical life of Australia; honoured with Queen's Jubilee Medal. Died 28 January 1992, Sydney. Sources: Brückner and Rock 1936; Gerigk and Stengel 1942; Brooks 1956; Trapp et al. 1999; LexM; NAA *A367, A435, MP1103/1–2*; Ilse Blair and Sibilla Baer (widows).

BAERWALD, WERNER BRUNO RICHARD: *b*.14 October 1914, Darmstadt. Son of Physics Prof Hans Baerwald (Jewish) and Ella, née Fiebrand (non-Jewish). Lutheran. (Father dismissed from University on racial grounds, 1933.) Studied piano at Leipzig Conservatorium, final exam 10 January 1939. After father's release from Buchenwald, escaped with him to Britain while his mother remained in Darmstadt. Arrested in Enfield 26 June 1940, and deported to Australia aboard *Dunera*. Interned in Hay (Camp 7, Hut 36 with Peter Stadlen). Released on 19 June 1941 and returned to Britain aboard *Largs Bay*. Lived in London, where he worked as a shorthand typist.

Naturalised 1948. Changed name to Vernon Barwood. Sources: Technical University Darmstadt; Goltz 2013, 92; NAA *MP1103/1–2*.

BEHRENS, MAX KURT (ALEX): *b*.27 December 1907, Altona near Hamburg. Son of salesman Bernhard Behrens and Frieda, née Auerbach. Jewish. Studied music (bassoon, piano, conducting, composition) in Hamburg and Leipzig. Piano teacher and conductor at Hamburg Volksoper; after 1933 in Jüdischer Kulturbund, Hamburg. In 1937 followed his sister Annemarie to London, where he appeared in concerts of Freier Deutscher Kulturbund [Free German League of Culture]. Arrested in London 27 June 1940 and deported to Australia aboard *Dunera*. Interned in Hay und Tatura, where he appeared as conductor. Departed 18 October 1941 for Britain. Military service until 1946. Naturalised 1947, London. Worked as conductor and music teacher. Received West German restitution. Died July 1998. Sources: Brückner and Rock 1936; Gerigk and Stengel 1942; Raab Hansen 1996; LexM; NAA *MP1103/1–2*.

BERG, KARL (CHARLES) JOSEF: *b*.28 March 1917, Charlottenburg near Berlin. Son of music critic Richard Max Berg and Rosina, née Blau. Jewish. Took violin and piano lessons with aim of becoming professional musician. Attended Augusta-Gymnasium, 1928–1934. Trained as bookkeeper in Berlin, continued from 1936 in London. On expiry of residence permit, settled in Australia in 1937. Sold violin and renounced musical ambitions. Married Grete Ladenheim 1943. Naturalised 1944. In addition to main job as bookkeeper and manager, worked from 1946 for Musica Viva Society of Australia: Secretary 1954–1968, President 1968–1974. Chairman of Australian Opera, 1974–1986. Awards: Order of the British Empire (1972), German *Bundesverdienstkreuz* [Federal Cross of Merit] (1973) and Order of Australia (AM) 'in recognition of service to music and the theatre' (1986). (His son Anthony was also awarded an AM in 1992.) Died 6 February 1988, Sydney. Buried in Jewish cemetery, North Ryde. Sources: Tribe 2007; NAA *A435, SP11/5*; Anthony Berg (son).

BERGER, EMMA: see Kimmel, Emmy

BISCHOFSWERDER, BOAS (BOJAS): *b*.25 February 1895, Lubien near Warsaw, Poland. Jewish. Names of parents unknown. Studied voice (opera) before attending Talmud school. Moved to Berlin, where he married Selma Manasse c.1920, mother of Felix (b.1922). After her early death (1926) he married Helene (Lea) Schwersenz, mother of Manfred (b.1929). Cantor of orthodox Wolfenstein Synagogue, then principal cantor at the synagogue at 33 Brunnenstraße. Invited to record Jewish music on account of his beautiful tenor voice. Left Berlin 1933. Last address: 5 Invalidenstr. Settled in London, where he became cantor at the Great Garden Street Synagogue and President of Association of Chazanim of Federated Synagogues. Song collection for Friday night liturgy published 1935. Arrested as enemy alien in 1940 and deported to Australia aboard *Dunera*, voluntarily accompanied by his son Felix; wife and second son remained in Britain. Deeply shocked by mistreatment aboard ship. Became ill and was placed in army hospital at Waranga, 1941; supported by Felix. Died 28 June 1946. Buried at Fawkner Cemetery Melbourne. Sources: Bergmeier 2001; Archive of Australian Judaica Sydney; NAA *MP1103/1–2*; Felix Werder (son).

BISCHOFSWERDER, FELIX: see Werder, Felix

BLACH (BLACK), KURT: b.5 February 1908, Rinteln, Westphalia. Son of merchant Robert Blach and Selma, née Rosenthal. Jewish. Studied piano at Bückeburg Music School; played coffeehouse music in Cologne. Escaped to Amsterdam in 1933. Settled in Singapore, 1935; worked at Raffles Hotel. Married Louisa Isaac. Deported to Australia in 1940 aboard *Queen Mary*. Interned at Tatura, where he participated in entertainment shows. Military service (8 Aust Empl Coy), 1942–1945. Naturalised 1946. From 1948 to 1977 played regularly at the Hotel Australia in Melbourne; then worked for bandleader Denis Farrington. Second marriage to Carmel Lorraine Lennox in 1958. Three children: Anthony, Michael, and Peter. Gave private tuition in piano and accordion at home studio (21 Valentine Street, Ivanhoe). Died 15 February 1983, Melbourne. Buried in Tempelstowe Cemetery, Melbourne. Sources: NAA *A435*, *B884*, *MP1103/1–2*; Michael Black (son), Denis Farrington, and Kurt Collinet, Cologne.

BLANKS, (FRITZ) FRED ROY: b.Fritz Mayer, 31 May 1925, Schwäbisch-Gmünd. Son of shoe manufacturer Josef Mayer and Beta, née Kahn. Jewish. Father died 1930. Moved to Stuttgart in 1936, where he attended Jewish school. Family escaped to Britain in 1938, taking separate routes. Arrived in Sydney 10 January 1939 aboard *Jervis Bay*. Attended several schools and Sydney Technical High School. Studied singing. Naturalised as Fred Blanks, 1946. Gained university degree in chemistry (1947) and worked professionally as industrial chemist. Wrote concert reviews for *Canon* magazine, 1949–1952. Spent 1952–1954 mostly in Britain. From 1952 music critic for *Australian Jewish Times*; correspondent for the *Musical Times*, 1955–1992. Married Christiane Hellmann. Two children: Stephen Joseph (*b.*1960) and Diana (*b.*1964). Wrote reviews for *Sydney Morning Herald*, 1963–1996. Retired as chemist in 1964. Awarded Member of the Order of Australia for services to music (1988). Created database of all concerts attended since 1944. Died 15 March 2011, Sydney. Sources: NAA A12508; interview Fred Blanks 21 April 2003; obituary *SMH* (21 March 2011); papers at NLA.

BLAU, HANS: *b.*31 January 1906, Vienna. Son of commercial clerk Emil Blau and Charlotte, née Winkler. Jewish. Trained as electrician 1920–1923 because father prohibited a musical career. First appearance as musician in 1926. Played accordion and piano and sang in several Viennese bars; also member of Splendid Club Orchestra. Married Nelly Helene Artner, 1933. Escaped to Switzerland in 1938 with Duke of Windsor's help. Arrived 16 January 1939 in Singapore, where he accepted engagement procured by Mischa Stiwelband. Appeared at Coconut Grove, and Cathay Ballroom and Roof Garden. Deported to Australia in 1940 aboard *Queen Mary*. Interned in Tatura (family camp) where he presented entertainment programmes. Military service (8 Aust Empl Coy), 1942–1945; many concert appearances. Married Ilse Baer after her divorce; abandoned plans for a return to Vienna. Performed at Claridges nightclub and Hotel Australia, Melbourne (with Kurt Blach et al.). Ceased daily appearances in 1986 after suffering a stroke. Died 12 March 1998, Melbourne. Sources: NAA *A435*, *B884*, *MP1103/1–2*; Ilse Blair (widow).

BLAU, OTTO: *b.*1 March 1893, Vienna. Son of Imperial Advocate Dr Mayer Markus Blau and Florentine, née Goldenzweig (a sister of Josef Weinberger, music publisher). Jewish. Wounded in WWI, 1915–1919. Studied law at Vienna University. Entered Weinberger publishing house in 1922; from 1928 executive of the business. Acquired extension of copyright for Johann Strauß in 1929. Address: 93 Grinzingerstr., Vienna XIX. Following Aryanisation of

Weinberger company in 1939, he escaped to London, where he had founded a publishing house in 1936. Arrested as enemy alien in 1940 and deported to Australia aboard *Dunera*. Interned in Hay and Tatura (Camp 4). Military service (8 Aust Empl Coy), 1942–1943. Met Victor Alberti in Melbourne. In December 1944 he returned on board *Glenstrae* via Panama and New York to London, where he rebuilt Josef Weinberger Ltd. Relocation to Switzerland in 1962. Died 27 January 1980. Sources: Brückner and Rock 1936; NAA *B884*, *MP1103/1*–2; Fetthauer 2004; LexM.

BONDY, EMMA: see Weiss, Emma

BRANDMANN (BRANDMAN), SALOMON (FRITZ/FREDERICK): *b.*25 July 1887, Berlin. Son of Juda Brandmann (Polish) and Lotte, née Bernstein (Austrian). Jewish. Known as Fritz Brandmann after conferral of German citizenship (1908). Jeweller. Married Charlotte Schirmeister in 1913. Five children: Fritz, Johanna, Hans-Joachim, Lieselotte and Eva. During 1936 Olympics he met Australian police officer William John MacKay, who assisted him with emigration. Family arrived in Sydney in 1939 aboard *Narkunda*. Translator for the police and cantor at Temple Emanuel, 1939–1946. Naturalised 1944. Died 14 June 1959, Sydney. Daughter Johanna/Joan was professional accompanist to many opera singers, including Joan Sutherland. Sources: NAA A435, *B884*, SP11/5.

BRENNER, ADOLF (DOLF): *b.*14 August 1905, Vienna. Son of salesman Moritz Brenner and Elsa, née Klein. Jewish. Studied at Vienna Academy of Music: piano, harmony, counterpoint and musicology (Guido Adler), 1922–1927. Teachers included Eusebius Mandyczewski, Hugo Reichenberger and Joseph Marx. Conductor at Gotha-Sondershausen and Arnstadt, 1928–1931; conductor and choirmaster at Municipal Theatre, Regensburg, 1931–1933. Lost position on racial grounds in April 1933 and returned to Vienna. Lived with his mother, whom he supported financially by giving piano and harmony lessons. Address: 39 Karl-Beck-Gasse, Vienna XVIII. Taken to Dachau after November pogrom. Moved to Britain in July 1939 (intended destination USA). Interned in 1940. Deported to Australia aboard *Dunera*. Interned in Hay and Tatura, where he participated in musical life, still hoping to proceed to the USA. In 1942, mother deported to Riga; father to Auschwitz. Military service (8 Aust Empl Coy), 1942–1945.

Married Herta Irma Jotkowitz (*b*.Hamburg) in 1945. Naturalised 1946. Music editor for Hector Crawford, 1946–1950. Conductor of St Kilda Philharmonic Society and Sandringham Choral Society. Conducted *Merry Wives of Windsor* (Otto Nicolai) at Albert Street Conservatorium of Music before abandoning conducting in 1951. Permanent clerk at Department of Immigration, 1951–1970. Awarded British Empire Medal (BEM) in 1971. Last address: 62 Riversdale Road, Camberwell. Died 1 July 1996, Melbourne. Buried at Chevra Kadisha Cemetery, Springvale. Sources: NAA *A367*, *B884*, *MP1103/1–2*; Felix Werder.

BYK, ELLEN: *b*.Ellen Cohn, 14 February 1887, Berlin. Daughter of merchant Siegmund Cohn and Sophie, née Byk. Jewish. Attended Busse's Girls School. As Ellen Cohn-Byk, studied violin with Issay Barmas at Stern Conservatory 1901–1904, then at Klindworth–Scharwenka Conservatory, where she later taught. First concert appearance under the name Ellen Byk (Berlin, 1911) followed by numerous other appearances. Was refused admission to Reichsmusikkammer in 1935. Forced to return teaching permit in 1936 and limited to Jewish pupils. Supported by her brother Walter. Last Berlin address: 10 Markgraf-Albrecht-Str. After unsuccessful struggle to obtain teaching position in Australia, invited as domestic servant by Prof. Robert Marshall Allan. Arrived in Melbourne 1 May 1939 aboard *Ormonde*. Home duties and factory work. Concerts with Mary Baillie. Advertised as a violin teacher after the war, and taught into old age. Subsistence supported by restitution from West Germany. Last address: 14 Spring Street, Prahran. Died 16 November 1968, Armadale. Cremated at Springvale Crematorium. Sources: Brückner and Rock 1936; Gerigk and Stengel 1942; NAA *A12508*, A261; LexM; Rosemary Pattenden, Cambridge.

CHLUMECKY-BAUER, JOHANNES: *b*.22 October 1920, Vienna. Son of landowner Dr Moritz von Chlumecky-Bauer and Margarethe, née von Remiz. Non-Jewish Catholic. From 1927 violin lessons with Rudolf Fitzner; from 1931 with Julius Winkler. Uncle deported to Dachau, where he died in 1938. Last address: 11 Geweygasse, Vienna XIX. Family escaped to Britain in August 1938; father and sons interned in 1940. Nikolaus deported to Canada, Johannes and his father to Australia aboard *Dunera*. Mother and sister remained in Britain. Interned in Hay and Tatura, where Johannes received violin lessons from M. Pietruschka, and participated in musical activities. Military service with his father (8 Aust Empl Coy), 1942–1946. Father applied in vain for their joint return to Britain; died 27 November 1945. Johannes moved to London, where he attended the Royal College of Music. Moved to Vancouver, Canada in 1948 because Czechoslovakia paid no restitution for expropriated property. Joined first violins in Vancouver Symphony Orchestra and played second violin in de Rimanoczy String Quartet. Married violinist Rowena Phyllis Miles. Conductor of Vancouver Youth Symphony Orchestra; also gave private violin lessons. Died 7 May 1981, Vancouver. Sources: NAA *B884*, *MP1103/1–2*; Nicholas Chlumecky (brother).

CLUSMANN (HENGHES), GUSTAV HEINRICH (HEINZ): *b*.20 August 1906, Hamburg. Son of August Theodor Clusmann and Luise, née Winterfeldt. Non-Jewish Protestant. Moved to New York in 1924. Returned to Europe in 1932 and lived as a sculptor in Switzerland, France and England. Following conscription to German army he struggled in vain for British citizenship. Arrested in London in 1940. Interned and deported to Australia aboard *Dunera*. Performed Negro spirituals and Gershwin songs on board ship and in internment camps. Returned in 1941 to Britain, where he taught at the Royal College of Art in London; changed his name to Henghes and obtained British citizenship. Died 20 December 1975, Bordeaux, France. Sources: www.henghes.org; NAA *MP1103/1–2*.

COHN, ELLEN: see Byk, Ellen

COHN (COLIN), ELISABETH (ELIZABETH): *b*. Lisbeth Bertha Caspary, 2 July 1883, Königsberg, East Prussia. Daughter of merchant Gustav Caspary and Johanna, née Bernstein. Jewish. Studied violin at Hochschule für Musik, Berlin with Heinrich Jacobsen, Gabriele Wietrowetz and Joseph Joachim, 1900–1903. Returned in 1903 to Königsberg, where she lived as a violin teacher. Married optometrist Dr Willy Cohn in 1911. Her son Ernst passed medical exams and settled in Edinburgh to prepare his doctorate. In 1938 he arrived in Melbourne and adopted the name Ernest Colin. Father taken to Buchenwald in October 1938, and died one month later. Elisabeth Cohn travelled via Britain to Australia, arriving in April 1939 aboard *Ascanius*. After struggling in vain for a position at the Melbourne Conservatorium she worked as private violin teacher. Naturalised as Elizabeth Colin in 1945. Applied for German restitution. Among her students were Susie Ehrmann, Abe Dorevitch and Herbert Feith. Last address: 331 South Road, Moorabbin (Brighton East). Died of a brain tumour, 8 December 1951, Melbourne. Sources: Brückner and Rock 1936; Gerigk and Stengel 1942; NAA A12508; Isabella Colin and daughter Eva; LexM.

COPER, FRITZ: *b*.28 March 1892, Berlin. Son of butcher Emil Coper and Paula, née Turk; brother of Willy. Jewish. Military service, 1912–1918. Singer in Czechoslovakia (1933–1934), Budapest and Poland (1935–1936). Migrated 22 April 1936 to London, where he became soloist and choirmaster at the Reform Synagogue in the West End. In May 1937 he arrived aboard *Moreton Bay* in Sydney, where he worked as a singing teacher. Married Mary Raine Stevens in November, and became choirmaster at Temple Emanuel and Maccabean Hall in 1938. Military service (3 Aust Empl Coy), 1942–1943. Naturalised 1944. Address: 15 Manion Ave., Rose Bay. Died after a traffic accident, 15 September 1961. Sources: Simmons 2003; NAA A435, B884, C123, SP11/5.

COPER, WILLY: *b*.24 March 1893, Berlin. [See F. Coper] Brother of Fritz. Jewish. Light entertainment musician (violin, drums). Was refused admission to Reichsmusikkammer in 1935. Taken to Sachsenhausen after November pogrom. Last Berlin address: 60 Fasanenstr. Arrived in Sydney 14 June 1939 aboard *Alster*. Worked as a chorister, peddler and cleaner. Military service (2 Aust Empl Coy), 1942–1945. Naturalised 1944. Address: 226 Longueville Road, Lane Cove. Died 22 December 1958. Buried in Macquarie Park Cemetery and Crematorium. Sources: Brückner and Rock 1936; Gerigk and Stengel 1942; LexM; NAA A435, B884, C123, SP11/05.

DANEMANIS (DANE), MORDCHAIS (MARIO): *b*.30 March 1911, Kuldiga, Lithuania. Son of Eta-Rose Danemanis. Jewish. Appeared from 1934 under the name Mario Dane as operatic tenor in Vienna. Last address: 2 Freundgasse, Vienna IV. His mother arrived in Fremantle, Australia aboard *Orama* in 1935. He arrived in Fremantle 23 August 1938, and in Melbourne 2 February 1939. Appeared as soloist in concerts and gave radio broadcasts. Military service, 1942–1943. In July 1945 he sang the title role in *The Tales of Hoffmann* under Hermann Schildberger. Naturalised 1949;

application showed profession as 'photographer'. From 1954 involved in radio programme 'Mobilsong'. Long-time soloist in Melbourne Hebrew Congregation choir. Last address: 9 Meadow St, E. St Kilda. Died October 1997, Melbourne. Sources: NAA A12508, SP173/1, *B78*; Felix Werder.

DREYFUS, GEORG (GEORGE): *b.* 22 July 1928, Elberfeld (today Wuppertal). Son of businessman Alfred Dreyfus and Hilde, née Ransenberg. Jewish. Family moved to Berlin in 1935 after selling the business. Attended Theodor Herzl and Leonore Goldschmidt schools. Last Berlin address: 6 Brümmerstr., Dahlem. Arrived in Melbourne on Kindertransport aboard *Orama* in July 1939. Attended Melbourne High School before studying music at the University Conservatorium. Took temporary work in carpet cleaning business belonging to his father, who abandoned plans to return to Europe in 1948. (Father died 1951.) First composition written 1947. Played second bassoon in Victorian Symphony Orchestra, 1953–1954. Further studies at Vienna Academy of Music, 1954–1955. From 1956 principal bassoon in Perth, where he continued composing. Returned to Melbourne in 1958; again second bassoon in VSO. Active with New Music Ensemble, 1961–1965. Owing to commercial success as a film composer, left orchestra in 1964 to become one of Australia's first freelance composers. Co-founder of ISCM Melbourne, 1965. Address: 6 Grace St, Camberwell. Comprehensive range of musical scores for film, television, opera and concert. Has received numerous grants and awards. Sources: Covell 1967; Dobson 1978; Röder and Strauss 1983; Dreyfus 1984, 1998, 2009; Traber and Weingarten 1987; Bebbington 1997; Dümling 2001; LexM; NAA *A12508*.

DULLO, WALTER ANDREAS: *b.* 26 November 1902, Königsberg, East Prussia. Son of Dr Andreas Franz Wilhelm Dullo (non-Jewish) and Alice Clara, née Japha (Jewish). Attended secondary school in Offenbach/Main where his father was Lord Mayor (1907–1919). Studied mathematics in Berlin, 1921–1924. Studied piano at Hochschule für Musik with Leonid Kreutzer, and took private lessons with Richard Buhlig, 1925–1927. Studied law in Münster, Heidelberg and Berlin, 1927–1933. Articled clerk, 12 January 1933. Dismissed from judicial service as 'half Jew'. Trained in massage and confectionery to prepare for emigration. Last Berlin address: 5 Goßlerstr., Friedenau. Married Annemarie, née Deutsch and travelled with her to

Sydney, arriving 11 September 1937 aboard *Rendsburg*. Opened chocolate shop at 479 New South Head Road, Double Bay. Worked for the Allied Works Council in Alice Springs, 1943–1944. Naturalised 1944. Founded Musica Viva Society of Australia together with Richard Goldner in 1945. Mother and sister arrived 1948. Wrote programme notes for concerts, composed cadenzas for Mozart concertos and completed Schubert sonatas. Vice President of Mozart Society. Contributed to radio station 2MBS-FM. Died 22 August 1978, Sydney. German *Bundesverdienstkreuz* awarded posthumously. Sources: Loewald 1996; Bebbington 1997; NAA A435, *A12508*, C123, SP11/5.

EDELMANN, HANS: *b.*22 April 1907, Vienna. Son of cantor Owse Leb Edelmann and Julie, née Lemberger (owner of piano shop in 30 Josefstädter Str., Vienna VIII). Jewish. Worked as piano tuner and at Alois Reichmann bookshop. Left Jewish religious community in 1936 to marry Helene Hammerschmied (non-Jewish). Dismissed from his position as a Social Democrat in April 1938. Escaped via Yugoslavia to Britain in October. His non-Jewish wife received no visa. Deported to Australia aboard *Dunera*, 1940. Interned in Hay and Tatura, where he appeared as solo tenor. Military service (8 Aust Empl Coy), 1942–1946. Returned to his wife in Vienna in 1946, and to Reichmann bookshop, which had been restored to its Jewish owners. Two children: Felix (*b.*1947), and Paul (*b.*1950). Died 1 June 1978, Vienna. Sources: NAA *B884*, *MP1103/1–2*; Felix Edelmann, Vienna (son).

EHRENFELD, ADOLF PAUL ALFRED: *b.*22 February 1893, Lemberg (today Lvov). Son of Anna Ehrenfeld, née Majulik, and her husband (first name unknown). Jewish. Lived in Vienna under guardianship of engineer Sigmund Fadenhecht. Studied law at University, 1911–1914. Military service, 1914–1918. Law degree completed with doctorate, 1920. Attended lectures in musicology and studied conducting with Felix Weingartner. Temporary assistant conductor of Philharmonic Society. Associate lawyer in Vienna. Address: 18/2/7 Ledergasse, Vienna VIII. Escaped in September 1938 to Britain, where he joined the Anglican Church. Interned and deported to Australia in 1940 aboard *Dunera*. Interned in Tatura, where he taught music theory and history, and conducted a choir. Worked in Melbourne from 1946 as conductor of Victorian Railways Institute Choral Society, and the Kew Philharmonic Society. Examiner and lecturer at Albert Street Conservatorium of Music; head of opera class at Melba Conservatorium; music director at Collins Street Independent Church, and conductor of Melbourne University Chorale Society. Address: 12, Lempriere Ave, Balaclava. Died 6 November 1953, Melbourne. Cremated at Springvale Botanical Cemetery. Sources: Archives of Kew Philharmonic Society; NAA A714, A997.

FAKTOR (FACTOR), ADOLF (ADRIAN) ABRAHAM JOSEF: *b*.18 January 1924, Plauen, Vogtland. Son of embroidery salesman Chiel Faktor and Dobra, née Scheiner. Polish Jew. (Father moved to Plauen in 1919 and married in 1923.) Received violin lessons in Falkenstein, together with his brother Helmut. Both boys' applications for Leipzig Conservatorium rejected on racial grounds. Father arrested in November 1938 and taken to Buchenwald for one month. Family escaped in December to Paris, where Adolf studied violin with Pepito Sanchez at the Conservatoire. Changed first name to Adrian. Family arrived in Melbourne 11 February 1940 aboard *Remo*. Military service (6 Aust Empl Coy), 1942–1946; founded a string quartet. Violinist and concertmaster for various orchestras, e.g. Victorian Ballet Company and ABC Melbourne Show Band. Also worked as a private teacher. Sources: NAA A12508, B884, *B6531*; interview Adrian Factor 11 March 2004.

FEIGL, LEONIE: *b*.25 November 1880, Vienna. Daughter of salesman Samuel Schlesinger and Franziska, née Pick. Jewish. Voice lessons with Johann Ress at Conservatorium. Married oil industrialist Leopold Samuel Feigl in 1898, and moved with him to Baku. Relocated to St Petersburg in 1908. Two children: Ernst (*b*.Baku), and Julie (*b*.St Petersburg). Returned in 1914 to Vienna, where she took voice lessons with Marie Brossement, gave lieder recitals and organised a music salon in her house in Hietzing. After husband's death she moved to 6/1/5 Boltzmanngasse in 1936. Escaped to Paris 16 November 1938, then travelled to Australia where her two children lived. Arrived in Sydney 5 August 1940 after hazardous crossing aboard *Commissaire Ramel*. Fruitless attempts to establish a concert career. Naturalised 1946. Address: 42 Raglan St, Mosman. Gave private tuition. Died 17 March 1959, Sydney. Ashes committed to grave of Leopold Feigl and his parents, Central Cemetery, Vienna. Sources: NAA *A435*, *A12508*, C123, SP11/5, SP173/1; Julie Kerner (daughter).

FISHER, ADOLF (ADDY): *b*.Adolf Frischer, 1 September 1910, Charlottenburg near Berlin. Son of salesman Salomon Frischer and Feigel, née Reiner. Brother of Emanuel. Polish Jew. Cello lessons with Edmund Kurtz. After secondary school, began apprenticeship in fur business. Worked as musician in several bars (saxophone, clarinet, double bass and guitar). Address: 65 Krumme Str., Charlottenburg. Engagements in Poland, Luxembourg and Switzerland, 1933–1934. Drafted to Polish Army in 1935, so returned to Berlin. Appeared as stand-in for Weintraubs Syncopators' Farewell Concert. Was refused admission to Reichsmusikkammer 19 August 1935. Began work in French club in Beirut, Syria on 1 September 1935. Married Hildegard Kurschner, and moved to Australia at his brother's invitation. Arrived in Sydney 20 May 1938 aboard *Largs Bay*; joined Weintraubs as Adi Normand. Following internment of German band members, he continued playing in Fisher's Sextet. Military service (2 Aust Empl Coy), 1942–1945. Naturalised 1943. Known as Addy Fisher from 1946. Began importing furniture from Britain in 1948. Business address: Noblewoods, 318 Oxford St, Bondi Junction. Bass player in Henry Adler Trio. Address: 35 Selsdon Flats, 16 Macleay Street, Potts Point. Died 15 July 2007, Sydney. Sources: Brückner and Rock 1936; Gerigk and Stengel 1942; NAA *A367*, *A12508*, *B884*, C123; Lloyd 2003; LexM; interviews Addy Fisher 2003 and 2004.

FISHER, EMANUEL (MANNY): *b*. Emanuel Frischer, 23 April 1913, Charlottenburg near Berlin. [See A. Fisher] Brother of Adolf. Attended Schiller-Gymnasium, played violin and trumpet and, inspired by Weintraubs Syncopators, founded student band, Charles Jazz Syncopators. Played in bands of Dajos Béla, Paul Godwin and Marek Weber while undertaking medical studies. Expelled from Berlin University in 1933 but continued studies in Poland. Invited to succeed Weintraubs Syncopators' trumpet player Ady Rosner during their guest appearance in Warsaw, and joined the band. Married Russian Lidia Gluszkow in Rostov-on-Don, July 1936; she was subsequently arrested and prohibited from leaving Russia. Tour of Japan, 1936–1937. Arrived in Fremantle on 14 July 1937. Parents arrived in Sydney,

October 1939. German members' internment during the war meant dissolution of Weintraubs Syncopators. Founded Fisher's Sextet. Naturalised 1942. Military service (2 Aust Empl Coy), 1942–1945. Having searched in vain for his Russian wife, he married Gwendolyn Mabel Christie. One child: Michael (*b*.23 May 1947). Together with a friend he opened a meat packaging company, Globus, in 1949. Music became a hobby. Participated in film documentation of the Weintraubs. Died 13 April 2006, Sydney. Sources: Obituary, *SMH* (18 July 2006); NAA *A12508*, *B884*, *C123*; interview Manny Fisher 22 August 2000; Michael Fisher (son).

FLEISCHER (FLETCHER), OSKAR: *b*.27 September 1910, Vienna. Son of salesman Friedrich Fleischer and Ilona (Helene), née Kolliner. Jewish. Last address: 19a/1/3/6 Sperrgasse, Vienna XV. Engaged as violinist with Mischa Stiwelband in Singapore (Coconut Grove, and Cathay Ballroom and Roof Garden). Interned as enemy alien in 1940 and deported to Australia aboard *Queen Mary*. Interned in Tatura, where he appeared with amateur pianist Arthur Fuhrmann. Military service (8 Aust Empl Coy), 1942–1945. Married Margarete Friedlich in 1943; she already had twins. From 1945 known as Oscar Harold Fletcher; played violin, trumpet, keyed bugle and trombone. Appeared until *c*.1956 with Hans Blau at Claridges nightclub, Melbourne. Because his wife suffered depression, he acquired a rural farm and commuted to Melbourne before abandoning his musical career. Died 21 September 1958, Woodend District. Fawkner Crematorium. Sources: NAA A997, B884, *MP1103/1–2*; Ilse Blair.

FORST, HANS RICHARD: *b*.1 May 1911, Vienna. Son of journalist Max Forst and Flora, née Grünwald. Jewish, Protestant convert. Studied piano from 1916, music theory from 1925 (with Anton Webern). Doctorate in law, 1934. From 1935 music critic of *Neues Wiener Tagblatt*, where his father was editor. Lost his job in 1938 because of Jewish ancestry. Last address: 55/5 Untere Viaduktgasse, Vienna III. Assisted by Alexander Kipnis, he escaped to Australia, where he arrived on 20 November 1938 aboard *Niagara*. Parents followed in June 1939. Worked as ABC employee, teacher and composer (songs, a musical). Military service (2 Aust Empl Coy), 1942–1944. Wrote reviews for *Sydney Morning Herald*, *Daily Telegraph*, *Australian* and *Northshore Times*. Established and directed music library for *Sydney Morning Herald*, 1946–1976. Published book *Opera Is Not Nonsense!* in 1987. Died 20 November 1997, Sydney. Private cremation. Sources: Obituary *SMH*; NAA A367, A435, B884; Eva Wagner.

FRENKEL, ERWIN: *b*.28 December 1921, Vienna. Son of principal cantor and rabbi Emanuel Frenkel and Hanni, née Weiss. Jewish. Received organ and piano lessons. Talmud student in Bratislava and Vienna, 1935–1936. Also played jazz. Last address: 7/3/13 Fugbachgasse, Vienna II. Escaped via Italy and Switzerland to Britain, arriving 22 November 1938. Following a denunciation, classified by Aliens Tribunal as Category A on 13 November 1939 and immediately interned. After surviving the *Arandora Star* tragedy, deported to Australia in 1940 aboard *Dunera*. Interned in Tatura and Loveday. Military service (8 Aust Empl Coy), 1942–1946. Married Ellen Lubasch, 1944. Naturalised 1946. Worked as piano teacher and jazz pianist. Two children: David (*b*.1947) and Miriam (*b*.1954). Unable to make a living from music, so became businessman in the building industry. Choirmaster of Hebrew Congregation in St Kilda. Editor of the monthly *Zionist* and weekly *Jewish Herald*; after abandoning Zionism, he wrote columns for the monthly *Australian Humanist*. Book publications: *The Third Way: Economics for the Layman* (1977), *The Press and Politics in Israel* (1994). Died 24 October 2000. Buried in Springvale Botanical Cemetery. Sources: Patkin 1979; Gillman 1980; Pearl 1983; obituaries in *Age* (6 December 2000) and *Dunera News* No. 51; NAA *A367, A435, MP1103/1–2*; interview Erwin Frenkel 22 July 2000.

FRISCHER: see Fisher

GOLDNER, RICHARD: *b*.23 June 1908 in Craiova, Romania. Son of merchant Avram Ber Goldner and Bertha, née Sachfer. Jewish. Family moved in 1909 to Vienna, where Richard took violin lessons. Began studies in architecture at the Polytechnic Institute before attending Simon Pullman's violin class at New Vienna Conservatory until 1930. Member of Pullman's Die Kammermusik [chamber music] ensemble; principal viola in Vienna Chamber Orchestra and from 1937 in Hermann Scherchen's Musica Viva Orchestra. After its dissolution in 1938 he struggled to acquire a visa for the USA. Married Marianne Reiss (died 1969). Arrived in Sydney with his wife and brother Gerhard aboard *Orama* on 23 March 1939. Worked in a jewellery factory, having tried in vain to secure an orchestral position. Parents arrived in 1940. In 1942 he turned to work as a strategic inventor for national defence. Naturalised 1944. News of Pullman's death in Treblinka in 1945 drove him to found the Sydney Musica Viva. Concert tours with Musica Viva Ensemble. One son: Peter. Founded Mittagong Chamber Music Camps, 1958. From 1966 to 1980 he lived in Pittsburgh, where he married violinist Charmian Gadd in 1970. Returned to Sydney in 1981. Died 27 September 1991. Sources: NAA *A435, A12508*; Goldner; obituary *SMH* (30 September 1991); Shmith and Colville 1996; Baker 2008; LexM; Charmian Gadd (widow) and Peter Goldner (son).

GRAFF, HORST: *b*.29 May 1905, Charlottenburg near Berlin. Son of merchant Hermann Graff and Friederike, née Masmon. Jewish. (Father opened Charlottenburg's first department store, 1905.) Buyer for machine factory, 1921–1923. Established the Weintraubs Syncopators with Stefan Weintraub in 1924, and began a professional career in music (clarinet, alto sax, flute, oboe, trumpet). Last address: 80 Wilmersdorfer Str., Charlottenburg. After stage ban, the band began touring. Married the dancer Margery ('Margo') Minna Graham in Moscow, 1936. Arrived with Weintraubs in Fremantle in 1937 aboard *Gorgon*. Managed concert tour of New Zealand, 1938. Interned as enemy alien 1940–1941; property confiscated. After dissolution of the band, worked as a mechanic and in 1942 applied in vain for military service. Naturalised 1945. Opened a refrigerator shop. Also worked as composer and musician for Bodenwieser Ballet and Kleines Wiener Theater. Married a piano teacher after divorcing Margo. Last address in Australia: Robertson Mews, Durham Close, North Ryde, Sydney. Moved with second wife to Spain (Girona). Died 4 January 1994. Sources: Bittman 1988; NAA *A435, A12508, MP1103/1–2*; Dorothy Graff (relative).

HACKER, GERTRUD: *b*.Gertrud Stern, 11 May 1915, Vienna. Daughter of merchant Moses Josef Stern and Emma, née Ranzenhofer. Jewish. Completed four years at Gymnasium before studying piano at the Academy of Music with Hedwig Andrásffy and Alexander Manhart (1931–1936). Took final exams 19 June 1936. Married lawyer Samuel Hacker in 1937 and moved with him to Ybbs an der Donau, where she worked as a piano teacher. Returned to Vienna in 1938. Address: 51 Stumpergasse, Vienna

VI. Husband temporarily arrested in November. Departure to Melbourne, where both arrived aboard the *Comorin* on 2 January 1939. Efforts to obtain teaching position at the Conservatorium unsuccessful. Various jobs, e.g. work in a milk bar. Naturalised 1944, following her husband's military service. One child: Sandra (*b*.1946). Worked as a saleswoman and also as piano teacher until hand injury *c*.1955. Last address: 71/46 Lansell Rd, Toorak. Died 26 December 1997. Springvale Crematorium. Sources: NAA *A12508*, A997; Sandra Hacker (daughter).

HAJEK-BODAN, OLGA: *b*.28 June 1899, Prague. Daughter of brewery director Eduard Hajek and Mathilde, née Grünhut. Jewish. Opera singer (soprano Olga Hajegg) at Vienna Volksoper. Married actor Karl Bodan and escaped with him to Shanghai. Arrived in Melbourne aboard *Cape Fairweather* on 30 December 1941. Tobacconist, actress and director. Husband first worked as a barber. Naturalised 20 September 1948. Address: 646 Malvern Rd, Armadale. From 1955 to 1956 the couple directed Melbourne's Kleines Theater [Little Theatre], which dissolved when they left Australia and returned to Vienna. Died 9 November 1979. Sources: Trapp et al. 1999; LexM; NAA A12508, *B78*; Website of Robert Schindel.

HARBAND, JANUSZ HANS (JOHN EDWARD): *b*.16 May 1914, Vienna. Son of banker Josef Harband and Laura, née Axelrad. Polish Jew. Early music lessons. Clerk for Canadian Pacific Railway Company. Last address: 61/3/14 Langegasse, Vienna VIII. Married Eva Susanne Abelis in 1938, after November pogrom. They travelled to Sydney aboard *Aorangi*, arriving on 8 April 1939. Name changed to John Edward Harband. Foreman for Radio Corporation, then professional music entertainer (piano and accordion). Invented an Audiolab lightweight tonearm for sound reproduction, and created many tunes. Worked as soloist and with his own jazz band until 1965; played mainly in Melbourne hotels, e.g. Oriental, Federal, Menzie's and Riverside Inn. Also played for Denis Farrington. Last address: 27 Glenbrook Ave, Malvern East. Celebrated his hundredth birthday. Died 20 June 2014. Sources: NAA *A435*, A659, *A997*; interview John Harband 22 March 2003.

HERWEG (HIRSCH), KURT: *b*.Kurt Hirsch, 11 May 1898, Landshut, Bavaria. Son of Abraham Adolf Hirsch and Cecilia, née Lissmann.

Jewish. Military Service 1916–1919. Member of Reich Federation of Jewish Front Soldiers (as Kurt Herweg). Studied at Munich Academy of Music. Conductor and pianist, from 1933 limited to Jüdischer Kulturbund, Berlin. Address: 31 Fasanenstr. Moved in 1936 to Britain, where he was pianist at Rippman School of Dancing, composer for Pepler Mime Group, singing teacher, arranger and conductor for the BBC. Engaged as pianist for dancer Anny Fligg; arrived with her in Sydney aboard *Orford* on 7 April 1938. Interned in Tatura 1940–1941. Recruited as mine worker, 1942–1943. From 1943 composer and conductor for J.C. Williamson, radio 2CH and George Patterson Pty Ltd. Musical director of Borovansky Ballet, 1945–1956. Married dancer Betty Warning, 1952. From 1957 directed ABC Department of Light Music. Composed songs such as 'The Australian Surf Life Savers' March' (1948) and 'Koala Lullaby' (1956), music for documentaries and advertising. Address: 10 William St, Double Bay. Died 9 November 1971, Sydney. Sources: Brückner and Rock 1936; Gerigk and Stengel 1942; NAA *A435*, *MP1103/1–2*; obituaries in *Musical Times* and *APRA Journal*; LexM.

HIRSCHBERG, GÜNTER: *b*.28 April 1920, Berlin. Son of Gymnasium teacher Walter Hirschberg and Edith, née Leschziner. Address: 20 Turmstr., Berlin N.W. 20. Arrived in Britain on a German-British exchange programme, 15 April 1937. After graduation studied theology at University of London and Jews' College. Last visited parents in Berlin in March 1938. Arrested and deported to Australia aboard *Dunera*, 1940. Interned in Hay and Tatura. Appeared there as bass baritone. Military service (8 Aust Empl Coy), 1942. Full-time cantor (Assistant Minister of Religion) at Temple Emanuel in Woollahra, Sydney (1943–1947). Naturalised 1944. Won Australian singing contest (1946) and second prize at Sydney Eisteddfod (1947). Performed Schubert's *Winterreise*. Moved to New York for further vocal study with Alexander Kipnis, December 1947. Cantor at Rabbi Schenk's synagogue in Brooklyn, 1952–1963. After completing studies at Columbia University he became rabbi of NY Rodeph Sholom Congregation and President of NY Board of Rabbis. Retained Australian citizenship. Died 18 July 1989, New York. Sources: NAA *A367*, *MP1103/1–2*; obituary *New York Times* (19 July 1989), quoted in *Dunera News* No. 15 (March 1990); papers in Leo Baeck Institute New York.

HITSCHMANN, EVA: see Wagner, Eva

HOFFMAN(N), ENDRE (ANDREW): *b*.26 November 1913, Budapest. Son of Ernest (Ernö) Hoffmann (mother's name unkown). Hungarian Protestant of Jewish origin. Studied violin in Budapest with Jenö Hubay, and formed his own string quartet. Arrived in Sydney aboard *Viminale* on 18 March 1940. Was refused membership of Musicians' Union, so worked in a shoe factory. Radio appearances. From 1941 member of Monomeeth String Quartet with Richard Goldner. Married Hannelore Tittmann (*b*.Frankfurt am Main), 1942. Concerts with Marcel Lorber (1943). Joined Union in 1945 and secured position with SSO (first violins), 1946. Naturalised 1946. Remarried after divorce. First concert with Hoffman String Quartet, 1956. Died *c*.2000, Sydney. Source: NAA *A446*; Henny Hoffman, Ronald Cragg.

HOLZBAUER (WOOD), HANS (JOHN): *b*.23 August 1909, Vienna. Son of manufacturer Hugo Holzbauer and Josefa Susanna, née Stroissnigg. Jewish. Last address: 12/19 Neubaugasse, Vienna VII. Left Vienna 25 June 1938 and travelled to Singapore for an engagement (clarinet and saxophone). Also worked as a language teacher. Interned in Kuala Lumpur (1940) and deported to Australia aboard *Queen Mary*. Interned in Tatura. Military service (8 Aust Empl Coy), 1942–1946. Numerous appearances, e.g. in Viennese Orchestra. Known as John Wood from 1945. Performed with Erwin Frenkel in Melbourne, e.g. in Maas' Cabaret and Restaurant. Employed as law clerk in public service. Last address: 22 Airlie Avenue, Prahran. Died 13 December 1965. Buried at Springvale Cemetery. Sources: NAA *B78*, *MP1103/1–2*; Ilse Blair.

KAISER, NED KURT JOHN: see Kay, Sydney John

KALB, JOSEPH: *b*.6 January 1890, Krzyrow, Poland. Names of parents unknown. Educated in Vienna as singer and as cantor by principal cantor Emanuel Frenkel. Main occupation watchmaker. Married Mindel Blaser, 1923. Address: 1 Konradgasse, Vienna VII. Arrived in Australia 10 February 1939 and became cantor of Melbourne Hebrew Congregation. Relocated to New York in 1941. Returned in 1948 to Melbourne, where he resumed work for the Hebrew Congregation and, together with Felix Werder, established a new male choir. Naturalised 1951. Died suddenly, 14 July 1959. Source: NAA *B78*.

KASSNER, EDUARD (EDWARD): *b.*28 February 1920, Vienna. Son of Hirsch Nuchim Kassner and Sabina, née Stern. Jewish. Early opera projects. Address: 166/17 Mariahilferstr., Vienna XV. Hazardous escape via the Netherlands to Britain in August 1938. Worked as composer in London. Arrested and deported to Australia aboard *Dunera* in 1940. Interned in Hay and Tatura. Returned in 1941 to Britain, where he joined the army as a translator. Established with his wife Eileen (married 1944) Edward Kassner Music Company, opened New York office in 1951. Successful merchandising of hits, e.g. Bill Haley's 'Rock Around the Clock'. Founded President Records Ltd in 1966. *The Edward Kassner Story* was broadcast by BBC 2 in July 1991. Died 19 November 1996, London. Sources: NAA *MP1103/1*; www.kassnermusic.com; Wikipedia.

KATZ, WERNER HANS: *b.*30 December 1898, Danzig, Germany (now Gdansk, Poland). Son of Louis Katz and Charlotte, née Friedländer. Jewish, Protestant convert. After military service (1914–1918), attended Hochschule für Musik, Berlin. Studied composition (Paul Juon, 1919–1920) and conducting (Rudolf Krasselt, Julius Prüwer, 1920–1922). Married Margarete Petersen (non-Jewish). One child: Brigitte (*b.*1925). Pianist and composer of chamber music, film scores and light music. Last address: 7 Wittstockstr., Schöneiche near Berlin. Taken to Dachau following denunciation in 1939. Escaped to Britain, leaving wife and daughter in Germany. Member of Church of England. Interned in Kitchener Camp. Deported to Australia in 1940 aboard *Dunera*. Interned in Hay (Camp 7, Hut 18) and Tatura, where he was the most experienced composer. Wrote music for the *Hay-Fever* show and gave harmony classes. Released from Tatura 12 August 1942. On his return trip to Europe aboard *Abosso*, the ship was torpedoed. Died 29 October 1942. Sources: Frank and Altmann 1936; Brückner and Rock 1936; Gerigk and Stengel 1942; NAA *MP1103/1–2*; Brigitte Goldstein (daughter).

KAUFMANN, ERNST NORBERT: *b.*10 October 1892, Aachen. Son of Heinrich Kaufmann (mother's name unknown). Jewish. Educated in music theory and composition by Johannes Naumann. First compositions. Qualified as medical doctor at Cologne University, 1920. Established himself as dermatologist and married Maria Meuffels. Last address: 12 Neustr., Herzogenrath-Kohlberg. Emigrated after deregistration from *Reichsarztregister* [medical register]. Arrived in Sydney aboard *Romolo* on

2 September 1938. Practised as a doctor until prohibited in 1940. From 1942 undertook medical studies at Sydney University. Address: 35 Darlinghurst Road, King's Cross. Naturalised 1945. ABC broadcast first movement of his Symphony in F minor Op. 5 (December 1944), and Piano Concerto Op. 8 in E minor (1948). Works include 12 Preludes for Piano Op. 6, String Quartet Op. 9 in A minor, Second Piano Concerto in B flat minor Op. 10, Symphonic Movement in C major Op. 11. Friendships with Alfred Hill, Charles Moses, Edgar Bainton and artist William Dobell. Amateur painter. Died 6 November 1958. Buried in Jewish Cemetery, Rookwood. Sources: *Reichsarztregister*; *New Citizen* (15 July 1948); NAA *A435*, SP827/2.

KAY, SYDNEY JOHN: *b*.Ned Kurt John Kaiser, 3 November 1906, Leipzig. Son of electrical engineer Moritz Kaiser (*b*.1872, Peru) and Grete, née Baum (*b*.1882, Zwickau). Peruvian Jew. (Father had relocated with parents and brother Paul from Peru to Leipzig, married and established an electric motor factory.) Graduated from Schiller-Gymnasium in Leipzig Gohlis; studied machine engineering at Polytechnic University in Berlin (1925–1928). Formed dance band Sid Kay's Fellows with fellow student Siegmund Friedmann (1926). Played trombone, saxophone and clarinet with Weintraubs Syncopators (from 1927). Wrote musical arrangements for film *The Blue Angel*. Last Berlin address: 20 Luitpoldstr. c/o Guttmann. Travelled to Manchuria after Berlin Farewell Concert (1935). Tour of Japan (1937). Arrived in Australia with Peruvian passport 14 July 1937. Founded own music publishing business, 1938. Appeared at Prince's Restaurant, Sydney, 1938–1940. Published own compositions under John Kay. Married Gerty Margarete Pfund (German). Denounced as spy during the war and interned June–November 1940. From 1942 music arranger for Colgate-Palmolive Radio Unit. Wife Gerty ran the Oriana Café, Mcleay Street, Potts Point. Ballet score *Lot's Wife* broadcast 1944, and *Fantasia* in D minor performed by SSO. Admitted to Musicians' Union following court decision. Manager, Theatre for Children and Stork Club (Princess Highway, Sylvania). From 1945 film composer (*Bush Christmas*, *The Back of Beyond* etc.). After divorce married Kathleen Lois Davidson, 1946. One child: Anthony. Naturalised 1947. Established and directed professional repertory company, Mercury Theatre, which closed in 1953 for financial reasons. Address: 51 Roslyn Gardens, Potts Point. Moved to London, 1955; wife and son followed, 1957. Film music includes *The Adventures of Long John Silver* and *The Invisible Man*. Participated in radio programme on Weintraubs (Zurich, 1964). Completed opera buffa, *Strategy* (based on Casanova), 1969. Suffered a stroke. Died 23 May 1970, Marylebone. Sources: Philip Parsons (ed.), *Currency Press Companion to Theatre in Australia* (Sydney: Currency, 1995); Vagg 2007; NAA *A261*, *A435*, A6126, *A12508*, *MP1103/1–2*; papers in NLA and State Library NSW (MLMSS 7164X); Anthony Kay (son).

KIMMEL, EMMA (EMMY): *b*.Emma Berger, 20 June 1895, Vienna. Daughter of butcher Ludwig Berger (mother's name unkown). Jewish, Catholic convert. Studied piano with Alfred Baumann at the Academy of Music (1909–1912). Appeared as coloratura soprano. Married lawyer Dr Jona Kimmel. Two children: Friedrich Georg (*b*.1925) and Elisabeth Charlotte (*b*.1933). Husband changed his first name to Hans, 1931. Residence: 57 Laudongasse, Vienna VIII. Emigrated to Australia. (Departure delayed because of husband's illness.) Arrived in Sydney aboard *Strathallan*, 19 July 1939. Husband temporarily committed to psychiatric clinic. Earned livelihood producing string bags and giving piano and singing lessons. Gave lieder recitals at the Sydney Conservatorium. Accidental death of son, 1947. Published brochure *The Art of Perfect Voice Production* (1947) and taught music (piano and voice) together with her daughter in Sydney and Pennant Hills. In 1957 she moved to London. Died 24 October 1965. Sources: NAA C123, ST1607/2; Hans Kimmel, *Sydney's Jewish Community: Materials for a Post-War (II) History*, compiled by J. Staedter and H. Kimmel, 2 vols (Sydney: H. Kimmel, 1953–1955).

KINSTON, STEVEN: *b*.Siegfried Kinsbrunner, 13 January 1908, Kolomea, Galicia. Son of Samuel and Josephine Kinsbrunner. Jewish. After growing up in Czernowicz, he settled in Florence, Italy, where he studied medicine at the university and piano at the Luigi Cherubini Conservatorium. Graduated in medicine and music, 1933. Winner of a national piano competition. Arrived in Sydney aboard *Ormonde* on 25 April 1939. Established a dental practice in Brisbane under the name Steven Kinston. Auditioned for the ABC and was accepted as soloist. Naturalised 1945. Supported Musica Viva Australia and founded Brisbane Branch. Died 1996. Sources: NAA A12508, *BP242/1*; Musica Viva Australia.

KOHN, KURT: see Martin, Ray

KOLBEN, ROBERT: *b*.Robert Schück, 16 January 1929, Prague. Son of factory director Ignaz Schück and Greta, née Kolben. Czech Jew, Protestant convert. (Father adopted the family name Schück-Kolben after his marriage.) Early piano lessons. After German invasion of Prague, father travelled to Britain to prepare departure; other family members arrived 27 April 1939. Father became factory director in Manchester, but lost position in 1940. Departed for Sydney aboard *Canadian Star* on 25 February 1941. Father acquired a dry cleaning business. Address: 9 Bulkara Road, Bellevue Hill. Attended Sydney Grammar School and studied engineering at Sydney University. Piano lessons with Laurence Godfrey Smith and Alexander Hmelnitsky. From 1949 prize winner in several ABC competitions. Gave farewell concert at Sydney Conservatorium, 13 April 1955. Further piano studies with Béla Siki (Geneva) and Emma Lübbecke-Job (Bad Homburg). Assistant to Hermann Scherchen in Gravesano, 1958. Pianist and piano tuner in Munich. Promoted compositions by Viktor Ullmann. Died 6 June 2005, Munich. Sources: NAA SP1011/1; interview Robert Kolben, 4 October 2003, Munich.

KOLOS, LILY (LYVIA): *b*.Lyvia Sperling, 16 January 1907, Budapest. Daughter of lawyer Karl Sperling and Blanka, née Guttmann. Jewish. Attended school in Budapest. Changed surname to Kolos after marriage. Trained as opera singer in Vienna. Concert singer at Radio-Journal in Bratislava, Slovakia. Lived with her sister in Prague after husband's early death. An Australian cousin facilitated her migration to Australia, together with siblings Juraj and Olga. Arrived in Sydney 18 March 1940. Married Eugen Gerofi, whom she met on board ship. From 1942 appearances as lied and opera singer, accompanied by Marcel Lorber, Henry Krips and Horace Keats. Opera engagement with J.C. Williamson. Co-operation with Kleines Wiener Theater. Also worked as a singing teacher. Died 15 May 2002, Sydney. Sources: NAA SP173/1, SP368/1; 'Lily Kolos: Opera and the Ocean' (ABC, The Listening Room, 1998); Tamara Sperling (relative).

KRAMER, FRIEDRICH (FREDERICK): *b*.12 December 1902, Prague. Son of Siegmund Kramer (mother's name unknown). Moved to Vienna in 1921. Worked as businessman (acetic acid wholesaler) and musician

(Kapellmeister). Address: 74 Lainzer Str., Vienna XIII. Arrived in Melbourne aboard *Orford* on 11 December 1938. Became an accountant after unsuccessful attempts to join Musicians' Union. Naturalised 1944. Subsequently joined Union and from 1945 member of MSO. Known as Fred Kramer. Member SSO (second violins), 1952–1954. Address (1954): 138 Burns Bay Road, Lane Cove. Married a friend from his youth (a doctor) in Sydney. Lived with her temporarily in Vienna and performed for the Union of Austrian Women's Association on 27 February 1967. Last residence in Terrigal, north of Sydney. No further information. Sources: NAA A12508, *A446*; Ronald Cragg.

KRIPS, HEINRICH (HENRY) JOSEF: *b*.10 February 1912, Vienna. Son of Dr Joseph Krips (Jewish) and Luise, née Seitz (non-Jewish). Studied at Vienna University and Conservatorium. Kapellmeister in Innsbruck, 1933. Operetta *Fiordaliso* premiered in Milan, 1934. Chief conductor at Municipal Theatre, Salzburg (1936–1937). Musical director of Vienna Volksoper (1935–1938). Married Luise Pauline Deutsch in 1938. Arrived in Sydney aboard *Viminale* on 18 November 1938. Was refused Union membership. Musical director of Cinesound Films, Sydney, 1940. Musical director of Kirsova Ballet, 1941. Military service (2 Aust Empl Coy), 1942. Established Krips-de Vries Opera Company, 1944. Naturalised 1944. Two children: Henry (*b*.1945) and Michael (*b*.1951). Musical director for Singers of Australia, 1946. Conductor West Australian Symphony Orchestra, Perth, 1946. Chief conductor South Australian Symphony Orchestra, 1949–1972. Trip to Europe, 1953–1954. Awarded honorary membership of International Gustav Mahler Society for introducing Mahler's music to Australia, 1963. Cancelled all Australian contracts and relocated to England, 1972. Compositions include: 'A Waltz Refrain', 'Land of Mine', *Revolution of the Umbrellas*, *Aboriginal Legend* etc.; film scores for *Sons of Matthew* and *Smithy*. Died 25 January 1987, Adelaide. Sources: NAA *A446*, A12508; Röder and Strauss 1983; Krips 1994; Sudrabs 2007.

KRUG, GÜNTER (GERALD): *b*.2 April 1932, Hamburg. Son of merchant Georg Krug and Irma, née Sander. (Family, originally from Poland, escaped to Spain in 1936. Migrated to Australia because of Civil War. Arrived on 2 April 1937. During his military service with 2 Aust Empl Coy, the father met Henry Krips and Curt Prerauer, who supported his son's musical interests.) After early training in piano, cello and bassoon, he undertook further study at Paris Conservatoire. Pupil of Igor Markevitch at Salzburg Mozarteum. Repetiteur in Gelsenkirchen, 1956. Kapellmeister in Biel, Switzerland, 1958. Returned to Australia. From 1967 resident conductor of Elizabethan Trust Opera Company; from 1990 Musical Director of West Australian Opera Company. Sources: NLA (biographical cuttings); interview Gerald Krug 7 June 2009.

KRUTSCH, MARTIN MICHAEL: *b*.24 June 1894 in Posen, Prussia. Son of upholsterer Hermann Krutsch and Bianca, née Bein. Jewish. Military service in WWI. Studied medicine in Heidelberg and Berlin, alongside vocal training. From 1920 dermatologist in Berlin. Address (residence and surgery): 24 Bülowstr., Berlin W. Married Helene Adler. Two children: Gretl (*b*.1924) and Heinrich (*b*.1928). Head Cantor at Synagogue Prinzregentenstraße. Arrived in Melbourne aboard *Franken*, 20 November 1938. From February 1939 cantor at Temple Beth Israel, St Kilda. Address: Jolimont Lane, Jolimont, East Melbourne. Worked as cosmetician when practising as doctor was forbidden. Naturalised 1944. Made recordings (vocal) for ABC. Collapsed during religious service and died suddenly, 6 December 1945. Buried in General Cemetery, Melbourne. Sources: German *Reichsarztregister*; NAA A435, A12508; Graff et al. 2005; John Levi; Henry (son) and Sylvia Krutsch.

KURTZ, EDMUND: *b*.29 December 1908, St Petersburg. Relocated in 1917 to Germany, where as thirteen-year-old cellist he was accepted as a student by Julius Klengel. Principal cellist at Bremen Opera (1926–1927). From 1930 member of Spivakovsky–Kurtz Trio. From 1932 principal cellist at Deutsches Theater, Prague, under Georg Szell. Brought to Australia with Spivakovsky–Kurtz Trio in 1933. Part-time lecturer in cello at Melbourne University Conservatorium, 1935–1937. Married Barbara Mitchell Bellair (Australian), 1936. Moved to USA in 1937. Until 1944 principal cellist with Chicago Symphony Orchestra, followed by solo career; works dedicated to him by Ernst Krenek, Alberto Ginastera and Darius Milhaud. Recorded Dvořák cello concerto with Toscanini, 1945. Collaboration with pianist William Kapell. Australian concert tours, 1946, 1950 and 1956. Moved to

London in 1951. Died 19 August 2004, London. Sources: NAA SP368/1; obituary in *Independent* (London; 23 August 2004).

LANDAUER, ALFRED: *b*.13 June 1910, Vienna. Son of Max Landauer and Wilhelmine, née Drucker. Jewish, Protestant convert. Escaped to Britain. Interned and deported to Australia in 1940 aboard *Dunera*, leaving his wife and mother behind. Commercial artist and musician. Interned in Hay (Camp 8) and Tatura (Camp 2). Participated in performances as guitarist, xylophonist and singer. Military service (8 Aust Empl Coy), 1942–1946. Returned to relatives in Britain. Died February 1971, Enfield, UK. Sources: NAA *B884*, *MP1103/1–2*.

LANGER, PETER: *b*.27 January 1905, Vienna. Son of bank manager Jacob Langer and Melanie, née Gallia. Jewish. Residence: 1 Lobkowitzplatz, Vienna I. Piano lessons. Graduated as Doctor of Laws (1928) and continued his musical education. Married Hertha Kary. Children: Susanne (*b*.1933) and Martin (*b*.1939). Arrived 7 November 1938 in Melbourne aboard *Nieuw Zeeland*. Worked as accountant; acquisition of saw-mill. Naturalised as Peter Edward Langer, 1944. Cellist with MSO (1946–1952). After losing position forced to sell his house (15 Knutsford St, Balwyn). Lessons with Pablo Casals in Prades, France for several months, 1953–54. Worked as cello teacher and as cellist in a ballet orchestra. From 1956 cellist in New Zealand Symphony Orchestra, Wellington. Died 15 September 1964 during a mountain walk. Buried in family grave, Central Cemetery, Vienna. Sources: NAA A12508; Susan Course (daughter).

LAQUEUR, RUDOLF (RUDI) SIEGFRIED: *b*.14 May 1922, Breslau. Son of solicitor Franz Laqueur and Rosalie, née Jakobowicz (widow of Böhm). Jewish. Attended Realgymnasium am Zwinger in Breslau, but had to leave prematurely. Received piano lessons. Address: 6 Kürassierstr., Breslau. Escaped in 1938 via Genoa und Leiden to London, where he studied piano and organ for ten months at the Royal Academy of Music. Interned and deported to Australia in 1940 aboard *Dunera*. Interned in Hay, where he accompanied Johannes Chlumecky and gave piano recital. Pianist and arranger for revue *Snowwhite Joins Up* in Tatura. Military service (8 Aust Empl Coy), 1942–1946. Married Dorothea Hildegard von Gizycki, 1945. Pianist at Studio of the Creative Dance, 1947. Later podiatrist and amateur musician. Occasionally organist at synagogue in St Kilda. Address: 2/72 Herbert Street, Mornington. Died 12 October 2012. Sources: NAA A997, B884, *MP1103/1–2*; Rudolf Laqueur.

LEMBERG, WALTER FRIEDRICH: *b*.5 July 1898, Breslau. Son of lawyer Dr Arthur Lemberg and Margarethe, née Wendriner. Jewish. Received violin and viola lessons, but trained as lawyer. Married Erika. Two children: Eckart (*b*.1929) and Gert-Joachim (*b*.1934). Disbarred in 1933 on racial grounds. Elder brother, biochemist Max Rudolf Lemberg, emigrated to Australia in 1935, was naturalised in 1937 and established the German Emergency Fellowship Committee together with Camilla Wedgwood. He facilitated Walter's emigration. Family arrived in Sydney aboard *Kitano Maru* on 18 May 1939. From 1947 listed as professional violinist and viola player by Musicians' Union, NSW Branch. Died 20 December 1972, Sydney. Sources: NAA A12508, B884; R. Bhathal, 'Lemberg, Max Rudolf (Rudi) (1896–1975)', *Australian Dictionary of Biography* Vol. 15 (Melbourne University Press 2000), 80–2.

LIFFMANN, ERICH (ERIC): *b*.22 September 1914, Beckrath near Mönchengladbach. Son of cattle trader Hermann Liffmann and Mathilde, née Kaufmann. Jewish. Worked as sign writer. Voice training with oratorio singer Ruth Kisch-Arndt. Last address: 63 Zietenstr., Düsseldorf. Escaped in April 1939 to Britain, where Union prevented him working for Gaumont-British. (Parents deported to Terezin and later killed in Auschwitz.) Deported to Australia in 1940 aboard *Dunera*. Interned in Hay and Tatura, where he appeared as solo tenor. Military service (8 Aust Empl Coy), 1942–1946. In May 1942 Melbourne-based radio station 3KZ rated him an 'overnight singing sensation'. Played Prince Charming in *Sergeant Snow White* (1943) and Tamino in the *Magic Flute* at the National Theatre. From 1944 concert appearances with songs and arias, accompanied by Herbert Voss and Rudolf Laqueur. Regular broadcasts with 'Happy Melodies'. Naturalised 1946. Travelled to West Germany in search of relatives. Returned to Melbourne. Married Patricia, née Kewish in 1949. Two children: Kurt and Karl. Performed in nightclubs, schools and Masonic Lodges as professional musician. Died 11 June 1987, Elwood, Victoria.

Buried in Trentham Cemetery. Sources: NAA *A435*, *MP1103/1–2*, SP173/1; papers at NLA; *Songs the People Love*.

LORBER, MARCEL: *b*.7 October 1900, Vienna. Son of merchant Josef Lorber (from Sieniawa, Galicia) and Chaje Ruchel, née Gabel. Jewish. Brothers Oscar (*b*.1892) and Jacques (*b*.1894). Studied piano (Prohaska) and harmony (Stöhr) at Academy of Music, 1919–1923. From 1920 pianist for Gertrud Bodenwieser dance troupe. Further studies at New Vienna Conservatory with Alfred Grünfeld et al. Last address: 7 Förstergasse, Vienna II. Moved to Czechoslovakia after the Anschluss in April–June 1938; then travelled with Bodenwieser troupe to Colombia. Arrived in Sydney aboard *Maunganui* on 23 August 1939, giving 'composer' as profession. Musical director for Bodenwieser, also piano teacher and accompanist. Address: 141 Brougham St, Kings Cross. Undertook tour of Japan with two dancers, 1947. Moved to Britain, where he married and worked as an accompanist. Part of his *netsuke* collection donated to Israel Museum, Jerusalem, 1982. Compositions include: *Die Masken Luzifers* (1936), *Cain and Abel* for violin, piano und women's chorus (1941), *Sphinx* (1939), *Gypsy Dance* (1940), *Diana, Goddess of the Hunt* (1940), *Greek Trilogy* (1941), *Form emerging from Chaos* (1943), *The Wheel of Life* (1944), *Trilogy of Joan of Arc* (1945). Died February 1986, London. Sources: NAA *A12508*, SP173/1; Crotty 1999; Vernon-Warren 1999; Gertrude Bodenwieser Archives, NLA; Vernon-Warren 1999; Bernard Keeffe.

MARTIN, RAYMOND STUART: *b*.Kurt Kohn, 11 October 1918, Vienna. Son of salesman Richard Kohn and Leopoldine, née Bachofner. Jewish. Studied violin (Moravec), piano, theory, orchestral studies (Krips) and music history (Graf) at the Academy of Music (1934–1938). Last residence: 15a/6 Esterhazygasse, Vienna VI. Moved in May 1938 to Britain, where he became solo violinist for the Carroll Levis Discoveries vaudeville show and member of the Stage and Radio Team 'Band Waggon', directed by Jack Hylton. Arrested in London in 1940 and interned on Isle of Man. Deported to Australia aboard *Dunera*. (Meanwhile, his parents were in Shanghai.) Interned in Hay, where as Ray Martin he wrote texts and melodies for songs like 'Hay Days' und 'Say Hay for Happy'. Returned to Britain in November 1941. Arranger and composer for Royal Air Force Central Band, and after the war for the British Forces Network in Hamburg, where he directed 'Melody from the Sky' show. Returned to London in 1949, where he was recognised as leading musical entertainer. Producer for Columbia Records and conductor of BBC Variety Orchestra. Toured USA with his own band, 1957–1973. Composed numerous songs and film scores. Moved to London (1973–1980), then to Johannesburg, South Africa. Died 7 February 1988, Johannesburg. Sources: NAA *MP1103/1–2*; Gammond 1991; The Robert Farnon Society Website; Wikipedia article 'Ray Martin (orchestra leader)'.

MATHY, MARIANNE: *b*.Marianne Kahn, 23 June 1890, Mannheim. Daughter of lawyer Dr Richard Kahn and Martha, née Fürth. Jewish. Married Colonel Erich Mathy, who was killed in WWI. Debut as coloratura soprano in Wiesbaden, 1918. Married architect Franz Martin Friedenstein in Berlin in 1921, but performed as Marianne Mathy. Banned from employment after 1933. Last Berlin address: 17 Jenaer Str. On Malcom Sargent's recommendation she emigrated to Australia, arriving in October 1939. Naturalised as Marianne Mathy-Frisdane, 1944. Worked as singer and vocal instructor. Published brochure, *The Singer's Companion* (1965). Died 18 October 1978, Sydney. Marianne Mathy Scholarship for young opera and classical singers established posthumously. Sources: Brückner and Rock 1936; Gerigk and Stengel 1942; NAA A446, SP173/1; Carmody 2000; LexM; Wikipedia.

MAYER, FRITZ: see Blanks, Fred

MEYER, MAX (PETER): *b*.3 November 1892, Munich. Son of Sigmund Meyer and Hedwig, née Weinberger. Jewish. Bank clerk. Married a Catholic in 1935 and converted to Catholicism. Moved to Sankt Gregor near Oberammergau, where he lived as music teacher and composer. Arrested in November 1938 and taken to Dachau. Escaped to Britain in 1939. Studied organ and composition at Royal College of Music, London; attained Associate and Licentiate diplomas. Deported to Australia in 1940 aboard *Dunera*. Interned in Hay, where he belonged to Catholic minority. Composed *Dunera Mass*. Released from Tatura on 30 November 1943 for return to Britain. Made unsuccessful attempts after the war to participate musically in Oberammergau passion plays. Died 18 November 1950

(Tutzing?). Sources: Brückner and Rock 1936; Gerigk and Stengel 1942; NAA *A367*, *MP1103/1–2*; Shapiro 2000; LexM.

NEUMANN (NEWMAN), KÄTHE (KATE): *b*.Käthe Weiss, 27 June 1897, Vienna. Daughter of Michael Max Weiss and Regine, née Deutsch. Jewish. Gymnasium education. Took private piano lessons with Prof Paul de Conne. Studied various subjects at Vienna Academy of Music, including harmony (Stöhr), piano literature (Fischer), organology (Mandyczewski), 1919–1920. Married industrialist Artur Neumann in 1922. Two children: Gerhart (*b*.1924) and Herbert (*b*.1927). Last residence: 1/7 Alserbachstr., Vienna IX. Arrived in Melbourne on tourist visa aboard *Oronsay* on 28 September 1938. Performed Eugen d'Albert's Piano Concerto in 1939 and gave further piano recitals. Parents arrived 1940. Worked as a piano teacher. Address: 274 Cotham Road, Kew. Died 7 March 1970, Kew. Buried in Boroondara Cemetery Kew. Sources: NAA A12508; *AMN*; family tree, <http://www.cs.technion.ac.il/~janos/FAM-TREE-04/regine.html> (accessed 28 November 2015).

PIETRUSCHKA, MAJER (MAX, IVAN): *b*.17 February 1901, Opatow near Minsk (Russia). Son of fur trader Alter Pietruschka and Rachel, née Kurlander. Jewish. Relocation to Warsaw and Łódź, where he was orchestral violinist. Continued his studies from 1919 in Berlin. Violinist and conductor in silent film orchestras, 1923–1932. From 1930 led Max Pietruschka Salon Orchestra. Was refused admission to Reichsmusikkammer in 1935. Learned tailoring and cutting (ladies' wear), 1935–1936. Last Berlin address: 33 Auguststr. Escaped to Britain in April 1939. Interned in Kitchener Camp, where he was soloist with camp orchestra. Deported to Australia aboard *Dunera* in 1940. Interned in Hay and Tatura, where he conducted orchestras and gave violin lessons. Military service (8 Aust Empl Coy), 1942. After discharge ironed clothes in a dry cleaning store. Married Australian composer Phyllis Batchelor in Anglican Church, 1946. Naturalised 1946. Violin teacher and violinist in Melbourne's 3DB Concert Orchestra under Vernon Williams, 1949–1951. Two children: Tanya (*b*.1947) and Maxwell Alexander (*b*.1952). Second violinist in VSO, 1952–1967. Died 24 December 1979, Melbourne. Sources: NAA A714, A997, *MP1103/1–2*; Tanya Makin (daughter).

PORTNOJ, ANNIE: *b*.Annie Gottlieb, 29 January 1900, Grulich, Bohemia. Daughter of merchant Leopold Gottlieb and Ida, née Auspitzer. Jewish. Child of first marriage born 1921. Moved to Vienna in 1922. Married Heinrich Portnoj. Completed training as milliner, 1926. From 1934 singing instructor. Arrived in Singapore on 24 October 1938. Deported to Australia with her husband aboard *Queen Mary* in 1940. Interned in Tatura; released 19 June 1942. Worked with husband as vocal teacher in Melbourne. Died 31 December 1972, Sydney. Buried with husband in Rookwood Cemetery. Sources: NAA *A367, MP56/10, MP1103/1–2*.

PORTNOJ, HEINRICH (HENRY): *b*.25 October 1895, Vienna. Son of singer Isidor/Israel Jankel Portnoj (from Podberez'ye, Vilnius) and Rosa, née Feigenblum. Jewish. Attended Gymnasium and completed matriculation. Private music lessons, 1905–1915. Repetiteur at Vienna Volksoper, 1915. Married Annie Gottlieb, 1922. Piano accompanist in bars and for revues. Musical director at Femina Theatre (1929–1938). Accompanist at Salzburg Festival, Summer 1937. Last residence: 71 Gumpendorfer Str., Vienna VI. From 1938 entertainment pianist in Penang. Relocation to Singapore to join his wife. Pianist in Coconut Grove, then Cathay Ballroom and Roof Garden. Pianist, accompanist, repetiteur and music teacher. Interned and deported to Australia in 1940 aboard *Queen Mary*. Director of *Tatura Melody 1940*. Military service (8 Aust Empl Coy), 1942–1945. Musical director at Studio of the Creative Dance, Melbourne, 1944–1947; then taught singing, piano and music theory. Address: 72 Stanhope Street, Malvern. Naturalised 1946. Conductor of Jewish male choir JMC Hazomir and co-director of Thea Philips School of Opera. Composition: 'A Skylark Sings' (1953). Lecturer in voice at Melbourne University Conservatorium, 1956–1959. Moved to Sydney, 1971. Died 19 December 1984, Sydney. Buried in Rookwood Cemetery. Sources: NAA *A367, A435, A714, B884, MP1103/1–2*; *AMN*; Bebbington 1997.

PRERAUER, KURT (CURT) EMANUEL: *b*.1 April 1901, Landeshut, Silesia. Son of factory owner Felix Prerauer and Gertrud, née Hammerschlag. Jewish. From 1921 after matriculating studied law and music in Munich (Hugo Leichtentritt, Adolf Sandberger et al.). Attained leaving certificate from Academy of Music. Opera repetiteur, Oldenburg, 1923–1924, opera choirmaster, Essen, 1924–1925. Repetiteur and organist at Berlin State Opera from 1925. Assistant to Leo Blech. Last Berlin address: 38a Kantstr. c/o Pagel. Lost position at State Opera in 1933. Arrived in England 18 June 1933. Assisted Adrian Boult with *Wozzeck*, 1934; accompanied Florence Austral on tour of the Netherlands. Conductor on Australia tour of Royal Grand Opera Company, 1934–1935. Remained in Australia and together with Maurice Abravanel organised opera season, 1935–1936. Naturalised 1938. Conductor of Royal Philharmonic Society Sydney, 1938–1939. Music critic for *Wireless Weekly*, *Tempo* and *ABC Weekly*. Teacher at Alfred Hill Academy of Music. Parents arrived 1939. Married Marea Wolkowsky in Anglican Church, 1942. Military service (2 Aust Empl Coy), 1942–1943. Private piano teaching and vocal coaching. Wrote music column for *New Citizen*, 1949. Musical director of NSW Conservatorium Opera School, 1949–1950. Address: 776, New South Head Rd, Rose Bay. European tour as accompanist and manager for his wife, 1950–1959. Failed to return to Berlin State Opera with Erich Kleiber in 1955. Music critic for the *Nation* and the *Sun*, 1960–1967. Australian correspondent for West German journals and radio stations. Translated Patrick White's *Riders in the Chariot* into German, together with his wife. Died 29 November 1967, Sydney. Sources: Frank and Altmann 1936; Gerigk and Stengel 1942; NAA *A446*, SP173/1; Bebbington 1997; Carmody and Bebbington 2002; Heer 2008; Maria Prerauer (widow); LexM.

REITHER, KARL (CARL, CHARLES): *b*.13 March 1907, Kassa, Hungary. Son of financial adviser Anton Reither and Gisela, née Katz. Non-Jewish Austrian. Moved to Vienna in 1919. Studied violin with Julius Stwertka at Vienna Academy of Music, 1921–1927. From 1925 bandleader for Atlantis Cinema and casual replacement violinist in several Viennese orchestras. Bandleader in Kitzbühel (1929–1931). Engagement in Bombay, India (1931–1932). Bandleader at Südbahn Hotel, Semmering (1932–34) and at Taj Mahal Hotel, Bombay (1934–1935). Married Kathleen Evelyn Pope in Bombay. Two children: Carl Michael (*b*.1936) and Derrick Geoffrey (*b*.1941). Engagements in Colombo, Calcutta, Rangoon and Singapore. Member of Manhattan Boys with Hans Bader in Singapore, 1939. Interned and deported to Australia aboard *Queen Mary* in 1940. Military service (8 Aust Empl Coy), 1942–1945. Numerous concert appearances, e.g. with the Viennese Orchestra. Member of ABC Variety Orchestra (1949) and second violin in Victorian String Quartet. Formed Viennese Trio with Kurt Blach (1950) and spent thirteen years in Victorian Dance Band. Violinist in VSO 1961–1972, then concertmaster of Camberwell Camerata Orchestra. Died 28 April 1995, Melbourne. Springvale Crematorium. Sources: NAA *A367*, *A435*, *A446*, *B884*, *MP1103/1–2*; Charles and Derrick Reither (sons).

ROTH, LEO: *b*.22 October 1921, Graz, Austria. Son of Polish merchant David Roth and Marie, née Feuerstein. Austrian Jew. Sent to England with Quakers' Kindertransport. Attended schools in London. Furrier training. Interned on Isle of Man in 1940 and deported to Australia aboard *Dunera*. Interned in Hay (Camp 8), where he sang in choir. Released from Tatura in 1941 and travelled to meet family in Shanghai. Studied biology there. Relocated to London *c*.1949. Cantor training at Jewish College. Cantor in Vienna, 1953–1957. Invited by Heinz Galinski to West Berlin, where he became one of the best-known cantors in the German-speaking world. Numerous radio broadcasts and recordings, including Viennese songs and musicals. Met Ray Martin in London. Died 29 March 2004, Baden-Baden. Buried in Jewish Cemetery Baden-Baden. Sources: NAA *MP1103/1–2*; Bartrop 1990; German Wikipedia; interviews Leo Roth 2000–2001, Berlin.

SCHILDBERGER, HERMANN: *b*.4 October 1899, Berlin. Son of merchant Michael Julius Schildberger and Clara, née Zweiger. Jewish. After matriculating, studied law, philosophy and musicology in Berlin, Frankfurt am Main, Würzburg and Greifswald. Graduated Doctor of Laws in 1920. Attorney and music critic in Gleiwitz, Upper Silesia, 1924–1927. From 1927 choral conductor of Jewish Reform Congregation Berlin; produced disc recordings of liturgy. Second bar exam, 1930. From 1931 directed Cultural Committee of the Prussian State Association of Jewish Congregations, and from 1933 Künstlerhilfe of Jewish community. Established Künstlerhilfe orchestra, 1934. Lost Reichsmusikkammer membership in 1934 because of dual professions. From 1936 organist of Reform Congregation. Married Ilse Wolff, 1937. Last Berlin residence: 43 Fasanenstr. One child: Michael (*b*.1938). Escaped in March 1939 to London, where he received the offer of position as musical director at Temple Beth Israel, Melbourne. Arrived in Melbourne aboard *Moreton Bay*, 7 August 1939. Established New Melbourne String Orchestra (1940), Brighton Philharmonic Society (1943) and Camberwell Philharmonic Society (1944). Conductor of Brighton Methodist church choir. Taught piano, organ and music theory. Associate conductor and choirmaster of the National Opera Melbourne. Naturalised 1945. Directed National Theatre Opera School (1949–1971) and State Service Orchestra (from 1951). Awarded MBE for distinguished service to music in 1970. Died 24 September 1974, Melbourne. Sources: Brückner and Rock 1936; Gerigk and Stengel 1942; NAA *A435, A12508*; Röder and Strauss 1983; Graff et al. 2005; papers at State Library of Victoria, Melbourne; John Levi; LexM.

SCHOENBERGER, THEODOR ISADOR: *b*.4 January 1874, in Kosten, Posen. Son of cantor Zemach Schoenberger and Bertha, née Friedland. Jewish. Studied piano (Heinrich Ehrlich and Felix Dreyschock) and music theory (Friedrich Gernsheim) at Stern Conservatory, Berlin. Piano teacher at Stern Conservatory, 1896–1936; Friedrich Hollaender was among his students. Married Emma Heine in 1910. Choirmaster of Jewish congregation, 84 Dresdener Str., 1913–1926; then at synagogue on Fasanenstraße. From 1934 he taught music at Jewish Teachers' Institute. After Aryanisation of Stern Conservatory, from 1936 piano teacher at private Jewish Hollaender Music School. Last Berlin address: 81 Motzstr. Arrived with his wife in Sydney aboard *Mooltan* on 7 July 1939. (His daughter Eva was already living in Sydney with her husband Dr Herbert Wohlmuth. When he joined the army in 1942, she moved in with her parents.) Address: 7 Windsor House, Stafford St, Double Bay. Gave private piano lessons. Organist at Temple Emanuel, 1939–1944. Accompanied Gunter Hirschberg for an aria competition, 1943. Died 10 February 1945, St Vincent's Hospital, Sydney. Sources: Frank and Altmann 1936; Brückner and Rock 1936; Gerigk and Stengel 1942; NAA *A12508*, C123; Schenk 1980; Simmons 2003.

SCHÖNZELER, HANS-HUBERT: *b*.22 June 1925, Leipzig. Son of mining engineer Dr Mathias Schönzeler and Charlotte Gertrud, née Seitz. Protestant. Received violin lessons from age five. (His father opposed the Nazis and sent him to the German School in Brussels in 1936 to prevent him from joining the Hitler Youth. Father then moved to Australia, where he was arrested as an enemy alien on 4 September 1939.) Arrived in Sydney with his mother aboard *Remo* on 29 September 1939. Attended Sydney Boys High School, but in 1942 was interned in Tatura, where he completed his education by correspondence. Released from Tatura March 1946. Attended NSW State Conservatorium in Sydney and studied conducting with Eugene Goossens. Naturalised 1947. Took private lessons with Rafael Kubelik. Further studies at Paris Conservatoire (1953–1954). Moved to London, where he directed Edition Eulenburg and established his own chamber orchestra. Met Wilhelm Furtwängler. Married. Freelance conductor and leading Bruckner authority. Book publications: *Bruckner: Leben, Werk, Charakter* (1970), *Of German Music: A Symposium* (1976). Died in London, 30 April 1997. Sources: NAA *MP1103/1*-2; Riemann-Lexikon, Ergänzungsband; *Gramophone* 75/891 (August 1997); obituary in *Independent* (8 May 1997); Wikipedia.

SCHULVATER, CYRIL: *b*.6 January 1907, Johannesburg, South Africa. Son of hotelier Robert Schulvater (*b*.Berlin) and Jenny, née Davis (*b*.London). Brother of Ernst. British Jew. Family relocated to Berlin *c*.1910 and adopted German citizenship. Trained as commercial artist and cellist. Lived in Paris 1921–1923. From 1924 member of several bands in Berlin. Reverted to British citizenship in 1926. Joined Weintraubs Syncopators (banjo, guitar, cello, trombone), 1928. Address: 25 Prinzregentenstr. International tours with Weintraubs to various countries including Russia, where his mother was imprisoned for illicit trading. Arrived in Australia aboard *Gorgon* on 14 July 1937. Left the band in 1938; opened a shop in Sydney and later a hamburger shop with his brother. From 1942 worked as turner in factory producing measuring instruments. Cellist in the SSO, 1946–1954. Married Alice Hochwald in 1956. Ran a delicatessen, later Cyril's Framing Studio on Sydney's North Shore. Died 5 December 1979. Buried in Rookwood Cemetery. Sources: NAA C123; Ronald Cragg.

SCHULVATER, ERNST (ERNEST): *b*.17 May 1905 in Johannesburg, South Africa. [See C. Schulvater] Brother of Cyril. British Jew. Lived in Berlin as German citizen from *c*.1910. Reverted to British citizenship in 1926. Musician (violin and saxophone). Saxophonist in Sid Barton's Orchestra, Leningrad, 1935–1938. Married a former ballerina, Antonia, in Russia and waited in vain for his mother to be released from prison. Arrived in Sydney with his wife aboard *Moreton Bay* on 10 August 1939. Opened a kosher meat shop, then a hamburger shop with his brother. Practised the violin daily and worked as a violin teacher for several decades. Address: 100 Victoria St, Malabar. Died June 1992, Sydney. Cremated 9 June 1992, Eastern Suburbs Memorial Park. Sources: Brückner and Rock 1936; Gerigk and Stengel 1942; NAA C123.

SILBERMANN, ALPHONS: *b*.11 August 1909, Cologne. Son of printing office owner Salomon Silbermann and Bella, née Eichtersheimer. Jewish. Took lessons in piano (Lazzaro Uzielli) and conducting (Hermann Abendroth). Studied law in Cologne and Freiburg. Junior lawyer in Cologne (1930–1931). Graduated as Doctor of Laws, 1933. Escaped to the Netherlands in 1935. Relocated in 1937 to Paris, where he worked as dishwasher, waiter and businessman. Arrived in Sydney aboard *Stratheden* on 13 October 1938. After parents' arrival in 1939, established fast-growing company, Silvers Food Bars. Refused to be drafted into Civil Alien Corps because of work 'essential to the war effort', 1942. Naturalisation delayed until June 1945. Address: 57 Ocean St, Woollahra. European lecture tour, 1946–1947. Published drama *Volpone or The Fox*; prepared broadcasts for the ABC and wrote music reviews for the *New Citizen*. Lectured in aesthetics at Sydney Conservatorium (1949–1950) and published lectures (*Of Musical Things*). Co-founded Sydney branch of ISCM, 1950. European tour, 1951–1952. Stage director at Kleines Wiener Theater, Sydney. Wrote articles for several journals. Left Australia in 1957 as a result of the Goossens affair. Lecturer at Musikhochschule, Cologne (from 1958) and at Cologne University (1960). Became tenured professor in Lausanne (1964–1969) before being appointed Professor in Sociology of Art, Cologne University. Regained German citizenship in 1970. Died 4 March 2000, Cologne. Sources: NAA *A435*, *A12508*; Röder and Strauss 1983; Silbermann 1989 and 2000; Lang 2006; Wikipedia; LexM.

SILBERSTEIN, OTMAR: *b*.16 August 1920 in Graz, Austria. Son of Mortka Fiszel Selbersztajn and Sura, née Tajtelbaum. Polish Jew. After Gymnasium he escaped to Britain. Interned in Kitchener Camp. Deported to Australia in 1940 aboard *Dunera*. Interned in Hay (Camp 7, Hut 4), where he performed J.S. Bach's Concerto for Two Violins in D minor with Pietruschka, and Tatura. Military service (8 Aust Empl Coy), 1942–1946. Friend of Walter Würzburger. Address: 392A St Kilda Road. Naturalised 1948. Played viola in VSO. Moved to New York, where his father and aunt were living. Sources: NAA *A435*, *A12508*, *B78*, C123; Eric Eckstein.

SPITZER, THERESE: *b*.Therese Schiller, 2 December 1900, Vienna. Names of parents unknown. Jewish. Address: Schmalzhofgasse 19, Vienna VI. Studied cello (2nd preparation class) with Friedrich Buxbaum at Academy of Music (1920–1921). Married pharmacist Dr Hans Spitzer. Two children: Erika (*b*.1929) and Georg (*b*.1933). After Aryanisation of the pharmacy they owned, they escaped from Vienna. Last address: 2 Traungasse, Vienna III. Arrived in Sydney aboard *Viminale* on 18 November 1938. Concert with soprano Anni Erhart, 1943. Naturalised 1944. Property in Mosman. Worked as music teacher. Died 2 July 1996 in Sydney. Sources: NAA C123, SP11/5; Norst 1988; USC Shoah Foundation Institute testimony, 1995.

SPIVAK (SPIVAKOVSKY), ADOLF: *b*.14 June 1891, Smila near Kiev. Son of synagogue cantor David Spivak and his wife Rahel. Russian Jew. Family moved to Berlin *c*.1908. Vocal training with Alfredo Cairati at Stern Conservatory. Restricted by asthma to teaching. Married Paula, née Perleberg (*b*.Berlin). Address: 75 Kantstr. Received visa for Australia 28 December 1933. Arrived in Adelaide with parents aboard *Orsova* on 10 March 1934. Chief study teacher of singing at Melbourne Conservatorium, 1935–1944. Naturalised 1939. Residence: 9 Riversdale Road, Hawthorn. Vocal lecturer at Conservatorium, 1947–1958. Pupils included Glenda Raymond, Kathleen Goodall, Sylvia Fisher and Stefan Haag. Died 19 August 1958. Buried in Springvale Botanical Cemetery. An Adolph Spivakovsky Scholarship for Composition of Music was established posthumously. Sources: Gerigk and Stengel 1942; NAA *A659*, D4880; *AMN*.

SPIVAK (SPIVAKOVSKY), ISAAC (ISSY): *b*.31 March 1902, Odessa. [See A. Spivak] Brother of A. Spivak. Disabled by polio. Studied violin (Issay Barmas, student of Joachim) at Klindworth-Scharwenka Conservatory and cello (Hugo Becker) at Hochschule für Musik in Berlin. Taught music at

Fürstin Bismarck School until 1933. German citizenship 1932. Arrived in Adelaide aboard *Orsova* on 10 March 1934. Taught violin, viola and cello privately and at Scotch College, Melbourne, 1937–1965. Pupils included Henry Wenig and John Glickman. Address: 26 Glendon Road, Toorak. Died 8 August 1977, Melbourne. Springvale Botanical Cemetery. Sources: Gerigk and Stengel 1942; NAA A446.

SPIVAK (SPIVAKOVSKY), JASCHA: *b*.18 August 1896, Smila near Kiev. [See A. Spivak] Brother of A. Spivak. First public appearance as pianist 8 February 1903, Odessa. Studied piano with Moritz Mayer-Mahr at Klindworth–Scharwenka Conservatory, Berlin. Concert with Berlin Philharmonic Orchestra in Scheveningen, 26 August 1911. Won Blüthner Prize, 1914. Interned when war began. Performed piano cycle with Berlin Philharmonic Orchestra, 1918. Australian tour (seventy-five concerts in seven months), 1921–1922. Married Australian Eleonore Crantz in 1926. Appeared with Furtwängler and Knappertsbusch, 1928. Tour of Australia and New Zealand, 1929. Debut of Spivakovsky–Kurtz Trio, 1930. Last Berlin address: 24 Berchtesgadener Str. Trio toured Australia in 1933. Remained as a result of political situation in Germany. From 1935 senior lecturer in piano at University Conservatorium, Melbourne. Students included Estelle Coady, June Epstein, Anna Jacobovich, Ilm McKenzie and Anny Rosenkranz. Numerous concerts and broadcasts for the ABC. Three children: Rahel (*b*.1933), David (*b*.1938) and Michael (*b*.1939). Naturalised 1938. No broadcasts during the war. Undertook tours of USA (1948), USA and Europe (1953). Withdrew from concert-life in 1960, but continued teaching privately. Died 23 March 1970, Melbourne. Springvale Botanical Cemetery. Sources: Frank and Altmann 1936; Brückner and Rock 1936; Gerigk and Stengel 1942; AMN; Röder and Strauss 1983; Spivakovsky 1985 and 1990; Bebbington 1997; J. Stevens 2002; Michael Spivakovsky (son); <http://www.jascha.com> (accessed 28 November 2015).

SPIVAK (SPIVAKOVSKY), NATHAN (TOSSY): *b*.23 December 1906, Odessa. [See A. Spivak] Brother of A. Spivak. Took private violin lessons with Arrigo Serrato, Berlin. First concert appearance at age eleven. Further studies with Willy Hess at Hochschule für Musik. Lived with family in 60 Sybelstr., Charlottenburg. Concertmaster of Berlin Philharmonic Orchestra, 1 February 1926–1930 April 1927; gave up this position for solo career. Made recordings for Parlaphone. Australian tour with Spivakovsky-Kurtz Trio, 1933. Married historian Erika Lipsker in 1934. One child: Ruth. Lecturer in violin at University Conservatorium, Melbourne, 1935–1939. Moved to USA in October 1939. Concertmaster in Cleveland, 1942–1945. USA premiere of Bartók's Violin Concerto No. 2, 1943. American citizenship 1946. Developed special bow technique for Bach's solo suites. Guest of Berlin Philharmonic Orchestra, 1959. Taught at Fairfield University, Connecticut and Juilliard School, New York. Died 20 July 1998, Westport, Connecticut. Sources: Frank and Altmann 1936; Gerigk and Stengel 1942; Röder and Strauss 1983; obituary *New York Times* (27 July 1998); Ruth Voorhis (daughter).

STADLEN, PETER: *b.*14 July 1910, Vienna. Son of lawyer Dr Max Stadlen and Hedwig, née Kunwald. Jewish, Protestant convert. From 1922 studied piano (Paul Weingarten) and harmony (Joseph Marx) at Vienna Academy of Music, followed by private lessons. Attended Hochschule für Musik, Berlin, where he studied piano (Leonid Kreutzer), composition (Walter Gmeindl) and conducting (Julius Prüwer, 1929–1933). Returned to Vienna in 1933. Last address: 78/7 Rechte Bahngasse, Vienna III. Escaped to Britain, spring 1938. Interned on Isle of Man and Huyton from June 1940. Deported to Australia aboard *Dunera*. Interned in Hay (Camp 7, Hut 36), where he performed *Israel in Egypt*. Mary Baillie provided a good piano. Released from Tatura on 18 October 1941 and returned to Britain. Gave further concerts from March 1942. Received British citizenship in 1946. Married Hedi Simon. Gave masterclasses at Darmstadt Summer Courses, 1947–1951. Numerous premieres, but rejected serial technique after 1958. Terminated stage career in 1959 to become music critic of *Daily Telegraph* (until 1986). Taught at All Souls College, Oxford et al., 1965–1969. Died 20 January 1996, London. Sources: NAA *B6531*, *SP173/1*, *MP1103/1*–*2*; Röder and Strauss 1983; Stadlen 1990; Raab Hansen 1996; Klaus Loewald.

STEINER, PAUL: *b.*10 January 1901, Vienna. Son of Hugo Steiner and Berta, née Leibel. Jewish. Studied violin and oboe at Innsbruck Conservatory (1911–1916) and at Breslau Conservatory (1917–1918); then in Vienna and Krems. Married Emma Schlemmer (non-Jewish) in Innsbruck in 1923 and converted to Catholicism. One child: Helga (*b.*1924). Toured with his own band across Austria, Germany and Switzerland, and also taught music. Moved to Salzburg, 1936–1938. Bandleader in Luxembourg (June–December, 1938). Travelled to Singapore in June 1939. Engaged in Ipoh (Hotel Majestic) and Singapore (Singapore Swimming Club). Deported to Australia aboard *Queen Mary* in 1940. Appeared in programme *Tatura Melody 1940* as 'One Man and Six Instruments'. Military service (8 Aust Empl Coy), 1942. Employed as instrument repairer by Allans Music store, 276 Collins St, Melbourne. Address: 20 Mary St, Kew. Naturalised 1946. Died 9 December 1964, Hawthorn. Buried in Booroondara Cemetery, Kew. His wife and daughter returned to Austria after his death. Sources: Gerigk and Stengel 1942; NAA *A367*, *A435*; Ilse Blair.

STERN, DOBRA ('DORY'): *b.*Dobra Torenberg, 2 January 1912, Belchatow, Poland. Daughter of merchant Josef Torenberg and Salomea, née Langnas. Polish Jew. Studied piano at Vienna Conservatorium. Father migrated to USA in 1925; raised by her mother. Appeared as concert pianist. Married engineer Egon Stern in 1934. Address: 6/1/9 Nestroygasse, Vienna II. Escaped to Luxembourg in July 1938. Arrived in Sydney aboard *Strathallan* on 19 July 1939. Worked as housekeeper for a language teacher. Mother deported in 1941. From 1943 pianist for Bodenwieser Ballet. Husband exempted from military service because of his strategic work as radio technician. Naturalised 1945. Tour of Africa with Bodenwieser, 1949. Moved *c.*1957 to Melbourne, where she was pianist for Elaine Valence ballet school until 1982. Gave private piano lessons. Last address: 45A Narrak Rd, Balwyn. Died 30 March 1990. Cremated at Springvale Crematorium. Sources: NAA *A435*, *A12508*, *SP11/5*; Norst 1988; Vernon-Warren 1999.

STIWELBAND, MISCHA: *b.*18 August 1896, Odessa. Son of Isaac Stiwelband and Anute, née Victorgaus (Wigdergaus). Russian Jew. Family moved in 1905 to Vienna, where father worked as factory hand, then merchant and hotelier. Studied violin (Prill), harmony (Stöhr), piano (Saphier) and chamber music (Rosé) at the Vienna Academy of Music, 1911–1916. Allegedly pupil and assistant of well-known violinist Otakar Ševčík. Played in Vienna's opera orchestra, 1917–1920. Married Margarete Wendlinger in 1920. Children: Erich (*b.*1921) and Oswald (*b.*1923). Toured Europe with his own band. Austrian citizenship from 1924. Engaged at luxury restaurant in

Bombay, 1937. After Anschluss he vacated residence and took his wife and son to Singapore. Last address: 8/5 Blechturmgasse, Vienna IV. Procured engagement for Hans Blau. Performed in Coconut Grove. Deported to Australia aboard *Queen Mary* in 1940. Interned in Tatura. Military service (8 Aust Empl Coy), 1942–1945. Participated in *Sgt Snow White*. Trained as cutter and designer. Naturalised 1946. Appeared as violinist with light music. Last Address: 619 St Kilda Road, St Kilda. Died 25 November 1972, Montefiori Home, East St Kilda. Buried in Fawkner Cemetery. Sources: NAA *A367, A435, MP1103/1–2*; Ilse Blair.

TICHAUER, SALO (SOLOMON) MAX: *b.*2 June 1898, Kattowitz, Upper Silesia (today Katowice, Poland). Son of shoemaker Fedor Tichauer and Lebl Rosa, née Pollak. German Jew. Military service 1917–1918. Violinist in own band, 1919–1923. Bandleader on US steamer *SS President Harding* (1923–1924), and in New York nightclub. Married Alma Weidner in Bielefeld, 1925. Violinist with own band, 1926–1933. After losing membership of Kapellmeister association in 1933, he performed only in Poland. Member of Federation of Jewish Front Soldiers, 1934–1938. Ran a grocery business, Breslau 1934–1938. Member of Jüdischer Kulturbund, 1936–1938. Last address: 77 Viktoriastr., Breslau. Arrived in Singapore on 24 January 1939. Bandleader in Café Wien (Singapore), Grand Hotel (Ipoh), Easter Hotel (Kuala Lumpur), Pavilion Theatre and Arcade Restaurant (Singapore). Deported to Australia aboard *Queen Mary* in 1940. Interned in Tatura, where he participated in *Laugh and Forget* programme. Military service (8 Aust Empl Coy), 1942–1945. Naturalised 1946. After death of first wife married Elly Armel, 1948. Continued as professional musician in light entertainment. Last address: 10 Landles St, McKinnon, Moorabbin. Died 22 December 1959, Royal Melbourne Hospital, Parkville. Buried in Fawkner Cemetery. Sources: NAA *B884, MP1103/1–2*; Ilse Blair.

VEIT, OTTI: *b.*14 October 1914, Emmendingen near Freiburg. Daughter of timber merchant Berthold Veit (mother's name unkown). Jewish. Received cello lessons from 1921. After matriculating (1934), she studied with Nicolai Graudan, principal cellist in Berlin Philharmonic. Moved to London in 1936 to continue lessons with Graudan; further study with Ivor James and Lauri Kennedy at Royal College of Music. In 1939 married mining engineer Kurt Robert Eisner, who obtained a position in Kalgoorlie (West Australia). Following her husband, she arrived in Fremantle aboard *Oronsay* on 27 January 1940. Solo cellist with West Australian Symphony Orchestra, Perth 1941. Two children: Miriam (*b.*1941) and Ruth (*b.*1946). Naturalised 1944. Moved to Melbourne (1948) to pursue solo career. Member of Paul McDermott String Quartet, 1951–1956. Performed with Hephzibah Menuhin and Walter Susskind. Lecturer in cello at Melbourne University Conservatorium, 1952–1981 and 1984. Last public appearance in 1995. Continued to play string quartets. Died 21 May 2000, Melbourne. Otti Veit Violoncello Scholarship established posthumously by her husband. Sources: NAA SP173/1; Foster 1986; Kurt Eisner.

WAGNER, EVA: *b.*Eva Hitschmann, 12 December 1912, Vienna. Daughter of patent attorney Dr Felix Hitschmann and Stella, née Forst. Jewish, Protestant convert. Parents divorced 1914. Received piano lessons from 1922. After matriculating in 1931, studied voice at New Vienna Conservatory, and had private vocal training with Prof. Rosner. Last address: 16/12 Skodagasse, Vienna VIII. From 1936 continued vocal studies in Rome, where she met her future husband, Dr Max Mayer. Studied medicine and after their marriage (October 1938) worked as a doctor in India. Arrested as enemy alien in 1940. Medical practice in Karachi, Pakistan, 1941–1946. In 1947 she divorced and moved to Sydney; met Wolfgang Wagner, whom she married in 1948. Ceased to sing after losing her voice, but assisted her husband with his music reviews. Three children: Peter (first marriage); Ruth and Hannah (second marriage). Died 20 December 2004, Sydney. Sources: NAA D4880; Bittman 1988; interview Eva Wagner 28 August 2000.

WAGNER, WOLFGANG: *b.*7 March 1904, Teplitz-Schönau, Bohemia. Parents unknown. Jewish. Received piano lessons. Worked as sports reporter. After leaving secondary school, employed by Albert Hahn steel works in Berlin. Married Charlotte in 1927. First child, Ruth, born in Vienna, 1932. Moved to Mährisch-Ostrau in 1937, where second child, Hannah, was born. Received Landing Permit for Australia in Prague in February 1939. Wife and three children arrived Sydney aboard *Oronsay* in May 1939. Bookkeeper for textile company. Naturalised 1944. Encouraged by Neville Cardus, wrote music reviews for the *New Citizen* (1946) and for *ABC Weekly* and *Musical America* (from 1947). After death of his wife met Eva Mayer and remarried in 1948. As co-editor of *Canon* magazine he organised special Arnold Schönberg edition, 1949. Music critic for the *Sun* and the *Australian*. Died 28 July 1969, Sydney. Sources: NAA *A12508*, SP11/5; obituary in *SMH* (30 July 1969); papers in State Library of NSW (MLMSS 6621); Eva Wagner.

WEINTRAUB, STEFAN: *b*.14 August 1897, Breslau. Son of Leopold Weintraub and Hulda, née Bandmann. Jewish. Piano lessons in Breslau. Moved to Berlin. After completing school trained in pharmaceutical sales from 1913. Military service 1917–1918 (awarded Iron Cross). Worked from 1919 as food retailer. Established the Weintraubs Syncopators with Horst Graff in 1924; contracted by Max Reinhardt, 1925. Transferred from piano to drums. Made first recording in 1928. Film music for *The Blue Angel*, 1930. Last Berlin address: 46 Barbarossastr., Schöneberg. Last appearance in Berlin, February 1935. International concert tours: Czechoslovakia, Sweden, Italy, Soviet Union. In Stockholm 1935 he met Gertrud Irene Bergmann, who joined the group. Tour of Japan, November 1936–June 1937. Arrived in Fremantle, Australia aboard *Gorgon* on 14 July 1937. New Zealand tour 1938. From December 1938 engaged at Prince's Restaurant, Sydney. Problems with Musicians' Union escalated during WWII. Married Gertrud Bergmann 11 September 1939. Arrested on 6 June 1940 following a denunciation. Interned in Orange and Tatura until 4 September 1941. Disabled after his release, so withdrew from musical profession and became a mechanic. Application for military service refused for reasons of 'security'. Naturalised 1945. Divorced and remarried. Worked as amateur pianist and composer for the Kleines Wiener Theater, Sydney. Travelled to USA and Europe. Address (from 1944 almost until his death): 10a Challis Avenue, Potts Point. Died 10 September 1981, Sydney. Sources: Brückner and Rock 1936; NAA *A12508*, *ST1233/1*, *MP1103/1–2*; Bergmeier 1982; Baer 1982; Kartomi et al. 2004; Lang 2006; Weintraubs Syncopators collection, Akademie der Künste Berlin.

WEISS, EMMA: *b*.Emma Bondy, 4 May 1885, Vienna. Parents unknown. Jewish, converted to Protestantism. Studied piano at Vienna Conservatorium with Prof. Hugo Reinhold, 1899–1904. Graduated in 1904; teaching degree

1905. Taught periodically in Britain, 1913. Piano teacher in Linz, 1917–1936. Married Julius Weiss, who apparently died young. Moved to Vienna, 1936–1939. Address: 13/2/15 Spittelauer Lände, Vienna IX. Arrived in Melbourne aboard *Strathnaver* on 21 March 1939. First accommodation with Dr Georgina Sweet (64 Mont Albert Road, Glenferrie), who had applied for her immigration. Gave piano lessons in Melbourne. Last address: 22 Glassford Street, Armadale. Contracted pneumonia. Died 8 December 1940, Alfred Hospital, Prahran. Buried in Springvale Cemetery. Sources: NAA A261, A997, *B6531*; *AMN*.

WEISS, LEO: *b*.17 February 1908, Berlin. Son of footwear representative Josef Weiss and his wife Ernestine. German Jew of Polish origin. After completing school, he worked at the stock exchange. Professional musician from 1926. Pianist for Marek Weber and Dajos Béla dance orchestras, and for Lud Gluskin's American College Band. Succeeded Franz Waxmann as pianist for the Weintraubs Syncopators in 1930. Last Berlin address: 4 Dahlmannstr., Charlottenburg. Received German passport in Venice on 16 July 1934. Concert tours throughout Europe, Soviet Union and Japan. Arrived in Fremantle, Australia aboard *Gorgon* on 14 July 1937. In spite of German citizenship, he was not interned during the war. In 1943 sent passport to the Department of the Interior with the request that he be regarded as stateless. Pianist in Fisher's Sextet after dissolution of Weintraubs Syncopators. Naturalised 1945. Married Betty Joan Tuck ('Miss Victoria' 1946). Composed songs such as 'I Shall Never Forgive You', 'I'll Always See you', 'Sleep Baby Sleep' and 'A-Mooning in the Moonlight'. Changed name to Leo White, 1947. Produced radio programmes 'Rendezvous with Leo White' and 'Caramba'. Leo White and his Orchestra were engaged at Prince's Nightclub until *c*.1955. Last job delivering engineering supplies. Died 1 January 1976. Sources: NAA *A435, A12508*.

WERDER, FELIX: *b*.Felix Bischofswerder, 24 February 1922, Berlin. Son of cantor Boas Bischofswerder and Selma (Sara), née Manasse. Jewish. Early music lessons from his father. Attended school of the Jewish Community in Große Hamburger Straße. Arrived 15 September 1933 in London, where his father also worked as cantor. After further schooling he studied architecture and art history at Shoreditch Polytechnic School. Arrested as enemy alien in 1940. Voluntarily accompanied his father to Australia aboard *Dunera*. Interned in Hay (Camp 7, Hut 4) and Tatura, where he wrote music for camp orchestra, and an essay on Jewish music in Babylon. Joined the army because of his father's illness. Military service (8 Aust Empl Coy), 1943–1946. Married Mena Waten in 1944. Arranger for radio network and repetiteur for Singers of Australia, Sydney, 1946–1947. Engaged by Sydney John Kay as bass player for Stork Club. After relocation to Melbourne in 1947, undertook teacher training at the University and spent *c.* five years as music teacher. His orchestral work *Balletomania* was conducted by Eugene Goossens on 17 October 1948. Musica Viva Portrait concerts. Choirmaster of Melbourne Hebrew Congregation, 1954–1969. Active in adult education. Music critic for the *Age*, Melbourne, 1960–1977. Lecturer in musical aesthetics at Melbourne University Conservatorium, 1966–1970. Opera *The Affair* performed at Sydney Opera House, 1974. Ensemble Australia Felix founded in 1976. Honorary degree from University of Melbourne conferred 2002. Died 3 May 2012, Melbourne. Sources: NAA A367, A435, *B884, B6531, MP1103/1–2*; Covell 1967; Murdoch 1972; Radic 1978; Traber and Weingarten 1987; Raab Hansen 1996; Bebbington 1997; several interviews; Werder 1991, 1994 and 2000; LexM; Papers in NLA.

WERTHER, RUDOLF THEODOR: *b.*21 January 1896, Berlin. Son of merchant Arthur Werther and Lisbeth, née Heimann. Jewish. Musical education at Klindworth–Scharwenka Conservatory, 1904–1913. Matriculated in 1913; studied economics and history in Edinburgh. Military service, 1915–1918. Continued studies in Berlin and Greifswald, gaining doctorate in economics. Private piano lessons with Moritz Mayer-Mahr. Worked in finance and export business. Married Hertha Lazarus in 1920. One child: Frank. From 1930 involved in import/export trade in Paris. Applied for French citizenship, 1935. Divorced in 1939. Married Anna Richert and arrived with her in Melbourne aboard *Oronsay* on 28 May 1939. Began musical career in Launceston, Tasmania. Conductor of Launceston Chamber Orchestra. Performance of Humperdinck's opera *Hansel and Gretel* planned for May 1940 cancelled owing to a defamation. Withdrew from public life for two years. Founded Tasmanian Musical Festival Society, 1942. Performances of *Hansel and Gretel*, Mozart's *Il Seraglio* (1943–1944), and *Der Freischütz* at National Theatre, Launceston (1945). Co-founder of Hobart Operatic Society. Naturalised 1945. Left Tasmania after conflict with Musicians' Union. Musical director of Cairns Light Symphony Orchestra, 1949. Interested in yoga and Hindu philosophy. From 1950 member of Guild of Australian Composers. Director of cultural activities at Cottesloe Civic Centre, Perth, 1951–1953. Composed numerous songs based on texts by William Blake, Christina Rosetti, R.A. Taylor, Tagore etc. Worked as language teacher (German). Died 13 October 1986, Perth. Sources: NAA A435, SP827/2; Rudolf Werther Music Fund at Wigmore Music Library, University of Western Australia; Daley 2003.

WOOD, JOHN: see Holzbauer, Hans

WÜRZBURGER, WALTER ERICH: *b*.21 April 1914, Frankfurt am Main. Son of private music teacher and synagogue organist Siegfried Würzburger and Gertrud, née Hirsch. Jewish. Three brothers: Hans, Paul and Karlrobert. Only Walter became a professional musician (saxophone, clarinet, accordion and piano). Attended Reform-Gymnasium Musterschule, 1924–1932. Studied music at Dr Hoch's Conservatory with Mátyás Seiber and Bernhard Sekles, 1932–1933. From 1933 jazz musician in Paris, Belgium, Luxembourg and Scandinavia. From 1939 worked as entertainer in Singapore. Theory lessons with Werner Baer. Deported to Australia aboard *Queen Mary* in 1940. Interned in Tatura, where he began serious composition. Taught counterpoint, jazz, arrangement and French at Tatura College. Military service (8 Aust Empl Coy), 1942–1946. Informed of his father's death in Poland, 1942. Undertook part-time studies at Melbourne University Conservatorium, 1942–1944. Naturalised 1945. Completed music studies at Conservatorium (1946–1948), where he then taught (1948–1950). Member of J.C. Williamson Theatre Orchestra with George Dreyfus. Moved to London to study clarinet with Frederic Thurston, 1951. Further composition studies with M. Seiber, 1952–1958. Operator for International Telephone Exchange, 1954–1968. Attended Darmstadt Summer Courses, 1963–1965. Married artist Hannah Gibianska in 1966. Two children: twins, Ruth and Madeleine. Conductor of Kingston Philharmonia, 1974–1991. Numerous unpublished works, mostly chamber music. Died 21 March 1995, Worcester Park, near London. Sources: NAA A997, B884, *MP1103/1–2*; Wurzburger 1996; LexM; Hannah Wurzburger (widow), Kenneth R. Ward (son).

ZANDER, HANS BERNHARD: *b.*12 January 1888, Berlin. Son of Louis Zander (mother's name unkown). Jewish. Kapellmeister and Artistic Director at Berlin Municipal Opera until 1931. Assistant to General-Intendant Heinz Tietjen at Berlin State Opera, 1931–1933. Administrative director of Jüdischer Kulturbund, Berlin, 1933–1938. Escaped to Britain in 1939. Interned on Isle of Man, 1940. Pianist for troop entertainment and Kurt Jooss ballet. Arrived in Sydney aboard *Johan de Witt* on 16 March 1947. Began work as piano teacher and repetiteur in Melbourne. Conducted *Bartered Bride*, *Martha*, *Eugene Onegin* and *Fidelio* at National Theatre, Melbourne from 1948. Later Director General and chief conductor of New South Wales National Opera in Sydney. Suffered from cancer. Died 23 December 1951. Buried in Jewish Cemetery, Rookwood. Sources: NAA *A435*, A12508, *B78*, ST1598/1; Straten 1994; obituary in *SMH* (24 December 1951); Röder and Strauss 1983; van Straten 1994; Raab Hansen 1996; Heer 2008; LexM.

Ship Arrivals

1933

12 April: Jascha Spivakovsky, Tossy Spivakovsky and Edmund Kurtz aboard *Oronsay* (from Naples) in Fremantle

1934

10 March: Adolf and Issy Spivakovsky aboard *Orsova* (from Toulon resp. Naples) in Adelaide
3 September: Curt Prerauer aboard *Maloja* (from London) in Melbourne

1936

29 August: Rabbi Hermann Sänger aboard *Viminale* (from Genoa) in Melbourne

1937

20 May: Fritz Coper aboard *Moreton Bay* (from Southampton) in Sydney
14 July: Weintraubs Syncopators aboard *Gorgon* (from Singapore) in Fremantle
(20 July: Comedian Harmonists aboard *Orford* in Fremantle)
11 September: Walter Dullo aboard *Rendsburg* (from Hamburg) in Sydney
20 September: Charles Berg aboard *Ormonde* (from London) in Melbourne

1938

7 April: Kurt Herweg-Hirsch aboard *Orford* (from London) in Sydney
20 May: Adolf Frischer aboard *Largs Bay* (from Port Said) in Sydney
23 August: Mario Dane aboard *Romolo* (from Genoa) in Fremantle

26 August: Heinrich Adler aboard *Aorangi* (from Vancouver) in Sydney
2 September: Ernst Kaufmann aboard *Romolo* (from Genoa) in Sydney
12 September: Antal Dorati aboard *Comorin* (from Marseille) in Melbourne
28 September: Käthe Neumann aboard *Oronsay* (from London) in Melbourne
13 October: Alphons Silbermann aboard *Stratheden* (from Marseille) in Sydney
7 November: Peter Langer aboard *Nieuw Zeeland* (from Colombo) in Melbourne
18 November: Henry Krips and Therese Spitzer aboard *Viminale* (from Genoa) in Sydney
20 November: Hans Forst aboard *Niagara* (from Vancouver) in Sydney
20 November: Martin Krutsch aboard *Franken* (from Bremen) in Melbourne
11 December: Fritz Kramer aboard *Orford* (from London) in Melbourne

1939

2 January: Gertrud Hacker aboard *Comorin* (from Colombo) in Melbourne
10 January: Fritz Mayer and Klopfer family aboard Jervis *Bay* (from Southampton) in Sydney
21 March: Emma Weiss aboard *Strathnaver* (from Colombo) in Melbourne
23 March: Richard Goldner aboard *Orama* (from London) in Sydney
8 April: Hans Harband aboard *Aorangi* (from Vancouver) in Sydney
13 April: Elisabeth Cohn-Colin aboard *Ascanius* (from Liverpool) in Sydney
13 April: Fritz Brandmann aboard *Narkanda* (from London) in Sydney
1 May: Ellen Cohn aboard *Ormonde* (from London) in Melbourne
18 May: Walter Friedrich Lemberg aboard *Kitano Maru* (from Yokohama) in Sydney
28 May: Rudolf Theodor Werther aboard *Oronsay* (from Toulon) in Melbourne
31 May: Wolfgang Wagner aboard *Oronsay* (from London) in Sydney
4 June: Vienna Mozart Boys' Choir (including Stefan Haag) aboard *Aorangi* (from Vancouver) in Sydney
14 June: Willy Coper aboard *Alster* (from Antwerp) in Sydney
7 July: Theodor Schoenberger aboard *Mooltan* in Sydney
19 July: Dory Stern and Emmy Kimmel aboard *Strathallan* (from Marseille resp. Colombo) in Sydney
23 July: Georg Dreyfus aboard *Orama* (from London) in Melbourne
7 August: Hermann Schildberger aboard *Moreton Bay* (from Southampton) in Melbourne
10 August: Ernest Schulvater aboard *Moreton Bay* (from Southampton) in Sydney

Ship Arrivals

23 August: Marcel Lorber with Bodenwieser dance company aboard *Maunganui* (from Wellington) in Sydney
29 September: Hans-Hubert Schoenzeler aboard *Remo* (from Genoa) in Sydney
1 October: Marianne Mathy-Friedenstein aboard *Stratheden* in Sydney

1940

27 January: Otti Veit aboard *Oronsay* in Fremantle
11 February: Victor Alberti and Andy Factor aboard *Remo* in Melbourne
18 March: Endre Hoffmann and Lily Kolos aboard *Viminale* (from Genoa) in Sydney
4 April: Goldner parents aboard *Esquilino* in Sydney
4 June: Ignace Friedman aboard *Strathmore* in Sydney
5 August: Leonie Feigl aboard *Commissaire Ramel* (from Marseille) in Sydney
3 September: Alfred Ehrenfeld and Erwin Frenkel aboard *Dunera* (from Liverpool) in Melbourne
6 September: Boas Bischofswerder, Felix Bischofswerder, Otto Blau, Adolf Brenner, Johannes v. Chlumecky, Hans Edelmann, Günter Hirschberg, Eduard Kassner, Werner Hans Katz, Kurt Kohn, Alfred Landauer, Rudi Laqueur, Erich Liffmann, Max Meyer, Majer Pietruschka, Leo Roth, Otmar Silberstein and Peter Stadlen aboard *Dunera* (from Liverpool) in Sydney
25 September: Hans Bader, Werner Baer, Kurt Blach, Hans Blau, Hans Holzbauer, Oskar Fleischer, Heinrich Portnoj, Charles Reither, Paul Steiner, Mischa Stiwelband, Salo Max Tichauer and Walter Würzburger aboard *Queen Mary* (from Singapore) in Sydney

1941

10 April: Robert Kolben aboard *Canadian Star* (from Liverpool) in Sydney
30 December: Olga Hajek-Bodan aboard *Cape Fairweather* (from Shanghai) in Melbourne

Sources and Bibliography

Archives and Collections

Australia

Brisbane:
    State Library of Queensland
Canberra:
    Australian National University (Noel Butlin Archives Centre)
    Australian War Memorial
    National Archives of Australia
    National Library of Australia (*i. al.* Australian Elizabethan Theatre Trust, Bodenwieser Collection Papers of George Dreyfus, Kenneth Hince, Sydney John Kay)
Hobart:
    Tasmanian National Library
Melbourne:
    Jewish Museum of Australia (Dunera Archive)
    Monash University (Australian Archive of Jewish Music)
    State Library of Victoria (Heinze Collection, Schildberger Papers)
    University of Melbourne Library (Faculty of Music)
Sydney:
    Archive of Australian Judaica (Cyril Pearl Collection, Max Joseph Collection)
    Australian Music Centre
    NSW Records Office
    State Library of NSW (*i. al.* Sydney John Kay, Wolfgang Wagner, Dunera Archive)
Tatura/Victoria:
    Tatura Irrigation & Wartime Camps Museum

Austria

Vienna:
   Archiv der Musikuniversität
   Israelitische Kultusgemeinde
   Österreichisches Staatsarchiv
   Orpheus Trust
   Stadt- und Landesarchiv
   Universitätsarchiv

Britain

London:
   Institute of Germanic Studies
   London Metropolitan Archives
   The National Archives, Kew
   The Wiener Library for the Study of the Holocaust and Genocide

Germany

Aachen:
   Stadtarchiv
Berlin:
   Archiv Akademie der Künste (Weintraubs Syncopators Archiv)
   Archiv Universität der Künste
   Bundesarchiv
   Entschädigungsbehörde
   Jüdisches Museum (Adam-Baillie-Sammlung [since 2006 at Tatura Irrigation
      & Wartime Camps Museum, Tatura/Victoria])
   Kassenärztliche Vereinigung
   Landesamt für Bürger- und Ordnungsangelegenheiten
   Landesarchiv Berlin
   Politisches Archiv des Auswärtigen Amtes
   Zentrum für Antisemitismusforschung
Frankfurt/Main:
   Deutsche Nationalbibliothek (Deutsches Exilarchiv 1933-1945)

Leipzig:
    Sächsisches Staatsarchiv
Lübeck:
    Stadtarchiv
Regensburg:
    Stadtarchiv (Sammlung Plank)
Zwickau:
    Stadtarchiv

Israel

Jerusalem:
    The Central Archives for the History of the Jewish People

Singapore

National Library Singapore

Interviews

Australia

Canberra: Klaus Loewald.
Melbourne: Ilse Blair, George Dreyfus, Eric Eckstein, Andy Factor, Erwin Frenkel, Susanne Gabor, Sandra Hacker, Rabbi John Levi, Leonard Radic, Felix Werder.
Sydney: Bob Adler, Henri Aram, Sybil Baer, Ronald Cragg, Charmian Gadd, Julie Kerner, Evelyn Klopfer, Eva Wagner.

France

Paris: Catherine Duncan.

Germany

Berlin: Leo Roth, Klaus Wilczynski.
Munich: Robert Kolben.

Database

Online-Lexikon verfolgter Musiker und Musikerinnen der NS-Zeit (LexM), Universität Hamburg

Bibliography

Abisheganaden, Paul, *Notes Across the Years: Anecdotes from a Musical Life* (Singapore: Unipress, 2005).
Akademie der Künste, ed., *Geschlossene Vorstellung. Der Jüdische Kulturbund in Deutschland 1933–1941* (Berlin: Hentrich, 1992).
Alderman, Geoffrey, *The Federation of Synagogues, 1887–1987* (London: Federation of Synagogues, 1987).
Alomes, Stephan, *When London Calls. The Expatriation of Australian Creative Artists to Britain* (Cambridge: Cambridge University Press, 1999).
Anderl, Gabriele, and Dirk Rupnow, *Die Zentralstelle für jüdische Auswanderung als Beraubungsinstitution* (Vienna: Oldenbourg, 2004).
Aster, Misha, '*Das Reichsorchester*'. *Die Berliner Philharmoniker und der Nationalsozialismus* (Munich: Siedler, 2007).
'Australien', *Jüdische Auswanderung. Korrespondenzblatt für Auswanderungs- und Siedlungswesen* (Berlin: Hilfsverein der Juden in Deutschland, 1937), 18–48.
Baer, Werner, 'Meine Erinnerungen als Organist der Synagoge Prinzregentenstraße', in Berlin-Museum, ed., *Synagogen in Berlin. Geschichte einer zerstörten Architektur* (Berlin: Arenhövel, 1983), 194–5.
Baer, Werner, 'Winding up the Weintraubs', *24 Hours* (September 1982), 18–19.
Baillie, Mary, 'In Memoriam: Artur Schnabel'. ABC Broadcast, 31 August 1976 (Adam–Baillie Collection L-2000/522/148).

Bair, Henry, 'Die Lenkung der Berliner Opernhäuser', in Hanns-Werner Heister and Hans-Günter Klein, eds, *Musik und Musikpolitik im faschistischen Deutschland* (Frankfurt/Main: S. Fischer, 1984), 83–90.

Baker, Suzanne, 'How a Zipper Came to Make Fine Music', *Australian Jewish Historical Society Journal* 19/2 (2008), 248–55.

Baker, Suzanne, *Beethoven and the Zipper. The Astonishing Story of Musica Viva* (Sydney: Suzanne Baker, 2010).

Bartrop, Paul R., *Australia and the Holocaust 1933–1945* (Kew, VIC: Australian Scholarly Publishing, 1994).

Bartrop, Paul R., 'Incompatible with security: Enemy Alien Internees from Singapore in Australia, 1940–1945', *Journal of the Australian Jewish Historical Society*, 12/1 (1993), 149–69.

Bartrop, Paul R., and Gabrielle Eisen, eds, *The Dunera Affair. A Documentary Resource Book* (Melbourne: Co-published by Schwartz & Wilkinson and The Jewish Museum of Australia, 1990).

Bebbington, Warren, ed., *The Oxford Companion to Australian Music* (Melbourne: Oxford University Press, 1997).

Benz, Wolfgang, *Das Exil der kleinen Leute: Alltagserfahrung deutscher Juden in der Emigration* (Munich: C.H. Beck, 1991).

Benz, Wolfgang, Claudia Curio and Andrea Hammel, *Die Kindertransporte 1938/39. Rettung und Integration* (Frankfurt/Main: S. Fischer, 2003).

Berghahn, Marion, *Continental Britons. German-Jewish Refugees from Nazi Germany* (Oxford: Berghahn, 1988).

Bergmeier, Horst J.P., *The Weintraub Story Incorporated. The Ady Rosner Story* (Menden: Der Jazzfreund, 1982).

Bergmeier, Horst J.P., Ejal Jakob Eisler and Rainer E. Lotz, eds, *Vorbei… Dokumentation jüdischen Musiklebens in Berlin, 1933–1938. Beyond Recall. A Record of Jewish musical life in Nazi Berlin 1933–1938* (Hambergen: Bear Family Records, 2001).

'Berlin Revisited: Werner Baer', *ABC Weekly* (7 October 1959), 7.

Bevege, Margaret, *Behind Barbed Wire: Internment in Australia during World War II* (St Lucia, QLD: University of Queensland Press, 1993).

Bindemann, Walter, *Doch die Wurzeln liegen in Deutschland. Erfahrungen und Erinnerungen Deutscher in Großbritannien* (Leipzig: Evangelische Verlagsanstalt, 2000).

Bischofswerder, Boas, 'The Stone' [Manuscript. Text in Hebrew, not dated] (Archive of Australian Judaica at the University of Sydney).

Bittman, Karl, ed., *Strauss to Matilda. Viennese in Australia 1938–1988* (Leichhardt, NSW: Wenkart Foundation, 1988).

Blakeney, Michael, *Australia and the Jewish Refugees 1933–1948* (Sydney: Croom Helm Australia, 1985).

Blakeney, Michael, 'Australia and the Jewish Refugees from Central Europe: Government Policy 1933–1939', *Yearbook of the Leo Baeck Institute* 29 (1984), 103–33.
Blanks, Fred, 'A School Reunion', *Northern Herald. Sydney Morning Herald Supplement* (19 June 1997).
Blanks, Fred, 'Credo of a Critic', *Sounds Australian* 35 (Spring 1992), 34–6.
Blanks, Fred, 'The Future (if any) of Music Criticism', *Musica Viva Bulletin* (July/August 1982).
Bodenwieser, Gertrude, 'Modern Dance and its Development in Australia', *New Citizen* (15 August 1946), 5.
Botstein, Leon, 'Sozialgeschichte und die Politik des Ästhetischen: Juden und Musik in Wien 1870–1938', in Leon Botstein and Werner Hanak, eds, *quasi una fantasia. Juden und die Musikstadt Wien* (Vienna: Wolke, 2003), 43–64.
Brooks, Lawrie, 'Werner Baer of the ABC, has had a Colourful Career in Music', *AMM* (December 1956), 15, 48.
Brückner, Hans, and Christa Maria Rock, eds, *Judentum und Musik: mit dem ABC jüdischer und nichtarischer Musikbeflissener* (Munich: Brückner, 2nd edn, 1936).
Bücken, Ernst, *Wörterbuch der Musik* (Leipzig: Dieterich, 1940).
Büttner, Ursula, *Die Not der Juden teilen. Christlich-jüdische Familien im Dritten Reich. Beispiel und Zeugnis des Schriftstellers Robert Brendel* (Hamburg: Christians, 1988).
Buzacott, Martin, *The Rite of Spring. 75 Years of ABC Music-Making* (Sydney: ABC Books, 2007).
Carmody, John, 'Mathy, Marianne Helene Sara (1890–1978)', in *Australian Dictionary of Biography. 1940–1980*, vol. 15 (Carlton, VIC: Melbourne University Press, 2000), 329–30.
Carmody, John, and Warren A. Bebbington, 'Prerauer, Kurt (Curt) (1901–1967)', in *Australian Dictionary of Biography*, vol. 16 (Carlton, VIC: Melbourne University Press, 2002), 28–9.
Cavanagh, Michelle, *Margaret Holmes: The Life and Times of an Australian Peace Campaigner* (Sydney: New Holland, 2006).
Christoffel, Udo, ed., *Berlin Wilmersdorf. Die Juden. Leben und Leiden* (Berlin: Kunstamt Wilmersdorf, 1982).
'Chronik der deutschen Internierungslager in Australien. II. Teil. Vom Juni 1940–15. Dez. 1940', in *Tatura-Liederbuch 1940* (Australian War Memorial Canberra).
Clarke, Alan, 'Theatre Behind Barbed Wire: German Refugee Theatre in British Internment', in Günter Berghaus, ed., *Theatre and Film in Exile. German Artists in Britain, 1933–1945* (Oxford: Berg, 1989), 189–222.
Corkhill, Alan, *Queensland and Germany: Ethnic, Socio-Cultural, Political and Trade Relations 1831–1991* (Melbourne: Academia, 1992).

Cottle, Drew, *The Brisbane Line. A Reappraisal* (Leicestershire: Upfront Publishing, 2002).
Covell, Roger, *Australia's Music. Themes of a New Society* (Melbourne: Sun Books, 1967).
Covell, Roger, 'Does Musica Viva's Past Guarantee its Future?', in Shmith and Colville, eds, 1996, 28–33.
Cracknell, Ruth, *A Biased Memoir* (Ringwood, VIC: Penguin, 1999).
Crotty, Joel, *Choreographic Music in Australia, 1912–1964: From Foreign Reliance to an Independent Australian Stance* (PhD Thesis. Monash University, Melbourne 1999).
[Cullen, Paul] Australian Jewish Welfare Society – A Short History (4 May, 1981) [Manuscript] (The Wiener Library London).
Cummins, Paul, *Musik trotz allem. Herbert Zipper: Von Dachau um die Welt* (Vienna: Lafite, 1993).
Cunneen, Chris, 'Magnus, Walter (1903–1954)', in *Australian Dictionary of Biography*, vol. 15 (Carlton, VIC: Melbourne University Press, 2000), 284–5.
Daley, Roberta, *Rudolf Theodor Werther – His Life and Music* (Master Thesis. University of Western Australia, Perth 2003).
Decsey, Ernst, *Musik war sein Leben. Lebenserinnerungen* (Vienna: Deutsch, 1962).
Dening, Greg, 'Adam, Leonhard (1891–1960)', in *Australian Dictionary of Biography*, vol. 13 (Carlton, VIC: Melbourne University Press, 1993) <http://adb.anu.edu.au/biography/adam-leonhard-9962/text17651> (accessed 20 October 2015).
Dobson, Elaine, 'George Dreyfus', in Frank Callaway and David Tunley, eds, *Australian Composition in the Twentieth Century* (Melbourne: Oxford University Press, 1978), 126–35.
Dokumentationsarchiv des österreichischen Widerstandes, ed., *Österreicher im Exil. Großbritannien 1938–1945. Eine Dokumentation* (Vienna: Österreichischer Bundesverlag, 1992).
Donner, Irmtraut, *Das Feuilleton des „Neuen Wiener Tageblatts" zwischen den beiden Weltkriegen* (PhD Thesis. University of Vienna 1951).
Dreyfus, George, 'Anpassen: Is There a Jewish Attitude to Music? (1996)', in *Being George – and Liking it! Reflections on the Life and Works of George Dreyfus on his 70th birthday* (Richmond, VIC: Allans, 1998), 42–7.
Dreyfus, George, *Brush off! Saving the Gilt-Edged Kid from Oblivion* (Melbourne: Three Feet Publishing, 2011).
Dreyfus, George, *Don't Ever Let Them Get You!* (North Fitzroy, VIC: Black Pepper, 2009).
Dreyfus, George, *The Last Frivolous Book* (Sydney: Hale & Iremonger, 1984).
Dreyfus, Kay, 'The Foreigner, the Musicians' Union, and the State in 1920s Australia: A Nexus of Conflict', *Music & Politics* 3/1 (Winter 2009) <http://quod.lib.umich.

edu/m/mp/9460447.0003.101/--foreigner-the-musicians-union-and-the-state-in-1920s?rgn=main;view=fulltext> (accessed 20 October 2015).

Dümling, Albrecht, 'Auf dem Weg zur "Volksgemeinschaft". Die Gleichschaltung der Berliner Musikhochschule ab 1933', in Horst Weber, ed., *Musik in der Emigration 1933–1945. Verfolgung, Vertreibung, Rückwirkung* (Stuttgart: Metzler, 1994), 69–107.

Dümling, Albrecht, 'Auf musikalischer Entdeckungsreise im fünften Kontinent. Zu verborgenen Beziehungen zwischen Berlin und Australien', *Philharmonische Blätter*, ed. Berliner Philharmonisches Orchester, No. 3 (1995/96), 1–19.

Dümling, Albrecht, 'Friedrich II, sein Lehrer Quantz und der deutsche Geschmack in der Musik', *Zeitschrift für Religions- und Geistesgeschichte* 56/2 (2004), 124–35.

Dümling, Albrecht, *Laßt euch nicht verführen. Brecht und die Musik* (Munich: Kindler 1985).

Dümling, Albrecht, *Musik hat ihren Wert. 100 Jahre musikalische Verwertungsgesellschaft in Deutschland* (Regensburg: ConBrio, 2003).

Dümling, Albrecht, 'Neue Volkslieder für einen erwachenden Kontinent. George Dreyfus: Film- und Fernsehkomponist in Australien', *Filmexil* 14/2001, 46–57.

Dümling, Albrecht, ed., *Zu den Antipoden vertrieben. Das Australien-Exil deutschsprachiger Musiker* [Verdrängte Musik – vol. 17] (Saarbrücken: Pfau, 2000).

Dullo diary, *Walter Andreas Dullo. Tagebuch, von seiner Mutter geführt* [diary, written by his mother], 3 vols (Archive Dümling).

Dullo, Walter, 'Important Contribution to Music in Sydney', *New Citizen* (15 April 1946), 3.

Dullo, Walter, 'Portrait of a Promising Young Talent: Henry Krips', *New Citizen* (15 May 1948), 7.

Dullo, Walter, 'Sydney John Kay. An Australian Theatre Pioneer', *New Citizen* (15 August 1948), 7.

Duncan, Catherine, 'Snow White Joins The Army. Novel Show as Pointer to Theatrical Future', *Listener In* (22 May 1943).

Dundy, Elaine, *Finch, Bloody Finch. A Biography of Peter Finch* (London: Magnum, 1981).

Durham, Lowel M., *Abravanel!* (Salt Lake City: University of Utah Press, 1989).

Elphinstone, Michael, and Wayne Hancock, *When Austral Sang. The Biography of Florence Austral* (Richmond, South Australia: Hyde Park Press, 2005).

Embacher, Helga, and Helmut Staubmann, *Österreichische Kulturschaffende im Exil. Das Beispiel Herbert Zipper und Trudl Zipper-Dubsky* (Innsbruck: Institut für Soziologie, 1996).

Evans, Allan, *Ignaz Friedman. Romantic Master Pianist* (Bloomington: Indiana University Press, 2009).

Fabian, Erwin, 'Rückblick', in *Max und Erwin Fabian. Berlin – London – Melbourne* (Berlin: Stiftung Stadtmuseum Berlin, 2000), 123–8.

Fahrmeir, Andreas, 'Immigration and Immigration Policy in Britain from the Nineteenth to the Twentieth Century', in Johannes-Dieter Steinert and Inge Weber-Newth, eds, *European Immigrants in Britain 1933–1950* (Munich: Saur, 2003), 43–54.

Faulkner, Trader, *Peter Finch: A Biography* (London: Angus & Robertson, 1979).

Fetthauer, Sophie, *Musikverlage im ,Dritten Reich' und im Exil* [Musik im ,Dritten Reich' und im Exil – vol. 10] (Hamburg: von Bockel, 2004).

Filmmuseum Potsdam, ed., *Im Reiche der Micky Maus: Walt Disney in Deutschland 1927–1945. Eine Dokumentation zur Ausstellung* (Berlin: Henschel, 1991).

Fischer, Gerhard, *Enemy Aliens. Internment and the Homefront Experience in Australia 1914–1920* (St Lucia, QLD: University of Queensland Press, 1989).

Fischer-Defoy, Christine, '"Wir waren schließlich durch das Schicksal verbunden." Die "Jüdische Private Musikschule Hollaender" in Berlin', *mr*[musica reanimata]-*Mitteilungen*, No. 64 (July 2008), 1–10.

Fishburn, Jonathan, 'Builders of the Jewish Future', *Jewish Quarterly* 197 (Spring 2005).

Flesch, Carl F., *'And Do You Also Play the Violin?'* (London: Toccata, 1990).

Flesch, Carl F., *'Where Do You Come From?' Hitler Refugees in Great Britain Then and Now: The Happy Compromise!* (London: Pen Press, 2001).

Forster, Frank M.C., 'Robert Marshall Allan (1886–1946)', in *Australian Dictionary of Biography*, vol. 7 (Carlton, VIC: Melbourne University Press, 1979), 37–9.

Foster, John, ed., *Community of Fate. Memoirs of German Jews in Melbourne* (Sydney: George Allen & Unwin, 1986).

Frank, Paul, and Wilhelm Altmann, eds, *Kurzgefaßtes Tonkünstler-Lexikon für Musiker und Freunde der Musik* (14th edn) (Regensburg: Gustav Bosse, 1936).

Freeden, Herbert, 'In Transit. Reminiscences of the Kitchener Camp', in *Dispersion and Resettlement. The Story of the Jews from Central Europe* (London: Association of Jewish Refugees in Great Britain, 1955), 18–20.

Frey, Stefan, *,Unter Tränen lachen'. Emmerich Kálmán. Eine Operettenbiografie* (Berlin: Henschel, 2003).

Fröhlich, Elke, ed., *Die Tagebücher von Joseph Goebbels*, Part I, vol. 5 (Munich: de Gruyter Saur, 2000).

Fröhlich, Elke, ed., *Die Tagebücher von Joseph Goebbels*, Part I, vol. 7 (Munich: de Gruyter Saur, 1998).

Frydman, Gloria, *Paul Morawetz. What A Life* (Adelaide: Wakefield Press, 1995).

Galliner, Peter, and Simone Ladwig-Winters, eds, *Freiheit und Bindung. Zur Geschichte der Jüdischen Reformgemeinde zu Berlin von den Anfängen bis zu ihrem Ende 1939* (Berlin: Hentrich, 2004).

Gammond, Peter, *The Oxford Companion to Popular Music* (Oxford: Oxford University Press, 1991).
Gedenkbuch Berlins der jüdischen Opfer des Nationalsozialismus (Berlin: Hentrich, 1995).
Geisel, Eike, and Henryk M. Broder, *Premiere und Pogrom. Der Jüdische Kulturbund 1933–1941. Texte und Bilder* (Berlin: Siedler, 1992).
Genée, Pierre, *Synagogen in Österreich* (Vienna: Löcker, 1992).
Gerigk, Herbert, and Theophil Stengel, *Lexikon der Juden in der Musik* (Berlin: Hahnefeld, 1942).
Gill, Alan, *Interrupted Journeys. Young Refugees from Hitler's Third Reich* (East Roseville, NSW: Simon & Schuster Australia, 2004).
Gillman, Peter, and Leni Gillman, *'Collar the Lot!' How Britain Interned and Expelled its Wartime Refugees* (London/New York: Quartet Books, 1980).
Goldner, Richard, *Musica Viva. Birth and Early Years. A Strange Tale Across The Ocean* (Typoscript n.d., in possession of Charmian Gadd, Sydney).
Goltz, Maren, *Musikstudium in der Diktatur. Das Landeskonservatorium der Musik/ die Staatliche Hochschule für Musik Leipzig in der Zeit des Nationalsozialismus 1933–1945* (Stuttgart: Steiner, 2013).
Goossens, Eugene, 'How Ban On Oversea Players Will Affect Music Here', *SMH* (17 January 1949), 2.
Göpfert, Rebekka, *Der jüdische Kindertransport von Deutschland nach England 1938/39: Geschichte und Erinnerung* (Frankfurt/Main: Campus, 1999).
Graff, Werner, Malcolm J. Turnbull and Eliot J. Baskin, *A Time to Keep. The Story of Temple Beth Israel: 1930 to 2005* (Melbourne: Hybrid Publishers, 2005).
Gyger, Alison, *Opera for the Antipodes: Opera in Australia 1881–1939* (Sydney: Currency Press and Pellinor, 1990).
Hammond, Joyce, *Walls of Wire. Tatura, Rushworth, Murchison* (Rushworth, VIC: Hammond, 1990).
Hanak, Werner, ed., *Papier ist doch weiss? Eine Spurensuche im Archiv des Jüdischen Museums Wien* (Vienna: Jüdisches Museum, 1998).
Hangler, Jutta, 'Schloss Fuschl. Beutegut des NS-Außenministers', in Robert Kriechbaumer, ed., *Der Geschmack der Vergänglichkeit. Jüdische Sommerfrische in Salzburg* (Vienna: Böhlau, 2002), 259–80.
Heer, Hannes, Jürgen Kesting and Peter Schmidt, eds, *Verstummte Stimmen. Die Vertreibung der ‚Juden' aus der Oper 1933 bis 1945* (Berlin: Metropol, 2008).
Heister, Hanns Werner, Claudia Maurer Zenck and Peter Petersen, eds, *Musik im Exil. Folgen des Nazismus für die internationale Musikkultur* (Frankfurt/Main: S. Fischer, 1993).
Helm, Everett, *Béla Bartók in Selbstzeugnissen und Bilddokumenten* (Reinbek bei Hamburg: Rowohlt, 1965).

Sources and Bibliography

Heyworth, Peter, *Otto Klemperer. Dirigent der Republik 1885–1933* (Berlin: Siedler, 1988).
Hippen, Reinhard, *Satire gegen Hitler. Kabarett im Exil* (Zürich: Pendo, 1986).
Hirsch, Lily E., *A Jewish Orchestra in Nazi Germany. Musical Politics and the Berlin Jewish Culture League* (Ann Arbor: University of Michigan Press, 2010).
Inglis, Kenneth S., *This is the ABC: The Australian Broadcasting Commission 1932–1983* (Carlton, VIC: Melbourne University Press, 1983).
Jacobson, Jacob, and Jacob Segall, eds, *Jüdisches Jahrbuch für Groß-Berlin auf das Jahr 1926. Ein Wegweiser durch die jüdischen Einrichtungen und Organisationen Berlins* (Berlin: Scherbel & Co, 1926).
Jahresberichte des Conservatorium für Musik und darstellende Kunst der Gesellschaft der Musikfreunde Wien (Archiv der Gesellschaft der Musikfreunde, Vienna).
John, Eckhard, *Musikbolschewismus. Die Politisierung der Musik in Deutschland 1918–1938* (Stuttgart: Metzler, 1994).
Jupp, James, ed., *The Australian People. An Encyclopedia of the Nation, its People and their Origins* (North Ryde, NSW: Angus & Robertson, 1988).
Jurgensen, Manfred, *Eagle and Emu. German-Australian Writing 1930–1990* (St Lucia, QLD: University of Queensland Press, 1992).
Kampe, Norbert, 'Sozialgeschichtliche Betrachtungen zur jüdisch-deutschen Akkulturation', in Akademie der Künste, ed., *Geschlossene Vorstellung. Der Jüdische Kulturbund in Deutschland 1933–1941* (Berlin: Hentrich, 1992), 13–24.
Kartomi, Margaret, John Whiteoak and Kay Dreyfus, 'Berlin to Bondi. The Flight of the Weintraub Syncopators', *Heat* 8 (2004), 15–33.
Kater, Michael H., *Gewagtes Spiel. Jazz im Nationalsozialismus* (Munich: Deutscher Taschenbuch Verlag, 1998).
'Kathe Neumann to Teach in Rubinstein Tradition', *AMN* (January 1940), 9.
Kay, Sydney John, 'Criticism – or Action?', *New Citizen* (15 March 1949), 4.
Kay, [Sydney] John, 'Music Life in Japan', *AMM* (1 January 1938), 25–6.
Kay, Sydney John, *A Selection of the Tunes of Bush Christmas. Film Music Composed and Arranged for Piano by Sydney John Kay* (Sydney: Chappell & Co., 1948).
Keussler, Gerhard von, *Autobiographie* (Estate Gerhard Keussler. Goethe and Schiller Archive Weimar).
Kieffer, Fritz, *Judenverfolgung in Deutschland – eine innere Angelegenheit? Internationale Reaktion auf die Flüchtlingsproblematik, 1933–1939* (Stuttgart: Steiner, 2002).
Kisch, Egon Erwin, *Landung in Australien* (Amsterdam: Allert de Lange, 1937).
Kolben, Heinz, 'Dr. h.c. Ing. Emil Kolben zum Gedächtnis', *Bohemia. Zeitschrift für Geschichte und Kultur der böhmischen Länder* 26/1 (1985), 111–21.
Krenek, Ernst, *Im Atem der Zeit. Erinnerungen an die Moderne* (Hamburg: Hoffmann & Campe, 1998).

Krieger, S.W., 'Resettlement in Australia', in *Dispersion and Resettlement. The Story of the Jews from Central Europe* (London: Association of Jewish Refugees in Great Britain, 1955), 27–9.
Krönung, Manuel, 'Gerhard von Keußler', in Ludwig Finscher, ed., *Die Musik in Geschichte und Gegenwart. Allgemeine Enzyklopädie der Musik*, Personenteil 10 (Kassel: Bärenreiter, 2003), 67–8.
'Kurze Chronik der deutschen Internierungslager in Australien für die 9 Monate vom 4. September 1939 bis 4. Juni 1940', in *Tatura-Liederbuch 1940* [Typoscript] (Australian War Memorial Canberra).
Kwiet, Konrad, 'Die Integration deutsch-jüdischer Emigranten in Australien', in Ursula Büttner, ed., *Das Unrechtsregime. Internationale Forschung über den Nationalsozialismus. Festschrift Werner Jochmann*, vol. 2 (Hamburg: Christians, 1986), 309–23.
Lafitte, Francois, *The Internment of Aliens. New Edition with an Introduction by the Author* (London: Quartet Books, 1980).
Lang, Birgit, *Eine Fahrt ins Blaue. Deutschsprachiges Theater und Kabarett im australischen Exil und Nach-Exil 1933–1988* (Berlin: Weidler, 2006).
Laqua, Carsten, *Wie Micky unter die Nazis fiel. Walt Disney in Deutschland* (Reinbek bei Hamburg: Rowohlt, 1992).
Lawson, Valerie, 'Baume, Frederick Ehrenfried (Eric) (1900–1967)', in *Australian Dictionary of Biography*, vol. 13 (Carlton, VIC: Melbourne University Press, 1993), 136–7.
Levi, Erik, 'Das britische Musikleben und die Polemik der Incorporated Society of Musicians gegen den Zuzug exilierter Musiker', in Michael Haas and Marcus Patka, eds, *Hans Gál und Egon Wellesz. Continental Britons* (Vienna: Mandelbaum, 2004), 70–85.
Levi, John S., *My Dear Friends. The Life of Rabbi Dr Herman Sanger* (Melbourne: Hybrid Press, 2009).
Levi, John S., 'Sanger, Herman Max (1909–1980)', in *Australian Dictionary of Biography*, vol. 16 (Carlton, VIC: Melbourne University Press, 2002), 176–7.
'Life Story of Mannie Fisher' [Typoscript] (Archive Dümling).
Loewald, Klaus, 'A Dunera Internee at Hay, 1940–41', *Historical Studies* 17/69 (1977), 512–21.
Loewald, Klaus, 'Broughton, Edward Renata (Muhanga) (1884–1955)', in *Australian Dictionary of Biography*, vol. 13 (Carlton, VIC: Melbourne University Press, 1993) <http://adb.anu.edu.au/biography/broughton-edward-renata-tip-9595> (accessed 10 January 2015).
Loewald, Klaus, 'Dullo, Walter Andreas (1902–1978)', in *Australian Dictionary of Biography*, vol. 14 (Carlton, VIC: Melbourne University Press, 1996), 43–4.
Loewald, Klaus, '"Man macht mich zum Bürger der Welt." Interview Dresden 1996', in Dümling, ed., 2000, 72–85.

Loewald, Klaus, 'The Eighth Australian Employment Company', *Australian Journal of Politics and History* 31/1 (April 1985), 78–89.
Loewald, Klaus, 'Zum Musikleben in den australischen Internierungslagern', in Dümling, ed., 2000, 66–71.
Lucas, James, 'Played Around the World. Story of the Weintraubs', *AMM* (1 November 1937), 19–20.
Lucas, Kay, 'George Dreyfus's *Garni Sands*: A Forward Step for Australian Opera', *Studies in Music* 7 (1973), 78–87.
Lühe, Barbara von der, 'Das große Glück, ein Orchester aufzubauen. Hermann Scherchen und sein Musica Viva Orchester Wien', *Das Orchester* 39/12 (1991), 1364–73.
Lühe, Barbara von der, *Die Musik war unsere Rettung! Die deutschsprachigen Gründungsmitglieder des Palestine Orchestra* (Tübingen: Mohr Siebeck, 1998).
Mahler-Werfel, Alma, *Mein Leben* (Frankfurt/Main: S. Fischer, 1963).
Malet, Marian, and Anthony Grenville, eds, *Changing Countries. The Experience and Achievement of German-Speaking Exiles from Hitler in Britain, from 1933 to today* (London: Libris, 2002).
Manning, Arthur, *Larger than life: the story of Eric Baume* (Sydney: A.H. & A.W. Reed, 1967).
Margis, Hans, 'In Memory of Erwin Frenkel', *Dunera News* 51 (February 2001), 14–15.
Martin, Peter, and Christine Alonzo, eds, *Zwischen Charleston und Stechschritt. Schwarze im Nationalsozialismus* (Munich: Dölling & Galitz, 2004).
McCredie, Andrew, ed., *From Colonel Light into the Footlights. The Performing Arts in South Australia from 1836 to the present* (Norwood, S. Australia: Pagel Books, 1988).
Menuhin, Yehudi, *Unvollendete Reise. Lebenserinnerungen* (Munich: Deutscher Taschenbuch Verlag, 1979).
Moore, Andrew, 'Scott, William John Rendell (1888–1956)', in *Australian Dictionary of Biography*, vol. 11 (Carlton, VIC: Melbourne University Press, 1988), 550–2.
Moser, Jonny, 'Die Apokalypse der Wiener Juden', in *Wien 1938. Historisches Museum der Stadt Wien. 110. Sonderausstellung* (Vienna: Österreichischer Bundesverlag, 1988), 287–97.
Mosse, George L., 'Personal Recollections', in *The Musical Tradition of the Jewish Reform Congregation in Berlin* (Tel Aviv: The Feher Jewish Music Center of Beth Hatefutsoth, 1999), 6–9.
Murdoch, James, *Australia's Contemporary Composers* (South Melbourne, VIC: Macmillan, 1972).
Musicians' Union of Australia, Rules (Melbourne: P.E. Hambly Pty. Ltd., 1929) (Archive Dümling)

Nachama, Andreas, and Gereon Sievernich, eds, *Jüdische Lebenswelten. Katalog* (Berlin: Jüdischer Verlag, 1991).
Nagel, Matthias, *Thema & Variation. Das Philharmonische Orchester Regensburg und seine Geschichte* (Regensburg: Pustet, 2001).
Naumann, Uwe, *Zwischen Tränen und Gelächter. Satirische Faschismuskritik 1933 bis 1945* (Cologne: Pahl-Rugenstein, 1983).
Neumann, Klaus, *In the Interest of National Security. Civilian Internment in Australia during World War II* (Canberra: National Archives of Australia, 2006).
Newton, Helmut, *Autobiography* (New York: Nan A. Talese/Doubleday, 2003).
Norst, Marlene J., and Johanna McBride, *Austrians and Australia* (Potts Point, NSW: Athena Press, 1988).
Okrassa, Nina, *Peter Raabe. Dirigent, Musikschriftsteller und Präsident der Reichsmusikkammer (1872–1945)* (Cologne–Weimar–Vienna: Böhlau, 2004).
O'Neill, Sally, 'Kruse, Johann Secundus (1859–1927)', in *Australian Dictionary of Biography*, vol. 5 (Carlton, VIC: Melbourne University Press, 1974), 44–5.
Palmer, Glen, *Reluctant Refuge. Unaccompanied Refugee and Evacuee Children in Australia, 1933–1945* (East Roseville, NSW: Kangaroo Press, 1997).
Palmer, Glen, 'Seventeen Children: Australia's Response to German Jewish Refugee Children 1933–1940', *Journal of the Australian Jewish Historical Society* 13 (1995), 88–96.
Patkin, Benzion, *The Dunera Internees* (Stanmore, NSW: Cassell Australia, 1979).
Paupié, Kurt, *Handbuch der österreichischen Pressegeschichte 1848–1959*, vol. 1 (Vienna: Braumüller, 1960).
Pear, David, 'Grainger on Race and Nation', *Australasian Music Research* 5 (2001), 25–48.
Pearl, Cyril, *The Dunera Scandal: Deported by Mistake* (Sydney: Angus & Robertson, 1983).
Peyser, Dora, *The Strong and the Weak: A Sociological Study* (Sydney: Currawong Publishing, 1951).
Pike, Andrew, and Ross Cooper, *Australian film 1900–1977: A Guide to Feature Film Production* (Melbourne: Oxford University Press, 1998).
Pollnitz, Emily, 'Writing the "Long-Haired Frustrates" Back into the History of the 'Wiener Schnitzel Society': Musica Viva, 1945–52', *Journal of Australian Studies* 30/88 (2006), 61–71.
Polster, Bernd, ed., *„Swing Heil". Jazz im Nationalsozialismus* (Berlin: Transit, 1989).
Portnoj, Annie, 'Memories of Salzburg', *AMN* (1 February 1947), 16–17.
Portnoj, Henry, 'The Art of Accompanying', *AMN* (2 May 1949), 33.
Prerauer, Curt, 'Australien meldet sich zum Wort', *Melos* 33 (1966), 428.
Prerauer, Curt, 'How Music Has Progressed in Australia', *ABC Weekly* (2 December 1939), 36–7.

Prieberg, Fred K., *Handbuch Deutsche Musiker 1933–1945*, CD-ROM, Version 1.2–2/2005.
Prieberg, Fred K., *Musik im NS-Staat* (Frankfurt/Main: S. Fischer, 1982).
Raab Hansen, Jutta, *NS-verfolgte Musiker in England. Spuren deutscher und österreichischer Flüchtlinge in der britischen Musikkultur* [Musik im ‚Dritten Reich' und im Exil – vol. 1] (Hamburg: von Bockel, 1996)
Rabinovici, Doron, *Instanzen der Ohnmacht. Wien 1938–1945. Der Weg zum Judenrat* (Frankfurt/Main: Jüdischer Verlag, 2000).
Radic, Thérèse, *Bernard Heinze. A Biography* (South Melbourne: Macmillan, 1986).
Radic, Thérèse, 'Felix Werder', in Frank Callaway and David Tunley, eds, *Australian Composition in the Twentieth Century* (Melbourne: Oxford University Press, 1978), 88–96.
Rave, Paul Ortwin, and Irmgard Wirth, *Die Bauwerke und Kunstdenkmäler von Berlin – Stadt und Bezirk Charlottenburg* (Berlin: Gebr. Mann, 1961).
Regan, Kerry, 'Peyser, Dora (1904–1970)', in *Australian Dictionary of Biography*, Supplementary Volume (Carlton, VIC: Melbourne University Press, 2005), 323–4.
Reichmann-Stieglitz, Birgitta, *Buch- und Antiquariathandlung Alois Reichmann* (Manuscript, n.d.) <http://www.murrayhall.com/files/referate/reichmann-stieglitz.pdf> (accessed 20 October 2015).
Reichsvereinigung der Juden in Deutschland, ed., *Jüdische Auswanderung nach Australien und anderen Gebieten des englischen Imperiums* (Berlin: Jüdischer Kulturbund in Deutschland, April 1939).
Renwick, William, 'Turnovsky, Frederick 1916–1994', in *Dictionary of New Zealand Biography* <http://www.teara.govt.nz/en/biographies/5t23/turnovsky-frederick> (accessed 20 October 2015).
Röder, Werner, and Herbert Strauss, eds, *Biographisches Handbuch der deutschsprachigen Emigration 1933–1945* (Munich/New York: de Gruyter, 1983).
Rössel, Karl, *Der Dunera-Skandal. Ein vergessenes Kapitel der deutschen Emigrationsgeschichte* [Radio Feature, 60 minutes]. Westdeutscher Rundfunk 5 and WDR 3, 1 October 1996.
Rubinstein, Hilary, *The Jews in Australia. A Thematic History. Vol. 1: 1788–1945* (Port Melbourne: William Heinemann Australia, 1988).
Rürup, Reinhard, ed., *Jüdische Geschichte in Berlin. Bilder und Dokumente* (Berlin: Hentrich, 1995).
Rutland, Suzanne D., 'Australian Responses to Jewish Refugee Migration Before and after World War II', *The Australian Journal of Politics and History* 31/1 (April 1985), 29–48.
Rutland, Suzanne D., *Edge of the Diaspora. Two Centuries of Jewish Settlement in Australia* (Sydney: Collins, 1988).

Rutland, Suzanne D., 'Falk, Leib Aisack (1889–1957)', in *Australian Dictionary of Biography*, vol. 8 (Carlton, VIC: Melbourne University Press, 1981), 464.
Sametz, Philips, *Play On! 60 years of Music-Making with the Sydney Symphony Orchestra* (Sydney: ABC Enterprises, 2001).
Scheit, Gerhard, 'Das sinkende Rettungsboot. Musik im Exilland Österreich', in Heister, Hanns Werner, Claudia Maurer Zenck and Peter Petersen, eds, *Musik im Exil. Folgen des Nazismus für die internationale Musikkultur* (Frankfurt/Main: S. Fischer, 1993), 215–34.
Schellenberg, Walter, *Invasion 1940. The Nazi Invasion Plan for Britain* (London: St Ermin's Press, 2000).
Schenk, Dietmar, 'Das Stern'sche Konservatorium der Musik. Ein deutsch-jüdisches Privatkonservatorium der Bürgerkultur Berlins 1850–1936', in Jürgen Wetzel, ed., *Berlin in Geschichte und Gegenwart. Jahrbuch des Landesarchivs Berlin 2000* (Berlin: Gebr. Mann, 2000), 57–80.
Scherchen, Hermann, 'Die gegenwärtige Situation der modernen Musik (1949)', in *Scherchen, Werke und Briefe. Bd. I Schriften* (Schöneiche b. Berlin: Peter Lang, 1991), 142–4.
Schildberger, Hermann, 'Jazz-Musik', *Die Musik* 17/12 (September 1925), 914–23.
Schildberger, Hermann, 'Jewish Music', *AJR* (April 1946), 5–7.
Schnabel, Artur, *Walking Freely on Firm Ground. Letters to Mary Virginia Foreman 1935–1951* (Hofheim: Wolke, 2014).
Schnierer, Irma, and Mark Siegelberg, 'Fünf Jahre Emigration in Australien', *Aufbau* (28 January 1944), 7.
Schrage, Dieter, 'Die totalitäre Inszenierung der Massen: Volksabstimmung vom 10. April 1938', in *Wien 1938. Historisches Museum der Stadt Wien. 110. Sonderausstellung* (Vienna: Österreichischer Bundesverlag, 1988), 98–113.
Schrieber, Friedrich, *Die Reichskulturkammer. Organisation und Ziele der deutschen Kulturpolitik* (Berlin: Junker & Dünnhaupt, 1934).
Schröder, Heribert, *Tanz- und Unterhaltungsmusik in Deutschland 1918–1933* (Bonn: Verlag für systematische Musikwissenschaft, 1990).
Schumann, Coco, *Der Ghetto-Swinger. Eine Jazzlegende erzählt* (Munich: Deutscher Taschenbuch Verlag, 1997).
Segaloff, Benjamin, *Jewish Choral Music in Victoria* (Melbourne: Published by the author, 1993).
Seyfert, Michael, '"His Majesty's Most Loyal Internees": Die Internierung und Deportation deutscher und österreichischer Flüchtlinge als "enemy aliens"', in Gerhard Hirschfeld, ed., *Exil in Grossbritannien: Zur Emigration aus dem nationalsozialistischen Deutschland* (Stuttgart: Klett-Cotta, 1983), 155–82.
Seyfert, Michael, *Im Niemandsland. Deutsche Exilliteratur in britischer Internierung. Ein unbekanntes Kapitel der Kulturgeschichte des Zweiten Weltkriegs* (Berlin: Das Arsenal, 1984).

Shapiro, James, *Bist Du der König der Juden? Die Passionsspiele in Oberammergau* (Stuttgart: Deutsche Verlags-Anstalt, 2000).
Shaw, Jennifer, 'Modernism, *The Canon* and Schoenberg Reception in Australia', *Australasian Music Research* 8 (2003), 31–58.
Shepherd, Naomi, *Wilfried Israel* (Berlin: Siedler, 1985).
Sherman, A.J., *Island Refuge. Britain and Refugees from the Third Reich 1933–1939* (Newbury Park: Frank Cass, 1994).
Shmith, Michael, and David Colville, eds, *Musica Viva Australia – The First Fifty Years* (Sydney: Playbill Pty. Limited, 1996).
Silbermann, Alphons, 'Apropos the Bodenwieser Ballet', *New Citizen* (15 June 1953), 12.
Silbermann, Alphons, *Verwandlungen. Eine Autobiographie* (Bergisch Gladbach: Lübbe, 1989).
Silbermann, Alphons, 'Zum Einfluß deutschsprachiger Emigranten auf das Musikleben Australiens', in Dümling, ed., 2000, 112–17.
Silbermann, Alphons, 'Zur Geschichte des Musiklebens in Australien', *Die Musikforschung* 12 (1959), 196–200.
Simmons, Lee A.M., *Kehillat Emanuel. A History of the Congregation of the Temple Emanuel Woollahra, New South Wales, Australia* (Adaminaby, NSW: Lee A.M. Simmons, 2003).
Smith, Bernard William, *Noel Counihan. Artist and Revolutionary* (Melbourne: Oxford University Press, 1993).
Smith, Herb, 'Werner Felix Baer 1914–1992', *2MBS-FM Program Guide* (May 1992), 22–23.
Smith, Michael, *Foley. The Spy Who Saved 10,000 Jews* (London: Coronet Books, 1999).
Snowman, Daniel, *The Hitler Emigrés. The Cultural Impact on Britain of Refugees from Nazism* (London: Chatto & Windus, 2002).
Solomon, Miriam, 'Music and Musicians of the Great Synagogue, Sydney (1878–1974)', *Australian Jewish Historical Society Journal* 11/6 (1993), 896–920.
Songs the People Love. A True Story of Laughter, Love, Tragedy and Tears. Narrated and illustrated by Eric Liffman, written by Patricia and Kurt Liffman (Fremantle, WA: Vivid Publishing, 2015).
Spivakovsky, Michael, 'Jascha Spivakovsky', *Music and the Teacher* 11/2 (June 1985), 3–10.
Spivakovsky, Michael, 'Jascha Spivakovsky. Continuing the Biographical Outline', *Music and the Teacher* 11/3 (December 1985), 3–9.
Spivakovsky, Michael, 'Jascha Spivakovsky – a Musical Life', *Journal of the Australian Jewish Historical Society* 9/1 (November 1990), 128–41.
Stadlen, Peter, '50 Jahre danach 1938–1988', *Österreichische Musikzeitschrift* 43/4 (1988), 194–6.

Stadlen, Peter, 'Österreichs Exilmusiker in England', in *Beiträge '90. Österreichische Gesellschaft für Musik. Österreichische Musiker im Exil – Kolloquium 1988* (Kassel-Basel–London: Bärenreiter, 1990), 125–33.

Steinert, Johannes-Dieter, and Inge Weber-Newth, eds, *European Immigrants in Britain 1933–1950* (Munich: Saur, 2003), 43–54.

Stent, Ronald, *A Bespattered Page? The Internment of 'His Majesty's most Loyal Enemy Aliens'* (London: Andre Deutsch Ltd, 1980).

Stevens, Catherine J., 'Spivakovsky, Jascha (1896–1970)', in *Australian Dictionary of Biography*, vol. 16 (Carlton, VIC: Melbourne University Press, 2002), 288–9.

Stibbe, Matthew, *British Civilian Internees in Germany: The Ruhleben Camp, 1914–1918* (Manchester: Manchester University Press, 2008).

Stölting, Walter, *Australien. Das Land von morgen* (Berlin: Deutsche Buch-Gemeinschaft, 1930).

'The Story of Addy Fisher – co-founder of AADA, as told to Dr Trevor Lloyd' [Typescript, 14 March 2003] (Archive Dümling).

Straten, Frank van, *National Treasure. The Story of Gertrud Johnson and the National Theatre* (South Melbourne: Victoria Press, 1994).

Stratowa, Hans von, ed., *Wiener genealogisches Taschenbuch*, vol. VII (Vienna: published by author, 1937).

Strauss, Herbert, 'Jewish Emigration from Germany. Nazi Policies and Jewish Responses (I)', *Leo Baeck Institute Year Book* 25 (1980), 313–61.

Stuckenschmidt, H.H., *Zum Hören geboren. Ein Leben mit der Musik unserer Zeit* (Munich: Deutscher Taschenbuch Verlag, 1982).

Sudrabs, Zaiga, 'Krips, Henry Joseph (1912–1987)', in *Australian Dictionary of Biography*, vol. 17 (Carlton, VIC: Melbourne University Press, 2007), 640–1.

Tagebuch von Kurt Lewinski [Kurt Lewinski's Diary] (Archive of Australian Judaica, University of Sydney (Shelf List 17)).

Tiemeyer-Schütte, Meike, *Das Deutsche Sängerwesen in Südaustralien vor Ausbruch des Ersten Weltkrieges zwischen Bewahrung von Deutschtum und Anglikanisierung* (Münster: Lit Verlag, 2000).

Thomas, Adrian, 'A Critic for the Times: Dorian Le Galienne in Melbourne, 1950–1963', *Australasian Music Research*, 2–3 (1997–1988), 111–27.

Traber, Habakuk, and Elmar Weingarten, eds, *Verdrängte Musik. Berliner Komponisten im Exil* (Berlin: Argon, 1987).

Trapp, Frithjof, Werner Mittenzwei, Henning Rischbieter and Hansjörg Schneider, *Handbuch des deutschsprachigen Exiltheaters*, 2 vols. (Munich: De Gruyter Saur, 1999).

Tregear, Peter John, *The Conservatorium of Music. University of Melbourne. An Historical Essay to Mark its Centenary 1895–1995* (Parkville, VIC: Centre for Studies in Australian Music, 1997).

Trevor, Allan, 'Werner Baer – Musician and Composer', *Broadcast* (25 February 1950).
Tribe, Kenneth W., 'Berg, Charles Josef (1917–1988)', in *Australian Dictionary of Biography*, vol. 17 (Carlton, VIC: Melbourne University Press, 2007), 88–9.
Trost, George F., 'Australische Eindrücke', *JR* (2 September 1938), 1.
Truman, Philip, 'The German-speaking Contribution to Australia's Post-War Musical Life', in Manfred Jurgensen, ed., *German-Australian Cultural Relations since 1945. Proceedings of the Conference held at the University of Queensland, Brisbane, from September 20–23, 1994* (Berne–Berlin etc.: Peter Lang, 1995), 286–308.
Turnbull, Malcolm, *Safe Haven. Records of the Jewish Experience in Australia. National Archives Research Guide* (Canberra: National Archives of Australia, 1999).
Vagg, Stephen, 'Finch, Fry and Factories: A Brief History of Mercury Theatre', *Australasian Drama Studies* 50 (April 2007), 18–35.
Vernon-Warren, Bettina, and Charles Warren, eds, *Gertrud Bodenwieser and Vienna's Contribution to Ausdruckstanz* (Amsterdam: Harwood Academic Publishers, 1999).
Vogel, Rolf, *Ein Stempel hat gefehlt. Dokumente zur Emigration deutscher Juden* (Munich: Droemer Knaur, 1977).
Voigt, Johannes H., 'Von deutscher Auswanderung nach Australien und der Rolle der Musik – eine Annäherung', in Albrecht Dümling, ed., 2000, 14–23.
Wagner, Wolfgang, 'Opera in Sydney', *Canon* 4 (1950–51), 452–7.
W.W. [Wolfgang Wagner], 'This Concerns Musical Australia', *Canon* 7 (1953–54), 35–6.
Walsh, Barbara Ann, *Forty Good Men: The Story of the Tanglin Club in the Island of Singapore 1865–1990* (Singapore: The Club, 1991).
Walter, Hans-Albert, *Deutsche Exilliteratur 1933–1950*. Vol. 3: *Internierung, Flucht und Lebensbedingungen im Zweiten Weltkrieg* (Stuttgart: Metzler, 1988).
Walzer, Tina, and Stephan Templ, *Unser Wien. "Arisierung" auf österreichisch* (Berlin: Aufbau, 2001).
Warren-Smith, Neil, *24 Years of Australian Opera* (Melbourne: Oxford University Press, 1983).
Wasserstein, Bernard, *Britain and the Jews of Europe, 1939–1945* (Oxford: Leicester University Press, 2nd edn, 1999).
Wasserstein, Bernard, 'Britische Regierungen und die deutsche Emigration 1933–1945', in Gerhard Hirschfeld, ed., *Exil in Grossbritannien: Zur Emigration aus dem nationalsozialistischen Deutschland* (Stuttgart: Klett-Cotta, 1983), 44–61.
Waters, Thorold, *Much Besides Music. Memoirs* (Melbourne: Georgian House, 1951).
Waters, Thorold, 'The Stranger Within the Gates. Refugees and the Musical Profession', *AMN* (March 1939), 3.
Webb, Peter G., *A Brief Account of the Tasmanian Musical Festival Society 1943 to 1962* [Typoscript] (Tasmanian National Library, Hobart, 2003).
Werder, Felix, '20th Century Rococo', *Opera Australia* (January 1974), 20–1.

Werder, Felix, 'Choices of Memories', in Mark Thomas, ed., *Images of Germany. Australian Insights* (Canberra: Embassy of the Federal Republic of Germany, 1993), 70–2.
Werder, Felix, 'German Jewish Expressionism', in Dümling, ed., 2000, 106–10.
Werder, Felix, *More or less Music* (Melbourne: Council of Adult Education, 1994).
Werder, Felix, *More than Music* (Melbourne: Council of Adult Education, 1991).
Werther, Rudolf, *Opera in Australia: The History Leading to the Australian Elizabethan Opera* (S.I., s.n., 1957 [NLA]).
Whiteoak, John, and Aline Scott-Maxwell, eds, *Currency Companion to Music and Dance in Australia* (Sydney: Currency House, 2003).
Wien 1938. Historisches Museum der Stadt Wien. 110. Sonderausstellung (Vienna: Österreichischer Bundesverlag, 1988).
Wilton, Janis, ed., *Internment. The Diaries of Harry Seidler May 1940 – October 1941* (Sydney: Allen & Unwin, 1986).
Wisshaupt, Walter, Das Wiener Pressewesen von Dollfuß bis zum Zusammenbruch (1933–1945) (PhD Thesis, University of Vienna 1951).
Wolfssohn, Michael, Deutsche Juden und andere Weltbürger (Jena: Glaux, 2004).
Wurzburger, Madeleine, and Matt Kelly, 'An Introduction to the life and work of Walter Wurzburger. Paper presented at the City University Study Day "Musical Refugees"', London, City University, 20 November 1996.
Zimmering, Max, 'Politische Bühne im Exil', in Max Zimmering, Der gekreuzigte Grischa. Begegnung mit Zeitgenossen (Rudolstadt: Greifenverlag, 1969), 63.
Zipes, Jack, *Fairy Tale as Myth, Myth as Fairy Tale* (Lexington: The University Press of Kentucky, 1994).
Zipes, Jack, *Happily Ever After: Fairy Tales, Children and the Culture Industry* (New York: Routledge, 1997).

Glossary

Anschluss: Nazi annexation of Austria, 1938
Arierparagraph: Aryan paragraph
Berufsverbot: work ban
Brüdervereinshaus: Jewish Fraternity Building (B'nai B'rith)
Bundesverdienstkreuz: Federal Cross of Merit
Central-Verein deutscher Bürger jüdischen Glaubens: Central Association of German Citizens of Jewish Faith
Deutsche Forschungsgemeinschaft: German Research Foundation
Deutsch-jüdischer Kulturbund: German Jewish Culture League
Freier Deutscher Kulturbund (London): Free German League of Culture
Fürsorge-Zentrale der Israelitischen Kultusgemeinde – Welfare Centre of the Vienna Jewish Community
Gestapo: Nazi Secret Police
Generalmusikdirektor: Director of Music
Gesellschaft der Musikfreunde: Society of the Friends of Music
Gesetz zur Wiederherstellung des Berufsbeamtentum: Civil Service Restoration Act
Gesetz gegen die Überfüllung deutscher Schulen und Hochschulen: Law Against the Overcrowding of German Schools and Colleges
Gleichschaltung: Nazi standardisation ('coordination') of institutions and politics, 1933
Gymnasium: secondary school
Hilfsverein der Juden in Deutschland: Aid Association of Jews in Germany
Israelitische Kultusgemeinde Wien: Vienna Jewish Community
Jüdischer Kulturbund in Deutschland: Jewish Culture League in Germany
Kammersänger: chamber singer
Kampfbund für deutsche Kultur: Combat League for German Culture
Kapellmeister: conductor
Kristallnacht: The Night of Broken Glass/November Pogrom, 1938
Künstlerhilfe der jüdischen Gemeinde: Artists' Aid of the Jewish Community
Kulturbund Deutscher Juden: Culture League of German Jews
Liedertafel: German male choir
Palästina-Amt: Palestinian Office
Rassenschande: racial defilement
Reichsbund Jüdischer Frontsoldaten: Reich Federation of Jewish Front Soldiers

Reichsfluchtsteuer: Reich Flight Tax
Reichskulturkammer: Reich Chamber of Culture
Reichsmusikkammer: Reich Chamber of Music
Reichszentrale für jüdische Auswanderung: Reich Centre for Jewish Emigration
Reifeprüfung: final examination at conservatories
S-Bahn: overground train
Scheunenviertel: Barn Quarter; Berlin district populated by many poor eastern European Jews
Schutzhäftling: Nazi term for prisoner in 'protective custody'
Singspiel: musical comedy
Technische Hochschule Berlin: Polytechnic University in Berlin
Volksgemeinschaft: Nazi term for 'Aryan population' (lit. people's community)
Zentralstelle für jüdische Auswanderung: Central Agency for Jewish Emigration

Index

Abarbanell, Hans 260
Abravanel, Maurice 34, 76–9, 83–5, 168, 171, 192, 345–6, 348, 392
Adam, Leonhard 253, 278
Adam, Manfred 253
Adler, Guido 349
Adler, Henry 39, 112–13, 184, 187, 243–4, 249, 285, 315, 317, 383, 388, 405
Adler, Hugo 380
Aeschylus 425
Ainsworth, Robert 76–7
Albers, Hans 18, 40, 406
d'Albert, Eugen 186, 367
Alberti, Gustav Victor 40, 100, 163, 235, 267, 307–8, 320
Alexander-Katz, Alfred 145
Allen, Robert Marshall 151–2
Allen, Woody 418
Almas, Josef 260
Altmann, Richard 95
Amadio, Clive 414
Anciano, Marcello R. 136
Anderson, Maxwell 434
Anderson, Sir John 220
Anouilh, Jean 434
Antill, John Henry 412–13
Aristotle 417
Arnold, Franz 38, 75
Arrau, Claudio 365
Ashbolt, Allan 431
Ashkenazy, Vladimir 365
Asmis, Rudolf 82, 215
Austral, Florence 75–6, 78

Bab, Julius 47, 64
Bach, Carl Philipp Emanuel 414, 417
Bach, Johann Sebastian 36, 49, 60, 135–6, 147, 167, 205, 226, 230, 263, 277, 331, 347, 365, 393, 397, 410–11
Backhaus, Wilhelm 165–6
Bader, Hans 29, 137–40, 156, 158, 271, 273, 299, 311–14, 316, 389
Baeck, Leo 129
Baer, Sybil 5, 336, 393, 436
Baer, Werner 4, 5, 15–17, 21, 35–6, 44, 46, 50, 91–3, 129–36, 158, 271, 273–6, 283, 286–9, 299, 306, 311–12, 316, 358, 374, 382–3, 387, 392–3, 410, 412–14, 430
Baerwald, Werner 256
Baillie, Julia Mary 5, 38, 58, 152, 166, 263, 265–8, 277–80, 282
Bainton, Edgar 78, 195–6, 217, 358
Bahr, Hermann 96
Bahr-Mildenburg, Anna 104
Baré, Rudolph 267
Barenboim, Daniel 4, 365
Barger, Heinz 196–7, 203, 436
Barmas, Issay 19, 22
Barrett, Sir James W. 84, 189
Barry, Keith 174, 347
Bartók, Béla 162–3, 414–16, 423
Baume, Frederick E. 215, 228, 235
Bausznern, Waldemar von 10
Bax, Arnold 84
Bayer, Anton 36
Beck, Karl 26, 37, 140–1

Becker, Günther 389
Becker, Hugo 22
Beecham, Thomas 165, 371, 393–4, 397–8
Beethoven, Ludwig van 6, 7, 35, 47, 49, 104, 172, 205, 230–1, 259, 263, 265–7, 277–8, 280, 329–31, 333, 341, 347, 367, 369, 372, 392
Behrens, Max Kurt 49, 221, 256, 266, 280
Béla, Dajos 21
Benatzky, Ralph 37, 301
Bendrodt, James C. 206–8, 228, 237, 249–51
Benjamin, Arthur 424
Benjamin, Rosemarie 431
Benz, Wolfgang 3, 7
Berent, Karl 360
Berg, Alban 34, 73, 372
Berg, Anthony R. 341
Berg, Charles 39, 74, 87–8, 321, 336, 338, 341, 378–9
Bergner, Elisabeth 14, 18
Bernell, Agnes 305
Berry, G.W. 179–80
Bertram, Georg 17, 133
Bertram, Hans 57
Bieber, Leo 260
Bikaner, Maharaja of 124
Bing, Rudolf 378
Bischofswerder, Boas 23, 42, 51–2, 221, 225, 266, 278, 307, 321, 406–8, 414
Bismarck, Otto von 82, 166
Bittman, Karl 337
Bizet, Georges 49, 78, 396
Blach, Kurt 125–6, 157–8, 271, 283, 286–8, 299, 311, 316, 363, 390
Blair, Ilse 4, 44, 93–4, 130–2, 137, 158–9, 307
Blanks, Fred 5, 45, 116, 396–8
Blau, Hans 4, 43–4, 101, 126–7, 140, 156, 159, 271–6, 283, 287–9, 299–301, 307, 390, 430

Blau, Otto 99–100, 283, 307–8
Blech, Leo 34, 73, 93, 154, 347, 373
Bloch, Ernest 365, 380
Boccherini, Luigi 278
Bodenwieser, Gertrud 122–3, 184, 384–7, 431
Bohnen, Michael 93
Bonynge, Richard 368
Borodin, Alexander 79
Borovansky, Eduard 384
Boulez, Pierre 418
Boult, Adrian 73, 347
Brahms, Johannes 27, 49, 172, 277, 287, 327, 340, 347, 368, 372–3, 388–9
Brandmann (Brandman), Solomon (Frederick) 149–50, 231, 380–1
Brandt, Willy 6
Braun, Alfred 18
Brecht, Bertolt 42, 276
Breisach, Paul 34
Brenner, Adolf 26, 36–7, 96, 102–3, 137–42, 221, 263, 280, 283, 311, 317, 348–9, 362, 375, 383, 429
Briner, Hans 376
Britten, Benjamin 365, 393, 416, 418
Bronhill, June 392
Brossement, Marie 27
Broughton, Edward R. 286, 298
Browne, Lindsey 326
Bruch, Max 17, 388
Bruckner, Anton 47, 353, 355–6
Brückner, Hans 40
Bruinier, Julius Ansco 18, 21, 41, 117
Brunner-Hoyos, Magda 123
Buchan, William 228–9, 244
Buchhalter, Ernst 155
Bücken, Ernst 59
Buhlig, Richard 11
Bumcke, Gustav 17, 273
Burstall, Tim 404
Burwood, Max 147
Busoni, Ferruccio 23

Index

Butterley, Nigel 418, 420, 424
Byk, Ellen 19, 92, 150–3, 184, 188, 315, 318, 392, 430
Byrd, William 136
Byron, Lord 54

Calwell, Arthur 316, 376, 411
Cameron, Archie G. 194–5
Cardus, Neville 333, 366, 372, 374, 394–5
Carrodus, Joseph A. 213, 233, 237
Casals, Pablo 165, 359
Casanova, Giacomo 426
Chamberlain, Houston Stewart 84, 96
Chamberlain, Neville 219
Chaucer, Geoffrey 255
Chekov, Anton 434
Chevalier, Maurice 128, 300
Chlumecky-Bauer, Moritz 106, 221, 223, 285
Chlumecky, Johannes von 106–7, 221, 223, 256, 262, 281, 283
Chopin, Frédéric 262, 277–8, 297, 300, 364, 367, 370
Churchill, Winston 124, 219–20, 222, 282
Clapham, Eric 378
Clusmann, Gustav Heinrich 225, 261–2, 280
Cockman, Edward 335
Cocteau, Jean 434
Code, Percy 411
Cohen, Sir Samuel 86–7, 456
Cohn, Sigi 260–1, 303
Colin, Elizabeth 19, 44, 149, 189, 392
Collier, Marie 392
Conne, Paul de 113, 186
Coper, Fritz 43, 73–4, 87, 186, 315, 380–3, 392
Coper, Willy 43, 73, 92, 188, 285, 315, 321
Counihan, Noel 171, 414
Covell, Roger 55, 341–2, 395, 416–17, 420–2, 424
Cowen, Frederic 363

Cracknell, Ruth 433
Crawford, Craig 207–9, 233, 249
Crawford, Hector 348, 389
Creighton, Walter 179
Crow, Sutton 168
Cubbin, David 420
Curtin, John 282

Dane, Mario 113, 321, 362
Davis, Herbert 349
Dawson, Peter 286
Dean, Brett 4, 430
Debussy, Claude 370
Decsey, Ernst 96, 104
Delibes, Leo 278
Delius, Frederick 84
Dempsey, Gregory 392
Descartes, René 417
Deutschkron, Inge 89
Dickens, Charles 434
Dietrich, Marlene 3, 18, 94, 202
Disney, Walt 289–92, 410
Döblin, Alfred 15
Dollfuß, Engelbert 95, 97, 107
Dorati, Antal 163, 328, 348, 371
Dorsch, Käthe 18
Dreyer, Arnold 16–17, 133
Dreyfus, Alfred 45, 109, 154–5
Dreyfus, George 1, 4, 44–5, 90, 109, 154–5, 321, 342, 359–60, 404–5, 417–22, 424, 426–8
Dreyschock, Felix 22
Dubsky, Edith 335
Duhan, Hans 124
Dullo, Andreas Franz W. 9
Dullo, Walter Andreas 6, 7, 10–12, 25, 31–3, 39, 44–5, 63–71, 88, 184, 240, 242, 244, 263, 285, 315, 321, 329–30, 332, 334–7, 342, 350, 352, 395, 432
Duncan, Catherine 7, 411–12, 471
Duncan, Constance 277

Dunlop, Shona 385–6
Durieux, Tilla 18
Dvořák, Antonin 136, 259, 278, 356
Dwyer-Gray, Edmund 316, 376

Ebert, Carl 34
Eddy, Jenifer 392
Edelmann, Hans 27–8, 43–4, 99, 118, 263, 281, 307, 352, 362
Edison, Thomas 159–60
Edwards, Ross 418
Ehrenfeld, Adolf (Alfred) 25, 220, 253, 271, 277, 362–3
Ehrenzweig, Anton 278
Ehrlich, Heinrich 22
Ehrlich, Max 50, 131, 133–4
Eichmann, Adolf 102, 311
Einstein, Albert 14
Einstein, Alfred 48, 82
Eisler, Hanns 402, 418
Eisner, Kurt 74, 235
Elgar, Edward 84, 147, 165, 333, 362–3
Elizabeth II 358, 416
Engelmann, Hans-Ulrich 428
Epstein, June 391
Eysler, Edmund 37, 301

Faber, Kurt 57
Fabian, Erwin 294–6
Factor (Faktor), Andy 38, 43, 235–6, 285, 361, 388–9
Falk, Erna 155
Falk, L.A. 259, 308, 379
Fall, Leo 100
Fanta, Robert 27
Feigl, Leonie 5, 27, 102, 137, 236, 317, 372, 392
Feuchtwanger, Lion 63
Feuermann, Emanuel 15
Feuerstein, Franz 266
Fichman, Hans 281, 303
Finch, Peter 402, 432–3

Fisher, Addy (Adolf) 20, 92, 204, 206, 210–11, 229, 239, 285, 311, 320, 388, 436
Fisher, Emanuel (Manny) 20–1, 43, 198–9, 201–2, 204, 207, 210, 213, 229–30, 239, 242, 285, 311, 315, 320, 345, 388, 436
Fisher, Sylvia 392
Fitzner, Rudolf 106
Fleischer, Oskar 25, 128, 156, 273, 276–7, 283, 286–7, 289, 317, 390–1
Flesch, Carl 15, 95, 104, 154
Fligg, Anny 88, 184, 384
Floyd, Alfred 368, 384, 411
Foley, Frank E. 72, 108–10, 142, 146
Foll, Hattil Spencer 213, 215, 235
Forst, Hans 96, 114, 184, 285, 315, 395–6, 406
Forst, Maximilian 96–8
Forster, Rudolf 18
Franz Joseph II (Kaiser) 106, 310
Freeden, Herbert 131
Freedman, David Isaac 82, 86
Frenkel, Emanuel 29, 121
Frenkel, Erwin 29, 117, 218–19, 222–3, 253, 271, 283, 286, 303, 311, 318, 390, 414
Frescobaldi, Girolamo 136
Freud, Alexander 115
Fried, Erich 262, 269
Friedman, Ignaz 366–7
Friedmann, Siegmund 21, 50
Friedrich II (Prussia) 20, 109
Friedrich Wilhelm III 55
Fry, Christopher 434
Fuhrmann, Arthur 277
Fuller, Sir Benjamin 76
Furtwängler, Wilhelm 35, 73, 154, 166, 347, 356

Gabrilowitsch, Ossip 22
Gadd, Charmian 339

Index 563

Gál, Hans 222, 429
Gardiner, Henry Balfour 84
Garmo, Tilly de 34
Garrett, Thomas Hugh 86, 178–82, 235
Gautier, Jeanne 287
Geck, Heinz 57
German, Edward 147
George, Heinrich 18
Gernsheim, Friedrich 22
Gerron, Kurt 18
Gershwin, George 225, 280, 405
Gifford, Helen 424
Gigli, Benjamino 124
Gilbert, Robert 196
Gilfedder, John 424
Gluck, Christoph Willibald 49, 376, 426
Gluskin, Lud 202
Gmeindl, Walter 25
Godowsky, Leopold 23, 367
Godwin, Paul 20–1
Goebbels, Joseph 40, 90, 97, 101, 291
Goethe, Johann W. von 260, 266, 291
Goetz, Kurt 18
Gogol, Nikolai 431
Goldberg, Szymon 334, 414–15
Goldman, Harry Aron 115
Goldmark, Karl 148
Goldner, Richard 30, 104–6, 184, 188, 195, 315, 327–30, 334–42, 431
Goldschmidt, Berthold 34, 429
Goodman, Alfred 146
Goossens, Eugene 353, 356–8, 368–9, 378, 401, 415
Göring, Hermann 33, 176
Gotsch, Carl 326
Gounod, Charles 278, 376
Gowrie, Lady Zara Eileen 237–9, 241, 251, 375
Graff, Horst 17–18, 21, 41, 117, 198, 203–4, 210, 212–15, 228–9, 231–5, 237–41, 246–9, 251–2, 269, 282, 285, 312, 315, 320, 345, 387–8, 436

Grainger, Percy 84–5, 170, 424
Granach, Alexander 18
Grant, Clifford 392
Grant, Madison 84
Graudan, Nicolai 20, 74, 372
Grätz, Paul 18
Grosz, George 21
Gruber, Georg 270, 356
Grünfeld, Alfred 104
Gurland, Hans-Heinrich 278
Guttmann, Oskar 93

Haag, Stefan 270, 285, 376, 378–9
Hacker, Gertrud 26, 137–8, 184, 188, 315, 321, 391
Haentzschel, Georg 41, 117
Hagel, Richard 51
Hajek-Bodan, Olga 321
Hamburger, Gerhard 280–1
Handel, George Frideric 47, 263, 266–7, 280, 330, 352
Hansen, Max 18
Hanson, Raymond 370
Harband, John 148, 390
Harlan, Veit 18
Hart, Fritz 424
Hartmann, Karl Amadeus 331
Hašek, Jaroslav 278, 298
Hauser, Heinrich 111
Haydn, Joseph 147, 161, 348, 355, 397
Heartfield, John 222
Heckroth, Hein 261, 292
Heine, Heinrich 47–8, 384
Heinze, Bernard 58, 62, 78, 84, 150–2, 154, 167–70, 175, 188–9, 195, 231, 263, 280, 326, 348, 350, 356–7, 363, 365, 367, 371, 395, 397–8, 416, 426
Helfgott, Samuel 358
Hendon, Hellmuth 162
Henze, Hans Werner 426
Herder, Johann Gottfried 89, 417
Hertz, Hugo 86

Herweg, Kurt 38, 43, 50, 74–5, 88, 184, 242, 246, 248, 269, 282, 285, 350, 384, 387, 411–12
Hess, Willy 23, 167
Hesse, Hermann 6
Hesterberg, Trude 18
Heyd, Kurt 57
Heydrich, Reinhard 176, 456
Heyer, John 403
Heymann, Werner Richard 196
Hill, Alfred 57, 78, 83–4, 347, 353, 424
Hince, Kenneth 396, 398, 424
Hindemith, Paul 273, 277, 326, 334, 418
Hinkel, Hans 46, 49, 130
Hirsch, Hugo 37
Hirschberg, Günter 44, 74, 221, 263, 281, 283, 308–11, 374, 381–3, 393
Hirschfeld-Mack, Ludwig 281
Hitchcock, Alfred 434
Hitler, Adolf 24, 31, 34, 56, 94, 97, 107, 165, 219, 238, 243, 270, 291, 297, 306, 347
Hitschmann, Felix 26
Hmelnitsky, Alexander 368
Hochberger, Simon 260–1, 305–6, 412
Hoffmann, Endre 163, 188, 195, 328, 357
Hölderlin, Friedrich 423
Hollaender, Friedrich 21–2, 304, 306, 434
Holmes, Margaret 277
Holst, Gustav 84
Holt, Harold 265
Holzbauer, Hans 27, 99, 273, 276, 283, 288–9, 311, 317, 345, 389
Honegger, Arthur 104
Hopkins, John 418
Horenstein, Jascha 348
Hörth, Franz Ludwig 35
Houseman, John 431
Hubay, Jenö 163, 188, 328, 334
Huberman, Bronislaw 165–6, 168–70, 192
Humble, Keith 417

Humperdinck, Engelbert 17, 375
Hutcheson, Ernest 57
Huttenbach, Alfred 278
Hylton, Jack 116–17

Ibsen, Henrik 416
Ippen, Evelyn 386
Isaacs, Sir Isaac 144
Israel, Nathan 39, 109, 112
Israel, Wilfried 109–10
Ivens, Joris 7, 480

James, W.G. 193, 346–8
Jandorf, Adolf 18
Joachim, Joseph 14, 19, 22–3, 57
Johann, A.E. 57
Johnson, Gertrude 377
Jones, Ivor 74
Jones, Maureen 335
Jooss, Kurt 145, 261
Joseph II (Habsburg) 28
Joseph, Max 246, 310, 383
Jurmann, Walter 40

Kaiser, Moritz 12
Kalb, Joseph 271, 383
Kallir, Erwin 267
Kálmán, Emmerich 37, 100, 281, 308, 390
Kandinsky, Wassily 417
Kanitz, Ernst 104
Kant, Immanuel 7, 94
Kassner, Edward 117, 219, 222, 256–8, 260, 280, 292
Kästner, Erich 306, 434
Katz, Werner Hans 139, 147, 219, 256, 260–2, 267, 278, 281
Kaufmann, Ernst N. 113, 188, 240, 413
Kay, Sydney John 12–13, 21, 40–1, 117, 199–202, 205, 210, 214, 230, 235, 239, 241, 244–6, 318–20, 358, 384, 388, 402–5, 410–11, 414, 431–6
Keating, Paul 4, 427

Index 565

Keefe, Inspector 230–1
Keeffe, Bernard 386
Keller, Hans 429
Keller, Otto 274
Kelly, Ned 13
Kelsen, Hans 33
Kennedy, Lauri 74
Kerner, Julie 5
Kerr, Alfred 14
Kestenberg, Leo 159
Keudell, Wilhelm A. von 464
Keußler, Gerhard von 58–60, 270
Kimmel, Emmy 186–7, 373–4, 392
Kinston, Steven 335
Kipnis, Alexander 95, 114, 374, 377
Kirsova, Helene 384
Kisch, Egon Erwin 56
Kitson, Frank 183, 192–5, 208, 212–14, 231–5, 237–9, 250–1, 318, 320, 351, 358
Kittel, Bruno 92–3
Kleiber, Erich 34
Kleist, Heinrich von 431
Klemperer, Otto 14, 34, 37, 146, 165, 168, 353, 381, 395, 430
Klopfer, Friedrich 41, 117, 335
Knepler, Paul 100
Koellreutter, Hans-Joachim 331–2
Kolben, Emil 159–61
Kolben, Robert 5, 160–2, 367–70
Kolisch, Rudolf 395
Kollo, Walter 36
Kollwitz, Käthe 67, 414
Kolm, Hanny 387
Kolos, Lily 162–3, 372–3
Körber, Hilde 18
Korngold, Erich Wolfgang 307, 333, 418
Kortner, Fritz 18
Kramer, Fritz 28, 116, 184, 188, 195, 318, 357–8
Kraus, Karl 30, 96
Kraus, Lili 334

Krauss, Werner 18
Kreisler, Fritz 165, 281
Krenek, Ernst 39, 96, 104
Kreutzer, Leonid 11, 25
Krips, Henry 25, 102, 114, 184, 193, 284–5, 315, 350–6, 358, 372, 374–5, 384, 393, 402, 406, 412, 414
Krips, Josef 25, 102
Krug, Gerald 356
Kruse, Johann 57
Krutsch, Martin 13, 114, 188, 273, 315, 379–80
Krützfeld, Wilhelm 129
Kubelik, Rafael 356
Künnecke, Eduard 225
Kurth, Ernst 154
Kurtz, Edmund 20, 61–2, 171, 189, 363, 430
Kurtz, Efrem 62

Laban, Rudolf von 122
Lach, Robert 25
Lachmann-Mosse, Hans 47–8
Lafitte, Francois 218
Lambert, Raymond 287, 367
Lamond, Frederic 146
Landa, Abram 321, 358
Landau, Anneliese 93
Landauer, Alfred 221, 278, 283
Langer, Peter 24–5, 98, 114, 187–8, 318, 358–9
Laqueur, Rudi 115–16, 219, 256, 262, 281, 283, 287, 292, 303, 387, 389
Lasker-Schüler, Else 14
Lasso, Orlando di 263
Layton, Julian 87, 181–2, 255–6, 267, 276, 313
Le Gallienne, Dorian 397, 404, 424
Lehár, Franz 37, 99, 117, 281, 287, 390
Lehmann, Lotte 165, 377
Leibowitz, René 395, 417

Leichhardt, Ludwig 54, 57
Leicht, Peter 260
Leicht, Walter 114
Lemberg, Max Rudolf 185
Lemberg, Walter Friedrich 318
Lenzer, Hyman 348
Leopold I (Habsburg) 28
Leschetizky, Theodor 11, 366–7
Lessing, Gotthold Ephraim 7, 416–17, 423
Levi, John 4, 380
Lewandowski, Louis 47, 380
Liffmann, Eric 221, 283, 299, 301, 303, 311, 374
Ligeti, György 421
Light, Alan 392
Lincke, Paul 281, 301
Linger, Carl 56, 412
List, Emanuel 377
Liszt, Franz 22, 364, 367
Loewald, Klaus 2–3, 5–6, 89, 221, 223, 225, 262–3, 265, 277, 283
Loewe, Carl 135
Lohde, Sigurd 299, 305, 470
Loos, Adolf 24
Lorber, Marcel 5, 29, 122–3, 184, 318, 372, 385–7, 391
Lorenz, Clarice 377
Luber, Cecil 382
Lueger, Karl 24
Lunzer, Fritz 27
Lyons, Joseph Aloysius 86

McCredie, Andrew 2–3
McDermott, Paul 371, 415
Macdonald, Alexander 247
McEwen, John 177
Mackay, William John 149, 231
MacMillan, Ernest 217
Magnus, Walter 465
Mahler, Gustav 36, 100, 166, 331, 355
Mahler-Werfel, Alma 331

Mandel, Fritz 335
Mandeville, W.M.R. 62
Mandyczewski, Eusebius 113, 349
Manifold, John 404
Mann, Thomas 6, 223, 265
Mannheim, Lucie 18
Mannix, Daniel 58–9, 270
Markevitch, Igor 356
Marshall-Hall, George 167, 424, 427
Marsick, Martin Pierre 104
Martin, Ray 116, 222, 225, 256–8, 260, 280–1, 292, 303, 406
Marx, Joseph 26, 349, 372
Masaryk, Tomáš 159
Masbach, Fritz 17, 133
Mascagni, Pietro 287
Massary, Fritzi 18
Mathy, Marianne 19, 372, 377, 392
Mayer-Mahr, Moritz 13, 22
Meale, Richard 396, 418, 420, 423–4
Mehring, Walter 18
Meitner, Lise 14
Melba, Nellie 60
Melchior, Lauritz 377
Mendelssohn-Bartholdy, Felix 47, 135–6, 166, 263, 352, 362, 364, 414
Mendelssohn, Eleonore von 18
Mendelssohn, Erich 50
Mendelssohn, Moses 7, 417
Menuhin, Hephzibah 326, 339–40, 370, 372
Menuhin, Yehudi 168, 174, 223, 326
Menzies, Robert Gordon 227, 237, 245, 247, 253
Meyer, Peter Max 44, 139, 221, 256, 260, 307
Meyer, Sir Manasseh 135, 137
Michaelis, Karin 94
Milhaud, Darius 326
Mitchell, Inspector 201, 212, 214
Mittler, Franz 27
Molière 432

Index

Moncrieff, Gladys 200, 215
Monti, Vittorio 261
Moodie, Alma 58
Morawetz, Paul 340
Morgan, Fred 359
Moser, Franz 26
Moses, Charles 167, 173–5, 192–5, 338, 357, 363
Mosse, George 48
Mozart, Wolfgang Amadeus 6–7, 16, 25, 49, 64, 93, 167, 205, 230, 263, 265–7, 278–80, 330, 348–9, 367, 375–6, 388, 393, 396, 426, 432
Murdoch, James 418
Mussolini, Benito 243, 306
Mussorgsky, Modest 60, 78

Nadel, Arno 23
Napoleon 161
Nathan, Isaac 54, 56
Neher, Carola 18
Neumann, Käthe 113–14, 121, 186, 366–7, 391
Newlin, Dika 395
Newton, Helmut 277, 408
Nicholas, Nola 326
Nicolai, Otto 349, 375
Nielsen, Asta 18
Nietzsche, Friedrich 274, 408–9, 423
Nikisch, Arthur 83, 165
Noé, Marcel 34
Nolde, Emil 414

Ochs, Siegfried 15
Öhlberger, Karl 360
Offenbach, Jacques 281, 362
Oistrakh, Igor 365
Olewski, Arno 41, 117
Olivier, Sir Laurence 432–3
O'Neill, Lieutenant 258
Oppenheimer, Lincoln 303

Orff-Solscher, Alice 58–9
Ormandy, Eugene 357
Ormonde, Francis 62
Paganini, Niccolo 54, 278
Pallenberg, Max 18
Palmer, Lilli 75
Paul, Tibor 368
Peart, Donald 418
Peček (Petschek), Julius 161
Penderecki, Krzysztof 421
Pergolesi, G.B. 373
Perkins, J.A. 83
Petö, Stefan 279
Peyser, Dora 44, 64, 66–7, 70–1, 87–8, 380
Pfitzner, Hans 274, 373
Pfund, Gerty 203, 230, 245
Philips, Thea 378
Pietruschka, Majer 5, 23, 92, 146–7, 256, 259, 261–3, 278, 281, 283, 299, 321–2, 360, 392
Pikler, Robert 334–5, 339
Pilcher, Charles Venn 187, 252, 465
Pilgrim, Volker Elis 427
Pirnitzer, Daisy 387
Plautus, Titus Maccius 433
Polatschek, Cornel 280–1
Pollack, Hubert 110
Polo, Danny 202
Porten, Henny 18
Porter, Eric 245, 434
Portnoj, Annie 378, 392
Portnoj, Henry 29, 43, 126–7, 156–8, 271, 283, 286, 299, 303, 312, 316, 318, 363, 378, 383, 387, 392
Post, Joseph 78, 413
Prentki, Horst 146
Prerauer, Kurt Emanuel 34–5, 37, 51, 73, 75–8, 285–6, 314, 318, 345–8, 356, 362, 366, 374, 391–2, 394, 396, 398, 418, 420, 423
Prihoda-Rosé, Alma 36

Prohaska, Emil 26
Prokofiev, Sergej 401
Prüwer, Julius 25, 146
Puccini, Giacomo 79, 287
Pullman, Simon 30, 104, 327, 329, 332–3, 340
Purcell, Henry 147, 330
Püttmann, Carl 3

Quantz, Johann Joachim 20
Quilter, Roger 84

Raabe, Peter 59
Rachmaninoff, Sergei 369
Radic, Leonard 425–6
Radic, Thérèse 62, 326, 425
Radok, Uwe 273, 277, 408–10
Rameau, Jean Philippe 266
Raphael, Günter 428
Rapp, Georg 262
Rathenau, Walter 1, 427
Rau, Johannes 4
Ravel, Maurice 85, 369, 416
Reger, Max 60, 148, 365, 410
Reich-Ranicki, Marcel 89, 473
Reinhardt, Max 14, 202, 307
Reither, Karl 123–4, 157, 271, 273, 283, 287–9, 360–1, 363
Reizenstein, Franz 429
Remiz, Gustav Edler von 107
Reynders, John 403
Ribbentrop, Joachim von 107
Riebensahm, Hans-Erich 11
Riefenstahl, Leni 291
Riemann, Hugo 273
Rich, Regina 338
Richter, Sviatoslav 365
Robitschek, Kurt 50
Romano, Orlando A. 251
Romberg, Sigmund 208
Roosevelt, Eleanor 223

Roosevelt, Franklin D. 110, 176
Rosen, Willy 50, 134
Rosenstock, Joseph 50
Rosenthal, Friedrich Jacques 122, 385
Rosner, Ady 21, 436
Rosner, Leo 389
Roth, Leo 5, 154, 219, 222–4, 280
Rothschild (family) 87, 102, 186
Rothschild, Fritz 106
Rubinstein, Anton 22, 113
Rubinstein, Artur 365
Rublee, George 176
Rüth, Ludwig 21

Sänger, Hermann 144–5, 379
Saint-Saëns, Camille 370
Salomon, Alice 66
Salomon-Lindberg, Paula 47, 93, 95
Salzmann, Theo 335, 339
Sarasate, Pablo de 259
Sargent, Malcolm 155, 167, 194, 397
Scarlatti, Domenico 49
Schacht, Hjalmar 176
Schalit, Hans 380
Schellenberg, Walter 220
Schenk, Max 308, 381, 383
Scherchen, Hermann 104, 330–2, 340–2, 368, 474
Schiff, Otto 181
Schildberger, Hermann 4, 13, 44, 47–9, 92, 133, 143–5, 183–4, 267, 273–4, 351–2, 362, 376–81, 392
Schiller, Friedrich 13, 423
Schindler, Oskar 389
Schmidt, Joseph 47, 95
Schmitz, Peter 299
Schnabel, Artur 15, 17, 37–8, 146, 154, 166, 168, 174, 263, 265, 270, 280, 381
Schneevoigt, Georg 168, 193, 371–2
Schneiderhan, Wolfgang 107

Schnitzler, Arthur 434
Schober, Franz von 9
Schoenberger, Theodor 22, 92–3, 95, 146,
    183–4, 321, 381–2, 391
Schönberg, Arnold 14, 28–9, 104,
    332–3, 395, 401, 414, 417
Schöne, Lotte 27, 34
Schönerer, Georg von 24
Schönzeler, Hans-Hubert 227, 355–6
Schönzeler, Mathias 227, 355
Schreker, Franz 15
Schubert, Franz 9, 47, 135, 147, 208, 230,
    254, 263, 265, 269, 277–8, 281, 333,
    337, 363, 369, 374, 386
Schück-Kolben, Ignaz 160
Schulvater, Cyril 21–2, 41, 117, 188,
    202–4, 206, 212, 229, 240, 242,
    248, 311, 320, 357–8, 436
Schulvater, Ernest 188, 212, 229, 240, 311,
    320, 392, 457
Schumann, Clara 22
Schumann, Coco 389
Schumann, Robert 9, 10, 13, 47–9, 230,
    262, 279, 362, 364, 367
Schuschnigg, Kurt von 97
Schuster, André 389, 478
Schuster, Hugo 260
Schwitters, Kurt 222
Scott, Cyril 84
Scott, Lieutenant Colonel W.P. 224
Scott, William John Rendell 231–2, 237
Scrimgeour, Colin 431
Sculthorpe, Peter 396, 417, 420, 423–4
Seiber, Mátyás 42, 429
Seidler, Harry 220
Selby, Mella 335–6
Seligsohn, Julius 179
Shakespeare, William 255, 434
Shostakovich, Dmitri 268, 418
Shaw, George Bernard 434
Shaw, John 392

Sherriff, Robert Cedric 298
Shostakovich, Dmitri 268, 418
Sikorski, Hans 100
Silbermann, Alphons 3, 12, 14, 33, 42–6,
    118–20, 184–5, 310, 312, 321, 323,
    395, 429–30
Silberstein, Otmar 147, 219, 254, 256, 263,
    283, 360
Simmons, Robert 392
Simon, Erich 332
Simon, James 109
Singer, Kurt 35, 45–6, 154
Sitsky, Larry 417, 424–6
Slezak, Leo 386
Smallbones, R.T. 72
Smart, Ralph 434–5
Smetana, Bedřich 49, 300, 348, 362
Smith, Lawrence Godfrey 368
Snowman, Daniel 429
Sophocles 94
Spender, Percy 246
Spinoza, Baruch de 417
Spitzer, Therese 98–9, 114
Spivakovsky, Adolf 22, 63, 113, 314, 378,
    392
Spivakovsky, Issy 22, 63, 83, 89, 392
Spivakovsky, Jascha 4, 7, 22, 60–3,
    170–5, 195, 287, 314, 363–6, 372,
    391, 430
Spivakovsky, Tossy 22–3, 36, 60–3,
    170–5, 189, 195, 363, 370, 430
Stadlen, Peter 2–3, 25–6, 96, 101–2, 116,
    221–3, 256, 262–5, 267–9, 278–81,
    332, 429–30
Stanislavski, Constantin 431
Stauffer, Teddy 389
Steele, James Arthur 167
Steiner, Paul 25, 121, 157, 271, 273, 283,
    299, 312, 316, 320
Steinrück, Albert 18
Stenz, Markus 4

Stern, Dory 122, 188, 387, 391
Sternberg, Max Kurt 262, 287,
    292–3, 299, 433
Steuermann, Eduard 395
Stevens, Bertram 86
Stiasny, Walter 376
Stiedry, Fritz 34, 395
Stierer, Maurice 30
Stiwelband, Mischa 29, 124–7, 156–8,
    271, 283, 286, 316–17, 390
Stockhausen, Karlheinz 418–19
Stoddard, Lothrop 84
Stöhr, Richard 27, 113
Stokowski, Leopold 368, 410
Stolz, Robert 99, 287, 390
Straus, Oscar 37, 100
Strauß, Johann 26, 99, 147, 276, 278, 287,
    364, 406
Strauss, Richard 13, 93, 231, 372, 410
Stravinsky, Igor 96, 269, 278, 401
Strindberg, August 434
Stuckenschmidt, Hans Heinz 51, 159, 163
Suchsland, Leopold 27
Sultan, Grete 11, 67
Sulzer, Salomon 47
Suppé, Franz von 99
Süßenbach, Jörg 2, 436–7
Susskind, Walter 372, 399, 415–16
Sutherland, Joan 392–3
Sutherland, Margaret 363, 424
Sverjensky, Alexander 369
Sweet, Georgina 150
Szenassy, Karoly 249

Tartini, Giuseppe 262
Tauber, Richard 117, 377
Taylor, Samuel A. 433
Tchaikovsky, Pyotr 61, 262, 372
Teichert, Curt 154
Tellkamp, Uwe 3
Terracini, Lyndon 392

Thomas, Rudolf 159
Thyssen, Fritz 107
Tichauer, Salo Max 49–50, 156–7, 283,
    286, 316, 390
Tietjen, Heinz 34–5, 73, 377
Tognetti, Richard 342
Toller, Ernst 306
Toscanini, Arturo 165–6
Trau, Sela 479
Tribe, Kenneth 338, 341
Tucholsky, Kurt 14
Turnovsky, Frederick 339

Ullmann, Viktor 5
Ullstein, Leopold 14
Urbach, Arthur 267

Valetti, Rosa 18
Valler, Rachel 368
Van Hien, Mark Gordon 136
Vaughan Williams, Ralph 84, 170
Vega, Lope de 431
Veidt, Conrad 18
Veit, Otti 19–20, 74, 235, 315, 370–2,
    392, 415
Velter, Joseph M. 57
Verdi, Guiseppe 49, 136, 346, 376
Verne, Jules 199
Vernon, Bettina 386–7
Volkmann, Oswald 276
Voss, Herbert 281, 283, 303
Vries, Sydney de 374, 393

Wagner, Eva 26, 124, 335, 336, 341–2, 395
Wagner, Richard 13, 33, 49, 75, 79, 84, 93,
    205, 230–1, 267, 404
Wagner, Winifred 35
Wagner, Wolfgang 162, 315, 339, 395
Wakehurst, Lord 237
Wallace, William Vincent 53–4

Walter, Bruno 14, 35, 37, 146, 162, 165–6, 188, 368, 381
Warburg, Gerald 106
Warren-Smith, Neil 392
Waten, Judah 414
Waters, Thorold 57, 165–7, 188–9, 230–1, 394–5
Waxman, Franz 434
Weber, Carl Maria von 172, 230, 376
Weber, Marek 21
Webern, Anton 96, 101, 332
Wedekind, Frank 434
Wedgwood, Camilla 185
Wegener, Paul 18
Weill, Kurt 42, 85, 276, 418
Weinberg, Jacob 380
Weinberger, Jaromir 34
Weinberger, Josef 99
Weinert, Erich 306
Weingarten, Paul 25
Weingartner, Felix 25
Weintraub, Irene 241, 252
Weintraub, Stefan 17, 18, 41, 43, 117, 198–205, 210, 229–34, 239–52, 269, 282, 285, 315, 320, 345, 388, 436
Weintraub, Zevi Hirsch Alter 465
Weir, Nancy 38, 58, 166
Weiss, Emma 150, 186, 320, 391
Weiss, Leo 198, 201–2, 205, 210, 212, 231, 239, 242, 250, 311, 320, 388, 436
Welles, Orson 431
Wellesz, Egon 25, 104, 154, 222, 429
Wenkart (family) 335–6
Werder, Felix 2–4, 52, 221, 266, 278, 283, 286, 307, 316–17, 337–8, 340–2, 349, 372, 383, 397–8, 414–17, 419, 423–4, 427–8
Werfel, Franz 96

Wertheim, Hugo 56
Werther, Rudolf T. 13, 120–1, 187, 311, 315–16, 351–2, 375–6, 391, 413
Wheeler, John 355, 412
Wheeler, Major R.H. 178–81
White, Thomas Walter 110–11
Whitlam, Gough 422, 436
Wigman, Mary 122
Wilde, Oscar 425
Wilhelm II 81, 165, 251
Williams, Neil 392
Williams, Verdon 360
Williamson, James C. 203, 206, 359, 378, 384
Wiltshire, John 431
Winkler, Julius 107
Winkler, Max 99–100
Winunguj, George 420
Wise, Freddie Gordon 21, 202, 204
Wittenberg, Emil 261, 292, 299, 470
Wohlthat, Helmuth 176, 456
Wolf, Hugo 27, 372, 374
Wolpe, Stefan 418
Wöss, Kurt 360, 418
Würzburger, Siegfried 410, 480
Würzburger, Walter 42, 157–8, 273, 276–7, 283, 287, 299, 317, 408–10, 414

Young, Simone 4

Zádor, Eugen 104
Zander, Hans 35, 37, 46, 133, 145, 222, 377–8, 411
Zeller, Carl 99
Ziegler, Hans Severus 39
Ziehrer, Carl 99
Zimmering, Max 260, 262
Zipper, Herbert 122
Zweig, Fritz 34

DIANA K. WEEKES

About the Translator

A former student of Jascha Spivakovsky, honours arts graduate from the University of Melbourne and recipient of a DAAD Scholarship, Diana K. Weekes began studies in musicology at Munich University before transferring to the Hochschule für Musik, where she completed a Master's degree in solo performance and pedagogy. A major prize winner in international competitions in Finale Ligure, Terni, Senigallia, Vercelli and Bolzano, she gave recitals and broadcasts in England, Germany, Italy and Switzerland before returning to Melbourne in 1974.

Since 1981 Diana has lived and worked in Adelaide, where she has performed for the ABC, Recitals Australia, the Adelaide Festival and the Barossa Music Festival. Formerly a lecturer in music at the Flinders Street School of Music, from 2002 to 2010 she was a full-time member of staff at the Elder Conservatorium of Music, where she was a Senior Lecturer in Keyboard, Coordinator of the Chamber Music program and Head of Undergraduate Studies. Widely experienced in the art of duo piano playing and accompanying, she also completed a PhD in musical composition in 2007.

Diana has lectured in Harmony, Accompanying and Keyboard Musicianship and until 2016 remained on the part-time staff of the Elder Conservatorium where, apart from her piano teaching, she supervised several PhD candidates and in 2013–2014 acted as Coordinator of the Honours Research Seminar. She now teaches privately and has become actively involved in the translation of books and articles from German into English for friends and colleagues. *The Vanished Musicians* is her first major published translation.

EXILE STUDIES

Edited by Franziska Meyer

A series founded by Alexander Stephan

Exile Studies is a series of monographs and edited collections that takes a broad view of exile, including the work and life of refugees of the Nazi period, and beyond. The series explores the different global and cultural spaces of exile as well as the specific historical, political and social concerns of exilic writers and artists. Of particular interest is scholarship that engages with recent theoretical approaches to exile to shed new light on the unique conditions of mass expulsion by Nazi persecution. A plurality of theoretical approaches is encouraged, featuring research that reaches beyond national frameworks or disciplinary boundaries and takes multi-directional, transcultural or comparative approaches. Themes include exclusion and delocalization, legacies of displacement and acculturation, migrating identities of the exile, the mutual impact of cultures, and the historical and political meanings of 'home' and 'homecoming'.

The series promotes dialogue among transnational, Jewish and memory studies, and among diaspora, Holocaust and postcolonial studies. It invites research that acknowledges questions of gender, race, class and ethnicity as indispensable tools for understanding the cultural processes connected to mass expulsions in the age of the refugee.

Vol. 1 Sonja Maria Hedgepeth, 'Überall blicke ich nach einem heimatlichen Boden aus': Exil im Werk Else Lasker-Schülers.
254 pp. 1994.
US-ISBN 0-8204-2219-3.

Vol. 2 Elfe Vallaster, 'Ein Zimmer in der Luft': Liebe, Exil, Rückkehr und Wort-Vertrauen.
278 pp. 1994.
US-ISBN 0-8204-2225-8.

Vol. 3   Waltraud Strickhausen, Die Erzählerin Hilde Spiel oder «Der weite Wurf in die Finsternis».
500 pp. 1996.
US-ISBN 0-8204-2623-7.

Vol. 4   Renata von Hanffstengel, Mexiko im Werk von Bodo Uhse: Das nie verlassene Exil.
251 pp. 1996.
US-ISBN 0-8204-2683-0.

Vol. 5   Harald Reil, Siegfried Kracauers Jacques Offenbach: Biographie, Geschichte, Zeitgeschichte.
159 pp. 2003.
US-ISBN 0-8204-3742-5.

Vol. 6   J. M. Ritchie, German Exiles: British Perspectives.
344 pp. 1997.
US-ISBN 0-8204-3743-3.

Vol. 7   Tibor Frank, Double Exile: Migrations of Jewish-Hungarian Professionals through Germany to the United States, 1919–1945.
501 pp. 2009.
ISBN 978-3-03911-331-6.

Vol. 8   Nicole Brunnhuber, The Faces of Janus:
English-language Fiction by German-speaking Exiles in Great Britain, 1933–45.
240 pp. 2005.
ISBN 3-03910-180-3 / US-ISBN 0-8204-6989-0.

Vol. 9   Lee Kyung-Boon, Musik und Literatur im Exil: Hanns Eislers dodekaphone Exilkantaten.
306 pp. 2001.
US-ISBN 0-8204-4938-5.

Vol. 10   Regina U. Hahn, The Democratic Dream: Stefan Heym in America.
150 pp. 2002.
ISBN 3-906768-53-8 / US-ISBN 0-8204-5865-1.

Vol. 11   Alexander Stephan (ed.), Exile and Otherness:
         New Approaches to the Experience of
         the Nazi Refugees.
         308 pp. 2005.
         ISBN 3-03910-561-2 / US-ISBN 0-8204-7588-2.

Vol. 12 Andrea Hammel, Everyday Life as Alternative Space
         in Exile Writing: The novels of Anna Gmeyner, Selma Kahn,
         Hilde Spiel, Martina Wied and Hermynia Zur Mühlen.
         264 pp. 2007.
         ISBN 978-3-03910-524-3.

Vol. 13 Axel Englund and Anders Olsson (eds), Languages of Exile:
         Migration and Multilingualism in Twentieth-Century
         Literature.
         336 pp. 2013.
         ISBN 978-3-0343-0943-1.

Vol. 14 Albrecht Dümling, The Vanished Musicians: Jewish Refugees
         in Australia.
         591 pp. 2016.
         ISBN 978-3-0343-1951-5.

www.ingramcontent.com/pod-product-compliance
Ingram Content Group UK Ltd.
Pitfield, Milton Keynes, MK11 3LW, UK
UKHW021837210426
5322IPUK00021B/341